Names on The Face of Montana

NAMES ON THE FACE

OF

MONTANA

THE STORY OF MONTANA'S PLACE NAMES

By
Roberta Carkeek Cheney

MOUNTAIN PRESS PUBLISHING COMPANY

MISSOULA

Library of Congress Cataloging in Publication Data

Cheney, Roberta Carkeek.
  Names on the face of Montana.

  Bibliography: p.
  1. Names, Geographical — Montana. 2. Montana — History, Local.
I. Title.
F729.C5   1983   978.6   83-15401
ISBN 0-87842-150-5

Preface

The first edition (1971) of *Names on the Face of Montana* was the result of two years of intensive research backed by a life-time interest in Montana place names. This second edition incorporates that information and in addition contains material that I have continued to collect in the decade between the two editions. The Bicentennial year inspired almost every county and some communities to delve into the past and publish a book about their history. A great many place-name origins surfaced in these books and have been added to those entries in the first book that had only post office dates. I am indeed grateful to every local historian who took the time to collect, publish, and thus preserve those segments of Montana history.

I am also most grateful to Dennis Lutz, president of the Montana Postal Cache, who with Meryl Lutz edited a journal which gave information about post offices in Montana. The lists and maps were of inestimable help to me in checking my material for accuracy and in adding names and dates that I did not have.

The major reference used in my original research was the *Record of Postmaster Appointments*. The five journals containing the records of the establishment and subsequent fate of all Montana post offices are found in the National Archives in Washington, D.C. These journals record the appointment of every postmaster between 1855 and 1930. The first journal includes all of the Western Territories but entries concerning the places that were later to be included in the State of Montana did not begin until 1862. The name of the county as well as that of the town and the postmaster were given in each instance. During the years when Montana's counties were expanding in number and shrinking in size, the journal keepers kept up with the changes by notations: ". . . Park County, late in Gallatin; . . . Now in Wheatland Co. . . .; name changed to Cataract, late Arklow; . . . Abe, madison Co. dis. send mail to Cameron." These records are also on microfilm and can be seen at the State Historical Library in Helena.

The records of postmaster appointments and establishment or discontinuance of offices since 1930 are found in the Bureau of Operations of the Post Office Department in Washington, D.C. The latest available Zip Code book was used to determine which towns had offices active in 1970 for the first edition and the 1980 edition used for this book. Each one that has an active post office as of this date is denoted by appearing in all capital letters in the body of the text.

Maps were my constant source of reference. The railroad maps, the highway maps, and specialized maps of specific areas, or of a particular phase of history were invaluable. The county maps in Ellis Waldron's book were used extensively to determine if a particular town in one of the newer counties could be the same one that was granted a post office years before in one of the original counties. He also kindly allowed his maps to be used as base maps for those that appear in this book. Three excellent illustrated maps by Ralph Shane gave pertinent facts about places and events in the history of the Blackfeet, Crow, and Cheyenne Indians in Montana. The maps that appear herein were designed and produced by William Mahoney of the University of Montana's Department of Geography.

The Montana Guidebook, written by members of the Federal Writers' Project and published by Viking and by Hastings contained valuable information about the existing towns, especially those along the main highways.

The two most extensive studies of Montana place names that I found were those by Frank Perrin of the Great Northern Railroad and by the late J. P. Rowe of the Department of Geology of the University of Montana at Missoula. Many of the towns were listed in both of these works, although Perrin's entries were railroad oriented, while Rowe's were geologically and geographically oriented. Mr. Perrin called his work "Statement of Origin of Station Names," and he very kindly sent me the 134 entries that referred to stations in Montana. Rowe's work, entitled "The Origin of Some Montana Place Names," contained 600 entries, about 500 of which were towns, and which was compiled in 1933. These were valuable resources for a study that hoped eventually to record every town name in Montana.

Besides scanning the new books that have come out in the past ten years, I have kept a clipping file of relevant newspaper articles and many people have sent information to me.

Two Montana historians, Dorothy Floerchinger and Mary Morsanny were especially helpful in sending information from their areas of Conrad and Ryegate. I am grateful to every feature story writer who has dug into the history of a specific locale and had it published in a Montana newspaper. The writings of Roberta Donovan and Kathryn Wright have been especially valuable. I am grateful to Robert Murray of Western Interpretive Services of Sheridan, Wyoming, for sharing his research about Montana, and to Merrill Burlingame, Ken Byerly, and other historians whose scholarly works were most helpful.

I continue to appreciate the many individuals who helped or sent material to me and are acknowledged in the first edition.

To people who sent me corrections and additional information, I give sincere thanks — to George Mueller and Robert J. Ege for clarifying locations in the historic Judith Landing area — and to my friend Philip St. George Cooke who sent information about his ancestor, Union General Philip St. George Cooke for whom Camp Cooke was named. William Ashton's "Corrections and Additions" list was carefully checked and changes were made in this edition when appropriate.

My sincere appreciation goes to University of Montana librarians Katherine Schaefer and Dale Johnson, who kept me informed of the new county histories and other information books as they came out and to the librarians at the Montana Historical Society who shared their files with me when I needed help on a particular place. The bibliographies, compiled by librarians, were a great help.

Finally I am indebted to the many people who wrote to say they found the first edition useful and interesting and to those who wanted a book but found it out of print. Those letters helped get a second edition published.

For several reasons I felt a second edition should be written. Both the publisher and I continue to get requests for the book and the first edition was sold out years ago. So much additional information about towns and their early histories became available with the publication of county histories during the Bicentennial year and that needed to be incorporated. There is an increased interest in researching our state's history and this edition gives the opening and closing date of every post office that existed in Montana, all 2,599 of them. Though some of them were of brief duration, they are listed. The latest available survey lists about 300 active Montana post offices in 1980.

More and more people are searching for their "roots" so, in this edition, I have listed the first postmaster in each town. In the first edition I gave the postmaster's name only if it had influenced the naming of the town. Another group who needs postal information in a readily available form are those who are collecting postmarks or cancellations.

"We speak the names, not thinking how they came to be, yet the names had grown out of the life and the life blood of all who had gone before," wrote George Stewart in *Names on the Land*. ". . . Our history, our tradition, our struggles are all in the names we put upon the land."

It is hoped that this book about place names will preserve even more completely the story of towns in Montana.

Roberta Carkeek Cheney

To my pioneer parents and grandparents
and to Truman, Karen, Maureen and Larry

Contents

Introduction

Place names impart an identity, almost an immortality, to a specific location. As men go to a new land, either to explore or to settle, they find a need to assign a name to each particular place so that it can be mapped, referred to in conversation, or even granted a post office. There is a need. There is also a pride and satisfaction in choosing an appropriate name and bestowing it upon a place. The story of Montana is reflected in her place names.

"There is a natural poetry in the sound of American names... read the names of the town and cities, of the creeks and rivers... read them aloud... there is a pattern that is a kind of folk music in itself, rich in human and historical associations, rich in humor, alive with a beauty that is sometimes smooth and singing and sometimes keen as a trapper's knife." (*Life*, Jan. 31, 1934)

Montana's names are like that. Read her history in *Adobetown*, *Wolf Creek*, *Red Eagle*, *Spotted Robe*; in *Abundance* and in *Chinook*, or *Snowshoe* and *Windville*. Follow her prospectors to *Gold Creek*, *Granite*, *Diamond City*, and *Copperopolis*. Remember historic events with names like *Custer*, *Alamo*, *Dunkirk*, and *Lincoln*. Honor government officials with *Jefferson*, *Edgerton*, and *Meagher*, and explorers at *Lewis and Clark Caverns*. Smile with the old timers at *Ubet*, *Hog-em*, *Jitney*, *Oka*, and *Whoop-up Trail*. Ride the open prairie and picture the cattlemen driving vast herds of longhorns in from Texas and turning their brands into place names like *Mill Iron*, *Two Dot*, and *Seventynine*.

Have compassion on the dry-land farmers who came to *Golden Valley*, *Gardenland*, *Richland*, and *Trouble*. The broad plains and free land of Montana beckoned to people from other countries who brought names with them to plant in the strange new land: *Zurich*, *Amsterdam*, *Glasgow*, *Haxby*, *Inverness*, *Kremlin*, *Plevna*, and *Silesia Springs*. Settlers from other states thought wistfully of towns they had left behind and called their new homes *Amherst*, *Ashuelot*, *Potomac*, and *Corvallis*.

The railroaders laid tracks over the trackless prairies and pushed through mountain ranges to cross the state. They named stations as they were established. Usually these names were chosen to honor a railroad official or a member of his family, but sometimes the names were romantic ones to attract travelers and settlers. *Glacier*, *Rising Wolf*, and *Fort Piegan* supplanted earlier and less colorful names as the Great Northern sought to settle the territory along its line.

In Montana there are more than 2,000 places that have, at some time in their history, reached the stature of a community with an established post office. In 1968 there were 398 Montana towns with active post offices; as of

May 1982 there are 363. I am most grateful to the editor of Montana Branch of the National League of Postmasters who made up a list of post offices and postmasters as of May 1982 and published it in the "Posthorn," and to Leonard McAtee of Cameron who made the list available to me.

In the very definitive list of Montana post offices prepared by Dennis Lutz, there are some 2,250 entries. Of these 88 names refer to places or post office appointments which were actually never activated. The notations from the *Record of Postmaster Appointments* indicate that the "order was rescinded," or "postmaster declined appointment," or simply "post office never in operation." There were also 454 entries where a name change had been indicated which means that one geographical place and/or post office would be listed twice, or in fifteen cases even three times, to accommodate changes. This leaves about 1800 post offices that were at one time active in Montana.... some for a brief period, some for more than a century. All of them are in this book with dates of establishment and the first postmaster's name. Many have a brief history included. It was difficult to find information about those places that "died aborning," but the name origin has been determined for most of the ones that survived for any length of time.

There is confusion in the matter of "name changed to" or "mail now sent to" notations in the National Archives records. For instance, in the case of *Adobetown* and *Nevada City* the postal records show a name change. Actually there were two separate mining camps, both of them near *Virginia City* in Madison County. First one camp had a post office and then the other, but the name did not change though the location of the area post office did. There may well be other errors of this nature that were impossible to identify. Often the notation of "send the mail to..." is the only clue to location of by-gone places. Therefore, it is given in the entry when it would seem helpful.

There are other "towns" that served only as a railway station, a side-track, or a meeting place. Each one, no matter how humble or how important its role in history of the state, had a name, an identity, and a part to play.

It is to locate these places in time, space, and nomenclature and to preserve their identity for the future that this book was written. There are nearly 2,500 entries exclusive of the material in the Appendix. Name origin has been determined for about two-thirds of them; bits of folklore or history is given for most of the entries and for everyone a basic date or fact.

The names of the railroads are briefed in the entries. Presumably, any student of Montana history will know that *Milwaukee* refers to the *Chicago, Milwaukee, St. Paul and Pacific Railroad*. The constant repetition of the whole names would have resulted in unnecessary bulk.

Counties are included because their names are significant in relation to the names of towns. It is also necessary to have a knowledge of the county boundary changes — of the breaking up of large counties into smaller ones — in order to understand the problem of locating towns in their proper and present counties. The nine original counties which were laid out by the Territorial Legislature in 1865 were divided, sub-divided, and had portions annexed to make changing boundary lines until 1925. In that year Petroleum County was established and brought the total number of counties to fifty-six, and an apparent end to the "county bustin' " that had gripped the state for years. Many towns have been in two counties, some in three. To trace the history of Red Lodge, for instance, one must look to the establishment of its post office in 1884 in Gallatin County. When Park County was created in 1887, *Red Lodge* was within its boundaries. In 1895

Carbon County was created from parts of Park and Yellowstone Counties. *Red Lodge* became the county seat of the new county. To find the origin of the town's name, one must go back even further to the time when it was a favorite spot for the Indians to camp and build their lodges. There seems to be no doubt that the town took its name from these Indian lodges, but residents disagree as to whether "red" was used because the Indians painted their teepees with the native red clay, or whether the white man, years later, used the term to indicate that the lodges belonged to the redmen.

Every effort was made in this study to locate each town within its present county boundary even though the town may have flourished and died while listed in the original county. The possibility of error in this is great, as is the possibility of error in spelling, because many names were taken from handwritten journals almost 100 years old. Mistakes resulting from handwriting even when it was new, were not unusual. Several errors in interpreting the handwritten applications for post offices which were sent to Washington, D.C. resulted in towns with names quite different from the ones intended. *Piniele*, in Carter County, was to have been named for the twin pinnacles directly north of the townsite. When the suggested name for the town was sent in, it was spelled "Pinicle" (which was at least a phonetic spelling). but the postal clerk red the "c" as an "e" and the town was officially named "Piniele" and has remained so to date. *Uebra* was supposed to be called "Nebraska" in honor of the home state of many of the settlers. However, an abbreviation (Nebra.) and a capital "N" that looked like a "U" on the application resulted in the strange name for the town in Garfield County.

Rivers and creeks are not included in the body of this book, but are handled briefly in the appendix. Many town names, however have come from the descriptive ones given to these town and other geographical features by the Indians, the explorers, trappers, and settlers. Some of the Indian names have been assimilated so thoroughly into our language that we have almost forgotten that words like "Missoula" and "Missouri" were from an earlier tongue. The different tribal names have been applied to towns, lakes, rivers, and counties. The two most used ones are "Flathead" and "Crow," but "Blackfoot," "Piegan," "Selish (or Salish)," "Bannack," "Assiniboine," and others appear as place names to reflect the Indians' part in the history of Montana. About four percent of the town place names in the state have an Indian origin. A larger percentage of the names assigned to topographical features are of Indian origin. These first inhabitants were concerned with the big rivers upon which they could travel. The Gros Ventres called the *Missouri* the "stream that scolds all others." The Crows called it the "big muddy." The name we use evolved from the Indian words used to describe it. "Yaak" is an Indian word for arrow. He saw the smaller river cutting across the "bow" of the Kootenai River in Northwest Montana and Canada, so called it the *Yaak River*. Streams, plains, valleys, mountains, and hills were designated in colorful, descriptive terms and a few of these have become a part of the white man's language.

Lewis and Clark continued the use of descriptive names such as *Dry River* and *Musselshell*, but they also assigned names to Montana rivers and landmarks in tribute to members of their own exploration party (*Pryor* and *Pompey's Pillar*), or to honor important men in government (*Madison*, *Gallatin*, and *Dearborn*). These explorers were fascinated with the new species of plants and animals in this wild new land and used such names as Big Horn and *Bitterroot* on the maps as they drew them. Sometimes they marked events by leaving names upon the land like *Fourth of July Creek, Blowing Fly Creek,* or *Travelers' Rest.* The former Northern Pacific Railway Company has named the recreation car on its old North Coast Limited train "Travelers' Rest" in honor of the explorers and that day in 1805 when they assigned that name to a comfortable resting place in Western Montana.

The French influence seems stronger than that of any other single ethnic group. The early French trappers left their mark on the maps of Montana. They left their names in the Indian tribes as they married the native girls and fathered half-breed children who were later to be instrumental in settling and name areas of the state. *Belleview, Bonaccord, Dupuyer, Argenta, Valleux, Chouteau, Teton, Wibaux, Pouchet* and many others are obvious remnants of French influence.

Later the miners came from England and from the South European countries. When the mines opened up, the impoverished coal miners from Cornwall and England proper came flocking to *Butte.* Some of them mined for awhile and then took up the land in one of the nearby counties — Madison, Jefferson, Beaverhead, or Deer Lodge.

The Slavic people came to work in the coal mines of *Stockett, Sand Coulee,* and *Giffin.* Hardy Highlanders from Scotland came to work as sheepherders and soon owned the flocks. Scottish names abound in the area around *Lewistown.* The Presbyterian Church, in cooperation with land development companies, sponsored groups of immigrants from Holland. The most successful of these groups was the one in Gallatin Valley, easily identifiable by the town names — *Amsterdam* and *Holland Settlement.* A group of Danish settlers named their town *Dagmar* in honor of their queen.

The gold rush led prospectors to Montana in the early 1860's. Many of them were rag-tags from the Civil War and they tended to use names from their past for the camps that sprang up around a rich "strike." *Unionville, Yankee Flats,* and *Springfield* competed with *Confederate Gulch* and *Varina.* According to one old-timer, "The blue and grey soldiers re-fought the Civil War in the saloons of Virginia City at regular intervals." (Harry Beauregard Daems, "Early Days on the Madison." Typed copy in author's possession.* Sometimes the prospectors named their camps for the metal that was to make them rich, sometimes for the man that discovered the mine, or for the topographical feature of the area: *White's City, Alder Gulch, Gold Run, Hughesville,* or *Grasshopper Creek.*

Religious origins accounted for one and one-half percent of Montana place names: *Mt. Horeb, St. Mary's Mission,* and *Mizpah.* The influence of the Catholic missionaries is indicated by names like *DeSmet, Ravalli, St. Ignatius,* and *St. Xavier.* "Brother Van," the famous and beloved Methodist circuit rider in the days of the open ranges and cowboys, almost had his name immortalized in a "town.' A post office to be named *Van Orsdell* was approved for a place in Fergus County in April 1924 but the order was rescinded.

The early day cowboys who rode the ranges for the big cattle pools made up a romantic and colorful chapter in the history of Montana. It is interesting to note that no towns were named for them, not even for the most famous one of all, Charlie Russell. They wintered in *Fort Benton, Utica, Chinook, Bullhook,* and *Landusky* but were not settlers. They worked the round-ups and slept wherever they unrolled their soogans. It is doubtful if any one of them ever thought of applying for a post office or starting a town.

Physical features of the land gave rise to about eighteen percent of the total number of town place names in the state. Many of them were named for a creek, a bluff, or a lake which had in turn been named for a person, an animal, or a topographical feature. It then becomes difficult to determine whether the name of a particular town should be included in the topographic category because it was named for a creek or taken one step back and listed with those towns named for an animal, a mineral, a person, etc. Red Mountain, Wolf Creek, Bearcreek, and Reese Creek are among the many names that present this problem. There are perhaps that many more towns that were named for the creek on which they were located but used only the creek's given name. This is especially true of the creeks that were named for a person, thus we find Armells, Burns, and Clancy are names assigned to post offices established along Armells Creek, Burns Creek, and Clancy Creek. The rivers and creeks were named first simply because they were in existence before the towns were laid out. They were landmarks and needed identifying names, so their names superceded town names and had a great influence on the future naming of settlements.

The category and percentage figures used here are necessarily arbitrary because so many names can easily fit into two or more categories. There is, however, a definite trend indicated. It would appear that the topography of the land was directly or indirectly responsible for 303 or some eighteen percent of the total number of names. Certainly a sampling of these descriptive names gives one a picture of the state: Alkali, Bald Butte, Basin, Bearmouth, Beaverhead, Benchland, Big Timber, Bozeman Hot Springs, Camas Prairie, Cascade, Chalk Buttes, Clasoil, Clear Lake, Dry Creek, Flatwillow, Four Buttes, Glacier, Great Falls, Milk River, Pinegrove, Rimrock, and Riverside.

The state itself was named for its mountain ranges. Sen. Stephen A. Douglas and Gov. James Denver were discussing names for that "territory up there in the mountains." They called on Mrs. Douglas who was a student of languages and confirmed the fact that "montana" was a Spanish word meaning a "mountainous country" and thus it seemed appropriate. Later, in Senate debate, it was stated that the name was a pure Latin word meaning "mountainous country" and that it had been used by Livy and other Latin historians. After much discussion, it was finally decided that the name did "suit" the new territory.

Lewis and Clark had called the Rocky Mountains, the "Shining Mountains," so Montana became known as the "Land of the Shining Mountains." The great mountain range that separated Atlantic headwaters from Pacific headwaters was officially named Rocky Mountains because of its topography.

Place names reveal that plants were native to Montana as towns were called Plum Creek, Rosebud, Greenwood, Pinegrove, Prickly Pear, Poplar, Primrose, Alder, Willow Creek, Cottonwood, Sagebrush, and Bitterroot.

Animals that were common to a particular area furnished inspiration for such names as Buffalo, Black Eagle, Trout Creek, Bearcreek, Bear Springs, Coyote, Porcupine, Wolf Creek, Wolf Point, and Rattlesnake. Plant and animal origins account for five percent of the place names that were given to towns.

Though mountains, rivers, and creeks were most often named for a natural feature, towns that began with a post office were more commonly named for people, often the first postmaster. Fourteen percent of all town names fall into this category. A rash of this kind of naming began in the 1900's and it was especially prevalent in dry-land farm communities that sprang up in eastern Montana during the land boom. In a great many cases, this naming for the first postmaster was done not so much as an honor or an ego-satisfying gesture, as it was a matter of convenience. As soon as the settlers had unloaded their wagons and gotten a few acres of sod plowed and seeded to grain, they began to be lonesome for news from home — from Iowa, from Kansas, from Norway, or Denmark. The nearest post office might well be seventy-five gumbo miles away, so one farmer would write to Washington and request a post office. He filled out the blanks, got signers for the petition, and agreed to be postmaster. In all probability, the "office" would be a corner of his kitchen or in a cigar box on the porch. As a matter of convenience in locating it, the new post office, hence the town," took the name of the postmaster, whether male or female. Many postmasters were farmer's wives.

The establishment of post offices in Montana began with the mining camps in Beaverhead and Madison Counties, and with *Hell Gate* in what later became Missoula County. This trading post in Washington Territory was granted a post office on November 25, 1862. Frank L. Worden was appointed postmaster. *Bannack City* was in Idaho Territory when its post office was established in November 1863. Both of these early towns became a part of Montana Territory when it was created on May 26, 1864. Other early offices were granted for *Adobetown, Nevada City, Sheridan,* and *Virginia City.*

"It was a great sight to see the stage coach of long ago bring mail to Virginia City. Half of the town people turned out. There were mail sacks inside the stage, mail sacks in the booth behind the stage. You would even see mail sacks hanging from the harness of the horses... The postmaster and his assistant worked hard to sort all the mail while anxious patrons waited outside. When he was through, he opened the door and people filed in one at a time to get mail at the window. Sometimes one had to wait two hours in line. The next stage would probably be coming in about three weeks." (Daems)

Helena, in Edgerton County (1965), and *Sun River,* in Lewis and Clark County (1868), were early day post offices that served other areas in the state.

Daniel Sylvester Tuttle, Bishop for the Episcopal Church in a missionary district that included Utah, Idaho, and Montana Territories, as well as parts of other states, wrote of Montana:

> At this time (1862-3) all the present area of Montana east of the main range of the Rocky Mountains was a part of Dakota. All west was part of Washington. In the winter of 1862-63 there were 373 men and 37 women residents in and near Bannack; and 37 men and two women in and near Fort Benton, making 410 men and 39 women in all, in that portion ... east of the mountains. In the same winter there were 69 men and eight women in Missoula County ... a total population, in all, for Montana, of 604 men and 65 women.

> The early days of Montana were such as to try men's souls. The Civil War was raging and its tempestuous billows threw not a few lawless men as driftwood into the mountain wilderness. The mines of California, Colorado and Idaho sent not only their restless and hardy, but also their reckless and hardened denizens upon stampedes to new diggings. A mining community is eminently excitable, unruly, defiant, without fear of God or man. Add to all this that Yankton, the capital of Dakota, and so the center of which restraint of civil authority must issue, was 2200 miles away from the Bannack mines, and it will readily be understood what a fierce and turbulent cauldron life in Montana in the early days must have been.

Bishop Tuttle established eleven churches in Montana but no town was named in his honor.

Forts played a major part in the development of Montana. The United States government established military forts to protect travelers and settlers from Indian attacks and to maintain an army whose purpose it was to subdue the redman. *Fort Assiniboine, Fort Carroll, Fort Logan, Fort Ellis, Fort Harrison,* and *Fort Maginnis* were among those that began as military posts. There were forty-six "forts" that had post offices. The majority of these establishments were trading posts rather than military ones. Generally these trading posts used "fort" as part of their name, though they were established strictly for trading. *Fort Owen, Fort Pease, Fort McKenzie, Fort Lucky,* and many others were set up by the big fur companies or by individuals who put in a store of beads, flour, coffee, whiskey, firearms, etc., and sought out the Indians who would bring in furs to exchange for these commodities. These trading posts were also fortified against the Indians. They had heavy outside walls so the Indians could not climb over or set fire to them. These strong walls were usually made of tree trunks set as closely together as possible. (At *Fort Carroll,* near the head of the Judith River the hardy cottonwoods took root and grew, leaving a natural enclosure long after the fort itself was abandoned.) At two corners, diagonally opposite each other, square blockhouses were built on top of the walls. These were equipped with guns and cannons which could be used to protect all sides of the blockade. The construction of the trading "forts" justified their name and in several cases, the towns that grew up around these early fortified posts have kept the descriptive and historic word is part of their name: *Fort Benton, Fort Peck,* and *Fort Shaw.*

Identifiable railroad associations accounted for eighty-six names or about five percent of all place names. *Hill* and *Hill County* for the famous "Jim" Hill of the Great Northern; *Harlowton* and *Maudlow* from the family of Richard Harlow of the old Montana Railroad; *Soo* and *Burlington* are among the most obvious names. A great many other towns were named for a conductor, an engineer, a construction superintendent, an official, or a member of the official's family. A few stations were given descriptive names like *Pacific Junction, Thompson River Spur,* and *Castle Junction* but the great majority of railroad-connected names were those of individuals.

Sweetgrass, Bonfield, Park City, Fishtrap, Gateway, Powderville, Stone Chack, Racetrack, Twin Bridges, and sixty-two other names describe either the town itself, or perhaps one outstanding feature in the area about it. Some four percent of all the names seem to fit comfortably in this group.

Government officials and army men account for about three percent of all town and county place names in Montana. Lewis and Clark, as a team of explorers, are immortalized in the name of a county and a state park. Custer and his officers, Benton and Keogh, were the inspiration for early day post office names. Governors Edgerton and Toole have counties named for them. Senators and representatives, both at the state and national level, have been honored by place-naming. Clagett, Carter Fergus, and McCone come in that category. Blaine, Lincoln, Coolidge, Garfield, Madison, Jefferson and Gallatin were among the national figures with namesakes in Montana.

The largest category of Montana place names is the one that includes the towns named for residents of the area or other local figures, exclusive of postmasters. Twenty percent of the names were taken directly from a local person's name. In most cases the name is used in its original form. Sometimes a suffix was added or two names were combined to make a suitable name for the community. From the long list, one can identify the nationalities that went into the frontier crucible to make Montanans: O'Neill and Kelly; McLeod and McDonald; Patterson and Andersonville; Story and Brooks; Reichle and Robare; Hauck and Kessler; Kilz and Gebo. The 333 names assigned to this category, in addition to the 246 that were in the postmaster list would indicate that almost one-fourth of all the towns in Montana were named for local people. In addition, practically all of the names in the list of 661 towns whose exact name origin could not be determined were obviously either surnames or given names of people. Since they were not recognizable as public figures, one can assume that they, too, would fall into the category of local people or possibly railroaders. This would bring the number of towns named for local people up to 1,240, or over half of the total figure.

Of the counties, twenty-six were named for men: Blaine, Broadwater, Chouteau, Custer, Dawson, Fallon, Fergus, Gallatin, Hill, Jefferson, Ravalli, Sanders, Sheridan, Toole, Wibaux, Carter, Daniels, Garfield, Lewis and Clark, Lincoln, McCone, Madison, Meagher, Phillips, Powell, and Roosevelt. Of the twenty-seven men thus honored, sixteen were national figures and eleven were prominent men within the state. Twenty-seven counties have names of geographic or idealistic origin: Beaverhead, Big Horn, Carbon, Cascade, Granite, Mineral, Musselshell, Park, Prairie, Rosebud, Richland, Silver Bow, Stillwater, Sweet Grass, Valley, Yellowstone, Golden Valley, Teton, Powder River, Treasure, Liberty, Lake, Glacier, Judith Basin (combination of a person's name and a geographical feature), Petroleum, and Pondera. The latter might be listed with the Indian names, since it was first the description of the shape of a lake (Pend d'Oreille or hanging ear), but it actually came to Montana as the name of a group of Indians. Teton, too, was the name of an Indian tribe belonging to the great Sioux or Dakota Nation. The name came from an Indian word ti-tan meaning "at or on land without trees." The most widely held opinion, however, is that teton, a French word meaning "woman's breast," was used by the early French fur traders to designate the Teton Peak and Teton Ridge, both in Teton County. Three counties have names of definite Indian origin: Flathead, Missoula, and Deer Lodge.

Idealistic names are found mainly on the land that was being promoted by the railroad companies to entice settlers (potential railroad users) to an area. Freewater, Golden Valley, Pleasant Valley, Pure Water, Richland, Treasure County, and Utopia fall into this group, and with similar ones, make up three percent of the place names in the state.

There was a tendency in mining-camp days to add "City" to the name of the town. Perhaps it gave a certain stature to a conglomeration of tents or log and mud huts; perhaps it indicated a dream for the future of a camp, though it was rough and primitive when the name was chosen: Bannack City, Virginia City, Nevada City, Cable City, Butte City, and Deer Lodge City were among the mining towns in western Montana thus named. All but Virginia City have dropped the word "city." There seemed to be an even stronger tendency in later years to add "ville" to a person's name to create a proper name for the settlement. Forty-four towns have this suffix as part of their names. Some are combined with a product or a natural feature, but the great majority use a name and the suffix: Barkerville, Coalville, Hughesville, Keplerville, Landville, Norrisville, Powderville, Salesville, and Walkerville. Nineteen town names use "ton" or "town" as an ending: Alberton, Comertown, Eagleton, Farmington. Eleven use either "burg" or "berg"; thirteen use "dale" as the suffix to make a person's name into a town name. Perhaps "ville" had a more sophisticated sound than "berg," "hill," or "dale." Whatever the reason, the French ending was favored four-to-one over any of the other suffixes for town names.

Neologisms account for at least twenty-five place names. Often two first names were combined: Isabell and May to make Ismay; Virgil and Ella to make Virgelle; Will and Sally to make Wilsal. Sometimes two parts of two last names were used to create a new name: Listo and Gamas to make Lismas; or a first and last name put together: Melvin Stone, shortened to Melstone; and Ole R. Field made into Rolefield. The name of the state was combined with that of a neighboring state for towns on or near the border: Monida and Mondak. Oilmont came from a product and part of the name of the state. "Mont" meaning mountain was also combined with products to create several names: Montbestos and Montaqua.

Postal records list 171 major name changes in the past century. These do not include minor changes or corrections such as Butte City to Butte; or Bell to Belle, or Bannock to Bannack. The reasons for the changes were numerous. Sometimes a new postmaster was appointed and he moved the "office" to his home or simply changed the name to his own; often a community changed its name to conform with the railroad station that had been established. In some cases a name was offensive or was not dignified enough. Finntown became Milltown; Last Chance Gulch became Helena; and One Horse became Florence. The Great Northern Railway changed many names along its route in northwestern Montana to make the area more alluring to travelers and settlers. Admus was changed to Gunsight; Arklow to Cataract; Carlow to Fort Piegan; Egan to Grizzly; Kilroy to Spotted Robe; and Lubec to Rising Wolf. Some changes were necessitated because another town in the state already had the chosen name. At least two "Hamiltons" had to be renamed because the one in the Bitterroot had been granted a post office under that name. When Marcus Daly laid out Anaconda, he called it Copperopolis, but had to change it because there was already a mining camp in Meagher County by that name. Morris in Carbon County had to be changed because shipments of freight and mail kept getting mixed up with Norris in Madison County.

This book is mainly concerned with the names and locations of towns and counties, but one cannot write of the place names in Montana without including such colorful ones as the "Jaw-bone Railroad," the "Whoop-up Trail," the "Horse Abattior," "Bone Trail," and "Chateau de la Fontaine!" There are a few entries put in merely for their name's sake.

The appelation "town" is used most loosely to indicate any place where a group of people gathered with enough permanence to feel the need of a post office or a name for their community. The word "station" is used with equal freedom to designate any stop on the railroad lines.

Emphasis has been placed upon the origin of each town and of its name, rather than upon the present state of each place. Hopefully, the origins will be historically valuable for all time, while the status quo could soon be obsolete.

It is to preserve a record of the names and places and their histories, which have been a vital part of the development of Montana, that this material has been assembled and written.

A

Abe (Madison) is south of Cameron near Wade Lake. The post office, granted in 1917, survived until 1938 to serve the few hardy homesteaders who stuck it out summer and winter, even though the thermometer in this Yellowstone Park area regularly dipped to 40° below zero. Herbert Ashley was the first postmaster but before he was appointed, homesteaders on the west side of the Madison River got their mail by a star route from Cameron; a cable was stretched across the river and mail for about twenty-five families on "Poverty Flats" went across it in a box pulled by a rope. **Abe** had a schoolhouse with summer sessions. Rural teachers often taught these four-month summer terms and then were hired for an eight-month winter term in another community. When Herb Ashley and others in the community were choosing a name for their post office, they wanted one that would be listed first in the "National Directory of Post Offices" and they succeeded with **Abe**.

ABSAROKEE (Stillwater), (pronounced Ab-SOR-kee), is fourteen miles south of Columbus. The town and the Absaroka Mountains bear an Indian name by which the Crows were originally known. Shane says, "The Crows are of Siouxan origin and were once part of the Hidatsa tribe around the Great Lakes. . . . In the Hidatsa tongue, the Crows were called *Absarokee* from the words *absa*, meaning "large-beaked bird", and *rokee*, meaning "children" or "off-spring." In the sign language, they were represented by the flapping of the arms like wings, interpreted as the raven — or crows." **Absarokee** was originally on Indian Reservation land. Its post office was established December 16, 1892, with Sever Simonsen as first postmaster.

Absher (Musselshell) was named for the first postmaster, Jacob Absher. The post office was active from 1910-1949.

Abundance (Yellowstone County), near Shepherd, had a post office from 1918-1919 with Nellie Furlong as postmaster.

Accola (Gallatin) was named for Louis Accola, a farmer who arrived there in 1887; he owned the land through which the Milwaukee Railroad ran a branch line.

Acorn (Rosebud), north of Forsyth, had a post office May-October 1903 with Jessie Franklin in charge.

ACTON (Yellowstone) is sixteen miles northwest of Billings. Its population was usually listed as 10; but this is cattle country, and the little town and post office served many people in outlying ranches. **Acton** began as a station on the Great Northern and its post office was opened in 1910 with Charles T. Robinson as postmaster.

Acushnet (Fergus) had a post office established in 1915. The settlers who named the town spelled this Indian name "Acuashnut," but the postal department spelled it **Acushnet**. But when the railroad came through, officials would not accept this Indian name for their station and instead called it Ware. Later the post office name was also officially changed to Ware. First postmaster was John Woolhiver.

Ada (Blaine), near Chinook, had a post office 1896-1917, serving farmers and ranchers between the Milk and the Missouri rivers, and providing a stop for the Chinook-Cleveland stage, which ran three times a week. Hart Nash was the first postmaster. In 1908 the office was moved to the Ramberg home, where Nettie Ramberg took care of the post office as well as her twelve children (Allison).

Ada (Rosebud), near Rosebud, had a post office August 1881-November 1882, with Ada B. Parker in charge.

Adams (Dawson) had a post office established 1906. The name was changed to Bloomfield in November 1907.

Adel (Cascade), near Cascade, had a post office 1896-1930. Bessie F. Burch was the first postmaster.

Adobetown (Madison) was located near another mining camp called Nevada City; both were close to Virginia City. The name describes the houses, which were made of dried mud and grass adobe bricks. **Adobetown** was said to be the oldest placer camp in Alder Gulch and it had one of the first schoolhouses in the state. The 1879 census gave its population as 175 whites and 250 Chinese. This was the richest section of the gulch — some $350,000 worth of ore was taken from the Adobetown-Nevada City area. A post office was established in Nevada City in 1865 with Nicholas Carey as postmaster; **Adobetown** took over the office in 1875 with Carey continuing; it was closed in 1907.

Agate (Rosebud), near Forsyth, had a post office February 1911-January 1912 with Frank Schmidt as postmaster.

Agawam (Teton), a few miles north of Choteau, was named after Agawam, Massachusetts. The Montana town was the terminus of the railroad in a land with great agricultural potential. A post office with George Boyd in charge was opened in 1913; it closed in 1956.

Agency (Lake) was an Indian agency when the post office was established in 1872 with George Mason as postmaster. It was discontinued in 1874.

Ahles (Rosebud), near Vananda, had a post office 1917-1920 with Peter Barthel as postmaster.

Ainslie (Custer), near Miles City, had a post office 1882-1883 with Silvanus Miner as postmaster. The office was open again from 1890-1893.

Ajerton (Valley), near Lustre, was named for postmaster Julius Ager, who served for the two years the office was open: 1918-20.

Alamo (Beaverhead), near Wisdom, had a post office 1889-1894. Mary Butch was the first postmaster.

ALBERTON (Mineral) is a railroad man's town. It seems to have been named for the Alberts family, who came from Canada in the late 1870s and settled at Frenchtown. They homesteaded the area when Indian trails were the only roads.

Albion (Carter) is in the extreme southeast corner of the state. This isolated community along the Little Missouri River had a post office

1914-64. Charles Crawford was the first postmaster.

Albright (Cascade) had a post office from 1898-1916. Presumably it was named for the first postmaster, William Albright.

Albright (Rosebud) was originally called Rosebud; the name was changed when William Albright became postmaster in 1884. The office was active until 1892.

ALDER (Madison) takes its name from the creek named by Henry Edgar in 1863. **Alder** was the terminus of a branch line of the Northern Pacific and served as a shipping point for Virginia City ore, livestock and farm produce from the Ruby Valley. The Confrey Placer Mining Company, which was operating an extensive dredging project, was influential in getting the railroad into **Alder** in 1901. Now tons of talc ore are loaded onto Burlington Northern trains and shipped to all parts of the world. The post office was established in 1902 with Orrin Wilcomb in charge.

Alder Gulch (Madison) contained some of Montana's richest placer deposits. Six prospectors led by Bill Fairweather struck gold here and started the stampede that was to make nearby Virginia City a boom town and a territorial capital. Henry Edgar, who was with Fairweather, wrote in his journal, "We were tired and hungry and all out of provisions . . . our supper consisted of antelope straight . . . 'What shall we call the gulch?' I asked. 'You name it,' Barney Hughes said. So I called it **Alder Gulch** on account of the heavy clump of alders along the creek." That was in May 1863 and before long small communities had sprung up all along the gulch; up the gulch from Virginia City were Beartown, Highland, Pine Grove, and Summit; down the gulch were Elkhorn, Central City, Nevada City, Slater's Bar, German Bar, Idaho Bar, Adobetown and Junction.

Aldridge (Park), on the upper Yellowstone River, was a little mining town which, like so many others, was short-lived. There was a post office from 1896-1910 with Frank Buttrey the first postmaster. The town was named for W. H. Aldridge, the director of the Montana Coal and Coke Company and later, manager of the smelter in Helena.

"**Aldridge** was born in 1896 on a blanket of coal. . . . In time there arose a post office, a school, several stores, boarding houses, and saloons. Within months 800 people were living in **Aldridge**. As it came into being it stretched and yawned, then shriveled and died. Fifteen years was its lifetime in the moments of eternity" (Bill and Doris Whithorn, *Photo History of Aldridge*).

Alger (Fergus) had a post office 1889-98. Rose Weldon was postmaster.

Alger (Sanders) was originally called Beaver. The name was changed when Henry Cullom took over as postmaster in 1914. The office closed in 1933.

Alhambra (Jefferson), near Helena, was part of the community that grew up around a natural hot springs that was developed into a resort. Wilson Redding was appointed postmaster when the office opened in 1885; it was discontinued in 1947. At various times the area post offices were known as Prickly Pear, **Alhambra**, and Clancy or Clancey.

Alice (Beaverhead), near Armstead, had a post office 1895-1899 (Horace McIntyre, postmaster).

Alice (Garfield) was named for the first postmaster Alice Hall. When the office was first established in 1914, the people of the community took turns going to Sand Springs once a week to bring the mail. The office was closed in 1934.

Alkali (Phillips), near the town of Phillips, was named for the type of soil predominant in the area. The post office was open 1915-1921 (Pearl Sabin, postmaster).

Allard, (Dawson), near Glendive, was named for a civil engineer who was accidentally shot on April 1, 1881, in a construction camp near the mouth of the Powder River. The post office, under E. L. Sperry, opened in 1884 and was active off-and-on until 1927.

Allen (Garfield) was named for postmaster John D. Allen and the office was active 1914-20.

Allen (Silver Bow) had a post office 1900-01 with Ronald Campbell as postmaster.

Allendale (Yellowstone) was named for Dr. W. A. Allen, who laid out the townsite.

Allerdice (Beaverhead) had a post office 1881-89 (L. Eugene Simmons, postmaster), when the name was changed to Lima.

Alma (Liberty) had a post office 1902-35. John Schauer was first postmaster. Its country store and post office served many homesteaders who settled north of Joplin.

Almberg (Rosebud) had a post office established in 1922 with Marie Nelson in charge. Later the name was changed to Rim Rocks and still later to Davidell.

Aloe (Toole) was formerly called Rimvale, according to postal records. The post office opened in 1913 under Frank Froemke and was discontinued in 1935.

Alpine (Carbon), in the Beartooth Mountains, is west of Red Lodge. Except for the years 1943-45 the office was open 1914-53. Christina Branger was the first postmaster; her family ran a hotel there for a long time. The head of the Branger family came from Switzerland and chose this name for a place on the shores of East Rosebud Lake in one of Montana's most rugged mountain canyons. A star route now serves summer home residents.

Alpine (Fergus) had a post office 1885-1904. Anna Coder was the first postmaster.

Alta (Jefferson) had a post office 1890-96. James E. Bush was the first postmaster.

Alta (Ravalli) had a post office 1898-1940. Charlie Stearns was the first postmaster. Early-day residents say the name came from the high altitude there.

"A one-room log cabin with a dirt roof and a dirt floor, located at **Alta** at the southern tip of the Bitterroot National Forest was the first ranger station constructed in the United States. It was built by two pioneering rangers, Thad Wilkerson and Hank Tuttle, in 1899. Wilkerson's journal records the fact that the homesteaders accepted Gifford Pinchot's idea of a Forest Service, but there was no organization of any kind at this early date. 'We didn't receive any instructions about anything much, so we did about as we pleased, and we built the **Alta** cabin on our own initiative. We paid for the nails, the hinges, for the door that we made, the four-paned window, and the U.S. flag we put on the tip of a twenty-foot lodgepole to float over our cabin on the Fourth of July, 1899. . . . We went down into our pockets for every cent and we never got any of it back. . . . Uncle Sam wasn't puttin' out a cent for a pair of hillbilly rangers to live while they took care of his woods.' " (Lois Kaiser, Stevensville High School) Now the **Alta** station is listed in the National Register of Historic Places and a sign identifies it as "The First Forest Service Building in the United States."

The site of **Alta** was known in early days as Hogum Junction. It was a flat at the junction of two creeks and a favorite overnight camping place for travelers between Montana and Idaho. After the discovery of gold on Hughes Creek, several cabins were built in the area. The creek was named for Barney Hughes, who claimed it was he who had discovered gold there. As many as a hundred men at a time were employed at the Hughes Creek mines, and it was estimated that a half million dollars worth of gold was taken from them.

Alton (Fergus), near Denton, had a post office 1909-16. George D. Dyer was first postmaster.

Altyn (Glacier) was established during the mineral boom on the ceded strip. Now only a few traces remain. The location is at the head of Sherburne Lake in Glacier National Park, very close to the Many Glacier Hotel (Jack Hayne).

Altyn (Teton), near Swift Current, had a post office 1900-06 with James Harris as first postmaster.

ALZADA (Carter) is almost on the Wyoming border in the southeast corner of the state. **Alzada** was originally called Stoneville, and a post office under that name was established in 1880. It was named for Lou Stone, who kept a saloon there 1877-78 during the time Gen. Nelson A. Miles was building a telegraph line from Fort Keogh (Miles City) to Fort Meade, South Dakota. The Stoneville station was a rock-covered dugout at the top of the hill. But because there was another Montana town with a similar name (possibly Stone's Station), there was some confusion with the mail, so the town was renamed in honor of Mrs. Alzada Sheldon, wife of a pioneer rancher who had come to the area in 1883. According to postal records, the name was changed in 1885.

Amazon (Jefferson) was first granted a post office in 1888 when John Currin was appointed postmaster. It was active then most of the time until 1931.

American Fork (Deer Lodge) developed at the mouth of a creek first known as Benetsee and then as Gold Creek. The first gold discovery in Montana was in this area, and people flocked in to settle and pan for gold. There were about sixty people in **American Fork** during the summer of 1862, "but only hope kept the settlement alive as there was no bonanza" (Toole). Granville Stuart reported in his journal that on ". . . July 14, 1862, we held an election. Great excitement, but nobody hurt except from an overdose of whiskey."

Amesville (Beaverhead), on Horse Prairie, was named for Dr. Azel Ames, who came to Montana from Massachussetts. **Amesville** had a post office 1884-97. Nancy Burnett was the first postmaster. After 1899 the post office was called Grant.

Amherst (Fergus) was named by C. A. Goodnow after his home town in Massachusetts.

Amos (Hill), about twenty miles northwest of Havre, had a post office from 1911-19. Amos Hardin was the first postmaster. A community — including a store and a dancehall — grew up around the office.

Amsterdam (Gallatin) was named by a group of Hollanders who settled there. It is still a thriving community of farmers who continue to use the customs of the old country. They get their mail at Manhattan (see **Holland Settlement** and **Churchill**).

ANACONDA (Deer Lodge) The name "Anaconda" has become a giant not only in Montana mining circles, but far beyond the state's borders. Not only the town, but also the mining company uses it. The story of the origin of the name — which stems from the word for a large, South American snake — is as interesting as the evolution of a mine into a company and finally a town.

Michael Hickey, an adventurous Irish miner and Union Army veteran, had read an editorial by Horace Greeley in the New York *Tribune* stating that Grant's army was "encircling Lee's forces like a giant anaconda." Years later, at Copper Camp, Hickey recalled, "That word struck me as a mighty good one. I always remembered it, and when I wanted a name for my mine, I remembered Greeley's editorial and called it the 'Anaconda.' " Hickey's famous property, discovered in 1882, led to one of Butte's richest copper veins, and later gave its name to the largest copper mining, smelting and fabricating organization in the world: the Anaconda Copper Mining Company.

The town of **Anaconda** is in the mouth of a narrow valley near the Continental Divide. When copper is in demand, both smelter and town prosper; but when the mines are quiet, so is **Anaconda**.

The company was started by Marcus Daly — the Copper King — who personally picked this spot for the smelter because it was near ample water and limestone. The story goes that Daly pointed out a cow grazing in the valley and said he wanted Main Street to run north and south right through the cow (*Copper Camp*). The city, platted in 1883, was first called Copperopolis, but when postmaster Clinton H. Moore learned of a Copperopolis already existing in Meagher County, he thought of the important mine in Butte and named the new city for it. The post office was also established in 1883.

Anad (Garfield) had a post office 1918-1930. M. C. Farrington was the first postmaster.

Anceney (Gallatin) is now a very small settlement and a railroad siding. It was named for Charles Leon Anxionnaz, a Frenchman who came to the United States and the Gallatin Valley to become a major landowner and prominent cattleman. Anxionnaz got involved in local politics, but friends could neither spell nor pronounce his name, so it was anglicized to "Anceney." He and his son, Charles L. Jr., obtained financing from H. W. Child of the Yellowstone Park Company to buy an additional 80,000 acres to start the Flying D Ranch. With 100,000 acres of deeded land and some 400,000 of leased land, their spread ran from the Gallatin River to the Madison. It was one of Montana's early-day cattle empires (*Pioneer Trails and Trials*).

Anderson (Silver Bow) had a post office 1896-1897 with William McKeevir in charge.

Andersonville (Meagher) is a ghost town near Lewistown. It was named for "Skookum" Joe Anderson, one of the discoverers of gold in the area. According to George Mueller, who has done extensive research on the subject, Anderson was not a half-breed as so often claimed, but a Canadian born of Norwegian parents who received his nickname from living with the Chinook Indians in western Washington. **Andersonville** had a brief revival when workers from an Air Force radar base lived there.

Andes (Richland) had a post office 1914-54. It was named for Samuel M. Andes, a lay minister with the Church of Latter Day Saints who dreamed of establishing a town for Mormons here. He built a home, a barn, a blacksmith shop, and later a church and schoolhouse; he was the first postmaster in an office in a corner of the sod blacksmith shop. Mail was brought in from Culbertson. The first school for the homesteaders' children was held in the granary on Harvey Neal's farm. The devastating hail storm of 1921 and the blowing dust of the "Dirty Thirties" — when only thistles thrived — discouraged most homesteaders, and they moved out so "a once up and coming community is now only a memory" (*Courage Enough*).

Andeville (Fergus) was named for the family of Mary Anderson, who was postmaster for the duration of the office April 1916-November 1918.

ANGELA (Rosebud), northwest of Miles City, is a crossroads post office established in 1913 (John Garvin, postmaster) with a store and a gas station serving a surrounding countryside that is harshly carpeted with cactus and low sagebrush.

Annis (Lewis and Clark), near Stemple Pass, had a post office 1916-17 with Frank Aagaard in charge.

Anslow (Rosebud) was granted a post office in 1918 with Anna E. Nelson to be postmaster; there is no further record of it.

Antelope (Rosebud) had a post office 1898-1902 with William Burton as postmaster.

ANTELOPE (Sheridan) is in extreme northeastern Montana twenty miles from Canada and the North Dakota line. The town and the stream were named for the graceful animal native to the area; large herds of antelope used to water at the stream. The earliest settlers at the present site of **Antelope** were the Richardson brothers, the Folsoms, Hedges, and Ators. The town was incorporated in 1913, three years after it had been granted a post office, and once had a population of 360. In 1967 a U.S. Navy gunboat was christened the "Antelope." Crew members came to visit **Antelope**, and in turn, twenty-eight citizens of **Antelope** went to Tacoma, Washington, to see the boat commissioned (David Friedrick, Antelope High School).

Antrim (Garfield), near Bruce, had a post office 1912-16, and was named for the homesteading family of Kirk and Nellie Antrim. The first postmaster was Thomas Antrim. The office was discontinued in 1916.

Apex (Beaverhead) had a post office off-and-on 1886-1925. James Haining was the first postmaster. The town was a station on the old Oregon Short Line Railroad, and got its name because it was located on the Divide between the Beaverhead and Big Hole Basins.

Apgar (Flathead) is in Glacier National Park at the lower end of Lake McDonald and two miles from the West Glacier entrance. Jessie Apgar was the first postmaster and the town was named for her family. This Flathead County post office was open 1913-30 and again 1942-44. In 1895 Dimon Apgar and others cut a road from Belton through heavy forests to Lake McDonald and homesteaded there.

Archer (Sheridan) had a post office 1914-57. It was named for William Archer, a homesteader, who arrived with many others after the coming of the railroad. James Michaels had a store and was the first postmaster. In addition to Michaels' store, there were two elevators, a section house, a depot, a school and a Lutheran Church.

Ardrum (Missoula) had a post office 1882-83 with C. C. O'Keefe as postmaster.

Argenta (Beaverhead) is a mining ghost town thirteen miles from Dillon originally called Montana City. It was chartered in 1865 and laid out at the mouth of Rattlesnake Canyon on the south side of the creek. In the 1860s the town flourished because of gold placers and silver quartz lodes and the name was changed to **Argenta** to emphasize its silver ore. The population was once listed at 1,500, but by 1874 the camp was nearly deserted, though a few settlers continued to live in the area. In 1882 a snowslide five miles above the town buried the entire Taggart family. The seven bodies were recovered in March and dragged into camp on rawhides. Mining claims were located on Watson and French creeks near **Argenta** (Wolle). The post office was established in 1871 with George French as postmaster; Elizabeth French served in the job soon after. The office was discontinued in 1904, but re-opened in 1906 and continued to serve the few remaining patrons until 1935.

Argo (Broadwater) had a post office 1907-10 (John Ryan in charge).

Arklow (see **Cataract**).

ARLEE (Lake) was named for Alee, a Salish chief. The spelling "'Arlee" is peculiar to English; the Indian word, which means"red night," has no "r." The town and post office (est. 1885) serve as a trading center for people of the Jocko Valley and Flathead Indian Reservation.

Charlo, chief of the Flatheads, refused to move to the reservation in conformance with the treaty of 1855 at Grass Valley. But some of the Indians decided to go despite Charlo's decree, and they chose Alee as leader.

Armells (Fergus) was named after Armells Creek, a stream which the Milwaukee Railroad followed through the area. A post office operated 1890-1891 under James Fergus and was open again 1899-1937. Fergus and his family located on Armells Creek in 1880 on the route of the old stage line which ran from Fort Maginnis to Rocky Point.

Armington (Cascade), near Belt, is a coal miner's town named for Jerould "Doc" Armington, on whose ranch property the little settlement was built. The post office was established in 1890 (William MacQueen postmaster) and closed in 1957. **Armington** was once the end of the railroad, where freighters with their wagons lined up to get groceries and supplies for Judith Basin settlers.

Armstead (Beaverhead), near Dillon, is in the country explored by Lewis and Clark. Lewis called the valley as he approached it, ". . . one of the handsomest coves I ever saw." It was there that he met a "lone Indian rider," a Shoshone, and it was the hope of the explorers that these friendly Indians could show them the route to the Pacific. The town was named for Harry Armstead, a miner who developed the Silver Fissure Mine at Polaris. In 1907 a survey was begun for the Gilmore and Pittsburg Railroad and this little railroad operated for thirty years. Many buildings were moved away before the Clark Canyon Dam flooded the area and put the site of **Armstead** under water. The post office was active 1907-62; Carl Decker was the first postmaster.

Arnold (Gallatin) is a railroad sidetrack and settlement named for George O. Arnold, a rancher.

Arp (Carter) was named for postmaster Charlie Arp when the office was established in 1909. It was discontinued in 1936, and the mail was ordered to Camp Crook, South Dakota.

Arrow (Judith Basin), near Geyser, had a post office 1905-09. It was named because of the many arrowheads found there.

Arrow Creek (Judith Basin) is located on a bench west of Coffee Creek and fifteen miles north of Stanford. Some stockmen settled there as early as the 1880s but most homesteaders came between 1907-10. The basis of the economy changed from livestock to grain, but many farmers had to move out following a severe drought in 1919. Those who stayed had larger holdings and managed to survive the dry years because they were balanced by years of bumper crops. In 1927 everyone pitched in and built the community hall. Huge petrified snails were found when a railroad tunnel was excavated here. The post office operated 1914-20. Charles Malone was first postmaster (Byerly and Byerly).

Arthur (Richland) was no doubt named for its first postmaster, Arthur O. Davis. The office was active 1911-15.

Ashdale (Sherdian) was a post office 1912-14 with James Lossing as postmaster. After that the mail was sent to Redstone.

Ashfield (Valley) had a post office 1903-08. Nathan A. Roch was the first postmaster.

ASHLAND (Rosebud) is on the Tongue River at the mouth of Otter Creek. The post office was established under this name in 1886; previously it had been called Birney and Strader. **Ashland** is division headquarters for the Custer National Forest, and it's possible the name comes from the abundance of ash trees. The town is a trade center for a group of cattle ranchers and for Indians from the Northern Cheyenne Reservation. St. Labre Mission is in **Ashland**.

Ashley (Flathead) was adjacent to present-day Kalispell. It had a post office 1884-91. Andrew Swaney was first postmaster. The town was named for Joe Ashley, the first settler in the upper Flathead (about 1857), and a trader who worked for Angus McDonald. A creek and a lake also bear his name. Though Ashley staked out a claim, he saw no future in the Flathead Valley and sold his claim for ten dollars. The town was promoted by Steve Lenneau, who located on Ashley Creek.

Ashley (Petroleum) was named for Eben L. Ashley, who homesteaded there. The post office was active from 1913-21 with Sadie Ashley as the first postmaster.

Ashmoor (Chouteau) had a post office 1913-27 with John Erickson as first postmaster.

Ashmore (Mineral) was a station on the Milwaukee.

Ashuelot (Teton) was a settlement named for a resident's home town of Ashuelot, Vermont.

Athlone (Toole), a station on the Great Northern, was abandoned by the railroad in 1925. The nearest post office was Galata.

Atina (Yellowstone), near Ballantine, had a post office for less than a year 1920-21. George Klein was postmaster.

Atkins (Gallatin) is a crossroads settlement named for a local farmer.

Atlanta (Flathead) had a post office 1903-05 with John Hibbard as postmaster.

Auburn (Fergus) had a post office 1913-34. Lizzie Williams was the postmaster.

AUGUSTA (Lewis and Clark), north of Helena, was named for the daughter of pioneer rancher J. D. Hogan, who also managed the holdings of Conrad Kohrs. The town was incorporated in 1883 and a post office was established the following year with Phil A. Manix in charge. **Augusta**'s place as a shopping and banking center area was briefly challenged by a new town, Gilman, which grew up around the railroad; the Great Northern bypassed **Augusta** and built its 1912 station a few miles to the north. But by 1942 this upstart town had faded, and **Augusta** was once more the school, shopping and banking center for the surrounding ranch area.

Aurora (Beaverhead) had a post office 1907-08 with M. Engelsgjerd as postmaster. Did some eager prospector or settler see this place as the Goddess of Dawn? or as bright and radiant? or did he simply come from the Illinois town by the same name?

Austin (Lewis and Clark) was a flag station on the Northern Pacific north of Helena near the once populous and prosperous placer camp known as Greenhorn. According to postal records, Peter Tostevin was appointed postmaster when the post office opened in 1901 in a place formerly known as Butler. The office closed in 1967.

Avery (Chouteau) had a post office 1903-09 except for a few months in 1908. Robert F. Murray was the first postmaster.

AVON (Powell), thirty-two miles from Helena, is a supply point where cattle and sheep ranchers rub elbows with prospectors and miners. It was named by a local Welchman. *Avon* means "river" in Welsh, and the river in this valley reminded him of his homeland. The post office under William Cramer opened in 1884.

Avondale (Valley), "Forty-five miles N. of Milk River and 4 miles NE of Snow Coulee Creek," according to the post office application, had an office 1915-35. In 1912 Atle Taerum came to Montana, found a place he liked, stayed, filed on some land, built a store and applied for a post office — he was the first man to maintain it. Taerum refused to allow his own name considered in a list of possible names for the settlement, and people decided to call it **Avondale**. Taerum built an addition onto the front of his store for the post office. Homesteaders came, the town boomed, and Bennie Sather brought the mail in from Baylor fifteen miles away. But then came drought and the Depression; the town faded as one by one homesteaders were starved out and left.

Axtell (Dawson) was named for its first postmaster, Charley Axtell. It had an active office 1912-17.

Aznoe (Chouteau) was named for Walter and Myron Aznoe. The post office was located on their homestead and Walter served as postmaster when the office opened in 1913; it closed in 1935.

B

BABB (Glacier) was named for C. C. Babb, district engineer in charge of the St. Mary's Irrigation Project. It has had a post office since 1905. Cicero Bristol was the first postmaster.

"By an Act of Congress, May 1, 1907, provision was made for a survey for the Blackfeet Reservation. By 1912, 2,750 allotments were made to Indians and sites were reserved for the towns of **Babb** and Browning" (Shane). The town now consists of a few houses, some tourist cabins, a general store and a post office. **Babb** is at the edge of Glacier Park, and in 1912 it became the headquarters for the Reclamation Service Project that diverted water from St. Mary's River (which drains into Hudson Bay) across the Hudson Bay Divide to the Milk River.

Bad Rock Canyon. In his memoirs Daniel Mumbrue (1867-1947) describes a treacherous "bad rock" in a channel at the junction of two great branches of the Flathead River; any boat floating with the current from either channel is naturally swept against this sharp, knife-like rock. And for anyone unfamiliar with the river, the rock cannot be seen in time to avoid it. The Sheldon expedition of 1885 was wrecked on this rock, as was another expedition that same year. The canyon is named for the rock. The Montana Historical Marker at Bad Rock Canyon on US Highway 2, two miles east of Columbia Falls, relates the story of an Indian attack, no date given, and suggests it was from this skirmish that the canyon was named.

Baeth (Phillips) was named for postmaster Henry Baeth when the office opened in 1902. In 1915 someone must have decided that the place needed a more attractive name and chose Goodsoil. Postal authorities at first accepted, then rescinded approval of that name; eventually the name Content was approved.

Bagdad (Madison) was a mining camp that grew up in the early 1860s in Bivens Gulch when the Ramshorn Mining Company was operating. It was about eight miles up the gulch from where the Bivens Road joins the Vigilante Trail. Gold nuggets valued at $1,000-$1,200 were found there. Residents got their mail at Cicero (*Pioneer Trails and Trials*).

BAINVILLE (Roosevelt) was named for postmaster Charles Bain when the office opened in 1904. Postal records state that the community had formerly been known as Kenneth.

Baird (Missoula) had a post office established in 1899 with Jacob Marsellis as postmaster; it was discontinued in 1934.

BAKER (Fallon), a county seat, was named for A. G. Baker, the construction engineer for the main line of the Milwaukee Railroad in eastern

Montana. It was first called Lorraine, but renamed in 1908 when the post office opened with Robert Pearce in charge. The town began as a camping place on the Custer Trail between Wibaux and Camp Cook, South Dakota, because surface springs and grass were abundant there; wagon ruts of the old trail are still visible near town. **Baker**, quietly serving as a market town for the grazing and farm area around it, boomed in 1915 when a driller seeking water for a well found natural gas. The well ignited and was a natural torch for six years. Many wells in the vicinity later produced oil in commercially important quantities.

Baker (Gallatin) was a post office name 1890-96. The name was later changed to Highlands and still later to Josephine.

Bald Butte (Lewis and Clark), near Marysville, was a mining camp with a post office 1891-1906; John Braun was the first postmaster.

Baldwin (Fergus) had a post office established in 1897 and named for postmaster Edward Baldwin. It closed in 1904.

BALLANTINE (Yellowstone) is northeast of Billings. It was started as a railroad station with the post office opening in 1907 under Lewis Chilson.

Balmont (Yellowstone) was formerly called Ballantine, after E. P. Ballantine, a farmer who settled here in 1905. The name was changed to **Balmont** (compounded from **Bal**lantine and **Mont**ana) when it was found there was a station on the Great Northern Railroad already named Ballantine.

Baltic (Teton) is an abandoned station on the Great Northern. The nearest post office is at Cut Bank.

Bannack (Beaverhead), near Dillon, is a mining ghost town rich in history. The town was named for the Bannack Indians who occupied this area before the white men came. A post office was established in 1863, but the name on the postal records was spelled Bannock until officially changed in 1898. The post office was discontinued in 1938.

While the Gold Creek diggings were being activated, large parties of Colorado prospectors bound for Idaho turned toward the Deer Lodge Valley when they learned that Idaho gold camps were being overrun by Californians; some went on to the Beaverhead River. On Willard's Creek (also called Grasshopper Creek), a tributary of the Beaverhead, William Eads made the first really big Montana strike on July 28, 1862, and **Bannack** sprang up overnight. Many of the gold-seekers were men who had left the East to escape the raging Civil War, but its echoes followed them; Confederate sympathizers named one gulch Jeff Davis Gulch, and **Bannack**'s residential district became Yankee Flats.

Henry Plummer was appointed sheriff of **Bannack**. He and his gang of highwaymen began their infamous operations in 1863 along the ninety-mile stretch of wagon trail between Alder Gulch and **Bannack**. They robbed stagecoaches of gold and killed more than a hundred men during their reign of terror. **Bannack** was the first capital of the Territory of Montana, and the largest city (pop. 8,000) in the new territory when it was separated from Idaho Territory in 1864.

In 1953 much of the **Bannack** townsite was bought at auction by C. W. Stallings, who donated it to the state. On August 15, 1954, **Bannack** was dedicated as a state park (Western Interpretive Services).

Barber (Golden Valley) was a crossroads hamlet along the Mussellshell

River. In 1920 **Barber** had a bank, hotel, general store, implement store, post office and a Lutheran church. The post office opened in 1910 with Nels Eklund as postmaster. Eklund and Henry Bartz, operating as the Minnesota-Montana Land Company, founded the town and encouraged other Midwesterners to come settle there. The railroad depot and post office originally serving this community were located on Elmer Crawford's ranch. Railroad officials wanted to buy more land, but the owner refused to sell, so the officials loaded the depot on a flatcar and moved it eight miles west, calling the new station Shawmut; the original Shawmut station was left with only a boxcar along the tracks. Someone quipped that they "had been given a clean shave and should change the name to **Barber** — and so they did. Years of hail and drought discouraged the homesteaders and one by one they moved away. Only one man stayed — he kept the store going for forty years. By 1978 only the little church was still in use.

Barcon (Deer Lodge) had a post office granted in January 1886 with Jacob Whitmire appointed postmaster. In April of that year the name was changed to Blossburg.

Barford (Valley) existed as a post office September 1910-September 1911 with Henry Downey as postmaster; at that time the Homestead post office was reopened to serve the area. The first name put on the boxcar depot was *Barford* because it was near where the N Bar N Cattle Company forded the Big Muddy. For a while the settlement was called Pederson because Peder Pederson was the first businessman there and at one time the postmaster. Then it was called Fort Peck, but that only caused confusion, so citizens settled on the name Homestead; this tiny, rural village near the North Dakota line has a long naming history.

Barker (Judith Basin), near Stanford, is a mining ghost town. In 1879 Patrick Hughes and E. A. "Buck" Barker made the first discovery of metals in the Little Belt Mountains. Barker was a colorful and well-known character, so the camp came to be known by his name, though the post office that served the camp was first called Clendenin. Gold Run, Galena, Meagher City, and Hughes City (later Hughesville) became rival camps. The first ore mined here was packed over the Kibbey Divide and on to Fort Benton, then shipped downriver to New Orleans and thence to a smelter in Wales. As new veins were located, two smelters were built, and the railroad built a line out from Great Falls. In 1893, **Barker** was considered the greatest transportation point in the Judith Basin. Soon afterwards, however, silver slumped, the railroad station closed for lack of business, and the death knell sounded for **Barker** as a town. **Barker** had established a post office in 1892 and maintained it until 1903.

Barkerville (Meagher) was named for "Buck" Barker, miner and prospector, who also had another camp named for him. This one had a post office March-June 1881. Frank Bucksen was postmaster.

Barley (Stillwater) was named for Lloyd Barley, the first postmaster. The post office was active 1911-1919. It was near Rapelje.

Barnard (Valley) was granted a post office in 1912 and Sidney Barnard was appointed postmaster; the office closed in 1933.

Barott, Barrotts (Golden Valley) was named for postmaster Luther Barott. The office was open 1885-1900.

Barr (Valley) was named for Isabel Barr, appointed postmaster when the office opened in 1903. When "Brother" Riggin retired from his work at the Epworth Piegan Indian Mission in 1912, he lived with his son Harry at **Barr** near the Canadian border, forty miles from the nearest railroad, so "the old soldier of the church ended his days again doing pioneer work, preaching some, marrying and baptizing when the occasion arose" (*When Wagon Trails Were Dim*). **Barr**'s post office was closed in 1934.

Barrial (Prairie) had a post office 1917-40. Anneta Vineyard was the first postmaster.

Barrows (Judith Basin), a station on the Great Northern, was named for Mrs. Alice Barrows, who lived about two miles from here at the old Ubet stage station.

Barzee (Meagher) had a post office 1920-33, and was named for the brand (the Bar-Z) of a cattle outfit there. Margaret Dreibelbis was the first postmaster.

Bascom (Rosebud) began as a station on the Milwaukee Railroad. Alex Holman was postmaster when the office opened in 1910; it was discontinued in 1936. **Bascom**, in its prime, consisted of four buildings: the railroad station, the one-room school, the combination store and post office, and the storekeeper's home.

BASIN (Jefferson), in the Boulder River Basin, was founded in 1880 by two miners named Lawson and Allport. The post office opened that year, too, with Julius Martin in charge. A small settlement called Cataract pre-dated **Basin**, when prospectors found gold there in 1862. Important mines were working and sending ore to Butte by 1880 and Lawson and Allport started a trading center. Most of the buildings are frame with the second-story false fronts which were common to nineteenth century camps. Most of the mining has ceased now, but the area is known for its radon mines, which are reputed to have healthful qualities.

Basinski (Custer), near Sabra, had a post office December 1888-July 1898. It was formerly called Younger. Monfort Bray was the first **Basinski** postmaster.

Battleson (Daniels) was granted a post office in 1916 and was no doubt named for the first postmaster, Benjamin Battleson. In 1926 the name was changed to Peerless.

Battrick (Fergus) was named for its first postmaster, Ellsworth Battrick, when the office opened in 1915; it was discontinued in 1929.

Batzel (Carter), near Ridgway, had a post office 1918-33; Leo Mitchell was the first postmaster.

Baxendale (Lewis and Clark) had a post office 1891-95. John Roy was first postmaster.

Baxter (Fergus) was named for the Baxter Ranch.

Bay Horse (Powder River) was named for a creek of that name which was so called because of a bay stallion who was the leader of a band of wild horses that ranged the area in the early days. The post office opened in 1917 under Perry Murphy; it was discontinued in 1955.

Baylor (Valley) had a post office 1911-43. Hopeful homesteaders petitioned for a post office and started a community. By 1933 the drought and the grasshoppers had devastated their crops and their hopes. Many moved away. The farms of those who stayed were saved by the rains that came in the late 1930s. **Baylor**'s first postmaster was Katherine Henderson.

Beach (Flathead) almost had a post office. One was approved and William Beach was appointed postmaster in November 1899, but the order was rescinded in March of 1900.

Bean (Carbon) was named for postmaster Jordon Bean when the office opened in 1894. The "office" was an apple box in his homestead cabin until it was discontinued in 1900. **Bean** was located on the southwest side of the Pryor Mountains near Piney Creek.

BEARCREEK (Carbon), east of Red Lodge, was named for the many bears that came along after berries — and sometimes are still seen in town along the creek. The town was founded 1905-1906 on the wealth of vast coal deposits beneath it. The Brophy Mine, International, Bearcreek, Foster, and Smith were the big mines in this area. A post office with Sarah Criger in charge was opened in November 1905. The Montana, Wyoming, and Southern Railroad, built in 1906, carried a hundred carloads of coal a day from the valley. **Bearcreek** declined in the late 1930s and early '40s as diesel and gasoline replaced coal as a primary fuel. A devastating explosion at the Smith Mine on February 27, 1943, killed 74 men in the first blast; others died from exposure and poisonous gas doing rescue work. After that tragedy, an exodus from **Bearcreek** left it almost a ghost town. A revival started in 1964 promises to at least partially restore this once-booming coal mining town. The **Bearcreek** *Banner*, published bi-monthly by the late Fay Kuhlman, predicted that **Bearcreek**'s comeback will be as an integral part in an area that is the heart of Montana's vacation land.

BEARMOUTH, BEAR'S MOUTH (Granite) began when a miner named John Lannen came to the country. Lannen traded his Helena claim for a cow, moved to the mouth of Bear Gulch with his wife and family in 1866, and ran a ferry across the river for travelers on the Mullan Road. The community became a stage stop and later a station on the Northern Pacific. There are two ideas on how the town got its name: one is that the physical features of the gulch resemble a bear's mouth; the other is that it was named because of incidents with the numerous bears in the mountains nearby — or was it just because the stage stop was conveniently located at the mouth of Bear Gulch? Except for a few months, the post office was in continuous operation 1875-1949.

Bearpaw, Bear Paw (Blaine) had a post office 1914-28, but the name "Bear Paw" was a part of Montana history long before that. The mountains were originally called the Bear's Paw. The town was named for the mountains, and they were named because "the mountains from their summit looked like a huge bear's paw spread out on the prairie." (*Adventure Trails in Montana*). A monument now marks the place where Chief Joseph of the Nez Perce Indians surrendered to Gen. Nelson A. Miles on October 5, 1877, after the six-day siege known as the Battle of the Bear's Paw. This area was the scene of a gold rush in 1888. Prospectors had been working here for years, but in that year the portion of the Indian land that was opened to whites brought miners stampeding to the area. The name was also given to a big cattle pool of the early days. When settlers and farmers came into the Judith Basin, the cattlemen there moved their 70,000 head across the Missouri into the Milk River and Bear Paw Mountain country; they reorganized the old Judith Basin Pool and called it the Bear Paw Pool. The mountains are in the southeastern corner of Hill County and extend into both Blaine and Chouteau counties.

Bear Spring(s) (Fergus) was settled in the years following 1909 when homesteaders came to the "lush Bear Springs country that is tucked in between the rugged badlands and breaks." About twenty-five families were there in the early days — one to each 160 acres. By 1970 only some five families were left and the original homesteads had been combined into large ranches. The shift was back to livestock along with grain crops.

Nora Teepell was postmaster when the office opened in 1914; it closed in 1933 as drought and depression reduced the population (Byerly and Byerly).

Bear Tooth. There was never a town by this name, but it is interesting regarding the naming of places. Explorers, plagued by wild bears, saw similarities in the natural features of the country and the animal, and the white limestone cliffs of a mountain range in Carbon County reminded them of a bear's tooth.

Beartown (Deer Lodge) originated in November 1865 when gold was discovered on First Chance Gulch, a tributary of Bear Creek. In a few weeks more than a thousand men were at the diggings. The settlement became **Beartown** and boomed until 1869. During its peak years, only pack trains could travel the rugged canyon (Western Interpretive Services). The post office under James McElroy opened in 1968. It was closed 1873-75 and then active until 1892.

Beatrice (Toole), near Galata in Toole County, had a post office 1898-1918. Susie Turner was the first postmaster.

Beaver (Sanders) was granted a post office in 1907 with Thomas Donlan in charge. The postal name was changed to Alger in 1914.

Beaver Creek, Beavertown (Broadwater), eighteen miles southeast of Helena, was in Jefferson County when its post office was established in 1872. The office was closed in 1876, reestablished in 1878, closed again in 1884, only to be reinstated in 1885. The first postmaster was Thomas Pauley. The town was named for a nearby stream, which in turn had been named for the animals that inhabited it. Beaver and trappers disappeared; the prospectors came, and the town's name kept pace: in 1887 the community moved up to the railroad siding and changed its name to Placer.

Beaverhead County, in the southwestern corner of the state, was organized as one of the original territorial counties on February 2, 1865. It was named for the rock which Sacajawea pointed out to Lewis and Clark, explaining that her people had called it that because it resembled a beaver's head. It was one of the smallest of the original counties, but is now one of the largest. **Beaverhead County** maintained its original area throughout all the county dividing, and the only change in its borders was made by an annexation of a part of Madison County in 1911. It contains Montana's oldest town, Bannack City, where a post office was established in November 1863. Dillon is the county seat.

Beaver Head Rock (Madison) is twelve miles south of Twin Bridges and eighteen miles north of Dillon near the line between Beaverhead and Madison counties.

From the journal of Capt. Meriwether Lewis, August 8, 1805: "The Indian woman recognized a high plain to our right which she informed us was not very distant from the summer retreat of her nation on a river beyond the mountains which runs to the west. This hill she says her nation calls the beaver's head from a conceived resemblance of its figure to the head of that animal." Postal records show an office opened in 1869 with Andrew McHesser as postmaster. It was first listed as being in Beaverhead County. The office was discontinued in 1871.

Beaverhill (Wibaux), a railroad station, got its name because of its location on Beaver Creek.

Beaverton (Valley) was one of the towns that sprang up as optimistic homesteaders moved in. Oscar Cutting was the first postmaster, appointed in 1908. By 1944 even the post office had discontinued.

Becket (Fergus) was a station on the Milwaukee between Grass Range and Lewistown. It was granted a post office in 1914 and Octavia Floaten was postmaster; the office closed in 1942.

  Becket is quiet now, but it was once lively with country dances and rodeos. "Fans came from miles around to root for the riders, ropers and bull doggers." Their admission ticket included a barbecue lunch. Dances were held in a barn loft. Ranchers loaded their cattle into railroad cars at **Becket**, bound for Midwest markets. Branding was a big event — often twenty or thirty neighbors came to help and at noon all would sit down to a ranch-style dinner (Byerly and Byerly).

Bedford (Broadwater) This post office was active 1879-95; Garris Johnston was postmaster, and the town was listed as "near Townsend."

  Granville Stuart wrote in his journal, "The infernal rocky road extending nearly to **Bedford** shook us up horribly. We had a good dinner at **Bedford** . . . and saw the abandoned mining town of 'Hog Em' in the distance . . . reached Radersburg about four p.m. by Stagecoach." The community was formerly called Springville. A local flour mill was producing high-qualty flour as early as 1874. A rival mill was built by Gavin Johnson, who also established a store, meat market and blacksmith shop; it was a stopping place for travelers using the ferry. The town's name was changed to **Bedford** for Bedford Maxwell, who with his brother built the Indian Creek Ferry (Western Interpretive Services).

Beebe (Custer) was once a ranch post office in a sparsely settled region between Miles City and Volberg. It was named for Elizabeth Beebe, the first postmaster, who was appointed in 1890; the office closed in 1935.

Beehive (Stillwater) had a post office 1910-53; Hattie Graves was the first postmaster.

Beeman (Custer) had a post office 1883-84 with James Hay in charge. The name was changed to Rosebud to conform with the railroad station name.

Been (Wibaux) was named for the family of first postmaster John Been when the office opened in 1912. It was closed in 1925 and the mail ordered to Burns.

Beisegel was a postal station named after the Beisegel brothers, who had a ranch on Beisegel Creek between Grassy Butte and the Little Missouri. The office was closed in the late 1930s (*Courage Enough*).

Belair (Powell) was for a brief time the name of a community with a post office that operated December 1913-May 1914. The name was then changed to Lake City, and Harry McNally continued on as postmaster.

Belfast (Dawson) was formerly called Sanford. It was near Jordan and Chester Patterson served the year the post office was open, April 1904-May 1905.

BELFRY (Carbon) was named for Dr. William Belfry. The town was platted in 1905 and the post office opened in 1906 with Mary Hall in charge. The Yellowstone Park Railroad Company built into **Belfry** in 1906 and planned to continue the road up the Clark's Fork Valley to the park, but this was never accomplished. **Belfry** was headquarters for the Montana, Wyoming and Southern Railroad.

Belgium Hill (Pondera) was settled by a colony of Belgian immigrants.

BELGRADE (Gallatin) was named by a Serbian capitalist from Belgrade (now Yugoslavia), who in 1883 was a special guest on the train taking president Villard of the Northern Pacific to Gold Creek for the ceremony of driving the last spike. The post office was established in 1887 with Thomas Quaw as postmaster. Quaw, a realtor, had purchased land along the railroad tracks ten miles from Bozeman and established a grain trading business. The Serbian investors were unhappy with their investments, but Quaw branched out to open a grocery store, promote a church, and in 1891 a school.

Belknap(s) (Chouteau) had a post office 1879-89. It was near Chinook. Presumably this was the first Fort Belknap trading post along the Milk River (see **Fort Belknap**).

Belknap (Gallatin) is a railroad sidetrack named for Robert L. Belknap, treasurer of the Northern Pacific railroad in 1879.

Belknap (Missoula) had its name changed to Enterprise to avoid confusion with Fort Belknap (*Weekly Missoulian*; May 9, 1884). Postal records show an Enterprise in Missoula County was granted a post office in March 1884.

Belknap (Sanders) had a post office 1901-64, when it became a rural independent station of Trout Creek. Harry Goetz was the first postmaster. The railroad came to **Belknap** in 1883 and the town grew to 3,000 by 1884. It was an outfitting point for miners, but most of the buildings burned to the ground later in 1884. A log building housed the Little Beaver School.

Bell Creek (Powder River) is near Broadus. The 160-acre townsite was bought in May 1968 by Sam Gary, an oilman. The town, named for the oil wells that brought it into being, continues to develop as a result of the rich oil fields discovered around there. The Bell Creek field produced more than a million barrels of oil in March 1968; in June alone it produced 1,707,436 barrels from 290 wells on 64 leases. In 1969 the spelling of the town's name was changed to Belle.

Bellealta (Phillips) was short-lived, if postal records are any indication. Its office, with Mary Sherard in charge, was open March-September 1918. It was near Regina.

Belleview (Teton), near Choteau, was granted a post office in 1885 with George Miller in charge. It was closed for a few months in 1903 and finally discontinued in 1910.

Belltower (Carter) was named for a butte in the vicinity which is shaped like a bell. The post office, established in 1918 with William Gross as postmaster, was discontinued in 1954.

Belmont (Chouteau) had a post office 1892-98 with Marvin P. Jones as postmaster.

Belmont (Golden Valley) was fourteen miles southeast of Ryegate and had a post office open in 1909; the postmaster was Ludwig Sandsmark. The town was settled by people from Viroqua, Wisconsin; one of them, T. A. Tolrude, was the first settler to take up residence, and he encouraged others to come. Tolrude invested in the promising town and by 1915 there were mercantile stores, hotels, churches, a bank, a school, and the railroad station. Little is now left of the town; fires destroyed many buildings, and drought and grasshoppers discouraged the settlers. The post office was closed in 1965.

Belmont (Lewis and Clark) had a post office 1879-82 with John Jurgens as postmaster.

BELT (Cascade) was named for Belt Butte, a nearby mountain that has a belt,or girdle of rocks around it. The Belt Mountains (once called the Girdle Mountains) also took their name from this butte. The town was originally called Castner, for its founder, John Castner. His coal mine, the first in Montana, supplied fuel for Fort Benton. In 1893 the Boston and Montana Mining Company began operations in the **Belt** coal fields and supplied fuel for the nearby smelter at Great Falls. The town was settled by Finnish and Slavic immigrants. In 1930 the smelters were converted to natural gas and the coal market slumped. The post office, with Eugene Clingan in charge, opened February 2, 1885.

Beltane (Chouteau), then in Meagher County, had a post office off-and-on 1880-83; E. Hackshaw was the postmaster.

Belton (Flathead) existed as a post office and community 1900-49, when the name was changed to West Glacier. Edward Dow was the first postmaster.

Belton (Missoula) was on the postal records 1892-95, but a notation reveals the office was never in operation.

Benchland (Judith Basin) is a fading wheat town named for the contour of the land in this expanse of wheatfields on the rolling benches, where only a few years ago fine prairie grass waved. A post office there was active 1909-64 and moved to seven different locations; Asa Herring was the first postmaster. The influx of settlers came in 1909 and following years, and the railroad set up a "depot" in a boxcar. The largest crowd ever to assemble in the community was about 1921 when Gus Hammer, a cowboy-turned-preacher, came to hold a church service. **Benchland**'s, heyday was about 1915, and there were still 200 people in the little community between Moccasin and Windham in 1920. But by 1975 only seven people remained. Houses were moved to neighboring towns and ranches; even the commercial buildings were moved. Two grain elevators are still operating.

Benrud (Roosevelt) was formerly shown in postal records as Camrud. The **Benrud** post office, with Ole Skaret in charge, was active 1923-38.

Benson's Landing (Park), on the Yellowstone River near Livingston, was named for a Mr. Benson who operated a boat landing there. It had a post office July 1878-April 1879, and again June 1879-August 1880, and a final active period December 1881-December 1882. James Baily was the original postmaster.

Benteen (Big Horn), a station on the Chicago, Burlington, and Quincy Railroad, was named for Captain Benteen, one of Custer's officers at the Battle of the Little Big Horn. It is south of Garryowen.

Benz (Prairie) was a settlement named for Fred Benz, a development agent for the NP known as the Potato King of the Yakima Valley. The railroad station, established in 1903, was originally called Zero.

Ben⁄ien (Garfield) is on a fork of Lodgepole Creek, shortly before it flows into the Musselshell River. A post office established there in 1916 (Nathan Sigman, postmaster) was discontinued in 1943. It was named for the Herman Benzien family, on whose homestead the post office was built. An early postmaster was Rose Cohen. Her brother-in-law and sister, Mr. and Mrs. Sol Kays, had a grocery store there from 1915 until the time when the homesteaders moved out and business was no longer profitable.

Benzien had only one store and a post office, but it had two newspapers! In 1916 David L. Watson, who had homesteaded on the South Fork of Lodgepole Creek, was running a paper in Sand Springs, and decided to establish the **Benzien** *Bugle* to protect his "final proof" territory. The fee paid by homesteaders, who were required to advertise that they were making final proof on their land, was the chief income of these little papers. Ed McRae put in a second paper, and the editors had a red-hot newspaper fight. Later McRae moved his press to Sand Springs and continued the competition with Watson's *Prairie Breezes*.

The Blue Ridge and Enterprise schools north of **Benzien** had good log buildings which were built by the men of the neighborhoods. Ingomar and Sumatra were the closest towns and they were sixty miles away, but they were on the railroad, so settlers from the **Benzien** area trailed their cattle and sheep to one of these stations for shipment to the East. On the return trip, they brought home supplies for the winter (*Big Dry County*).

Bercail (Wheatland), near Halbert, had a post office 1882-97 and again 1899-1947. Phillip Moule was the first postmaster.

Bernice (Jefferson) began as a station on the Great Northern. It was named in honor of Bernice Cannon, daughter of Charles W. Cannon of Helena, vice-president of the Montana Central Railroad. S. F. Pratt was the first postmaster and the office was opened and closed four times between 1890-1910. In earlier days, a stagecoach station named Calvin was at this location.

Bervie (Petroleum) had a post office 1922-32. The community had formerly been known as Fort Musselshell, but when John Town became postmaster in 1922, he moved the post office three miles up the river and renamed it for a town in Ontario, Canada, where his mother had grown up. **Bervie** was abandoned when Fort Peck waters covered the area.

Berwind (Carbon) was a coal mining operation of the Montana Coal and Iron Company located on a spur of the Montana, Wyoming and Southern Railroad.

Bew (Yellowstone) had a post office 1914-1926. It was near Custer, and James E. Patten was the first postmaster.

Bickel (Lewis and Clark) began as a station on the Great Northern. It was named for Paul Bickel, a civil engineer.

BIDDLE (Powder River) is an isolated settlement near the Wyoming border on the Little Powder River. H. H. Hunt, in a letter to *Montana Magazine* (Summer, 1958), wrote, "I went to Montana in 1916 and at that time there were many Highlander cattle in the Little Powder River area. I learned that the Biddle ranch imported them from Scotland in the 1890s. The Cross Ranch was owned by the Philadelphia Biddles." **Biddle**'s post office was established in 1916 with Charles Schofield as postmaster.

Biem (Roosevelt) had a post office 1919-25 and again 1927-34. Albert Biem was the first postmaster.

BIG ARM (Lake) is twelve miles north of Polson on a "big arm" of Flathead Lake. The post office opened in 1911 with Marion F. Lamb as postmaster.

Big Dry (Garfield) was named for Big Dry Creek. Lewis and Clark had called it Big Dry River in their Journal for May 6, 1806, "on account of its having a bed of a large river 200 yards wide, yet not a drop of water." The **Big Dry** post office was operated by Jessie McCune 1911-13 in the five-room log house shared with her brothers. Sherman and Fred McCune ran a gasoline-powered ferry boat, the "Eloise," back and forth across the Missouri near where the Big Dry empties into the river. The whole area took the descriptive name of the creek and much of Garfield County is known as the "Big Dry."

Big Elk, Bigelk (Wheatland) was a part of Meagher County when the post office was established in 1882 with Ozias Hatch as postmaster. "Two Dot" Wilson came to this area in 1870 and began raising cattle and horses along the Musselshell north of **Big Elk**. The community, which was named for the large elk herds found there, was moved when the Montana Railroad came through the valley. The new location was on a part of Wilson's original ranch. According to Stearns, **Big Elk** had a schoolhouse consisting of one room in a lean-to. Miss Walker, the teacher, and her pupils put on a program for Fourth of July celebrations. School was held only during the summer months. The post office at **Big Elk** was closed in 1885 and then active again 1888-1913.

BIGFORK (Flathead) got its name from its location on the fork of Swan River. It has had a post office since 1901; Everit Sliter was the first postmaster. The town has been described as "A huddle of little grey houses in a hollow just below the dam and powerhouse" that supplies electricity for Kalispell and much of Flathead County.

Big Hole is an area rather than a town, but it cannot be left out of a history of the Montana place-names. The Battle of the Big Hole was fought here in August 1877 when Gen. John Gibbon found the Nez Perce in the Big Hole Basin. Chief Joseph withdrew and took flight across Montana. "Hole" was a term used to describe a basin or valley which had been cut for a river bed in ages past. This area in extreme southwestern Montana produces fine hay crops and livestock.

Big Horn (Custer) was the name originally given to a post office established in 1877 with Theodor Borup as postmaster. In 1878 the name was changed to Fort Custer.

BIG HORN (Treasure) had a post office 1903-05 with Walter Ayres in charge; the office was reinstated in 1907. **Big Horn** is near the Yellowstone County border where the Big Horn River flows into the Yellowstone. Granville Stuart in his journal speaks of a **Big Horn** post office in 1880 at the junction of these two rivers — but that doesn't quite fit with postal records. **Big Horn** is on ground that has been occupied almost continuously by white men since explorer William Clark camped there in July 1806. Manuel Lisa built a trading post there in 1807. In 1822 Col. W. H. Ashley built another post, Fort Van Buren, two miles below the mouth of the Big Horn River, where many west-bound travelers stopped for a rest. General Gibbon with 450 men crossed the Yellowstone at this point in June 1876 as he was hurrying south to aid General Custer in a battle that had already been lost.

Big Horn was one of the original nine counties laid out by territorial legislators in 1864. It included almost a third of the area of Montana, a wide stretch of land from Canada to the Wyoming border. By 1889 this county had been divided into two relatively equal-sized counties called Dawson and Custer. There was no Big Horn County in Montana then until 1913, when a new one by that name was created out of parts of Rosebud and Yellowstone counties (see **Big Horn County**).

Big Horn County is in eastern Montana along the Wyoming border. Like the mountains, the river, and the town, it takes its name from the Big Horn sheep that ranged its steep hillsides. These animals were first described by Lewis and Clark, to whom they were great curiosities: "They walked about and bounded from rock to rock with apparent unconcern where it appeared to me no quadruped could have stood firm." Next to the buffalo, this was the most sensational animal reported by the explorers: ". . . wild sheep, its head and horns weigh about eighty or ninety pounds . . . this one was caught in the Rocky Mountains." Lewis and Clark's fascination with this strange, regal animal inspired them to name the mountains and the river. Urbanek says that the Indians called the area Ah-sah-ta, for the great droves of Big Horn sheep found there.

The county was organized from parts of Rosebud and Yellowstone counties in 1913. Hardin is the county seat. The county contains most of the present-day Crow Indian Reservation and some of the Northern Cheyenne Reservation. The Little Big Horn (Little Horn) River and the Big Horn River flow through the county on their way to the Yellowstone. The Battle of the Little Big Horn, the Custer Battlefield National Monument, and a town named Garryowen indicate the history of this area.

Big Sag (Chouteau) was a station on the Milwaukee Railroad named for a topographical feature here. A large sheep company known as the Big Sag Outfit ran their stock here.

BIG SANDY (Chouteau) was named for a creek near the town. The Indians called the creek Un-es-putcha-eka, which translated from the Blackfeet language as "Big Sandy Creek." A post office has been in operation since December 22, 1887; Leigh Marlow was the first postmaster.

Big Sandy is one of the storied towns of the Old West. Charlie Russell worked on ranches near here. Rusty Brown's saloon and other old-time buildings are gone, but the region remains a meeting ground for fact and fiction. **Big Sandy** was the prototype for "Dry Lake," the town B. M. Bower featured in her *Flying U* novels. The novelist lived in this town in the middle of the open range country. In John Willard's notes is this statement: "**Big Sandy** was a cow town of long tradition and a freighting center when goods were unloaded at the Coal Banks Landing just south of here on the Missouri River. Materials for Fort Assiniboine were delivered at Coal Banks by river steamer, then freighted overland to the fort." According to Allison, a saloon was opened in a tent near McNamara and Marlow's freight depot in 1886, and then another saloon, the Log Cabin, was put up. The railroad came and located its depot and water tank near the water source and the McNamara freight depot. In 1887, **Big Sandy** consisted of those two depots, a warehouse, a boxcar for the section foreman to live in, and nine saloons which, except for the Log Cabin, were tents with wooden floors or small shacks. In 1889 the Spokane Hotel was built to accommodate increased business — cowboys, settlers and railroad men. By 1912, it had become a homesteaders' boom town and the GN moved its depot into town. Before that a horse-drawn bus met all trains. For 50c a passenger could ride the 1½ miles to Big Sandy. The depot was moved overnight on a flatcar and the Mackton Coal Mine was a going industry, but by 1919, many of the homesteaders were broke and left. Big farm units absorbed the inadequate homestead acreages and by 1928, the country was prosperous again.

BIG SKY (Gallatin) is a resort complex forty miles down the canyon from Bozeman and forty-seven from West Yellowstone. **Big Sky** was the dream of television commentator Chet Huntley, and its development, backed by Chrysler Realty Company, occupied his final years after he retired. Huntley was born in Cardwell, Montana, and grew up in small Montana towns wherever his railroading father's work took the family. His book *The Generous Years* and **Big Sky** were his tributes to his native state. A post office was opened in **Big Sky** in 1973.

BIG TIMBER, BIGTIMBER (Sweet Grass), a county seat, took its name from the large cottonwood trees along the banks of the creek. There is little of the natural timber left near the town now, but some of the state's biggest cottonwoods were in the area in the early days. The name was first applied to the stage station at the mouth of Big Timber Creek a few miles from the site of the present town. **Big Timber**'s post office with Ella Burns as postmaster, opened in 1880, closed in 1881 and re-opened in 1882.

Bilakin (Custer) was one of several Montana towns that hardly came to life. A post office, with August Theade as postmaster, was approved in September 1916, but in January 1917 the order of establishment was rescinded.

BILLINGS (Yellowstone), a county seat, is a major trading center for a vast area of southeastern Montana. It was named for Frederick Billings, lawyer, railway promoter, and philanthropist. He was one of the original stockholders of the Northern Pacific Railway and secured the right-of-way for that line to cross Montana. In 1879 he became president of the company. The original townsite of **Billings** was platted in 1882, and a post office was established that year with Lucius Whitney as postmaster.

In the winter of 1876-77, Mssrs. P. W. McAdow, J. J. Alderson, Joseph Cochran, Henry Colwell, Clinton Dills, Milton Summers, and others founded the town of Coulson around McAdow's store where the Northern Pacific bridge now spans the Yellowstone River. The village looked promising, so in 1878 the Minnesota and Montana Improvement Company attempted to purchase sites for more ambitious development, but they were unable to make satisfactory arrangements with the Coulson people. The company then laid out the village of **Billings** a short distance up the river. It soon surpassed Coulson.

Bird (Cascade), near the town of Cascade, had a post office November 1895-May 1896 and 1897-99; Robert McCollim was the first postmaster.

Birdseye (Lewis and Clark) had a post office granted in 1898 with William J. Tobin as postmaster. The community and post office were formerly called Clough. The office was discontinued in 1916. J. P. Rowe gives two versions of why it was so named: "After a freighter who ran a line of freight wagons through that territory years ago" and "Probably named for Charles G. Birdseye, a prominent resident of this section in the early days." Maybe they are both right — even a mule-skinnin' freighter *could* settle down and become a prominent citizen.

Birdtail (Cascade), near Simms, was named for Birdtail Divide, a spur of hills in this country, one peak of which has a remarkable resemblance to a bird's spread tail. The post office, under Alfred H. Dear, operated 1916-18.

BIRNEY (Rosebud) is about twenty-five miles south of Ashland on the Tongue River at the mouth of Hanging Woman Creek. Postal records show that the present town of Ashland was previously called **Birney** and before that Strader. Under the **Birney** name and at that location, there was a post office 1881-86 with Arthur M. Birney as postmaster. The present day **Birney** has had a post office since December, 1886; Edward Brown was the first postmaster. Ralph Shane, in his "Early History of the Northern Cheyennes," notes in an illustrated map that **Birney** was the scene of a battle on January 7, 1877: "Two Moon's band of the Cheyennes and Crazy Horse's band of Ogalalla Sioux spent the summer of 1876 in the valleys of the Rosebud and Tongue Rivers. Late in the summer they moved to the mouth of Otter Creek near the present townsite of Ashland. Here they were attacked by General Miles in January 1877 and they moved on up the Tongue River to the mouth of Hanging Woman Creek (near the present side of **Birney**) where General Miles and his men attacked again on January 7, 1877. Four women, three children, and one young warrior were captured. On January 8 a fierce battle was fought here as the Indians tried to recover the captives." This was the Battle of Wolf Mountain. The soldiers returned to Fort Keogh and the Indians moved to winter camp on the Big Horn River at the mouth of Rotten Grass Creek, near the present town of St. Xavier.

Bisher (Fallon) is near Baker. It had a post office 1914-18 located on what later became the Art Massage place. Florence Bisher was the first postmaster.

Bison (Liberty) was a station on the Great Northern formerly called Buelow. That name, along with several others along the line, was changed in an effort to make them more appealing and thus encourage travel and settlement. The **Bison** post office operated 1918-36; Charles Haigh was the first postmaster.

Bitter Root as a name is an integral part of the story of Montana — of her beauty, her history, her valleys and mountains. The verdant valley that bears this name was first called that by the Indians, who named the northern end of it "Place of the Bitter Root." The roots of this plant were harvested by the Flathead (Salish) Indians in spring and summer, for use as a general food, and as an appetite restorer in the winter. The Flatheads called the plant "*Spet-lm*" (plant with bitter-tasting root), and the original name of the Bitterroot River was *spet-lm-seulko* (the water of the bitter-root). The name is spelled both as one word and as two.

The following recipes for the use of the bitterroot appeared in the *First Ladies Cookbook*, edited by Mrs. Tim Babcock, Montana's First Lady, in 1963. The recipes were submitted by Mrs. Alfred Olson of Billings, who had gotten them from Julia Rock-above, a Crow Indian woman living in Pryor. Julia's recipes were given to her by her mother and grandmother, who had in turn gotten them from their ancestors.

Bitterroot Soup

Boil dried roots in buffalo, elk, or bear broth until tender.

Bitterroot Sauce

Boil the roots until they are tender. Sweeten and serve.

Bitterroot Pudding

Use about one-half cup of roots per serving. Parboil roots for a few minutes. Drain and add fresh water. Cook until tender. Sweeten with wild honey to suit taste. Add 1 teaspoon of bone marrow per serving. Thicken with scrapings from the inner side of a fresh skin.

Lewis and Clark applied the name "Bitterroot Valley" to the whole valley where the plant grew profusely. Lewis took specimens of it back to St. Louis with him. The botanical name *Lewisia Rediviva* comes from the explorer's name, and the plant's tenacity to live, as well as from its color. Lewis first collected the plant in September of 1806 on the way from Lolo Creek to Hell Gate Pass. A year later the plants were still alive. The Bitterroot was officially designated as Montana's State Flower by the legislature in 1895.

Bitter Root (Ravalli) had a post office July 1915-May 1916 with Herbert Stockholm as postmaster. It was a short-lived town, "founded" in 1910 and located at the present-day site of the Bitter Root Inn.

BLACK EAGLE (Cascade) almost adjoins Great Falls. It was named for the Black Eagle Falls on the Missouri, which in turn were named because of the many eagles seen in the area by Lewis and Clark. August Cor was the first postmaster and the office was established in 1917. The town was once nicknamed "Little Chicago" because it is an industrial area where many workers from refineries and smelters live; many are of Balkan birth or descent, and for many years they retained the habits and customs, as well as the dialects, of Slavic countries.

BLACKFOOT (Garfield) was a settlement on Seven Blackfoot Creek near the place where the creek (now called simply "Blackfoot") empties into the Missouri. According to a *History of Garfield County*, written in 1947 by a high school "Montana Life" class, the creek was named because there were seven Blackfeet Indians hanged to the limb of a cottonwood tree and left there to rot away; it is said that white men hanged them after the Indians had stolen their gold. This was cattle country and Granville Stuart was one of the men who ranged his herds here. As late as 1947, his son, Charlie "Patch Eye" Stuart, was still living in the Blackfeet country.

Blackfoot (Glacier) is a few miles east of Browning. It was named for the Blackfeet Indians, but conflicting legends are told to account for the name of that tribe. Some of the Blackfeet adhere to the old Sun faith; according to one legend, an old man with three sons had a vision that caused him to send the sons to the far plains of the North Big River (Saskatchewan) in search of game. There they saw great herds of buffalo, but could not approach to kill them. But in another vision, Sun told the old man to rub the feet of the eldest with black medicine which Sun provided. With this aid the young man easily overtook the fleeing buffalo, and his father decreed that this son's descendants should be called Blackfeet.

Another legend says that the Blackfeet were given their name because their moccasins were blackened in crossing the burnt prairies between

Lesser Slave Lake and the Montana plains. The Indian name *Siksiksa* is said to translate "Blackfoot" but the constitution under which the tribal council operates gives the name as "Blackfeet", so both names have been used. A post office for **Blackfoot** was established in 1908 with James Perrine as postmaster.

Blackfoot City (Powell) Life was rich, raw and lusty for a few short years in **Blackfoot City**. The first miners to arrive worked the earth in a frenzy, piling their waste tailings in front of the mines or along stream banks; then the Chinese came by the thousands to mine the tailings.

"**Blackfoot City** reached its brawling fingers west up Ophir Gulch, north to Butcher Ridge and south into Carpenter Gulch as far as you wanted to call it 'town.' It was subdivided into Lower Town, Upper Town, Chinatown, Carpenter City. It existed without incorporation in a land that wasn't even a part of the United States" (Beverly Badhorse, Billings *Gazette*; Nov. 14, 1976). For sixty years Clay Moore has been marking Montana's anonymous frontier dead with his crudely lettered signs; he has also tried to restore **Blackfoot City** — where he was born — but fire has destroyed his efforts. A sign marks Centennial Street:

Blackfoot City —
Founded 1865 by
Col. Pemberton,
A. Nagle,
Hugh Bratton
and others in Party unknown

Blackfoot City had a post office 1866-96; after that the Ophir office served the area. Silas Crounse was the first postmaster in **Blackfoot City**.

John Clarkson Moore arrived at the mining camp in 1866 to work in the mines. His wife Flora was a "doctor and angel of mercy" to the camp. A thirty-foot water wheel still survives in Carpenter Gulch, a few stones remain to mark a basement, and the flume holds rushing water just as it did a hundred years ago (Beverly Badhorse, Billings *Gazette*; Nov. 14, 1976).

Blackhawk (Meagher) had a post office 1890-93. Hiram K. Edwards was postmaster.

Blackleaf (Teton) was formerly called Raymond. The name was changed to **Blackleaf** in 1910 and William Lillard served as postmaster. This office was discontinued in 1936.

Blackmon (Dawson County) was named for postmaster Thomas Blackmon. This post office near Oswego was open 1902-05.

Black Pine (Granite County) had a post office 1887-90 with Ewing Tasseville as postmaster.

Blacktail (Flathead) was a station on the Great Northern along the border of Glacier National Park. It was named for the abundant blacktail deer there, and is another example of the GN's efforts to make the names along its route sound enticing to Easterners.

Blackwood (Gallatin), southwest of Bozeman, was named for Edward L. Blackwood and A. B. Blackwood, who settled there in 1890, and whose farms adjoined the townsite.

Blaine (Madison), south of Twin Bridges, had a post office from 1893-1935. Records show Benjamin Pidgeon as first postmaster.

Bessie Mailey Gratton, a pioneer resident of Sheridan, wrote in a letter dated November 6, 1973: "Point of Rocks was a mail drop between Bannack and Virginia City. When the old fellow that owned the Point of Rocks stage station sold it, my mother became postmistress. We lived about a mile over the hill from the station. At this time Blaine was running for president and she had it named after him. She retired after fifty years (*sic*), then the post office was discontinued."

James Blaine was defeated for the presidency by Grover Cleveland in 1884, but he tried again for the Republican nomination in 1892. Just who was Benjamin Pidgeon remains a mystery.

Blaine County is in the eastern half of the state along the Canadian border and contains the Fort Belknap Indian Reservation. The county was named for James G. Blaine, American statesman and politician. It was created in 1912 from a part of Chouteau County. The Bear Paw Mountains form part of the eastern border, and the wide prairies spreading out from these mountains between the Milk and Missouri Rivers were early day cattle ranges. **Blaine County** rose to its population heights during the boom of dry land farming; many hopeful homesteaders came and settled, but the majority of them gave up in the face of drought, hail, and grasshoppers. Many post offices in the southern part of the county that once served ranchers and farmers are old landmarks now, but they too are gradually being removed. Offices have closed at Caraco, Nelson, Ada, Maddux, Kabo, Riedel, Rattlesnake, Bear Paw, Sand Cliffs, Ramberg, and Cleveland. Chinook is the county seat.

Blaine Springs (Madison), near Varney, now supplies water for the federal fish hatchery known as the Ennis Hatchery. In earlier days a Mr. Blaine operated a milk ranch here and sold milk and butter to residents of Virginia City. This community is home to what is reputed to be one of the largest springs in Montana.

Blair (Roosevelt) was named for Sidney D. Blair, a resident.

Blakeley (Yellowstone) is listed in postal records as having an office 1886-97, and the location is given as Yellowstone County — Indian Reservation. Henry Ebert was the first postmaster.

Blakeslee (Petroleum) was a community first known as Minnesota Bench, because so many homesteaders came from that state. The Charles Blakeslee family got a post office started in 1914, so the office and later the community took their name. The post office was moved from one home to another as various members of the community took their turns at being postmaster; salaries were based on cancellations. Lumber was hauled in from Lewistown to build the homesteaders' houses (Fleharty, Winnett *Times*). The post office was closed in 1937.

Blanchard (Missoula) was named for Louis Blanchard, the first postmaster. The office was established in 1901, and the name of the town was changed to Evaro in 1905.

Blatchford (Prairie), near Terry, was named for Judge Blatchford of the United States Circuit Court, who had come from New York, according to one historian; another says it was for John Blatchford Collins, once the assistant postmaster at Miles City and later a member of the Montana legislature. It was a station on the NP established in 1882, and was possibly first called Morgan. A post office was established in 1885 with John E. Kennedy as postmaster; it was closed 1889-91, then reopened at the Kalfell ranch. By 1915 the postal name for the area had been changed to Zero. The

Chapin School south of **Blatchford** was in a remodeled granary (*Wheels Across Montana's Prairie*).

Blodgett (Flathead) had a brief postal history with an office open September 1903-July 1904 with Daniel Whitaker as postmaster.

Bloomdale (Custer) had a post office for less than a year, August 1889-May 1890; Fred Middleton was in charge.

BLOOMFIELD (Dawson) is twenty-three miles north of Glendive. It was formerly called Adams and a post office under that name was established in June 1906. The name was changed to **Bloomfield** in 1907.

Blossburg (Powell), very near the Lewis and Clark County line, was a station on the Northern Pacific. The name was chosen by Mr. Wicks, a mining engineer, after a Pennsylvania coal mining town named Blosburg. The railway information sheet on names says that the area had once been called Mullan, after the trailblazer, but that shipments were going astray to Mullan, Idaho, so the name was changed. Postal records show a **Blossburg** post office in Deer Lodge-Powell County established in 1886 with Jacob Whitmire as postmaster. A notation indicates it was formerly Barcon; that office was closed in 1902. Another **Blossburg** is listed in Powell County with an office opening in 1950 with Edna Medsker as postmaster. The notation says that this one was formerly called Schatz; that office was discontinued in 1957.

Bluffer (Big Horn), near Becker, had a post office 1921-23 with Albert Adams in charge.

Bluffport (Prairie), a station on the Milwaukee, is in the bluffs between Fallon and Terry and named for its location and scenery.

Blum (Carbon), between Edgar and Rockvale, was a station on the Northern Pacific named for Bernard Blum, the engineer for maintenance. Large gravel pits near here furnished material for construction.

Blythe (Cascade) is a settlement named for J. W. Blythe, a settler and landowner.

Bog Coulee (Valley) had a post office 1913-16 with Effie Poston as postmaster. The name was no doubt descriptive.

Bogut (Richland) was named for postmaster Leo Bogut. The office was in operation 1914-15.

Bohemian Corners (Fergus) is a service station and restaurant at a major highway junction. The first homesteaders moved into this area in 1912 shortly before the railroad came to nearby Roy. By 1928 Bohemian Hall had been built, but the area continued to be quite isolated until the Fred Robinson Bridge was constructed across the Missouri. With that, travel increased and Perry and Marge Kalal developed the stopping place at the corners (Byerly and Byerly).

Bold Butte. "In 1885 Rodney Barnes made a strike in the Sweet Grass Hills near the Canadian border and dug out $125,000 worth of placer gold. **Bold Butte**, springing up as a prosperous village, is now a ghost town" (Mockel).

Bole (Teton) was formerly called Limington. The post office opened in 1914 with Peter Stoltzman as postmaster and closed in 1943. **Bole** was a station on the Great Northern.

Bombay (Glacier) was a station on the Great Northern near Browning formerly called Carlow and eventually named Fort Piegan.

Bonaccord, Bon Accord (Beaverhead) had a post office March-December 1899; William Bray, Jr., was postmaster. It was located at the site of White's Bar, where gold was discovered in 1862. The Bon Accord Dredge used there was made by an English corporation in 1897; but the dredge was top-heavy and capsized and the town faded (Western Interpretive Services).

Bone Trail (Garfield) is a trail which dropped off Slaymaker Ridge and angled steeply down for three miles to the mouth of Blackfoot Creek. The lower part of the trail is now beneath Fort Peck Reservoir waters.

After the buffalo were gone from this area, the Indians gathered great quantities of buffalo bones and stacked them into piles on Snow Creek. From there the Indians took the bones down the **Bone Trail** by red river carts and travois to sell them to steamboat captains. The bones were then taken to St. Louis to be made into fertilizer. The Indians called the steamboats the "fire canoes." (*Big Dry Country*).

Bonin (McCone) was named for postmaster Emil C. Bonin when the office opened in 1917. It remained active until 1933.

Bonita (Missoula), on the banks of the Clark Fork River, once had a population of 3,000. The word *bonita* is Spanish for "pretty" or "beautiful," and the town's name is attributed to Mexican section hands working on the Northern Pacific tracks nearby in 1884. This designation was not used locally until NP officials put up a sign indicating that would be the name of the station. It was formerly called Cramer Station in honor of Charles Cramer. The post office was established in 1886 with John Lovall as postmaster; it closed in 1942.

BONNER (Missoula), east of Missoula, had one of the state's first large sawmills. The town was named for E. L. Bonner, an early settler in Missoula and first president of the Missoula and Bitter Root Valley Railroad (1888). The post office opened in March of that year with Lane Paskill in charge. Bonner's Ferry, Idaho, was also named for this Montana lumber magnate.

Boots (Custer) had a post office October 1908-July 1909. It was near Baker and the postmaster was Curtis Shreve. Was it so named because this was cowboy country?

BOULDER (Jefferson) is a county seat and was named for the massive stones strewn about the valley. The town was established in the early 1860s as a stage station on the Fort Benton-Virginia City route. Later it became the trading center for a mining and agricultural area, once serving the mining districts of Elkhorn, Comet, and Baltimore. The Great Northern Railway came through in 1888. The state schools for the deaf, blind, and feebleminded were established here in 1892. The town was first called Boulder Valley, and its first post office operated under that name 1866-97. William Barkley was appointed postmaster in 1866. When the name was changed to **Boulder** in May, 1897, Alonzo Foster was postmaster.

Boundary (Valley) had a post office for just two years: October 1906-October 1908. Edith Howard was postmaster.

Bowdoin (Phillips) is on the Great Northern line near the Larb Hills. Lake Bowdoin, just north of town, and the area around it have now been developed into a wildlife refuge. A post office under the **Bowdoin** name operated 1911-14 with Lion Hoag as postmaster. After the Wooldridge office closed in 1917, the post office for this area was again known as **Bowdoin**. It closed in 1943. The Bowdoin National Wildlife Refuge has had as many as 2,700 adult pelicans as summer residents. In the fall the birds fly back to the Gulf of Mexico or the California coast.

Bowen (Beaverhead) in the Big Hole Basin, had a post office 1890-1924. Elba Pember was the first postmaster.

Bowers (Powder River) had a post office 1928-56. LaNora Allen was the first postmaster.

Bowler (Carbon) was named for first postmaster John Bowler. A trading post was established there after the opening of the Crow Reservation in 1892. The post office was active 1894-1936. The Burlington and Missouri River Railroad had a station near **Bowler**, but the line was discontinued in 1911.

Bowman Lake (Flathead) had a post office from 1924-26 with Fred Gignilliat as postmaster. After that residents and summer visitors got their mail at Polebridge.

Bowmanville (Garfield), the North Fork of Lodgepole Creek, was named for Ella Bowman, who was the first postmaster. The office was established in 1913. In 1915 Margaret McGlumphey was appointed postmaster and the office was moved to her home. The name was changed to Bright Star in 1916, and later that same year to Dilo.

BOX ELDER, BOXELDER (Hill) was named for the creek, which in turn was named for the box elder trees that line its banks. The town serves as headquarters for the Rocky Boy Indian Reservation. The Rocky Boys are often called "the landless Indians;" they came from Canada in the 1870s and lived first around Assiniboine and the Bear Paw foothills. Later they scattered over other parts of Montana. These Indians, also called Metis, come from a northern tribe of Chippewa-Cree.

The townsite of **Box Elder** was laid out by Jonas Breemer, leader of forty Ohio families that were brought in by the railroad company to settle. These homesteaders asked Mr. Cowan to move his store from Cypress, which he did in June 1889. The hot, dry summers of 1889 and 1890 discouraged most of the Ohioans, and all but two families left (*Trial and Triumph*). Cowan bought buffalo bones from the Indians for $6 a ton and shipped them to East St. Louis for use in refining sugar. The post office was established in 1889 with William McGraw in charge.

BOYD (Carbon), near Roberts, was named for John Boyd, a homesteader on Rock Creek. The post office was established in 1909 with Roland Doughty as postmaster. It became a rural independent station in 1965. This is an irrigated area with crops watered by melting snow from the Beartooth Mountains. Most of the farmers are of Finnish stock. Many homes have log house steam baths similar to the ones they had in Finland. Steam is created by throwing water on heated rocks. **Boyd** serves as a trading center for farmers in the wide countryside up to Shane Ridge. Livestock, grain, and sugar beets are shipped from the Northern Pacific depot (Maryott).

Boyd (Valley) was named for the first postmaster, James Boyd. The office was open 1898-1902.

BOYES (Carter) is a roadside store, gas station, and post office. It was named for Arthur Boyce, who homesteaded the southern part of the county. The post office was established in 1906 with John E. Johnston in charge, and the name spelled **Boyes**. Boyce was an early day mail carrier who gave up on homesteading, returned to his native England, married and stayed there.

Boyle (Custer), near Miles City, was named for the family of the first postmaster, Mary Boyle. The office was active 1892-1902.

BOZEMAN (Gallatin) lies in a narrow valley that is almost entirely surrounded by the Rockies. The town is named for John Bozeman, who blazed a trail across Wyoming and in 1864 guided the first train of immigrants into the Gallatin Valley. Jim Bridger guided another train into the area that same year, using a different pass; the two were friendly rivals. Bozeman was killed by Piegan Indians in April 1867 as he was coming through an especially narrow part of the valley. He was buried there, but his body was later moved to the town that became his namesake. The town for a time called Missouri because of the number of Missourians among the settlers. In 1867 **Bozeman** became the county seat of one of the nine original territorial counties. The town started in 1864 and the post office opened in December of 1868 with John Roth as postmaster. Montana State College (now University) was established in 1893.

Bozeman Hot Springs (Gallatin) is a settlement that grew up around a natural hot springs. A big public plunge was built there. It was named after the springs and its nearness to Bozeman. It is now a highway crossroads.

Brackett (Gallatin) is near Clyde Park (Park County) and had a post office 1910-11 with Clara Anderson as postmaster.

Bradford (Lewis and Clark) was an early office post office 1891-83; Ezra Clemons was postmaster.

Bradley (Powell) was a station on the Northern Pacific named for Lieutenant Bradley, an Army officer killed at the Battle of the Big Hole.

BRADY (Pondera) is the grain marketing and distribution center for 5,000 acres of farm land that is watered by the Bynum Irrigation Project. Water is conveyed to **Brady** ranches and farms through Muddy Creek from a reservoir thirty miles to the west. There are two ideas about the origin of the town's name: one, according to some residents, is that it was named in honor of Doctor Brady, who was employed by Tohey Brothers Contractors while they constructed a narrow gauge railroad from Shelby to Great Falls about 1885; when an epidemic of smallpox broke out at the construction camp just as the steel was being laid, Brady came from Great Falls to treat the sick and check the disease (*Montana, a Guide Book*). The other idea is that **Brady** was named for the attorney for the Great Falls-Canada Railroad, who was also the father of Mrs. Kranz of Great Falls (Floerchinger). At any rate, the post office was established in 1910 and Charles Johnson was the first postmaster.

Brandenberg (Rosebud) had a post office 1881-1957. It is on the Tongue River and George Liscom was the first postmaster.

Brandon (Madison) was a mining camp east of Sheridan at the mouth of Mill Creek. It was incorporated in 1865, the sixth town in the territory. The area was first prospected in 1862 by James Bradley. **Brandon** saw three major mining booms, and while it never had a post office, it *did* have several saloons, a boarding house, a dance hall, a schoolhouse, and was home to 300-400 people at times. Frank B. Linderman built a log house and lived in **Brandon** with his family from 1897 to about 1901. His daughter, Norma, was born there (*Pioneer Trails and Trials*).

Brassey (Meagher), near Cottonwood, had a post office 1881-84 with Edward Brassey as postmaster.

Brazwell Summit (Yellowstone), near Laurel, had a post office 1914-17 with Julia Woods as postmaster.

Bredette (Roosevelt) had a post office 1915-43. Anna Gribble was the first postmaster.

Breeston (Chouteau), near Dutton, was named for postmaster Percy Brees. The office was open August 1919-October 1920.

Bremer (Hill) was on postal records only for October-December 1889. Warner Bremer was postmaster.

Brenizer (Wibaux), was almost on the North Dakota border. In fact, when the post office was first approved it was listed as North Dakota. The Montana office was established in 1909 (Herman Gregory, postmaster). After it closed in 1919, residents got their mail at Beach, North Dakota.

Brenner (Beaverhead) had a post office 1910-1913 with Charles C. Fife in charge. Finan McDonald, with a company of sixty-five trappers, came to this area in 1822. They lost seven men in a battle with the Piegan Indians and later, in revenge, set fire to the brush in which the Indians were hiding and nearly annihilated the whole band (Western Interpretive Services).

Brewer's Springs (Meagher) was for a time called Brainerd Springs. The post office was established in 1875 with Henry Brainerd as postmaster. The official name is for James Brewer, who started the resort around a natural hot springs. The mineral qualities of the water evidently won out, because the name was changed the next year to White Sulphur Springs.

BRIDGER (Carbon) Jno. (sic) Babcock is listed as the first postmaster when this office opened in 1898. **Bridger** is south of Billings twenty-one miles from the Wyoming line. It was named for Jim Bridger, one of the first white men to explore Yellowstone Park. Bridger was born about 1795, worked for the Rocky Mountain Fur Company, and in 1842 built a trading post, Fort Bridger, on the Black Fork of the Green River. He scouted many trails, including the one that still bears his name. Army officers vied with each other to hire him as a guide. There was popular belief that he could map any part of the Rocky Mountains from memory, and Bridger himself boasted he could smell his way when he couldn't see it.

On one journey, Capt. J. L. Humfreville started to read *Hiawatha* to Bridger to settle him down. Bridger was fascinated at first, but he couldn't stand Longfellow's idealizing the Indians. But Bridger heard about Shakespeare's plays and decided he wanted to know more about them, so he sat for days on the Oregon Trail stopping every wagon that came by until he finally found a family that had a set of Shakespeare. Bridger bought the books and hired a boy for $40 a month to read to him. He liked the earlier plays and listened attentively, even memorizing many parts, but when the boy began to read *Richard III*, Bridger grabbed the book and threw it into the fire. "No man," he shouted, "could be that mean" (*Montana, A Guide Book*).

One of the first activities in **Bridger** was a coal mine opened up by

George Town; for a while the locality was known as Georgetown because of him. Later an adjoining cluster of houses called Stringtown became a part of another, nearby mining camp. Jim Bridger guided a wagon train bound for Virginia City in 1864 and forded it across the Clark Fork River near this place. The spot came to be known as Bridger's Crossing and eventually the name **Bridger** was adopted for the town. East Bridger was a stop on the Burlington Railroad with loading facilities and a side track. A county bridge over the Clark Fork River connects it with **Bridger**.

Briggs (Liberty) was named for postmaster William Briggs. The office was open 1911-17. It was near Lothair.

Brighton (Teton) was the post office for an area that also included the old narrow gauge railway station at Collins. The office opened in June 1890 with Aeneas McDonald as postmaster; it was closed in 1891, opened again in 1895 and closed in 1903 after which patrons got their mail at present day Collins in practically the same location. The name has since been changed to Collins.

Bright Star (Dawson) was the name used for a few months for a town formerly called Bowmanville. The name was changed to **Bright Star** in 1916 and later the same year it was changed to Dilo. Postal records list an office under each of these names.

Brightview (Garfield) was named because the post office was in the home of Margaret Bright. The office was active 1916-20. The Brights had a little store as well as the post office in their home. A school district was formed and a schoolhouse built by homesteaders, but all of them gave up and moved away before even one term could be held in it.

Briley (Sweet Grass) had a post office 1917-37. Carroll Johnson was the first postmaster.

Brinkman (Hill) had a post office established in 1913 with George Bridges as postmaster. It closed in 1937. These years spanned the homestead era, and many little communities sprang up and then faded around this time. This town was possibly named for Johnny Brinkman, an early-day cowboy with the Bear Paw Pool.

Brisbin was a station on the Yellowstone Park branch of the Northern Pacific, and was named for Major Brisbin of the U.S. Army.

Briston (Beaverhead), near Wisdom, had a post office 1899-19. Alfred Shaw was the first postmaster.

BROADUS (Powder River) is a county seat in the southeast corner of the state near the junction of Powder and Little Powder rivers. It was named for the Broaddus family, settlers on the Powder River; one of the "d's" was left out by mistake in Washington, D.C. when the post office was established in February 1900. **Broadus** is often called one of the "biggest little towns in the West." It was a cow town until the nearby Belle oil fields were developed — now truckers and oil men are as numerous as cattlemen. The high school in **Broadus** is the only one in the county, and the nearest railroad is 87 miles away, but good highways from Miles City and Billings funnel into the community. Many three-generation families like the Pembertons have operated cattle ranches on the Powder.

Julia Allen was the first postmaster and probably had the office in her ranch home. In 1907, the office was moved to the Troutman ranch; Mrs. Troutman offered eighty acres for a townsite and suggested more land be sold by the county to finance a courthouse. **Broadus** is known today for its cattle, oil and an outstanding school system.

BROADVIEW (Yellowstone) is northwest of Billings. Dr. Sudduth (Suddith), a ranch owner in the area, requested that the post office and the town be so named because of the view from his home, which was three miles out in the country. A post office was established in 1908 with Rebecca Meyer as postmaster.

Broadwater County is in the western half of the state about midway between the northern and southern borders. It was named for Col. Charles Broadwater, president of the Montana Central 'Railroad in 1887 when, in spite of opposition from the Northern Pacific, it was brought into Helena. At noon on November 19 of that year, the track layers finished laying the rails in Last Chance Gulch. There was a formal welcome on November 21, and a triumphal arch at Main and Edward streets bore the inscriptions: "Manitoba-Montana," "J. J. Hill and C. A. Broadwater," and "Hail to the Chiefs" (*Montana Pay Dirt*). Broadwater built an elaborate resort at the hot springs near Helena and for many years the Broadwater Hotel and plunge was the vacation spot for Montana's social elite: *Michelen's Guide* even gave it a three star rating.

Broadwater County was organized in 1895 from parts of Jefferson and Meagher counties. Townsend is the county seat.

BROCKTON (Roosevelt), thirteen miles east of Poplar, has been described as a "wind-swept village on the prairie." A few miles north of **Brockton** are the Twin Buttes, named because two of them rise dramatically from the flat, rolling plains below. The buttes are a famous landmark because of a battle there between Crow and Sioux Indians. Terry Boyd, a Sioux Indian high school student who lives near here, sent this account of it: "Five Crow Indians stole about 150 horses from a Sioux camp and from Fort Kipp during the time that the fort was occupied by the U.S. Cavalry. The Sioux took out after them. The Crows, probably intending to circle around the Sioux, crossed Big Muddy and followed it for 25 miles to Rocky Point. They stopped to rest at Twin Buttes and the Sioux were waiting for them there. The Sioux warriors were in better shape than the Sioux are now. The Sioux were hiding behind the west butte and the Crows were camped on a small knoll between the two buttes. In the ensuing battle, all the Crows were massacred and the horses recaptured."

Brockton's post office opened in 1904 with Fred Anderson as postmaster.

BROCKWAY (McCone) is twelve miles southwest of Circle. It was named for James Brockway. Mary Brockway was appointed postmaster when the office opened in 1913. The town is a railway center for the vast inland stock and grain country surrounding it. A two-story frame boarding school was built and maintained because long distances and inadequate roads made day school impractical for most students.

Brooklyn was a mining camp near Helena so named because it was also near York, which had been named for New York City.

Brooks (Fergus) was named for the owners of the Brooks Brothers Ranch located in the area. The town began when the railroad came in 1910, and developed the usual pattern of two general stores, a blacksmith shop, livery stable, saloon, two grain elevators and a post office which opened in 1912 with David Milne as postmaster. It followed, too, the oft-repeated pattern of decline as homesteaders moved away and the post office was discontinued in 1953. There were never more than a hundred people in town, but older citizens can remember when it was lively. And they remember a kindly grocer who let the farmers have things on credit when they had no money (Byerly and Byerly).

Brookside (Phillips) was established as a post office in June 1903 with Robert Coburn as postmaster; it closed in 1937.

Brorson, (Richland), northwest of Sidney, was settled by Danish descendants. They were good farmers and strong members of the farmers union because they were cooperative-minded. The post office was open 1910-16 (Neils Damskov, postmaster).

BROWNING (Glacier), near the entrance to Glacier National Park, is the agency headquarters for the Blackfeet Indian Reservation, and roads from all parts of the reservation converge here — so do tourists. A museum here preserves Indian artifacts and culture. The Blackfeet are the year-round patrons of the stores and businesses in **Browning** and add local color for tourists in the summer. The town was named for a U.S. Commissioner of Indian Affairs. The post office was established in 1895 with Thomas Magee as postmaster.

Brown's Trading Post. In 1880 Granville Stuart wrote in his journal: "Traveled about 18 miles up Flat Willow Creek to Brown's Trading Post near Big Horn and Yellowstone River Junction."

Bruce (Garfield) had a post office established in 1913. Musetta Stephenson, postmaster, made room for the office in the one room dugout home she shared with her husband, two daughters and a son. The office was discontinued in 1919 and patrons got their mail at Anad.

Bruckman (Yellowstone) was named for Louis Bruckman, postmaster for the office that was open 1884-86.

Bruffeys (Park), near Livingston, operated 1902-14 and was named for postmaster George Bruffey.

Brunelda (Garfield), in the southern part of the county, is near Sand Springs. The post office operated 1914-36. Frank Bennett was the first postmaster and the mail came in three times a week from Ingomar. Bennett also published a newspaper, the **Brunelda** *Banner*. This was buffalo country; the old-timers used to say, "'No matter which way you looked, there were buffalo on every hill and in every valley." Dan LeValley was one of the early-day hunters, called "skinners." Hides brought from $1.50 to $4.50 each and a tongue was worth 25c a pound — the rest of the animal was left to rot. In later years, large bands of sheep roamed the land and were wintered near Smoky Butte. In the spring they trailed the sheep to Sand Creek to be sheared and summered (*Big Dry County*).

BRUSETT (Garfield) is northwest of Jordan. The post office was established in 1916. There was no post office to serve the settlers on LongTree Creek for many years, and homesteaders had to go to Bruce for their mail. When it was learned the Bruce office would be closed, Mrs. Glen Smith applied for a post office to be established in her community. She made many trips with a team and buggy to consult with the Bruce postmaster, Musetta Stevenson. When Mrs. Smith got word from Washington that the post office would be moved to her home, she was also told that it must have a new name. **Brusett** was the name the postal authorities chose from the list sent in — it was Mrs. Smith's maiden name. As the other north Garfield

County post offices closed one by one, the **Brusett** office handled mail for as many as 136 scattered families. Most roads around here were built after 1920; before that the people used trails. **Brusett** is now one of only six towns shown on the map in the vast area of Garfield County.

Bryan (Park) had a post office active 1897-98 with Alton Shafer as postmaster.

Buckey (Musselshell) was named for postmaster James Buckey. The office was open 1906-15.

Buell (Custer) was named for H. S. Buell, president of the H. S. Buell Land Company. The post office operated 1879-84, with James Kennedy the first postmaster.

Buelow(s) (Hill) was named for first postmaster Mary Buelow. The office was open 1911-1918, when the name was changed to Bison.

BUFFALO (Judith Basin) is almost on the Fergus County line. It was named for the great, shaggy, native Montanan that served as a source of food, shelter, and tools for the Plains Indian. "A buffalo robe was the Indian's bed; dressed skins covered his lodges; braided strands of rawhide and twisted hair served as ropes; a green hide provided him a vessel in which to boil meat or, when stretched over a frame of boughs, a boat in which to cross a river. Moccasins and leggings were often made from the tough hides" (*Montana, A Guide Book*).

Lewis and Clark, in their journals for July 11, 1806, describe this strange new animal. When this was written, the explorers were near the present town of Logan: "A gangue of buffalow . . . the bulls keep a tremendous roaring we could hear them many miles and there are such numbers of them that there is a continuous roar . . . I sincerely beleif that there are not less than 1,000 buffalow within a circle of two miles." Lewis also described a buffalo jump near the Judith River, saying there were a "vast many carcasses of buffalow . . . they created a most horrid stench" . . . and that there were ". . . great many wolves in the neighborhood of these mangled carcases" which were fat and ". . . extremely gentle." It seems appropriate that a settlement in this rich grazing land once filled with buffalo should be named for this first occupant.

The town began with a post office in old Fergus County in 1890. Oka William Shiell, who had homesteaded on Buffalo Creek, chose the name. The first postmaster was Emery Philbrick, member of a pioneer family. Other early settlers in the Twin Peaks area were John A. and Lydia Dover. He came West in 1888, and by 1893 had chosen his Montana home in a valley he called Doverdale, after his old home in Missouri. Before settling here, he taught school in Martinsdale and Philbrook. In 1894 his college friend, Lydia Layman from Kentucky, came West to teach in Garneill. They were married the following year, and spent the rest of their lives in the shadow of the Twin Sisters; outstanding pioneer ranchers and church leaders — five sons and their families carry on the tradition.

The post office was discontinued 1890-93 and patrons had to go to Ubet for their mail. But when the Great Northern Railroad extended its line to Billings in 1908, **Buffalo** came to life again as a railroad station, and the post office was reestablished that year. Few people live in **Buffalo** now, but the rolling green hills still support prosperous cattle ranches.

Buford (Mineral) was named for an old prospector who lived up St. Joe Creek in the early days.

Bullhead Springs (Pondera) were named because many times cattle were caught in soap holes here and found with only their heads protruding (Floersinger).

Bundane (Fergus), near Roy, had a post office 1917-18 with Roy Sinclair as postmaster.

Bundy (Musselshell) is hardly a wide spot in the road now. When the post office opened at this location in 1909, the name was Waldheim. By 1919, and influenced by World War II, citizens decided they didn't want a German name for their community, so Wahoma was suggested and submitted to Washington, D.C. When that name was found unacceptable, the name **Bundy** was chosen in honor of Marine Corps Gen. Omar Bundy, who had rendered exceptional service at Chateau Thierry. The **Bundy** post office (William E. Davies, postmaster) was active 1919-35.

Burch (Dawson), near Wolf Point, had a post office for a little over a year 1912-13 with Mabel Jackson as postmaster.

Burgeton (Petroleum), near Winnett, was named for postmaster Charlie Burge. The office was open 1917-19.

Burgoyne (Golden Valley), near Ryegate, had a post office 1911-13 with John Fitch in charge.

Burlington (Silver Bow), near Butter, had a post office 1885-1901; William Master was the first postmaster. It may have taken its name from the Chicago, Burlington, and Quincy Railroad that built a short line between Butte and Anaconda. Woole says that a town by that name grew up around the Bluebird Mine and that a silver mill was built there in 1885. It was one mile from Rocker and at one time had a lodge hall, stores, school, and a church.

Burnham (Hill), near Fresno, was a station on the Great Northern and a post office 1914-1916. Martha Moss was the first postmaster.

Burns (Richland) was named for Burns Creek, which had been named for an Irish pioneer who lived along it. The post office, with Elmer Turner as postmaster, was established in 1906; it was discontinued in 1943.

Burnt Pine (Beaverhead) had a post office 1874-82; Daniel Parker was the first postmaster.

Burt (Custer) A post office under this name was applied for before the name was changed to Ismay in 1908.

Burton, Burtonville (Teton), near Choteau, had a post office 1894-99 with Ulysses Allen as postmaster. It was named for Z. T. Burton, who founded the town.

BUSBY (Big Horn) is on the Crow Indian Reservation twenty-six miles east of Crow Agency. The post office was established in 1904 with Sheridan Busby as postmaster. Ralph Shane says that "Custer's last camp on June 24, 1876, was on the Rosebud near the present townsite of **Busby** — they broke camp at midnight to start for the Indian camp on the Little Big Horn." The Busby Day School for Indians was started by the U.S. government in 1902.

Busch (Gallatin) started as a station on the Chicago, Milwaukee, St. Paul and Pacific Railroad. It was named for A. J. Busch, an assistant superintendent for the railroad.

Busteed (Stillwater) was named for the Busteed family, and Thomas Busteed was the first postmaster when the office opened in 1903.

Maggie Busteed had a team and a buckboard that she had fixed up to handle "bum" lambs. When the big sheep outfits with bands totaling between 15,000 and 18,000 ewes lambed out near Painted Robe and **Busteed**, Maggie drove along and gathered up the "bums." She had a milk cow tied to trail behind the wagon so she could have fresh milk for the lambs. When the buckboard was crowded she drove home and unloaded but repeated the process until she had fifty lambs to raise. "This deal used to drive Tom Busteed half crazy, as he was an ex-'79 outfit cowman at heart" (*They Gazed on the Beartooths, Vol. II*).

The **Busteed** post office was closed in 1933.

Butler (Lewis and Clark) was a post office name 1891-1901. Thomas Coulter was postmaster. After that the mail address was Austin.

BUTTE (Silver Bow), a county seat, was first called Butte City. A post office was granted under that name in July 1868 — Anson Ford distributed the mail from his drug store. Miners dubbed the city, taking the name from the nearby sentinel-like peak (Big Butte) which stands 6,369 feet above sea level. The first recorded visit by white men to this hill was in 1856. Judge C. E. Irvine and a party from Walla Walla, Washington stopped there on an exploration trip. They found a prospector's hole that later led to the Original Lode and some elk horns lying about which they figured had been used to dig the hole.

"Gold was discovered there in July 1864 by G. O. Humphrey and William Allison. By 1875 the name had been changed to **Butte**; silver was bringing riches, and copper was beginning to be seen as **Butte**'s fortune" (*Copper Camp*). Beneath the city lay one of the world's richest mineral deposits. There are some 250 miles of streets on the surface of Butte Hill, and more than two thousand miles of underground corridors and tunnels.

Marcus Daly (1841-1900), an Irish immigrant, learned about ores and mining while in Nevada; he rushed to **Butte** when the rich strikes of 1874 were reported. There he drilled, and at four hundred feet found not the silver that he anticipated, but the richest vein of copper known. The vein was fifty feet wide, and in twenty years Daly became the head of one of the world's most powerful monopolies, the Anaconda Copper Mining Company.

A townsite patent was issued for **Butte** in 1876 and the city was incorporated in 1879. By 1885 **Butte** had a population of 14,000 and the copper boom was on. The Montana School of Mines was established in 1900 (*Montana, A Guide Book*).

Open pit mining in recent years has scarred the face of the hill and eliminated hundreds of homes, buildings and even the famous and beloved Columbia Gardens. Residents have moved to the "flats."

Butte Creek (Garfield) was named for the creek it was on, which in turn had been named for a landmark butte nearby. The post office, established in 1913, was in the home of Mr. and Mrs. Frederick Kinney. Patrons came to this post office from the Blackfoot, Billy, Moonlight, and Snow Creek areas — At one time there were a hundred homesteaders served by this office. By 1936 they and the post office were gone.

Byford (Fergus) was named for postmaster Byford Wagstaff. The office was active 1915-18.

BYNUM (Teton) was named for the Stephen Bynum family, early settlers in the region. It is fourteen miles north of Choteau. The country store and post office (1885, George Fry in charge) was located on the banks of Muddy Creek for the convenience of stock growers.

C

Cabin Creek (Fallon) was the name of a post office 1911-13 and 1915-31. Elma Krema was the first postmaster. It has been suggested (*Wheels Across Montana's Prairie*) that the creek was named because many early trappers built cabins of cottonwood logs as they trapped for beaver. After the office closed in 1931, the mail went to Ismay.

Cabinet (Flathead) This post office was established in 1901 and Angus Hutton was postmaster. The office closed in 1905.

The Historical Society of Montana publication for 1896 mentions a steamboat, the "Cabinet," which was "the second river boat to navigate the waters of western Montana. Operations began in 1862 and were profitable for two or three years. The 'Cabinet' ran up the Clark's Fork River from the upper end of Cabinet Falls to the Rapids of Rock Island." There are also Cabinet Mountains, but whether they were named for the boat or vice versa is uncertain.

Cabinet Landing, (Missoula) had a post office February-May 1867 with M. B. Koontz in charge.

Cable (Deer Lodge) was named for the Atlantic Cable Mine discovered in 1866. It was first called Cable City and a post office was established under that name in 1868 with William Kelley as postmaster. The office was closed July 1869-July 1870 and then active until 1918 when the mail was ordered to Southern Cross.

Cadmus (Glacier) near Cut Bank, had a post office 1921-23 with Leon LaBarge as postmaster.

Cady (Park County), near Springdale, had a post office 1916-1920 with William Sincock as postmaster.

Calabar (Custer County) This post office opened in 1909 with Mrs. Stine Dunlap as postmaster. It was formerly called Lock; in 1929 the name was changed again, this time to Sheffield.

Caldwell (Phillips) was named for postmaster Andrew Caldwell when the office opened in 1914; it closed in 1935. These were the homestead years — years of great hope followed by despair.

Calkins (Meagher) was a station named for R. M. Calkins, vice-president of the Milwaukee Railroad. The post office opened in 1915 under Otto Randler, and closed in 1930 with orders to send the mail to White Sulphur Springs.

Callaway (Madison) had a post office 1871-72 with Ovide P. Laurin as postmaster, and again 1873-74. It was named for a prominent pioneer family. Col. James E. Callaway, his wife Mary, and son Llewellyn arrived in Virginia City in 1871 after Callaway had been appointed Secretary of Montana Territory by President Grant. He served in that capacity for six years, was a member of the Constitutional Conventions of 1884 and 1889, and was the first Republican Speaker of the House. His son, Llewellyn Callaway, was Chief Justice of the Supreme Court of Montana 1922-35 (*Trails and Trials*).

Calumet (Fallon) eighteen miles south of Plevna, served homesteaders as a post office 1911-35. Lydia Hugg was first postmaster and had the office in her all-stone home.

Calvert (Cascade) was named for the first postmaster, Sidney Calvert. The office was open 1908-34 and the mail then sent to Stockett. Previous to 1908, mail had come once a month from Evans. Calvert rode horseback to circulate a petition for a post office and later partitioned off part of his living room for the office.

Calypso (Prairie), near Terry, was a station on the Milwaukee Railroad; before that it was a ferryboat crossing on the Yellowstone. The ferry was operated by a block and tackle using gravity. When one end was raised, it propelled the ferry across the river. During World War II, the operator, Reno Walters, camouflaged it lest the Germans bomb it (*Wheels Across Montana's Prairies*).

Camas (Sanders) is near the border of Lake County. An early day post office was established in 1898 with Telesphore Demers as postmaster; it closed in 1957. The town was named for the abundant camas plant, a member of the lily family with an onion-like flavor. The Kootenai and Salish Indians used to come regularly to dig the bulb, which formed a staple in their diet.

Camas Prairie (Sanders), a few miles out of Camas, is on the Flathead Indian Reservation. The name is descriptive. A post office operated 1910-29; William Boberick was the first postmaster.

CAMERON (Madison) was named for the pioneering Cameron family. The settlement was originally known as Bear Creek. Addison Bovey Cameron and his brother James took up desert claims here in 1886. Add Cameron had the first post office in his home 1890-93. Later he and Josie had a store and post office on the ground floor of a building and a dance or community hall on the upper floor. At different times the post office was in the home of Frank Kirby and the Boardmans. In 1919 the **Cameron** store building was purchased by Frank Falbaum, who moved it six miles down the road to take advantage of the highway business generated by tourists traveling between Ennis and Yellowstone Park. This angered Bear Creek settlers, and for years none of them would trade at the **Cameron** store.

The mail came by rural delivery. The ranchers who now use the post office as headquarters have rich hay and pasture lands spreading up to the foot of Sphinx Mountain (elev. 10,860 ft.). The mountain was officially named by geologists because of a supposed resemblance to the Great Sphinx of Giza, but natives affectionately call it "Old Red" because of the beautiful red rock cliffs that glisten in the sunset.

Camp Baker (Meagher) had a post office 1872-79 when the name was changed to Fort Logan. John Hammell was the first postmaster.

Camp Cooke (Fergus), named for Gen. Philip St. George Cooke, was established in 1866 on the Missouri River above the mouth of the Judith River — the first U.S. Army fort in Montana. It was garrisoned until 1869 and was constructed of adobe with rock around windows and doors, and cottonwood logs for corner supports. The site, chosen by the War Department, was opposed by many military officers serving in Montana. Brevet Maj. Gen. William Hazen reported, "The post at the mouth of the Judith River is at a point where neither white nor red men ever go, and the location is subject to ridicule wherever I go" (*Military Posts of Montana*). By 1869 the garrison at **Camp Cooke** had been reduced to three officers and twenty-seven enlisted men; by March 1870 they too were gone. "To reach the site of the fort now, one must ford the river . . . and it takes a lot of imagination to see the fort. . . ." Actual destruction of the fort was accomplished by settlers, who built short-lived Judith City and Fort Claggett (*Oscar Mueller*).

Camp Lewis was located at what is now the edge of Lewistown. It was established in 1874 and garrisoned only during the summers of 1874 and '75.

Campsite (Cascade), near Monarch, had a post office 1922-37.

Camp(s) Pass (Powder River) had a post office 1917-55. Alta Camp was postmaster, so it would seem this was a pass or trail that went by the Camp family's place. In 1935 the post office was moved to Orville Cunningham's ranch and in 1940 it was moved to the Weichman ranch.

Camrud (Roosevelt) was granted a post office in 1921. Early in 1923, the name was officially changed to Benrud, and Ole Skaret continued on as postmaster.

Canton (Broadwater) was an old town in original Meagher County. The rich farm land around here supported some of the area's oldest settlements. The post office, established in 1872 with William Tieney as postmaster, was discontinued in 1935. When the Canyon Ferry Dam was built and the lake filled, all Canton Valley went under water.

Canyon (Yellowstone) had a post office 1880-83. Sidney Erwin was postmaster.

CANYON CREEK (Lewis and Clark) was formerly called Georgetown. It takes its present name from the creek that flows through a canyon to the Missouri River. The town, which has had a post office continuously since August 1871, now serves as an outpost for the ranches of the Prickly Pear Valley. The general store and filling station are located a few miles northwest of Helena. William Negus was the first postmaster.

Canyon Ferry (Lewis and Clark), near Helena, had a post office 1868-1907 (Joseph Stafford, postmaster); the office was active again 1910-22 and 1949-57. Early travelers found this a convenient place to ferry across the Missouri as it runs through the canyon. A later boom came with the building of the Canyon Ferry Dam here.

CAPITOL (Carter) was once known as Capitol Rock. It is on the Little Missouri River, where it crosses the state line into South Dakota. The post office was established in 1891 with Bernt Anderson as postmaster.

Carasco (Blaine) had a post office from 1890-92 with Samuel McLeod as postmaster.

Carbella (Park) is on the Northern Pacific line in the southwest corner of the county. It had a post office 1915-1936 (Alexander Stewart, postmaster).

Carbert (Daniels) was probably a name coined from postmaster Albert Carter's two names. The post office was active 1920-44.

Carbonado (Carbon) was named for the early coal mining activities in this area, near Joliet. A post office, opened in 1898, was discontinued in 1902; Lucius Whitney was postmaster. A Northern Pacific track ran up to the mine. Later, farm irrigation waters flooded the mines and they closed. Many of the houses were moved to Red Lodge.

Carbon County borders Wyoming and is centrally located in the state from an east-west view. It was named for the abundant coal deposits within its borders. **Carbon County** was created in March 1895 from parts of Park and Yellowstone counties. Red Lodge is the county seat. Agreements with the Crow Indians opened portions of what was to be **Carbon County** in the years 1882-92 for settlement by homesteaders and for locating mineral claims. The first road through the county was the old Meeteetse Trail.

Cardinal (Gallatin) was first called Crane. The name was changed when it was found there was another Crane, Montana, in Richland County.

CARDWELL (Jefferson) is 37 miles east of Butte on the Jefferson River. It was named for Edward Cardwell, an extensive property owner when the town was started. Chet Huntley, famous for his television news broadcasts and development of the Big Sky resort, was born here. **Cardwell** was a station on the Northern Pacific Railroad and is just across the river from Jefferson Island. It flourished when the Mayflower Mine was operating. A post office was established in 1909 with Agnes Johns as postmaster. Before that, area residents got their mail at Jefferson Island, an office which opened in 1872.

Carl (Sheridan) had a post office 1913-14 with Martha Bledsoe as postmaster. The name was changed to Flaxville.

Carlow (Glacier) was later called Fort Piegan. The new name was chosen by the railroad to revive the memory of old Fort Piegan, a trading post set up by the American Fur Company.

Carlton (Ravalli) is nine miles north of Stevensville. It was named for Mrs. Robert Carleton, an early settler. The "e" was somehow dropped from the name when the post office was granted in 1883 with Lizzie Young as postmaster. The community is located on Carlton Creek where it now meets US Highway 93. **Carlton** grew up along the railroad and once consisted of several houses, a post office, and a Methodist church. The railroad brought groceries and supplies needed by the settlers. A school was built in 1888 to serve both the Florence and **Carlton** communities, and they have come to be known as one community, Florence-Carlton. The post office at **Carlton** was discontinued in 1908 (Dennis Werner, Stevensville High School).

CARLYLE (Wibaux) is near the North Dakota border. It was named for the son of Arthur C. Knutson, who had a store and was postmaster when the office opened in 1907.

Carpenter Creek (Musselshell) had a post office 1915-18 John Donovan as postmaster. A big coal mine operated there for several years.

Carpenters Bar (Powell) briefly a post office June-December 1872.

Thomas Pounds was postmaster.

Carperville (Big Horn) had a post office 1920-22 with William Chapman as postmaster.

Carroll (Chouteau) Postal records show an office under this name operating 1874-77 in what was then Dawson County. Later entries under Chouteau County were for April-June 1880, and May 1881-November 1882 (County borders were a bit uncertain and often changed as Montana developed as a state).

"The Diamond R, one of the largest freight outfits, and the Missouri River Transportation Company, which owned several steamboats, after negotiations with the Northern Pacific, promoted a freight road through the Judith Basin from a point on the Missouri 25 miles west of the mouth of the Musselshell River. The little town here was called **Carroll** and the new road was known as the Carroll Trail. . . . **Carroll** had military protection during the summers of 1874 and 1875. During 1875 and 1876 a mail stage route operated over the Carroll Trail" (*Big Dry County*).

There were hopes that this point on the Missouri would rival Fort Benton because of its more advantageous location downstream, but it flourished only briefly in the 1870s (*A History of the Upper Musselshell Valley of Montana*).

"This short-lived port near Cow Island on the Missouri River was named for one of the promoters, Matthew Carroll. He, along with E. G. Maclay, C. A. Broadwater, and George Steel of Helena, formed the Diamond R Freighting Company. This new port was below the rapids in the river and even during low water, boats could get as far upstream as Cow Island and the plan was to transport the goods overland by team and wagon the 225 miles to Helena. As early as 1866 delegates to the Montana Constitutional Convention petitioned Congress for a good wagon road, but no interest was shown. The Northern Pacific Railroad in 1873 signed a contract with the Kountz Steamboat line and the E. G. Maclay Co. in an attempt tó appropriate the Missouri River trade in advance of the extension of its tracks. The railroad would bring goods to Bismarck, the steamboat would convey goods to a point below the rapids, and the wagon company would freight goods to Helena. All plans were calculated to divert the trade then going to Fort Benton.

"The Carroll Road built by the Diamond R Company was fraught with trouble from the beginning. It passed through Indian-held lands, spring rains and muds mired its wagon wheels, and the river boats failed to arrive on schedule. . . . By September 1874 Carroll Landing had become a modest commercial center of 75 to 200 people, depending on the time of year. . . . George Clendenin operated a general mercantile store surrounded by a protective wood stockade. . . . The freight road, except for local traffic, was used for the last time on November 1, 1875. The town itself was washed away by the Missouri in the 1880s" (Silliman, *The Carroll Trail, Utopian Enterprise*).

Matt Carroll, the freighter, later became General Gibbon's wagonmaster and hauled supplies for the Montana column during the Battle of the Little Big Horn (*Cabins and Campfires in Southeastern Montana*).

Carroll (Deer Lodge) had a post office 1888-1902 with Aaron Staton as postmaster.

CARTER (Chouteau) is a few miles southwest of Fort Benton, near the Missouri River at a spot where a ferry operated for many years. The town was originally called Sidney, but in 1905 the Great Northern Railroad changed the name to honor a U.S. Senator (see **Carter County**). The post office was established in 1910 with Marie Worth as postmaster.

Carter (Mineral) had a post office 1890-94 with William Bryan as postmaster. The office was open again 1902-04; after that the mail was ordered to Superior.

Carter County occupies the southeast corner of the state, bordering on South Dakota and Wyoming. The county seat is Ekalaka, which is located at the edge of a patch of Custer National Forest. Except for this and one other piece of forest land, the county is prairie land. Box Elder Creek and the Little Missouri River run through it. **Carter County** was named in honor of U.S. Senator Thomas Carter, who was also Montana's first congressman. The county was created in February 1917 from parts of Fallon County.

Cartersville (Rosebud) was named for U.S. Sen. Thomas Carter (see **Carter County**), one of the owners of the town plot, who was instrumental in reclaiming and irrigating a large tract of land there. **Cartersville** was a station on the Milwaukee Railroad near the mouth of the Rosebud River. The post office operated 1909-57; John Johnson was the first postmaster.

Casady (Blaine), eighteen miles northwest of Havre, had a post office 1914-29. Wilda Casady, with his four motherless daughters and his brother Ben, left Missouri for Montana. Wilda opened a store, served as postmaster after the office opened in 1914, and proved up on a homestead. When he eventually got discouraged and went back to Missouri, the post office was moved to his brother's homestead (*Grits, Guts and Gusto*).

CASCADE (Cascade) was a rival for the honor of being the county seat. It is a much older town than Great Falls. It was named for the cascades or falls in the Missouri River, although it is not very close to them. Postal records say the area post office was originally called Dodge. The **Cascade** office was established in 1887 with Thomas Gorham in charge. Charlie Russell lived here for a while.

Cascade County is in the north-central part of the state. It was organized in September 1887 from parts of Chouteau and Meagher counties; another part of Meagher County was annexed to **Cascade County** in 1898. It was named for the falls in the Missouri River in the northern part of the county. Great Falls is the county seat.

Castagne (Carbon) is near Red Lodge. It had a post office 1919-35 which served the settlers along Red Lodge Creek. The community was named for Frank Castagne, reportedly the first Carbon County casualty of World War I. John Kelly was the first postmaster.

Castle (Meagher) has a history typical of many mining boom towns in Montana. It took its name from the mountain on whose side it sprawled. An unusual rock formation, which can be seen as one approaches White Sulphur Springs, resembled a castle atop the mountain and gave rise to the name Castle Mountain. One of the mines was appropriately named the Princess; it and the Yellowstone were among the most lucrative. Most of the 1,500 mining claims in this area were discovered and worked between 1886 and 1890. The Castle Land Company platted eighty acres for the townsite, and within two months $100,000 worth of building lots had been sold. A post office under Hanson Barnes was established in 1887. **Castle**

reached its peak in 1891, the year it was incorporated; by then there were nine stores, one bank, two barber shops, two livery barns, two hotels, a photo gallery, and a dance hall, as well as churches, a schoolhouse, a fancy jail, fourteen saloons, a justice of the peace, a deputy sheriff, and a brass band. Stage lines powered by four-horse teams provided daily mail plus passenger and freight service between **Castle** and Martinsdale, White Sulphur Springs, Townsend, and Livingston. **Castle**'s streets were jammed with freight wagons and bull teams hauling in mining machinery and coke for the smelters. Methodists, Congregationalists, Episcopalians, and Presbyterians all held services there. During its brief life, **Castle** had four newspapers, each also short-lived.

Castle's three smelters were built between 1889 and 1891. The Cumberland Mine here was the highest single producer of lead ore in the state. Bars of bullion weighing a hundred pounds were shipped by ox team to Livingston. By 1892 the stockholders were jittery and sold out to a New York firm. Operations were closed down in 1893, awaiting the arrival of the railroad to make transportation more economical. Richard Harlow finally got his "Jaw Bone" railroad extended to Leadboro two miles below **Castle** in the fall of 1897, but it was too late to save the town (*Montana Pay Dirt*). A cluster of tumbledown log and frame buildings are now the ghosts of a once-booming camp.

Castle Buttes (Yellowstone) had a post office 1916-24. Walter Harris was the first postmaster.

Castle Junction (Broadwater) was the original name of Lombard. Nearby Castle was in the center of an important mining areas, and **Castle Junction** was a railroad connection which aided in the shipping of ore from the Castle mines (see **Castle**).

Castle Rock (Rosebud), near Forsyth, had a post office 1910-26 (George Binkerd, postmaster).

Castner (Meagher) was named for postmaster John Castner. The office was open only April-June 1883; the mail was then sent to Beltane.

Cataract (Jefferson) had a post office 1880-81 with George Gallahan as postmaster. It was no doubt named for a cataract or falls in one of the large rivers that flow across this county.

Cataract, a station in Glacier National Park, was formerly called Arklow. The new name, chosen by the railroad, suggests the many beautiful waterfalls in the mountains near here.

Cat Creek (Petroleum), near Dovetail, was a "raw, roaring oil camp" in the early 1920s. There were tar paper shacks for families and company bunkhouses for single men. There was a company cook house and a recreation hall. Many of the 200-300 men working at **Cat Creek** were homesteaders who worked to support families left on often impoverished farms. The post office was opened in 1922 with Orville Canfield as postmaster and storekeeper.

Cat Creek was the site of Montana's first commercially successful oil strike, in 1920. A four-inch pipeline was built to the railroad at Winnett. There were about 150 producing wells at the peak. By 1975, thirty-five of them were operating "on pump" and the employment boom was over. In 1963 the post office was made a rural branch of the Winnett office. It has been estimated that about 23 million barrels of oil have been produced in **Cat Creek**'s 54-year history.

Cathmere A post office was established here on May 12, 1914, with William G. Heisler as postmaster. It was discontinued in 1930 and mail was sent to Cartwright (*Courage Enough*).

Catlin (Meagher) was named for the Catlin Brothers, ranchers who settled there in 1900 and were influential in developing the area.

Cato (Prairie), near Terry, was named for an old Texas family that went north with a cattle herd and became prominent in Miles City. O. C. Cato was a cattleman, range foreman, and manager for the XIT outfit, and at one time, sheriff.

Cavendish (Beaverhead), near Bannack, had a post office 1891-93 with John Fleming as postmaster.

Cavern (Jefferson) was named for the caves now called Lewis and Clark Caverns. The post office was open 1909-36 (Eugene Woodward, postmaster). Woodward was one of the three men who made the original exploration of the caves in 1898.

Cavetown (Lewis and Clark) was established as a post office in 1878 with Court Sheriff as postmaster. The office closed two years later.

Cecil (Lewis and Clark) had a post office 1884-86 with DeWitt Holbrook as postmaster.

Cedar (Wibaux) had a post office 1901-11. The first postmaster was Samuel Bovee.

Cedar Junction (Mineral) had a post office 1870-71 with Andrew J. Simmons as postmaster.

Cedarview (Gallatin) had a post office 1898-1901 with Ella Kinney as postmaster. The mail was then sent to Manhattan. Presumably this settlement and the two above were named because cedar trees flourished in each area.

Ceekay (Phillips) had a post office 1932-37; Nettie Morgan was the first postmaster.

Centennial (Madison) had a post office 1889-92 with William Reed as postmaster.

Centennial Valley (Beaverhead) was named in 1876 in honor of the nation's centennial by two prominent stockmen of the area. William C. Orr and Philip H. Poindexter established the P&O Ranch along Blacktail Creek. The ranch later became the Matador Cattle Company, and the **Centennial Valley** became a renowned federal bird sanctuary on the edges of the Red Rock Lakes.

Center City (Madison) was a mining camp in Alder Gulch.

Centerville (Madison) was a community near Twin Bridges midway between Pageville and Point of Rocks and had a schoolhouse which served not only for classes but as a community center. It was active for thirty-eight years, from the 1870s on.

CENTRAL PARK (Gallatin) is famous for its cheese products. "There is some discussion as to the relationship of Creamery, Fly, and the two **Central Parks**. About 1889 a small settlement was established approximately three miles south of the present site of **Central Park** along US Highway 10. This city was known as **Central Park** also, and was on the west side of the West Gallatin River. A gentleman named H. C. Cockrill built a bridge across the river and named it Cockrill's Bridge. The main body of the 'city' was then moved to the east side of the river, and an extra bit of enthusiasm was created over the building of a city there. In 1882, a man named William Fly purchased the property, which consisted of the bridge, a hotel, and some other small buildings. In 1884, William Fly was appointed postmaster of his little domain of Fly. Not too long after the Northern Pacific went through the valley in 1883, a station was established at the present site of **Central Park** and this place was also named **Central Park**. Just a half mile from it, H. C. Cockrill had a dairy farm and a creamery. Then when William Fly died in 1887, Cockrill became postmaster and the post office was established on his farm. This post office took the name of Creamery. In the meantime, a store, hotel, and other buildings had been moved from old **Central Park** to the new **Central Park**, and the old spot became known as Fly or Fly's Bridge. It is not known just when Creamery gave up the ghost, but it was probably when Cockrill resigned from the postal business. The post office was then moved to **Central Park**, and Creamery ceased to exist" (Iverson).

Postal records show a **Central Park** (Centralpark) with a post office established in 1871 with Vardamon Cockrill as postmaster. It was closed in 1887, reopened in 1891, and closed again in 1901 with the notation that it was formerly called Creamery. The office was open again 1902-09, and I'm sure the authorities in Washington were as confused as this author until Mr. Iverson sent the above information.

Centreville (Broadwater) was located on the east side of the Missouri River just across from the mouth of Indian Creek. It had a post office 1872-74 with John Robinson as postmaster, and again December 1874-83. The town faded when the railroad came in and built a station at Townsend.

Chadborn (Park) was a station on the Northern Pacific Railroad named for A. W. Chadborn, from whom the right-of-way for the railroad was acquired. There was a post office in **Chadborn** 1914-34; Joseph Webber was the first postmaster.

Chaffinville was a short-lived settlement named for the Chaffin family, who were early settlers in the Bitterroot Valley.

Chaldia (Garfield), near Cohagen, had a post office 1915-16 with George Azoo as postmaster.

Chalk Buttes (Carter), named after the white-colored buttes nearby, is located on Cabin Creek in a small mountain range southwest of Ekalaka. The post office was open 1910-42. Gabriel Bradshaw was the first postmaster.

Chamberlain (Fergus) is near the town of Grass Range. It was a stopping place on the main road from Custer Junction, past Mussellshell and the Flatwillow post office. A log cabin still stands on the Tynan place to mark the site of **Chamberlain**, northwest of old Fort McGinnis (Bard and Ann Teigen).

"Frank Chamberlain came to Montana as a wolfer and trapper. . . . The Hudson Bay Fur Company had a large trading post at Fort Benton run by John Jacob Astor in the 1860s and '70s and bought furs from Indians and trappers. Chamberlain joined up with the Crow Indians and married one of their young squaws and made some money by hauling all their furs and hides. He bought 2,000 ewes, filed on some land on McDonald Creek, and

47

started a sheep ranch. He built two log cabins — one was the post office, saloon and stage stop, where drivers could change mules and eat dinner for 75 cents" (Degner). Since postal records do not list **Chamberlain**, it is probable that the stage station was just a mail drop, rather than an office.

Thomas Cruse of Helena trailed a band of yearling ewes to the Little Snowies in 1880, looking for a place to start a sheep ranch. He liked Chamberlain's spread and made a deal for the two of them to run sheep together. In 1884 a man called Timer Line was killed in Chamberlain's saloon. Chamberlain sold all his holdings to Cruse, took his squaw and family, left and was never heard of again. That was when the famous N Bar Ranch was started." (Winnett *Times*). Cruse had the post office (?) moved to Charter's store 1½ miles south of **Chamberlain**.

Champion (Deer Lodge) had a post office 1889-93. William Molthen was postmaster, and the settlement was near Deer Lodge City.

Chance (Carbon) was named for Nathan Chance, a stockman and early settler. In 1890 Chance built a tall bridge at what later became the Clark's Fork River; previously a ferry was used. **Chance** was a stop on the Old Meeteetse Trail to Wyoming. "Buffalo Bill" Cody traveled this route to his enterprises on the Shoshone River until the Burlington and Missouri River Railroad built into Cody, Wyoming, in 1901. Lillie B. Chance, Nathan's daughter, was appointed postmaster when the office opened in 1898; it was closed in 1921 and the mail was sent to Belfry.

Chapman (Gallatin) was named for John Chapman, a farmer whose land adjoined the townsite (Rowe).

Chapman (Phillips), was a station on the Great Northern Railroad. It had a post office 1929-55; Ivan Barker was the first postmaster.

Chappell (Chouteau) was a station on the Great Northern Railroad. The Post Office Department uses the name Loma — and so did the railroad company for many years, but in 1915 or '16 the station name was changed to **Chappell** to avoid confusion in handling shipments consigned to Lohman. The name **Chappell** was chosen to honor Edward Chappell, who homesteaded the area in 1888 and owned the land on which the town and railroad were later built. Before Loma and **Chappell**, the little settlement was known as Marias.

CHARLESBURG (Powell) was named for postmaster Charles Anderson but the office was only active February-September 1920. Mail was then handled at Elliston.

CHARLO (Lake) was originally a trail crossing for freighters hauling grain and other goods from the rich Ronan Valley to the railroad at Dixon. The place was first called Big Flat, then Charlotte, and later **Charlo**, in honor of Chief Charlo of the Flatheads, one of the few chiefs who refused to sign Special Commissioner James A. Garfield's order (August 27, 1872) removing all Indians of the region to the Jocko reservation. Joseph Dixon, a governor and U.S. Senator, was instrumental in establishing the name **Charlo**.

Johnny Chilcott of Stevensville High School sent this quote from his grandfather's diary: "The Indians all left this morning, poor souls, it was sad to see them. They took their horses, packed some wagons, took their cattle and all their belongings." Chief Charlo left his war blanket to Johnny's grandfather, Lee Bass, who had described Charlo as a good-sized

Indian, a man of few words and a strong arm. "He was looked up to by the other chiefs of the Flathead Nation. He knew the value of peace and tried to live as peaceful a life as he could. He was a man of strong will and wise thoughts. He refused for many years to leave his beloved valley of the Bitterroot and pleaded with the government agencies to let them stay. Finally he had to go; his people were sick, weak and hungry. Charlo was defeated in peace as Chief Joseph had been defeated in war."

The **Charlo** post office was opened in 1918 with Pontus Haegg as postmaster.

Chateau de la Fountaine (Ravalli) was never a town; there was never even a post office by that name, but it *was* a community gathering place and it has such a delightful name that it cannot be left out of a book about names. **Fountaine,** a French word, means not only fountain, but also spring or well, and **Chateau** brings to mind a castle or large manor house, so "Castle of the Spring" is a descriptive and romantic name for this three-story grist mill on Burnt Fork Creek. The earliest available record has an entry about grain being brought to the mill on January 5, 1871. Actually, the mill was built by a Frenchman named Peter LaFountaine and another man named Clairmont. The mill probably started out as the Mill of LaFountaine, and its unusual three-story structure and French owners developed the name into "chateau."

The grist mill pulverized grain from as far away as Fort Benton and Great Falls until the arrival of the railroads spelled its end. Stones which were used to grind the grain into flour are now preserved on the Stevensville school grounds. The huge three-story mill has hand-hewn timbers and wooden augers brought in by steamboat which are still in place. The mill was operating until the beginning of World War I (Vickie Thoft, Stevensville High School).

Chausse (Carter) was named for the family of Mary Chausse, postmaster when the office opened in 1915; it closed in 1927.

Chautauqua (Flathead), reminiscent of the popular traveling shows that crossed Montana in the early 1920s, was also a post office active 1901-05 with John Stover as first postmaster. Entertainers in Model A Fords braved summer rains and gumbo roads to get from one little town to the next — to Opheim, Plentywood, Kremlin, and Brockton. Chautauqua programs were planned to be educational, entertaining and culturally enriching and they were popular. Then came the movies and radio; by 1928 the hey-dey of **Chautauqua** was over and soon after that the big brown tents folded for the last time and were trucked away (*Montana Magazine*, Summer 1976)

Cheadle (Fergus) grew up along the proposed Great Northern line from Lewistown to New Rockford, North Dakota. Construction workers built two tunnels and completed a graded roadbed for track that was never laid. A narrow gauge construction track and small engines were used in the work. The post office lasted 1915-23. Nellie Snider was the first postmaster. Only a few buildings remain, but there once was a schoolhouse and two teachers handling forty students in eight elementary grades and one year of high school. The homesteaders who came about 1914 were mostly miners and stonecutters from Yugoslavia.

The community was named for Judge F. K. Cheadle, who homesteaded about a mile east of the general store and post office. Now the small homesteads have been combined into huge ranches (Byerly).

Checkerboard (Meagher), was a highway store and gas station. The entire area was owned by the Bair Livestock Company, the control of which later passed into the hands of Bair's two sisters. Bair was one of the biggest sheep ranchers in Valley County around 1910; it was said he owned about 60,000 sheep which he brought into the Judith Basin for wintering (see **Lismas**).

Chelt (Valley), near Ophein, had a post office 1916-18 with Maud Bubb as postmaster.

Cherry Patch (Blaine) had a post office 1914-19; Gunde Gulseth was postmaster. The mail was then sent to Twete.

Cherry Ridge (Blaine) is near Zurich. The post office opened in 1913 under John Jones and closed in 1935. Early-day homesteader George Jacobsen writes in a letter to *Montana Magazine*: "In 1913 I filed on a homestead north of Zurich and about six miles northeast of a store and post office called **Cherry Ridge**. . . . My land bordered on the Canadian line. . . . Hauling my living equipment and building material to the site took two wagon loads. It was October; snowflakes were falling. I was alone on the north prairie with no sign of neighbors as far as one could see. . . . I could hear a coyote crying in the still night. . . . In 1915 I took Marjorie Peelman of Havre for my wife. . . . I made skis for each of us from one-by-four foot flooring and turned the ends up by boiling them."

Cherry Springs (Carbon) was between Roberts and Bridger. The schoolhouse served as community center and voting place.

Chesley (Fergus) was granted a post office in 1917, but the order was rescinded.

CHESTER (Liberty), on the High Line 57 miles west of Havre, is a county seat. **Chester** is located on the banks of Cottonwood Creek at the place where ranchers in the 1880s paused to rest on the long drive to the railhead at Minot, North Dakota before the Great Northern Railroad was built. The name was chosen by the first telegraph operator there in honor of his hometown in Pennsylvania.

The **Chester** post office was established in 1895 with Brown B. Weldy as postmaster.

Chestnut (Cascade) was an early day town near St. Clair. The post office was opened in 1878 with R. N. Sutherlin as postmaster. It closed in April 1890.

Chestnut, Chesnut (Gallatin) was named for Col. J. D. Chesnut. The name was erroneously spelled **Chestnut** when the post office was established in 1894. It was open until 1906 and again 1907-14; Leonard Barrott was the first postmaster. This early coal mining town is now deserted and mail is handled out of Bozeman.

Chico, Chico Hot Springs (Park) was originally just **Chico**. It began when miners from Yellowstone City moved up the gulch and established a new camp. Some of them took up farming. The settlement was constantly plagued by attacks from Crow Indians, especially in the spring of 1868, when the Crow Reservation extended much farther west. Indians persisted in stealing horses. During winters many families left the area and traveled up the Yellowstone by boat to spend the cold months in a warmer part of the state. In 1880 **Chico**'s mining area was described as ten miles long, principally deep underground. The town supported a hotel, meat market, store, blacksmith shop, schoolhouse, sixty cabins, and a post office, which opened in 1874. John Cone was the first postmaster. The office closed in 1919 and mining operations ceased in 1933. **Chico Hot Springs** takes its name from the warm water bubbling up here some twenty miles north of Yellowstone Park.

Childs (Sanders) was a station on the Northern Pacific. The post office on the highway near there is known as White Pine.

Chimney Rock (Park), near Livingston, had a post office 1893-1919; Asa Merrill was first postmaster. It was named for an interesting rock formation nearby that resembles a chimney.

CHINOOK (Blaine), a county seat, is located on Lodge Creek near where it empties into the Milk River. According to Perrin, the first name for this settlement was Belknap, and the railroad station's name was Dawes. But the latter name was unsatisfactory to settlers, and upon the suggestion of E. R. McGinnis, Great Northern immigration agent, the name **Chinook** was adopted. The name comes from an Indian word meaning "warm wind," and it is this wind, melting the snow in January and February, that makes it possible for cattle to reach the rich bunch grass and survive — chinook winds have saved many a cattleman from disaster. It was Charlie Russell's postcard picture of a starving range cow, "Waiting for a Chinook" (also called "The Last of Five Thousand"), that first won him recognition as an artist. Willard says that seventeen miles south of **Chinook** is the site of the battlefield where on October 4, 1877, Chief Joseph, with 87 warriors and 147 women and children of the Nez Perce tribe, finally surrendered to Gen. Nelson A. Miles on the banks of Snake Creek.

The **Chinook** post office opened in 1889 with Thomas O'Hanlon as postmaster. Lizzie Curtis was the first schoolteacher.

CHOTEAU (Teton) is a county seat and one of the oldest still-active towns in this part of Montana. It began as a trading post and was called Old Agency when the post office was established in 1875. In January 1882 the name was changed to **Choteau** to honor Pierre Chouteau, Jr., president of the American Fur Company, who brought the first steamboat up the Missouri (Perrin). Chouteau's father was a founder of the Missouri River Fur Company. The county which was also named in honor of this family uses the original French spelling (Chouteau), but the town name has dropped the first "u." Alfred Hamilton was the first postmaster.

Chouteau County was one of the original nine counties established by the territorial legislature in 1865. It encompassed the north-central part of the state and is still one of Montana's largest counties, even though several smaller counties have from time to time been created out of its original area. The county was named for Auguste and Pierre Chouteau, American pioneers, fur traders, and founders of the city of St. Louis. Fort Benton, the county seat, was famous as a shipping point for riverboats that could come up the Missouri only this far. In 1883 **Chouteau County** extended from old Missoula County on the west to Dawson County on the east, or more than one-third the length of the state. It also extended from the Canadian border to more than one-third of the way to the southern border. Parts of **Chouteau County** were taken to form Teton County in 1893; Blaine and Hill in 1912; and parts of Liberty and Pondera in 1919. Another part was annexed to Teton in 1921.

Christensen (Fergus), near Roy, was named for first postmaster, Niels

Christensen. The post office was active 1915-21.

CHRISTINA (Fergus) is a prosperous farm and ranch community north of Lewistown. It was named for Christina Hilger, wife of David Hilger, who was postmaster when the office opened in 1885. Postal records say the place was formerly called Saltbrook and that the office was closed 1896-99, then open until 1907, then closed again until 1914.

The homesteaders arrived about 1906 and until the one-room schoolhouse was built in 1913, some summer terms were held in a homesteader's shack. The first teacher got $35 a month and taught 35 to 40 pupils in all eight grades. Upper-grade kids helped teach the younger ones (Byerly).

Christina hit its peak in 1915 with the usual stores, businesses and even a six-room hotel. Neighbors pitched in to serve meals at the Central Montana Fair for two or three years to raise money to build the community hall.

Churchill (Gallatin) is a part of the Holland Settlement, which also includes Amsterdam, a shopping center, and a railroad station. Churches were built on the hill and the houses form a cluster around them, so this part of the settlement was called **Churchill**. The community began after the West Gallatin Irrigation Company, in conjunction with the Reverend Wormser — a Presbyterian minister — brought a group of settlers from Holland. The first came in 1893. The language was strange, the dry land was different, and even the church was different from the one they had left back home. These settlers tended to remain in a tight little group, associating very little with people from other communities. They finally established a Christian Reform Church and the Presbyterians moved out. Later a Protestant Reformed Church was introduced into the community and caused a rift among the townspeople. The Manhattan Christian High School is located in **Churchill**.

Cicero (Madison) had a post office under that name 1869-74, with Jean Laurin as postmaster. In 1874 the name was changed to Laurin (Lah-RAY).

Cinnabar (Park), just north of Yellowstone National Park, was named for the the Cinnabar Mountains, whose vertical reefs are made of intense red rock. The red coloring is the result of the presence of iron, but the cause was originally thought to be cinnabar (red oxide of mercury). The post office, with Leander Hoppl as first postmaster, was open 1892-1903.

Dick Randall — pioneer rancher, guide and dude wrangler — writes in his memoirs, "**Cinnabar** was a coal town founded by Harry Hare. The Conrad Company of Great Falls found it was good coking coal. The railroad built what they called the National Park branch from Livingston and they got as far as **Cinnabar**, near where Gardiner sits now. The land was owned by Mrs. McCutcheon and she wouldn't give them the right-of-way, so the road stopped at **Cinnabar** — that was about 1884 and a little hamlet sprung up there. The railroad unloaded the passengers here and 'staged' them with six-horse stages the five or six miles to the Park." A 1902 photo shows President "Teddy" Roosevelt arriving at the **Cinnabar** station for an inspection trip of the park (*Montana Magazine*; Summer, 1976).

CIRCLE (McCone) is a county seat situated halfway between Glendive and the Fort Peck Reservoir. It was named for the circle brand of one of Montana's first cattle outfits, which was owned by Cross and Twiggly. Records show a post office approved in 1902 with George Cross to be postmaster, but it was never activated. In 1905 the post office did open and Marie Rorvik was postmaster. Old-time cow punchers used this cow town as headquarters and could usually find a job in the spring with one of the cattle pools that grazed their stock on the lush ranges nearby. South of **Circle** are the Big Sheep Mountains, once home of the Audubon Mountain Sheep, a species made extinct in the homestead days by hungry settlers who liked the tasty meat.

Citadel (Flathead) was a station on the Great Northern. It was originally named Coram. The name was changed by railroad officials to make it suggestive of the mountain formations in Glacier National Park.

Clagett, on the east side of the Judith River, was a trading post later known as Judith Landing. It was named for William Clagett, one of Montana's first congressmen. Clagett's political career began when he was a camp cook. When the election was held at what is now **Clagett** to choose a delegate to Congress for Montana Territory, the vote was unanimous for Billy. Five voters turned out — just enough to hold a legal election, with three judges and two clerks (*In the Land of Chinook*).

"T. C. Power Co. operated a commissary at Camp Cooke until the fort was closed in 1869. They finally bought the remnants from the government and continued there until 1872 when they built the new trading post called Fort Clagett on the east side of the Judith River. . . . The Stevens Treaty was held on the north side of the Missouri on the flat below the PN Ferry crossing in 1855. The PN Ferry crossing continued to operate though the trading post and the army were there only a few years. The post office was opened in 1872 with Abel Quaintance in charge of that along with a store and stopping place for cowboys. The office closed in 1878" (George Mueller).

More futile attempts at settlement were made at or near **Clagett** than at any other place in the entire territory, according to Elizabeth Cheney; her husband "Kid" Amby was one of five cowboys who swam great cattle herds (25,000 at a time, about 70,000 in all) across the Missouri here to greener pastures in the Bear Paw Mountains and along the Milk River. The Judith Basin was being taken up by settlers, so the Judith Basin Cattle Pool decided to move their stock and reorganize as the Bear Paw Pool. In the summer of 1890 Judith Landing came alive again as bellowing herds, 1,500 to 2,000 at a time, were driven into the big river and forced to swim across.

CLANCY, CLANCEY (Jefferson), a few miles south of Helena, was named for Clancy Creek; the creek, in turn, was named for a colorful old-timer known as "Judge" Clancy. Postal records show an office open 1872-85 (Henry Hill, first postmaster) and includes the notation that the place was first called Prickly Pear. In 1885 the name was changed to Alhambra, and an office under that name was active until 1947. Also in 1885, postal records show establishment of another **Clancy** office with Frances Harvey as postmaster. This new location was at the railroad station a short distance from the hot springs resort of Alhambra.

The area was a famous silver camp in the late nineteenth century and the ore from the **Clancy** district was so rich that even after it was hauled by bull team to Fort Benton and shipped by river and ocean to Swansea, Wales, for smelting, it still netted a profit.

Clara (Golden Valley) was a post office originally in Fergus County 1905-35. It was named for the only daughter of the first postmaster, William Victor Lewis. A former pharmacist, Lewis came to Montana in the late

'80s to go into the sheep business with the Raw family, who were early ranchers over an extensive area around Hobson, Ubet, Straw and Garneill. Later, he married their daughter, Kathryn Raw, and they moved to the Little Snowies in April of 1905 while Bill Lewis continued on his own as a sheepman. After living for a time in their log cabin home at the base of the mountains, Lewis decided to build a large rock house adjoining it. His three oldest sons brought immense slabs down on a stone boat with horses; a skilled stonemason who had moved to Montana from Scotland was hired to build the imposing two-story house.

For five years Bill Lewis rode twenty-five miles west to get his mail at the Irene post office on Swimming Woman Creek. Beginning in 1910, William Evans carried mail on a new route from Pine Grove to Lavina. Once a week he would make the fifty-five-mile trip one way. Evans lived five miles from the first post office, so he would start out on horseback at two o'clock in the morning to get the mail sacks, come home for breakfast, then hitch his team and start out in a three-seat spring wagon. In good weather he would arrive by 6 P.M. and spend the night in Lavina. The next day the mail run would be heavy and homesteaders would send letters out and receive catalogs and packages in return. His salary from the government was $700 a year.

The rock house at **Clara** has played a central role down through the years. In 1938 the notorious Lee Simpson — who then owned the old Bill Lewis ranch — fired on two Golden Valley County officers from an upstairs window. He killed a deputy sheriff who was trying to hide behind his car parked at the gate, and after hours of gun-play, the sheriff, in the dark, reached a ranch on foot two miles away, carrying a bullet hole in his hat. After a spectacular trial in which Wellington D. Rankin was the prosecutor and most of the detective magazines of the day printed the lurid details, the judge set December 30, 1939, as the day of Simpson's hanging — the first and last in Golden Valley County. Borrowed gallows were brought in from Miles City, and on that cold winter evening, a large number of people gathered in front of the courthouse in Ryegate, and because of liquor flowing freely, a hundred of them had to be appointed as deputy sheriffs to preserve order. (Mary Morsanny)

Clarence (Meagher) was a post office 1887-88. William Heaton was postmaster.

Clark (Park) was named for the explorer. A post office was granted under this name in October 1882 but the name was changed to Livingston the next month. Oscar Phillips was postmaster.

Clark (Richland) had a post office 1910-29. Charlie Clark was postmaster.

Clarkston (Gallatin) was named for the family of the first postmaster, W. Guy Clark. The office opened in 1910; it closed in 1958.

Clarkston (Lewis and Clark) had a post office 1873-78 and again 1883-84. Bradford Woods was postmaster.

Clasoil (Jefferson) was named for the type of soil around the little store and post office at the crossroads. The office was open 1917-43. John Broberg was the first postmaster. The store and gas station enjoyed a brief boom during the building of Canyon Ferry Dam as workers turned off the main highway at this junction. The Northern Pacific siding here was called Louisville.

Clayton (Chouteau) A post office was authorized but soon rescinded here in 1903. John Meyer was to have been postmaster.

Clearcreek (Blaine) had a post office 1903-13 (Winfield S. Young, postmaster). It was near Ada.

Clear Lake (Chouteau) was near Graceville and had a post office 1911-19. Frank Fisher, the first postmaster, owned a coal company that imported coal from the Roundup mines. He kept the post office in the front room of his home. The community was named for a body of water about two miles from the Clear Lake schoolhouse, which also served as the community social center. Chautauquas came in the summer.

Clearwater (Missoula) Postal records show an office authorized in what was then Deer Lodge County in 1889 but it seems never to have gotten into operation until 1902. It was active then until 1926.

Cleiv (Teton) had a post office during homestead days, 1915-36. Margit Fjeld was postmaster.

Clemons (Lewis and Clark) was an early settlement with a post office 1898-1925, except for a few months in 1901. Frank Eberl was the first postmaster. **Clemons** is near Wolf Creek.

Clendenin (Judith Basin) This office is shown opening in old Meagher county in 1882 with Fred W. Reed, postmaster, and a notation that the office was formerly called Goldrun. In 1892 the name was changed to Barker. **Clendenin** was a mining camp active at the turn of the century named for Col George Clendennin, who built one of the smelters and later died in a rock slide.

Clendenin (Meagher) had a post office open 1881-82 with James Matkin as postmaster.

Cleora (Park) This post office was open 1891-97, and had William Potter as postmaster.

Cleveland (Blaine), in Milk River country, had a post office 1893-1957.
    James Roberts was the first postmaster in those years of open ranges and big cattle herds, followed by the homesteading days and still later, the consolidation of little farms into large ranches.

Cliff (Powell) Postal records show this office opening in 1900 with Daniel Heyfrom in charge. It was closed in 1905.

Cliff Lake (Madison), near Yellowstone National Park, takes its name from the surrounding topography of lake and mountains. Cliff and Wade lakes were early well-known fishing spots, and the area around them abounded in fur-bearing game, but it was not until the Missouri homesteaders arrived that it had a particular name. After the Missourians settled it became known as Missouri Flats. The post office was established in 1912 with Jesse Connor in charge. The schoolhouse became the community center, and rodeos, picnics, and races became a part of Sunday outings. By 1942 most of the homesteaders had starved out or been frozen out — finally they sold out. The post office lasted until 1953. Now it is an important recreation area, and only a few cattle ranches and ranges remain as reminders of the agricultural days.

Clifford (Missoula) was the name chosen by postmaster John Clifford when the office opened in 1888. The name was changed to Demersville in 1889.

Clifton (Yellowstone), near Huntley, had a post office for only six months in 1914-15. Ruth Cleveland was postmaster.

Climax (Carter), near Piniele, had a post office established in 1913 with Ross Hedrick as postmaster; the office closed in 1920.

CLINTON (Missoula) is an old mining and lumber town. Ore deposits were discovered in 1889 and the Charcoal Mine yielded thousands of dollars worth of lead and silver. The name **Clinton** was chosen that year in honor of Henry Clinton. Originally the place had been known as Betters' Station. It was started as a stage station on the Mullan Road in 1883 and named for Austin Betters, a homesteader. The Northern Pacific railroad men first called this place Wallace, but the name was unacceptable to the Post Office Department. At different times the settlement was also called Pine Grove (which was very descriptive) and Blossberg. The **Clinton** post office, with Samuel Scott in charge, opened in 1892.

Clipper (Madison), a mining camp near Pony, had a post office September 1902-04. It has been claimed that the Clipper, Boss Tweed, Old Joe and Garnet mines produced over $4 million in gold. Daniel Welch and William Umspaw were the two postmasters.

Clough (Lewis and Clark) was a station named for Col. J. B. Clough, principal assistant engineer for the Northern Pacific. Postal records show an office 1894-98 with Mary Brien in charge and note the name was changed to Birdseye.

Clow (Broadwater) was a station named after Frank Clow, an engineer who lost his life when Train Number 2 was held up by highway robbers.

CLYDE PARK, CLYDEPARK (Park), north of Livingston, was originally called Sunnyside, which was also the name of "Madame Bulldog's" stage stop and travelers' rest station; when the post office was established at her place in May 1885, it also took the name Sunnyside. The postmaster is listed as Sarah Robinson. In 1887 the office was moved to the ranch of Messrs. Harvey and Tregloan, who were raising Clydesdale horses imported from England. The name was changed to **Clyde Park** after these horses and the park-like appearance of the valley. This name followed the post office as it moved from one ranch to another with each new postmaster appointment. In 1900 it was moved to the present site of **Clyde Park**, at a four-way crossroad. The branches led to farms and ranches — one to Rock Creek Ranch, one to Brackett Creek, one to White Sulphur Springs, and one to Livingston. Supplies in the early days were hauled into **Clyde Park** by Jim Bowen, known as the "Cayuse Kid," who freighted with a twenty-four horse jerk line. By 1914 the Northern Pacific Railroad was making its run up Shields Valley past **Clyde Park** six times a week (Dorothy Pattyn, Park County News).

Coalcreek (Daniels) had a post office 1909-April 1921. Ella Dodge was the first postmaster.

Coalridge (Sheridan) is in the extreme northeast corner of the state near the North Dakota border. Old Coalridge is an abandoned mining town about a mile from the present town. It was named for a tunnel mine begun along the ridge in 1906. George Onstad bought the mine and built a general store with two stories. The upper part served as a church when the Reverend Hegge, a circuit-riding minister, came by, and as a community hall when there was need for one. A law office, bank, school, drugstore, and a newspaper called the **Coalridge** Call were established, and the town band played on holidays. A post office was opened in 1907 with Charles Ballack as postmaster; it closed in 1974. The town moved to its present site in 1924 (Gary Boles, Antelope High School).

Coalville (Carbon), according to postal records, was originally called Gebo; the name was changed in 1907 and Henry Griffith was appointed postmaster. The office closed in 1912. Information from local historians indicates that both Gebo and **Coalville** were mining camps which were later incorporated into Fromberg.

Coalwood (Powder River) is between Broadus and Miles City. John W. Janssen opened the post office there in 1912, and also had tobacco, paper, pencils, pens and ink to sell. By 1915, his place had become a regular merchandise store. The name for the town was suggested by W. C. Hocking and approved by a vote of the settlers because they had "plenty of coal, plenty of wood, and plenty to be thankful for" (*Echoing Footsteps*). The region around it was once Cheyenne Indian hunting ground. Tepee rings, arrowheads, and stone knives have been found on old campsites along the creeks.

Coberg, Coburg (Blaine) is near Savoy. A post office was active 1902-36; the spelling of the name was changed in 1917. John Burnett was the first postmaster. The homestead rush hit **Coburg** about 1910 as the dry land farmers moved in. There was a school, depot, and post office, as well as a hotel, cafe, and pool hall. The following advice was printed in the local newspaper, the **Coburg** *Times*: "The ambitious young man who aspires for the top of the ladder by starting at the bottom will find **Coburg** the place to come to" (Allison).

Coberly (Deer Lodge) was briefly the name of a settlement that later became New Chicago. A post office under the **Coberly** name was active only for January-November 1872. It was named for the Coberly family.

Coburn (Big Horn), on the Crow Indian Reservation, had a post office 1902-05 with Zoe D. Sipe as first postmaster.

COFFEE CREEK (Fergus) was named for the creek whose water had a dark, coffee-brown color. In early days this was a favorite stopping place for cowboys riding the open ranges around it. The town itself began as a station of the Milwaukee Road and the post office opened in 1914 with Robert Cox as postmaster. Two grain elevators and an International Harvester farm machinery store indicate this is now grain, rather than range country.

COHAGEN (Garfield) is in the southeastern section of the county. A post office, started there in 1905, was given the maiden name of postmaster Harry Harris's mother. The Harrises were the first settlers in the area and the post office was in their home on the old LU Ranch about a mile southwest of the present site. By 1915 **Cohagen** was booming: Mrs. Fleming ran a little roadhouse and her husband worked as foreman on the LU Ranch. There were three stores, a schoolhouse, a doctor and a dentist, two hotels, and a restaurant. "Later on a high school was built. The first teacher was a redhead from New York. She didn't stay a second term," wrote the students in the "Montana Life" class at Garfield High School in a booklet that has been preserved in the library. In 1948, the students wrote, "**Cohagen** today is one of Garfield County's many little has-been towns. Most of the buildings are gone and its population has greatly decreased."

This is good sheep country if the winter isn't too tough, but hard winters have devastated entire bands. In 1903-04 one man had five thousand wethers on Phillips Creek west of **Cohagen**, and after the storm not a single one was left alive. The N Bar Company brought 15,000 sheep down from the Musselshell country to winter in the Blackfoot and around Smoky Butte; after the blizzard only seven thousand were left (*Big Dry Country*). Teams of horses pulling crude snow plows were used during the severe winter of 1903 in an attempt to clear some land so the sheep could graze. Often the horses' legs were cut and bleeding from the crusted snow. Some ranchers skinned dead cows and used the hides to make leggings for the horses.

Cokedale (Park) had a post office 1889-1900 with Joseph Daily in charge. The office was open again 1903-06.

Cold Spring(s) (Jefferson), near Boulder, had a post office 1872-1924. B. F. Myers was postmaster.

Cole (Phillips), near Saco, was a station on the Great Northern where the railroad crossed the Milk River. It had a post office March-October 1929; Mary Palm was postmaster.

Colgate (Dawson) was named for Colgate Hoyt, director of the Northern Pacific Railroad 1887-93. **Colgate** was the first station south of Glendive.

Collegedale (Lewis and Clark) was the name of a post office which only existed February-September 1900. Eugene Peck was postmaster.

Collins (Teton) was named in honor of Timothy E. Collins, a resident of Fort Benton, who was a stockholder and director of the Great Falls and Canada Railroad, a narrow gauge line built about 1890 from Great Falls to Lethbridge. The settlement was formerly called Brighton. A post office under Aeneas B. McDonald was in operation 1891-93; it reopened 1903-61.

Coloma (Granite), near Garnet, was a mining camp with a post office opened in 1895 and Anna Richards as postmaster. The office closed in 1908.

Colony Bay (Chouteau), near Loma, had a post office 1913-34; Josephine Sutherland was the first postmaster.

COLSTRIP (Rosebud) is a town whose name is a composite of the words "coal" and "strip." In recent years **Colstrip** has become synonymous with the controversy over strip mining and power generating plants. The coal bed here is nearly flat with only a small amount of rock covering it. The rock is stripped off and coal is mined with steam shovels. A thirty-foot vein of lignite just under the surface supplied much of the coal used by Northern Pacific locomotives in the heyday of the trains. A post office opened in 1925 with George Nash as postmaster.

"The largest single investment by private capital in the history of Montana was celebrated Saturday at this mining community when nearly 3,000 people ... attended dedication ceremonies for the $295 million steam generating units No. 1 and No. 2" (Billings *Gazette*, September 19. 1976).

Today it seems almost prophetic that this little mining community chose a name that combined the two words "coal" and "strip" — words that were to be bombarded from Montana to Washington, D.C., as strip mining became a national issue.

Colter's Hell was the first name given to what is now Yellowstone National Park. John Colter, who had been with Lewis and Clark in Montana, later joined the Manuel Lisa Fur Company. During the hard winter of 1807-08, Colter was sent out to bring the Indians into the fort rather than have the trappers go out to them. Westward he came upon the Clark's Fork of the Yellowstone River and from there to present Yellowstone Park. Colter's journey — and the fiery geysers and boiling mud pots that he discovered — gave the park its first name. Colter was the first recorded white man to explore the park region (Toole).

COLUMBIA FALLS (Flathead) One story is that, when the Great Northern Highline was built, the town of Columbia was proposed as a division point, but when property owners demanded exorbitant prices for land, Jim Hill rechristened the town **Columbia Falls** and the new town of Whitefish was made division headquarters. The town had been platted on a scale that proved too generous when it failed to get the railroad division point. Excellent sidewalks extend some distance beyond the built-up area. J. P. Rowe says that the townsite was originally planned for a place near a falls in the Flathead River which is a part of the headwaters of the Columbia River — hence the name **Columbia Falls**. Postal records say an office was established under this name in 1891 with James Kennedy as postmaster, and that it was formerly known as Monaco.

COLUMBUS (Stillwater), a county seat, began as a stage station on the Yellowstone Trail and is now a shipping center for the rich farm and ranch lands around it. Its greatest flurry of prosperity came when the Columbus Quarry was chosen to furnish the stone for the state capitol building in Helena. This project and other contracts for the fine stone kept the quarries and the railroad busy for several years. The *Montana Almanac* (1958) says that the town may have been named for Christopher Columbus or for Columbus, Minnesota.

"There is probably no town in Montana that had a more spectacular career in finally 'lighting' on an incorporated name than did the county seat of Stillwater. Until its incorporation in 1907, its name changed every time the whims of a merchant moved his stock of merchandise or a new business appeared. First it was Eagle's Nest, about two miles west of town; then an Indian trading post was listed as Sheep Dip, a descriptive reference to the kind of whiskey sold there, and it was not until the Northern Pacific built a station there in 1882 and named it Stillwater that the town's location attained permanence. Even this name didn't last long, however, as the Northern Pacific had already listed a Stillwater, Minnesota, on their main line and the similiarity of Minnesota and Montana led to misdirected shipments, so the name of **Columbus** replaced Stillwater" (*They Gazed on the Beartooths*, Vol. II).

The **Columbus** post office was established in 1893 with Rosanna Garrigus as postmaster.

Comanche (Yellowstone) was a station on the Great Northern Railroad. It was named for the famous horse that was the only living thing found on the battlefield after the Battle of the Little Big Horn. The post office was opened in 1909 with Lola Dell Helm as postmaster; it was discontinued in 1942. Only the station, a few houses and some deserted buildings remain.

Combination (Granite), a mining camp near Philipsburg, had a post office 1892-1900; James Rhoads was the first postmaster.

Comertown (Sheridan) boomed with the arrival of the Soo Railroad in 1913. It was named for a resident, W. W. Comer. The post office was active

1914-57; William Vezina was the first postmaster. Now cattle roam the streets and the town looks forlorn.

Comet (Jefferson) was the name of a mine. A post office by that name had as many ups and downs as the prospectors. Between 1877 (John Russell, postmaster) and 1894, it was opened and closed four times. In 1917, application was made for a Comet Mine post office but Nora Quinlan declined the appointment as postmaster and the office did not open.

Como (Ravalli) was granted a post office in 1882 with Wilson Harlan appointed postmaster; it closed in 1935.

Concord (Toole) petitioned for a post office in 1901 but it was not established until 1908. Anne Gardner was postmaster. In 1912 the name was changed to Devon.

CONDON (Missoula) has had a post office since 1952,when Russell Conkling was appointed postmaster.

Confederate Gulch (Broadwater) is fifteen miles from Townsend by a dirt road. Confederate soldiers captured in Civil War battles near Lexington, Missouri, were banished up the Missouri River by the Union commander. Two of the exiles, Washington Baker and Pomp Dennis, came from Fort Benton in the fall of 1864, prospecting as they went, toward Last Chance Gulch (Helena). In this **Confederate Gulch**, which is part of the Big Belt Mountains, they made a strike and prospectors began to pour in. Montana Bar and Diamond City were two of the richest areas in the Gulch — an estimated $15 million worth of gold was taken out before 1870. Nothing is left now except a few mounds of earth which indicate where the buildings were.

Conley (Chouteau) was named for the postmaster, James Conley. The post office operated September 1906-December 1907.

Conlin (Dawson), near Fallon, had a post office September 1907-February 1908. Peder Undeim was in charge.

CONNER (Ravalli) is 25 miles south of Hamilton. Its post office was established in 1906 with Robert McLaughlin in charge.

Conrad (Chouteau) (see **Fort Conrad**).

CONRAD (Pondera) was granted a post office in 1903 with Mary Wilson as postmaster. A postal notation says that the place was first called Pondera, but actually the latter was a little community near the present site of **Conrad** (see **Pondera**). W. G. Conrad was the moving figure in the Conrad Investment Company, which owned a large part of the land in this vicinity, so the town was named for him. It was a station on the Great Northern branch line that ran from Great Falls to Shelby and on to the Canadian border.

Constance (Chouteau) is in the record books for a post office 1905-1907 (Marie Archer as postmistress), but the office was never active.

Contact (Sweet Grass) had a post office for a few months in 1892 with Samuel Cowan in charge. It was active again 1895-1933.

Content (Phillips) was formerly called Baeth, then for a brief time Goodsoil, and finally in 1915 the optimistic homesteaders and the post office department agreed on **Content**. The office survived until 1945.

Contact (Sweet Grass) had a post office for a few months in 1892 with

Samuel Cowan in charge. It was active again 1895-1933.

Content (Phillips) was formerly called Baeth, then for a brief time Goodsoil, and finally in 1915 the optimistic homesteaders and the U.S. Postal Service agreed on **Content**. The office survived until 1945.

COOKE CITY, COOKE (Park) is one of the entrances to Yellowstone Park. It was named for Jay Cooke, Jr., who was interested in mining claims in the district. **Cooke City** began as a prospect hole in the early 1870s. Weathered cabins with moss-covered roofs can still be found behind the myriad gasoline pumps that now mark it as a tourist town. Before the railroads came in, **Cooke City** was the receiving point for goods shipped by boat up the Missouri and Yellowstone rivers and then forwarded by stage and pack train over the winding trail through Red Lodge. Here, Buffalo Bill's Indian trade goods were shipped to Cody, Wyoming. In 1877 Chief Joseph and his retreating Nez Perces swept through **Cooke City** and burned the gold mills. New ones were built but the ore was too poor in grade to be mined commercially, and the miners left for richer fields. The post office, with William Randall as postmaster, opened in February 1882.

"**Cooke City** in the New World Mining District was discovered by Bart Henderson. With him were 'Horn' Miller and 'Pike' Moore, as they were drifting back from the '49 California gold rush. They were from Pike County, Missouri. Horn had a big powder horn, a .50 calibre rifle that he packed with his own powder. If you heard his gun go off, you knew who it was. Horn was a dead shot" (Dick Randall).

Coolidge (Beaverhead) was named for the thirtieth president of the United States. "A million dollar mill," considered one of the state's largest, was built at **Coolidge** and was still standing when Don Miller, author of *Ghost Towns of Montana*, took a photo of it in the 1970s. Since then the mill has been mostly torn down by a salvage company. It was near Wise River and had a post office 1922-32. Evan Woolman was the first postmaster.

Coombs (Stillwater), near Big Lake, began in earlier days as a station on the Rapelje branch line of the Northern Pacific, and was named for a farm family in the area. In 1970 there was only one resident left: Mrs. Earl Linger, Sr., who came as a bride to Coombs Flat in 1918 and stayed on amid the deserted houses that gave mute evidence of the broken dreams of homesteaders.

Cooney Recreation Center (Carbon) is on the Cooney Reservoir, which was named for Gov. Frank Cooney, under whose administration this water storage and flood control dam was constructed.

Copper (Meagher), a mining camp named for its product, was a post office 1899-1903 (William Harris, postmaster). The office was again active 1914-19, when World War I brought a rebirth of activity to many mining areas.

Copper Cliff (Deer Lodge) was a company mining town. Copper was discovered in 1890 by W. P. Shipley and the mine was later sold to an English firm (Western Interpretive Service).

Copperopolis (Meagher), possibly the same place as Copper, had a post office granted in 1881 with John Sutherlin in charge. It was because of this town that Marcus Daly could not name his new smelter town "Copperopolis" and had to settle instead for "Anaconda." **Copperopolis** was a lively mining town in the 1890s, but now only one cabin remains to mark the place northwest of White Sulphur Springs which was once a stage station between that city and Martinsdale. It became more important in 1866 when J. Hall and his partner Hawkins, discovered copper veins in the area north of Castle Mountain. They packed out five tons of the rich metal ore by jack train to the Missouri River and shipped it to Swansea, Wales, for smelting. The discovery of copper brought prospectors to the region and customers to Elizabeth Scott's hotel and stage station. Miners and stockmen from the Judith Basin kept the town going, but it boomed when Marcus Daly bought up the copper prospects in 1900. **Copperopolis** flourished and grew as a company town with large-scale mining operations. An estimated quarter of a million dollars worth of ore was taken out before the economic depression in Germany of 1901 caused the price of copper to fall. By 1903 no copper was wanted for export and all the mines closed (*Montana Pay Dirt*). Stearns says that the town was sometimes referred to as Fort Ben Stickney because "General" Stickney had established a small camp and stables there.

Cora (Meagher) This post office was established in 1882. It was a stage station on Cora Creek near the present Judith Basin county line. The stage line ran from Great Falls to Lewistown. The post office was open, except for a few months in '83, until its final closing in 1905.

CORAM (Flathead) is south of West Glacier. John Crossthwaite was postmaster when the office opened in 1914. The post office is called **Coram**, but as a station on the Great Northern, the town was called Coram-Nyack.

Corbin (Jefferson) was named for D. C. Corbin, pioneer prospector, and builder of the Spokane and Northern Railroad in Washington state. The post office was opened in 1887 with Emma Trimble as postmaster; it closed in 1943.

Cordova (Teton) was formerly named Plummerton and had a post office under that name established in 1917. The name was changed to **Cordova** in 1924 and a post office under that name operated until 1938; Louis St. Mars was the first postmaster. **Cordova** was a station on the Great Northern Railroad.

Corinth (Big Horn) had a post office 1915-53 (William Crooker, postmaster).

Corlett (Missoula) was named for Margaret Corlett when she was appointed postmaster and the office was opened in 1912. In 1918 the name was changed to Seeley Lake.

Corral Coulee (Blaine) had a post office 1915-24; John Bagan was the first postmaster.

CORVALLIS (Ravalli) was named for the town of Corvallis, Oregon, by people who had come from there to settle in the rich Montana valley. The name originally came from two French words: *coeur*, meaning heart, and *vallee*, meaning valley.

"The wagon trains began coming to the valley in 1862. . . . Some of the people settled there. . . . A Frenchman by the name of Herron named **Corvallis** in 1869, and was the first to build a house on the townsite" (Luther Stanley and Rozella Olson). Later there were three stores: Cowan's, Curtiss,' and one begun by the Missoula Mercantile. A post office was established in 1870 with Tom Rollins as postmaster.

Corwine Center (Phillips) was named for the family of first postmaster William Corwine. The office was open 1928-43.

CORWIN SPRINGS (Park) is seven miles north of the Gardiner entrance to Yellowstone Park. The post office was started in 1909 with John Holliday in charge. The town was named for Doctor Corwin, who built and operated a hotel resort here.

Cosier (Sheridan) had a post office for only six months, June 1917-January 1918; Abraham Buller was postmaster.

Cottonwood (Fergus), a stage stop, was first approved for a post office in 1883 with William DeWitt as postmaster. It was closed 1894-96, then active again until 1904. "Cottonwood" is also the name of a valley and a creek. The original buildings for the community hall and school were built in 1898 and have since been moved. There are about fourteen families now in the Cottonwood Valley, near the Snowy Mountains, with "ranches just about the right size."

Cottonwood (Hill), twenty-two miles north of Havre, had a post office 1911-29 (Thomas Connolly, postmaster). Connally located here about 1901 in a deep coulee which was named Cottonwood after the trees. He began hauling the mail in his buggy from Havre since there was no local post office. He kept the mail in a large desk and neighbors called for it when they could. The arrangement became official in 1911 when the post office was approved.

Cottonwood (Powell) was the name given by gold miners to the camp that eventually became the town of Deer Lodge.

Coulson (Yellowstone) is an old town named for a firm named Coulson which built and owned a line of steamboats. The townsite lies near the present site of Billings. **Coulson** grew up around P. J. McAdow's store. It was laid out in the winter of 1876-77 by McAdow, J. J. Alderson, Joseph Cochran and others at the place where the Northern Pacific bridge later spanned the Yellowstone River. **Coulson** is mentioned as a trading center in the journals of Granville Stuart and others long before and even after its rival and neighbor, Billings, had been platted as a town. **Coulson** had a post office 1877-82; Samuel Alexander was the first postmaster.

Council Grove (Missoula) was a trading post and early settlment near the old town of Hell Gate. In 1968 the few remaining buildings were moved away. It was the scene of a council between Indian tribes and Isaac Stevens, who wanted to buy their land.

Courts (Gallatin), near Springhill, had a post office 1980-91; Dan Harris was the first postmaster.

Cowans (Gallatin) was named for postmaster Andrew Cowan. The office was open less than a year in 1876-77.

Cow Creek (Dawson) was the name of a post office 1911-13 with George Reynolds, postmaster. The name was changed to Hamblin, according to postal records, for the new postmaster. Now it is in McCone County. Another **Cow Creek** post office was established in McCone County in 1930 with Emma Carr as postmaster; it was active until March 1934.

Cow Creek (Rosebud) is the end of the line for the Northern Pacific branch line serving Colstrip.

Cowels, Cowles (Park) was an early day post office 1899-1904 with

Murray Gilbert as postmaster.

Cow Island (Chouteau) briefly had a post office April-August 1880. It was just below Judith Landing on the Missouri River where the Judith River dumps into the "Big Muddy." During low water steamboats were unable to navigate the mouth of the Judith so all freight had to be unloaded at **Cow Island** and freighted to Fort Benton. Guards protected the piles of cargo from Indian raids. **Cow Island** contained several hundred acres of land and in the early 19th century some traders found a lone cow on the island hundreds of miles from any other cattle. Her source remained a mystery but the island was named for her (James Murphy, *Half Interest in a Silver Dollar*).

Coyle (Valley) was granted a post office in September 1895 and named for James Coyle, who was to serve as postmaster. However, the office was never in operation and was officially discontinued in April 1896.

Coyote (Fergus) was named for the creek on which it was located, and this creek, like many in Montana, was named for a native animal. There was a post office at **Coyote** 1909-14, with Francis Jones as first postmaster. It was near Stanford.

Crabtree (Beaverhead) was the name of a station on the old Oregon Short Line. The community was later known as Kidd.

Crabtree (Custer) This post office was active 1910-12; Isaac Crabtree was postmaster.

Cracker Box (Dawson), near Glendive, had a post office 1917-20 with William Kirkham as postmaster.

Crackerville (Silver Bow) is a little settlement just off the highway near Gregson.

Craig (Lewis and Clark) was named for Warren Craig, a pioneer resident, In 1886 Craig built a log house, with a stone fireplace, which he had to defend many times from the Indians (Perrin). The house is a half mile from the Great Northern depot. In 1890 his son, John Craig, also settled here and Mrs. John Craig later served as postmaster. Postal records say the name was formerly Stickney, but actually the Stickney post office was on the other side of the river. It closed in 1888. Service was resumed at the **Craig** office with Benjamin Stickney continuing as postmaster. For some years a ferry ran across the Missouri between the two places. The **Craig** post office was closed in 1953.

CRANE (Richland) is ten miles south of Sidney, and about the same distance from the North Dakota border. It was named for the owner of Crane's Ranch, which is shown on a map dated 1881. The post office opened in 1910 with Severt Knutson as postmaster. Another little settlement in Gallatin County was first named Crane, but changed to Cardinal when it was found there was already a Crane in the state.

Craney (Flathead) was to have a post office in 1901 with George Dempsey in charge, but the order was rescinded.

Crawford (Madison) was a mining camp with a post office 1872-73. Charles Gideon and Charles Stiles were postmasters.

Creamery (Gallatin) was named for its extensive dairy industry. The post office under this name existed 1885-91; the first postmaster was H. C. Cockrill, who also owned the dairy farm and creamy — the post office was on his place. In 1891 the office was moved to Central Park (see **Central Park**).

Crescent (Jefferson), named for a mine, had a post office 1890-93 with William Sprague as first postmaster.

Creston (Flathead) had a post office 1894-1956 when it became a rural station out of Kalispell. Charles Buck was the first postmaster.

Crevasse (Park) was a post office 1892-93 with John Edgerton in charge. The office was open 1894-96.

Criswell (Park) had a post office February-September 1937; the postmaster was Mae Terry. Postal records say it was formerly called Rockcreek.

CROW AGENCY (Big Horn) is a trading center and agency headquarters for the Crow Indian Reservation. There were two earlier locations of **Crow Agency**: the first was seven or eight miles east of Livingston near the junction of U.S. Highways 90 and 89; the other was about three miles south of Absarokee (Ralph Shane). Originally the Crow Reservation extended this far west, but as it was cut down the agency moved to keep within the new boundaries. The **Crow Agency** post office was established in 1881 and listed as on the reservation. Charles Babcock was postmaster. In 1884 the office was closed in September and reopened in November, probably in the new location, because it was then listed as being in Big Horn County.

Crow Coulee (Chouteau), near Eagle, had an active post office 1928-32 with Edwin Jones as postmaster.

Crowley (Prairie) was named for first postmaster Henry Crowley when the office opened in 1914; it closed in 1920. The mail was ordered to Watkins.

Crown (Beaverhead) was to have a post office in 1898 with Matilda Brown in charge, but it was never in operation.

Crow Rock (Prairie), near the mouth of Hay and Crow Rock Creek, takes its name from the creek. In 1869 the Crow and Sioux Indians had a fight atop the large rock where about thirty Crows had taken refuge. The Sioux killed them all.

In 1897 a man named Naylor lived in a dug-out there beside a spring and ranged his sheep for thirty miles in every direction. An English Canadian named Penman built a huge stone house into the hill with rock walls two feet thick and huge cottonwood logs for beams; Penman ran sheep and started the business that later became the Crow Rock Sheep Company. A post office was established at **Crow Rock** in 1913 with Mons Ringreide as postmaster; it closed in 1945. Mail came from Miles City until a route was set up out of Terry. The first school in the **Crow Rock** area was held in a sheep wagon near the head of the creek about 1910.

Crow's Nest (Big Horn) was never a town or even a settlement, but it was historically important. The exact location of the original crow's nest is uncertain, but it was a high point in the Reno Creek area from which Custer's Crow Indian scouts first spotted an Indian camp on the Little Big Horn. Later, Henry Weibert, a Garryowen rancher and Custer biographer, was able to find and verify the spot using a 1919 photo. Weibert and Walter Boyes erected a concrete-and-stone marker on the **Crow's Nest** site with a bronze plate inscription:

CROW'S NEST
So named by General Custer's Crow scouts
because there was a crow's nest here.
This marker, erected in 1972, goes on to detail the events of that June 1876 morning.

Cruse (Lewis and Clark) was named for Tommy Cruse, discoverer of the Drum Lummon Mine and later a banker and philantropist, who financed the Roman Catholic cathedral in Helena. **Cruse** was also the name of a railroad siting on the Musselshell River. After Cruse had made his fortune in mining he came to the Flatwillow area in Petroleum County and went into the sheep business.

Cuerth (Blaine) was named for the family of first postmaster Minnie Cuerth when the post office opened in 1916. The name was changed to Rattlesnake in 1917.

CULBERTSON (Roosevelt) was named for Alexander Culbertson, an early fur trapper and mountain man. He was the chief factor of the American Fur Company at Fort Union and was also instrumental in establishing a number of other trading posts on the upper Missouri and Marias Rivers. In 1840 he married Matawista Iksana, daughter of a Blood Indian chief. In 1879 Culbertson's son Jack started a ranch near the present town which seems to have come into existence sometime between 1888 and 1892.

The discrepancy arose over the definition of "town." A certain Lucy A. Isbel is supposed to have stepped off the train in 1892 and spent some time looking for **Culbertson** — two log cabins were not regarded as a "town" where she came from. A post office was established in January 1892 and the railroad had come in 1887. The postmaster was James Skinner.

As county boundaries continued to shift, the townsite of **Culbertson** has been in five different counties: Big Horn, Dawson, Custer, Valley and Roosevelt. It was first chosen to be the county seat of Roosevelt County, but the offices were transferred to Poplar and later to Wolf Point.

Culbertson is one of the oldest towns in eastern Montana. It was founded in June 1887 when Montana was still a territory. The area was first viewed by white men in May 1805 when Lewis and Clark came up the Missouri River. They were amazed at the abundant grassland and wild game. Fur traders came in 1807, but the Blackfeet Indians didn't cooperate until Major Culbertson took charge; his fair dealings with the Indians quickly won their respect and fur trading began. Later, **Culbertson** became a trade center for the cattle industry. Cowboys rode into town (sometimes they even rode their horses into the saloons), whooping and yelling, but cowboys were men of honor and they always came back to pay for any damage they had done. At one time there were thirteen saloons open for business twenty-four hours a day in this little town. Famous outlaws who made **Culbertson** their hangout were "Dutch" Henry, Sam Hall, and Tom Reed.

The first depot in **Culbertson** was an 8- x 30-foot boxcar. The first agent, James Skinner, began work September 1, 1890. He was robbed, murdered, and burned with the depot on February 1, 1894. The first school was in a one-room log building built in 1897. **Culbertson** developed into a prosperous eastern Montana town with a unique industry — a safflower mill.

Cull (Blaine) had a post office 1915-20 with Ira Phillips as first postmaster.

Cultay (Chouteau) had a post office 1890-93 with William Zimmerman as postmaster. It was near Fort Benton

Cummings (Carbon), near Bowler, was named for Blanche Cummings, the postmaster. The office was open 1910-11.

Curry (Dawson) was a station on the Northern Pacific near Glendive named for Howard Curry, general mechanical superintendent of the railroad when the town was started.

CUSHMAN (Golden Valley) was named for a local rancher, cowboy, and at one time, conductor on the Montana Central Railroad (Rowe). The post office opened in 1909 with Ernest Skinner as postmaster.

Cuskerton (Roosevelt) was established in 1917 with Frank Coney as postmaster. The settlement was formerly served by the Oakno office. The **Cuskerton** office closed in 1910.

Custer (Yellowstone) was named for Gen. George Armstrong Custer, who was killed in 1876 at the famous Battle of the Little Big Horn. The town was started after Junction, a little village on the opposite bank of the Yellowstone River, was washed away by floodwaters. **Custer** was a freight station for traders bringing supplies to the Crow Indian Reservation. Earlier this spot had been a favorite campground for those traveling to and from Fort Custer, which had been established at the junction of the Bighorn and Little Big horn Rivers. The post office opened in 1905 with Herbert Higgins as postmaster.

Custer County, in southeastern Montana, was named for Gen. George Armstrong Custer. It was created in 1877 from a part of old Big Horn County; parts of it were taken in 1901 to form Rosebud County and in 1913 to form Fallon County; a part of **Custer County** was taken to form a part of Prairie County in 1915; also, Powder River County in 1919 and Carter County in 1917 were created from parts of **Custer County**. Miles City is the county seat. The area is famous as early-day cattle country.

CUT BANK (Glacier) is a county seat about halfway between Browning and Shelby, and about the same distance from the Canadian border. The town was named for the deep gorge near it that was made by Cut Bank Creek. The Blackfeet Indians had described the stream that flows through this area as "the river that cuts into the white clay banks." John Stauffer was appointed postmaster when the office opened in 1892. Anna Wilkes took over in 1901.

The population of **Cut Bank** jumped from 845 in 1939 to 4,539 in 1960 as the oil and gas fields were discovered and continued to produce. Gas piped from this region is used in the homes of Great Falls, Helena, Butte and Anaconda, and has replaced coal in the copper reduction plants.

Cutler (Custer) was named for the first postmaster, George Cutler. The office was open 1882-91. It was near Etna.

Cyanide (Lewis and Clark) For many years a large plant operated here which treated ore with cyanide.

Cypress (Blaine) is a settlement which was laid out on Big Sandy Creek north of Fort Assiniboine and the railroad station.

"Lots were sold and **Cypress**, catering to the soldiers' trade, boomed to thirty-two saloons, two houses of prostitution, a Chinese restaurant, and in June 1888, Cowan's General Store. In two or three months, however, the commanding officer at the fort ruled **Cypress** out of bounds. **Cypress** withered at once to two saloons, the restaurant, a few homes, and Cowan's store" (*Trial and Triumph*).

Presumably **Cypress** was so-named because it was located in an area watered by West Fork and North Fork Creeks that come down from the Cypress Hills in Canada to flow into the Milk River. By 1889 Louis Shambo (Chambeau) was tending bar there — and that was the only activity left in **Cypress**.

Cyr (Mineral), near Alberton, was a station named for A. Cyr and E. Cyr, from whom the right-of-way for the Northern Pacific was acquired. The post office opened in 1908 with Mary Stringham in charge and closed in 1914.

D

DAGMAR (Sheridan) is near the North Dakota line and the Canadian border. It is the trade center for a community of Danish-Americans who have for a long time successfully conducted various cooperative enterprises. These include a store, a coal mine, a telephone exchange, a fire insurance company, and a burial association providing funerals for $45. The original name of the town, Dronning Dagmar's Minde, was chosen by E. F. Madsen to honor Queen Dagmar of Denmark. Madsen was appointed postmaster when the office opened in 1907 under the shortened name of **Dagmar** (Duane Ibsen, Antelope High School.)

Daleview (Sheridan) had a post office 1907-14, with Robert Dickey as first postmaster. Another listing for **Daleview** in Sheridan County in postal record shows an office open 1915-43 and a notation that it was formerly called Ranous. A high hill near **Daleview** contained the hideout of "Dutch" Henry and his outlaws.

Daly's, a station on the Oregon Short Line, was named for Marcus Daly, the mining king who ran a spur from the main railroad to here to get out the rock that was used for the Anaconda smelter.

Dama (Custer), near Beebe, had a post office 1901-1905 with George Redman first postmaster.

Dane Valley (Valley) had a post office 1898-1912 with August Fryling as first postmaster.

Daniels (Powell), near Race Track, had a post office 1902-04 with Dora Lingo in charge.

Daniels (Sheridan) was named for postmaster Mabel Daniels when Old Scobey changed its name to **Daniels** in 1915; the new community that had grown up around the Great Northern station wanted to shorten its name from East Scobey to Scobey. The **Daniels** office lasted only a year, December 1915-December 1916.

Daniels County, in the far northeastern part of Montana, borders on

Canada. It was named after Mansfield A. Daniels, a pioneer rancher and storekeeper. Scobey is the county seat. **Daniels County** was created on August 28, 1920, from parts of Sheridan and Valley counties. The land within its borders was once a rich cattle range; now it is used for farming.

Danmore, (Jefferson) a station on the Northern Pacific, was named for Dan Morrison, discoverer of the nearby Lewis and Clark Caverns (formerly Morrison Cave).

Danton (Custer) had a post office 1879-81 with Daniel Harris as postmaster. The suffix "ton," a brief form of "town," was often used in combination with a person's name to create a place name.

DANVERS (Fergus) was a station on the Milwaukee between Lewistown and Great Falls. It was named by C. A. Goodnow after an old Massachusetts town. The community was first called Warwick. The post office was established in 1914 with Frank Linhart in charge. The town was bustling then; by 1975 only 5 residents and the grain elevator remained.

DARBY (Ravalli) was named for its postmaster, James Darby. It is located on the Bitterroot River and was the terminus of the Northern Pacific Line. Crumbling log buildings with two-story false fronts attest to its life in the gold dust days. The post office opened in 1889.

Darling (Beaverhead) was named for a family of pioneer settlers by that name. A post office was in operation 1872-81.

Darrel (Fergus) had a post office 1913-34. Agnes Koons was the first postmaster.

D'Aste (Lake), near Ronan, started as a station on the Dixon-to-Polson branch line of the Northern Pacific. It was named for a Jesuit missionary who had been sent to work with the Indians. The post office operated 1914-17 with Thomas Quinn serving as first postmaster.

Davidell (Rosebud) had a post office 1928-38. Marie Nelson was the first postmaster. Postal records say the place was formerly called Rim Rocks.

Davidson (Chouteau) had a post office 1888-89 with Thomas Harwood as postmaster. It was near Randolph.

Dawes (Blaine) was the original name of a Great Northern station that later became Chinook.

Dawson (Silver Bow) was a railroad station west of Butte.

Dawson County is in the extreme eastern section of the state. Glendive, the county seat, accounts for most of the population. It was named for Maj. Andrew Dawson of the American Fur Company. The county was created January 15, 1869; later, parts of the large, original county were taken to form Valley County in 1893, Richland County in 1914, a part of Wibaux in 1914, a part of Prairie in 1915, and a part of McCone in 1919.

DAYTON (Lake), on the shores of Flathead Lake, is the embarkation point for Wild Horse Island. This island, which is seven miles from the shore, was once famous for its 4,500-acre dude ranch, but is now owned by the state and under the management of the Department of Fish, Wildlife, and Parks. Clarence Proctor was postmaster when the office opened in 1893.

Deadman's Basin (Wheatland) is a government reservoir near Shawmut. There is also a Deadman's Basin in Madison County, among others.

Several creeks also have this name — a reminder of the hardships and tragedies of exploration in pioneer days when men went out alone in bitter winter weather over unmarked trails and all too often never returned.

Dean (Stillwater) is near Fishtail. Except for a few months, a post office was in operation 1902-51. Bessie Haskin served as first postmaster.

Dearborn (Lewis and Clark) was named for the river, which had been named by Lewis and Clark, the explorers, on July 18, 1805, to honor Henry Dearborn, then Secretary of War. **Dearborn** had a post office 1876-77 with Hubert Milot in charge. The office was opened again 1878-98.

DEBORGIA, DE BORGIA (Mineral) was a station on the Northern Pacific twenty miles from Lookout Pass, which separates Montana and Idaho. The town derives its name from the St. Regis de Borgia River, named in 1841 by Father de Smet in honor of Saint Francis de Borgia, who had been a member of the Jesuit order to which Father de Smet belonged.

The post office was established in 1900 with Elizabeth Wence as postmaster.

DECKER (Big Horn) is along the Tongue River near the Wyoming line. The first post office was in a cabin on Badger Creek and Badger was the name suggested by the people who signed the petition for an office, but somehow the name got changed in Washington and the official name was sent out as **Decker**. That was in 1893 and Morris Shreve was postmaster. Since then, **Decker** has become famous for its coal deposits. Except for a quirk of fate, we might now have the Badger Coal Company digging the black treasure (Cathie Monroe in *The Market Place*).

Deepdale (Jefferson) had a post office 1882-83 with Burt Skinner as postmaster.

Deerfield (Fergus) had a post office most of the time beween its opening in 1888 (Emory Huson, postmaster) and its final closing in 1917.

DEER LODGE, (Powell) a county seat, is located in the valley that was once called the "Lodge of the White-Tailed Deer" by the Indians. The French trappers called it *La Loge Chevreuils*. There was a natural salt lick in the valley to which the deer came in droves. The Clark Fork River bisects the town. The settlement was once called Cottonwood by gold miners because of an abundance of that kind of tree. Later it was called LaBarge City in honor of Capt. LaBarge, who arrived in July, 1802, to start a trading post. In 1863 the citizens formed the Deer Lodge Town Company, had the town platted, and changed the name to Deer Lodge City. The post office opened in 1866 with Romulus Percy in charge. In 1896, the name was shortened to **Deer Lodge**.

"While **Deer Lodge** was still known as the "Little Village on the Trail to Bear," the Montana Collegiate Institute, first college in the Territory, was born. The school began in 1878 or '79 with two teachers, one for music and chemistry, the other to teach languages — French, German, and the classics. . . . Remnants of the school finally merged with Montana Wesleyan in 1923 to form Intermountain Union College of Helena" (*Montana Standard*; July 6, 1976).

In this town, with its complicated naming history, one can still find the "castles" built with mining and ranch money standing side-by-side with log cabins from an earlier era. The gray walls of the state penitentiary dominate the west side of town. The prison, which pre-dates the statehood of Montana, was built with federal funds and opened in 1871 under federal control. **Deer Lodge** is surrounded by an area rich in mining and cattle ranching history.

Deer Lodge County is in southwestern Montana, one of the smallest counties and one of the nine original counties created by the first legislature of Montana in 1865. A map from that era shows it as a long, narrow county extending from the Canadian border on the north to Beaverhead County on the south. Divisions have cut the area down to 746 square miles. Parts of it were taken to form Granite in 1863; a part was given to Silver Bow in 1881; a part was given to Lewis and Clark County in 1894; a part was taken to form Flathead in 1900; a part was taken to form Powell County in 1901; and a part of Silver Bow was annexed in 1903. Anaconda is the county seat. The county, like the town by this name, was in a section of the state frequented by deer because of natural salt licks.

Deer Park (Gallatin) was a settlement originally named by the Indians because deer used to come here in large numbers every winter to drink at the small lake and to graze around it. The natural growth of trees gave rise to the second part of the name.

Deever (Park) was a station near Gardiner named for a Mr. Deevers, who owned a stockyard there.

Degrand (Prairie) was near Watkins and named for the family of Emma DeGrand, first postmaster. The office was open 1914-24, spanning the homestead years.

Dehart (Sweet Grass) was a station on the Northern Pacific west of Big Timber. It was named for H. A. Dehart, rancher and stockman.

Del Bonita (Glacier) had a post office 1939-42 with Francis Lovall as postmaster.

Delight (Valley) was open only briefly, 1920-21. Lily Steams operated the office formerly served by the Milks post office.

DELL (Beaverhead) was a station on the Union Pacific between Kidd and Lima. This trading center for valley ranchers was named because of the topography of the area — a country dell or secluded valley. The post office was opened in 1890 with Elizabeth Dowling as postmaster.

Delos (Fergus) had a post office 1903-05 with Andrew MacDonald in charge.

Delphia (Musselshell) was a station on the Milwaukee Railroad east of Roundup. Nora Spenddiff was a postmaster when the office opened in 1908. In 1959 **Delphia** became a rural station out of Roundup.

Delpine (Meagher) was near Martinsdale and had a post office 1899-1929. George Williams was the first postmaster.

Demers (Toole) had a post office during homestead days, 1914-32. John Fitzpatrick was the first postmaster.

Demersville (Flathead), near Kalispell, came into being in 1888 when large boats began using Flathead Lake. Telephase J. Demers, a skinner with a freight outfit in the early 1880s, was heading for the placer mine diggings in British Columbia when he heard of the rich Flathead country, stopped off and decided to stay. He set up a trading post on part of Betty Gregg's homestead. Thus in 1887, Demers began mercantile operations at the head of navigation, which was the boat landing on the Flathead River. Settlers were arriving by stage, covered wagon and river steamer. Building materials were easy to get; lumber mills were nearby. This river town grew fast; by 1890 it had a population of 300. Demers Department Store later sold out to the Missoula Mercantile Company. Demers, a Canadian by birth, died in Butte City in 1889.

Steamboating here reached its peak in 1890. Among the big boats coming into **Demersville** were "The Klondike," with a capacity of 110 tons and 425 passengers; the "U.S. Grant;" and the "Pocahontas." The latter capsized, sank, was raised, restored, and renamed the "Dora." "The Cresent" was a stern-wheeler (most of the boats were propeller driven) — it had two state rooms and stables for ten horses. The "State of Montana" was 150 feet long, 26 feet wide and carried a crew of 25.

Postal records show an office established in **Demersville** in 1889 and notes that it was formerly known as Clifford. John Clifford was the postmaster in 1889 and probably until the office closed in 1892. It was reopened in 1893 and active until 1898.

Addison Bragg (Billings *Gazette*, March 31, 1974) says that Bar Rock (or **Demersville**) was listed in the Dun report in 1892 as a Montana town with men of financial status. **Demersville** was located one mile above the big bend in the Flathead River called Foy's Bend. Its demise came with the news that the railroad would bypass the river town. People moved their houses and stores into Kalispell. **Demersville** and the river boats were a short-lived but exciting chapter in Montana's history (*Yesterday was Demersville*).

Dempsey (Powell) was named for Dempsey Creek which in turn was named for Robert Dempsey, a Montana pioneer who built up a ranch on that creek in the 1860s. Granville Stuart says: "I went to Dempsey's Ranch today (south of the present day town of Deer Lodge) and found everyone drunk and three strangers there with fifteen gallons of Minnie Rifle whiskey [made of] one part alcohol; ten parts water with a considerable quantity of tobacco and cayenne pepper to strengthen it."

Dennis (Fallon) was named for postmaster Harvey D. Dennis when the office opened in 1910. In 1913 Eva Dennis took it over. Only the foundation stones of an elevator remain to mark the spot.

DENTON (Fergus) was named for two brothers named Dent, stockmen who owned the land on which the original townsite was located. "Dent" was considered too short a name for a town, so it was changed to **Denton**. Harry Dent was appointed postmaster when the office opened in 1888. It's a farming community where modern methods have increased grain yields from an average of 20 to 25 bushels to 35 or 40 bushels per acre. Cattle and hogs are also important products.

Depew (Flathead) was a station on the Great Northern named for William Depew, a train dispatcher.

Desmet (Missoula) was named for the Jesuit missionary, Father Pierre Jean deSmet, famous for his work with the Indians. His mission at Stevensville was established in 1841. The **DeSmet** post office operated 1901-07. Thomas Shaughnessy was the first postmaster.

Devee (Wheatland) was a post office 1886-87 and named for postmaster James Devee.

DEVON (Toole) is between Chester and Shelby. This station on the Great Northern was formerly called Concord. The post office was opened in 1912 with Annie Gardner as postmaster.

Dewey (Beaverhead) is a mining ghost town. It was named for D. S. Dewey, early rancher who is said to have built the first cabin in the area. The original townsite was south of the Big Hole River and above the present location. Butte fishermen in the early days rode horseback to Dewey's Flats to fish the Big Hole. Lumbering was the first industry, then Quartz Hill lode was discovered and a mining boom gave the town its best years from 1877 to 1895. The post office was open 1878-88, and 1890-1913. John Heldt was first postmaster.

DeWitt (Meagher) almost had a post office in 1884. W. W. DeWitt was to have been postmaster but the order was "held up."

Diamond City began with the discovery of gold there December 3, 1864, by four ex-Confederate soldiers. It grew to a peak population of 5,000 in 1867. By 1880 most of the gold and the people were gone. A booming mining camp in Confederate Gulch, it was one of the state's richest gold strikes, located in the range of mountains that separates Broadwater and Meagher counties. Now a ghost town fifteen miles from Townsend, only mounds of earth show where the log cabins were. William Meek was postmaster when the office opened in 1867. It was active through December 1908 and then again for a few months in 1909. Mockel says that **Diamond City** was named for the pattern of the trails in the snow that joined the four claims in the narrow gulch. It was known as the wealthiest, gayest, and toughest place in Montana.

Diamond Springs (Lewis and Clark) had a post office 1885-86 with J. Underhill as postmaster.

Dick (Rosebud) is near Sanders and was named for postmaster Charles Dick. The office was open from 1908-09.

Dickey (Yellowstone) is near Pineview and had a post office 1914-15 with Mabel Maas as postmaster.

Dickson (Custer) is near Miles City and had a post office March-September 1883. Flora Woodliff was postmaster.

DILLON (Beaverhead), a county seat, was named for Sidney Dillon, president of the Union Pacific Railroad, who directed the completion of the line from Utah to Butte. The location of the town was determined by accident. Construction on the Utah and Northern Railroad was suddenly brought to a standstill in 1880 when a rancher owning the land refused to give it up for a right-of-way. A few enterprising men engaged in business at or near the terminus banded together, bought the ranch and gave the railroad the right to go through. They continued their partnership by executing a trust deed recorded on December 4, 1880, and the Town of Terminus was established. A post office under this name was granted in 1880 with Thomas Warren as postmaster. The name was changed to **Dillon** in March 1881. Adams (*When Wagon Trails were Dim*) says that in 1869 the place that is now called **Dillon** was known as Black Tail. There was a little Sunday School there led by Sister Selway of the Methodist Church. He also speaks of services "held in the Poindexter School House (now called **Dillon**). . . . There were a number of Indians gathered quietly about the windows and doors anxious to look and listen." A letter dated September 10, 1880, from Mrs. Eddy Ferris at Red Rock, Montana, describes the founding of **Dillon** on Blacktail Deer Creek; she says that the town was to be called Washington City in honor of Washington Dunn, constructor of the roads. Three weeks later Mrs. Ferris wrote that the new town had been named **Dillon**. By January 1881 she was living there and wrote, "Of all the dreary looking places I ever saw, **Dillon** is about the worst."

But it improved and at one time was the largest wool shipping point in Montana. The tree-shaded streets became country roads leading to ranches that are much older than the town. Montana's Normal College was moved from Twin Bridges to **Dillon** in 1892 and continues to be a part of the greater University of Montana system.

Dilo (Garfield) is located on Lodgepole Creek. The post office was moved to Margaret McGlumphey's home in 1915. It was formerly called Bowmanville and for a brief period Bright Star. It was officially named **Dilo** in 1916. The Wisehart Hall, which had been built by Dr. Wisehart, Mrs. McGlumphey's brother, was moved from his homestead to her place and added on to the house, so is became a community meeting place and thus a "town" originated. Alice Johnson was later appointed postmaster and served until she moved away. By 1935 most people had moved away, and the post office was discontinued in January of that year.

Dilworth (Carbon) was named for the first postmaster, James R. Dilworth. Established in 1884, it was the earliest post office in what is now Carbon County. Dilworth started a horse and cattle ranch there and was postmaster until the office closed in December 1891. He was shot to death at Bull Springs, a couple of miles east of **Dilworth**, after an argument with a "squatter" about the neighborhood water spring. Mail came in by stage over the Old Meeteetse Trail from Red Lodge to Meeteetse, Wyoming — about 100 miles. This road was called the 100 Mile Route.

Discord (Custer) was near Mizpah. One wonders if its name has anything to do with the fact that the post office survived only from May to August in 1919. Kirby MacKenzie was postmaster.

Discovery Butte (Chouteau) was originally called Sturgill. It was near Colony Bay and the post office only operated 1915-16, with Emma Larsen as postmaster. In the Bear Paw Mountain area, there are many descriptive names using the word "butte:" Squaw Butte, Saddle Butte, Eagle Butte, and others.

DIVIDE (Silver Bow) gets its name because it is near the Continental Divide, where waters on the west side end up in the Pacific and streams from the east slope wind toward the Gulf. This station on the Union Pacific served as a distribution and stock shipping point for the Big Hole Valley. The post office opened in 1873 with Charles Wunderlich as postmaster.

DIXON (Sanders) was a division point on the Northern Pacific Railroad. The post office opened in 1904 with Charlie Shelledy as postmaster. The community, which was formerly known as Jocko City, was renamed to honor Gov. Joseph Dixon.

Dodge (Cascade) was the original name of the community that became Cascade. A post office under the name **Dodge** operated August 1886-November 1887 with Thomas Gorham in charge.

Dodgeton, Dodgetown (Musselshell) was named for postmaster Henry Dodge. The office was open in 1883-84.

DODSON (Phillips), on the Milk River, was named for a merchant who operated a well-patronized trading post and saloon there before the Great Northern Railroad came through.

A legend commemorates one of **Dodson**'s characters, "Peanut" Parson, a bachelor who ate his peas with a knife ground to the keenness of a razor blade. An Easterner who spent two weeks with Peanut in 1911 was about to object to the dangerous habit when Peanut leaned across the table. "Pardner," he protested mildly, "Every time you put that there fork in your mouth, I shiver in my boots for fear you'll punch a hole plumb through your tongue."

A post office was opened in **Dodson** in 1891 with Richard Garland as postmaster. It closed in October of that year, but reopened in 1894.

Donald (Madison) was a settlement named for Donald McIntosh, one of the brothers who were general contractors for the construction of the Milwaukee line east of Butte.

Donlan (Sanders) was named for Ed Donlan, lumberman and state senator from Missoula.

Donovan Ranch (Beaverhead) was a country post office near Grant named for its location. Cora Rand was the first postmaster and the office was open from 1916-26.

Dooley (Sheridan) This post office was established in 1914 with Peter Hegseth handling the mail from his homestead shack. Postal records say the place was formerly called Jenkins. The Soo Railroad line came in 1913 and a town was platted in the northeast corner of W. D. Dooley's homestead. Forty buildings went up and business thrived. The first baby born in the town was to Hegseth and his wife — the little girl was named "Dooliette". An old homestead shack was moved in to serve as a schoolhouse in 1913. The post office closed in 1957, the homesteaders are gone, and now little is left of the townsite.

Dorsey (Meagher), near Ringling, had a post office 1915-18; James Puckett was the first postmaster.

Dory, (Fergus) near Roy, had a post office from 1915-1918. James Puckett was the first postmaster.

Doty (Meagher) was named for postmaster Edwin Doty. The office survived only from February to November of 1892.

Doughty (Fergus) This post office operated 1918-19. It was named for postmaster Roland Doughty, and was near Grass Range.

Dovenspeck (Petroleum) is a settlement between Teigen and Dovetail.

Dover (Judith Basin) had a post office 1911-1950; Richard Cox was the first postmaster.

Dovetail (Petroleum) Dovetail Creek was named for the way the creek branches in two separate directions, then comes together to form the shape of a dove's tail. The large butte just north of the creek was given the same name, as was the community. Tom Iverson, sheepman, and E. J. Sanford, cattleman, both hunting open range and good grass for their stock, were two of the first settlers in the early 1900s. The homestead boom soon followed, with a homesteader on every 160 acres. Martin Rigg and his brothers came from Valentine — thirteen miles to the east — to start the first store and post office. The office was opened in 1916 with Rigg as postmaster. Later Lois, Mary, and Alfred Coffey served in turn as postmasters. The Milwaukee Railroad had a line to Roy, and the mail was brought from there by stage to Valentine, where another stage picked it up for the trip to **Dovetail**. It was a rugged trip for man and horses alike in the bitter cold and deep snows of winter. The office was discontinued in 1945.

The Dovetail-Valentine area was once a land of homesteads and hardships, of neighborhood picnics and dances; now it is home for a few large, progressive cattle ranches.

Dowd (Roosevelt) was named for postmaster Charles Dowd; the office was open 1919-40.

Dowlin (Rosebud) is a station on the Colstrip branch line named for state senator Charles Dowlin.

Downieville (Meagher) was an early post office 1868-69. Thomas J. Favorite was the first postmaster.

Dracut was a station on the Great Falls-Agawam branch of the Milwaukee Railroad. It was named for Dracut, Massachusetts.

Dragseth (Fallon), originally in Custer County, was named for postmaster Stinus Dragseth; the office was open 1900-04, and was near Knolton.

Dreamland remained just that, but in 1895 a group of "citizens and taxpayers" residing "on Capitol Hill, which is the corner of Lewis and Clarke, Jefferson, and Deer Lodge counties at a point distant six miles from Rimini" petitioned the postmaster general for a post office, claiming that eighty people now lived there and there were 250 more within a radius of 2½ miles. A tenstamp milling plant had been built; two more soon would be, and rich discoveries of gold promised permanence of the settlement. A daily mail service was requested out of Helena. But the ore proved not to be gold-bearing and the hopes of **Dreamland** came to naught (Rex Martin, *Montana, Magazine of the Northern Rockies*; Spring 1975).

Drexel (Mineral) opened a post office in 1928 with Christian Dall as postmaster; it closed in 1953.

Drulett (Fergus) had a post office 1917-21 with Robert Wright as postmaster.

DRUMMOND (Granite) is on the Clark Fork River and was named for a trapper by this name who operated a line of traps in the territory and made his camp about where the railroad station now stands. The first camp at this site was established in 1871 and called Edwardsville for John Edwards, a local rancher. It was renamed for Hugh Drummond in 1883; when the post office was established in 1884 the name was shortened from Drummond Camp to **Drummond** (Western Interpretive Services).

Dry Creek (Dawson), near Wolf Point, was a post office 1882-83, with Gilman Norris as postmaster.

Dry Creek (Gallatin) Postal records show an office by this name open only from June-July 1874 with Thomas Mulvaney as postmaster.

Dryhead was the name chosen when citizens petitioned for a post office on an "Indian Reservation" in 1908. Charles Phelps was to have been postmaster, but the order of establishment was rescinded.

Dryhead (Carbon) was established in 1919 with James Ellis as postmaster. The area was named for the many dried buffalo skulls found at the bottom of a buffalo jump here. **Dryhead** is in the eastern portion of Carbon County in the foothills of the East Pryor mountains. The mail carrier came twice a week when roads permitted. There was a voting precinct in **Dryhead**, but quite often bad roads made it impossible to get results to the county seat at Red Lodge for a week or more.

Dubuque (Judith Basin) was named for Dubuque, Iowa. An office under that name was established by the postal department in 1886; it closed later that year to be reopened in 1890. Thomas Morgan was the first postmaster. In 1892 the name was changed to Stanford. Old Stanford, a nearby post office, had been discontinued in 1891 and several buildings as well as the post office were moved to **Dubuque**, which later became Stanford.

Duclair (Blaine) was a post office near Cherry Ridge that was active 1916-18 with Katherine Baritell as postmaster.

Duderanch (Park) couldn't have had a more appropriate name, because that is just what it was. James Norris "Dick" Randall was known as "Mr. Dude Rancher" in Montana. Randall established the OTO ranch near Yellowstone Park, where he kept three hundred head of horses ready for saddle or pack on 5,000 acres. He often lodged a hundred guests on the ranch, guiding them on horseback trips and delighting them with his stories. His wife Dora supervised the kitchen and food operations, salting down enough butter in the spring to last through the dude season. She made cheese, preserved garden vegetables, and saw to it that all guests were well fed. She also served as postmaster. The ten years from 1927-37 while the office was open were also the high point years for dude ranching.

Dudley (Fergus) is near Lewistown and had a post office 1888-91 with John Powell as postmaster.

Duffy (Lewis and Clark) was a tiny settlement named for John Duffy, an early settler.

Duncan (Gallatin) was named for its first postmaster, Scott Duncan. The office was open 1890-1900 and the mail was sent to Gallop after that.

Dundee (Richland) was presumably named for Dundee, Scotland, as there were many Scottish-descendant sheepmen in the area. The post office was only active September 1884-January 1885, and the mail was then ordered to Glendive — which must have been a "fur piece" to go for a letter.

Dunkirk (Toole) was a station on the Great Northern Railroad east of Shelby. There seems to be a disagreement as to when the post office was established — one record says 1910, another 1914. Cassius Johnson was the first postmaster.

Dunkleberg (Deer Lodge), near Warm Springs, had a post office 1890-91 with Reuben Conn as postmaster.

DUPUYER (Pondera), midway between Browning and Choteau, takes its name from Dupuyer Creek. The latter's name came from the French word *depouilles*, which trappers and explorers used to describe the back fat of a buffalo, a delicacy esteemed by both Indian and white man. **Dupuyer**, a supply point for stock ranches, came into existence as a stage stop on the bull team freight route between Fort Benton and Fort Browning. The post office, with Julian Burd in charge, was opened in 1882.

Durant (Silver Bow) was a train station named by M. S. Dean, traffic manager for the Anaconda Copper Mining Company at Chicago. Dean had a friend in New York by the name of Durant and he named the station in his honor.

DUTTON (Teton) was named for a Great Northern freight and passenger agent who was stationed at Helena in 1905. The **Dutton** post office was established in 1909 with John Menzie as postmaster. This is a wheat-producing area which began with a cowboy-turned-homesteader named "Sinker Bill" Frixel, who made final proof on his homestead in September 1909 — **Dutton** now stands on what was his property. Bill's nickname came from his days as a cook for roundup crews, who described his biscuits as "sinkers." George Sollid had the idea of getting people to locate in this area, even though land was free and open in all directions. Sollid set up shop near the old Frixel ranch and an old reservoir and began locating homesteaders sent to him by his brother at Conrad. According to the **Dutton** Jubilee booklet, newcomers were told: "Just go down to the depot and sit around looking like a sucker. It won't be long before George will show up." "Brother Van," the famous frontier Methodist minister, promoted the building of a church here and dedicated it in 1913.

Dwyer (Roosevelt), a town near Bainville, was named for Jack Dwyer, postmaster when the office opened in 1911; it was closed in 1915.

E

Eagle Butte (Chouteau) is near the Missouri River northeast of Fort Benton. It is named for nearby Eagle Butte, a landmark, which in turn was named for the many eagles that were found there. The post office opened in 1913 with John Zimmer as postmaster. The mailman came three times a week and also brought supplies for residents. The office closed in 1935.

Eagleton (Chouteau) is near Eagle Creek and Eagle Butte, so the suffix "ton" was added to indicate the town. A post office opened in 1914 with Celia Hawkins as postmaster and closed in 1951. It seems that prior to 1914 the settlement was called Richfield.

East Bridger (see **Bridger**).

East Fork (Rosebud) was named for the creek on which it was located. The post office opened in 1915 with Alice Steele in charge; it closed in 1923.

East Gallatin (Gallatin) had a post office 1869-73 and 1877-81; Daniel Maxey was the first postmaster.

EAST GLACIER PARK (Glacier), formerly called Glacier Park, had a post office established in 1950 with Cleola Ralston as postmaster. It is thirteen miles southwest of Browning on the Blackfeet Indian Reservation.

Eastham (Teton) was a railroad station named for Eastham, Massachusetts.

EAST HELENA (Lewis and Clark) was named for its location in relation to Helena. It is a smelter town for the Anaconda Copper Mining Company.

Many of the first settlers came from the Balkan countries shortly after 1900. The post office opened in 1888 with Henry Clark in charge.

East Portal (Mineral) was a station on the Milwaukee named because it is at the east end of the St. Paul Pass Tunnel at the summit of the Coeur d'Alene Mountains.

East Roundup (Musselshell), a suburb of Roundup, had a post office of its own March-May 1908 with George Osborne in charge.

East Scobey (Daniels), near old Scobey, was a train station. In 1914 it was granted a post office with Patrick Burke as postmaster. In 1917 the post office at the train station location took the name Scobey.

Echo (Flathead), near Creston, had a post office 1901-05. William Kelsey was the first postmaster.

EDDY (Sanders) was a station on the Northern Pacific. There was a section house, a watertower, and from 1900 on, a post office. John McKay was the postmaster and later a schoolhouse was built on a corner of his homestead. A lumber mill and a camp for workers were also built. The town was named for Dick Eddy from Missoula, one of the early promoters of the area. In 1960 it became a rural postal station out of Thompson Falls.

Eden (Cascade), south of Great Falls, first got a post office in 1900 with Robert Meisenbach as postmaster. It was opened and closed three times before the final discontinuance in 1960. A post office named Truly was established in 1884 and served patrons of the area. Someone made the long trip by horseback or with horse and buggy to get the mail. Neighbors chipped in to buy a mailsack, which was kept at Meisenbach's place; folks left their outgoing letters and urgent grocery and medicinal orders there. Anyone going to Stockett picked up the sack, filled the orders, and brought back everyone's mail. In 1899 a group of early homesteaders petitioned for a post office. They met at Pribyl's shack to select a name from the list the government office had sent, and chose **Eden** because they thought it appropriate for their beautiful surroundings. At first the post office was in the upstairs part of Meisenbach's blacksmith shop, but in 1909 it was moved to a back room of the Eden Creamery.

EDGAR (Carbon County) is in the lower valley of the Clark Fork River. It was named for Henry Edgar, one of the discoverers of gold in Alder Gulch in Madison County. According to one old-timer from that area, the town was started and laid out by a man named Thornton, who owned the land where the town now stands — he wanted to have one town without a saloon in it.

Edgehill (Wibaux) had a post office 1909-16 and 1917-28; Karl Meichkley was the first postmaster.

Edgerton (Beaverhead) had a post office October 1879-October 1880; James Kirkpatrick was postmaster. It was named for Gov. Sidney Edgerton.

Edgerton County was one of the original nine counties set up by the Territorial Legislature in 1865 and named for Montana's first territorial governor, Sidney Edgerton. The county name was changed in 1867 to Lewis and Clark.

Edgewater (Fergus) had a post office 1900-08; Susie McMahon was the first postmaster.

Edilou (Gallatin) was a sidetrack on the Bozeman-Menard branch line named for the son (Edward) and daughter (Louise) of C. F. Allen, the resident engineer then engaged in construction of the Milwaukee Railroad.

Edna (Prairie) had a post office 1914-16 with Anna Goodard in charge.

Edsel (Dawson) was granted a post office, but it was never in operation. This was in 1916; George Coyl was to have been postmaster.

Edwards (Garfield) was near Gumbo Flat and Sand Springs. It was named for John E. Edwards, resident and former cowboy with the old 79 outfit. Later he served as state senator from Rosebud County. The story of **Edwards** starts as far back as 1897, when Mr. Sanford and Glen Webster moved into the Big Dry country and settled at the head of Sand Creek. They brought in sheep from Mereno and the Upper Musselshell and raised them here. When the homesteaders came, a post office was established in 1913 with Joseph Scott as postmaster. A store and schoolhouse were built near the headquarters of the old 79 outfit. There was also a newspaper, the **Edwards** *Times*. The town was once a contender for the county seat.

Maj. John F. Edwards settled in Forsyth in 1902 with the honorary title given to all Indian agents. Edwards was a cowboy with the N Bar outfit owned by the Newman Brothers (Fulmer).

Carroll Graham, later a state senator, recalls the dugouts that some homesteaders lived in when wood was not available for building: The "house is right over there where the blanket is hanging up on that bank . . . the cave house had no support, it was dug in very hard material and had 3 small rooms that were arched into a clay bank . . . the lady was extremely friendly . . .and I learned afterward that she was a mail order bride . . . later she became very lonely and unhappy, so her husband took her only pair of shoes with him when he went to get the mail and groceries so she couldn't run away . . . one day in the spring he came home to find her gone . . . the weather was warm enough for her to go barefoot" (*Not in Precious Metals Alone*). The post office closed in 1945.

Egan (Missoula) had a post office 1888-92. Jessie Yume was postmaster.

Egly (Chouteau) was a post office 1915-33 and was named for first postmaster Margaret Egly. Mrs. Egly, a widow, came from Iowa in 1912 to be a pioneer homesteader. Her home was the post office and the community center.

Eight Mile (Ravalli) is a settlement on Eight Mile Creek. The creek was named because it empties into the Bitterroot River eight miles from Stevensville. The White Cloud Mine operated at **Eight Mile** from 1880 to 1890, according to Rodney Todd of Stevensville High School. Early residents tell of a post office there named Pyrates after the iron ore pyrite. Postal records show an office named Pyretees 1890-1907 in Ravalli County. **Eight Mile** once had a school and a church.

Eight Point (Valley) had a post office established in 1916 with Peter Wittmayer in charge. The office closed in 1936.

EKALAKA (Carter) is a county seat named for an Indian girl, the niece of Sitting Bull. Her Indian name, Ijkalaka, means "swift one" in the Sioux language. **Ekalaka** was often nicknamed "Puptown" because of the great number of prairie dogs around. The town began as a saloon for cowboys. Claude Carter was a buffalo hunter and bartender. He was on his way to another building site when his broncos balked at pulling the load of logs through a mudhole. "Hell," he said, "any place in Montana is a good place to build a saloon," so he unloaded the logs and erected the Old Stand Saloon. For more than fifty years, he bartended profitably to Carter County cowpunchers. David Harrison Russell was the first homesteader in the area and in 1875, he married Ijkalaka. In 1881 he brought her to the little community that had grown up around the Old Stand. She lived there until her death in 1901. **Ekalaka** now has a high school and students come from as far away as ninety miles to attend. The high school museum contains many well preserved specimens of prehistoric marine life, all excavated in Carter County. The post office opened in 1885 with Charles Cartwright as postmaster.

Eldridge (Gallatin) had a post office 1903-40; George Dean was the first postmaster.

Electric (Park) was named for Electric Peak, which in turn, was named because of the unusual electricity felt by a group of people during a storm in 1872. The settlement was formerly called Horr. The post office was active 1904-1915 and the mail then ordered to Corwin Springs. John Cleave was the first postmaster.

Elgin (Carter) had a post office 1911-38; John Howe was the first postmaster. It was near Ekalaka.

Elizabeth (Teton) had a post office 1898-1910; John Kellogg was the first postmaster.

Elk Basin (Carbon), on Silver Tip Creek, is the site of the first permanent oil well tapped in Montana (1915) by the Ohio Oil Company. The workers' housing village was moved to a high bench in Wyoming on account of gas pollution in the air.

Elkhorn (Jefferson) is an old mining town near Boulder. It has been designated one of the most important historical sites in the West and renovation has been undertaken by the Western Montana Ghost Town Preservation Society. **Elkhorn** flourished in the 1880s and '90s, when millions of dollars worth of gold and silver were mined. Reportedly the town had 2,500 residents, with 500 woodcutters, mostly of French and Norwegian descent, were employed to supply wood for the town and the mill. Several of the original buildings still stand. One of the most interesting is Fraternity Hall, a two-story structure with an exterior balcony protruding from the second floor. There was a large hall with a raised stage in one end on the first floor which served for all kinds of meetings and entertainment. The second floor contains small rooms and a large hall used for lodge meetings and dances. Two notable hotels were the Commercial and the Metropolitan. The post office opened in 1884 with William Healty as postmaster and was discontinued in 1924. Residents had long since moved away and the remaining buildings are left to the ghosts of rambunctious mining days.

Elkhorn City was a telegraph station on the east bank of the Powder River for the line that ran from Fort Keogh (later Miles City) to Fort Meade near Sturgis, South Dakota. The ford at **Elk City** provided a crossing for the Powder River on the stagecoach road between the forts. Later, Powderville was built on the other side of the river and the army telegraph line fell into disrepair after only two years of use.

Elk Park (Jefferson County) had a post office January 1889-November

1899 and again 1900-30; Charles Cunningham was the original postmaster. **Elk Park** was a station on the Great Northern between Boulder and Butte. It is in a wooded or "park" area which once had abundant deer and elk.

ELLISTON (Powell) is near the Continental Divide twenty-five miles from Helena, on the other side of McDonald Pass from the capital city. It began as a trade town in a gold, quartz, and placer mining district. Later a lime quarry and a mill supported the economy of the town. The post office was established in 1884 with S. N. Nicholson as postmaster.

Elloam (Blaine) had a post office 1916-1935; Eliza Hopkins was the first postmaster. **Elloam** is north of Chinook and seven miles from the Canadian border. Hopkins coined the post office name from three neices — Elizabeth, Lois and Marjorie. When the office was granted, the Hopkins family set aside a corner of a room in their home. The salary for a postmaster, based on the number of stamps cancelled, never exceeded $75 a year. The mail carrier ran errands and made purchases for **Elloam** residents on his weekly trips to Chinook. Sometimes passengers went with him on Tuesday and came back when he brought the mail on Saturday. When snow drifts blotted out roads and trails, the mailman had to make the frozen river his route. The 1930s were hard on homesteaders, and most people left **Elloam**, including Adeline Wagner, who was postmaster then, so there was no one left to keep the office after 1935.

Ellsmere (Cascade) was active 1890-1893. George Currie was postmaster.

Elmdale (Richland) had a post office 1908-1944. Levi Turner was the first postmaster.

Elmer (Rosebud) was south of Brunelda near the Garfield County line. It was named for Ralph Elmer, the first postmaster. The office was open 1914-1935.

ELMO (Lake) is on the Big Arm of Flathead Lake on the Flathead Indian Reservation. A post office here in 1911 with Aaron Stuckman as postmaster.

Elso (Mussellshell) was near Roundup. The post office was active 1891-1916; Henry Willis was the first postmaster.

Emery (Powell) had an off again, on again postal history between its opening of an office in 1896 (James Sullivan, postmaster) and the final closing in 1937. The post office had been inactive since 1906 when a petition for reestablishment was approved in 1936, but then rescinded in 1937.

EMIGRANT (Park) is on the Yellowstone River halfway between Livingston and Gardiner. It gets its name because the town is at the base of a mountain range containing Emigrant Peak, which rises to an altitude of 10,960 feet. Thomas Curry discovered gold in Emigrant Gulch in 1862. Early trappers and prospectors bathed in crude vats built around a natural hot springs here. Emigrant trains arriving near the narrow entrance to the gulch in 1864 found a lone pine tree in which eighteen or twenty elk horns had been embedded. Jim Bridger asserted that he had placed them there 25 years earlier. **Emigrant** (then in Gallatin County) had a post office 1872-1876. Postal records show the establishment of a Park County **Emigrant** office in 1911 with August Anderson as postmaster.

Emory (Golden Valley) is in the northeastern part of the county on Cameron Creek and the Lavina star route. The **Emory** post office was established in 1911 in a store run by Mr. and Mrs. Jim Lynch as a branch of the Slayton Mercantile in Lavina. Many of the homesteaders who settled here came from Emory, South Dakota, and brought the name to Montana. The first postmaster was John M. Oliver; the office closed in 1933.

Empire (Lewis and Clark) had a post office off-and-on 1886-1895: Joseph C. Pyle was the first postmaster.

ENID (Richland) is on Redwater Creek west of Sidney. It was named in honor of Enid Montana Dawe, the infant daughter of L. A. Dawe, an early settler and postmaster when the office opened in 1898. The office was originally at the Lassie Dawe Ranch on Burns Creek, but was moved to the Oakley ranch in the sand hills a half mile north of present-day **Enid**. Oakley had a general store which featured dry goods, tobacco and candy. In 1915 the post office was moved to the present site of **Enid**. The town boomed as homesteaders moved in. By 1916 there was a new railroad depot, a two-story schoolhouse and all kinds of shops and stores.

ENNIS (Madison), on the Madison River, was named for William Ennis, who was one of the first three men to locate in the Madison Valley. Ennis was born in County Down, Ireland, in 1828. He came to the United States when he was fourteen and to Montana in 1863. For awhile he lived in Bannack, then came to the Madison, where in 1879 he built a store. He became the first postmaster when the office opened in 1881, and for the next eighty-six years **Ennis** postal service was in the hands of his family; his daughter, Jennie Ennis Chowning, was postmaster 1898-1940; a granddaughter, Winifred Chowning Jeffers held the office 1940-67. In 1873, Ennis took his family through Yellowstone — these were the first white children to see the Park. William Ennis was shot on June 18, 1898 — while standing in front of the Madison House in Virginia City — by a neighbor who was angry because of an unfounded rumor that Mr.Ennis had maligned his character. He died of his wounds on July 4th.

Enterprise (Daniels) had a post office 1908-1916. Charles Coryell was postmaster. **Enterprise** was near Froid.

Enterprise (Missoula), near Missoula, had a post office March-November 1884, with Ezra Baker, postmaster. Mrs. Ludwig Browman tells of evidence that a place named Belknap had its name changed to **Enterprise** because the postmaster feared confusion with Fort Belknap (*Weekly Missoulian*; May 9, 1884).

Eplin (Sanders) was named for Martha Eplin, who was appointed postmaster when the office was approved in 1915. However, the order was rescinded and the office was never in operation.

EPSIE (Powder River) is nine miles west of Broadus. It was named for a rancher's wife, Epsie McAllister. **Epsie** has a somewhat violent history: in 1940 Frank Peterson, the postmaster, moved his shack and the post office to the highway; sometime later neighbors found the shack on fire and Peterson in front of it, dying of gunshot wounds. In 1954 the **Epsie** store and post office were held up at gun point. The proprietors, Mr. and Mrs. Marston, were tied and gagged. Two men took $100 from the till and some cigarettes. From the post office they took money orders — which proved to be their undoing, because they were arrested when they used them to try to buy a car. (*Echoing Footsteps*). The post office was established in 1916 with Rose Trowbridge in charge. At one time there were seventy patrons, but deep winter snows made regular travel impossible, so Archie Kelly delivered mail pulling a contraption on two poles behind a horse, Indian style. After twenty-four years, the isolated little office moved up to the highway and civilization.

Ericson, Erickson (Custer) had a post office established in February 1890; Levi Norgord was postmaster. The office was discontinued in January 1914, and the mail ordered to Camp Crook, South Dakota.

Erlice (Gallatin) was a station on the Bozeman-Menard branch line named for the daughter of Taylor Hamilton, a farmer who settled there in 1885.

Eskay (Chouteau) is in the extreme southeast corner of the county between Birch Creek and the Missouri River. It had a post office 1917-36. Clara Colton was first postmaster.

Esper (Teton) had a post office established in 1916 with N. Esper Norman as postmaster. The name was changed to Ledgerwood in 1917.

ESSEX (Flathead) is twenty-five miles south of the West Glacier entrance to the Park. It was on the Greater Northern line that bordered Glacier Park on the south. The post office, established in 1898 (William Glazier, postmaster), is called **Essex**; the railway station is named Walton.

Etchetah (Custer) had a post office 1877-1892 (except for a few months); Madison Black was the first postmaster. When the office closed the mail was sent to Blakely.

Ethel (Musselshell) was near Waldheim (Bundy). The post office operated 1914-1919. George Williams was the first postmaster.

ETHRIDGE (Toole) is between Shelby and Cut Bank. The post office opened in 1912 with Adam Cyr as postmaster.

Etna (Custer), near Miles City, had a post office 1882-1913. Ellen Adams was the first postmaster.

Etna (Ravalli)had a post office March 1872-January 1875. Renee Lipelt of Stevensville High School reports on the first school at **Etna**, as recalled by old-timers who attended the school. The first school was built in 1871 or '72. It was made of logs and served until it burned down. The first pupils made their own desks and brought their own books and slates from home. When slates were full of writing, they were washed in a pail of water that was kept warm by placing it on the heating stove. A pencil was a rare thing. Transportation to and from school was by wagon or sleigh with straw in it, and the children were covered with buffalo robes. The usual school term was three months (Rene Lipelt, Stevensville High School).

Eudora (Flathead) is near Elmo. The post office opened in 1912 with Printha Troutwine as postmaster; it closed in 1919.

EUREKA (Lincoln), in the extreme northwest corner of Montana, was first named Deweyville, after Ed Demers' wife's maiden name. The first buildings were on the banks of the Tobacco River. The town began building up the hill. A large sawmill which supported the economy of the town burned down in 1923; since then, the residents have developed a flourishing Christmas tree market. Huckleberries grow in abundance on the hillside. The post office opened in 1904 with Emma Dimmick as postmaster, who suggested the new name of **Eureka**.

Evans (Cascade) was named for Captain John Evans, an early settler. The post office was established in 1889 with Zinia Wainer in charge. It closed in 1937 and mail was sent to Giffin.

Evaro (Missoula), formerly Blanchard, was a station on the Northern Pacific named in honor of a French count who journeyed through this territory in the early days. Now it is a small Indian town near the edge of the Flathead Indian Reservation. The post office opened in 1905 with Reisin Otis as postmaster; it closed in 1953.

Evelyn (Ravalli), near Darby, had a post office April 1895-April 1899; Adam Koch was the first postmaster.

Everson (Fergus) is in the fertile benchland northeast of Denton. It was named for the postmaster, Herman Evers, when the office opened in 1900. There were five one-room schools in the area in the early days, and 75 or 80 families lived on their 160-acre homesteads. Twelve or fifteen ranchers live there now, with holdings of several thousand acres each. **Everson** never had a store or a church; religious services were held in a schoolhouse. The post office closed in 1927.

Ewalt (Custer) was named for postmaster Mildred Ewalt when the office opened in 1905. The name was changed to Ridgeway in 1911.

Ewing (Carbon) was named for postmaster Erastus Ewing when the office opened in 1898. **Ewing** was near Barry's Landing on the Big Horn River, and this was the only possible crossing for many miles in Big Horn Canyon. The office closed in 1908 and mail was sent to Pryor. "Rasmus" Ewing was a homesteader on Hough Creek, but the land was too lean to support farming, and settlers who had come with hope gave up and moved away. The Big Horn Gold Dredging Company worked gravel bars near here for gold about 1906.

Excie (Custer) was a post office 1901-06; Maude Hardesty was postmaster. It was near Ewalt.

Exeter (Dawson) had an active post office 1888-90; R. M. Trafton was postmaster.

Expanse (Sheridan), near Wolf Point, operated a post office 1917-18 with Agnes Christenson as postmaster.

F

Fairbanks (Carbon) was formerly called Tony. The post office was listed as **Fairbanks** only for June-August 1906. Joel Hutton was postmaster and when the office closed the mail was ordered to Linley.

Fairchild (Hill) was six miles north of Lilacs. The post office opened in 1913 in the home of postmaster Florilla Miller. It was closed April-November 1930, and then open until October 1941. The office was just across the road from the famous Peter Johnson sheep ranch and was named for an early governor of Wisconsin. Later, a general store was built and the post office was moved there. Mail came in three times a week by wagon from Gildford (*Grit, Guts, and Gusto*).

FAIRFIELD (Teton) began as a station on the Milwaukee, and is between Great Falls and Choteau and near Freezeout Lakes. **Fairfield** serves as a trading center for the farmers of Greenfield Bench. Irrigation now assures crops, but in earlier days a dry summer made the grass scarce and the name "Freeze-out Bench" was applied to the area. "Greenfield Bench" and **Fairfield** are now descriptive of the hay and grain fields surrounding the town. The post office opened in 1908 with John Zimmerman as postmaster.

FAIRVIEW (Richland) is north of Sidney, and part of it is across the North Dakota border. L. E. Newton located a homestead where **Fairview** now stands; he had the first store and was the first postmaster (1904). Newton named the town because he had a "fair" or beautiful view of the lower Yellowstone Valley from his home. A lignite mine on the edge of town furnishes fuel for local consumption. **Fairview** was a station on the Great Northern. Just north of **Fairview** are the remains of Fort Union, the most famous frontier trading post of all time.

FALLON (Prairie) is between Miles City and Glendive. It was a station on the Northern Pacific and one of the old towns along the Yellowstone River named for Benjamin O'Fallon, Indian agent, Army officer, and nephew of William Clark, the explorer. O'Fallon's report of the slaughter of 29 members of the Jones-Imenell party of the Missouri Fur Company by 400 Blackfeet in May 1823 presents one of the most vivid pictures of Indian warfare in the West. **Fallon** is now in the middle of rich grain fields. In the early days the land was covered with a nourishing buffalo grass that supported millions of bison. Cattle and sheep grazing cut the grass down too far and let the rich topsoil blow away during the Dust Bowl years. A post office for **Fallon** was active October-December 1884 and then reestablished in 1890. Cyrus Mendenhall was the 1884 postmaster.

Fallon County borders North Dakota. Baker is the county seat. The county was created in December 1913 from a part of Custer County. A part of **Fallon County** was annexed to Wibaux County in 1914; a part to Prairie County in 1915; and a part to Carter County in 1917. Wibaux County and **Fallon County** annexed parts of each other in 1919. Oil and gas resources have made valuable land that was once only a vast prairie.

Family (Glacier) was on Two Medicine River and took its name from the Holy Family Mission there, a Catholic boarding school for Indian children. The post office was active January 1900-July 1901 with Ignatius Vasta as postmaster. The office was open again 1902-40. It is east of Browning near old Fort Piegan.

Faranuf (Valley) must have been named by weary homesteaders who had come across the plains looking for a place to settle. And many of them must have given up in the bad years because the post office was discontinued in 1935. It was established in 1929 with Myrtle Burke in charge.

Farlin (Beaverhead), near Apex, had a post office 1905-06 with Gertrude Black as postmaster.

Farmington (Teton) was a station on the Milwaukee's Great Falls-Agwam branch line. The name was chosen by the first settlers because of the surrounding, rich farmland. A post office opened in 1899 with Martin

Monson as postmaster and closed in 1951.

Farralltown (Mussellshell), on the edge of Roundup, has a legend of cave dwellers — relatively modern ones. When trouble was brewing in Europe prior to World War I, many people fled to America. The Milwaukee Railroad brought hundreds of these immigrants to work in the coal mines at Klein. Work was plentiful, but housing was scarce. In 1909 Dominic Finco used his mining skills to enlarge a cave, and his talent as a stonemason to wall up the entrance. Wooden door frames, glass windows, and a bright coat of paint completed the abode. Other immigrants followed Finco's lead and soon a collection of cliff dwellers lived beneath the rim of **Farralltown** (Billings *Gazette*; Nov. 25, 1973).

Farrell (Madison) This post office was probably located on the early-day stock ranch of Varney-Farrell. Thomas Farrell, an Irish immigrant, served with the Confederate army and came to Virginia City when the war ended. There he ran a freighting business, a livery stable, and finally a ranch that supplied horses for General Howard's cavalry, which tried to subdue Chief Joseph and his tribe of fleeing Nez Perces. In 1873 Farrell was elected sheriff of Madison County. The post office by this name operated February-March and May-July of 1881.

Fattig (Musselshell) began as a stage station on Fattig Creek around 1880. A log building serving as home, post office and grocery store was operated by Henry Ostrander and his family. The post office was active 1903-16. In renovating the old log house recently, the new owners found the marriage license of the Ostranders, dated November 1, 1899 (Billings *Gazette*; November 14, 1971).

Febes (Madison) had a post office 1892-93, according to Lutz's list. James Febes is shown as postmaster. But no record of this is found in other Madison County listings.

Feeley (Silver Bow) was named for John F. Feeley, an early settler. Its post office was open off-and-on again 1888-1904.

FERDIG (Toole) is between Sunburst and Shelby. It was formerly called Red Deer. **Ferdig**'s post office was opened in 1926 with Cora Grass as postmaster. The new name was to honor an oil man who had extensive property in the area.

FERGUS (Fergus) began as a station on the branch line of the Milwaukee Railroad, and was named for Andrew Fergus, a cattleman and one of the first settlers in the area. The county was named for his father. The post office for this town, located near the headwaters of Box Elder Creek near Roy, was opened in 1899 with William Fergus as postmaster. The post office and store were moved in 1959 to a point along the highway. The community hall and schoolhouse still stand on the original site (Byerly).

Fergus County was named for James Fergus, an early-day miner in the Bannack area who was later elected to the territorial legislature. Fergus was vocal and influential, a cattleman and first president of the Montana Pioneers Society. The county was created in December 1886. Lewistown, the county seat, is located in the exact center of Montana. A part of **Fergus County** was taken in 1920 to form part of Judith Basin County; a part was taken in 1925 to form Petroleum, and another part in 1911 to form part of Musselshell County.

Ferguson (Madison) had a post office 1896-1905. Three members of the

Ferguson family served as postmasters: Andrew, Roland, and Jennie.

Fermus (Musselshell) had a post office 1915-16 with Otto Hill, postmaster. It was near Roundup.

Ferris (Powder River), formerly in old Custer County, had a post office 1893-1902. Walter Shy was the first postmaster.

Fiedler (Chouteau) was named for the family of Camille Fiedler, the first postmaster, 1917-18. It was near Big Sandy.

Fielding (Flathead) was near Essex and had a post office 1909-14 and 1915-19. Joseph Cremans was the first postmaster.

Fife (Cascade) was a station on the Great Northern east of Great Falls. Some residents of the area say that the town was named for the variety of wheat grown on the ranches. Fife wheat continues to be an important crop. Charles Russell said that Tommy Simpson named it for "his village in Scotland that he was run out of as a youth for poachin'." A post office in **Fife** was established in 1914 with James Prodger as postmaster; the office closed in 1963.

Fin (Jefferson) had a post office 1890-94 with Richard Swarbrick serving as first postmaster.

Finch (Rosebud) is almost on the border of Treasure County. It was named for F. N. Finch, one-time superintendent of a division of the Northern Pacific (a Frances Finch was postmaster at Lisle, also in Rosebud County, 1911-12). The **Finch** post office was established in 1914 with Walter Thayer as postmaster. It closed in 1940.

Findon (Meagher) was probably named after Findon, Scotland, by Mary Grant, who settled this area in 1881. However, a handwritten note on a scrap of paper on file at the Historical Library says that Lewis Cameron named it for his hometown in Scotland. At any rate, it is certain that the name came from Scotland. There was a post office at **Findon** 1892-94 with John Cameron as postmaster. The office was reopened 1912-37.

Finger Butte (Garfield) had a post office in the home of Mr. and Mrs. William McCants. The mail came once each week from Jordan. The office was discontinued in 1934. **Finger Butte** was named for a tall, slim hill nearby that resembles a finger. Time and erosion have worn it away, and the resemblance is no longer apparent. The hill was a landmark for persons who lived on Hall Creek (Highland).

Finn (Jefferson) was a railroad station named for J. D. Finn, a superintendent of the Northern Pacific. It had a post office 1900-02 with James Ryan as postmaster.

Finn (Powell) was named for Luke Finn, who operated the only saloon. It was a halfway stop between Avon and Helmville. The post office opened in 1910 with Edwin Graver as postmaster; it closed in 1941.

Finntown was the original name of Milltown (see **Milltown**).

Finrock (Fergus) had a post office established in 1916. The name was changed to Merino in 1917.

First Creek (Phillips) had a post office 1918-35. It is between Regina and Sun Prairie. The first postmaster was Florence Knapp.

Fish Creek (Madison) had a post office established in 1870, taking over the postal service formerly known as Jefferson Bridge. The little settlement was at the bridge which crossed the Jefferson River. The **Fish Creek** office was discontinued in 1896; the first postmaster was Harrison Jordan. George Comfort, the only itinerant Methodist minister in Montana from 1868 to 1869, served many communities in the Madison and Jefferson valleys — including **Fish Creek** — until he, too, followed the stampede to the richer strikes at Last Chance Gulch.

Fishel (Musselshell) had a post office 1915-16 with Maurice Curtin, postmaster.

FISHTAIL (Stillwater) is twenty-five miles southwest of Columbus. It was named for a Mr. Fishtail who resided in the area. A post office was established in 1901 with Charles Sullivan as postmaster. A new mail route was laid out to service many new homesteaders of the Fiddler, **Fishtail**, and Rock Creek areas. Stressley Tunnell set up a store and later served as postmaster. The Columbus Mercantile bought out his store in 1908, and Benny Banks took over the operation. A saloon, blacksmith shop, hotel, and livery barn completed the business section of town. The streets were laid out and the town was platted in 1913 (Annin).

As to the origin of the name, some residents say that the Indians point to a local mountain formation that looks like a fishtail. There is also a Fishtail River.

Fishtrap (Deer Lodge) was named because a man named LaMarsh built a trap for fish on the creek here and peddled his catch to the mining camps. The office operated 1901-40; George Groun was postmaster.

Fisk (Chouteau) was to be named for R. Clarke Fisk, but the 1906 order to establish a post office was rescinded.

Fivemile (Carter) had a post office 1898-1907. It was near Alzada.

Flandrem (Valley) was the name of a post office 1906-07 with Edward Stubban, postmaster. The name was changed to Medicine Lake in 1907, but Stubban continued in the office.

Flat (Musselshell), near Wheaton, had a post office 1914-23. Ezra Young was postmaster.

Flathead (Missoula) This post office was active 1867-68 with John T. Hanks postmaster.

Flathead County is in the northwestern part of the state, bounded on the east by the Continental Divide where it bisects Glacier National Park. Kalispell is the county seat. It was named for the Flathead, or Salish, Indians. The name "Flathead" seems to have been given to the tribe by Lewis and Clark, but there is no evidence that these Montana Indians ever adopted the practice of flattening their children's heads as did some tribes further west. Clark drew a sketch to show a wooden device used by Indians living near the mouth of the Columbia River to flatten the heads of infant females. W. F. Wheeler, in a very old handwritten article (Montana Historical Library Collection), says that the Flathead Indians denied this was ever a practice of their tribe. Wheeler quotes Coues (*History of the Lewis and Clark Expedition*): "The remarks upon the Flatheads presented in this statistical view are vague and merely rest upon information gotten from the Minnetarees who had taken (captured) some Flathead persons. . . . It must be through some such second-hand source of information that Lewis and Clark were induced to publish the story." Debbie Reynolds of Stevensville High School suggests that the Flatheads are known by that name since their home was at the "flat" head of the river as contrasted with the deep canyons below.

The county was created in February 1893 out of Missoula County. It annexed part of Deer Lodge County between then and 1900; part of **Flathead County** was taken to form Lincoln County in 1909, and another part was taken to form Lake County in 1923.

Flat Head Indian Agency (Missoula), had a post office (Ludger Tuott, postmaster) 1882-85 when the name was changed to Arlee.

Flat Head Lake (Missoula) This post office opened in 1873 with Valentine Coombes in charge. It closed in 1875, and postal records state that it was originally called Scribners.

Flatwillow (Petroleum) takes its name from Flatwillow Creek, named for the willow trees along its banks. A post office operated here most of the time between 1883-1946. John Dochter was the first postmaster. The settlement was first called Flatwillow Crossing, and began as a trading post. In 1903 a regular store was opened there and by 1918 **Flatwillow** was thriving as it served homesteaders for miles around. The first schoolhouse was a log cabin built in 1900; by night it was used as a saloon. **Flatwillow** was once a town catering to many homesteaders; later it became a community of prosperous ranchers and stockmen as the 160-acre units were bought up and combined into economically sound ranches.

Flax (Fergus) had a post office 1912-15 with Flora Wheeler as first postmaster.

FLAXVILLE (Daniels) was so named because flax was about the only grain grown in this territory in the early days. The original settlement was located about 2½ miles southwest of the present townsite and was called Boyer. The town was moved to its present location when the Great Northern came through. The post office was established in 1914 with Martha Bledsoe as postmaster.

Flesher (Lewis and Clark), near Wilborn, was named for first postmaster Gideon Flesher. The office was open 1902-28 except for a few months in 1916-17. **Flesher** is also the name of a pass at the Continental Divide north of Helena.

Fletcher (Glacier), near Babb, had a post office 1913-15 with Hugh Gallegher as postmaster.

Flint (Meagher) was named for the family of Calla Flint, first postmaster. The office was open 1903-17 and 1918-19. It was near White Sulphur Springs.

FLORENCE (Ravalli) was named for Florence Abbott Hammond, wife of A. B. Hammond, prominent Missoula resident. The post office was established in 1888 with Gilbert Strout as postmaster.

The settlement was first called One Horse, and was settled in 1889 by Irish immigrants; later, German settlers joined them. **Florence** in the early days had a good general store, a blacksmith shop, post office, railroad station, greenhouse, saloon, and cheese factory. At one time as many as 100 carloads of wheat a day were shipped out during the harvest season. The first schoolhouse, built in 1889, was made of hand-hewn logs. The first church was also built that year. The new school is called Florence-Carlton, as it serves both communities (Pam Nixon, Stevensville High School).

Florence Springs (Lewis and Clark) was originally called Florence and named for Florence Lippincott Fuller (Rowe). A post office operated there February-April 1879. Florence's father, Ed Lippincott, was postmaster.

Floweree (Chouteau) is near the Missouri River northeast of Great Falls. It was a station on the Great Northern. "From Texas in 1873 came Daniel Floweree with a herd of 1500 cattle followed by another large herd from Oregon the next year" (Mockel). The post office was opened in 1910 with Arthur Martin as postmaster. In 1974 it became a rural station out of Great Falls.

Flume (Teton) was once a station on the Great Northern. It was named for the large irrigation flume that crossed the line of the railroad at that place.

Fly (Gallatin) (see **Central Park**).

Flynn (Rosebud) was a station near Forsyth. It was named for T. M. Flynn, then superintendent of the Northern Pacific Railroad.

Foley (Prairie) had a short-lived post office, May 1881-April 1882, with Albert Long, postmaster.

Folsom (Golden Valley), near Lavina, had a post office 1890-96 with Dalon Salyton as first postmaster. The office was active again 1897-1905.

Ford (Custer) was a post office 1911-12 with Ethie Smith as postmaster.

Forest City, Forest (Missoula) had a post office 1871-1908; Thomas Williams was postmaster. When the office closed, mail was directed to Iron Mountain.

FOREST GROVE (Fergus) is Hereford and Angus country now, but no doubt it was Texas Longhorn country when the post office was established in 1899 with Thomas Frost as postmaster. The office was discontinued in 1900 and reopened in 1904. There were small coal mines worked in this area in the 1920s and '30s. Each mine had a mule to pull the ore cars. Coal was shipped out on the Milwaukee. **Forest Grove**'s peak population was 525 in 1918, when homesteaders were still hanging on. Now only the post office and the wool shop of postmaster May Charbonneau are left (Byerly).

Forks (Meagher) had a post office 1891-93; William Lee was postmaster.

Forks (Phillips), in the northeastern part of the county, was named for its location near the confluence of North Fork Creek and East Fork Creek where they join to form Whitewater Creek. The post office opened in 1919 with Ella Simonson as postmaster; it closed in 1951.

FORSYTH (Rosebud) is a county seat. It was named for Gen. James W. Forsyth, who landed here from a river steamer before there was a town. Later he wrote *A Report of an Expedition Up the Yellowstone River in 1875*. Forsyth was the first U.S. Army officer to come by steamer to this Yellowstone River landing. The post office was established in 1882 with Fred Henning in charge. Indians from the Tongue River Reservation come here to trade and visit.

Fort Alexander was built on the north bank of the Yellowstone River, opposite the mouth of Rosebud Creek (Mockel). It was built in 1842 by Charles Larpenteur and named for Alexander Culbertson.

Fort Andrews was built in 1862 on the Missouri River fifteen miles above the mouth of the Musselshell. It was named for Andrew Dawson.

Fort Assiniboine (Hill) was an old fort and military reservation named for a tribe of Indians whose name signifies "stone boilers." The name is said to have been given to them because of their singular manner of boiling their meat by dropping heated stones into the water with the meat until it was cooked. Many of the old fort buildings are still standing. "On May 4, 1879, the 18th Infantry arrived at Coal Banks, Montana, from stations in Kentucky. Their commander, Col. Thomas H. Ruger, lost no time establishing the site of Montana's most substantial fort, **Fort Assiniboine.**" Much of the work on the fort was done by the troopers. From May through September, the troops escorted load after load of building materials from Coal Bank to the site of the fort. The fort was built mainly of brick. Kilns were built near the post to manufacture brick. The result was the largest military installation built in Montana — 104 buildings. A fort the size of Assiniboine was not needed anywhere in Montana by 1879. The duties were mostly patrolling the Canadian border for stray Indians, mainly Crees. In 1896 the Tenth Cavalry, a Negro regiment, was stationed there with Lt. John Joseph Pershing, later, World War I Supreme Commander (Koury).

There was a post office at the fort 1879-1911; H. B. Hill was the first postmaster.

Fort Belknap (Blaine) was a station on the Great Northern Railroad named in honor of Robert L. Belknap. This is also agency headquarters for the Fort Belknap Indian Reservation in the eastern half of Blaine County. The Gros Ventre (Fr.: "big bellies") and the Assiniboine (a mountain branch of the Sioux), who were former enemies, have lived together on the reservation since it was set aside for them in 1887. The old Fort Belknap trading post was established on the other side of Milk River from Fort Browning, after it was forced to close, and about fifty miles upriver, or almost due north of the gap in the Bear Paws marked by needle rocks (Allison). St. Paul Mission church was established in 1885.

FORT BENTON (Chouteau) was named for Sen. Thomas H. Benton, an early-day senator originally from Missouri, who did a lot for the West. The town, now county seat of Chouteau County, was originally a trading post. It is one of the oldest communities in Montana, having been established in 1850. It was also one of the most important early-day trading posts, because it was built at the head of navigation on the Missouri River. Steamboats brought supplies up the river this far, but because of rapids could go no further and all cargo had to be unloaded here and taken by freightwagons to the gold camps at Helena and Virginia City and other places in western Montana. Supplies came by riverboat for Idaho and Canada, for the cattlemen and the settlers. This post was the point of debarkation for thousands of tenderfeet anxious to reach the gold fields. **Fort Benton**'s hotels, with their high ceilings, plush furniture, and glittering chandeliers were the last word in fashion in the 1870s and '80s. The first steamer to arrive at Fort Benton was the "Chippewa" in 1860. The peak year was 1867, when somewhere between 39 and 47 boats came in. When the Great Northern reached Helena in 1887 the steamboat days were over. The last boat came to Fort Benton in 1922, but the lucrative trade had long since gone to the railroads.

Ruins of the old trading post and blockhouse are in a five-acre tract west of the present-day tourist park. The fort was 250 feet square and built of adobe, under the supervision of Alexander Culbertson. It had bastions at two corners. There was no stockade. A wall said to be 32 feet thick formed the back of the buildings, all of which faced an inner courtyard. A large gate and a small one faced the river. The fort was built about 1856 and was originally called Fort Lewis for Meriwether Lewis (*Half Interest in a Silver Dollar*). The first commander was also named Lewis — Maj. William H. Lewis. The American Fur Company closed out its business in 1870 and leased the fort to the government. The Seventh Infantry, under Maj. Lewis, occupied it briefly.

The town became headquarters for cowboys and cattlemen as the big cattle pools ranged their herds on the open country toward the Judith and Milk rivers. The post office was established in 1867 with Isaac Baker as postmaster.

Fort Browning (Glacier), a station on the Great Northern, was named for the trading post by that name in Phillips County.

Fort Browning (Phillips) was south of the present town of Dodson. It was named for O. H. Browning, Secretary of the Interior in 1868. J. H. Willard says it was at the mouth of Peiole's Creek, which flows out of the Little Rockies, and that on Thanksgiving Day, 1868, Maj. John Simmons invited his friend Nepee, the Gros Ventre chief, to the fort, along with some other Indians, to enjoy a feast of buffalo, venison and antelope, topped off with strong whiskey. Nepee showed the major a sack of gold that he had gathered, but no amount of coaxing or trade whiskey could pry out of the Indian his secret of the source of the gold. **Fort Browning** was abandoned as a trading post in 1871 because the Sioux moved into the area to hunt buffalo and prevented the weaker Gros Ventre and Assiniboine from trading there. In 1893 gold deposits were discovered by white men, and the rush was on to Zortman and Landusky.

Fort Buford. In 1868 the U.S. Government bought old Fort Union, which had been established as a fur trading post near the junction of the Yellowstone and Missouri rivers, and dismantled the buildings. The materials were then used to build **Fort Buford** eight miles down the Missouri.

Fort Campbell, a trading post, was built in 1846 near Fort Benton, and named for Robert Campbell.

Fort Carroll. The landing place on the Missouri known as Carroll was occasionally referred to as **Fort Carroll**.

Fort Cass was built in 1832 three miles below the junction of the Yellowstone and Big Horn rivers. It was a trading post for barter with the Crow Indians (Mockel). It was built by Samuel Tullock and named for Lewis Cass of Michigan.

Fort C. F. Smith (Big Horn) was Montana's second military post. In 1863 John M. Bozeman blazed a wagon road from the Oregon Trail to the Montana gold camps. Travelers on the road were constantly attacked by Sioux, Cheyenne, and Blackfeet — this was their prime hunting ground and they fought to protect it. To guard the trail for the invading white men, **Fort C. F. Smith** was set up by the army in August 1866. It was the northernmost post of the three established for this purpose. The original building, supervised by Captain N. C. Kenney, was a 300-foot square stockade. It was a crude and isolated post, and so hated by the Indians that they renewed their attacks and the government withdrew its troops two years later. It was named for Maj. Gen. Charles Ferguson Smith, who died in 1868. It was first called Fort Ransom. The Bozeman Trail was too dangerous and little used after the troops were withdrawn. Little is left of **Fort C. F. Smith**, but a marker indicates the spot where 25 soldiers stood off

1,000 Sioux warriors.

Fort Chardon. Following the abandonment of Fort MacKenzie, Francis Chardon and Alexander Harvey, two fur traders, set up a new trading post across the Missouri from the mouth of the Judith River. This post was located on the north bank of the Missouri for protection from the Blackfeet Indians, with whom they hoped to trade. It was never a successful post, because the Blackfeet were Plains Indians and refused to cross the Big River to trade, especially in times of high water. To hold their trade it was necessary to return to the north bank of the river. This was done in 1846, and Fort Lewis was built (Abbott). Large herds of buffalo and many beaver in the streams made traders risk their lives to hunt and trap in the Judith country. **Fort Chardon**, built in 1843 by the American Fur Company, was maintained for only a year.

Fort Clagett was built on the site of defunct Camp Cooke above the mouth of the Judith River. The new name honored William Clagett, a delegate to Congress from Montana Territory in 1872 (see also **Clagett, Camp Cooke**, and **Judith Landing**). Settlers took logs from the old fort to make new buildings but they, too, found this was a poor location and **Fort Clagett** was short-lived (Oscar Mueller, *Military Posts of Montana*.)

Fort Connah was built in 1846 or 1847 by Angus McDonald, who was in the employ of the Hudson's Bay Company. It was a few miles south of Flathead Lake. Angus was married to an Indian girl, and their son, Duncan McDonald, told historians in 1916 that his father had been told in 1849 by Benetsee, an Indian, that there was gold in the area that later became known as Gold Creek. According to Duncan McDonald, the Hudson's Bay Company wanted to suppress any such rumors because the company feared that a gold rush would ruin their lucrative fur trade. Burlingame and Toole say the fort was built in 1846 by Neil McArthus and Angus McDonald and named for the River Connen in Scotland (*History of Montana*).

Fort Conrad was built by Charles Conrad where the Whoop-Up Trail crossed the Marias River. It was a lively spot in 1875, when bullwhackers prodded their teams, hauling supplies and whiskey to posts in Canada and returning with fine furs and buffalo hides. Joe Kipp described the fort as two rows of connecting log cabins with stables and corrals at the west end. There were warehouses for storing merchandise, furs and hides. The post office opened in July 1884 with Kipp as postmaster of a bi-monthly mail service. The last bull train traveled the trail in 1892. The buildings burned in 1888 and the river has washed away the site. A map drawn by the famous author James Willard Schultz places the fort just west of the railroad bridge. The post office closed in 1888 (Floershinger).

Fort Custer was a cavalry post built at the junction of the Bighorn and Little Bighorn Rivers in 1877. Lt. Col. George Buell had chosen the spot and General Sherman agreed it was a good location "in the very heart of Sioux country." The site of the post was well chosen, but it came too late. It was only twelve miles from the scene of Custer's disaster. The fort sat on high bluffs, commanding a fine view of the Valley of the Little Big Horn. It was a large and impressive fort, well constructed and attractive. Originally called the Big Horn Post, the name was changed to **Fort Custer** in November 1877 (Koury). Except for the Crow Rebellion of 1887, the troops had little to do except patrol duty. Some turned to amateur theatricals for amusement, and on one occasion, when a traveling impressario visited the fort, the company, with his help, presented the story of Capt. John Smith, using Crow Indians in the cast. At the point where Pocahontas was pleading for the life of Smith, a Crow Indian burst into the theater saying that a band of Sioux had stolen all the horses that had been hitched to the rack outside. The bugler blew "Boots and Saddles," Plenty Coups called a hurried war council, and the Indians joined the cavalry in pursuit of the thieves (*Montana, A State Guide Book*). The fort was officially abandoned April 17, 1898. A post office operated 1878-97 and 1900-01; Theodor Borup was the first postmaster. Nothing is left at the site now, except one monument with a few pertinent facts.

Fort Dauphin was a fur trading post on the Missouri at the mouth of the Milk River, built in 1860 by Louis Dauphin, a Creole trapper who operated posts at several locations between the Poplar and Milk Rivers during the late 1850s. He was killed by Sioux at the mouth of the Milk River in 1865.

Fort Elizabeth Meagher was established in May 1867. It was located eight miles east of Bozeman at the mouth of Rock Creek and was under the command of Brig. Gen. Thomas Thoroughman and Col. Walter W. DeLacy of the Montana Volunteer Militia. A "picket post" was also erected on the approach to Bridger Pass. Settlers in the Gallatin Valley were fearful that the area was about to be invaded by a large band of hostile Sioux and Crows following the murder of John Bozeman in April 1867. The posts were designed to block the passes through the mountains into the valley. The fort probably consisted of a stockade. It was named for the wife of Thomas F. Meagher, secretary and at one time acting governor of the territory (Fraser). Fort Ellis was built on the same site.

Fort Ellis This military post was completed near Bozeman August 27, 1867, and was strategically located to command Bozeman, Bridger and Flathead passes. The local citizenry demanded a stockade and Colonel Brackett described the post, built under the supervision of the Thirteenth Infantry: "The fort is made of logs and surrounded with palisades with two block houses at diagonal corners. It is small, compactly built, and seems well adapted for frontier protection. The stockade was put up at the request of the citizens to serve as a place of refuge in case of an Indian invasion." By 1867 the stockade had disappeared . . . there were quarters for 400 men, a two-story hospital with ten rooms and other buildings (Koury).

Fort Ellis was abandoned in August 1886 and the post office, which had opened in 1880 (Winfield Larcey, postmaster), was also discontinued.

But back in 1877, a correspondent for *Harper's* magazine wrote of arriving at the "old straggling cavalry station of **Fort Ellis** with its low squatty log houses," but he found the inside of the commandant's house had "comfort and even elegance." He also wrote of a theatrical performance by the Fort Ellis Troupe — "one of the best variety companies we have ever seen" — and of a soldiers' ball in a beautiful decorated barracks dining room. Of course, the protocol of the time insisted that enlisted soldiers and their wives be careful never to exchange even a glance with commissioned officers and their wives. A young lieutenant who danced one set with the pretty daughter of a laundress was severely reprimanded (Western Interpretive Services).

Fort Ellis was named for Col. Augustus Van Horn Ellis of the 124th New York Volunteers. It was built on the spot where Capt. William Clark and his exploration party had come on July 14, 1806. For nineteen years, **Fort Ellis** played an important part in the taming of the frontier in the Gallatin area. The Washburn-Langford expedition, whose report of the geysers, hot springs, terraces, paint pots, and other marvels of the Yellowstone region led to the creation of Yellowstone National Park, outfitted at **Fort Ellis** in August of 1870. Remains of the old fort can still be found.

Fort Fizzle is about five miles west of Lolo in western Montana. Built by the Army, it was intended as a barricade to keep Chief Joseph and his Nez Perce warriors bottled up long enough to prevent their flight into Canada. But the Indians merely rode up the hills and around the obstacle, and the entire defensive plan fizzled. Capt. Charles Rawn, Seventh Infantry, with four officers, five enlisted men, and many volunteers, built and occupied the fort in July 1877. A forest fire destroyed the old log fort in 1934.

Fort Floyd was the original name of the fort that was renamed Fort Union in 1828 (see **Fort Union**).

Fort Gilpin (Blaine) was named for an old Indian trader. A Fort Galpin, built in 1962 on the north side of the Missouri twelve miles above the mouth of the Milk River, is also shown as a Montana fort. No doubt this was just a variance in spelling.

FORT HARRISON This post, near Helena, is officially known as **Fort William Henry Harrison**. Established in May 1892, it was originally named for Pres. Benjamin Harrison, since the establishment of the fort coincides with his term of office. However, there was also a fort by that name in Indiana, so in 1906 the name of the Montana post was changed to **Fort William Henry Harrison**. The latter Harrison was born in Virginia in 1773, joined the Army in 1791, and made a gallant showing during Gen. Wyne's expedition against the Indians of the Northwest. He served in Congress in 1799 and was made governor of the Northwest Indian Territory the following year. He died one month after taking the office of President of the United States. **Fort Harrison**'s post office opened in 1899 with Martha Hodel as postmaster. It was inactive 1902-24. **Fort Harrison** was discontinued as an army post but was used for a while by the Montana National Guard. Most of it is now a hospital administered by the Veterans' Administration.

Fort Hawley This was a trading post for buffalo hides and beaver skins located near the mouth of the Musselshell River.

Fort Henry was built in 1822 at the mouth of the Yellowstone River and abandoned in 1823; later, Fort Union was built near the site of this short-lived fort. On March 20, 1882, William H. Ashley advertised for a hundred "enterprising young men" to engage in the Missouri River fur trade — with this the Rocky Mountain Fur Company was born. Jim Bridger, Hugh Glass and Mike Fink, a superior boatman, were among those who responded. Ashley was a brigadier general who had served during the War of 1812, and Maj. Andrew Henry was his associate in fur enterprise. They left St. Louis in April 1822 but encountered hostile Arikara Indians and Ashley turned back. The rest of the party continued up the Missouri and established **Fort Henry** where the Yellowstone empties into the Missouri. Henry pushed up the Missouri as far as Great Falls but there was turned back by Blackfeet. The company, led by Henry, operated for twelve years; it was never as successful as some others, but it is estimated that some $500,000 worth of beaver hides were shipped out by Henry and his men.

Fort Howes Levi S. Howes directed the building of a rock-walled redoubt on a hill above the Howes ranch buildings south of Ashland. Neither a military nor trading post, it survives as one of the few of its kind in the United States. Howes was foreman for the Howes, Strevelle, and Miles, Circle-Bar outfit that ran about a thousand head of cattle and horses on Otter Creek. With the help of his cowboys he built the edifice now known as **Fort Howes** as a civilian defense against a threatened outbreak of Cheyennes in 1897. The "fort" is located at the head of Otter Creek in Powder River County. The Circle-Bar men dug off the point of a hill down to hard rock for the floor. Rocks from the side of the hill were piled up to make the walls. The roof was of heavy pine planks covered with earth. Portholes in the walls were shoulder high so there would be no injuries to those inside — The Indians would have to shoot upwards and their bullets could only reach the soft, overhanging roof. The "fort," rounded in the shape of a hill, was ten by eighteen feet and was supplied with barrels of water, food, arms and ammunition. For some time a guard was posted there at night.

No attack was ever made on **Fort Howe**, but later some Indians climbed the hill, looked over the edifice, and pronounced it "heap good" (Fulmer).

Fortine (Lincoln) is twelve miles south of Eureka. It was named for Octave Fortine, an early settler. This station on the Great Northern was near Harrisburg. The post office was established in 1905.

Fort Jackson was built in 1833 at the mouth of the Poplar River by F. A. Chardon (Highland). It was named for Andrew Jackson, who was president at the time.

Fort Keogh (Custer) was actually the beginning of Miles City. It was established as an Army post in 1876 and named for Capt. Myles Keogh, the fighting Irishman who died with Custer at the Battle of the Little Bighorn. Keogh's horse, Comanche, survived the battle and became a revered, living symbol of all the men who lost their lives that June day in 1876. **Fort Keogh** was built a year after the battle and was used as a base for troops engaged in subjugating Indians who had rebelled at the destruction of their food supply. Gen. Nelson A. Miles commanded the fort until 1880. By then most of the buffalo and many of the Indians had died.

"After the Two Moons band surrendered to General Miles at **Fort Keogh**, many of the Northern Cheyennes joined the Army as scouts. White Bull was the first to join up. John Two Moons, son of the chief, and High Wolf were the Northern Cheyenne scouts who located the Chief Joseph camp in the Bear Paw Mountains" (Ralph Shane).

Fort Keogh remained an army post until 1900. Later it became a remount station where horses were trained for the Army. Still later the fort and military reservation were converted to a livestock experiment station. **Fort Keogh**'s post office was originally listed as Tongue River (1876). Nelson Miles was the first postmaster and William O'Toole the second. In January 1878 the name was changed to **Fort Keogh** on the postal records, but the office was discontinued in 1908. Efforts are now being made to restore and preserve some of the old buildings as historic landmarks and establish a museum.

Fort Kipp (Roosevelt) is ten miles east of Brockton and two miles from the Missouri River on the edge of the Fort Peck Indian Reservation. It was named for Capt. James Kipp, who commanded the fort for many years. Kipp was a fur trader, respected by the Indians, and married to an Indian woman. The fort was built in 1860 on the Missouri River above the mouth of the Big Muddy. The old buildings are gone, but a community of houses has grown up around the place where they once stood.

"In the 1960s **Fort Kipp** was formed into a small community. . . . We have two churches, a community hall and a rodeo grounds. Most of the people who live here are Sioux Indians. Others are half Sioux and Assiniboine. There are some other tribes here, too. We get along the best we can. All the Indian people speak English. The older folk speak in Indian when visiting one another. The younger people understand but speak very little of the Indian language. . . . The children go to school in Brockton. . . . Our community is quiet and beautiful" (Cecilia Long Hair, Brockton High School).

(Fort) Kootenai Post was built in 1808 on the Kootenai River opposite Libby for the use by Northwest Fur Company. A second **Kootenai Post** was built in 1811 opposite Jennings.

Fort Lewis was the name of a trading post built in 1845 on the south bank of the Missouri, eighteen miles above Fort Benton. It was also called Fort Cotton, Fort Honore, Fort Henry and Cotton Bottoms. It was built by Honore Picotte (Burlingame and Toole).

Fort Lewis This post was built in 1846 on the north bank of the Missouri River. The name was changed to Fort Benton in 1850. Its first commander was Maj. William H. Lewis. (See **Fort Benton**).

Fort Lisa (see **Fort Manuel Lisa**).

Fort Logan (Meagher) was built in 1869 and called Camp Baker, though Maj. Eugene M. Baker, for whom it was named, felt the new fort was completely unnecessary. It was established at the insistence of miners at Diamond Gulch and built by members of the Thirteenth Infantry, who had already built several other Montana forts. There were quarters for 100 men, officers' quarters, a hospital, laundry and post office — all made of logs. The post office was established in 1872 and the name was changed to **Fort Logan** in 1879; William Gaddis was postmaster. In 1870 the original Camp Baker was moved ten miles upstream on the Smith River (Koury). The new name was in memory of Capt. William A. Logan, who lost his life when Baker's garrison joined Col. Gibbon in the hard-fought Battle of the Big Hole. By 1880 the fort was closed and the military reservation was sold the following year. The post office was discontinued in 1929. Much of this fort still stands.

Fort Lucky (Petroleum), also called Lucky Fork, was a trading post set up by Pike Lundusky on Flatwillow Creek (See **Landusky**).

Fort Mackenzie (Chouteau) was named for Kenneth Mackenzie, the famous and successful factor at Fort Union, but it was located more than halfway across Montana from it, between Fort Benton and Loma. Mackenzie skillfully won over the Blackfeet and Assiniboine Indian trade for the American Fur Company. He was even able to get the two tribes, traditional enemies, to sign a treaty in 1830, agreeing that the Milk River was to be the boundary between the two. For his own part, he agreed to build them a "trade house" at a convenient place in the land of Blackfeet; this he did in the fall of 1831 with the establishment of Fort Piegan. After it was abandoned in the spring of 1832, the company built a new post six miles above the old fort because the Blackfeet trade was too lucrative to be lost; this new post was called **Fort Mackenzie**. The American Fur Company carried on a successful business with the Blackfeet for eleven years from this fort. Much of its success was due to the ability and fair dealings of Alexander Culbertson, who managed the company's affairs in the Upper Missouri. Culbertson was absent from the fort one time and Chardon and Harvey, who were left in charge, antagonized the warlike Blackfeet; the resulting violence forced the abandonment of **Fort Mackenzie**. The men went downriver to a place a few miles above the mouth of the Judith River and built Fort Chardon (Abbott).

Fort MacLeod (see McLeod).

Fort Maginnis was first a trading post located within the confluence of Badger Creek and Two Medicine River on the Blackfeet Reservation. It was about one mile west of the point where the two streams joined. This post was closely connected with the T. C. Power firm of Fort Benton. The post office for this place was established on March 16, 1875 and discontinued February 9, 1876.

Later a new trading post still called **Fort Maginnis** was located on the north bank of Birch Creek. This was just inside the new southern border of the Blackfeet Reservation when the boundary line was moved north to Birch Creek. It was still connected with the T. C. Power firm. A post office named **Fort Maginnis** was re-established on January 14, 1878 and discontinued on June 16, 1879 at this new location (Jack Hayne).

Fort Maginnis was a military post established in July 1880 by Capt. Dangerfield Porter to protect settlers and stockmen from Indian attacks. It was laid out on ground that was part of the land used by the DHS cattle company. Soldiers lived in tents; officers and their families resided in log cabins. The fort was near Maiden and Gilt Edge, both early-day mining camps in the Judith Mountains. **Fort Maginnis** was named for Maj. Martin Maginnis, a territorial delegate to Congress. When it was abandoned in 1890 the buildings were torn down and the logs were carried away by ranchers and others from Lewistown. Beset by widespread cattle rustling, stockmen charged that the Army, due to "indolence, ignorance, or official delay," offered them little protection, and turned to the Montana Stock Growers Association, under the leadership of Granville Stuart, for help. In 1884 the problem was summarily solved when the vigilantes, under Stuart, caught and hanged most of the rustlers.

On September 18, 1882, Frank Burke wrote his mother from **Fort Maginnis**: "**Fort Maginnis** lies in the midst of an almost untraveled wilderness at the eastern base of the Judith Mountains. . . . This place is one of the most important posts on the frontier. It is garrisoned by three companies of cavalry and three of infantry. These troops are held in constant readiness to take the field against the hostile Indians north of here. . . . I have been made manager of the telegraph line from here to Fort Buford, a distance of 400 miles. . . . Society here is not exactly what it is in New York or 'aesthetic' Boston. There are more than 500 men here and only about ten women. . . . The belle of the garrison is the daughter of an Irish washerwoman, and the court that is paid her would excite the envy of the fairest damsels of Saratoga or Newport" (*Montana, the Magazine of Western History*; Winter, 1969).

Postal records show a post office under the name of **Fort Maginnis** in Meagher (then Fergus) County opening in 1881 with Charles McNamara as postmaster. During the previous year a post office called Parker served this area. The **Fort Maginnis** office was discontinued in 1938.

Fort Manuel Lisa has also been known as Fort Ramon, Fort Lisa, Lisa's Fort, and Fort Manuel. It was Montana's first trading post, built by Manuel Lisa, a Spaniard who lived in Louisiana before he went to St. Louis and became associated with William Clark, who had recently been appointed Indian agent for all the Upper Missouri region. In 1807 Lisa outfitted an expedition of forty men and started up the Missouri, planning to establish a fur trading post on the Yellowstone. En route he met John Colter and George Drewer (Droillard), both former members of the Lewis and Clark expedition, who were now headed for St. Louis with a load of furs which they and two companions had gotten by hunting and trapping the Yellowstone Valley. Lisa persuaded Colter and Drewer to join his party and they returned to the Yellowstone country together. They built the fort at the mouth of the Big Horn River in the summer of 1807. Drewer stayed to help Lisa with the construction, while Colter and his Indian guides were dispatched up the Yellowstone to find the Crow Indians and tell them about the new "trade house" in their country. Colter traveled far into the mountains, but failed to find the Crows. Colter's guides deserted him when he came to the land of the Shoshones in the mountains east and south of Yellowstone Park, so he struck out alone in the direction of **Fort Manuel Lisa**. On the way he came upon the geysers, the boiling mud pots, and the breathtaking waterfalls that have made Yellowstone National Park world famous — Colter was the first white man to see what is now the park, but no one believed his strange tale when he returned to **Fort Manuel Lisa** or later, in St. Louis.

Lisa and a group of capitalists founded the Missouri Fur Company, a profitable enterprise carried on from his location at the Yellowstone and Big Horn rivers. Lisa knew how to handle the Indians; he brought seeds and taught them how to grow plants; he brought a blacksmith who sharpened their weapons; he married an Indian woman; and he gave the Indians good count and fair measure. They came to trust and respect him. Colter and a companion named Potts were sent to the Three Forks region in 1808 to explore and trap; Potts was killed by hostile Blackfeet, but Colter made his way alone back to **Fort Manuel Lisa**.

Another party was sent out from this fort to try to establish a post at the three forks of the Missouri. They returned with three thousand beaver skins, but the Blackfeet had killed five of the men and captured all the guns, horses and traps — effectively ending the idea of a trading post at the headwaters of the Missouri. **Fort Manuel Lisa** operated for less than a year. It might have become permanent, but the War of 1812 was causing unrest among the Indians and the fort was abandoned about that time. Later it was burned by the Indians. No trace remains to indicate the exact location, but it is known that it was a few miles southwest of the present town of Hysham in Treasure County. Lisa first named the fort for his son, Ramon, but the men knew it as Lisa's Fort or Fort Manuel.

Fort Missoula (Missoula) was established in response to a request for protection by residents of Missoula — Chief Joseph and his Nez Perce Indians were spreading fear across the mountains as they began their strategic retreat. The fort was built 2½ miles southwest of the city and Capt. C. C. Rawn was put in command of fifty regulars and a hundred volunteers. Lolo Pass was fortified. Chief Joseph was granted free passage down the Bitteroot Valley when he promised no harm to citizens, so Rawn and his men, who had gone on to Lolo, returned to the fort. For many years **Fort Missoula** was the only garrisoned post left in Montana; it was manned by two battalions of the Fourth Infantry. Buildings erected in 1910 contrast with the remnants of log buildings and stone powderhouses from the earlier era.

Fort Missoula's postal record begins with an opening in 1879, when John McCormick was appointed postmaster. It was closed in 1882; open again 1888-94; and active again 1911-18.

Fort Mortimer was a trading post built in 1842 on the Missouri River just below the mouth of the Yellowstone on the old Fort William site.

Fort Musselshell In the 1860s and '70s this was an important post for fur trade with the Gros Ventre Indians. The fort was located some thirty-five miles north of Mosby at the mouth of the Musselshell. Traders, a few wolfers, and woodchoppers who sold fuel to Missouri River steamboats, were the only white men in this part of the country for a long time. The Gros Ventre were glad to exchange a buffalo robe for ten cups of flour or six cups of sugar. The Sioux and Assiniboine harassed the post constantly and finally forced its abandonment. The Indians sometimes brought gold dust and nuggets to **Fort Musselshell** when Mr. and Mrs. Walter Fletcher established a store, saloon, and ferryboat service. The post office opened in June 1913 with Mollie Fletcher as postmaster. It closed in 1915, reopened in 1917. In 1922 John Town took over and moved the post office three miles upriver. He changed the name to Bervie, after a little town in Ontario, Canada, where his mother had spent her childhood.

Fort Owen (Ravalli) is near Stevensville. St. Mary's Mission was the forerunner of this trading post. In 1841 Father DeSmet and his helpers erected a small chapel and built a sawmill and a gristmill. The saw was made from the iron bands of wagon wheels, and the millstones were imported from Antwerp, Belgium. Oxen carts brought in tools and plows, and by 1842, there were vegetables in the mission garden.

In 1850 Maj. John Owen established one of the most successful and long-lasting trading posts in early-day Montana. Owen was born in Pennsylvania, joined the army at Fort Leavenworth as a sutler under Lieutenant-Colonel Loring, and with his regiment followed the Oregon Trail to the West. Owens resigned his sutlership to carry on free trade with the Indians and emigrants. He brought his Indian wife Nancy (from the Snake tribe) and purchased all the mission property except for the chapel. Then he built a trading post that was sturdy and well fortified, because the Blackfeet Indians continued to raid in the valley. For the next decade, the fort grew in trade and importance. Because of its rich grass and mild weather, the Bitterroot Valley was a favored winter camp for traders, survey crews, and others. **Fort Owen** continued as a trading post for gold miners after the fur trade had vanished. Owen prospered and kept daily records; the **Fort Owen** Ledger is the earliest known record of trade kept by any free trader in Montana (Luther E. Stanley). Figures indicate the steadily imporving volume of business done at **Fort Owen**: in 1850, $1,880; in 1854, $2,567; and in 1859, $9,571 (Paula Fillmore). Owen dealt fairly with both red and white men and played a large role in the building of the Bitterroot. A new trading post established at Hell Gate eventually drew away much of Owen's business. The only official record found of a post office at **Fort Owen** is one for July-December 1868, with John Chatfield in charge. A picture sent by Beverly Lunceford shows Major Owen's post office: it was an upright box with sixteen pigeon holes — one for each family or person getting mail in this area of Montana at the time — perhaps Owen maintained an unofficial mail service for his store patrons and took care of any letters that came to his post from the states. Owen's "post office" was later presented to Matthew Whaley, who was for many years the agent at Jocko Indian Agency. Now one crumbling wall remains to mark the spot where **Fort Owen** once stood.

Fort Parker was a little settlement at the great bend of the Yellowstone River at the mouth of Mission Creek on the north bank of the river. "Buckskin" Williams ran a saloon and trading post here. By 1873 the area had become known as Benson's Landing, after a man named Benson who ran a ferry across the river. Later it was a stage stop and for a while was called Clark City. When the railroad came through and built a station at what is now Livingston, the riverfront residents moved to the new town.

Fort Pease actually never came into being except as a post office named Peasefort, which was established in 1879 with F. D. Pease as postmaster. The name was changed to Junction in 1880. Fellow D. Pease was employed as an Indian scout under General Harney in 1856, and in the following years, Pease became the dean of frontiersmen, renowned for his knowledge of the country and his life-long friendship with the Indians. He was married at Fort Union in 1859 to Margaret Wallace, daughter of a Crow woman whose husband was of Crow-French descent. Major Pease and others planned to form a colony to be known as **Fort Pease** on the Yellowstone River at the mouth of the Big Horn River as a head of navigation. General Forsyth thought that owing to its gravel bed and stable banks the Yellowstone River offered a much better route of commerce from Fort Buford to the settlements of western Montana Territory than did the shifting and dangerous Missouri River from Buford to Benton. The Custer Massacre and constant Indian raids led to the abandonment of the project.

FORT PECK (Valley) is a planned city built by government engineers as headquarters for construction and operation of the huge Fort Peck Dam, which began as a WPA project in October 1933. The dam stretches across the Missouri from bluff to bluff, a distance of over 3½ miles, and is crossed by a highway 100 feet wide. The estimated length of the lake eventually to be created is 175 miles with a shoreline of 1,600 miles. A post office was opened at **Fort Peck Dam** in 1934 with Mrs. Peter Peterson as postmaster. The modern town takes its name from the old trading post which was located there. In 1867, Col. Campbell K. Peck and Comdr. E. H. Durfee established an Indian agency and trading post a few miles from the present dam site. The fort was named for Colonel Peck, who with Durfee undertook to pacify the Indians with goods and gifts. Favorite trade goods were the 100-pound sacks of flour emblazoned on each side with great red circles composed of Durfee and Peck. The Indians adopted the sacks for a war dress, merely cutting holes for the arms and head. The Hunkpapa, a branch of the Sioux Nation, especially valued the bright red circles as "good medicine." **Fort Peck** enjoyed a monopoly of fur trade with the Assiniboine and Sioux and rivaled old Fort Union in importance. Peck went to Washington in the first attempt to get federal aid for the development of Missouri navigation; he died on his way back in 1869. His post was abandoned in 1879 and was later swept away by the river. The original **Fort Peck** was built in 1867 for Durfee and Peck by Abel Farwell, a veteran of more than a hundred Indian battles (Willard).

102

Remains of herbivorous and carnivorous dinosaurs, armored fishes, and swimming reptiles are among the fossils preserved in the foyer of the **Fort Peck** theater. These and segments of palm trees and petrified figs indicate the area was once subtropical and under water.

Records show a **Fort Peck** office operating 1879-81 in "county unknown" with Charles Gould as postmaster.

Fort Piegan (Glacier) This was once a station called Carlow; the name was changed by the Great Northern to revive the memory of old Fort Piegan, which was the first trading post established in Blackfeet Indian territory by the American Fur Company.

Fort Piegan was the "trade house" that Kenneth Mackenzie promised to build for the Blackfeet Indians at a place convenient for them. On October 1, 1831, James Kipp — with an armed party and a supply of trade goods — arrived on the north bank of the Missouri where the Marias River flows in. There he built **Fort Piegan**, naming it after the branch of the Blackfeet that lived in the area. It was a good location and trade was brisk throughout the winter; during the first month, over 3,000 beaver skins were brought in. By spring the supply of trade goods was exhausted and it was necessary for Kipp to go downriver to Fort Union to turn in the furs and replenish supplies. The Blackfeet Indians were so hostile that the men were afraid to stay at the fort without Kipp, so the post was abandoned in the spring of 1832. After that it was burned by the Indians and all signs of it have now vanished. Fort Mackenzie was built the same year six miles above the site of **Fort Piegan** so the lucrative trade with the Blackfeet could continue. In 1877 a post office under the name Piegan was established in old Chouteau County.

Fort Poplar was built in 1861 by Charles Larpenteur on the Missouri River near the mouth of the Poplar River (Highland).

Fort Ramon (see **Fort Manuel Lisa**).

Fort Reeds, Reed's Fort (see **Lewistown**).

(Fort) Salish, Saleesh House was a trading post built in 1809 on the Clark Fork River near Thompson Falls by David Thompson for the North West Fur Company. A second Saleesh House was built in 1824 near Eddy for the Hudson's Bay Company.

Fort Sarpy was on the Yellowstone River west of Forsyth in Rosebud County. It was built in 1850 and abandoned in 1853. "A band of Crow Indians hoping to drive the white men from their country set up tepees and posted warriors around the fort so that no one could leave. Without firing a shot, they soon had whites in a bad way. Fur traders, like Indians, lived on fresh meat. When the hunters could not get out, they ate all the jerked meat, pemmican, and killed and ate the few dogs they had. The Crows had stolen their horses or they would have eaten them" (Towne). But at least they had a well inside the fort for fresh water. Finally the men boiled and ate old buffalo hides. But they were still starving, so Maj. Alexander Culbertson, who was in charge of the post, warned the Indians that if they did not leave by noon, he would shoot. The warriors laughed, but precisely at noon, Culbertson shot his big cannon into the tepees, tearing several to shreds, and wounded several warriors. The Indians figured this was "big medicine" and left within five minutes. **Fort Sarpy** was built by Culbertson and named for John B. Sarpy. The second **Fort Sarpy** was built on the Yellowstone, twenty-five miles below the mouth of the Big Horn River.

FORT SHAW (Cascade), on the Sun River, is twenty-four miles west of Great Falls. Built in 1867, it was first named Camp Reynolds, then changed to honor Col. Robert Shaw, a Civil War soldier. It was established as a military post to protect travelers on the Mullan Road and early settlers from raiding Blackfeet. General Gibbon rode out from **Fort Shaw** in 1876 with the Seventh Infantry with orders to join Perry and Custer.

Fort Shaw has been called the "Queen of Montana's Posts" (Koury); it boasted one building that was 125 feet long. Many "brilliant theatrical functions" were held here, including the first professional stage performance in Montana. The theater had log benches with no backs for the seats; these were moved out for dances on the floor of hard-packed earth. During a play, if it were necessary to dim the lights, the orchestra arose in unison to turn down the kerosene lamps that lined the stage apron.

A post office operated 1867-91; it was opened again in 1902. Nathaniel Pope was the first postmaster. **Fort Shaw** was abandoned as a military post in 1890, but later served as an Indian school. The name **Fort Shaw** was revived when it became a station on the Vaughn-Augusta branch line of the Great Northern Railroad.

Fort Sherman was the first building in the Judith Basin. Nelson Story and a man named Hoffman established a trading post here, expecting that Crow Agency I, near Livingston, would be relocated. **Fort Sherman** was erected below the mouth of Big Casino Creek, along the south bank of Big Spring Creek, in 1873. Peter Koch was in charge. In the summer of 1874, "Major" A. S. Reed and Jim Bowles bought **Fort Sherman** from Story. They dismantled it and moved it some two miles downstream. The Crow agency had not been moved to Judith Basin, so the fort ended its brief existence" (Western Interpretive Services).

(Fort) Three Forks Post. Two unsuccessful attempts were made to establish a trading post at the headwaters of the Missouri (see **Fort Manuel Lisa**).

Fort Union was built in 1828 on the banks of the Missouri near the mouth of the Yellowstone. It was actually not within the confines of present-day Montana, but was 500 feet east of the contemporary Montana-North Dakota border. But for the men who lived at **Fort Union**, it was a trading headquarters for the area to the west and into Montana proper (Abbot). The American Fur Company, owned by John Jacob Astor, sent James Kipp, an experienced frontiersman, to found a fur trading post near the junction of the Missouri and Yellowstone rivers. The fort that was established that year was first called Fort Floyd, but later the name was changed to **Fort Union**; the name was appropriate, since from here the American Fur Company could draw together all its areas of work. From here they were able to send trappers and traders to remote Indian tribes by easy water routes stemming from this location. To **Fort Union** came bands of Crow and Assiniboine Indians to trade their furs for blankets, guns, beads, tools, and whiskey. Independent trappers and traders also came to trade their furs for supplies. **Fort Union** was strategically located on the north bank of the river at the edge of a level plain. There were few trees to obstruct the view, and the Missouri River here was about a hundred yards wide, so it was a perfect defensive location.

Kenneth Mackenzie was the first factor (manager) at **Fort Union**, and was in charge of the company's trade in all of the tributary regions of the two rivers. Mackenzie's task was to win both trust and trade of the Assiniboine and Blackfeet Indians from the Canadian traders across the border. He was so successful he won the complete confidence of the Assiniboine, and in 1830 even induced the Blackfeet to sign a treaty with their old enemies, establishing the Milk River as the boundary line between the two tribes. In 1832 a fort near the present site of Fort Benton was built and named for Mackenzie.

Life at **Fort Union** was much more refined than at most trading posts. There was dignity, formality, and pomp as distinguished visitors continued to visit the fort. George Catlin, the famous Indian portraitist, came to **Fort Union**, as did Audubon and several European dignitaries.

Fort Union was the post office name for the Mondak community 1925-28. Soren Clevenger was postmaster during that time, and the location was very near the old historic fort.

Fort Van Buren. In 1835 Samuel Tullock (who had built Fort Cass in 1832) built a new post at the mouth of Rosebud Creek and named it **Fort Van Buren**, for the U.S. president. The fort was burned by Charles Larpenteur, who then proceeded to build Fort Alexander. In their quest for furs, traders searched every valley with a stream looking for beaver (Western Interpretive Services).

Fort Wagner (see **Wagner**).

Fort William was built in 1883 on the Missouri just below the mouth of the Yellowstone, and was named for the man who constructed it, William Sublette.

Foster (Big Horn) was named for a son of J. M. Hannaford, according to Rowe, but the name of the first postmaster was James Foster. The office was active 1907-20; the mail was then sent to Hardin.

Foundation (Custer) had a post office 1925-36; Marie Myers was first postmaster.

FOUR BUTTES (Daniels), ten miles west of Scobey, was a station on the Great Northern Railroad. The name describes a nearby formation of four rounded mountains, or buttes, which are visible for many miles; oldtimers called them Whiskey Buttes. The post office opened in 1927 with Hans Kjos as postmaster.

Fourchett(e) (Phillips), located near a large fork in the Missouri River, had a post office 1922-37. Sven Tallakson was postmaster. The name is French for "table fork."

Fowler (Pondera) was started in 1908 and named for B. R. Fowler, a pioneer sheep and cattleman with large holdings on the nearby Dry Fork River. The post office was established in 1910 with Oscar Flutto as postmaster; it was closed in 1945.

Fox (Beaverhead) was a Big Hole Basin post office established in 1891 with Walter Fox as postmaster. It was named for his family. The office was discontinued in 1918 and the mail was sent to Wisdom.

Fox (Carbon) was a siding on the Northern Pacific Railroad six miles north of Red Lodge. At one time it was an important grain and hay shipping station and had two elevators. It was named for J. M. Fox, the first manager of the Rocky Fork and Cooke City Railroad. Finnish immigrant miners settled here, and as late as 1920 their children still spoke Finnish at home and on the playground, and English only in the classroom.

Fox Lake (Richland) had a post office established in 1910 with Mary Cummings as postmaster. The name was changed to Lambert in 1914.

Foy's Lake. Three small lakes near Kalispell are named for the pioneering Foy family. In 1883, John Moroni Foy brought his large Mormon family into the Flathead Valley and settled at the foot of the present Foy's Lake Hill. He built a lumber mill and operated it along with his ranch. The McCarthy and Dodge families also settled here.

Frances Heights and Lake Frances (Pondera) were named for the wife of W. G. Conrad.

Francis (Gallatin) had a post office 1939-62; Charles Hoff was the first postmaster. Postal records say the name was formerly Josephine.

Franklin (Golden Valley), originally in Musselshell County, was six miles north of Ryegate in a fertile irrigated area. The post office opened in 1910 with Edna Dunlap as postmaster and remained active for forty-three years. **Franklin** was named when the branch line of the Great Northern railroad built southeast from Great Falls in 1907-08. After acquiring the right-of-way to cross Bill Jenisen's ranch, the company built a tower for its huge wooden water tank along with a water treating plant for the steam engines. At the time it was felt that a depot wasn't needed at this particular site; however, to everyone's surprise, one did arrive by mistake that had been ordered for Franklin, Minnesota. The depot was not moved and the name was switched. That was the beginning of **Franklin**, Montana, which Jenisen tried to develop south of the tracks on his ranch. He set up a land office but his efforts proved futile when Addie Dunlap, a surveyor, laid out lots for the townsite just north of the tracks. Dunlap's parents built a general store where the post office was authorized, and from the leftover lumber and trestles, a lumber company was founded which did a flourishing business. Across the street was the two-story Andy Fitch Hotel and north of the tracks were the Rocky Mountain and Farmers Grain Elevators (Mary Morsanny).

Franklin (Powder River) had a post office established in 1889. During 1891 the office was at the George Mitchell ranch. "About every Sunday that the weather was nice the neighbors would gather here to pick up their mail and visit. Sometimes they came to race their horses, as Mr. Mitchell had a straightaway and a racetrack laid out near the house. He loved horses and had some of the best, finally building his herd up to a thousand head, many of them from thoroughbred stallions" (*Echoing Footsteps*). The post office was discontinued in 1902.

Fraser (Valley) is between Glasgow and Wolf Point on the Missouri River not far from Fort Peck Dam. It began as a Great Northern station and was named for the foreman of a grading crew when the railroad was being built through here. The post office opened in 1907 with James Ivey as postmaster. Towering grain elevators indicate it is now a grain shipping center.

Freedom (Garfield) had a post office 1914-33; Walter White was the first postmaster. Some patrons wanted it called Freeman, for an early settler in whose home the post office was maintained for many years, but the final choice was **Freedom**. Mail came by carrier once a week from Jordan. Later it came twice a week, often by sled team. **Freedom** was luckier than most homestead communites because a Scottish-born and educated physician, Dr. Thomas A. Mackenzie, filed on a homestead near the **Freedom** post office. He was constantly being called to the homes of sick neighbors during the year that he lived there. The early 1930s saw discouraged homesteaders leaving.

Freeman (Broadwater) was to have been the name of a post office with Jefferson Doggett the postmaster. But the office that was approved in 1898 was never in operation.

Freewater (Phillips) had a post office 1916-27. The mail was then sent to Malta. Richard Garland was the first postmaster.

Freeze Out Lake Area is now a bird management preserve. The name comes from a stagecoach station that was established here in 1885, halfway between Choteau and Sun River. Legend has it that some soldiers stationed at Fort Shaw were caught in a blizzard while coming through the flat and the area was called **Freezeout Flat**. The basin was known by that name as early as 1870.

French Bar (Lewis and Clark) had a post office opened in 1869 with William Jares as postmaster; it closed in 1876.

French Gulch (Deer Lodge) had a post office established in 1869 with Michael Larkin in charge. The office was closed in 1881 and then open again 1901-13. An original drawing by Granville Stuart in 1869 shows **French Gulch** as a mining camp consisting of a cluster of log houses around the base of a hill. Mortimer Lott began mining gold here soon after the Stuarts began operations at Gold Creek.

Frenchman's Ford. Andy Adams has left us a vivid description of a place by this name: "The trail followed the Sweet Grass down to the Yellowstone. . . . The next day Flood rode on ahead to **Frenchman's Ford**, and late in the day returned with the information that the Ford was quite a pretentious frontier village of the squatter type. There was a blacksmith and a wheelwright shop. . . . The town struck me as something new and novel, two-thirds of the habitations being of canvas. Immense quantities of buffalo hides were drying or already baled. Large bull trains were encamped on the outskirts of the village, while many such outfits were in town, receiving cargoes or discharging freight. . . . The population was extremely mixed, and almost every language could be heard spoken on the streets. The men were fine types of the pioneer, buffalo hunters, freighters, and other plainsmen . . . typical specimens of northern Indians, grunting their jargon amid the babel of other tongues. The only civilizing element to be seen was the camp of engineers, running the survey of the Northern Pacific railroad. . . . The sole product seemed to be buffalo hides. Every man in the place wore the regulation six-shooter in his belt, and quite a number wore two" (Log of a Cowboy). The primitive law of nature known as self-preservation was very evident in August of 1882 at **Frenchman's Ford**.

FRENCHTOWN, FRENCH TOWN (Missoula) is sixteen miles northwest of Missoula. Early inhabitants were mainly French Canadians, hence the name. They came from Quebec and Ontario and settled in the area about 1864. Many contemporary residents are descended from the Brunswick French of eastern Canada, some have intermarried with the Indians, and others are descended from the Quebec French. The holiday of the year in **Frenchtown** was St. John's Day, which was noisily celebrated on June 24 in honor of the town's patron saint. The Indians called Frenchtown Valley qua elth, meaning "state of tranquility." A post office was opened in 1868 with Charles Cusson as postmaster; it closed in 1869 and was reopened in 1870. In March 1873, Hyppolite Lassere was appointed postmaster. The St. John's Day celebrations were discontinued in the 1960s, but lately residents have been planning to revive them (*Frenchtown Valley Footsteps*). In 1869 Louis Barrette discovered gold and staked out a claim for his Discovery Mine. A stampede followed and 3,000 prospectors wintered in the gulch.

Fresno (Hill) had a post office 1913-41 but the name is more familiar for the Fresno Dam. The dam, which is north of Havre, forms a reservoir to supply irrigation water for the Milk River Valley. The lake is also popular with boaters and fishermen. Frank McSloy was postmaster back in 1913. By 1916 the town had a population of 75, with stores, cafes, churches, a school and a newspaper.

Fridley (Park) was named for the first postmaster, Frank Fridley. The office was open 1885-1911; when it closed mail was sent to Emigrant.

Friel (Garfield) was named for Mr. and Mrs. Myles Friel, who lived on Dry Creek. Bessie Friel was postmaster; the office was open 1925-29.

Frog Springs (Valley) For five months between May-October 1912 there was a post office by this name. Peter Schumacher was postmaster.

FROID (Roosevelt) is near Medicine Lake and the North Dakota border. One theory is that the name was suggested by division engineer Charles Walker, who selected it from an old map of Nebraska (Perrin). *Froid* is a French word meaning "cold" and was no doubt appropriately applied to this spot in northern Montana. **Froid** does not appear on modern Nebraska maps, but it is listed in *Nebraska Place Names* by Lillian Fitzpatrick, who says it was in northeast Deuel County on high table land. **Froid**, Montana, was the home of John W. Schnitzler, whose wheatfields covered thousands of acres, and whose enthusiasm for aviation led to the establishment of an excellent airport at **Froid**. Schnitzler was killed in 1932 when his private plane crashed against a high butte near Glasgow. The **Froid** post office opened in 1910 with Fred E. Price in charge.

FROMBERG (Carbon) was formerly called Gebo, after a man who opened the coal mines here. There are many Slavic-Americans in this area, and **Fromberg** is a Slavic name. It is an agricultural village and trade center for a fruitful section of land that is now under irrigation. Before there was water, the area was often referred to as Poverty Flats because settlers nearly starved to death trying to make things grow in the arid land while waiting for the promised irrigation system. Now wild rice grows in roadside ditches and redwing blackbirds come in flocks to feed on it. The O% Cattle Company had its winter camp where **Fromberg** now stands in the winter of 1893-94, which was also the year that the Gebo Coal Mine was opened. The post office opened in 1903 with Abraham Pierson as postmaster.

Frontier (Chouteau) was a post office 1890-91 with Charles La Breche as postmaster.

Fullerton (Fergus) was named for Frank Fuller, a local rancher who was also postmaster when the office opened in 1904. It was across the Judith River from Everson, though the mail was directed to the latter town when the **Fullerton** office closed in 1914.

Fulton (Lewis and Clark) was a settlement with a post office 1888-1914; Lottie Woodruff was the first postmaster.

Furness (Broadwater) Postal records show a post office under this name

March-May 1887; the name was then changed to Toston. William Austin was postmaster.

G

Gaffney's Station, Gaffney (Madison) was a stage stop with a post office under that name operating 1871-75. Owen Gaffney ran them both. So optimistic was he about the future of this spot that he had his Planters Hotel moved there from Virginia City. The stage stop thrived until the railroad passed it by. Gilmore and Salisbury also ran a famous stage line through this area, and in 1875 the name was changed to Salisbury. The original name was Pollinger.

Gage (Musselshell) was a station on the Milwaukee Railroad east of Roundup. Its post office operated 1908-40; George Mills was the first postmaster. Sheepmen from surrounding ranches shipped their lambs and wool from the **Gage** station, which in 1877 also served passengers and drivers on the Bozeman-Miles City stage line on the ranch of Horatio Gage near Hunters Hot Springs.

GALATA (Toole), east of Shelby, is near Willow Creek, one of the streams that flows into the reservoir created by Tiber Dam. It was a trading point and cattle shipping station on the Great Northern's High Line. In 1901 David R. McGinnis, first immigration agent of the Great Northern Railroad, was so impressed by the beauty of the spot that he filed a claim for the land near the railroad where it crossed dry Galata Creek. McGinnis hired a surveyor to lay out a town and the following year brought carpenters and lumber from Kalispell to build a two-room house. A post office was installed and officially opened in 1902. Cattlemen from the Marias River ranges brought their cattle to **Galata** for shipment to eastern markets. On cold winter days they were glad to have the protection of the two little rooms in the only building in "town." The house burned down in 1904, but in 1905 McGinnis began rebuilding **Galata**. He built a two-room real estate office and an eight-room hotel, and eventually induced a storekeeper to set up shop in one of the rooms of the real estate office. Ranchers would drive in with a chuckwagon and load up $500 — sometimes even $1000 — worth of supplies, pay in cash and return home for the long winter. After a few years, **Galata**'s only merchant closed shop and the hotel was abandoned; McGinnis gave up his dream of a town and moved to Kalispell. One day he was surprised to receive a check in the mail. It was marked "back rent," and was from a cowhand who had moved into the deserted **Galata** store and had done a good business with dryland farmers who were then settling on the old-time open range. By 1910 **Galata** had four lumberyards and five stores.

Galbraith (Rosebud) was once a siding on the Milwaukee Railroad in an area used for pasturing cattle. "Fred LaRocque tells of being the roundup cook for the men trailing a thousand head of cattle from Missouri River breaks to **Galbraith**, near Sumatra (Highland)." The blizzard of 1919 struck them when they were three miles from the loading pens. The herd drifted and six men spent three nights and two days in a small tent. After the storm was over they gathered the stock and moved on to **Galbraith** — only to find that the railroad was blocked by snow.

Galen (Deer Lodge) was named for a Dr. Galen, who was a specialist in the treatment of tuberculosis. The State Tuberculosis Sanitarium is located here. **Galen** was a station on the Northern Pacific. A post office was approved in January 1921, but the order was rescinded.

Galen (Meagher) Postal records show a **Galen** post office 1891-96. William Lackie was postmaster.

Gallatin City (Gallatin) was the "first town located in Gallatin County. It grew and for a time, flourished at the mouth of the Gallatin River, a few miles north of the present town of Three Forks." The townsite was laid out in 1863. To attract settlers, pictures were circulated showing riverboats lying at theoretical wharves in **Gallatin City**; but that dream vanished when it was found that river steamers could go up the Missouri no further than Fort Benton. Gov. Sidney Edgerton appointed officers and **Gallatin City** became the first county seat of Gallatin County. But in the 1867 election this town lost out to Bozeman and the county seat was moved. The flour mills, the homes, the stores and schools have all disappeared now. Postal records show a **Gallatin** office active 1867-90; Gordon Campbell was the first postmaster (Harvey Griffin, Billings *Gazette*; Feb. 19, 1970).

GALLATIN COUNTY is in the southwestern part of the state. Its long, narrow contour roughly follows the Gallatin River, which heads in Yellowstone Park and flows into the Missouri at Three Forks. **Gallatin County** was one of the original nine counties created by the territorial legislature in February 1865. The county tooks its name from the river, which was named by Lewis and Clark on July 27, 1805, in honor of Albert Gallatin, then Secretary of the Treasury. Parts of **Gallatin County** were taken to form Yellowstone in 1881, and Park in 1887.

GALLATIN GATEWAY (Gallatin) is twelve miles southwest of Bozeman on the Gallatin River. It is located at the mouth of the canyon on the road leading to Yellowstone National Park, hence the **Gateway** part of the name. It was originally called Salesville, for Alan Sales, a storekeeper, and his brother, Zach Sales, who had a mill here in the late 1860s. Logs were sawed and floated down the river. In more recent years the town's economy has depended upon tourist trade and fine dude ranches such as the Elkhorn, that provide a taste of Western life for Eastern visitors. The post office was established in 1927 with Joseph Williams as postmaster.

Gallagher (Yellowstone) is north of Billings. It was named for an engineer who worked on the Billings branch line of the Northern Pacific; he was also depot master at Missoula at one time.

Gallop (Gallatin) was named for postmaster James Gallop when the office opened in 1885. The office closed in 1908 and mail was ordered to Maudlow.

Gallup City (Pondera) is southwest of Conrad. Its post office was opened in 1928 with Violet Seekins in charge. The office was discontinued in 1939. It was named for one-time governor Hugo Aronson, according to chroniclers of Pondera County history. While Aronson was a truck driver in the oil fields, he was nicknamed "The Galloping Swede."

Galpin had a post office 1908-12; Charley Chervenka was the first postmaster.

Gardenland (Meagher) was the name given to a post office which was open 1880-81 with Frank Bassett as postmaster. The office was open again October 1881-January 1882.

GARDINER (Park) is the northern entrance to Yellowstone National Park. It was named for Johnston Gardiner, a trapper and mountain man who worked along the upper Yellowstone and its tributaries in the 1830s. Early efforts at settlement here were frustrated by the hostility of Crow Indians who hunted the area. A dispute over the location of the townsite also caused a twenty-year delay in getting the railroad into the town. The Northern Pacific came to Cinnabar, a few miles to the north, in 1883, but it was not extended to **Gardiner** until 1902. The post office opened in 1880 with James McCartney in charge. Placer gold was discovered at the mouth of Bear Gulch by "Uncle Joe" Brown and two other prospectors during the winter of 1865-66. "Uncle Joe" is said to have taken $1800 worth of gold out of the mouth of the creek in May 1866. He put in a system of ditches and erected the first quartz mill. In July 1883, gold was discovered in placer mines within "city limits." Robert "Buckskin Jim" Cutler claimed the diggings and got into an argument with McCartney over ownership and townsites, which delayed bringing in the railroad. The population in June 1883 was listed as 200, with six restaurants, five general stores, two hardware stores, two fruit stands, two barber shops, one newsstand, one billiard hall, two dancehalls, four houses of ill fame, one blacksmith, twenty-one saloons, and one milkman. Since there was no sawmill in the area, the "houses" were tents and log shacks made of hand-hewn logs. Pres. Theodore Roosevelt came to **Gardiner** in April 1903 to dedicate an arch made of basaltic rock through which travelers could go on their way to the "Yellowstone Wonderland." "**Gardiner** has matured and grown to meet the needs of today's visitor with churches, motels, cafes, trailer parks, lounges and a pleasant picnic area" (*Madisonian*, July 1973).

Garfield (Custer) was a post office May-June 1881 with Frank Zahl as postmaster. That was the year President Garfield was assassinated.

Garfield (Garfield) was between Cohagen and Mosby. It had a post office 1914-23 under the direction of Frances Carey.

Garfield (Gallatin) was the name of a post office from 1867-1868 with John Culver as postmaster.

Garfield County is in the eastern part of the state, bordered on the north by the Missouri River and the expanding waters of Fort Peck Dam. The 1960 census lists its population as 1,981 in an area of 4,812 square miles. The county was created in April 1919 from a part of Dawson County, and was named for James A. Garfield, the assassinated U.S. president. For many years, one doctor with an office in Jordan was the only medical person to serve an area of over 5,000 square miles. No railroad has ever come through **Garfield County**; surveyors came through, but concluded it would not support a railroad, and transportation has ever been a problem. The first route was the Missouri River. Indians in bull boats and later, white men in steamers and rude boats, used the "road that runs." Buffalo hunters used carts and wagons and chose the smoothest part ahead as a "road." Goods were freighted by bullteam from steamboats landings to Fort Benton when the river was too low to float the big boats on to Fort Benton. In 1866 the Rocky Mountain Wagon Road Company made ambitious plans for a road from Virginia City to Kercheval, but it fell through.

The Northern Pacific Railroad owned a lot of land in the county and issued plenty of propaganda and publicity to entice settlers to come and buy it. Many farmers did come, paying from $5 to $25 per acre for the dry land homesteads. In 1919 there were thirty settlements in **Garfield County** with post offices; by 1968 there were only four in addition to the county seat, Jordan. The land that had once been open grazing range for cattle and sheep was cut into small farms. Later the dry years drove most of the farmers away. The land went for taxes or for fifty cents an acre (Highland).

Garland (Custer), on the Tongue River, had a post office 1890-1950. Mari Reich was the first postmaster.

GARNEILL (Fergus) is between Lewistown and Harlowton. It was named for Garnet Neill, wife of an early-day rancher. It was already a trading post when the Central Montana Railroad established a station here in 1903. The railroad named its station Ubet in memory of the famous old stage station a few miles to the west. Three towns were laid out because of a division of sentiment on a moral issue: There was Ubet around the railroad station; there was North (which was dry) Garneill, which still survives; and there was South (or wet) Garneill, which consisted of a pretentious hotel, saloon, blacksmith shop, and stores. The railroad in time changed the name of its station to **Garneill** to conform to local wishes. At **Garneill** is the Ubet and Central Montana Pioneers Monument, a 2½-ton granite rock. In its concrete base are embedded pieces of ore, Indian relics, petrified wood, and other objects. Carved in it are the names of important pioneers and the dates of their arrival in Montana. A post office was opened in 1899 with Edwin C. Hill as postmaster.

Garnet (Granite), near Drummond, was named for the garnet rock found there (Woole).Gold was also discovered and placer mining began in the 1860s. In the 1880s there were some 4,000 men in **Garnet**; by 1916 it was practically deserted. The post office, which opened in 1896 with Sue Woods as postmaster, closed in 1928, and the mail was ordered to Bearmouth. The office was open again 1935-42. A restoration project was undertaken by the Bureau of Land Management in 1960 to restore **Garnet** because it is representative of early Montana mining towns and because many buildings were left standing, though vandals had taken many things which would have made the restored ghost town more authentic. The Nancy Hanks mine structure and shafts are reminiscent of the golden days of **Garnet** (Dale Burke, *The Missoulian*).

GARRISON (Powell) is named for William Lloyd Garrison, an anti-slavery leader. Perhaps some Yankee veteran from the Civil War had come for the gold rush and settled in the valley and named it after the man he most admired. It developed into a railroad town tucked in between the Clark Fork River and a high bluff. The Northern Pacific trains from Butte and Helena met there and continued on to Missoula as one line. The post office was established in 1883 with William Facer as postmaster.

Garry (Flathead) had a post office January-October, 1923, with James Beardsley as postmaster.

GARRYOWEN (Big Horn) is on the Little Big Horn River a few miles south of the Custer Battlefield and a part of the area involved in that famous confrontation. It was a station on the Chicago Burlington and Quincy Railroad; now even the new highway has passed it by. **Garryowen** is within the boundaries of the Crow Indian Reservation. A post office was established in 1931 with Grace Eggart as postmaster.

Garryowen was named for the marching song of the old Seventh Cavalry. Myles Keogh, one of Custer's officers, brought the tune and the words from Ireland. It had been the marching song for the Royal Lancers, a famous British unit, of which Keogh's father was an officer (Fifth Royal Lancers), at Garryowen, Ireland. In 1876 the stirring notes of the same song echoed down the Little Bighorn River Valley and are now commemorated in the name of this town.

We are the pride of the army,
And a regiment of great renown,
Our name's on the pages of history
From Sixty-Six on down.
If you think we stop or falter
While into the fray we're goin'
Just watch the step with our heads erect,
When the band plays, "Garry Owen"

Many years later, and halfway around the world, the "Garryowen" marching song made history once again. On the eve of World War II, a regiment of Scottish and English soldiers who called themselves the "Garryoweners" was stationed in Japan. After the bombing of Pearl Harbor, the Japanese told this contingent that they were to be shot at sunrise and to prepare themselves to die the next morning. At daybreak the command was given to muster and march out to the parade grounds. The British soldiers, attired in ceremonial kilts, marching in formation, and playing their famous song loudly on their bagpipes, swung along proudly. The skirl of the pipes so terrified the Japanese that the British won the day as the enemy fled for cover (Jean Mitchell).

Gary (Cascade) was originally an old settlement called Sunnyside. It was rebuilt in 1930 into a dude ranch known as Gary Cooper Ranches, Inc.,or the 7 Bar 0 Ranch. The name was changed to **Gary** that year in honor of the Western movie star who had grown up in this area and had maintained an interest in it for many years. The **Gary** post office was active 1930-34; May Hansen was postmaster. After that the mail went to Craig.

Gaspard (Missoula) was named because the right-of-way was acquired from Gaspard Deschamps, who came from Canada to Missoula in 1877 and opened a blacksmith shop. The place was first called Mellady, in honor of a parish priest who was serving at Frenchtown. The name was changed to Shilling after a pulp mill was built, and Mr. Shilling, the company president, began using the siding for shipping out his products.

GATES (Toole) was named for the first postmaster, Jasper Gates. The post office was open 1912-20 and after that the mail was handled at Fowler.

Gates of the Mountains (Lewis and Clark) is on the Missouri River in Lewis and Clark County. On July 19, 1805, the explorer Meriwether Lewis named the place: ". . . these cliffs rise from the waters edge on either side perpendicularly to the hight of [about] 1200 feet. every object here wears a dark and gloomy aspect. the tow[er]ing rocks in many places seem ready to tumble on us. the river appears to have forced it's way through this immence body of solid rock for the distance of 5¾ miles and where it makes it's exit below has thrown on either side vast vollumns of rock mountains high. the river appears to have worn a passage just the width of it's channel for 150 yards. it is deep from side to side nor is there in the 1st 3 Miles of this distance a spot except one of a few yards in extent on which a man could rest the soal of his foot . . . from the singular appearance of this place I called it the gates of the rocky mountains . . . ." (*Montana Magazine*; summer, 1966).

Gateway (Lincoln) is a border town and so named because it is a "gateway" to Canada. The post office operated 1902-50. William Smith was the original postmaster.

Gauglersville (Meagher) was one of the forerunners of Martinsdale. "Two Dot" Wilson came here in 1870 and settled along the Musselshell River, and Frank Gaugler's store was the first polling place in Musselshell Valley (in the election of 1878, twenty-one votes were cast). Gaugler's nephew, Herman Gaugler, was the first merchant in Straw, Montana, and in 1893 Frank Gaugler took over the store in Ubet. In a feature story for the Billings *Gazette*, Roger Clawson writes of "Gogglersville," a community in the Musselshell Valley; it seems possible that since **Gauglersville** was on the south fork of the Musselshell River, that this is just a variation in spelling. "Ida Pound came to Montana via sidewheeler and prairie schooner. On the riverboat "Far West" she entertained passengers by playing her huge Chickering grand piano that she was taking to her new home. She married C. T. Busha, and became the first teacher in Gogglersville."

Gaylord (Madison) was the name of an early mining camp with a post office under that name (Hardman Fleming, postmaster) 1896-97. According-ing to postal records the name was changed to Parrot.

Gearing (Lewis and Clark) was a station on the Great Northern named for Thomas D. Gearing, an early-day rancher.

Gebo (Carbon) This was the first name of a coal mining settlement not far from Fromberg. It was named for a miner named Gebo who opened the first mines there. A letter written about 1885 mentions "a Frenchman named Mose Gebo" who was on his way to Silver City. The post office was called **Gebo** 1897-1907 (Ida Manger was first postmaster); thereafter it was known as Coalville.

Geddes (Custer) was a post office 1894-97; George S. Geddes was postmaster.

Geer (Judith Basin), "up Dry Wolf Creek," was in Fergus County when the post office was established in October 1895. It was named for Thomas Geer, the postmaster, and when the office was discontinued in 1903 the mail was sent to Stanford. Geer came before 1890, ran a sawmill, and built his home and ranch near where the old ranger station was later built. Now nothing is left but a tiny, fenced cemetery where Geer, his wife, and an infant are buried. The family spelled its name "Greer" in later years (Elizabeth Cheney).

Genevieve (Valley) had a post office 1916-42; Arthur Moen was first postmaster.

Genoa (Fergus) had a post office 1891-93 with Frederick Awe as postmaster.

Genou (Chouteau) Settlers had become weary of going once a week on foot or horseback to Lytle for their mail, so they petitioned to have the mail route extended to their community. This was granted in 1911 and the post office was housed in the store belonging to postmaster Lester Urton. Urton's wife, who was of French extraction, named the little village

Genou, which is French for "knees"; the surrounding buttes were known as the Knees because of their topography. The office was open until 1954 (Ephretta Risley, Meagher County News; 1975). There is an Indian legend that in earlier times an Indian giant had been buried in what is now Montana with his head in the Sweet Grass Hills and his knees in this locality.

Genou farmers suffered a drought in 1914 but in 1916 there was a healthy crop, with wheat production at 59 bushels to the acre. In 1917, hopes of discovering oil gave new impetus to **Genou**, but wildcatters eventually gave up and left. Now it is a prosperous wheat-producing area with large acreages and modern machinery paying off where 160-area homesteaders failed.

George (Liberty), near Chester, was named for the first postmaster, Elva R. George; the office was open 1913-24.

Georgetown (Deer Lodge) was named for George Cameron, an early miner. Nearby Georgetown Lake accommodates many summer homes.

Georgetown (Lewis and Clark) had a post office established in September 1869. The office was closed in 1871 and the postal area became known as Canyon Creek.

GERALDINE (Chouteau) is the center of a huge wheat-producing region. It was named for Geraldine Rockefeller, the wife of William Rockefeller, who was director of the Milwaukee Railroad which ran through the town; the name was bestowed with the friendly sanction of the Rockefeller family. It had no particular sugnifigance to the town, "but it is well to have some powerful interests at court" (*Spokes, Spurs and Cockleburs*). The **Geraldine** post office opened in 1913 with William Welch as postmaster.

The land that became the **Geraldine** townsite adjoined Winchell Springs, which for many years had been a stopping-off point for travelers. The springs, named for a homesteader, were **Geraldine**'s water supply until artesian wells were drilled in 1959. The stagecoach stop was called the Dew Drop Inn; Steve Clark made the long stage trip from Benton to Graceville three times a week.

Gerber (Cascade) was a station on the Great Northern.

Gerhard (Fergus) had a post office 1915-20; Nellia Gerhard was postmaster. The town was near Winifred.

German Gulch, German's Gulch (Deer Lodge) was a post office 1869-75.

GEYSER (Judith Basin) was named for the nearby bubbling mud springs. "The mud geysers at Old Geyser were very active during the dry years of the 1930s and dried up when the rains returned. Nobody knows why. We could push long poles into the geysers and they just disappeared and never came back up . . . ." At the turn of the century, the area around **Geyser** was dominated by the J. B. Long sheep company. Homesteaders, many of them Finnish, came later; often they had been coal miners at Belt and were lured here by offers of free land. **Geyser** hit its peak about 1920 (Byerly and Byerly). The old town was moved to its present site when the Great Northern was built from Great Falls to Billings and **Geyser** became a station. In the very early days, it was a stagecoach overnight stopping place on the trail from Lewistown to Great Falls. The post office was established in 1892 with Mary McCarthy as postmaster.

Giant Springs (Cascade), near Great Falls, is one of the largest fresh-water springs in the world. It was noted by Lewis and Clark when they explored the area. In 1805 Lewis wrote, "I think this fountain the largest I ever beheld." He went on to describe it as a natural fan-shaped fountain 300 feet wide. It is now a park and picnic area. The clear waters of the giant fountain boil out of the earth and then cascade down to dissolve into the muddy Missouri.

Gibbons (Beaverhead) was named for Gen. John Gibbons, and is near the site of the Battle of the Big Hole, where Gibbons and his men beseiged Chief Joseph in 1877. The post office was established in 1907 with Anton Christiansen as postmaster. It was closed in 1935 and the mail ordered to Wisdom. There is also a Gibbon's Pass over the Continental Divide between Beaverhead and Ravalli counties near the Idaho border.

Gibson (Cascade) applied for and was granted a post office in May 1902, but the order was rescinded in August. Clara Epperson was to have been the postmaster.

Gibson (Sweet Grass) had a post office 1905-42; Stephen Gibson was the first postmaster.

Gidley (Richland) had a post office 1928-29 with Maude Gidley as postmaster.

Giffin (Cascade), near Stockett-Sand Coulee, was named for the Nat McGiffin family (postal records show the name as Giffen). In 1882 McGiffin left Iowa and came to Montana to prove up on a homestead and go into ranching with his brother, Abner. A few months later he drove a wagon to Corinne, Utah, to meet his wife May and infant son, who had come that far by train. The McGiffins settled in what is now the Stockett-Sand Coulee area some twenty miles from the present site of Great Falls, although that city was then only a crossroads settlement. The McGiffin's daughter, Elizabeth, was the first white girl born in the area (1885), and the McGiffin children attended the first school that was established in Great Falls. Elizabeth married "Kid" Amby Cheney and spent most of her life on a ranch at the foot of Wolf Butte in Judith Basin County. When coal was discovered in the Stockett-Sand Coulee area, miners poured in. **Giffin**, too, became a mining town when the Cottonwood Coal Company bought up the old McGiffin ranch property and opened a coal camp from which several thousand people prospered for awhile. Nothing is left now of the camp that was active for some twenty years. **Giffin** had a post office 1933-38; Mildred Klasner was the first postmaster.

Gilbert (Powell) was named for F. W. Gilbert, general superintendent of the Northern Pacific Railroad.

GILDFORD (Hill) was a station on the Great Northern High Line named for Guildford (Surrey) England. (Willard). Modern **Gildford** is a grain marketing town for Northern Plains farmers who raise excellent hard spring wheat. The **Gildford** post office opened in 1903 with Bessie Schwartz as postmaster, though the office and settlement were actually at Dayton, then at the Sage Creek Crossing a mile west of present-day **Gildford**. Trappers wintered at Sage Creek Crossing where there was good feed and water for their horses. When Sage Creek ran freely from the spring thaw, they loaded their furs on crude rafts and floated them to Fort Benton. G. Fred Mundy built a flour mill and during the hard days of poor crops and low grain prices, he found grain for impoverished homesteaders,

116

which gave them cereal to eat and some feed for animals. The mill has become a landmark and **Gildford**'s primary industry.

Gile (Meagher) was named for postmaster Erastus Weus Giles. The office was active 1901-02.

Gilman (Lewis and Clark) had a spurt of life after the Great Northern built a depot here in 1912. The town was named for L. C. Gilman, vice-president of the railroad. It had the usual stores, shops and even cement sidewalks. The September Fair was the big celebration. **Gilman** challenged the already established town of Augusta for status as an area banking and shopping center. A battle ensued when the new town demanded a school, which they eventually succeeded in getting. But the tragic year of 1919 started business on the downhill trend for the new community; the railroad ordered its depot building moved to Augusta, and by 1923 **Gilman**'s bank had closed, and in 1926 the big, new school building stood empty, though an elementary school continued until 1955. The post office, which opened in 1912 with George Nash as postmaster, closed in 1942. In 1950 a local rancher bought title to all of **Gilman** for $81 (*Montana Magazine*; Spring, 1976).

Gilman Ranch (Carter) had a post office 1927-33. Lorin Gilman was postmaster, and when the office closed the mail was sent to Teedee. Gilman's ferry conveyed new settlers and their belongings across the Clark's Fork River.

Giltedge (Fergus), northeast of Lewistown on Ford's Creek, was a mining camp when the post office was established in 1894 with Louis Beaupre as postmaster. The camp was sometimes called Whiskey Gulch, but officially it was named for a mine worked by "Limestone" Wilson. In the fall of 1883 Wilson found an ore lead in limestone around the edge of a ridge, so he called his mine the Gilt Edge. A mill was built and an estimated $1,250,000 in gold was processed. Granville Stuart's vigilante committee formed in **Giltedge** and went forth from here to arrest and hang cattle rustlers and horse thieves. The post office closed in 1948. A March 1981 fire destroyed several buildings, including the old two-story Gilt Edge Hotel that had served miners at the turn of the century, and the little log post office.

Girard (Richland) had a post office 1907-43. The first office was located on the William Pinkley farm; his wife, Lydia, was postmaster. The name came from Girard Butte, about two miles southwest. There is a story that the butte was named for Girard Whistler, an army officer at Fort Buford (*Courage Enough*). After Pinkley's death in 1910, the post office moved frequently from one homestead cabin to another, to a store building and once to the section house. In 1928 Ruby Daniels took the over the job as postmistress, and the office as well as the local store moved to the Daniels farm. After 1943 the patrons got mail by a rural route.

Gird's Creek (Missoula) had post office 1870-71 with Anthony Chaffin as postmaster.

Glacier (Flathead) had a post office 1909-13; Olive Lewis was appointed postmaster the year it opened. Earlier, the place was called Snyder, and after 1913 a station in the area was known as Lake McDonald. The name is derived from its nearby proximity to spectacular glaciers.

Glacier County This northern Montana county borders Canada, Glacier National Park, and encompasses the Blackfeet Indian Reservation.

It was created in April 1919 from a part of Teton County. Cut Bank is the county seat.

Glacier National Park This spectacular park straddles the Continental Divide from Canada on the north to Marias Pass to the south. Heavy snows keep its streams full in summer and the snow, along with the glaciers, feeds the many crystal-clear streams. The presence of many mountain glaciers accounts for the name. There are sixty large glaciers and many smaller ones, all remnants of ice rivers; each year they recede very slightly. The park is encircled by roads and one, Going-to-the-Sun Highway, crosses it. The first white man to see Glacier Park was probably Hugh Monroe, a Hudson's Bay Company trapper known to the Blackfeet as "Rising Wolf." Monroe arrived about 1815 and later married a Piegan woman. The Blackfeet say that Father DeSmet visited the region in 1846 and gave the name St. Mary to the two mountain lakes pointed out to him by Monroe.

Explorers had long sought for the gap through the mountains that the Indians often described. Major Baldwin discovered it — Marias Pass — in October 1889, but John Stevens was the first to record it officially, and it was Stevens who walked into the pass on December 11 that year. Dr. Lyman B. Sperry explored the park, penetrating as far as Avalanche Lake, and reached the glacier that now bears his name. He also saw the beautiful lake that is now called Lake Ellen Wilson. Sperry convinced the Great Northern's Jim Hill of the lucrative tourist potential for a railroad around the park. The GN completed its road in 1892, and in 1895 settlers cut a narrow trail through heavy timber from Belton to Lake McDonald. George Snyder shipped a steamboat to the lake and built a log hotel there. On May 11, 1910 **Glacier National Park** was created by an Act of Congress. Though in the state of Montana, it is under federal jurisdiction.

Glacier Park (Glacier) is near the entrance to the park. The town was formerly called Midvale. The name was changed in 1913 and Isabel Dawson was appointed postmaster. Located on the Great Northern Line, it is often called East Glacier Park because of its location near the east entrance. Since 1950 the post office has been officially listed as East Glacier Park.

Gladden was a way station on the Whoop-Up Trail on land later owned by Albert Stordahl east of Conrad. A man called "Froggie" and his Indian wife lived there when ox and mule teams took supplies from Fort Benton to Canada. It is said that "Froggie" once killed some teamsters, took the freight for his own use, and buried the bodies along the creek bank. Mail was received at Lucille.

Gladys (Carter), near Alzada, had a post office May 1903-May 1904; Hiram C. Groat was postmaster.

GLASGOW (Valley) is on the Milk River seventeen miles north of Fort Peck. It is one of the oldest communities in northeastern Montana, and since the beginning of construction on Fort Peck Dam, one of the busiest. The town was created in 1887 during the building of the Great Northern Railroad, which at first called it Siding, because it was the 45th siding west of Minot, North Dakota. When the town was platted the following year it was named after Glasgow, Scotland. The first buildings were four tents housing saloons and a restaurant. By 1889, Mrs. Frank Fryburg had started a Sunday School, which she held first in a boxcar, then in a schoolhouse, later in the Lewis Brothers store, and finally in a little Methodist Church built in 1890 (Glasgow Womens Club, 1925). The post office opened in

1888 with Charles Hall as postmaster.

"**Glasgow** was not much of a town at this time (1894), but it was the county seat of newly-created Valley County — taken out of Dawson County in 1893 — and it had a courthouse. Lewis Wedium and J. L. Truscott had a general store; General Coleman had a hotel, and the rest of the buildings were mostly log cabins. . . . The only occupations for the vicinity then were railroad work, cowboying, sheepherding and gambling" (Highland).

The sleepy little shipping station for cattle, sheep and grain woke up when workers on the Fort Peck Dam began to pour into town. The first issue of Life magazine (1936) presented a pictorial record of the revival of a Wild West atmosphere. At the peak of construction in 1936-37 some 7,200 men were employed at the dam, and "demands for housing led to a series of boomtowns not unlike the gold rush camps of the previous century." In 1935 Orlo Misfeldt wrote a "final listing of the mushroom towns" for the **Glasgow** Courier: Park Grove, New Deal, Wheeler, Delano Heights, McCone City, Lakeview, Idlewild, Valley, Martinville, Sorensons Place, Parkdale, and Midway; there were also the towns of Cactus Hill, Hiland, Roosevelt, Square Deal and Wilson — all with quite transient populations (Not in Precious Metals Alone).

Glasston (Sweet Grass), near Big Timber, had a post office 1914-24; Leon Shaw was the first postmaster.

Glaude (Missoula) was the name of a post office 1897-98; the name was then changed to Huson. It was originally named for postmaster Napoleon Glaude (see **Huson**).

GLEN (Beaverhead) has had a post office since 1950, when Louise Boucher became postmaster. Once a Union Pacific station, it was named because it is in a glen between the Big Hole and Beaverhead rivers. The rocky hillsides nearby are a retreat for rattlesnakes, and area residents conduct occasional snake hunts during which they blast the rattlers from their dens. The community began as Willis Station (post office under that name 1878-79); the name was shortened to Willis and still later changed to Reichele. Presumably the town moved to be on the railroad.

Glen (Flathead), near Flathead Lake, now has a general store and service station. Summer homes and cottages dominate. The post office opened in 1898 with William Bohannon as postmaster. It was closed in 1903 and then open again 1910-14.

Glenberg (Jefferson), near Wickes, had a post office 1909-12 with Fred Jenkins as postmaster.

Glencoe (Rosebud), near Forsyth, had a post office 1898-99 with Nettie Shriver as postmaster.

Glendale (Beaverhead) is a mining ghost town. The post office opened in 1875 with Louis Schmalhausen as postmaster; it was active for 25 years.

Alma Coffin and two of her sisters arrived here in 1878 to join their father. In 1879 she wrote: "Glendale is located on Trapper Creek. . . . (Here are) many of the buildings of the Hecla Mining Company including the smelter, a large roaster office, assay office, warehouse, blacksmith shop, sack-house, iron house, powder houses, coal sheds, stables, and dwellings for the officials. The Hecla Hospital is a clean up-to-date institution. . . . Glendale has one main street winding up a gulch and a number of little frame houses and log cabins scattered along the stony hillside. The only vegetation is the prickly pear cactus and a scant growth of low bushes. The smelter gives employment to the community. It reduces the copper and silver ore brought down by freight wagons from the Trapper Mountain mines nine miles above. . . . Dancing and card playing are the chief amusements. A little Sunday School is maintained and church services are held once or twice a month by Rev. W. W. Van Orsdel or Rev. Duncan, both of the Methodist Episcopal Church. Bishop Tuttle of the Episcopal Church visits and conducts a service in each community once a year. Father taught the Glendale school last winter and . . . the only stipulation made by the trustees was that 'the teacher must not get drunk in school hours.' In this instance the teacher had always been a total abstainer." Alma taught school in Beaverhead Valley that fall and spent the rest of her life in Montana (*Not in Precious Metals Alone*). There is a legend that when the first citizens needed a name for their town, two were suggested: **Glendale** and Clinton. The names were written on opposite sides of a sheet of paper which was then thrown up in the air. **Glendale** landed on the upside, so it became the official name. The town was near Butte and an active one in its day. There were Masonic and IOOF lodges, a racetrack, a two-story schoolhouse, a roller skating rink, a church, and an opera house. There was also a brewery which at one time laid in a supply of 50,000 pounds of hops. The town mansion, owned by Henry Knippenberg, boasted six fireplaces and Brussels carpeting. The outside of the house was ornate with cupolas.

Glendale (Musselshell), near Emory, had a post office 1911-19; William Johns was the first postmaster.

Glendive (Dawson) is a county seat. The town was named for Glendive Creek, which name was said to be a corruption of Glendale, the name originally given it by Sir St. George Gore.

The geographical term "glen" is common in the homeland of this wealthy Irish sportsman, who was involved in an episode in 1854 which was perhaps the last wild explosion of color during Montana's hunting and trapping era. Sir Gore arrived with some companions, forty servants, 112 horses, a dozen yoke of oxen, fourteen hunting dogs, and an arsenal of arms and ammunition; he also had six wagons and 21 carts loaded with every luxury of the times. Gore engaged Jim Bridger as a guide to hunted the Powder River region, and they slaughtered so much game that the Indians became resentful. In 1856 Gore drifted down to Fort Union where he burned his equipment rather than pay the price demanded by Major Culbertson for transport to St. Louis. Instead he wintered at Fort Berthold and returned to St. Louis in the spring of 1857.

"**Glendive** took form as the Northern Pacific track pushed westward late in 1880. Nine hundred people crowded into the railroad camp during its first two years." The post office opened in 1881 with Nelson Lawrence as postmaster. **Glendive**, formerly the metropolis of a cattle empire, is now the trading and shipping center of an area that produces sugar beets, grain and forage crops.

Glengarry (Fergus) was a station on the Milwaukee a few miles southwest of Lewistown. The settlement was named by Angus MacMillan, a pioneer who came in 1880 and wanted to honor his native home in Scotland. The post opened in 1909 with Samuel Lewis as postmaster; it closed in 1924. There were a couple of stores, a grain elevator, a Presbyterian Church and a school. Most of the kids rode horseback and tied the horses in the school barn during the day. At one time there were four passenger trains a day through **Glengarry**. Farmers sent cream to town on the early morning train and the empty 5-gallon cans came back from Lewistown at night (Byerly).

Glenrock (Carter) had a post office most of the period 1891-1901; Grace Senderling was postmaster.

GLENTANA (Valley) is ten miles from the Saskatchewan border. It was a station near the end of the branch line of the Great Northern that went up to Opheim. The post office opened in 1913 with William O'Connor as postmaster.

Glenwood (Broadwater), near Townsend, had a post office 1898-1911; Richard Clendenin was postmaster.

Gloster (Lewis and Clark) had a post office 1882-95; Hiram McAllister was the first postmaster.

Goforth (Missoula) was a siding on the Milwaukee between Bonner and Sunset.

Goldbutte (Toole) had a post office established in 1895 with Peter Hughes in charge. "Rodney Barnes made a strike in the Sweet Grass hills near the Canadian border and dug out $125,000 worth of placer gold. **Goldbutte**, springing up as a prosperous village, is now a ghost town" (Mockel). The post office was closed in 1945.

Goldcoin, Gold Coin (Deer Lodge), near Anaconda, had a post office 1897-99 with Charles Beaton as postmaster.

Gold Creek, Goldcreek (Powell) On September 8, 1883, Henry Villard, president of the Northern Pacific Railroad, came here to drive the iron spike that completed the line linked the West Coast with the East.

This spot, at the junction of Gold Creek and the Clark Fork River, is claimed to be the scene of the first gold discovery in Montana; however, "no one has been able to establish exactly who discovered the first gold in Montana or where. Francois Finlay, a half-blood better known as Benetsee, is said to have brought a teaspoon of gold dust into Fort Connah to Angus McDonald in 1850 and reported that he had gotten it at the present site of **Gold Creek**, near Garrison" (Toole). The Gold Creek area was originally called the Benetsee Creek area. Nothing was done to develop it until James and Granville Stuart began working there. On May 8, 1862, they set up the first sluices in Montana near the head of Gold Creek. A letter written by the Stuarts to their brother Thomas, in Colorado, advising him to join them, started a small rush to Montana. A post office was opened in 1886 with Francis Bird as postmaster; it closed in 1894. The office was open again 1898-1901. Postal records show the name spelled as one word. The office reopened in 1903.

Gold Dust (Jefferson) was the name of a short-lived postal service during gold mining days. The office was open 1891-92 with Lizzie Rich as postmaster.

Golden (Carbon), between Bridger and Belfry, had a post office 1898-1912 and again 1916-19. It was reportedly named for a man named Golden who settled there. **Golden** was a shipping point on the old Montana, Wyoming, and Southern Railroad near the Gold Dome oilfields.

Golden Valley County is a little east of the center of the state. It was named because the soil is rich and there are plenty of streams for irrigation. Promoters hoped that the name would attract more settlers to the area.

Golden Valley County was created in October 1920 from the western part of Musselshell County and the northern part of Sweet Grass County. Ryegate is the county seat.

Gold Medal (Valley), near Nashua, had a post office 1916-17 with Philip Edman as postmaster.

Goldrun (Meagher) This post office operated briefly January-April 1882, with Thomas Maddock as postmaster. The name was changed to Clendenin.

Gold Stone (Hill) is twenty-five miles north of Rudyard and eight from the Canadian border. Frank Novak was appointed postmaster when the office opened in 1911. He named the place because once as he was walking across the prairie he picked up a rock that looked like gold. Novak opened a store; settlers moved in. At one time there were 147 mailboxes with deliveries from Inverness twice a week. Coal from Canadian Coulee kept homesteaders warm, but dry years drove them out. The old schoolhouse still stands, a lone sentinel to this once prosperous and hopeful community. All other buildings have burned to the ground. The post office closed in 1954.

Goodale, (Cascade) near Portage, had a post office from June 1911 to August 1912.

Goodsoil (Phillips) had a post office under that name February-April 1915. Joseph Dyer was postmaster. The name chosen to attract settlers. The area was formerly called Baeth; later, it was known as Content.

Goosebill (Chouteau), near Eagleton, had a post office May 1914-June 1919 and June 1922-September 1923. Lena Stevens was the first postmaster. **Goosebill** had a store, a post office, and a dance hall, all under one roof. The first school was held in Fred Alson's shack. The name in early days was Bisque d'Outard, French for "goosebill." *Outard* was the name the French gave to the common wild goose of Canada. The Blackfoot called the goose *mis' ops pe chris.*

Goosehead Bay, at Flathead Lake, was the home of Frank B. Linderman. "I borrowed a horse and an axe and went into the mountains to cut a set of house logs," he recalled; in 1917 he built a comfortable home of tamarack, and after many restless years of trapping, hunting, merchandising, newspaper work and politics, he settled down by the lake to write twelve of his thirteen books. He died there in 1938. (See **Brandon**).

Gopher (Rosebud) had a post office 1917-33. Glenn Heaton was the first postmaster, and this community, like several others, was named for a prevalent wildlife specie.

Gordon (Pondera) was named for a Mr. Gordon who was foreman of the T.C. Power Company, an "outfit" with extensive holdings in this area. The post office was open only 1910-11 with George Berthaume as postmaster; the mail was then sent to Dupuyer.

Gore Field, the Great Falls airport, was named for James D. Gore. In 1890 Gore filed on a 320-acre homestead which covered most of the east slope of the hill where the airport is now located. A contractor, carpenter, and general handyman, he built the three-story stone business block which was later occupied by the Park View Hotel. On his homestead he built a large house, a fine barn, and planted some trees, which he watered with a windmill. The buildings burned down about 1900; only a few foundation stones and the trees remain.

Gorham (Cascade) had a post office 1885-89. John Dyas was the first postmaster. The postal name for this area went from Ulidia to **Gorham** and then to Saint Clair.

Gorus (Ravalli) is near Darby. It was named for G. D. Gorus, one of the first successful raisers of McIntosh Apples. He shipped them out of the Bitterroot Valley in carload lots.

Gossett (Richland) had a post office 1905-13. Susie Bone was the first postmaster, and she named the community for Dan Gossett, an old roundup boss from South Dakota. Gossett came here in 1900 and bought a ranch on 101 Creek. When the **Gossett** office closed, people had to go to Clark, across the river, for their mail. Charley Clark kept the office in his home. Later, **Gossett** residents got their mail at Skaar.

Gould (Lewis and Clark) was named for the Jay Gould Mine, which in turn was named for the famous financier. **Gould** was near Wilborn. The post office opened in 1888 with Otis Allen as postmaster. It was closed 1891-93 and then open again until 1917.

Graber (Prairie) was named for Elizabeth Graber, first postmaster. The office was open 1917-31; after that the mail was sent to Crow Rock.

Grace (Silver Bow) is along the Jefferson County border. It was named for Grace Penfield, wife of W. H. Penfield, Engineer for Maintenance of the Milwaukee Railroad. The post office opened and closed four times between 1882-1926. William McCall was appointed postmaster when it was inaugurated.

Graceville (Chouteau) had a post office 1911-23, which roughly spans the homesteading years. In 1912, Lottie Payne's family owned and operated a store and post office located on their homestead. Florence Payne was the postmaster. Lottie made newcomers and patrons feel welcome; she always had the coffee pot on and a box of penny candy to give to children. At one time there were sixty homesteaders getting mail at the **Graceville** office. There was a spirit of neighborliness, of helping each other, but even that could not make up for the stark realities and hopelessness of most homesteading. Sue Howells and her husband Joe located in Chouteau County several miles from **Graceville** and she vividly recalls that homestead life was often monotonous and lonely. New settlers usually lived in one-room tar paper shanties that were cramped, stark, dusty and cold. Entertainment was sparse, since families usually lived miles from any community center. When they went to town — and then only to buy absolute necessities — they found little more than a tiny settlement. Sometimes dances were held on the Ledstone Ferry Boat. "The resourceful homesteaders thus provided their own diversions, meeting at someone's home. Dances, literary groups, and picnics constituted many of the social gatherings" *(Not in Precious Metals Alone)*.

Grafton (Judith Basin) opened its post office in 1887 with Annie Frost as postmaster; it closed in 1894. **Grafton** was a stage station east of Stanford between Surprise Creek and Geyser. K. W. Hay recalls, "My first home was on the 'Lone Tree Ranch' at Grafton, Montana, a spot long since forgotten. It was on Arrow Creek and the stage stop and post office there (were) named after a Scotch sheepherder named Grafton Frost" *(Montana Magazine; Autumn, 1971)*.

Graham (Powder River) had a post office 1894-1943. Frederick Williams was the first postmaster.

Grain (Valley) could not have been more appropriately named, for in 1916, when the post office opened, it was grain that would make or break the settlers. Joseph Weber was the first postmaster; the office closed in 1920.

Grandview was undoubtedly an inspired name bestowed on the community by an optimistic homesteader when the post office opened in 1910. Martin Bergsven was in charge. The office closed in 1933 as homesteaders gave up and moved away.

Granite. (Granite) In the early 1880s, when **Granite** was a boom town, the mining companies furnished water to residents for $1.50 a month. It was hauled in barrels mounted on sleds or carts and ladled out at the rate of two or three buckets a day to each housewife — a little more was allowed for wash day. The post office opened in 1886 with Carlton Hand as postmaster; it was closed 1897-98, then open until 1908. **Granite** grew up as a mining town when Charles D. McClure, who had been foreman of the Hope Mine in Philipsburg, persistently prospected Granite Mountain and finally found "bonanza ore". The Granite Mountain Mine proved to be one of the richest of its kind and the little town sprawled on the hillside became a booming mining camp. According to Abbot, "There was no night . . . every day was 24 hours long; . . . But there was little disorder, the folks were all too busy. During the years it worked, this mine contributed over $25 million to the mineral wealth of Montana." The Census of 1890 listed 1,310 inhabitants; it was then eleventh in size in the state. When silver declined, the mine closed and people moved away. Today it is a ghost town.

Granite County has a land area of 1,728 square miles. It is north and west of the Continental Divide. The area was originally called Flint Creek Valley. The first settlement sprang up in 1866, when the Comanche Quartz Lode was located. The county is named for the celebrated Granite Mountain Silver Mine; the mountain is named for the granite rock found in it. **Granite County** was created in March 1893.

Grannis (Park) was a station on the Northern Pacific and was also called Grannis Crossing. The right-of-way for this part of the railroad's Wilsall branch line was secured from Mrs. Thirza Grannis.

Grant (Beaverhead) is on Prairie Creek and was formerly known as Amesville. The **Grant** post office opened in 1899 with Joseph Nesley as postmaster; it was discontinued in 1967. The name origin is uncertain: "Jonni" Grant was a famous prospector and rancher, but available information indicates it was probably named for Gen. Ulysses S.Grant (Western Interpretive Services). Today a store and the Horse Prairie Hilton (a motel), dominate **Grant**.

Grant Creek (Missoula), near Missoula, was once a thriving community. Now it's a pleasant valley that one drives through on the way to the Snow Bowl ski resort.

In early days it was important because the famous Mullan Road was built through here. Capt. Richard Grant, after his service on the U.S. Military Road project, returned to the Missoula area and established a horse ranch, supplying animals needed for work on the Mullan Road. After the railroads came West, the road was little used. John and Olive Rankin settled in

Grant Creek Valley in 1884 and established a sawmill, furnishing lumber for the first Higgins Avenue bridge and many buildings in Missoula. Their children — Jeannette Rankin, first woman congressman; Harriet Rankin Sedman, Dean of Women at the University of Montana; and Wellington D. Rankin, big-time cattleman and landowner — were all important figures in Montana's history.

GRANTSDALE (Ravalli) is three miles from Hamilton. It was named for H. H. Grant, a landowner who built the first flour mill and kept the first store in this area. The post office opened in 1888 with Thomas Owings as postmaster. The postal area was formerly called Skalkaho.

Grasshopper Creek (Beaverhead) was near Bannack. On July 28, 1862, John White and other prospectors from Colorado discovered a bonanza of placer gold along this creek. News spread and within a month a thousand people had arrived. In 1862, at the confluence of the Beaverhead River and Rattlesnake Creek, stood the only signpost in the vast wilderness of Montana Territory. On one side of a rough-hewn board this message was daubed in axle grease:

Tu grass Hop Per digins
30 myle
Kepe the trale nex the bluffe

On the other side was written:

To Jonni Grants
one Hundred & twenti myle

The "grass Hop per digins" were near Bannack. "Jonni" Grant was a rancher in the Deer Lodge Valley who got his start by trading for worn-out cattle along the Emigrant Trail in Utah in 1850. He would drive the cattle to Montana, fatten them up, and take them back to the trail for resale at a profit. By 1858 the Grants — Capt. Richard Grant, a former employee of the Hudson's Bay Co., and his two sons John and James had several hundred head of cattle and horses. Conrad Kohrs bought the Johnny Grant ranch in 1868 (Western Intepretive Services).

Grasshopper Glacier (Park) is in the mountains west of Red Lodge and was named because of the many grasshoppers that have been found frozen in the ice here.

GRASS RANGE (Fergus) is east of Lewistown. It existed as a village, post office, and trading center before the Milwaukee Railroad made it a station on the branch line to Winnett. The post office opened in 1883 with John Chamberlain as postmaster, with the name spelled Grassrange. The town grew up in the middle of some of the finest open grassland used by the early cattle pools and was named for this range grass, which was eventually turned under by homesteaders' plows. Elaine French of **Grass Range** summed up the story of many dry-land families: "People came to **Grass Range** in 1913-14 with lots of money and went out broke."

Grass Valley (Missoula) was an early post office 1887-95. John Cyr was the first postmaster. The name is descriptive.

Grayling (Jefferson) was a station on the Oregon Short Line named for the river fish.

Grayling (Gallatin) was a post office in a ranch home near Hebgen Lake in the extreme southern tip of the county. The office was open 1898-1951; Lulu Kerzenmacher was the first postmaster. It was named from the specie of fish that was caught here.

125

GREAT FALLS (Cascade) is a county seat. Lewis and Clark wanted to be sure that the south fork was the main channel of the Missouri River, so they set out from this fork above Fort Benton — where the Marias flows into the Missouri — on June 11, 1805, to find the "great falls" in the river that the Indians had described to them. They arrived at the first falls about noon on June 13. Lewis said he longed for the pen of an artist that he ". . .might be able to give the enlightened world some just idea of this truly magnificent and sublimely grand object which has from the commencement of time been concealed from the view of civilized man." The highest falls is about eighty-seven feet and the series of five cascades that the party explored brings the Missouri River down some four hundred feet. One of the falls was described by Lewis as "pleasingly beautiful" and the other as "sublimely grand." About the time the romantic Lewis was dreaming about the scenery, a grizzly bear charged him. Lewis plunged into the water, readied his spear, and finally the bear left. Lewis and Clark had to portage around the falls, and it took them ten days to go 17 miles. A severe storm and cloudburst caught them between the river and a cliff; Sacajawea and Clark almost drowned.

Nearly eighty years later, on July 10, 1884, the **Great Falls** post office opened with Paris Gibson as postmaster. Authorities agree that **Great Falls** owes its beginning to Gibson who, as far back as 1881, saw possibilities in the vast resources of water power running "to waste." He and a friend filed on the land in 1882. The first house in town was a log structure built by John Woods in the autumn of 1883. The coming of the Manitoba Railroad in 1887 was the beginning of a larger life for **Great Falls.** It was incorporated as a city in 1888. Tom McGiffin was the first graduate of Great Falls High School. Nat McGiffin was the first assessor of Cascade County.

Green (Teton), near Choteau, had a post office 1894-95 with Charles F. Green as postmaster.

Greene (Fergus) was named for postmaster Alexander C. Greene. The office was in his ranch and operated 1900-08. It was near Straw. Greene was a school teacher, county commissioner, legislator, and owner of a large sheep ranch.

Greenhorn (Lewis and Clark) was once a prosperous and populated mining camp.The post office was open 1871-73 with John Reynolds as postmaster. The office reopened in November 1882 but in April of the following year the territorial governor of Montana telegraphed postal authorities in Washington, D.C.:

"VIGILANTES AT GREENHORN MONTANA HAVE REMOVED
POSTMASTER BY HANGING OFFICE NOW VACANT"

Evidently he wasn't replaced, because the post office was ordered discontinued and the mail was sent to Helena.

GREENOUGH (Missoula) is a little town some twenty-five miles east of Missoula. It was named for one of the area's most successful early settlers, T. L. Greenough, whose mansion in Missoula is still a showplace for the city. The luxurious grounds that once surrounded the mansion are now Greenough Park, and the mansion has been moved to another part of town.

Greenspring (Sanders) was named for the first postmaster, Frank Green, and probably for a natural spring there. The post office opened in 1910 and closed in 1916 with orders to send the mail to Perma.

Greenville (Valley) was a short-lived post office 1909-10 with Walter

Parrish as postmaster.

Green Wood (Deer Lodge) had a post office 1868-75; the first postmaster was Henry S. Clark.

Greenwood (Gallatin) was a post office name 1902-05; Joseph Theobald was postmaster.

Gregory (Jefferson) had a post office 1881-83 with Lionel Nettre as postmaster. The office was open again 1885-88.

Gregson, Gregson Springs (Silver Bow) was one of the early recreation areas between Butte and Anaconda. The natural hot springs there were used for the swimming pool, and an extensive picnic grounds was built around the indoor pool. The post office was established in 1897 with Con Hayes as postmaster, it was closed in 1937.

Greve (Phillips) was named for the family of first postmaster Katherine Greves. The office was open 1914-36.

GREYCLIFF (Sweet Grass) is ten miles east of Big Timber and is named for a cliff east of town which is comprised of grey-tinted conglomerate rock. The post office was open 1885-87 and again in 1891. Julia Wirst was the first postmaster.

Grisdella (Garfield) was a post office in the Griswold home and Myrtle Griswold was postmaster when it opened in 1927. The office closed in 1937. Presumably the name is a compound of the first part of "Griswold" and the Christian name of some family member.

Gunderson (Silver Bow) was named for the first postmaster, Louis Gunderson. The office opened in 1883 and the name was changed to Meaderville in 1903.

Gundlach (Teton) had a post office 1916-17 with Edgar A. Gundlach as postmaster.

Gunsight (Glacier) was a station on the Great Northern near Cut Bank. It was named for Gunsight Mountain and Gunsight Pass in Glacier Park. The station was formerly called Admus.

Gunton (Fergus) was named for Anna Gunton, who was postmaster when the office opened in 1896. In 1903 the name was changed to Halbert.

Gwendale (Deer Lodge) had a post office established in 1872 with Morgan Evans as postmaster. In 1878 the name was changed to Morristown.

Gypsum (Fergus) was a station east of Lewistown on the Milwaukee Railroad named for the gypsum mine and plant there. It is now called Heath. There was a post office at the plant 1926-28 with Christina Van Duser as postmaster.

———————— H ————————

Hackamore (Richland) sounds like a good Western, horse-oriented name, but the post office by that name never got into operation, even though a 1916 petition was submitted by residents. Lizzie Lamberton was to have been postmaster.

Hailstone (Sweet Grass) suffered the same fate as Hackamore; the 1917 effort to establish a post office came to naught. John Chattin was to have been postmaster.

Halbert In 1882 the Halbert family came to Billings on the first run of the Northern Pacific, located a cattle ranch on the Benton Trail, and ran the **Halbert** post office and stage station 1885-1902. The location was about ten miles northeast of present-day Hedgesville. Thomas Halbert, one of the sons, was the first postmaster. The office was moved to the George Pirrie ranch and finally to Rothiemay Flat, where the name was changed to Rothiemay and Annie W. Pirrie became postmaster. The other Halbert son, Willard ("Will"), bought some land on Careless Creek and took over the Bercail (Gunton) post office. Postal records show this Fergus County office operating under the name **Halbert** with Alice Halbert postmaster 1903-05. A biography of Willard Halbert written by his daughter states that he took over the Gunton post office from Harry Giltinan in 1910 and that his wife, Lillian, was soon named postmaster, serving for thirty-eight years, until the office closed.

Early Montana post offices usually moved to the postmaster — to his ranch or to the general store in a mining camp or to a stage station. There were **Halbert** post offices in two locations, both of them named for and operated by members of this 1882 pioneer family.

Halfmoon Pass, (Musselshell) near Rothiemay, had a post office in operation from 1916-17 with Alice Covell as postmaster.

HALL (Drummond), south of Drummond, was named for Henry Hall, from whom the Northern Pacific Railroad secured the right-of-way. The station became a livestock shipping point. **Hall**'s post office was established in 1896 with Ella Engle as postmaster.

Halpin (Missoula) was named for Michael Halpin, who was postmaster while the office was in brief service April-August 1883.

Hamblin (McCone) was originally called Cow Creek. The name was changed in 1913 when a post office was established and Charles Hamblin was appointed postmaster. The office was closed in 1928.

Hamilton (Gallatin) had a post office established December 1868 with Daniel Small as postmaster. Postal records show the name was changed to Moreland in September 1884; the Northern Pacific had completed its line across Montana the year before and a station on its branch line through Ravalli County was also named Hamilton. In 1891 the name was changed again, this time to Manhattan. This name was chosen because a large Manhattan (New York) investment company had bought up a lot of land and was operating the holdings in the area.

HAMILTON (Ravalli) is a county seat named for J. W. Hamilton, from whom the right-of-way for the Northern Pacific line was secured. The post office was established in 1890 with Lewis Williams as postmaster. **Hamilton** is a business center for the Bitterroot Valley and owes much of its early development to Marcus Daly. The "Copper King" toured the valley and liked it, so he bought a large stock farm and built a mansion, furnishing it with the finest of everything and surrounding it with terraced lawns; he also built a swimming pool and even a lake, which he stocked with trout. He called his barn Tammany Castle, in honor of one of his finest racing horses. Daly was instrumental in getting the county seat moved from Stevensville to **Hamilton**. Located in **Hamilton** now is a large government-owned laboratory which was established in 1901 for the study of Rocky Mountain Spotted Fever and the tick that carries it (Jane Lloyd, Betsy Maeir).

HAMMOND (Carter) is a cluster of cabins and a general store. The post office for the area was moved from Piniele to **Hammond** in 1934 so it would be on the highway. Charles Bates Eccles was the first postmaster in the new location.

Hampton (Custer) had a post office April 1900-December 1901 with Martha Newell as postmaster.

Hanover (Fergus) was a station which opened after the construction of the railroad, when gypsum rock deposits were found and quarries opened up. Plants were set up for the manufacture of gypsum products. It was named by C. A. Goodnow, assistant to the president of the Milwaukee Railroad, after the town in Massachusetts. The post office opened in 1916 with Blanche Bickel as postmaster. It was discontinued in 1957.

Harb (Phillips) had a post office 1915-19 with John Hunter as first postmaster. The office was open again 1928-33.

HARDIN (Big Horn) is a county seat on the edge of the Crow Indian Reservation. It was named by C. H. Morrill, president of the Lincoln Land Co. of Lincoln, Nebraska, the company which purchased and platted the present townsite, in honor of Samuel Hardin, a personal friend. Hardin was an old-time settler and cattleman who lived near Ranchester, Wyoming, south of **Hardin**. The area was opened to settlement in 1906 and a post office was established in 1907 with Edwin Spencer as postmaster. **Hardin** is a farmers' and ranchers' town, which chiefly serves residents of the Crow Indian Reservation.

Hardy (Cascade) was a station on the Great Northern Railroad near the Lewis and Clark County line. There was a post office there 1888-1915. Stephen Carman was the first postmaster.

HARLEM (Blaine) is about halfway between Havre and Malta. It was founded in 1889 and grew up as a trading center for the Fort Belknap Indian Reservation. The first post office was a shoe box in Smith's General Merchandise Store; when the volume of mail outgrew the box, an empty beer case fitted with pigeon holes took its place. The depot was a box car. For a long time an annual Sheepherders Convention was held in **Harlem**.

At the last one, in 1922, they formed a union. According to Malta newspaper, **Harlem** was one of the towns named by officials of the Great Northern Railroad in St. Paul. To find names for the new stations along the High Line, they spun a globe of the world and, blindfolded, put a finger on a spot. This time, according to the article, the finger landed on Haarlem in the Netherlands.

The post office was officially established in 1890 with John Manning as postmaster. Mrs. J. A. Wise came here in 1888, the first white woman in the area.

Harley (Dawson) had a post office June 1899-December 1900; mail was then sent to Tokna. May Dawson was postmaster.

HARLOWTON (Wheatland) is a county seat. It is named for Richard Harlow, who built the "Jaw Bone" Milwaukee branch to Lewistown by way of **Harlowton**. The town was originally called Merino because of the many sheep of that breed raised in the area. **Harlowton** became a division point on the Milwaukee Railroad, whose electrified section began here. A flour mill serves the large wheat-growing area. Several buildings, notably the Graves Hotel, are made of stone from a nearby quarry. The Merino post office was established in 1881; the name was changed to **Harlowton** in 1900 and Joseph Labrie was appointed postmaster.

Haro (Philips) was a Great Northern station at first called Eureka; the name was changed to **Haro** in 1900, and there was a post office 1915-17 with William Kelsey as postmaster. Near Dodson, it was named Survant in 1941 and abandoned as a GN station in 1956.

Harrigan There seems to have been an effort made in 1891 to have the name of Kalispell changed to **Harrigan**, with Charles Harrigan as postmaster, but the change never took place.

Harris (Custer) had a post office 1888-99. Wilson Harris was the first postmaster. It was near Sabra.

Harrisburg (Flathead) had a post office 1903-05 under Claude Bradley. It was replaced by the office at Fortine.

Harrisburgh (Deer Lodge) was named for first postmaster Benjamin Harris. The office was open 1869-73 and 1874-75.

Harrison (Madison) is a ranch town with a single street and a cluster of houses. It was named for the Henry C. Harrison family, which settled at Willow Creek in 1865 and became known for their Morgan horses, shorthorn cattle, and large steam dairy. A post office was first opened in 1870 or '71 with H. S. Paul as postmaster. The office opened and closed three times before 1905, when Frank Warburton was appointed postmaster and has been continuously open since then. Between 1889-1905 the area was served by a ranch post office at the Ferguson place.

Harte (Missoula) was named for Carl Harte, postmaster when the office was established in 1913. The name was changed to Round Butte in 1920.

Harvey (Valley) had a post office 1910-11 with Henry Thomas as postmaster. According to postal records the name was changed to Monota; perhaps this name was chosen because of the town's location on the North Dakota border. The name Monota is a combined word from "Montana" and "Dakota."

Hasmark (Granite), near Philipsburg, had a post office April-August 1880 and again 1892-97. Samuel Silverman was the first postmaster. It was named for two men, **H. A. S**tyles and Mr. **Mark**le.

Hassel (Broadwater) was famous for its huge Diamond Hill Stamp Mill, which was operating at full capacity in 1898. **Hassel** is near Townsend. It had a post office established in 1895 with Willis Eversole as postmaster. The office closed in 1905 but was open again 1909-11. **Hassel** was formerly called Saint Louis. It had a rebirth when new quartz mines were discovered above town, and some mines were still producing as late as 1910. Postal authorities insisted the name be changed because both Missouri and Montana were often abbreviated "Mo.," thus leading to missent mail and freight. A town meeting was held to decide on a new name; it was a tie between Lowery and **Hassel**, both names of early-day miners. Charlie Moffet was home drunk, but he was pulled out of bed to come vote and break the tie (Western Interpretive Services).

HATHAWAY (Rosebud) is between Miles City and Forsyth. It was a station on the railroad, and named for Major Hathaway, a U.S. Army officer. Now it is only a cluster of tumbledown, unpainted houses around a post office and gas station. The post office opened in 1887 with Albert Huffey as postmaster. Postal records say it was formerly called Putnam.

Hauck (Judith Basin) was a station on the Great Northern named for rancher John C. Hauch. An elevator was built to serve the rich wheatfields that surround it.

HAUGAN (Mineral) is about five miles from the Idaho border. The town was named for H. G. Haugan, land commissioner and comptroller for the Chicago, Milwaukee, St. Paul and Pacific Railroad. **Haugan** was established and maintained as a pusher station for trains ascending the Coeur d'Alene Mountain grade. The post office opened in 1911 with Lavina Emmert as postmaster.

Hauser Lake (Lewis and Clark) was named for an early banker-stockman who was part owner of the DHS outfit (Davis, Hauser and Stuart). Postal records show an office established as Hauserlake in September 1905 and adds that the name was changed to Holter in 1908. Hauser Dam was completed in 1911; Holter Dam is some fifteen miles down the Missouri and was completed in 1918 — so it was a new location, not a name change.

Hausman (Hill) was named for John Hausman, who was appointed postmaster when the office opened in 1915; it closed in 1918 and mail was sent to Hingham.

Havana (Madison) had a post office 1873-74 with John Thomas as postmaster. It has to be a mining camp.

HAVRE (Hill) is a county seat. This area was first called Bull Hook Bottoms, after a stream by that name that flows out of the Milk River. The town was founded in the fall of 1891, when the original railroad station at Fort Assiniboine on the St. Paul, Minneaplis and Manitoba Railway was abandoned. The new station was given the name Bull Hook Siding. James J. Hill sent his construction crew out in 1887 and, finding plenty of good water in the area, he decided to build a branch line south to Great Falls from here instead going on towards the West Coast. The name of the town was changed to **Havre** (pronounced HAV-er) in honor of the birthplace (in France) of Simon Pepin and Gus DesCelles, the original homesteaders on land that was later used as the townsite (Havre *Plaindealer*; Jan. 13, 1906). **Havre** was one of those towns named by a twirl of the globe in St. Paul (Phillips County News). (See **Harlem**).

Havre was a true "cow town" of the Old West: cowboys from the Bear Paw Pool and other big cattle outfits used it as a trading center and a place to "hole up" for the winter. Years later, **Havre** gained national publicity when a dispute arose as to whether or not it was legal to tie horses to the parking meters; the cowboys who rode into town maintained that as long as they put money in the meter, the horses had as much right to the space as any car. The post office opened in 1890 with William Connors as postmaster.

In a recent history written by Hill County residents, it is recounted that when Jim Hill decided to run his railroad through Bull Hook Bottoms, he insisted on a better name. The first meeting called to select one ended in a brawl, so another meeting was held. Several interested persons attended, including Louis Shambo. It was agreed that only five of the homesteaders there were entitled to vote. Joe DeMars suggested the name "France," since most of them were Frenchmen. The others wouldn't agree to that, but Guy Decelles (DesCelles) suggested the name **Havre** for his parents' hometown in the old country. The three Frenchmen voted "*oui*," and with that, Bull Hook Bottoms became **Havre**.

Hawarden (Chouteau) was named by settlers from Iowa for their hometown in that state. The post office opened in 1910 in the homestead shack of Lucy Brady, postmaster. Mail came in a gunny sack carried by the stage driver. The office closed in 1916 because no one was willing to be the postmaster.

Hawk's Home, (Carter) was named because there was a large hawk's nest near there. The post office was open from 1916-1920. From the diary of Violet Martin Hafer: "In 1916 we moved to the Montana homestead. We got our mail twice a week. Dad (Fred Martin) had built an extra room on our house that year for a store and a post office. We were granted the name "Hawk's Home." He went to Albion, Montana thirty miles away for the mail. All building materials and also our food had to be freighted by team from Belle Fourche, S.D. which was our nearest railroad point. It was 75 miles from our home. Food was ordered twice a year from Sears Roebuck in Chicago." The post office was originally housed in the home of Mrs. Anna Weiss who served as postmaster. It was then moved to Fred Martin's place and his wife Delia Bruner Martin was postmaster. When that office closed the mail was handled at Ridgeway.

Hawkwood (Park) had a post office from 1896-1903. Edith Pemberton was postmaster.

Haxby (Garfield) is in the "V" formed by Fort Peck Reservoir. Harry Conklin moved in and took up a homestead at the head of Box Creek and took the lead in getting a post office started. Many names were suggested, but none of them was accepted by the postal department and the citizens. It was finally called **Haxby** in honor of a town by that name in England. The post office was established in 1915 and operated until 1959. The first cattle ranch in this region was one belonging to Land, Tomb, and Lennon. They claimed to have the largest fenced pasture anywhere — 865,000 acres of leased land on the Standing Rock Indian Reservation. That was in 1902. Besides the large herd of cattle, their outfit ran 400 head of horses. Before the post office was established, anyone going across the river to Lismas picked up the mail for everyone on the south bank of the Missouri and kept it at his house until each neighbor rode over on horseback to pick it up.

Hay Coulee (Garfield) is now under the water of Fort Peck Reservoir. The name was descriptive and the post office was in the home of Mr. and Mrs. Orr who had built their home in a grassy coulee with a water supply. The office was discontinued in 1925. It had opened in 1916 with Frieda Tillotson as postmaster.

Hay Coulee (Liberty) had a post office from 1928-1936. John Dalimata was the first postmaster.

Hayden (Flathead) had a post office from 1902-1905. Peter Gavin was postmaster. It was near Rexford.

Hayden (Gallatin) had a post office from 1874-1883. It was near Bozeman; Rhoda Ferrel was the first postmaster.

Hayes (Missoula) was a station on the Northern Pacific so named because the right of way was bought from Elizabeth Hayes.

Haymaker (Meagher) was a post office from 1912-1914. Luna Parlasca was postmaster. It was near Two Dot.

HAYS (Blaine) is on the Fort Belknap Indian Reservation and at the edge of the Little Rocky Mountains. The post office was established in August 1899 with George Heath as postmaster. Highland says: "Another horse ranch was started near Hays, Montana, and was operated by Rufus Warrior for eight years. Then the horses were trailed across the Missouri and a ranch headquarters was established at Sand Spring." **Hays** is an Indian town that comes to life in September each year when the Indians hold their fair, with dancing, racing, and games.

Hazel (Prairie) was a post office that spanned the homestead years between its opening in 1914 and its closing in 1935. It was named for the postmaster's daughter Hazel (Clement). Jessie Smith was the first postmaster.

Hazny (Gafield) was formerly named Trouble. The **Hazny** post office was active from 1918-1934. Bert Duncan was the first postmaster, after the office was moved to the Tom Fullerton ranch.

HEART BUTTE (Pondera) is near the Continental Divide. The post office opened in 1815 with Fannie Crim as postmaster. It is an Indian town near the Rocky Mountains and is named for some inverted heart-shaped mountains.

Heath (Fergus) was formerly called Gypsum. The post office was active from 1910-1926 and from 1928-1963. The new name was for the family of postmaster Perry C. Heath. The gypsum deposits and processing plants located there gave rise to the original name.

Heckman (Wibaux) was a station named for Frank Heckman, an old Northern Pacific employee and dispatcher on the Yellowstone Division.

Hecla (Beaverhead) was named for the Hecla Mining Company. It was near Melrose and only a trace of the buildings remain. A post office first opened there in 1881 with James Parfet as postmaster. It was closed in 1892 and then opened again from 1894-1900 and from 1913-1914.

Hedges (Wheatland) was named for a local rancher W. A. Hedges. It was a station on the Great Northern. The post office which was first located on the old Hedges ranch (1888) was called Yale. Ida Hedges was the postmaster. In 1910 the station and the post office both became known as Hedgesville.

Hedgesville (Wheatland) was named for W. A. Hedges and the post office was located on his ranch when it opened in April 1888 under the name of Yale. In 1910 the name was changed to **Hedgesville** as was the name of the railway station which had originally been called Hedges. The first building in **Hedgesville** was a tiny depot for the Billings and Northern Railroad (later taken over by the Great Northern). The first business establishment other than the station was a saloon. Angus McKay from Garneil moved over, pitched a tent, lived in one side of it with his family and dispensed drinks from the other side. In 1909 the *Hedges Herald* announced that "no less than 200 families of Holland Dutch" were planning to come to **Hedgesville** to settle and raise sugar beets. Two small groups did come under the auspices of the Montana Holland Colonization Co. They came by ship and by train, but they came with no money and no possessions and only ten stayed. Nellie Ashley was the postmaster in 1910.

Hedstrom (Dawson) was named for postmaster Ole Hedstrom when the post office opened in 1903. When it closed in 1906, the mail was sent to McMillan.

HELENA (Lewis and Clark) (pronounced HEL-en-a) is the county seat as well as the capital of the state. It owes its existence to the gold discoveries in Last Chance Gulch (now Main Street) in the summer of 1864. Main street follows the trail by which bull and mule team freight outfits entered the lusty young city. In October 1864, it was decided that Last Chance Gulch was not a suitable name for the rapidly growing camp. A meeting was called to select a more dignified name. John Somerville dominated the meeting and pushed through the adoption of **Helena** after his home town in Scott County, Minnesota. The miners and the bullwhackers didn't like the way the Minnesotans prononced the name (Hel-E-na), so shifted the emphasis to the first syllable and slurred the second "e" and that has become the accepted pronunciation for the Montana town. A post office was established in August 1865 with John Potter as postmaster. **Helena** soon became one of the most important towns in the Territory, so in 1870 a patent for its townsite was requested and granted. The discovery of placer gold and quartz gold and silver, as well as lead, in the nearby areas boomed the city. It was incorporated in 1881 and a railroad reached it in 1883. In 1875 **Helena** became capital of the Territory, taking the post away from protesting Virginia City. On November 8, 1889 when Montana became a state the question immediately arose as to where the permanent capital should be located, because in Territorial days, Bannack, Virginia City, and **Helena** had all served in that capacity. Back in 1875, Colonel Broadwater's Diamond R Freight Company, whose bull trains had for years hauled mechandise into **Helena** from Fort Benton, was engaged to move the Territorial Capital from Virginia City to **Helena**. The papers and records were loaded up on April 2 and arrived in **Helena** on April 11. The second floor of Black Block at 105 Broadway had been rented ($650 per year) for Territorial Headquarters. The Lewis and Clark County Courthouse was completed in 1885, and Territorial offices moved into it in 1885. With the change to statehood in 1889, these headquarters automatically became those of the state and the courthouse became the State Capitol. The fight for a permanent location of the state capital pitted Marcus Daly and his backing of Anaconda against William A. Clark who supported **Helena**. **Helena** won and in October 1898, ground was broken for the new Capitol buildings which were to be dedicated on July 4, 1902.

Hellgate (Granite) had a post office from 1907-1909. It was near Bearmouth; George Snyder was postmaster.

Hellgate was once a thriving trading post near the present city of Missoula. The post office was established November 25, 1862 (Washington Territory), with Frank Worden as postmaster, and was moved to Missoula Mills in 1866. Long before the white man came this area was familiar to both the Flathead and Blackfeet Indians. The Flathead had to pass through the canyon east of the Missoula Valley to reach the plains for their periodic buffalo hunts, and they were often attacked by Blackfeet near the entrance to the canyon. "The reputation of the place caused French-Canadian trappers to call it *Porte de l'Enfer* or, the Gates of Hell" (Salisbury). Dimsdale, in his famous history, *The Vigilantes of Montana* (1866), says the vigilantes "knew that the robbers were to be found at **Hell Gate**, which

134

was so named because it was the road which the Indians took when on the war path, and intent on scalping and other pleasant little amusements, in the line of ravishing, plundering, fire raising, etc. for the exhibition of which genteel proclivities the Eastern folks recommend a national donation of blankets and supplies to keep the things up. . . . If the Indians were left to the Vigilantes of Montana, they would contract to change their habits at small cost." Christopher P. Higgins, a member of the July 1855 treaty-making party, took a special interest in the **Hell Gate** region; he saw it as an ideal place for a trading center because of the meeting of trails there and the friendliness of the Flatheads. In 1860 Higgins returned to **Hell Gate** with his partner, Frank L. Worden, to found a trading center; they located the new store on the Mullan Road, which was then under construction. East-west travel stopped at the Higgins-Worden store for supplies. And the store attracted other enterprises: a blacksmith shop, a livery stable, a "refreshment center," and a traveler's hotel. The store prospered, but by 1866 the rush was over and people were moving to Missoula Mills five or six miles to the east.

HELMVILLE (Powell), is in the mountains near where Nevada Creek empties into the Blackfoot River, and is a gathering place for scattered farmers and ranchers in the large surrounding valley. Its annual Labor Day Rodeo is widely known. The town was named for Henry Helm, a pioneer settler. The post office was established in 1872 with Alvin Lincoln as postmaster.

Henderson (Gallatin) was on postal records July-November 1875 with Stokes Henderson designated as postmaster.

Henderson (Mineral), near DeBorgia, was named for Benjamin Henderson, the owner of the townsite, a saw mill operator, and a businessman influential in the lumber industry. The post office opened in 1904 with Alice Dugal as postmaster and closed in 1930. **Henderson** was primarily a logging community which claimed a population of 1,400 in the early 1900s. A dam was built at **Henderson** on the Clark Fork River in 1907. Much of the material for the dam came from a cyclone-ravaged jack pine forest with plenty of uprooted trees. Heavy winter snows curtailed all winter activity. **Henderson** was once a station on the Northern Pacific; little is left there now.

Henkel (Fergus) was named for the postmaster, Delia Henkel. The office was established in 1919 but has since been discontinued.

Hepler (Cascade) was near Sun River and had a post office 1894-1903; Charles Walker was the first postmaster. In later years Roy and John Hepler had cattle ranches in Madison and Jefferson counties.

HERON (Sanders) is almost on the Idaho border. The post office for this town on the Clark Fork River opened in 1884 with William Quirk in charge; it was closed in 1888 and reopened in 1891. By 1915, Henry Schwindt's fine frame general merchandise store also housed the post office. A log building served for the River Echoes school.

Hervin (Chouteau) had a post office 1917-21 with Melvin Nelson in charge. The office was open again in 1922 and 1923.

Hesper (Yellowstone) adjoins the old Hesper Ranch, which was named for Hesper or Hesperus, the evening star. In classical mythology, this star was the king of western lands — one wonders what pioneer dreams went into the naming of places! A post office was active at **Hesper** (Fred Heitkamp, postmaster) 1912-34.

Hibbard (Treasure) was named for George Hibbard, general passenger agent for the Milwaukee Railroad at Seattle. The post office opened in 1912 with Sadie Rasque in charge and closed in 1924.

Hicks (Park) had a post office 1892-94 with Burt Crandal as postmaster.

Hidden Lake A hidden lake of great beauty and interest is the source of the name of this station in Glacier National Park (Rowe). The station was originally called Garry but was changed in 1926 when the Great Northern was seeking enticing names for the places along its line.

Highfield (Fergus) had a post office 1890-1905; Donald Fowler was the first postmaster. It was near Limegrove.

Highland (Madison) was a mining camp in Alder Gulch.

Highlands (Gallatin) was originally called Baker, and in 1900 the name was changed to Josephine. The **Highlands** post office operated 1896-1900; Fannie Cowan was postmaster.

High Line is a much-used Montana term which indicates both the route laid out by the Great Northern Railroad and US Highway 2 where it traverses the windswept, glaciated plains and shallow valleys of northern Montana. Much of the **High Line** follows the Missouri and Milk rivers, extending roughly from Poplar past Fort Peck Reservoir, to Glasgow and Malta, Chinook and Havre, and on to Shelby, Cut Bank, and Browning, ending up in Glacier National Park.

Highview (Silver Bow) was named by the Northern Pacific for its location at the summit of the Continental Divide.

HIGHWOOD (Chouteau) is some twenty-five miles east of Great Falls in the center of early cattle-grazing land. Cowboys from here went to Fort Benton for supplies that were shipped up the Missouri by riverboat — a journey of about twenty miles as the cowboys rode. It has been suggested that the town, mountain, and creek were so named because in this plains district trees grew high upon the old, volcanic Highwood Mountains (Rowe). A post office established in March 1881 was discontinued and reestablished three times before 1886, when it was reopened and has remained so to date. Isaac McCord was postmaster back in 1881.

HILGER (Fergus) is north of Lewistown and was named for David J. Hilger, early resident and prominent citizen of the area. For many years Hilger was secretary of the Montana Historical Society at Helena. The town was originally known as Kendal, after a mining camp a few miles to the west. The post office opened in 1911 with Jesse Wicks as postmaster. In 1913, three heavy gold bars were put on the train at **Hilger**, the last gold shipment from the Kendal Mine, according to the Wells Fargo messenger, Frank Kowatch, who was there to deposit the gold in the train's special safe.

Hilgersville (Lewis and Clark), named for postmaster Nicholas Hilger, was a post office 1886-87 and April-May 1890.

Hill (Liberty) had a post office 1898-1954; James Hamilton was the first postmaster.

Hill (Missoula) had a post office 1890-93 with John Bowen as postmaster.

Hill County is in the northern part of the state, bordering Canada and encompassing part of the Rocky Boy Indian Reservation. Havre is the county seat. **Hill County** was originally part of Chouteau County. "Havre had.become the center of such a thriving area by 1911 that the citizens began campaigning to get a separate county carved out of old Chouteau County. The movement finally succeeded, and on February 24, 1912, **Hill County** was formed and named after James J. Hill, the 'empire builder' (Havre *Daily News;* March 26, 1937)." In 1920-21 parts of **Hill County** were taken to form Liberty County. In 1915 there were forty active post offices; sixty years later only a dozen remained.

Hillcrest, Hill Crest (Custer) had a post office 1915-35; the first postmaster was Julius Watkins.

Hillman (Gallatin) was a station on the Bozeman-Menard branch line named for A. J. Hillman, commercial agent for the Milwaukee Railroad.

Hillsboro (Carbon) is near the border of Big Horn County. When the post office was opened in 1915, it was in the log cabin of postmaster G. William Barry; when the office closed in 1945 the mail was ordered to Kane, Wyoming, the nearest post office. Yellowtail Reservoir has now put Kane under water. The crumbling remains of **Hillsboro** are near Barry's Landing on the man-made lake in Big Horn Canyon.

Hillsdale (Gallatin) had a post office most of the time from its opening in 1881 (Benajah Morse, postmaster) to its closing in 1897.

Hillside (Garfield) had its post office established in 1914 and was located in the home of Mr. and Mrs. Ole Johnson for many years. Homesteaders came to the area about 1910; before that it was occupied by the small "cow outfits." The only way to get to or from Miles City and the railroad was by stagecoach; it carried mail, passengers and items ordered by the isolated residents of Garfield County. Passengers were often asked to hold breakable items on their laps. A halfway house was located near **Hillside** in the extreme southeastern corner of the county, a good day's journey from Miles City. The halfway house served as a kind of hotel, eating place, and post office for travelers and residents of the area. The post office was discontinued in 1945.

HINGHAM (Hill), on the High Line, is a shipping and storing station for stock and grain. The post office opened in 1910 with Peter Carrier as postmaster.

The **Hingham** *Review* reported, "We now have a thriving town in which 20 firms are doing business . . . this time last year, there was no semblance of a town here. Peter Carrier had come in on the Great Northern in 1909, bought some real estate and began developing a town. By 1912 elevators were built, Dr. Arthur Husser came and a hospital and drug store opened. **Hingham** was perhaps the best town on the Hi-line in those early days. It was euphemistically known as 'the progressive city, a city built on the square.' "

HINSDALE (Valley) is north of Glasgow on the Milk River. According to one writer, it was named for a town in New Hampshire after a "spin of the globe;" but according to another source, it was named for a town in Illinois (see **Harlem**). North of **Hinsdale** on Rock Creek are some of the most spectacular and little-known badlands in Montana. "It is sort of a pint sized Grand Canyon with an Old West atmosphere thrown in" (Willard). The post office was established in 1891 with Thomas Peacock as postmaster.

HOBSON (Judith Basin) was named for S. S. Hobson, an early-day cowboy and rancher who lived between **Hobson** and Utica on the Judith River and owned the Campbell and Clendenan ranches. He later became a state senator from Judith Basin County. The post office was moved from Philbrook to the new town of **Hobson** when the Great Northern branchline was built in 1907-08. For a short while, the office in its new location continued to be called Philbrook and the railroad station was called **Hobson**. In 1912 the railroad name prevailed and the post office was established under that name, too. Thomas Nicholson was the postmaster (*Furrows and Trails in Judith Basin*).

Hockett's, Hockett (Custer) was named for the family of first postmaster Martha Hockett. The office opened in 1889 and was closed for a final time in 1912 when the postal area name became Kimball.

Hodges (Dawson) is halfway between Glendive and the North Dakota border. This was a station on the Northern Pacific named after Leonard Hodges, superintendent of tree planting for the railroad. The post office was open 1898-1968; Charley Anderson was the first postmaster.

Hodson (Jefferson) was briefly the name of a Jefferson County post office February-November 1887; John Baldwin was appointed postmaster.

Hoffman (Park), near Chimney Rock, was named for George Hoffman, the first postmaster. The office was open 1900-1904 and 1909-18.

Hoffmanville (Richland) came into existence in 1917 when the 'Great Western Sugar Company located a plant here. The town was first known as Midway, but the name was changed to honor Albert Hoffman, a farmer who donated the land to the Northern Pacific for a station.

Hogan (Lewis and Clark) had a post office 1887-1919; Joseph Embody was the first postmaster. It was near Augusta.

HOGELAND (Blaine) is twelve miles from Canada. It was named for A. H. Hogeland, who was for many years chief engineer for the Great Northern Railroad. The boom for this homesteading area came with the railroad in 1928. The post office was established that year with Stener Wiprud as postmaster; the office from Twete also moved to **Hogeland**. Buildings sprang up, and at one time **Hogeland** consisted of a hotel, three restaurants, two general stores, two pool halls, two garages, a filling station, a butcher shop, three elevators, a lumberyard, a blacksmith shop, confectionary, hardware store, implement dealer, a weekly newspaper, a church, school, and a dairy. By 1960 the population had dwindled to 80. **Hogeland** was at the end of the Great Northern spur that took off from the main line at Saco.

Hog-Em (Broadwater) was once a mining camp between Radersburg and Bedford that was later the village of Springfield. The colorful name was originated by disappointed miners, who found that a few men had "hogged up" the pay claims in the area. (Western Interpretive Services). Two other camps there had equally descriptive names: Cheat-Em and Rob-Em.

Holland, Holland Settlement (Gallatin) was settled by a group of Dutch colonists, who persistently held on to Old World customs and traditions. It was also a station on the Milwaukee Railroad (see **Amsterdam** and **Churchill**.).

Holland Lake (Powell) was named for the first settler, B. B. Holland.

Hollandville (Blaine) was settled by Dutch immigrants. The post office opened in 1918 with Martin Vande Ven as postmaster; it has since been discontinued.

Holmes (Chouteau) was named for Warren Holmes, the first postmaster. The office was open 1904-11; the mail was then sent to Cleveland.

Holt (Flathead) was near Big Fork and had a post office 1890-1908 and 1912-15; Eugene Sears was the first postmaster.

Holter (Lewis and Clark) was named for Anton M. Holter, a prominent pioneer resident and Helena businessman. Holter and his partner, Alexander Evenson, came to Virginia City in 1863 and set up a water-powered sawmill to supply the demand for lumber of Alder Gulch miners. Since the mill was primitive and the demand was great, larger mining companies sometimes waylaid loads of lumber belonging to Holter and Evenson and intended for another mine; though they took every board, they were always careful to pay according to the bill of lading that was with the load (*Not in Precious Metals Alone*). When the **Holter** post office was established in 1908 with Albert J. Reed as postmaster, it took over the postal area formerly served by the Hauserlake office. The **Holter** office was discontinued in 1918.

Holter Dam (Lewis and Clark), on the Missouri River, was completed in 1918.

Home Creek Butte is a landmark so named because early range riders could find their direction by it — it is nearly a mile high near where the Stacy post office used to be (*Fanning the Embers*).

Home Park (Madison), near Alder, had a post office 1879-94 and 1895-1919; James Snapp was postmaster. The office was located on the Home Park Ranch, which is now a part of the Gilbert Livestock Company.

Homestake (Jefferson), on the Continental Divide southwest of Butte, was a station on the Northern Pacific named for an old mining camp there. "Stake" was a popular term with prospectors: one used a stake to mark a claim, thus "staked out a claim;" you borrowed enough money for a "grub stake" or enough food to survive while you prospected. When you struck "pay dirt," you made your "stake," and the ultimate in success was to find enough gold for a "homestake," meaning you could now afford to take your "stake" and go home to the States from Montana Territory or other mining areas (Mildred Fielder, Homestake Mine, Lead, South Dakota). The **Homestake**, Montana, post office opened in 1899 with Rosey Garrity in charge; it closed in 1956.

Homestead, (Jefferson) near Whitehall, was an old town along the railroad but supported by mining activity in the early days.

HOMESTEAD (Sheridan) had a post office from 1907-1910, and again from 1911 to the present. It was reopened to take over the postal area formerly served by the Barford office. **Homestead** is on the Big Muddy, south of Medicine Lake in Sheridan County. It was a station on the Great Northern and when the boxcar depot was set down along the tracks the name of Barford was put on it because it was near the place where N Bar N cattle were forded across the river. The area was once called Pederson and then Fort Peck but the name of **Homestead** was finally decided upon as suitable because this area owed its beginning to the homesteading settlers.

Honor, (Hill) near Rudyard, had a post office from 1913-1915 with Lula

Ladwig as postmaster.

Hoosac (Fergus) was a station on the Milwaukee named for the nearby tunnel. C. A. Goodnow had called the tunnel after one by that name in the Berkshire Mountains. **Hoosac** is near the headwaters of the Judith River. It had a post office from 1914-1919; James Finney was postmaster.

Hoover (Meagher) had a post office from 1879-1880 with William Buchanan in charge.

Hope (Jefferson) was the name of a post office from 1887-1891. Ellis Elmer was postmaster there.

Hope (Yellowstone) was also the name of a post office from 1896-1898. B. H. Brown was postmaster.

Hopp (Chouteau) was named for first postmaster Wilhelm Hopp. The office was active from 1914-1944.

Hoppers was a station on the Northern Pacific between Bozeman and Livingston and was named for John Hoppe who settled near there in 1877.

Hopsonville, (Rosebud) near Forsyth, was named for a rancher; Estelle Hopson was the first postmaster. The office operated from 1915-1925.

Horr (Park) was a post office from 1889-1904 when the name was changed to Electric. Laura Pinkston was the first postmaster. It was named for Harry Horr and Major Joseph Horr, who were associated with the coal mining industry there.

Horse Abattoir (Powder River) was never a town, but it was an establishment, and for a brief period, was important to the economy of Montana. Located near the place where U.S. Highway 212 crosses the Powder River, it was a profitable venture when thousands of horses cluttered the range after farm mechanization reduced the market for horses. It was fully equipped with modern slaughterhouse machinery. Horses were driven in from large corrals, shot, skinned, boned, and converted into a kind of corned "beef," much of which was shipped to Belgium. When there were no longer herds of surplus horses, the abattoir closed and the government took over the plant to use as a tannery for hides and pelts.

Horse Creek (McCone) was a post office in service from 1912-1925; Samuel Strecker was postmaster. The mail was then sent to Circle. Postal records say the post office was formerly called St. Joe. There was also a Horse Creek settlement in Sheridan County. The CS ranch was there and was most active between 1910-1914.

Horse Plains (Sanders) had a post office from 1869-1883 in old Missoula County. L. R. Hilleary was the first postmaster. The name was changed to Plains. The lush grass and comparatively mild winters made this a good area to pasture horses.

Horse Prairie (Beaverhead) is a mining ghost town near Bannack and Dillon. It was named for a creek of that name. A mining district was organized at **Horse Prairie** in 1863 by eleven men. The first permanent settlers were Barretts and Stinebergers, who began to farm the land about 1875. The Indians were especially troublesome to the settlers. A post office was established in 1869 with Joseph Yeanan as postmaster. The office was closed from 1871-1875 and then open until 1888; the mail was then sent to Amesville.

Horton (Custer) was a station on the Northern Pacific near the western border of the county. It had a post office from 1899-1904 with Nils Kildahl in charge. The office was open again from 1915-1945.

Hosey (Blaine) was named for the family of the first postmaster, Vida McHose. It was near Warwick. The office was open from 1927-1935.

Hotchkiss (Carter) was named for the first postmaster, Stephen Hotchkiss. The office was open from 1885-1892. It was near Beebe.

HOTSPRINGS (Sanders) is at the edge of the Flathead Indian Reservation. It was named for the natural hot springs found there. Montana, being "next door" to the boiling geysers and underground fireholes of Yellowstone Park, has many natural hot springs, most of them in the southwestern part of the state. Others are: Alhambra, Anderson, Barkell, Boulder, Bozeman, Chico, Cowin, Elkhorn, Gregson, Hunter's, Lolo, Medicine, Pipestone, Potosi, Quinn's, Sleeping Child, Sun River Medicine, Thompson and Siegler's. The post office for the Sanders County **Hot Springs** opened in 1913 with Henry E. Smith as postmaster.

Houskin (Cascade) was a post office from 1899-1911. William Irwin was the first postmaster.

Howard, (Rosebud) near Forsyth, had a post office established in 1883. Conflicting ideas relate to the origin of the town's name. One is that it was named for William A. Howard, land commissioner for the Northern Pacific Railroad in 1872. Samuel Newnes was the first postmaster and the office had a final closing in 1924.

Howie, (Sweetgrass) near Big Timber, had a post office from 1892-1915. Waborn Harrison was the first postmaster and postal notes say the area was formerly called **Sweet Grass**.

Hoyle (Fergus) was named for the family of postmaster Mary Hoyle. The office was open from 1916-1918.

Hoyt (Dawson) was a station south of Glendive. It was named for Colgate Hoyt, director of the Northern Pacific Railroad from 1887-1893. A post office was active there from 1892-1895; Edward Delano was postmaster. It was open again from January 1905-January 1906.

Hubbart (Flathead) was near Marion and had a post office from 1905-1917. William Frederic was the first postmaster.

Hubble (Sweetgrass) had a post office from 1914-1933; Solomon J. Craft was postmaster.

Huffine (Gallatin) was a station on the Bozeman-Menard branch of the Milwaukee. It was named for Francis M. Huffine, a farmer who settled there in 1890. The road between Bozeman and Bozeman Hot Springs is still called Huffine Lane.

Hughesville (Judith Basin) was named for P. H. Hughes, co-discoverer with "Buck" Barker, of ore deposits that developed into the Barker Mining District. Rich silver and lead ore from this region was hauled by bull team to Fort Benton, shipped down the Missouri River to the Mississippi and thence to New Orleans, where it transferred to ocean steamers for shipment to smelters in Swansea, Wales. Postal records show a post office in **Hughesville** (then Meagher County) from 1881-1883 with Charles Mix as postmaster, and from 1891-1892. The records also show a **Hughesville** office (Cascade-Judith Basin) operating from 1912-1938; Henry Daniel was postmaster. It was open again from 1942-1943.

The mine was near Clendenin and according to newspaper accounts the "elite" of Great Falls society occasionally took excursion trips by rail and coach to visit the mining camps. An "annual" ball was held at the Clendenin Hotel. The mines were reactivated in the early 1900s.

Hungry Hollow (Blaine) is a small community southwest of Lloyd. The "Hollow" had been settled in the spring of 1901 when everything was green and beautiful. "The settlers were homesteading on small acreages, not knowing that the soil was too shallow for farming and having no idea how long the winters were. Most of them starved out the first year. . . . The community was first christened **Hungry hollow** because there was so much hunger there that first winter of 1901-2." (Allison) Maddux was the nearest post office.

HUNGRY HORSE (Flathead) is at the mouth of the lake formed by a government dam, completed in 1952, which also bears the name "Hungry Horse." The post office opened in 1948 with Ellis Strong as postmaster. In 1947, Joseph Kinsey Howard wrote, ". . . Up in Northwestern Montana, just south of the western entrance to Glacier National Park is **Hungry Horse**, site of a long-projected dam development on the Flathead River. . . . On and around the dam site a group of "boom towns" living solely on beer and hope have sprung up. There has been no actual work on the dam due to recent Congressional economy campaigns, God knows when there will be. . . . Nevertheless, the towns of **Hungry Horse** and Martin City are booming. . . . The area is among the most beautiful in the Northwest, with several mountain ranges in close proximity and two or three big lakes." (*Not in Precious Metals Alone*).

Hunter's Hot Springs (Park) is a resort town named for Dr. Andrew J. Hunter. He was the first white man to discover the medicinal qualities of the springs. He came there in July 1864 and also served as postmaster when the office was established in 1878. It was discontinued in 1932. The following is from the *Yellowstone Journal* of October 9, 1879: "Dr. A. H. [sic] Hunter of Hunter's Springs has raised sugar cane this season with stalks over six feet in height." His Crow Indian neighbors did not resent his coming and often came to bathe in his springs.

HUNTLEY, (Yellowstone) is ten miles north of Billings. It was named for S. S. Huntley, a pioneer stockman. The town "boomed" as the administrative center for the Huntley Irrigation Project. This project was completed in 1907, the first, and one of the most successful in Montana. It was made possible by the Reclamation Act of 1902 and led to large scale irrigated farming in the area. The post office was established in 1877 with Omar Hoskins as postmaster. It was cattle country then. That office closed in 1886, and was open again from 1890-1892. It was opened again in 1895 and has remained so to date. S. S. Huntley set up a store in 1876 and ran a ferry boat across the river. It was a stage stop on the Bozeman-Miles City line and headquarters for trappers.

Hurst (Meagher) had a post office 1884-1891 with Robert McClatchey as postmaster.

HUSON, (Missoula) a station, post office, and store, was named for H. S. Huson, engineer on construction for the Northern Pacific Railroad. The post office opened in 1898 with Napoleon Glaude, operator of the lime kiln, as postmaster. The postal name for the area was formerly Glaude, as the town began when Glaude built his hotel there, though the first activity in the Huson area was in 1872 when Eusebe Scheffer opened his road house and stage station for the convenience of the Cedar Creek miners. Beyond here the road was impassable for anything but pack strings and small wagons. Lime was hauled to Missoula and Huson grew to meet the needs of lumberjacks and miners — in fact most of the needs were met by Glaudes Hotel. In the basement were a wine cellar, a lime kiln, a root cellar and general storage. The ground floor consisted of businesses and living quarters. The second story had hotel rooms and a dance hall in it (*Frenchtown Valley Footprints*).

Hutton (Big Horn) is on Rosebud Creek about half-way between Cache Creek and the mouth of Big Thompson Creek. It was named for Joel W. Hutton, a rancher and the first postmaster. The post office, established in September 1889, was discontinued in February 1901, and the mail sent to Kirby. **Hutton** was found to be within the boundaries of the territory declared Indian Reservation. "Major James McLaughlin negotiated in behalf of the Northern Cheyenne in 1898. He bought out and removed all settlers from within the Reservation given to the Cheyennes by the Executive Order of November 26, 1884. For the sume of $151,000, he bought out all valid white claims including the town of **Hutton** (Ralph Shane). Arthur Dickson of Dayton, Wyoming wrote: "We were running a general store at **Hutton**, Montana, in the '90s. One night in the fall of 1897 we were wakened by a neighbor who reported there was trouble with the Indians. A sheep herder by the name of Hoover surprised a couple of Indian youths butchering a beef. They shot Hoover and his dog 'and the fat was in the fire.' " Families hurriedly packed up and went to Sheridan (Wyoming) or to Crow Agency or the OD ranch. This and other scares led to the establishment of Ft. Mackenzie in Sheridan, Wyoming.

Hyde, (Custer) near Etchetah, had a post office from February-July 1883; George Hyde was postmaster.

Hyde (Gallatin) was also named for the first postmaster; this one was Herbert A. Hyde. The office was open from 1892-1911; it was near Logan.

Hydro (Blaine) was near Norheim and had a post office from 1914-1926. John Stuckle was the first postmaster.

Hyfield, (Musselshell) near Wheaton, had a post office from 1912-1914 with Mary Redfield as postmaster.

Hylent (Sanders) was formerly called Trout Creek. The post office was established as **Hylent** in May 1910 with Nerus Hurst as postmaster. In December of the same year the name was changed back to Trout Creek.

HYSHAM, (Treasure) the county seat, had a post office established in 1907 with James Lockard as postmaster. Charles J. Hysham, a Texas trail herder, was connected with the Flying E ranch that ran several thousand head of cattle on the Crow Indian Reservation land south of the Yellowstone River. A crossroads store stood where the town now stands. Mr. Hysham was one of the best customers, putting in large orders that often had to be filled with shipments from the East. After he moved away, the developing town was named for him (1963 booklet, Hysham High School).

I

Ida (Cascade County) had a post office from June 1888 to August 1889 with Edward Reinicke as postmaster. It was near Great Falls.

Illiad (Choteau) near Big Sandy had a post office from 1914 to 1944. Virginia Donnell was the first postmaster.

Independence is a mining ghost town south of Big Timber in Sweet Grass County. It was part of the Boulder mining district in the Absaroka Range where claims were made and ore discovered. The region was almost inaccessible and could be gotten to only by difficult trails. During the height of the mining boom in 1893 a tri-weekly stage from Big Timber did come in to bring mail, express, and passengers. Bits of rusting machinery and logs from an old cabin are all that remain. **Independence** had a post office from 1892 to 1895 with John Anderson as first postmaster.

Inga (Chouteau County) had a post office established in 1915 with Hattie Jackson as postmaster. It was closed in 1935.

INGOMAR (Rosebud County) is a trade center for the surrounding sheep raising area. It has one of the largest sheep shearing plants in the state. The post office opened in 1910 with Simon Sigman as postmaster. In the early days **Ingomar** and Sumatra were the chief trading towns for the homesteaders in western Garfield County. Freight wagons were often caught in the Gumbo Flats — a wide strip of land south of Sand Springs that can't be crossed when it's wet.

Intake (Dawson County) north of Glendive, it came into being when the irrigation dam was built across the Yellowstone River. It is the location for the "intake" of the irrigation system. The post office was opened in 1911 as the homesteaders came in. Gilbert Woodwick was the first postmaster. In 1965 **Intake** became a rural station out of Glendive.

INVERNESS (Hill County) is on the Highline west of Havre. It was named by "Scotty" Watson, pioneer stockman in memory of his native town in Scotland. The Scottish town is located on the inlet to Loch Ness, famous for the Loch Ness monster. A post office was opened in **Inverness**, Montana in 1909 with Adolph Gesche as postmaster. The homesteaders were beginning to arrive. Many of them who were to settle in this area came to **Inverness** by train and from there went out to look for a suitable location. The majority of them came from Minnesota and North Dakota — the greatest number arriving in 1910-12. There were good years like 1915 and 1916 but they were to be followed by extreme drought and by 1918 many homesteaders gave up and moved away. The tar paper shacks disintegrated and the tumbleweeds took over. Those who stayed bought up more land and built up larger and more economically sound units than the 160 acre homesteads. (Information from *Tumbleweeds and Tar Paper Shacks* published by the Minneota Club.)

Iona was a station on the Northern Pacific in Dawson County.

Irene, northwest of Ryegate in the area that was to become Golden Valley

County, had a post office established in 1894. It was named by Allison P. "Old Ike" Brewington for his wife Emma Irene who served as postmaster and maintained the office on his ranch until 1910 when the postal service was moved to Rothiemay. "Old Ike" was a veteran of the gold fields at Alder Gulch and Last Chance Gulch and by 1869 returned to Kansas financially successful. He brought his family back to Montana Territory in 1882, camping in a slough where the Billings Fairgrounds now stand. Later they lived in a log cabin with dirt floors covered with buffalo hides located near Lavina and near his timber claim. In 1884 the family settled on Swimming Woman Creek below the Central Snowy Mountains. (Information from Mary Morsanny.)

Iron Mountain (Mineral) was a station named for the Iron Mountain Mine, which was really a lead and zinc mine. The mine was discovered in 1888 by J. K. Pardee. The name of the station was changed to Superior in 1929 (according to J. P. Rowe) to agree with the town and county seat which was just across the Clark Fork River from the station. Postal records show an **Iron Mountain** office from 1891-1949 with Charles Beall as the first postmaster.

Iron Rod (Madison), "strung along both sides of the river" and connected by a swinging footbridge, was first known as Upper Silver Star and then as Ragtown. There were a number of cabins and larger houses, a long, dirt-roofed barn used as a relay station for stage horses, sleeping accommodations for travelers and a saloon. Freight rates from Corinne, Utah (the end of the railroad), to **Iron Rod** were $3.75 per hundred pounds. According to George Carkeek, a pioneer rancher of Madison County, the town took its new name when a big bridge was built across the Jefferson River and its iron rods were painted red. Carkeek used to ride horseback out from Butte to go fishing here. There was a post office 1869-72 and 1876-82.

On May 14, 1873, the Philadelphia *Ledger* carried the following article concerning postal facilities in Montana Territory: "An agent . . . officially visiting various offices in Montana Territory for the purposes of correcting any irregularities of postmaster, stopped at **Iron Rod**. Going into the post office he found the room divided into three sections; first a saloon, next the post office, and last a faro bank. The mail bag was brought in and a rough looking customer opened it up and emptied the contents on the floor. The entire crowd at once got down on their hands and knees and commenced overhauling letters . . . and selected such as they wanted. After they were through, the remaining letters were shoveled into a candlebox and placed on the bar. The special agent, thinking the office needed regulating, asked the bartender if he were the postmaster. . . . He answered, 'No, he's gone to Hell's Canyon, and by thunder Bill Jones has got to run this office next week. It's his turn.' The government official . . . demanded the keys to the 'office.' The bartender . . . placed the candlebox on the floor, gave it a kick sending it out the door, saying, 'There's your post office and now get.' The agent says 'Knowing the customs of the country, I lost no time following this advice and got.' The office was discontinued" (*Montana Magazine of History*, January 1953).

Ironton (Fergus) had a post office approved but the order was rescinded in 1898. John Gray was to have been postmaster.

Irwin (Deer Lodge) had a post office approved and a postmaster, Charles Dobson, was appointed, but the office was never in operation. The name was carried on postal records 1896-99.

Isabel (Powell) had a post office December 1885-January 1888; John Fitzpatrick was the first postmaster. It was near Junction.

ISMAY (Custer) began as a Milwaukee station on O'Fallon Creek. One story is that it was named for Isabelle and Mary Peck, daughters of George W. Peck, general counsel for the railroad (Rowe); however, elsewhere the names are given as Isabel and May Earling, daughters of another railroad official (*Wheels Across Montana's Prairies*). **Ismay** was on the old stage line that ran from Fort Lincoln at Bismarck to Fort Keogh (Miles City) 1878-83. The old trail came down the ravine in the north part of town and crossed O'Fallon Creek here. The town originated with the building of the Milwaukee Railroad in 1907. The first school was established by Edwin Stanton in a tent on Mr. Cass's place; the Union Sunday School met in a lumber office. By 1910 the homesteaders were coming. Many lived in tents until shacks could be built. In October Addie Stewart wrote: "We do not take the *Democrat* now. We had to cut out every expense that was not absolutely necessary. We are facing the hardest winter we ever did. I am sure I don't know how we will come out. I'll tell you better in the spring" (*Not in Precious Metals Alone*).

Ivanell (Rosebud), near Ingomar, had a post office 1915-26; Clara Buck was the first postmaster.

--------------- **J** ---------------

JACKSON (Beaverhead) is on the Big Hole River twenty miles from Idaho by snowshoe and forty-five by automobile. The area, now a famous winter sports resort, was named for Anton Jackson, who also served as first postmaster. The office opened in 1896.

Japan (Musselshell) was once a siding on the old Puget Sound Railroad, later the Milwaukee, between Musselshell and Melstone.

Jardine (Park), near Gardiner, was named for A. C. Jardine, secretary of the Bear Gulch Mining Company when a post office was approved in December 1898. **Jardine** has been called the "most wide awake gold camp in the state" in 1900, and Jardine's wife was said to be the only "highly cultured lady" in Bear Gulch. The mines were last operated during World War II but the little mountain community, which is accessible only by a steep gravel road, has taken on new life as a recreation area. In recent years the Blankenship family turned an old mine building into a ski lodge, refurbished some of the old log homes, and built a ski run (Billings *Gazette*; February 28, 1971).

Java (Richland), near Mondak, had a post office 1907-13 named for Anton Jevnager, the first postmaster, who owned the grocery and hardware store. The town was half in North Dakota and half in Montana; the Blind Pig Saloon operated on the Montana side.

Jaw Bone Railroad was officially known as the Montana Central; the nickname **Jaw Bone** was given to it because of the generous use of "jaw-bone" (i.e., promises or talk) in the promotion of its construction. But its builders seemed to have little basis for their hopes, and after its completion, the Northern Pacific requested a timetable of the new road to incorporate in its own. "There were no towns on the line," said Richard Harlow, president of the **Jaw Bone**, "Nor . . . any provocation for towns . . . but I drew up a schedule and located plenty of them. Two young ladies (Fan and Lulu) were visiting at my house. On the timetable you will find . . . Fanalulu just below...Ringling" (Stearns). The Chicago, Milwaukee, St. Paul and Pacific began construction in 1906, entering Montana near Baker, following a route through the Musselshell Valley and reaching Harlowton in 1908. From Harlowton to Lombard and to Lewistown, it used tracks of the old "**Jawbone**" line (it was sometimes spelled as one word, sometimes as two). The "**Jawbone**" was plagued with snow during its short life; one train was stalled in drifts from late February to early April.

Jeffers (Madison) is just across the Madison River from Ennis. The ranches that surround it are some of the oldest in the valley. It was named for Myron D. Jeffers, a New York native who worked his way west as a miner and civil engineer. In 1864 he came to Madison and freighted for the gold camps, in 1869 he trailed a herd of cattle up from Texas and sold them at Bannack, and in 1871 he trailed in another herd from Texas and noted in his diary that 1,894 cattle and 37 head of horses were "road branded." With this herd he started the Yellow Barn Cattle Ranch. His wife Florence (nee Switzer) was the first postmaster at **Jeffers** when the office opened in 1903; the Switzer Store served as post office and general merchandise headquarters for many years. From 1940 until the office closed in 1975, Helen Wonder served as postmaster and community storekeeper.

Jefferson Bridge (Madison) was named because it was near the bridge that crossed the Jefferson River. The post office opened in 1866 with Charles Flanagin as postmaster. In 1870 the postal name for the area was changed to Fish Creek.

JEFFERSON CITY (Jefferson) is twelve miles north of Boulder. It began in 1864 as a stage station on the freight and passenger line between Virginia City and Fort Benton. There was some mining activity here. The town took its name from the nearby river, which was named by Lewis and Clark for President Thomas Jefferson. A post office was established in 1866 with William Rutan as postmaster; the office was closed 1868-69 but reopened later that same year.

Jefferson County is in southwestern Montana and was named for the river that forms part of its southern boundary. The Continental Divide is its western boundary. The Jefferson River was named by Lewis and Clark in honor of Thomas Jefferson, who was President when they made their journey of exploration. **Jefferson County** was created February 2, 1865, one of the smallest of the original counties in Montana Territory. A part was taken to form Broadwater County in 1897. Boulder is the county seat.

Jefferson Island (Jefferson) took its name from an island formed by the slough or channels of the Jefferson River. A post office was opened in 1872 with Joseph Gans as postmaster. The postal name was changed to Cardwell in 1909, when the office moved across the river to the railroad station.

Jefferson Island (Madison) had a post office 1912-54 serving the area formerly called Lahood. Arthur Shaw was postmaster in 1912. For a ways, the Jefferson River forms the boundary between Jefferson and Madison counties.

Jenkins (Sheridan) had a post office established in 1912 with Peter

Hegseth as postmaster. In 1914 the name was changed to Dooley.

Jenks (Richland) was a Great Northern Railroad station named in compliment to C. O. Jenks, the company's vice-president.

Jennings (Lincoln) had a post office 1892-1952; Andrew Wigen was the first postmaster. The railroad line was completed from Kalispell to Jennings in 1892 and went on to the Cascades. Later the main line was rerouted but a spur line ran from **Jennings** to the Canadian oilfields. It also was finally abandoned.

Jens (Powell) was named for an area resident whose first name was Jens. A post office was open 1915-52; Jessie Madesen was the first postmaster.

Jerusalem (Beaverhead) was the name of a gold mining camp on Grasshopper Creek. Ore mined here was taken to the quartz mill at Centreville. This suburb of Bannack was apparently laid out by Thomas Holmes, who led the Holmes Train into the gold fields. A St. Paul newspaper reported that Holmes was founding New Jerusalem, where the streets were paved with gold.

Jessup (Flathead), near Creston, was named for Herbert Jessup, who was appointed postmaster when the office opened in 1909; it was discontinued in 1918.

Jimtown (Rosebud) is between Lame Deer and Colstrip in the Wolf Mountains. It used to be on the Indian Reservation, but was moved across the line. A bar and filling station make up the town.

Jitney (Petroleum) was a homesteaders' post office which came to life during the years that Henry Ford was revolutionizing the travel habits of Montana homesteaders; the town was named for the Model T, which was commonly known as a "jitney" or "tin lizzie." A post office opened in 1916 and was housed in the O. K. Hough home with Thomas Norton as postmaster. When the Houghs moved away, the office was moved to the Coxon place; Henry Coxon had come from Northumberland, England, in 1910 and landed in the Judith Basin. From there he traveled to Cat Creek Basin with a team, a sheep wagon, and one cow. He spent the rest of his life there except for the times he had to hire out to make enough money to keep his homestead going. The post office was discontinued in 1934.

Jocko (Lake) was named for the river which flows across the county, and the river was named for Jacques (Jocko) Raphael Finley, a trader and trapper for the Northwest and Hudson's Bay Fur companies (see **Rivers** section). The post office office opened in 1890 with Mary Dade in charge; it closed in 1914. **Jocko** is near Arlee, and the Jocko Valley is on the Flathead Indian Reservation. In 1872 the government ordered all Indians in this region to move to the Jocko Reservation. But Chief Charlo of the Flatheads refused to leave his beloved Bitterroot Valley, so tribal members who did move chose Arlee as their new leader.

Johns (Lewis and Clark) was named for William Johns, who had a ranch there in the early days.

Johnson (Broadwater), near Townsend, had a post office 1900-13; William H. C. Hale was postmaster.

Johnstown (Cascade) to quote from the *River Press*, Fort Benton, January 2, 1884. . . . "Following down Sun River to its confluence with the Missouri we come to a bran new burgh, which has been christened Johnstown;

after that staunch old pioneer, John Largent. This is a beautiful location for a large city, as the Missouri has no cut banks at this place, but the land gradually raises on both sides of the river. . . . E. B. Largent and Co., dealer in general merchandise, have all the business here to themselves. A substantial ferry has been put in here and does a good business in the summer months. Great Falls, just across the river, is still a paper town. . . ." (Jack Hayne).

Johnstown, Johnston (Chouteau) was an early post office originally listed in Lewis and Clark County. Edward Sargent was postmaster and the office was open 1884-87.

JOLIET (Carbon) is on Rock Creek. It was the shipping point for the rich produce area around it, as grains and garden products flourished in this irrigated valley. The post office was established in 1893 with Maud Smith as postmaster. "**Joliet** was reportedly named by a Northern Pacific Raiload official as he had come from Joliet, Illinois. The old Joliet stage road to to Gebo and Clark's Fork Valley is a very scenic drive" (Maryott).

Jones (Fergus) was named for William Jones, an early settler. Benjamin Jones was the first postmaster when the office opened in 1906; it closed in 1919 and mail was sent to Lewistown.

Joplin (Liberty) is a High Line train station where hopeful homesteaders arrived to settle on "free land." The post office opened in 1910 as they arrived, most from Missouri, Minnesota or North Dakota. Joseph Rehal was the first postmaster. This part of Montana, formerly a battleground of Piegan, Blood, and Gros Ventre Indians, became a land where homesteaders battled the elements and grasshoppers.

"Harvey filed on land 30 miles north of Joplin in 1912. He built a 12x14 shack, established residence and returned to Tulsa to get his family . . . we came by train to Inverness in December. . . . On a nice sunny day in January of 1913 we started on the long bumpy road to our claim in a lumber wagon. . . . Harvey had furnished this shack with a small cook stove, table made from a 20 pound cracker box with 1x4s for legs, one bed and a pair of springs hinged to the wall which could be folded down into a bed at night. The next day Harvey and Billie Adams went 20 miles . . . for a load of coal and enough water to last me and the three little girls while Harvey went to Havre, 84 miles away. He bought a team, wagon, more supplies and lumber for a barn and outhouse. . . . Spring came and we started breaking sod. . . . In 1914 neighbors went together and bought a house and moved it to a central location for the North Star school . . . also used for church services . . . we gathered tubsful of buffalo berries for jelly and jam . . . we hauled grain to market 32 miles away (Joplin) with teams and wagons. . . . I went to town three times in ten years and two of these were to Havre with toothaches. . . . In 1922 we decided to take a trip and see about some other way to earn a living . . . we sold everything except the land. . . . In 1932 we returned to the homestead . . . it was depression and the land had been rented but sadly uncared for, so with determination we started again. We broke more land, purchased more, bought tractors and machinery" (Adams). Those homesteaders, like these, who somehow managed to hold on to the land through the bad years could make a comeback and expand. But many more just had to give it up and leave.

JORDAN (Garfield), on Big Dry Creek, is the county seat of Garfield County. It began as a cow town in the late 1890s. The post office was established in 1899 with Arthur Jordan as postmaster.

There is some confusion concerning the name. County librarian Doris M. Hart says that the following version is accepted locally: The town was founded by Arthur Jordan, who requested that it be named for a friend of his who operated a big ranch supply house in Miles City. The friend's name was also "Jordan." Arthur Jordan "squatted on land there in 1896. His first home was a tent. Later he opened a general store and his customers were cowboys, who wanted not only tobacco, groceries, and range land supplies like lariats and new saddle cinches, but also the mail from back home. So Arthur Jordan applied for a post office and when the mail came in, he dumped it on the floor and patrons hunted out their letters. Later a small corner of the store was partitioned off for the post office, and still later even pigeon holes were installed. **Jordan**'s store was partly a dugout into the hill. In early days, the mailman came by horseback from Forsyth. One time he had to swim his horse across flooding Porcupine Creek and the first class mail sack got so wet that all letters written in ink were smeared, but the ones written in pencil were still legible. When the mail was finally brought directly to **Jordan** from Miles City, there was still no bridge over either Big Dry or Sand Creek. In good weather the mail was carried by horses and light spring wagon. On one trip, a young lady who was to teach in the local school was a passenger. The Big Dry was roaring high and the spring wagon upset as the driver tried to ford the stream. A young cowboy happened by and jumped in to rescue the teacher, but the mail floated downstream. A rancher, who had ordered a pair of cowboy boots, found one of them months later hung up on the branch of a tree. A new sewing machine was also washed away by the muddy water on that trip" (Highland).

Joppa (Rosebud), near Hathaway, was a siding on the Northern Pacific. An itinerant worker on the Billy Merrill ranch here killed Mrs. Merrill and was lynched on Main Street in Forsyth in 1911 (Fulmer).

Josel (Deer Lodge) had a post office 1892-93.

Josephine (Gallatin), is a siding between Three Forks and Harlowton named for a member of the family of R. A. Harlow, president of the Montana Central Railroad. The postal area was formerly called Highlands. From 1900 to 1939 (Fannie Cowan, postmaster) the office operated under the name of **Josephine**. In 1939 it became Francis. The original postal name was Baker.

Joslin (Fergus) is near Roy. A post office opened in 1915 with David Kelker as postmaster; it closed in 1921.

Judith (Fergus) had a post office established in 1880 with James Wells in charge. Postal records show it was discontinued the same year; open again 1882-83 and 1884-1919.

Judith Gap (Wheatland) is seventeen miles north of Harlowton. Its location in a gap between the Little Belt Mountains and the Snowies gave rise to the name. The gap offered the easiest way to get to the Judith Basin. **Judith** was once a busy grain shipping center and its roundhouse, coal chute, and water tanks are reminders of the time when it was a division point on the Great Northern. The gap in which the town sits is a funnel for northern blizzards but it was once a vital part of the route used by freighters, prospectors, cattle drivers, hunters, and settlers who passed northward into the Judith Basin or southward toward the Yellowstone or Musselshell valleys. These travelers followed the path made years before by

Indian hunters and warriors seeking or defending the rich hunting ground of the Judith Basin. The name came from that of the river, as named by Lewis and Clark. The post office opened in 1908 with George Haynes as postmaster. The Ubet office formerly served the area.

Judith Basin County was created in central Montana December 12, 1920, out of Cascade and Fergus counties. Its name comes from the Judith River, which flows through rich basin grazing and farm land. Meriwether Lewis named the river in 1805 for his cousin, Judith Hancock of Faircastle, Virginia. The open range gave way to homesteaders who fenced the land and raised wheat. The big cattle pool here took its herd across the Missouri to the Milk River country. When Granville Stuart traveled across the Musselshell country on his way to the Judith Basin, the country was "black with buffalo." In 1881 David Hilger went to Dog Creek to establish a ranch. He and Andrew Fergus amused themselves by killing buffalo, which were competing for the grass wanted by ranchers for their livestock. The area around the Judith Mountains had been prime buffalo hunting grounds for the Indians. Some mining of sapphires, silver and other metals added to the wealth of the region. Now Stanford, the county seat, serves as trading center for farmers and ranchers.

Julian (Daniels), near Whitetail, had a post office 1911-21; Carrie Erickson was the first postmaster.

Junction, Junction City (Madison) is a mining ghost town near Alder Gulch on Granite Creek. It was laid out in January 1865, but began to fade as a mining camp within two years; by 1872 the population was down to 100. It had a post office 1869-76.

"The Chinamen of Junction had a war with the Chinese of Virginia City. The Chinese of V. C. bought all the rifles, shotguns, cleavers, and butcher knives that they could lay their hands on from the hardware stores of V. C. From there they went down the Gulch after the Junction orientals. . . . Several Chinamen were killed in the battle. . . . The V. C. combatants were the victors and peace was declared between the two warring people" (Daems).

Later settlers in this area turned to farming and found a market for their vegetables in the mining camps.

Junction City, Junction (Yellowstone) was originally called Peasefort. The post office opened in 1880 with Henry Keiser as postmaster; it closed in 1907. **Junction City**, Montana, was on the Yellowstone River across from where Custer, Montana, is now located. The Crow Reservation was on the south side of the river (Elsa Spear Byron).

"The town of **Junction City** was in sight of where the Custer battle was fought. All supplies for the cow camps came from **Junction City**. Paul McCormick owned the big store there. He took along a lot of silver dollars when he started out on a trip and everytime he met an Indian squaw, he'd slip her a dollar. That's how he got along so well with the Indians and could get anything he wanted on the reservation. He had a lot of cattle and the Crow Reservation was the cream of Montana. McCormick ran cattle in the Shields River Valley, too, and all over eastern Montana. This country all belonged to the Crows; their agency was on Mission Creek" (Randall).

Actually, **Junction City** probably began when a man named Basinki set up a general store in a tent near the ferry landing on the north side of the river. A military depot on the south bank of the Yellowstone two miles above the mouth of the Big Horn showed signs of becoming a permanent settlement. It was called Terry's Landing, but in 1877, when Basinki opened his tent store, the town grew up around him. By 1882 it was a thriving town and head of navigation on the Yellowstone. Most river steamers stopped here. A fire in 1883 started in a saloon and spread out to destroy most of the town and that was the end of it. Nothing remains; most of the original townsite has been washed away by the river.

Junction Ranch (Beaverhead) was the name of a post office that opened in 1871 with George Phifer as postmaster. It closed in 1873.

Juneaux's Trading Post (Judith Basin) was at the mouth of Frenchman's Creek, where it served a colony of Metis, or half-breed Indians. Metis is apparently an Indian word meaning "mixed bloods;" in their sign language, the Crees called these people "half man, half wagon." When they realized they could no longer depend on the buffalo for their needs, the Metis sought to settle independent colonies in Canada and northern Montana. Granville Stuart, while seeking suitable range for his cattle, noted the Metis quite often in the Judith Mountain area; he once mentions some "Red River half-breeds" that were camped at Chamberlains, near present-day Grass Range. On May 19, 1880, he wrote that **Janeaux's Fort** (the spelling varies) was 100x150 feet; "It is neatly fixed up and on the inside neat and in contrast to most of the posts of the white men. There is quite a settlement of Red River half-breeds here who are plowing and planting a crop." There were Metis settlements near Fort Benton, Lewistown and Helena; the Lewistown colony had a high level of education. Because the Metis were nomadic, they called the carts they made "Red River carts;" they had solid wheels made from a three-foot cross section of a tree. The whole cart was made of wood so it would float. Later wheels were wooden rims held with thongs and spokes. They were never greased, so they screeched and creaked when they were pulled by ponies or oxen. The Metis people farmed along the Red River but made two trips each year to hunt buffalo. Between 1850 and the 1870s they established colonies on the Milk River, the Marias, and along Spring Creek. They were fervently religious Catholics; a priest was part of every hunting expedition and women always wore a silver cross.

K

Kabo (Blaine) is on the Raglan Bench. It was settled by dry land farmers, many of Slavic descent. A school was started in 1916 with 13 pupils meeting in a homesteader's shack. The post office opened in 1916 with Mary Hamilton as postmaster; it closed in 1938.

Kachia (Fergus) had a post office 1915-20; William Rose was the first postmaster.

Kahle (Daniels) had a post office established in 1917 with Lillian Krause as postmaster; it closed during the hard times of 1932.

KALISPELL (Flathead) is a county seat named for the Kalispel Indians, who are related to the Flatheads. The town is in a setting of awesome beauty with the Whitefish Range to the north and the Swan to the east, and is only a few miles from Montana's largest lake, Flathead Lake. The Indians called the Flathead Valley the "Park Between the Mountains." The first permanent settlement was in 1881 when Angus McDonald of the Hudson's Bay Company established a post. When the Great Northern Railroad completed its track to this point, the little settlements of Demersville (a steamboat landing on the Flathead river 4½ miles away) and Ashley (a half mile away) were gradually moved to the new location and became a part of **Kalispell**. The post office opened in 1890 with Charles Harrigan as postmaster.

Kalma (Teton) was a post office 1915-19; Mary Wanish was the first postmaster.

Karch (Garfield) was named for the family of postmaster Marie Karch; the office was active only for 1916-17.

Karst Kamp (Gallatin), near Big Sky on Highway 191, was originally a dude ranch founded in 1901 by Pete Karst, who was awarded the property in lieu of back pay owed him by the Cooper Tie Company. Karst started with one cabin and built it up to 25 cabins to accommodate 100 people. In 1937 he installed a rope tow and thus became a pioneer in recreational skiing. He operated this popular stopping place for fifty years before he retired, but the resort is still in operation.

Keatingville (Broadwater) was named for the Keating Mine, one of the best ore producers in the area. Elisha Terrell was postmaster during the life of the office, 1872-73.

Keefer (Valley), near Saco, had a post office 1915-16 with Edward Hudspeth as postmaster.

Keene (Powell), near Garrison, was named for postmaster Hiram M. Keene when the office was open 1883-84.

Keith (Dawson) was the first name of a post office established in 1882. The name was changed to Mingusville in July 1884 in 1895 to Wibaux. William Fountain was the postmaster.

Kelley (Petroleum) had a post office established in 1913 with Charles A. Roth in charge; it was closed in 1938. The place was named for "Mike" Kelley.

Kellog (Richland) was a post office 1913-18; Arthur Poulson was the first postmaster

Kelsey (Custer) was named for Samuel Kelsey, postmaster. The office opened in 1901 and closed in 1902.

Kemmis (Richland) was named for the family of Fredda Kemmis, postmaster. The office was open 1919-20.

Kendall (Fergus), near Hilger, was named for Harry T. Kendall, developer and owner of the Kendall Gold Mining Company. The camp got underway in the 1890s, after a strike was made. In 1901 the big **Kendall** mill was erected and a post office was established with Ethel Robinson as postmaster. By 1902 **Kendall** was thriving and the output of ore was profitable. Freighters were kept busy; gold shipments were often hidden in kegs of nails or otherwise disguised so stages wouldn't be held up. In 1913 Fergus County was the foremost gold producing section of the state, but when the Barnes-King Development Company ceased operations in 1920 the town collapsed. The post office was discontinued in 1923 and the area is now served by the Hilger office (Woole).

Kenilworth (Chouteau), near Big Sandy, had a post office 1911-28 with Edwin K. Johnson, postmaster.

Kenneth (Custer) This post office was open 1892-93. It was named for the postmaster, Kenneth McLean.

Kenneth (Valley) was the first name given to an area that later became Bainville. The post office operated under as **Kenneth** 1902-04 and Otis Forte was postmaster.

Keplerville (Garfield) was on the Big Dry south of Jordan and was named for Mr. and Mrs. Perry Kepler, who kept the post office when it was first established in 1914. The office closed in 1945 (Highland).

Kercheval (Petroleum) was a "hoped for" town that was to be located where the Musselshell River flows into the Missouri, probably on the east side. It was named for an old steamboat captain, some say; others insist it was named for F. B. Kercheval, a prominent territorial figure and member of the Rocky Mountain Wagon Road Company. This company built one cabin and laid out a townsite in 1865; their plan was to unload goods from the river steamers here instead of having them go on to Fort Benton. Sometimes the water was so low that boats could not go beyond the mouth of the Musselshell. The plan also called for building a toll road from **Kercheval** through the Judith Basin and on to the gold mines around Virginia City. The idea was bitterly opposed by the freighters and merchants of Fort Benton but supported by people in the western part of Montana. Toll gates were set up and as much as $2 every forty miles was charged, but the "road" remained an unimproved trail. When steamboat captains refused to unload at **Kercheval** the whole project was dropped.

Kevin (Toole) is a town twenty-five miles from the Canadian border near the first gusher that was drilled in the rich Sweetgrass Arch in 1922. The Kevin-Sunburst oil fields are among the richest of Montana's natural gas and oil fields. **Kevin**'s post office was established in 1910 — during homestead days — with Rudolph Lehmann as postmaster. The town was named for Thomas Kevin, an official of the Alberta Railway and Irrigation Company, which once ran from Lethbridge, Alberta, south into Montana. It was a narrow gauge railroad built in 1887 and nicknamed the "Turkey Track".

Keystone (Mineral) is near Superior and had a post office 1913-25; Eugene Keesey was postmaster.

Kibbey (Judith Basin) is fifteen miles from Monarch. The post office opened in 1883 with William Sellew as postmaster. The area was formerly called Lessard. The office closed in 1909 and mail was sent to Raynesford. The **Kibbey** schoolhouse was for many years used for community dances and gatherings. The building has now become "a ragged beggar sunning" but it is surrounded by fine ranches on green, rolling foothills.

Kidd (Beaverhead) was a railroad station between Lima and Dillon on the old Union Pacific line. It was named after a passenger train conductor who was murdered about 1910 by a highwayman who had robbed a saloon at Monida and boarded the train in an attempt to get away.

Kiehl (Carbon) was named for the family of postmaster Maggie Kiehl; the office was open 1902-03.

Kila (Flathead), in the lake country, is on Smith Lake and only a few miles from the north end of Flathead Lake. When the post office was applied for the name of Kiley was suggested to honor an old-time settler by that name, but the postal department changed it to **Kila** when the office was approved in 1901. Harry Neffner was the first postmaster.

Kimball (Custer) was named for Jennie Kimball, first postmaster. The office was open 1912-20 when the mail was ordered to Mizpah. The area was formerly called Hockett.

King (Hill), near Alma, was the name of a homesteaders' post office established as new settlers rushed in to take up the 160-acre plots. Mrs. Wallace Hunt writes: "When we first came, the post office, Alma, was the closest place to get mail or groceries. . . . That was about 15 miles and neighbors took turns going. After a few years another store and post office, **King** (1915), was built up about 5 miles from our place. The mail came from Joplin to Alma on Tuesday, Thursdays and Saturdays on a star route. Then on to **King** on Monday, Wednesdays and Fridays. The mail carrier was errand boy for everyone. He did your grocery shopping and gave your list to the other driver and he did it in Joplin if Mrs. Jack Keith didn't have it at Alma. She was the postmaster and storekeeper there. Oscar Hultin was the **King** postmaster and storekeeper" (*Tumbleweeds and Tar Paper Shacks*). This post office, like so many others, closed in 1919 after the dry years.

Kingmont (Fallon) This station was "named because it is at the summit of the climb out of the Little Missouri Valley" (Rowe). Presumably the reference was to a stage or freight station, as no railroad has ever run through the Little Missouri Valley, which is now in Carter County. Carter County was created from a part of Fallon County in 1917.

Kingsley (Custer) was named for the family of first postmaster Annie Kingsley. The office opened in 1902, closed in 1907 and was open again 1911-29.

Kingston (Fergus), a station on the Great Northern, was named for Anton and Joseph King of the King Brothers Land and Livestock Company.

Kinread (Liberty) was named for first postmaster Emilie Kinread or her family when the office was opened 1915-33, spanning the homestead years.

KINSEY (Custer) had a post office 1898-1906; Hiram Gilmore was first postmaster. It was opened again in 1909. **Kinsey** is fifteen miles northeast of Miles City on the opposite side of the Yellowstone River from the highway. It was named for a Mr. Kinsey who owned a ranch there.

Kintla (Flathead), named for Kintala Lakes in Glacier National Park, had a post office 1916-25; Mary Schoenberger was first postmaster. When the office closed the mail was sent to Polebridge.

Kipp (Glacier), near Browning, was named for James Kipp, who opened the upper Missouri River area to Blackfeet fur trading when he traveled up the Missouri with a 44-man party in the fall of 1831 and established Fort Piegan at the mouth of the Marias River. In 1892, when the **Kipp** post office was established with Joseph Kipp as postmaster, both that settlement and the remains of Fort Piegan were in old Chouteau County. The office closed in 1905.

Kippen (Toole) had a post office 1911-33 with U. S. G. Pettycrew as postmaster, spanning the homestead years.

Kirby (Big Horn) **Kirby**'s 1960 population was listed as 5. It is located on Rosebud Creek in the extreme eastern part of the county only a few miles from the Tongue River Indian Reservation. The post office opened in 1895 with George Carroll as postmaster. The settlement was named for George Kirby, a prominent stockman of the area who first worked for the "79" outfit. He and his cousin, J. P. McCuistan, built a cabin and wintered on Lodgepole Creek; later he went ranching for himself along the Yellowstone. There was a one-room school at **Kirby**. Billy Porter came to Montana with a trail herd of cattle in 1890 — two-year-old steers with a few "threes" and "fours" thrown in made up the 3,600 head count. There wasn't much to do that winter at the **Kirby** ranch where Billy was staying, so he decided to go to school; he was twenty-one and his teacher, Leila Buffington, was eighteen.

Kirtzville (Petroleum) A. J. Noyes quotes Joseph Mosser as saying, "I went to the mouth of the Musselshell, then called **Kirtzville**, at that time supposed to be the seat of Dawson County. James Brewer, who was afterwards at White Sulphur Springs, was sheriff. There were two stores, George Clendenning's Montana Hide and Fur Company, and Jacob Smith's." Mosser's description indicates he was probably talking about Kercheval. (see **Kercheval**)

Kismet (Garfield) is at the mouth of the Musselshell River on the east. It had a post office 1901-06 and again 1908-09; after that the mail was sent to Leedy. Mail was carried to the **Kismet** post office from Jordan. In 1908 a devastating flood swept down the river bottom, washing everyone out. The postmaster, who also ran a ferry about a mile below the mouth of the Musselshell, was drowned while trying to cross the swollen river in his boat. He had also run the **Kismet** store and had been getting supplies by steamboat. When the flood came, some of the cowboys dived in under the door of the store and rescued some Stetson hats from a top shelf. The water was near the top of the door by the time they got out.

A favorite story in the area concerns the sale of water-damaged goods conducted by the widow of the drowned storekeeper. Everyone from above the Musselshell gathered at the UL Ranch across the river; then the steamboat came along and picked everyone up along the riverbank and took them to the **Kismet** store for the sale. Later the steamboat took everyone back up to the UL Ranch for a big chicken-and-dumplin' dinner. Upon arrival at the UL, the guests found a large boiler filled with chickens cooking with about half their feathers still unplucked. The two cooks, George Bickles (Beckler) and "Dad" Hickman, were both drunk and stretched out on the floor. The ladies dug out the chickens, finished dressing them and eventually served the chicken-and-dumplin' dinner (John Town, Winnett *Times*). The **Kismet** post office was moved to the UL Ranch and Arthur Lewis took over as postmaster. Ranchers took turns carrying the mail from Leedy.

Klein (Musselshell), near Roundup, was named for Mike Klein (Margaret Lewis Moness). George Klein was postmaster at Atine and Mary Klein was postmaster at Roundup. The **Klein** office opened in 1909 with Nellie Cherry as postmaster and closed in 1957. **Klein** is a coal miners' town in the foothills of the Bull Mountains. The Monarch Mine there once employed 500 men and furnished much of the coal used by the Milwaukee Railroad. It was a thriving town with a high school and a big mine payroll. When the demand for coal declined the mines closed and people moved away. There were many workers of Italian and Slavic descent here, but there was also a goodly number of Scots, who annually put on a Bobbie Burns celebration that was the social event of the year.

Knels was a settlement in Sheridan County.

Knerville (Judith Basin) had a post office 1898-1915 in what was then the extreme western edge of Fergus County, with Maggie Edwards, postmaster; the mail was then sent to Geyser.

Knobs (Fallon) was named for a topographical feature repeatedly found in this area. A post office opened in 1913 with Hannah Green as postmaster. Later, while Barney Heyings was postmaster, he ran a grocery store and meeting place that was as near to being a town as **Knobs** ever became.

Knowlton (Custer) This post office opened in 1892 and was named for postmaster Rotus(?) Knowlton. The office closed in 1944. The Knowltons were old-timers in the area.

Kolin (Judith Basin) is off the main highway between Stanford and Lewistown. Many people of Bohemian descent settled here, so the settlement was named after a city in Bohemia. The post office opened in 1913 with Frank Rau as postmaster; it closed in 1972.

Kohr (Powell) was a station named for Conrad Kohrs, from whom the right-of-way for the railroad was purchased. Kohrs was a prominent businessman in Helena who had extensive cattle interests in eastern Montana.

Kootenai is a name frequently used in the extreme northwest corner of Montana, particularly in Lincoln County. It comes from an Indian tribe, also known as Deer Robes, who lived in this region and were credited with being the finest deer hunters and tanners of hides among the western Indians. The **Kootenai River** crosses the county after rising in the **Kootenai National Forest**. Close to where Pipe Creek (Indians used the fine white sand there to make their clay pipes) runs into the river is the site of the **Kootenai Ceremonial Sweat Baths**. The place is marked by thousands of pieces of rock which cracked when they were thrown red-hot into shallow pits to heat the water. The pits were six to eight feet square and after the Indian bather had steamed himself in the very hot water, he emerged to take a plunge in the icy waters of the **Kootenai River** to close his pores. **Kootenai Falls** is near the highway and consists of a spring, a rock fountain and a campground with a view of the cascading waterfall. **Kootenai** is also the name of a station on the Great Northern. In 1896 a post office by this name was approved which remained on the postal records until 1899, but a note in the record adds, "never in operation;" it was in Flathead County. **Kootenai Gorge** is heard as a hollow roar before you reach the viewing site, which is over the iron railing of the railroad.

Korn (Blaine), near Chinook, had a post office 1914-17; Nellie Fulton was first postmaster.

Korner (Glacier) had a post office 1921-38; Ernest Anderson was first postmaster.

Koyl (Teton) was a station on the Great Northern branch line between Choteau and Bynum Lake. A post office operated for just a year January 1916-January 1917 with William Levy as postmaster.

Kraft (Daniels), near Scobey, operated as a post office for a little over a year, 1915-16. William Kraft was postmaster.

KREMLIN (Hill) is a Great Northern station surrounded by nutritious buffalo grass that still grows on the plains. The post office was opened in 1910 for the many Russian settlers who had come. Two ideas persist concerning the towns name: "It is said to have been named because the Russian settlers saw the citadel of Moscow in the mirages that appear on the surrounding prairie" (*Montana, A State Guide Book*). And, "Russian settlers in this wheat country named their town for an old-country term meaning fortress" (Willard). At any rate, many of the early settlers were Russian and the name is certainly Russian, but the first postmaster's name was Archie Parsons. There are many other Scandinavian names in the list of early settlers. In 1913 the Great Northern constructed a depot there to handle the implement and equipment shipments coming in for home-steaders who were pouring in. "It is a bustling, booming, growing trade center for the hundreds of homesteaders who have filed on 600,000 acres of highly productive chocolate loamsoil" (Matt Casey, *Kremlin Chancellor*).

Kruger (Powder River) had a post office 1916-33; George O'Connor was the first postmaster.

L

LaBarge City (Powell) For a brief time the town that is now Deer Lodge was known by this name. The original camp was named Cottonwood by the gold miners. Then in July 1862 a Captain LaBarge arrived to start a trading post and the camp was called by his name. In 1863 the citizens formed the Deer Lodge Town Company and again the name was changed (see **Deer Lodge**).

Lacy (Chouteau), named for the family of first postmaster Ella F. P. Lacy, had an office 1890-98; when it closed the mail was ordered to Highwood.

LaHood (Madison) is between Whitehall and Lewis and Clark Caverns, and Lahood Park is on the Jefferson River, which for a way forms the boundary line between Madison and Jefferson counties; it was a popular stopping off place for travelers and freighters between Butte and the Madison River, and for many years was a crossroads store. Shadan LaHood was born in Lebanon and came to America in 1899 and to Montana in 1902. That year he built a covered wagon and bought a horse. From 1902 to 1919, he canvassed for a dry goods firm, travelling to Butte, Dillon, Missoula, and all around Madison County. It was rough going, especially in winter, when he had to walk and clap his hands trying to keep warm. In 1909 LaHood and his wife opened a general merchandise store at Jefferson Island and petitioned for a post office. The office operated under the name **LaHood** 1909-12 with Charles Black as postmaster. It then became Jefferson Island. LaHood built the park that bears his name.

Laird (Liberty), north of Chester, was named for John Laird, the first postmaster; the office was open 1905-20.

Lake Basin (Stillwater) had a post office in 1913 with Robert Grout as postmaster. The topography of the land and a nearby lake gave rise to the name. It was changed to Rapelje in 1917.

Lake City (Lincoln) was near Lake Creek, which comes out of Bull Lake to the south. Established in the 1880s as a mining camp and headquarters for the grading crews preparing the roadbed for the Great Northern, **Lake City** was full of saloons and tough characters. The town dwindled and died when the railroad surveyor chose the present site of Troy for the round-houses, freight yards, and a division for the Great Northern. During the moving process, Tom Dobson, who ran the grocery store at the dying camp, was seen walking along the road to the new townsite carrying a teakettle. Asked what he had, he replied, "The **Lake City** post office." In the kettle were letters, cash, and stamps, all of which Dobson handled in his grocery store in lieu of a proper office (Wolle). The **Lake City** office operated under that name 1891-93.

Lake City (Powell) was near Helmville. It was originally called Belair and under that name had a post office established in 1914. The name was changed to **Lake City** the next year and Harry McNally continued as postmaster. The office was discontinued in 1917.

Lake County is in northwestern Montana and is so named because massive Flathead Lake comprises much of the northern part of the county. It was created in 1923 from parts of Flathead and Missoula counties. Polson is the county seat.

Lake Five (Flathead) is very near Belton and Glacier National Park. A post office under this name operated 1920-28; Margaret Gafaney was first postmaster.

Lake McDonald is on the edge of a lake by the same name in Glacier National Park. The town is busy during the tourist season, and the population figure depends entirely upon the time of year. The town was formerly known as Glacier, and before that as Snyder. A post office was opened in 1913 with Olive Lewis as postmaster; in 1944 it was discontinued but reopened in 1946. In 1966 **Lake McDonald** was made a rural station out of West Glacier.

LAKESIDE (Flathead) is on the west shore and near the north end of Flathead Lake. It exists mainly to entertain tourists who come to Flathead Lake and Glacier Park. A post office was opened in 1948 with Raymond as postmaster.

Lakeside (Roosevelt), near Bainville, was located on a very sharp bend in the Missouri River where the water almost doubles back in its channel and forms a "lake" there. The post office opened in 1907 with Ora Waterman in charge; it closed in 1920.

Lakeview (Beaverhead) is a hamlet in the extreme southern tip of the county near Red Rocks Lakes. The post office was established in 1897 with George Shambow as postmaster; it closed in 1938.

LaMarsh (Silver Bow) had a post office 1896-99 with Bertha Etheredge in charge.

LAMBERT (Richland) was a station on the Great Northern branch line west of Sidney. The post office was originally known as Fox Lake and was located on Fox Creek. The **Lambert** office was established in 1914 with Edmund Bronson as postmaster.

LAME DEER (Rosebud) is between Broadus and Hardin on Deer Creek and the Cheyenne Indian Reservation. It was named for Lame Deer, an

Indian chief. It was to this village that Dull Knife (also known as Morning Star) returned with his few straggling followers from their long march home after being held in Oklahoma. The story is told in Mari Sandoz's book, *Cheyenne Autumn*.

An Indian historian gives the following account of a much earlier event and the story of Chief Lame Deer: "Lame Deer's camp of 51 lodges of Minneconjou Sioux refused to come in (as per government order) and moved over to the Rosebud to hunt buffalo. On May 7, 1877, General Miles attacked Lame Deer's camp on the Lame Deer Creek tributary to the Rosebud. Lame Deer and Iron Star were separated from the band, and General Miles rode up to shake Lame Deer's hand. Just when it looked like all might be settled peacefully, a soldier rode up with a rifle drawn. Lame Deer, suspicious, dropped back and fired at General Miles but missed and killed another soldier. A hot fight ensued in which both Lame Deer and Iron Star and many others were killed. The soldiers then looted and burned the Indian camp" (Shane).

The sheer cliff 22 miles southeast of **Lame Deer** is one of the most classic of buffalo jumps. Fragments of buffalo bones can still be found at the base. **Lame Deer** today is a reservation town, serving as a meeting place and headquarters for the Indians who live in the area. The post office was established in 1887.

Lanark (Roosevelt), near Bainville, tried for a post office in 1905 and finally got one in 1909; Ora Bond was postmaster. The office was open until 1931.

Lance (Carter) existed briefly as a ranch post office in the extreme southeast corner of the state. The office was open 1918-19 with Maggie Beeman as postmaster. The mail then went to Albion.

LANDUSKY (Phillips) has a quiet present but a roaring past. Near the Lewis and Clark National Forest, where it clings precariously to the side of the Little Rocky Mountains, it was born "a-boomin' " in the early 1890s. Powell, better known as "Pike" Landusky, and Bob Orman discovered gold deposits here in August 1893 and named their mine after the month. At first they took their ore out by night because they thought the claim was on the Fort Belknap Indian Reservation and feared government interference; however, the mine proved to be a few miles south of the reservation line. News of it leaked out; prospectors poured in and a settlement was established in 1894. Pike, for whom the town was named (presumably no one cared to argue with him about the name), was a raw kid at Alder Gulch in the late sixties when Virginia City and Alder Gulch were roaring mining camps. Pike got his nickname because he boasted that he came from "Pike County, Missouri, by God" — quickly won a reputation as one of the toughest fighters in the West. In 1868 he went to the mouth of the Mussel-shell River to trap and trade with the Indians, but was captured by a war party of Brules. Landusky angrily beat one of the braves with a frying pan, then ripped off the warrior's breechcloth to continue the lashing. The awed Indians withdrew and left two ponies to placate the wild captive. Later he set up a trading post on Flatwillow Creek and called it Lucky Fort; it was located in what is now Petroleum County. There Landusky was shot by a Piegan brave. His jaw was shattered; he tore out the loose fragments of four teeth and threw them away.

Five miles south of **Landusky** lived the Curry brothers. "Kid" Curry and his brothers used **Landusky** as a trading center. The following story about

160

the confrontation between Pike and the Currys comes from "Kid Amby" Cheney, a cowboy working for the Bear Paw Pool, who also made **Landusky** a stopping off place for supplies both wet and dry: "Pike was known as a mean devil. He always carried a gold headed, weighted cane and he used it often, sometimes hitting a bystander at the bar whether he was making trouble or not. Pike owned the Landusky Saloon and he had a business rival just across the street named 'Jew Jake,' a one-legged guy who had lost the other one in a shooting scrape in Great Falls. Jew Jake used his rifle as a crutch when he walked and kept it slung around his neck when he sat down. He used to sit out on the porch of his saloon waiting for some trouble with Pike. One day Kid Curry and Pike got into an argument: some say it was over a woman, others that it was over a plow that the Currys had borrowed from Pike and returned badly broken. The Kid was standing at the bar in Pike's saloon when the argument began. Pike reached for his gun, but Curry was quicker on the draw and killed Landusky with the first shot. Curry escaped and by the time the sheriff had come from Fort Benton (200 miles away) the smoke had cleared away and the officer told the boys in **Landusky** that if they ever happened to see the Kid to tell him to come on in and give himself up. They wouldn't do much to him because of Pike's quarrelsome reputation. After Landusky's death, Johnny Curry, one of the Kid's brothers, sort of throwed-in with Mrs. Landusky."

Landusky's post office, which opened in 1894 with John Hiroop as postmaster, is still operating, but the rest of the action has pretty well died down. The post office now is the information center for announcements.

Lane was a station on the Great Northern between Enid and the end of the line at Richey. Its post office was established in 1925 with Stephen Reynolds as postmaster; the office closed in 1944.

Lantis (Custer) was a turn of the century post office with Daniel Lantis postmaster February 1900-January 1901.

Lantry (Rosebud) was named for T. H. Lantry, general superintendent of the Northern Pacific Railroad.

Larb (Valley) was a post office during homestead days 1919-33 with Orilla Taylor serving as postmaster.

Larchwood (Sanders), near Trout Creek, had a post office 1911-23; Duard Brown was the first postmaster.

Laredo (Hill) was a station on the Great Northern line that goes from Pacific Junction to Great Falls and on south. There was a post office 1917-57; John Barry was the first postmaster.

Largent (Cascade) was the original name of Sun River. John Largent built a bridge over the Sun River in 1867-68.

Larslan (Valley) is about halfway between Fort Peck and the Canadian border. The post office opened in 1918 with Otho B. Moore as postmaster, who had applied for an office the year before, requesting the name Hyatt in honor of the Bill Hyatt family. But for some reason postal authorities crossed out Hyatt and wrote in **Larslan**; no one seems to know why. Mrs. Moore drove a team and buggy twice weekly to Avondale to get the mail. The office was in the Moore's sod house.

Many Mennonite families settled this area as homesteaders around 1916. A church building was started in 1929 but drought, dust storms and the depression caused many to leave and it wasn't until 1957 that a full-service church was completed.

Many other settlers were of Scandinavian ancestry, and a Lutheran church was organized in 1919. Like other prairie homesteaders, most farm families lived in tar-paper shacks.

In 1919 the post office was moved to **Larslan's** present location in the Bollinger store, which also served as the community gathering place, seldom closing before 11 or midnight, due to the many lonely bachelors and homestead families who enjoyed visiting there. As in most homestead areas, the attempt to make a go of it on 160 acres proved to be hopeless. Some settlers left; others stayed and bought more land, knowing it was necessary to have a very large spread in order to make a living (*Since Homesteading Days*).

LaSalle (Flathead), near Kalispell, had a post office 1900-05; the first postmaster was Walter Jellison.

Lat (Park) was the name of a post office 1898-1918 with brief closures in 1902 and 1917; Annie Stephens was the first postmaster.

LAUREL (Yellowstone) "straggles on both sides of an intricate pattern of railroad tracks." Through the center of town runs the joint trackage of the Northern Pacific, Great Northern, and the Chicago, Burlington, and Quincy railroads. Much of Montana's wheat, hay, copper, zinc, livestock, wool, lumber and other products were routed to the Midwest or the South through **Laurel's** yards. At the edge of town is a huge oil refinery.

No one knows for sure the origin of the name. Mrs. Gehrett, who came to **Laurel** in 1911, thinks it was named by a railroad man for a member of his family; Mrs. Moran heard that a railroad man named it for his hometown of Laurel, Mississippi; Elsie Johnson, who has written a book about **Laurel**, says it was originally named Carlton, and that no one can explain the change. There is a Carlton in Ravalli County, but the connection, if any, is unclear. Still another suggestion is that it was named after the laurel plant; however, no shrub even remotely resembling that species grows here.

Many early settlers here were of German descent, and in 1973, along with other residents, they inaugurated an annual *Herbstfest*, after the traditional German celebrations.

Long before the trains or settlers came, Lewis and Clark camped at the forks of the river near **Laurel**. And even earlier, Chief Joseph and his band of Nez Perces crossed the Yellowstone here, an event commemorated in a painting by Bernard Thomas (O. K. Chapman). The post office opened in 1886 with James Ashbaugh in charge.

Laurin (Madison) (pronounced Lah-RAY) was a station on the Northern Pacific between Sheridan and Alder. It was named after John Baptiste Laurin, who operated a trading store near here, having acquired much of the surrounding agricultural land. Before Laurin's arrival the settlement was known as Cicero. Laurin's store prospered as he carried supplies for the miners and traded furs with the Indians. He continued to buy land and was in the mercantile and livestock business in Madison County for forty years. Laurin was born in Canada, the sixth of thirteen children in a devoutly religious French-Catholic family. John and Adeline LaGris Laurin had no children of their own, but they raised fourteen who had in various ways been left to their care. The couple built and donated to the community a magnificent Catholic church of native stone; now, a century later, it remains standing "resolute and strong."

Less than a half mile from **Laurin** is Hangman's Tree, where Erastus "Red" Yager and G. W. Brown, messenger and secretary of the Plummer outlaw gang, were hanged on January 4, 1864.

The **Laurin** post office opened in John Laurin's store in 1874; he served as postmaster until 1886. Postal records use the French spelling of his first name "Jean" (*Pioneer Trails and Trials*). The office was discontinued in 1972.

LAVINA (Golden Valley) began as a trading post and stage station on the route between Billings and Lewistown. The Adams Hotel here served travelers for many years, and a post office was established in 1883 with Walter Burke as postmaster. Burke and Clate Warner put up a few stage stables and some other shacks at the town's original location circa 1882. Burke, who was superintendent of the stage line, blazed trails, blasted stumps, and built bridges on the 220-mile run of the Billings-Benton stage line — the first north-south route to carry mail on coaches. It was Burke's job to establish stage stops, build barns and corrals, and stock them with hay and oats for the horses; he also provided an eating place, bar, and bunkhouse for drivers and passengers. None of the stations pleased him as much as the one on the south bank of the Mussellshell, and Burke named it **Lavina**, in memory of a former sweetheart (*Dawn over Golden Valley*). By 1883 fine Concord coaches were rolling out of **Lavina** in three directions: north to Lewistown, east to the log post office at Roundup, and south to Billings. The town was often called the "White City" because so many of the buildings were painted white. Old **Lavina**, a mile downstream from the present townsite, was originally an Indian campground. The railroad bought the holdings of Louis Lehfeldt and built a depot; the first train pulled into the new station in February 1908. The stage stop gave way to a more modern train station as settlers arrived and the town was born (Bicentennial Project of Golden Valley County).

Lawrence (Petroleum) "When Fred Lawrence first started his trading post is unknown. In early 1860, when Jim Duffy first saw Flatwillow Creek, he said there was a lively place called **Lawrence**, and a log saloon connected" (Edward Degner, the Winnett *Times*).

Lazy Day (Park) was the name of a post office 1938-46; Amanda Welch was first postmaster. The origin of the name is unknown.

Leadboro (Meagher) got its name from its mining activity. It was a camp and post office 1898-1900 with William Twohy, postmaster.

Lebo (Meagher) was along Cottonwood Creek near the Crazy Mountains. The post office opened in 1913 with Mandius Teig as postmaster — the office was probably at his ranch — and closed in 1933.

LEDGER (Pondera) grew up on the Great Northern. The name was chosen in honor of Dan Ledgerwood, a farmer and county commissioner. Postal records show a Ledgerwood post office established in Teton County in 1916; before that the community was known as Esper. The original townsite was laid out in 1914 and named for N. Esper Norman, who became postmaster when the Esper office opened in 1916. The office became Ledgerwood later that year and remained so for three years, when the name was changed to Sterrenberg and John Sterrenberg replaced Norman. For much of this period the railroad station was called Price, after a local merchant, Jack Price. There was also a North Dakota community called Ledgerwood; the inevitable confusion prompted the 1919 change. Eventually the townspeople got together and on settled **Ledger**. The post office under this name was established in 1923 with Frank Stuart as postmaster (Floershinger).

Ledgerwood (see **Ledger**).

Lee (Rosebud) had a post office in 1885. Mary Lee was first postmaster; however, J. P. Rowe says it was named for Lee Austin, the nephew of Orson Merritt. The office was discontinued in 1936.

Leedy (Phillips) was named for Schyler Leedy, who was appointed postmaster when the office opened in 1903. Leedy, who ran a trading business along the Missouri, brought in much of his goods by boat from Fort Benton; he also kept a small boat to bring customers across the river to his store. People sometimes summoned this unique taxi service by shooting a gun into the air to attract Leedy's attention. The first school opened in 1904; each term lasted for two or three months, or until the money ran out. Still, **Leedy**'s children fared better than some. "**Leedy** was on the north side of the river in Valley (now Phillips) County; the Gallinger school was in Dawson. When money for one school was exhausted, the other school on the opposite side of the river would hire a teacher, usually the same one, and the teacher would move to the other school. The children from the school just closed would cross the river daily by boat, as the other children had done before" (Highland).

"The spot where the **Leedy** post office stood is under 100 feet of water now, since the Fort Peck Dam went in" (Agnes Buffington Leedy). The office closed in 1938.

Legg (Phillips) was named for the family of John Legg, the first postmaster. The office was open 1917-36.

Lehigh (Judith Basin) is nearly a ghost town now. The post office opened in 1915 with Albert Hazen as postmaster. When the Stockett coal mines played out, the Cottonwood Coal Company moved its operation to **Lehigh**. The mines flourished in the early twenties, but when they closed there was nothing to keep the town going. People moved away, the post office closed in 1924, and most of the houses were moved to Windham or Stanford. During the good days, a payroll clerk brought $10-12,000 cash for the miners each payday.

Leiterville (Madison) was a thriving mining camp located on Wisconsin Creek about nine miles from Sheridan. The mines operated 1892-98. and were owned by L. %. and T. Benton Leiter.

Leland (Valley) was very briefly a post office May-September 1910 under Jay Hull. Later the name was changed to McCabe.

LEMHI PASS was the ancient road on the Continental Divide, through which the Shoshones tracked down to the headwaters of the Jefferson River and buffalo country. "Emence Ranges of mountains still to the west of us," said Lewis as he stood on the Divide looking into the Salmon River country; he rested there for a few minutes,then descended into the ravine ". . . to a handsome bold running creek of cold clear water. Here I first tasted the water of the great Columbia Rivers." Here Lewis and Clark met a large party of friendly Shoshones with horses. The natives came forward to greet the whites and Lewis ruefully recorded that the motive was more agreeble than the manner: ". . . we were all carressed and besmeared with their grease paint until I was heartily tired of the national hug." **Lemhi Pass** now marks the dividing line between Montana and Idaho.

Lennep (Meagher) Despite the fact that its 1960 population was down to a mere 25, **Lennep** remains an important livestock center. The post office opened in 1903 with Inger Nelson postmaster and closed in 1962. The town was a station on the Milwaukee Railroad in the southern part of the county. The first Lutheran church service in Montana was held in **Lennep** on January 10, 1891 (Stearns). For 1900-03 records show the name spelled Lennop.

Leon (Lake), near St. Ignatius, had a post office 1912-16; Lottie Lee was the first postmaster.

Leona (Flathead) This post office was open 1896-99; Frank Stryker was the first postmaster.

Leroy (Blaine) had a post office in 1915 with Lois Westover as postmaster, which served the farmers of Lone Tree Bench and settlers between Black Coulee and Cow creeks in the southern tip of the county. A school was started on the bench in 1916 with 6 pupils. From their homes on the open bench settlers could see the Bear Paw Mountains to the north; the Little Rockies to the east; and off to the southwest, Square Butte. Nearby the ferryboats carried settlers and travelers across the Missouri River (*Montana Postal Cache*; August, 1975). The post office closed in 1964.

Lessard (Judith Basin) was a post office February-March 1883. The name was then changed to Kibbey.

Leta (Rosebud) was a post office 1917-19 with Ethel Fisher as postmaster.

Levengoods (Deer Lodge), near Anaconda, was named for the family of first postmaster Peter Levengood. The office was open 1879-84.

Lewis (Madison) had a post office 1873-83 with Paul Hayward and John Scanlan, postmasters. **Lewis** was a mining camp near Norris, but nothing more is known abut it. When the office closed the mail was forwarded to Red Bluff.

Lewis (Meagher) was named for the family of Len Lewis, the first postmaster. The office, which was near Fort Logan, was open 1897-1918. Records also show an office by this name in the same county 1883-84 with Joseph Roads postmaster.

Lewis and Clark Caverns (Jefferson) were originally called Morrison Cave after Donald A. "Dan" Morrison, the developer. The cave was discovered in 1892 by two ranchers, Thomas Williams and Bert Pannell, while deer hunting. Six years later they explored part of the cave with E. C. Woodward with the help of ropes and candles. Later, Williams contacted Morrison, a prominent miner and promoter, and in 1902 the latter began clearing passageways and building trails. Though Morrison spent a lot of time and money, he was never able to get title to the cave, and in 1911 it was declared federal property with the name changed to **Lewis and Clark Caverns**. In 1927 it was opened to the public and in 1941 the surrounding area was dedicated as Morrison State Park. **Lewis and Clark Caverns** have been called "the most beautiful limestone cavern(s) in the world."

Lewis and Clark County is in the western part of the state and was first called Edgerton in honor of first territorial governor Sidney Edgerton. It was one of the nine original counties established in 1865. The name was changed in 1870 to Lewis and Clarke, but the "e" was later dropped. Parts of Deer Lodge and Meagher counties were annexed to **Lewis and Clark** in the years 1890-1900; parts of **Lewis and Clark** were taken to form Cascade in 1887; another part of Cascade was annexed to **Lewis and Clark** in 1941; and a part of **Lewis and Clark** was annexed to Cascade that same year. Helena is the county seat, as well as the state capital. At one time the county courthouse also served as the capital building.

LEWISTOWN (Fergus) is a county seat at the geographical center of Montana. The town was first called Reed's Fort, after Maj. A. S. Reed, who opened the first post office here in 1881. It began as a small trading post on the Carroll Trail between Helena and the mouth of the Musselshell River. When the town was incorporated the name was changed to honor Maj. William H. Lewis, who had established Fort Lewis in 1874 near the present location of the city swimming pool. The Central Montana Railroad — the "Jawbone" — reached **Lewistown** in 1903. **Lewistown** is a pleasant little town, neatly laid out, its streets lined with shade trees, but its origin was boisterous. Cattle rustlers were rampant in the area, causing serious economic damage to ranchers. The problem grew more serious until ranchers took matters into their own hands; on July 4, 1884, a couple of suspected ringleaders, Edward "Longhair" Owen and Charles "Rattle-snake Jake" Fallon — described at the time as "villainous looking" — rode into town. After they had lost most of their money on a horse race and had become roaring drunk, they started shooting up the town. Some locals armed with Winchesters took up positions in stores along the only street. During the fight that followed, Rattlesnake Jake made a break to get out of town, but seeing that his cohort was wounded, fought his way back. The pair kept firing until they could no longer pull their triggers. Jake was hit nine times — Longhair eleven. Their last stand was made in front of a tent set up by an itinerant photographer, who took pictures of the bodies and sold them at a profit. **Lewistown**'s post office was established under its current name in 1884 with Nicholas Erickson as postmaster.

LIBBY (Lincoln) is named for a daughter of George Davis, an early settler. The town is in the northwest corner of the state twenty miles from the Idaho border and about fifty miles from the Canadian line. **Libby** is a lumberjack's town, and lumberjacks pour in from the surrounding logging camps; they don't all wear bright-checked shirts, black beards and caulked boots, but they are a distinctive breed just the same, and anyone can tell just by walking down the streets of **Libby** that this is Paul Bunyan country. **Libby** has one of the largest sawmills in the state. The post office opened in 1891 with Robert Cantwell as postmaster.

Liberty County is an oblong section of Montana tucked in between Toole and Hill counties and bordering on Canada. **Liberty** was created in 1920 from parts of Chouteau and Hill counties; more of Hill was annexed in 1921. When Chester lost its fight to become the county seat of Hill, the citizens began agitating for a new county. They were assisted in their efforts by Dan McKay, champion "county-splitter," and the new county was approved by the legislature February 11, 1920, at the expense of Hill County. Chester became the county seat (Burlingame and Toole).

Lilacs (Hill), near Fairchild, had a post office 1911-14; Mabel Claviter was first postmaster. A poet said that "lilac bushes were the footprints left behind by pioneer women;" it was the one flowering shrub that seemed to survive hot, dry summers and long, cold winters. Even after homesteaders' shacks had tumbled down, one could often find a lilac bush still alive.

LIMA (Beaverhead) is on the Red Rock River some fifteen miles from Monida Pass, which separates Montana from Idaho. The community was originally called Allerdice; then, when a station of the Utah and Northern (Union Pacific) was built there, it was called Spring Hill. The name **Lima** was chosen by Henry Thompson for his home, Lima, Wisconsin. The post office opened in 1889 with William Bernstein as postmaster.

Lime Spur (Jefferson) was a post office 1891-1908 and a station on the Northern Pacific. Daniel Morrison, a key figure in the promotion of Lewis and Clark Caverns — then called Morrison Cave — was the first postmaster.

Limestone (Stillwater) got its name from the common limestone deposits found throughout the county. It is in the mountains near the Sweet Grass County border. The post office operated 1910-5?; Mabel Wright was the first postmaster.

Limington (Teton) was briefly the postal name of a community later known as Bole. The post office operated as **Limington** March-November 1914 with William Withraw as postmaster.

Linair (Phillips) had a post office April-September 1918 with Everett Mitchell in charge. The mail was later sent to Malta.

LINCOLN (Lewis and Clark), near the border of Powell County, is about seventy miles east of Missoula "as the crow flies," about fifty miles northwest of Helena, and near Stemple Pass on the Continental Divide. The town is surrounded by some of Montana's largest pine trees and is buried under heavy snows in the winter. During the summer it becomes a haven for Helena citizens, many of whom have vacation homes here. **Lincoln** used to be an important placer mining camp a few miles from its present location. It took its name from two mining companies that operated here: Lincoln Placers, Inc., and Lincoln Associates, Inc., which were named for the first mine, located August 31, 1865, at Abe Lincoln Gulch. The camp was first called Springfield, presumably for Springfield, Illinois; many Civil War veterans were coming West at the time, and Springfield was widely hailed as the home of the famous president. A post office has operated here almost continously since 1869; the first postmaster was named Alfred Pose.

Lincoln County forms the northwest corner of Montana, bordering Canada to the north and Idaho to the west. Libby is the county seat. The county was created in 1909 from a part of Flathead County.

LINDSAY (Dawson) was named after the Hon. William Lindsay, U.S. Marshal, who settled in Dawson County in 1883 and became a sheep rancher. **Lindsay** is a prairie town between Glendive and Circle. The post office opened in 1908 with Wendel Fellows as postmaster.

Lindstrom (Fergus) was named for first postmaster Emil Lindstrom. The office was open 1912-18. **Lindstrom** was near Roy.

Lingshire (Meagher) had a post office 1920-37; the first postmaster was Bessie Rubison.

Linley (Carbon) had a post office open in 1902 with Walter Linley, postmaster. Linley, who settled on West Red Lodge Creek, ran a general store there. The office closed in 1907 and Luther, a nearby "twin city", handled the mail.

Lion City, Lion Mountain got their names because a prospector named Gerry Grotevant had been frightened by what he thought was a lion. It turned out to be just a white mule grazing peacefully. Now **Lion City** is a mining ghost town.

Lippard (Chouteau) was a station on the Great Northern between Fort Benton and Virgelle.

Lisle (Rosebud), near Forsyth, had a post office 1911-12 with Frances Finch as postmaster.

Lismas (Valley) was on the north bank of the Missouri River. Most of the country between the Missouri and the Yellowstone rivers was occupied by sheep and cattle ranchers who had to ferry across the Missouri in order to trade at Glasgow or summer their stock on the verdant northern ranges. The first ferryboat at **Lismas** was run by Bill Kirkland, who had a flat-bottomed boat, much like a tub, which was attached to a rope cable. Kirkland crossed the river where it made a bend and was sufficiently narrow so that the strong current propelled the boat to the other side. He also had a ferry made of two cottonwood poles and a platform; this could transport a team of horses and a wagon. Sometimes people had to wait several days to get across the river because ". . . Mr. Kirkland did not really attend to his work very diligently." Glasgow merchants wanted the trade of the settlers south of the river, so they urged Horace Gamas to buy the ferry business, which he did in 1903. Gamas's partner was Julius Listo(e). The pair applied for a post office and, required to furnish a name, they devised a compound word using the first three letters of **Lis**to and the last three of Ga**mas**. The ice gorge of 1905 broke up the ferryboat and cable, so businessmen from Glasgow helped finance the installation of a 1500-foot steel cable, with a sixty-foot tower on the south side of the river, and a forty-foot tower on the north. This new arrangement made it possible to haul a four-horse team and wagons, or twenty cattle, or more than 200 sheep. The big cattle outfits swam their herds across the river, but sheep had to be ferried. Gamas eventually bought out his partner and continued to haul sheep until the hard winters of 1907 and later broke many sheepmen. In 1910 Gamas "crossed" 60,000 head of sheep for Mr. Bair at a penny a head. The sheep that grazed the open range from Malta to the North Dakota line were brought into the Judith Basin for winter feeding and had to cross the Missouri to get there. At **Lismas**, travelers could put up the team for the night, sleep, eat, and have a drink, as well as get the mail (Highland). The post office opened in 1903 with Gamas as postmaster; it closed in 1920.

Little Crooked (Fergus) was named for the creek of the same name. The post office was open 1916-30; after that the mail was sent to Wilder. Montgomery Marshall served as first postmaster.

Little Jewell (Blaine), near Turner, had a post office 1913-25; Frank Allen was the first postmaster.

Living Springs (Wheatland) is at the edge of the Big Snowy Mountains. The post office opened in 1916 and likely took its name from an area spring fed by mountain waters. John Wecklerly was the first postmaster; the office closed in 1951.

LIVINGSTON (Park) is a county seat twenty-five miles and one mountain pass east of Bozeman. The post office was established November 1822 with Frederick Wright as postmaster. **Livingston** began in 1882 when railroad surveyors camped on the site and called it Clark City, for the famous explorer who traveled down the Yellowstone River while his associate, Lewis, explored the northern branches of the Missouri. Clark and his men came down Billman Creek and arrived at the Yellowstone just south of **Livingston**'s present site on July 15, 1806. The first settlement here, called Benson's Landing was started about 1873 as a ferry crossing four miles north of the present town. Throughout its development, the town has depended greatly on the railroad. Its present name is in honor of a director of the Northern Pacific, Crawford Livingston of St. Paul, Minnesota. The annual **Livingston** Rodeo helps keep the spirit of the Old West alive.

Lizard (Toole) was the name of a short-lived post office near Devon; it was open 1920-21 with Sophia Seitz in charge.

Lizzott (Silver Bow), named for first postmaster Frank Lizzott, was a post office 1888-93.

LLOYD (Blaine) is near the Bear Paw Mountains on Snake Creek, where Chief Joseph made one of his great stands. In 1890, when the Judith Basin began to be invaded by homesteaders and farmers, the Judith Basin Cattle Pool decided to move its thousands of cattle to the rich range along the Milk River and the Bear Paw Mountains. The new headquarters for the reorganized pool, called the Bear Paw Pool, was on a ranch owned by L. B. Taylor near the present town of **Lloyd**. Herds of cattle varying from two to three thousand head were rounded up and driven across the Missouri River at Judith Landing.

"Any community feeling the need for postal service had to prove the need by financing a six-month trial period of carrying the mail. The **Lloyd** patrons did this by bringing the mail to Pat Murphy's place on Snake Creek. Mrs. Murphy dispensed the mail, and then the people receiving letters were expected to pay one dollar a piece for them. This arrangement continued until 1890 when a post office was established and Alice Murphy became the official postmaster" (Allison). For several years the Dolans ran a store and handled the office at **Lloyd**. Besides serving **Lloyd**, the office there supplied the offices at Leroy, Riedel, Maddux, and Bear Paw near Star Route three times a week. Mail and supplies for the store in **Lloyd** had to be hauled by four-horse teams from Chinook.

Locate (Custer) is twenty-seven miles east of Miles City where the highway crosses the Powder River. The post office opened in 1925 with William Bradshaw as postmaster and closed in 1974.

Lock (Custer) was named for first postmaster Christina Lockie; the office opened in 1895. In 1909 the postal area here became known as Calabar.

Lockhart (Jefferson), near Bernice, had a post office 1891-1906 and was named for first postmaster William Lockhart.

Lockwood (Yellowstone), a Northern Pacific station, had a post office 1906-10 with Ava Crombie, postmaster.

LODGE GRASS (Big Horn), which is on the Little Big Horn River and the Crow Indian Reservation, is the trading center for ranchers whose herds graze the rich, grass-covered uplands where buffalo used to range. In the early days the Crows made their summer hunting camps here. The town was named for Lodge Grass Creek, which empties nearby into the Little Big Horn. The Indians called the stream "Greasy Grass," because the grass was so nourishing that it made their animals greasy fat. The words for "grease" and "lodge" are so similiar in the Crow language that an interpreter mistakenly translated the phrase as *Lodge Grass* (Rowe). The post office opened in 1900 with George Pease as postmaster.

Lodgepole (Blaine) Local historians say that this post office was in operation 1899-1916 with Col. William H. H. Healy postmaster for this entire period; postal records, however, report his tenure as 1906-19. But Nettie Walsh, Healy's daughter, insists that when her father died in 1916 he had been postmaster for seventeen years: "We had the post office in **Lodgepole** when the subagent, Maj. William J. Allen, was shot and killed by Charles Perry on March 28, 1902" (from a letter belonging to Ralph Shane). **Lodgepole** is on the Fort Belknap Indian Reservation.

Loesch (Powder River), near Stacey, was named for first postmaster Marion Loesch; the office was active 1916-50.

"This was cattle country in the days when herds were trailed in from Texas. The ranchers living along Pumpkin Creek built a sod shanty or a log house; they were pretty much of one breed; weatherbeaten, hard-working, sometimes hard living cattlemen. Women were scarce (Theodore Roosevelt said 'The frontier is hard on women and horses.') and the wives of these settlers ran the gamut; some were retired prostitutes, some were Indian, some came from the states as 'mail order brides;' some came with their husbands from the East, all were ladies who had to adapt to the rigors of blizzards, drought, and Indian attacks" (*Before Barbed Wire*). The **Loesch** post office was first located on Valentine Loesch's ranch and moved in 1919 to the Edwin Lockwood ranch. Jew Hall was on a hillside overlooking Pumpkin Creek; it was a frame structure originally intended as a store. Later the storekeeper and owner left and gave the building to the community for a recreation center. It needed no remodeling; the large front windows let in plenty of light, and the shelves served as childrens' beds while their parents danced in the hall. Dances and socials of all kinds were held in Jew Hall and the ranchers remained deeply appreciative of this gift from their Jewish friends. Later the building burned.

Logging Creek (Cascade) was a post office 1893-99. It was located on the creek by the same name, which is a tributary of Belt Creek. The community was formerly called Morris. **Logging Creek's** post office was open 1893-99 with Hattie Dodd, postmaster.

Logan (Gallatin) is a railroad town. The right-of-way was acquired from Odelia Logan in 1885. The community was originally called Cannon House, but the name was changed in 1889. The post office opened in 1891 with Owen Thomas as postmaster. It became a rural station out of Manhattan in 1960.

Logie (Blaine) was a dry-land farmers' community. One year an invasion of army worms ate every green-growing thing in the area; this disaster, added to other hazards and the elements, was the last straw, and many discouraged settlers moved away (Allison). A post office with the tentative name **Logie** was approved for Lewis and Clark County in 1896 but was never in operation. William Logie was to have been postmaster.

Lohman (Blaine), a few miles west of Chinook, was a station on the Great Northern with a post office 1916-64, and named for the family of Lillie Lohman, first postmaster.

"A. S. Lohman opened banks, too. In 1916 he built a ranch house at

Yantic. That same year his good friend, Louis Hill, son of James J. Hill, renamed the community **Lohman**" (Allison).

LOLO, LO LO (Missoula) is near the Montana-Idaho border and Lolo Pass, which was so eagerly sought for — and eventually located — by Lewis and Clark. The post office was established in 1888 with John Delany in charge. The creek was originally called Travelers' Rest Creek, because men using the trail there found it an ideal spot to stop, rest, hunt, and repair their gear and clothing before tackling the trip over the pass. The natural hot water springs also helped made it a favorite stop. There has been much conjecture concerning the origin of the name. One idea is that the Indians named it for Lewis, but that in their language it came out Lou Lou and finally Lo Lo. Another suggestion is that it was named by early French traders for LeLouis, and that the present form is a corruption. Still another is that *lolo* is a Nez Perce word meaning "muddy water." Omundson concluded that it is an Indian rendition of Lawrence, the name of an old French trapper, and that the Flathead Indians, unable to sound the "r", replaced it with an "l".

Lolo Hot Springs (Missoula) was originally called Boyles Springs at the suggestion of William Clark, who wrote in his journal for September 13, 1805: ". . . (I) tasted the water . . . found it boiling hot . . . put my finger in water . . . could not bare it but a second." The Lolo post office was first established under the name **Lolo Hot Springs**. A fine indoor plunge which uses the natural hot water is popular with residents of the county. There is also an outdoor swimming pool.

LOMA (Chouteau) is northeast of Fort Benton where the Marias River joins the Missouri. Lewis and Clark camped here on June 3, 1805, and named the smaller river after Capt. Lewis's cousin, Maria Wood. In 1831 Fort Piegan, a trading post, was established here by James Kipp of the American Fur Company. A year later the post was abandoned, burned by the Indians, and replaced by Fort McKenzie. Ferryboat service was available for many years at **Loma**. The post office opened in 1911 with Robert Lee as postmaster. The Great Northern station there was called Chappell.

Lombard (Broadwater) was a railroad town in its early days. The station was at the crossroads of the Northern Pacific and the Milwaukee. For many years there was no automobile road into town and all citizens had to go and come by train. The name was chosen to honor A. G. Lombard, chief engineer of the Montana Railroad during its construction. The original name was Castle Junction. In 1900 the community was dominated by the "Jaw Bone" Railroad. Billy Kee (Kie), the Chinese mayor, hotel proprietor, and man-about-town was famous for his two-story High Point Inn, which he opened in 1897, serving good meals and featuring a bathroom with hot and cold running water. Kee ran his hotel with flexibility: when he went to bed he left a light burning and the register open; late-comers simply scrawled their names in the book, chose a key, and raced the bedbugs to the rooms (Stearns). The post office operated 1896-1957; George Walker was the postmaster.

LONEPINE (Sanders) is west of Polson on the Flathead Indian Reservation. The post office opened in 1911 with William Whiteside as postmaster.

Lonesome (Phillips) was no doubt exactly that out on the high plains of this county. The post office was in operation 1919-23 with Nettie Bell as first postmaster. It was near Midale.

Lonetree (Chouteau), formerly Steele, was north of Conrad and named for a lone cottonwood on Bullhead Creek. The office operated 1914-15 with William Sullivan as postmaster.

"The Lone Tree Stage Stop between Fort Benton and Lewistown was a welcome sight in 1908 as travelers jostled about in the stagecoach, descending from a high rock outcropping to this place in the valley. The building, which dates back to 1889, is still occupied and has been preserved by the Tanner family" (Roberta Donovan: Billings *Gazette*, December 28, 1975). Originally built of sandstone by homesteaders Kit and Ed Wilsow, the building was multi-purposed. It was a stage stop, a school, post office, and candy store as well as a home. It was also the starting point for cattle roundups and a community center for people from the Square Butte and Big Sag areas.

Long (Wheatland) was on Careless Creek east of Judith Gap and was named for first postmaster Norah Long. The office opened in 1905 and closed four years later with orders to send the mail to Bercail.

Lookout (Mineral) This station got its name from its location at the summit of the Coeur d'Alene Mountains 38 miles northwest of St. Regis. Both the Northern Pacific Railroad and the highway used this route over Lookout Pass.

Loomont (Madison) seems to have been in the Waterloo area near Twin Bridges. It is possible that a part of "Montana" was combined with a part of "Waterloo" to create the name, but this is pure conjecture. Alfred C. Farr was postmaster when the office opened in 1912; others were Aralan Kirby, Alba Warn and Harry Mellott. Lena Carney, who was appointed in 1920, was the last; she was probably related to Patrick Carney, who lived in **Loomont** and was known as the Potato King because he was the supply source for the Northern Pacific's famous baked potatoes before Idaho took over the market.

LORING (Phillips) is sixteen miles from Canada. The post office was established 1929 under Wallace Mead. **Loring** was a station on the Great Northern spur line that ran from Saco to Hogelund.

Lost Lake (Chouteau) was a post office 1904-07 with James Patterson as first postmaster. It was near Geraldine and a group of little lakes north of the Highwood Mountains.

Lost Lake (Phillips) was the name of a post office 1915-17 with Emma Forward the first postmaster.

LOTHAIR (Liberty), on the High Line between Chester and Shelby, is surrounded by promising oil and gas fields. The post office opened in 1910 with Morgan Reip as postmaster.

Lothrop (Missoula) was named for L. R. Lothrop, engineer for construction for the Northern Pacific. The post office was established in 1900 with Julia Lashell, postmaster; it closed in 1913.

Louisville (Missoula) was a post office 1870-71 with Franklin Decker as postmaster.

Louscot, (Rosebud) near Rosebud, seems to have had a post office from January-November 1917 with Leonard Franks as postmaster.

Lovejoy (Phillips) was a rural post office between the Milk River and the Canadian border named for the Lovejoy family, and E. P. Lovejoy was postmaster when the office was in operation 1886-87. Harry Lovejoy was postmaster when the office reopened in 1910; it closed in 1933.

Loweth was a station on the Milwaukee named for chief engineer C. F. Loweth at the summit between the Castle and Crazy mountains; it was first named Summit. **Loweth** was between Lennep and Ringling.

Lowrane (Phillips) was a post office 1921-37. The postal area here was originally called Nielsen. The first postmaster was Sadie Buck.

Lowry (Teton) was an early post office 1897-1943. The postmaster was William Flowerree, the son of Daniel Flowerree, who trailed cattle from Texas to Montana in 1873 and built up one of the state's largest herds.

Lozeau (Mineral) is between Alberton and Superior. The post office opened in 1921 with Chris Chulufas in charge, closed in 1925, was reestablished in 1927, and remained active until 1963, when it became a rural station out of Superior.

Lubec (Teton) had a post office 1906-07 with Thomas Carr as postmaster. It was near Glacier Park.

Lucerne (Liberty), near Chester, had a post office 1914-18; Chauncey Sweeney was the first postmaster.

Lucille (Toole) had a post office 1888-95 and December 1895-1901; William Turner was first postmaster. The community was a way station on the old Whoop-Up Trail near Shelby and was named for a daughter of the man stationed there when the office first opened.

Lump Gulch (Jefferson) was named by Fred Jones and William Sprague in 1864 because of the single large lump of gold they found on a prospecting trip in the gulch. A post office **Lump** operated from 1895-1898 with Charles Goble as the first postmaster.

Lundville (Roosevelt) was between Dowd and Bredette and was named for E. A. Lund. A post office opened in 1921 with Agodt Berg as postmaster; it closed in 1930.

Lupfer (Flathead) was a station northwest of Whitefish named for an engineer who was in charge of construction for the Great Northern Railroad. The post office was open briefly in 1917 with Hubert Harmon as postmaster; it was also open 1924-25 and 1930-34.

Lusk (Missoula) was a siding east of Huson named for Frank S. Lusk, president of the First National Bank in Missoula 1910-19 and a landowner in the area. Lusk was also responsible for the establishment of Lusk, Wyoming (Omundson).

Lustre (Valley), twenty miles north of Wolf Point, was settled by people of Dutch descent, most of them Mennonites, around 1916. The Homestead Law, cheap land, lots of grass, and a chance to raise their children away from towns were the main motives for their move to **Lustre**. Worship services were first held in homes; later, five churches were built — there is now a Lustre Bible Academy. A post office opened in 1917 with Henry Dick as postmaster; in 1959 it became a rural independent station out of Frazer.

LUTHER (Carbon) is in the mountains northwest of Red Lodge. The post office was established 1907 and served the nearby Linley area after that office closed. The town was named for the Luther family; Grace Luther kept the post office in one corner of her husband's general store. At one time there was also a blacksmith shop, a lumberyard and a saloon. Linley and **Luther** were sometimes called the "twin cities."

Lux (Gallatin) was a station named for John T. Lux, a farmer who settled there in 1896 (Rowe).

Lyon (Madison) is thirty-five miles upriver from Ennis between Cameron and West Yellowstone. The settlement had its first post office in 1887 in the home of George Barnard, the postmaster. Later it was moved to the Lyon home, and still later to the Hutchins place, which was at the bridge across the Madison River. The office served these three families for many years, a rural route out of Cameron with mail arriving three times a week. All three families were engaged in cattle ranching, but the Hutchins home also became a stopping place for other cattlemen, who had to cross the river here as they drove their herds to summer ranges in the West Fork Range, which extends into Idaho. The post office was closed in 1935.

Lytle (Pondera) had a post office 1901-21; it was named for the family of first postmaster Thomas Lytle.

M

Mabel (Hill), near Rudyard, had a post office 1913-15 with John Heider as postmaster.

Mackenzie, (Fallon) named for postmaster John McKenzie, had a post office from 1912-1943. McKenzie settled there in homestead days and owned the land and log cabin where the post office was located. He also ran a store that was a gathering place for early-day cowboys.

Maddux (Blaine), in Milk River cattle country, was named for postmaster Clara Maddux when the office opened in 1898. The mail was sent to Lloyd when the office closed in 1940.

Madison (Gallatin) was a post office 1870-73 with James Shed as postmaster.

Madison County is in the southwestern part of the state, and is an original county created by the territorial legislature in 1865. Virginia City is the county seat. The county was named for the river which flows its length in the eastern section. The Madison, which empties into the Missouri at Three Forks, was named by Lewis and Clark for then-Secretary of State James Madison. The scene of some of the earliest and richest gold-mining activity in Montana history, **Madison County** has remained almost unchanged in its boundaries while most of the nine original counties have been repeatedly divided. In 1911 the extreme lower portion of **Madison** was annexed to Beaverhead County, which now extends across **Madison's** southern border; otherwise, the boundaries of **Madison County** are much the same as they were in 1865.

Madoc (Daniels) was originally called Orville, and a post office was established under that name in 1910. The name was changed in 1915 and Mary Lockrem was appointed postmaster. The office closed in 1963.

Magdalen (Madison) was a post office 1892-97. Postmasters were Emma Williams, Gene Williams and Herman Fisher. The area was formerly served by Shambow.

Magnolia (Meagher) seems a strange name for a Montana post office, but there it was, open 1880-81 with Nelson Bump as postmaster.

Magpie was a stagecoach station in a two-story frame building near Canyon Ferry.

Maiden (Fergus) was said to have a population of 6,000 in 1881. Settlers and miners came to the area from Coulson, near Billings, by bullteam. Prospectors had planned to call the camp Groven after an Indian woman, presumably a Gros Ventres, but in April 1881 Mrs. James H. Connely visited the camp and, asking why they didn't give a white woman a chance, suggested they name it after her little girl. **Maiden**, sometimes called Maidenville, rivaled Lewistown for the honor of being the county seat in newly-created Fergus County. The miners held out for **Maiden**, but stockmen and ranchers lobbied for the new settlement of Lewistown and finally won. A disastrous fire swept **Maiden** in 1905 and leveled the buildings, but business had already dwindled and there was no point in rebuilding (Woole). **Maiden** had a post office 1882-1921; Fred Dunton was the first postmaster. Frank Burke, writing from Fort Maginnis, Montana Territory on October 20, 1882 is quoted: "Near here . . . is the little mining community called Maidenville. It consists of about one hundred rough log shanties and is a fair specimen of a frontier settlement. . . . A most delightful social affair in which two men lost their lives took place there last Sabbath" (see *Montana Magazine*, winter 1969). The *Mineral Argus*, a newspaper published at **Maiden**, reported on November 27, 1884 that the Crows were raiding the Musselshell for horses. Then, ten days later, the same paper reported that in a gulch some twenty or thirty miles east of Musselshell there were seven Blackfeet Indians hanging from cottonwood trees.

Main, (Teton) near Altyn, was named for the first postmaster, Henry Main. The office was open from 1899-1902.

Makoshika is a state park in the badlands southeast of Glendive. Improved roads and hiking trails now lead to campgrounds and make the rugged grandeur of the place accessible to visitors. The area was once a Sioux hunting ground; they gave it a name meaning "hell cooled over." It was also once the home of prehistoric lizards, and fossil hunters now comb the formations for specimens.

MALTA (Phillips), a county seat, was named for the Mediterranean island by an official of the Great Northern Railroad — another time when a spin of the globe determined the name of a Montana station. For the years 1870-1900 **Malta** was the hub of a cattle empire that reached from Glasgow to Havre, from the Missouri Breaks to Canada. The Bear Paw Pool and owners of four famous brands — Phillips, Coburn, Matador, Phelps — controlled the range. For years **Malta** was the Saturday night haven for cowpokes from the Canadian border to the Missouri. Robert Trafton was postmaster when the office opened in 1890.

Mammoth (Madison) was a post office near Jefferson Island 1877-1908 and 1930-31 with William Marr, postmaster.

Manchester (Cascade), near Great Falls, was a station on the Great Northern named after the Manchester Woolen Mill in Vermont, which established a mill in Montana. The town was settled by a colony of Mormons. The post office opened in 1904 with Florence Haugh as postmaster, closed in 1905, was open again 1906-11, and possibly opened for a final time in 1915, but has since been discontinued.

MANHATTAN (Gallatin) is twenty miles northwest of Bozeman. The name was chosen by a group of New York investors who had bought a lot of land in the area and also operated the Manhattan Malting Co. Previous postal names were Moreland and Hamilton, though the latter community was about a mile south of the present town. **Manhattan** eventually moved to the site chosen by the railroad for a station. Prohibition ended a profitable twenty-three years in the malting business for **Manhattan**, but the stone malt house still stands. The post office was opened in 1891 with Robert Chisholm, Jr. as postmaster.

Manicke (Lincoln) was named for first postmaster Augusta Manicke. The office was open 1915-35.

Mann (Judith Basin) was near Geyser. Edgar Mann was postmaster when the office opened in 1888; it closed in 1892.

Manrock (Richland) was a station on the Great Northern. The name is derived from a large rock a short distance southeast of the station that resembles a man.

Manson (Pondera) is now a ghost town on an irrigation project named for Dr. F. M. Manson's nephew, who surveyed the area for the project. The post office opened in 1911 with Robert Stormont as postmaster; it closed in 1922.

Marco (Dawson) was a station on the Northern Pacific along the Yellowstone River north of Glendive. The post office opened in 1909 and was named for George Marco, the postmaster; it closed in 1918.

Marewell (Custer) briefly had a post office January-June 1884. The postmaster was Joseph Kastner.

Margana (Madison) existed as a postal name July 1886-January 1887, when the name was changed to Revenue. **Margana**'s postmaster was James Harvey Johnson, who continued in the position when the name was changed.

Marias (Liberty) was named for the Marias River which flows through the lower section of the county. Meriwether Lewis named the river for his cousin, Maria Wood. Recent historians have concluded that this is the river that the Indians called *ah-mah-tah-ru-shush-sher*, or "the river that scolds all others" (*Montana Magazine*, summer 1976). A **Marias** post office was opened in 1898 with John George, postmaster. It was closed in 1940.

MARION (Flathead) is southwest of Kalispell on Little Bitterroot Lake. The post office, established in 1892 with Charles Mitchell as postmaster, has served summer visitors to the cabins and campgrounds as well as year-round residents. The area is also knows as Swan, and from time to time the post office has been under that name. The office was closed 1894-1906.

Mariposa (Missoula) This office was open 1873-74 with David Simmons, postmaster.

Marne (Stillwater) was a post office 1922-24; Rudolph Stark was postmaster.

Marsh (Dawson) was named for F. H. Marsh, who was trainmaster for the Northern Pacific in 1882. The first building was erected near the railroad siding in 1910 by N. A. Folger and used as a general store and post office. A ferryboat crossed the Yellowstone at **Marsh** 1914-18 — the boat was later destroyed by an ice gorge. A telephone line was built in 1918 to the John Meidinger farm using barbed wire fence for line. The post office opened in 1910 with Noble Folger as postmaster; it closed in 1962.

Marshall (Lewis and Clark) was a post office April-August 1875 with August Kruger as postmaster. The office was open again 1914-15 under Claud Lockwood.

Marston (Flathead) was a post office 1895-1907 and named for first postmaster Cyrus Marston.

Martina (Missoula), near Frenchtown, was a gold miners' camp that came to life when Louis Barrette made a strike there in 1869. It was nearly deserted by 1880.

Martina (Missoula) When this post office opened in 1875 John Rains, the saloonkeeper, was postmaster. The office was mostly open until 1918.

MARTIN CITY (Flathead) boomed when the Hungry Horse Dam project started. The post office opened in 1947 with Clara Frederick as postmaster. In that same year Joseph Kinsey Howard wrote, "These towns are the youngest and brashest boom towns I ever saw. **Martin City**, for instance, is busily planning a 'Pioneer Days' fete in the spring to honor its 'oldtimers;' the town will be one year old then. . . . **Martin City** occasionally sings hymns of praise to its pioneer 'business men' — barkeeps; it has seven bars and that's about all it has. . . . The county in which all this is happening is high and remote, pretty well isolated all winter. Nearest town of any size is Kalispell" (*Not in Precious Metals Alone*). In spite of government red tape, the Hungry Horse Dam was built and **Martin City** settled down to being a regular Montana town.

Martinsdale (Meagher) was named for Maj. Martin Maginnis, territorial delegate to Congress for several terms. **Martinsdale** is a sheepman's town; to the west is the Smith ranch of 86,000 acres and to the east the Bair spread of 80,000 acres — two of the biggest sheep outfits in the state. In 1910 Bair shipped out forty-four carloads of wool, said to be worth $500,000 and the largest single shipment of wool that ever left Montana. False fronts on the buildings along Main Street reflect the era of the 1880s. The Milwaukee depot is quiet for most of the year, but it was a bustling place when cattle and sheep were brought in for shipping. George Clendenin, Jr., was appointed postmaster when the office opened in 1878 and the ranges were still filled with cattle.

MARYSVILLE (Lewis and Clark) was once a famous mining town. It is some thirty miles northwest of Helena and popular with skiers. **Marysville** was one of the state's leading gold producers 1880-90. Thomas Cruse, who discovered the Drumlummon Mine there, named his strike after his home in Ireland and the town for Mrs. Mary Ralston, the first white woman to arrive. It has been estimated that the total output from this mine was around $50 million. Much of it was mined while Drumlummon was owned by an English company. "Tommy" Cruse was converted to Catholicism shortly before his death, and much of his fortune went toward building the beautiful Gothic cathedral in Helena. The **Marysville** post office opened in February 1881 with Michael Lane as postmaster.

Maschetah (Big Horn) had a post office 1915-37; first postmaster was Stella Schultz.

Mason (Broadwater) was a post office 1905-09 near Townsend; William Tierney was the first postmaster.

Mason (Carbon) was a loading place near Laurel named for S. D. Mason, engineer for the Northern Pacific.

Matador (Blaine) was a Great Northern station originally called Montauk. The name was changed in 1915 for the Matador Land and Cattle Company, a large Texas outfit that ran cattle in the area.

Mathus (McCone) had a brief post office May-October 1915. The name was changed to Pattonhill, presumably for Ruth Patton, first postmaster.

Matthews (Gallatin) was named for Thomas Matthews, a farmer who settled there in 1898.

Maudlin (Rosebud) was named for postmaster Lloyd Maudlin when the office opened in 1916. When it closed in 1926 the mail was ordered to Angela.

MAUDLOW (Gallatin) was a post office 1898-1905 with George Dodge as postmaster; it was reopened in 1905. It was named for a member of the family of the Montana Railroad's president, R. A. Harlow; presumably her first name, Maud, was combined with the last part of Harlow.

Mauland (Fergus) was named for Claus Mauland, a stockman. The post office was open 1905-08.

MAXVILLE (Granite) is south of Drummond on Flint Creek and the Northern Pacific spur that went to Philipsburg. Originally called Flint, the name was changed to honor storekeeper and postmaster R. R. MacLeod. But due to an error in recording the name on national postal records, the name that was supposed to be Macville became **Maxville**. The post office opened under that name in 1912 and Henry Bauer was appointed postmaster.

Maxwell (Park) was briefly on the postal records July-November 1893 with Joel Gaylor as postmaster.

McALLISTER (Madison) is seven miles north of Ennis. The general store and post office are located almost on the shore of Ennis Lake. It was named for the family of a local rancher. **McAllister** was established as a town, in a slightly different location, in December 1896 on land bought by Alex McAllister from the Northern Pacific Railroad. McAllister's parents had settled here in 1871. One of the first churches in Madison County, a Methodist frame building, was built here in 1887 and is still used occasionally. The post office was established in 1902 with Davis Lindsay as postmaster. However, the area had been known as Meadow Creek, and a post office under that name a few miles to the east opened in 1869 and served residents until the **McAllister** office opened.

McCABE (Roosevelt) was named for the first white man who settled on the creek that was later named McCabe Creek, between the Big Muddy

River and the North Dakota border. The post office opened in 1910 with Jay Hull in charge. The community was formerly called Leland.

McClain (Missoula) was named for T. A. and J. P. McClain, from whom the right-of-way for the Northern Pacific was acquired. The McClains had an apple orchard of a hundred trees, and a siding was built here so they could ship their apples, cider and vinegar.

McClave (Fergus) was named for Charles R. McClave, who at one time was manager of the Montana Flour Mills. The town lies at the foot of the Big Snowy Mountains and almost on the Judith Basin County line. **McClave** began as a station on the Milwaukee.

McClellan Gulch (Deer Lodge) had a post office 1869-1890; Charles Peyse was the postmaster. In 1890 the postal area was called Rochester.

McCone (Dawson) was a post office 1916-20 with Elsie Good as postmaster. The office opened in 1923 and closed a year later. **McCone** was between Circle and Brockway.

McCone City (McCone), on the Missouri River, had a post office 1935-41; Nora Witt was first postmaster. The community was active during the construction of Fort Peck Dam.

McCone County is in northeastrn Montana. The county seat is Circle. The name is in honor of Dawson County's Senator McCone, who worked to create **McCone County** in 1919 from parts of Dawson and Richland counties. Waters from Fort Peck Reservoir reach into the arid acres of **McCone County**.

McCracken (Yellowstone) is a settlement named after a local rancher.

McDermott (Toole) was formerly called Westbutte. The name was changed in 1924 to honor Peter J. McDermott. The post office was discontinued in 1933.

McDonald (Sanders) got its name because it was near the ranch of Duncan McDonald, the son of Angus McDonald and an Indian woman. In 1916 Duncan told historians that the half-breed Benetsee had told Duncan's father as early as 1849 that there was gold in the Gold Creek area. Duncan, who was employed by the Hudson's Bay Company, had built Fort Connah in 1847, and the company, fearing a gold rush would ruin the lucrative fur trade, hoped to suppress word of the discovery. Lake McDonald in Glacier Park is named for the same family.

McDowell (Custer) This post office was in operation 1883-84 with William Jacobs as postmaster. When the office closed, the mail was ordered to Brandenburg, so **McDowell** must have been near where the Rosebud, Custer, and Powder rivers now join.

McElroy (Sheridan) was named for first postmaster John McElroy. The office was open 1914-19 and 1924-50. **McElroy** was on the Milwaukee near the North Dakota border in the northeast corner of Sheridan County.

McElroy (Yellowstone) This settlement was named for a Billings contractor.

McGowan (Chouteau) was named for Francis McGowan, the first postmaster. The office was open 1912-13; after that the mail was sent to Highwood.

McHessor (Madison) was a post office 1915-34; postmasters were

Martha Page, Alfred Whitney and Mable Holzmiller. McHessor Creek and this settlement were southwest of Twin Bridges almost on the Beaverhead County line.

McIntire (Broadwater) had a post office 1913-17 with William McIntire as postmaster.

McKay (Custer) had a post office 1899-1903 and was named for first postmaster Charley McKay.

McKenzie (Fallon), named for postmaster John McKenzie, had a post office 1912-43. McKenzie, who settled the area in homestead days, owned the land and log cabin where the office was located. He also ran a store that was a gathering place for early day cowboys.

McLEOD (Sweet Grass), on the Boulder River south of Big Timber, was named for W. F. McLeod. Originally a trading post, the post office opened there in 1886 with Elijah Fowler the first postmaster. The office closed in 1918 but reopened in 1920.

McMillan (Prairie) was in old Dawson County when the post office was open 1898-99 with Alexander McMillan as postmaster. The office was open again 1900-07 and 1908-09.

McNamara (Missoula), at the confluence of Union Creek and the Blackfoot River, was named for Mike McNamara, who owned a saloon and two or three other buildings there in the early 1900s. The community is now abandoned (Omundson).

McNulty (Sheridan), named for the family of first postmaster Elizabeth McNulty, had a post office 1911-14.

McQuarrie (Missoula) was a Northern Pacific siding named for Daniel McQuarrie, a resident at Bearmouth as early as 1893 and a farmer near Clinton in 1898 (Omundson).

McRae (Big Horn) is near the Treasure County line in a fork of Sarpy Creek. The post office opened in 1916 with Alice Warren in charge and closed in 1953.

McTwiggin (Garfield) had a post office 1917-35; Clara Turner was the first postmaster.

Meaderville (Silver Bow) was originally called Gunderson, then renamed for Charles T. Meader, a forty-niner who came to California via Cape Horn and arrived in Butte in 1876. **Meaderville** was on "the richest hill on earth," and was a busy Butte suburb when the mines were flourishing. Its post office was open 1903-08; Frank Lyons was postmaster. Open-pit mining in recent years has removed the last vestige of **Meaderville**.

Meadow (Flathead) had a post office established in 1901. The name was changed to Pleasant Valley in 1903 — both names are obviously descriptive. Charles Lynch was the first postmaster at **Meadow**.

Meadow Creek (Madison) had a post office opened in 1869 with Waity Walton in charge; the office served the area later taken over by McAllister. The **Meadow Creek** office closed in 1883 and reopened 1886-1908. Ranches in the area ranged from the Tobacco Root Mountains to Ennis Lake.

Meagher County (pronounced MAR) is located a little southwest of the center of Montana. It was created in 1867 from parts of Chouteau and

180

Gallatin counties; a part of **Meagher County** was taken to form Fergus County in 1885, and a part to form Broadwater in 1897; parts were annexed to Cascade and Lewis and Clark 1890-1900, a part of Fergus was annexed to **Meagher** in 1911, and parts of **Meagher** were taken to form parts of Sweet Grass in 1885. White Sulphur Springs is the county seat. **Meagher County** was named for Gen. Thomas Francis Meagher, an Irish patriot and Civil War "hero" who was a federal official when he arrived in Montana. Kenneth Richard Meagher of Antelope High School, a descendant drawing on family records, says, "Before coming to the United States, Meagher joined a band of men in Ireland who were trying to separate Ireland from England by violent means. When put to trial he was sentenced to death for treason, but the sentence was changed to life imprisonment in Van Diemen's Land, now called Tasmania. On his way to Van Diemen's Land he managed to escape and come to the United States, where he became a general leading a Union band called the Irish Brigade. After the Civil War and his release from the Army, he became a writer and lecturer. Failing at this, he took his chances and came to Montana and was acting governor of the territory during the Blackfeet trouble. He became known as 'Meagher of the Sword' because he once stated in a speech that the only way to freedom was by bloodshed. Meagher disappeared from a riverboat on the Missouri at Fort Benton." What happened to Thomas Francis Meagher remains one of the mysteries of pioneer Montana. Some of his staunch supporters declared him a martyr to the Irish cause and erected a statue of him on the capitol grounds in Helena. Elizabeth Lake and Elizabeth Falls in old Missoula County were named for his wife.

Mecaha (Garfield) had a post office 1915-41. The mail was brought to this office from as far away as Melstone until post offices were opened at Mosby and Ross. The name (pronounced MUH-kay-haw) means "racoon" in the language of one of the Southern tribes (Highland) and was chosen by M. J. Carron, the U.S. Land Commissioner on the Musselshell. During the hard winter of 1919 a cattle outfit that used an "X" brand was wintering 1,100 head in the area; when the snow got too deep for grazing, freighters — in fifty-degrees-below-zero weather — hauled in cracked corn to try to save the cattle, but 700 died. The first postmaster was Tina Busic.

Medhurst (Granite) had a post office 1884-85 with John Easton as postmaster. There was a family named Medhurst in Montana around this time.

MEDICINE LAKE (Sheridan) takes its name from the nearby lake, which was so named by Indians because they found many of their medicinal herbs and roots on its shores. They also believed that the water itself had medicinal qualities. Located in the northeast corner of the state, the lake is now the center of a federal migratory waterfowl reserve. The post office opened in 1907 with Edward Stubban as postmaster.

Medicine Rocks (Carter) were considered holy by the Indians. Their medicine men often went to visit them on the eve of big occasions. The rocks are strange sandstone buttes covering about a square mile and tower like sharp peaks or ridges eighty feet above low, sandy hills. They were described as "fantastically beautiful" by Theodore Roosevelt, whose stock ranch at Medora, North Dakota was a day's ride, and whose name was carved into the stones — they have since been worn away by erosion. "The rocky buttresses appear chalky white above the flowing sands in bright sunlight; in moonlight they appear as molten silver. The crannies in the rock appear as black lines and give it all an air of eerie unreality" (*Montana, A Guide Book*).

Medicine Lodge (Beaverhead), near Armstead, had a post office 1909-14; Lora Guyaz was the first postmaster.

Meeteetse Trail began at Billings, went the length of Carbon County and on to Meeteetse, Wyoming, and was reportedly located by the army in 1881 as one of its routes. In August 1882 the Northern Pacific Railroad reached Billings, which was on the trail, and that city at once became the main distribution center east of the Rocky Mountains. Supplies were carried by wagon train through Laurel, Park City, Roberts, Red Lodge, Chance and on into Wyoming. The **Meeteetse Trail** is one of the most historic and scenic of the old stage and freighter roads and was used from 1881. "Buffalo Bill" Cody used it while he was developing "Cody County" in northwestern Wyoming. Lesser trails branched off to connect Bridger and Fromberg to the main trail (Maryott). Stout teams of four and six horses, motivated by salty drivers, pulled tough coach-type wagons and had to be changed every fifteen or twenty miles. Stages traveled sixty to eighty miles a day, tying together cattle ranches and army posts.

Meharry (Valley) is almost on the Canadian border in the northwest corner of the county. The post office opened in 1920 under Martin Brown and closed in 1937.

Mellady (Missoula) was a railroad station named for a parish priest in Frenchtown. The station was also known as Gaspard; now it is called Schilling.

MELROSE (Silver Bow) is on the Big Hole River halfway between Butte and Dillon. It is famous for its trout fishing. The post office opened in June 1881 with Charles Shively, postmaster.

MELSTONE (Musselshell) began as a Milwaukee Railroad station and was named for Melvin Stone, an Associated Press reporter who was aboard the train with the railroad's president, his daughter, and a friend, all of whom were naming towns along the line. The station was a freight division and promised to be important. The post office opened June 18, 1908, with Robert Wilson as postmaster. Dry land farmers followed the railroad but the surrounding acres proved too dry, and now they are dotted with producing oil wells; while other towns around it are decaying, **Melstone** has begun a new lease on life.

MELVILLE (Sweet Grass), on the Sweetgrass River, was named by H. O. Hickox for Lieutenant Melville of arctic exploration fame. It is a supply point for sheep camps in the Crazy Mountains as well as headquarters of the Cremer Stock Ranch, which not only breeds bucking horses and other stock for Western rodeos, but once even supplied them for Madison Square Garden. The post office was established in 1883 with Hickox as postmaster. **Melville** ranchers also raised good cattle, mostly Herefords, but during the lean years they — like so many Montana ranchers — found prices low, money hard to borrow, and government regulations making them spend more time "with bureaucrats than with cows." Some of them went into small-scale dude ranching for extra income (*Not in Precious Metals Alone*). "Spike" Van Cleve, one of those who did, has presented a vivid· picture of **Melville** in his book *Forty Years Gatherings*.

Melz (Chouteau) was named for first postmaster Albert Melz. The office was open 1897-99.

Menard (Gallatin) was named for Telsford Menard, an area farmer. The town consisted of a few houses, a store, and a station for the Milwaukee spur from Bozeman. The post office operated 1915-46; Amos C. Curtis was the postmaster.

Mendon (Fergus) is between Buffalo and Hobson. When the Great Northern built the spur line connecting Billings with Great Falls, it was the railroad's policy to have a siding about every seven miles where trains could pass. Some were actual depots, others only a name. At its height **Mendon** had a store, lumberyard, grain elevator, and a post office which operated 1909-13 under postmaster William Hersch. The mail bag was thrown off as the train went by. If there was a passenger wanting to board, he stood in the middle of the tracks and waved his arms. The engineer would toot his whistle twice to indicate he would stop. Citizens were called upon to name the siding. Some felt Murder would be both descriptive and appropriate, as two or three Negro construction workers had been killed in a fight. Instead of burying the slain men, workers threw them into the railroad grade and simply covered them up. But other citizens thought Murder was too undignified and everyone finally agreed on **Mendon** (*In the Shadow of the Twin Sisters*).

Meredith (Custer) was named for Meredith Neil, postmaster when the office opened in 1912; it closed in 1933.

Merino (Judith Basin), between Geyser and Stanford, was named because large bands of Merino sheep were raised here. The settlement was originally called Finfrock. When the name changed in 1916 a post office was established as **Merino** with Henry M. Johnson as postmaster; it was discontinued in 1955.

Merino (Wheatland) had a post office 1881-82 with Delphaett Scaurmont as postmaster. The office reopened 1885-1900 when the name was changed to Harlowton. Merino sheep were raised extensively here. **Merino** was a stage station on the east-west route between the Judith Basin and Big Timber and consisted of one building and a combination stage stop-post office-general store and saloon.

Meriwether (Glacier) was formerly called Bombay. The name was changed to honor Capt. Meriwether Lewis, who camped here July 1806.

Meriwether Camp (Lewis and Clark) is in the Gates of the Mountains area, which is now a recreation development. It was named for Capt. Meriwether Lewis, who first described it; Lewis said there was hardly a spot "large enough that one could rest the soul of his foot" between the mountain cliffs and the river. Gass, who was with Lewis, called it "a howling wilderness."

Merrill (Sweet Grass), near Columbus, had a post office 1890-1910; Mathew Miller was the postmaster.

Merriman (Park) was named for W. H. Merriman, an official of the Northern Pacific Railroad.

Meyersburg (Park) had a post office in 1887 with Sam O. C. Brady as postmaster; it closed in 1911. It is sometimes spelled Myersburg.

Midale (Phillips) was a post office 1919-38; the first postmaster was Caroline Sanders.

Midasburg (Madison) was a short-lived mining camp less than a mile from Sterling, where in 1867 a group of New York businessmen built the Midas Mill. The fifty men employed there refused to be a part of the Sterling settlement, so they named their community of cabins and tents **Midasburg**, because they were grouped around the $40,000 Midas Mine. There was a school at the confluence of Hot Spring and Pony creeks 1888-1902. Presumably the Eastern promoters named their gold mine in honor of the legendary King Midas. Several buildings are still standing.

Midby was a station on the Great Northern branch line that ran from Bainville to Scobey. It was near Plentywood. The post office opened in 1914 with Laura Robertson as postmaster and closed in 1922.

Mid Canon (Cascade) was a station on the Great Northern almost on the Lewis and Clark County line. It is one of the few places in Montana with a name of Spanish origin, and no doubt derived its name from its position in this mountainous area. The office opened in 1890 with Eliza Wantz as postmaster and closed in 1905.

Middle Creek (Gallatin) had a post office 1869-71 with George Austin as postmaster. It was also active 1872-73.

Middle Fork (Valley) was a post office 1913-14 with Tena Bachlund as postmaster. It was about twenty miles from the Canadian border almost directly north of Glasgow.

Midland (Carter), near Ekalaka, had a post office 1894-1914; Margaret Simmons was first postmaster.

Midvale (Glacier) had a post office December 1892-March 1893 with John Larkin as postmaster. The office was open again 1901-13 when the name was changed to Glacier Park.

Midway (Pondera) got its name because it was halfway between Conrad and Brady.

Mifflin (Yellowstone) is a community between Hardin and Billings on Pryor Creek.

Mikado (Fergus) This post office was operating 1888-1889 with James Crouse as postmaster.

Mike Horse (Lewis and Clark) was a post office 1943-52. The first postmaster was Elizabeth Klugman.

MILDRED (Prairie County) is on O'Fallon Creek 20 miles southeast of Terry. The station was named for a daughter of a Milwaukee Railroad official. The post office opened in 1908 with Edward Harper as postmaster. **Mildred** was a thriving little town on the Old Yellowstone Trail with many tourists traveling through. The town hall was the scene of wrestling matches, basketball games, spelling bees, and dances. A cyclone carried away most of the building but left the piano unharmed and sheet music still in place on it. Children from the Lacomb and Whitney areas came to school by train each day. When the highway was changed, the town lost population. During the drought years, the country folk left and business places had to close. (*Wheels Across Montana's Prairies*)

MILES CITY (Custer) This county seat was named for Gen. Nelson A. Miles and first called Milestown. The **Miles City** post office was established in 1877 with Louis Payette as postmaster. The 5th Infantry set up camp at the mouth of the Tongue River on the Yellowstone following the

1876 campaign of "rounding up hostile Indians." The commanding officer was Col. (he was later promoted) Miles and the camp was the beginning of **Miles City**. Fort Keogh was built there the following summer. The location at the mouth of the Tongue was excellent for fording the Yellowstone and for trading; it soon became an important stopping place for the long cattle drives from Texas. The Northern Pacific came as far as **Miles City** in 1881 and thus made the town accessible by rail. This was cattle country and each year the Montana Stock Growers Association met in **Miles City**. Sometimes wives came too, for what was often the only trip away from an isolated ranch house for the year. In 1876 the first sheep were introduced by John Burgess from his ranch near Red Bluff, California. One morning, Miles and his men looked out from the stockade and saw a band of sheep grazing the rich grass of the surrounding prairie. There was nothing to do but let them stay, and besides, the soldiers were glad to have a winter supply of mutton. In the spring Burgess sold the band to George M. Miles, then a quartermaster's clerk, and Capt. Frank Baldwin, and the sheep business was launched in eastern Montana (Brown and Felton).

Milk Ranch (Jefferson) was a post office 1867-69 with Orville Branch the postmaster. When the office was moved to the large, white ranch home of E. G. Brooke the name was changed to Whitehall. Brooke's home was a few miles from present-day Whitehall.

Milk River was a Great Northern station on Milk River between Glasgow and Oswego. It tooks its name from the river, which Lewis and Clark said looked like "a cup of tea with a spoonful of milk." The **Milk River** post office operated 1902-10 under Warner Colwell; the name was then changed to Wiota.

Milks is shown in postal records as having an office established in 1920 with Lily Stearns as postmaster. A notation adds that the name was changed to Delight.

Millegan (Cascade) was named for Ruben Millegan, an early settler and postmaster when the office opened in 1887. It closed in 1928.

Miller (Hill) was a post office 1912-20 during homestead days. The first postmaster was storekeeper James B. Miller. The Millers — mother, father, five sons and their families — came by Emigrant train in 1910 and took up homesteads. Hard times and no crops made them all decide to move to Havre (*In Years Gone By*).

Millersville (Lewis and Clark) was a post office 1875-76 with Alexander Loyd as postmaster.

MILL IRON (Carter) was named for the Mill Iron Brand of the Harris-Franklin Cattle Outfit. The settlement grew up on a ranch connected with the Hashknife (brand) spread, which ranged 65,000 cattle in Montana. **Mill Iron** is near Box Elder Creek at the edge of Custer National Forest and about five miles from the South Dakota border. The post office opened in 1916 with Willard Meyer as postmaster.

MILLTOWN, (Missoula) near Bonner, was called Riverside when it was established in 1893 because of its proximity to the Clark Fork and Blackfoot Rivers. The name was changed to avoid confusion with a community of the same name near Butte. At first, in recognition of the many persons of Finnish descent living there, a new name of Finntown was chosen, but later residents disapproved and changed it to **Milltown**. A lumber mill was erected here about 1886 by A. B. Hammond, who sold the mill to Marcus

Daly in 1898. By 1912 the post office was officially listed as **Milltown** and Oscar Hemgren was the postmaster.

Milner, named for the family of first postmaster Anna Milner, was an old Fergus County post office 1898-1907. **Milner** was near Musselshell.

Minden (Meagher) was a post office 1896-03 with Mary Diefendorf the first postmaster. When the office closed the mail was sent to Dorsey.

Miner (Park) is near the Yellowstone River a few miles from Yellowstone National Park. It was a land of prospectors and miners when the post office opened in 1898 with Maggie Morrison the postmaster. The office closed in 1920 but was open again 1921-67.

Mineral (Missoula) had a post office July-December 1886.

Mineral County is a long, narrow county bordering Idaho. Superior is the county seat. The county was named for the many mines and mining prospects in its mountains. **Mineral County** was created in 1914 from a part of Missoula County.

Mingusville (Dawson) started out as Keith; the **Mingusville** post office opened in 1884 with Gustave Grisy the postmaster. In 1895 the name was changed to Wibaux. "Wibaux was first named **Mingusville**, and I had a hand in changing its name. It was a little old railroad town, and to begin with the company had named it after a section foreman and his wife. Her name was Minnie, his was Gus, consequently **Mingus(ville).** In the fall of 1894, while the ox wagon was camped on the flat near the town, shipping beef, Pierre Wibaux and some other fellows rode out to our wagon with a petition to change the town's name to Wibaux. Though there weren't actually a dozen houses in the whole place, old Pierre had a string of names as long as his arm. He'd been meeting all the wagons that came in there, and of course, we all signed his petition, too. He must've got enough names to get the job done, for the next time I went there the town was Wibaux. By wintering cows on brush and cropped green cottonwood limbs, Wibaux brought most of his cattle through the terrible winter of '86-'87 (John Leakey in *The West that Was, From Texas to Montana*).

Mink (Dawson) was a post office southeast of Circle that opened in 1915 with Guy Owen as postmaster; it closed in 1936.

Minnehaha (Cascade) had a post office 1893-94 with Charles Whitman as postmaster. It was near Armington.

Minneota (Hill) was a community of homesteaders who formed a club, built a hall and, in choosing the name of their settlement, remembered their home states of Minnesota and Dakota. They got their mail at Sage or Alma.

Mission (Park) was a station named for an old mission that had been built there to serve the Crow Indians; at that time the Crow Reservation extended that far west. The post office was in operation 1882-85 with Jesse Thompson postmaster.

Missoula, (Missoula) a county seat, was first called Missoula Mills because the town was built around flour and sawmills. The origin of the name **Missoula** has never been agreed upon, but several ideas have found their way into print: Salisbury says, "Indians used to call Hellgate Canyon 'Issoul' meaning horrible. From this the growing city got its name." Rowe insists it is a "Salish Indian word meaning 'River of Awe;'" Duncan

McDonald claimed it is from an Indian word meaning "sparkling waters;" according to *Montana, a Guide Book*, "Missoula takes its name from a Salish Indian word, 'lm l sul a,' meaning 'by the chilling waters.'" And Stout agrees with Rowe that the name is from the Salish 'In mis sou let ka,' which translates into English as the 'river of awe.' The **Missoula** post office was established in 1866 with Charles Shaft as postmaster. The new town soon took much of the trade away from nearby Hellgate. The University of Montana, established in **Missoula** in 1895, greatly influenced the city's economic and cultural growth of the city. Episcopal services were first held in **Missoula** July 10, 1870 by the Rt. Rev. Daniel S. Tuttle, who recruited a brass band to furnish the music and be the choir. In a letter to the Board of Missions in New York Tuttle wrote, "In **Missoula** . . . only the world, the flesh and the devil with mighty helps, and the Holy Spirit unhelped are at work" (Holy Spirit Parish bulletin).

Missoula County is in the western part of Montana. It was established as a county even before Montana Territory was created. The legislature of Washington Territory set up **Missoula County** and included in it a large part of what later became western Montana. Hell Gate was the county seat. Later it was one of the original territory counties created by the Montana legislature in 1865. Its area then extended from the Canadian border to Beaverhead County and formed the western border of the state. Flathead County was created from part of Missoula County in 1893 as was Ravalli County in the same year. Part of Powell County was annexed to **Missoula** in 1915. Lake County was organized from a part of **Missoula County** in 1923 and part of **Missoula** was annexed to Granite in 1943. A part of Granite County was annexed to **Missoula County** also in 1943. **Missoula County** was named before the city of Missoula was named and the same confusion as to origin of the name exists in this case. (See **Missoula**.) The scholarly Father Lawrence Palladino, revered priest of the Missoula parish, concluded that the words the Indians used to describe this place would seem to translate "at the stream of surprise or ambush."

Mitchell (Lewis and Clark) was named for Martin Mitchell, a ranchowner at the time this Great Northern station was built. It was first known as Mitchell's, and Mitchell was postmaster when the office opened in 1888, only to close later that same year. The office was open again in 1898 with Mary Burfield as postmaster; it closed in May 1899, opened again in December, closed in 1922, and was open again 1924-25. The name was then changed to Sieben.

Mizpah (Custer) is southeast of Miles City at the conjunction of the Mizpah and Powder rivers. *Mizpah* is a Biblical word meaning "look out" or "watch tower." It was the meeting place of Jacob and Laban at the watering place in Gilead. According to *Echoing Footsteps*, the stream was named by Brig. Gen. W. F. Raynolds, who wrote in his journal for July 27, 1859: "While on the hill today, and as I was riding in advance of the (wagon) train with a view of finding a route by which we could return to the valley, I lost a much valued seal, and, as this mishap occurred near the source of the branch we had discovered by leaving the river, I named the creek after the motto on the seal. 'Mizpah' is a Hebrew term meaning, 'The Lord watch between me and thee when we are absent one (from) another.'" However, Dr. Marvin Shaw, Asst. Prof. of Religious Studies at Montana State University, says that the word *mizpah* is not an acronym, but that Mizpah in Gilead was named by Jacob in memory of his pact with

Laban, which was sealed with the words, "Yahweh watch between me and thee. . . ." and that there are six places mentioned in the Old Testament called Mizpah. The little Montana town was named for the river; the post office was established at this "watering place" in 1892 with Lucy Hill as postmaster. It was opened and closed four times before its final closing in 1941.

Mobridge (Phillips) was born in 1959 when a bridge across the Missouri was completed and a road opened up for traffic; suddenly the once-isolated farming area had easy access to the rest of the state. The **Mobridge** area has been described as one of "wild harsh beauty" and "a land of stark beauty and violence." Settlers remember devastating floods when the Big Missouri went on a rampage, sizzling summers with thermometers reaching 120 degrees, and feeding cattle in bone-chilling 58-degree-below-zero weather; but they also remember the annual June celebration when the government steamship took advantage of high water and came by, en route to Fort Benton (Byerly and Byerly). **Mobridge** is now inside the Charles M. Russell National Wildlife Range and next door the the James Kipp Recreational Area, so the residents have learned that the neighborliness of frontier life must be adjusted to include campers, travelers, and the demands of a wildlife preserve.

MOCCASIN (Judith Basin) was named after a mountain range, but these mountains with low, rounded summits and densely-forested with lodgepole did look a little like Indian moccasins. The post office was open 1896-97 with Charles Maloy as postmaster; it reopened in 1909. **Moccasin** has been plagued with destructive fires — in 1916, 1919, 1922 and 1955. The town never really recovered from the 1919 blaze, the biggest of all, which burned an entire block of buildings. **Moccasin** is in the productive wheat-raising area of Judith Basin County and was once a station on the Great Northern. Postal records show the establishment of a **Moccasin** post office in Chouteau County in 1891 with William Vannest appointed postmaster. Though it was on the postal books until 1895, there is a notation that it was never in operation; this appears to be the same **Moccasin**.

Moccassin (Meagher) had a post office 1884-85 with John Arnold as postmaster.

Mock (Flathead) had a post office 1921-39 with Peter B. Wiggen, postmaster.

Moiese (Lake County) is near the National Bison Range and was named for a Flathead Indian subchief. The post office opened in 1918 with James Sloan as postmaster. In 1960 it became a rural station out of Charlo.

MOLT, (Stillwater) a Northern Pacific station, is twenty-two miles west of Billings near Big Lake and named for Rudolph Molt, who donated land for the townsite and from whom the railway purchased its right-of-way. The post office for the area was originally called Stickley. The office was moved to its present location and the name changed to **Molt** in 1918. Roy Ege was the postmaster.

Mona (Richland) was a post office some ten miles from the Missouri River. The office opened in 1910 with William Holt as postmaster; it closed in 1944.

Monaco (Flathead) had an office January-July 1891 with James Kennedy as postmaster. The settlement later became known as Columbia Falls.

MONARCH (Cascade) is an almost deserted mining town in the mountains at the junction where two gulches join Belt Creek. From here prospectors with "some grub and an extra pair of socks" still go out to look for paydirt in the hills. Some coarse and fine gold can be caught in the sluice boxes and nuggets worth up to a dollar have been found in recent years. The Great Northern built a branch line from Great Falls to **Monarch** in 1890 so ore could be shipped to the Great Falls smelter. "Three adjacent mining claims at the time were known as 'King,' 'Czar,' and 'Emperor,' " and this may account for the name of **Monarch**. The post office opened in 1889 with Charles Martin as postmaster.

Mondak (Roosevelt) is near Fort Union on the border of North Dakota; thus the two state names were combined. The post office operated 1904-25 with Jacob Deel as postmaster. "Personal liberty and personal restraint met in a head-on clash at the Montana-North Dakota line 1904. The rendezvous was named **Mondak** ... the clash lasted twenty years ... it involved people and the forces of good and evil. ... North Dakota entered the Union as prohibition state; Montana entered the same year (1889) as a wet one. ... The idea of establishing a town on the border, but mostly in Montana so liquor could be sold, was originated by George Stevens, manager of a ranch on Tongue River. ... The ranch was owned by Hamm's Brewing Company of St. Paul, Minnesota. ... **Mondak** was a planned town. ... Stevens proposed the idea to Luke Sweetman. ... Jacob Seel owned some property on the North Dakota border ... it was ideally located on the Great Northern Railroad, on the banks of the Missouri and near the site of the famous old Fort Union. ... In 1904 lots were laid out, buildings began to rise ... ample hitching posts were planned for parched throats from Dakota. ... Prohibition went into effect in Montana in 1920 and there was no longer a reason for **Mondak** and the once wild town became a quiet village" (Alice Sweeetman: *Montana Magazine*, Autumn 1965).

Monida (Beverhead) is so named because it lies close to the boundary line between Montana and Idaho; the name is composed of the first three letters of each state. The highway goes through Monida Pass and crosses the Continental Divide. The town had a post office 1891-93 with William Culver as postmaster. The office was open again 1896-1964 when it became a rural independent station out of Lima.

Monota (Valley) was a post office from 1911 to 1913 with Henry Thomas as postmaster. It would now be in Sheridan County and was practically on the North Dakota border. Again the name came from combining parts of each state's name. The area was formerly called **Harvey** and was near Dagmar.

Montague was a station on the Great Northern near Geraldine and a little cluster of lakes named for Montague, Mass. The post office opened in 1914 with Ferderick Whitmore as postmaster. In 1962 it became a rural independent station out of Fort Benton.

Montana was the name chosen for "that territory up north" because it was the Spanish word for mountain, which seemed appropriate for such a rugged area dominated by the Rockies (for the complete story of how the state was named, see **Introduction**). Robert Dalton Harris, who writes and publishes a postal history quarterly, has long been interested in the fact that three early-day **Montana** post offices had cancellation stamps that spelled the state's name "Montano." Harris has searched diligently for evidence that there might have been some move during the infancy of Montana Territory to promote the "o" spelling. The only clue so far is that during the discussion about the name someone remarked that *Montana*, under Spanish grammatical rules governing gender, was the feminine rendering for "mountain." So possibly a few hardy men in Virginia City, Bannock and Helena sought to use a masculine form of the name in 1865-67.

Montana (Beaverhead) was a gold and silver mining boom town. A post office was established there in 1866 but the name was changed in 1871 to Argenta. H. D. Weed was the postmaster.

Montana City (Jefferson) was a station on the Great Northern only a few miles from Helena. A post office operated there 1887-90; the postmaster was John Geiger.

Montaqua (Carbon) An oil exploration well was drilled here but the result was mineral water, not oil, so it was decided to develop a mineral water resort. The 1959 earthquake shut the water off and the resort closed. The name appears to be a combining form of either "mountain" or "Montana" with "aqua" (water). Sugar beets are loaded at the nearby railroad siding at **Montaqua**. The town is about three miles from Joliet.

Montbestos (Madison) was near Cliff and Wade Lakes. Israel Ameron Hutchins, who owned a cattle ranch on the upper Madison, explored the nearby mountain and located an asbestos mine. He took out a patent but did little actual mining. In the late 1920s a mining company leased the claim and began a huge promotional campaign, selling stock to people all over Montana and even some to citizens of Idaho and Utah. The company built a big mill, established a post office which operated 1929-31 with David Hamilton as postmaster, and then went out of business, leaving the mill to be sold for taxes and the stockholders with nothing. As in Montaqua, here the name of the state or the word 'mountain' was combined with a product to produce a place name.

Montford, (Flathead) near Creston, had a post office 1900-10. Arthur Lindsey was the first postmaster.

Montreal was a gold camp that sprung up thirty-five miles from Frenchtown after gold was discovered there in 1869 by Louis Barrette. As mining activity increased in the Nine Mile area, restaurants, saloons, grocery stores and a blacksmith shop appeared in **Montreal**. By 1875 most of the miners had moved to Frenchtown and very little was left of the camp.

Montrose, (Chouteau) near Gates, had a post office 1914-16 with Isaac Duncan as postmaster.

Monument, (Beaverhead) near Grant, was a post office 1907-10. Samuel Howell was the first postmaster.

Moon Creek (Custer) had a post office 1931-42. Lee Bennett was the first postmaster. The creek for which it is named is in the western part of the county and runs into the Yellowstone River between Miles City and the Rosebud County line. Its contour suggests the shape of a new moon.

MOORE (Fergus) was named after a Mr. Moore of Philadelphia who rendered financial help to Richard A. Harlow when he was building the "Jaw Bone" Railroad from Harlowton to Lewistown. Later Lady Catherine Harlow Moore of Wateringbury, England, visited this part of Montana, indicating a relationship between the Harlows and the Moores that may have been personal as well as financial. The Moore brothers operated a large ranch near here in 1884 and may have been part of the same family. The post office opened in 1904 with Patrick Tooley as postmaster.

Moorehead (Powder River) was named for first postmaster William Moorehead. The office was established in 1890 and closed in 1958. "**Moorehead** was called Franklin from 1892 to 1898. Annis P. Moorehead homesteaded at the present site of the town in about 1900. He was dedicated — the "promoter" type and it is believed he lived in Montana four or five years just for the novelty of it. Between 1917 and 1920, the **Moorehead** post office was moved down the river to the Wimpy family home; this put the post office five miles from the store" (*Echoing Footsteps*).

"Dry wind weathers the logs of a saloon and general store deserted for half a century. . . . The ghost town of **Moorehead** is a relic of the homestead era imposed on wild, arid badlands by Eastern politicians who thought anyone ought to be able to make a living on 160 acres. As the homesteaders dried out or blew away, cattle and sheepmen bought their holdings and adapted to this old buffalo range — knowing what the Easterners didn't, that the land would never adapt to them. Upriver is the site of abortive Moorehead Dam," wrote Clark "Speck" Ritchie (Billings *Gazette*; Nov. 30, 1975), who's been shooting down dams proposed for Powder River for thirty-five years and points to the deserted Moorehead Dam site as an example of foolhardy planning by politicians.

Moose Creek (Deer Lodge) had a post office 1875-82 with William Burgh as the first postmaster. The settlement took its name from the creek which, like so many others in Montana, took its name from the wildlife around it.

Moreland (Gallatin) had a post office 1884-91 with Mark Ledbeater as postmaster. The area was originally called Hamilton; after 1891 it became Manhattan.

Morgan (Madison) was a post office 1892-93 with Thomas Park as postmaster; all this is according to a single surviving postal record, but no other mention of **Morgan** can be found.

Morris (Carbon) was the name of a post office 1901-05 named for Robert O. Morris, the first settler on the Big (East) Rosebud River. **Morris** was near Crow Agency and served as headquarters for Indian service 1875-83. The confusion in sorting mail for **Morris** and Norris in Madison County led to a request for a name change, and it was subsequently called Roscoe after a favorite horse of Morris's wife. Mrs. Morris was postmaster at the time, but when the office reopened in 1901 Timothy George was appointed.

Morris (Cascade) had a post office established in August 1891. The name was changed to Logging Creek in 1893. Peter Morris was the postmaster.

Morris,(Dawson) southwest of Glendive, was a post office 1911-12 with Edward Jacobs as postmaster.

Morrison (Beaverhead) had a post office which was discontinued in 1907 and the mail was ordered to Argenta. The office opened in 1905 with Matt Thomas postmaster.

Morrison Cave (see **Lewis and Clark Caverns**).

Morristown was in Deer Lodge County when the post office operated briefly under this name May-September 1878 with Daniel James as postmaster. The area was formerly known as Gwendale.

MOSBY (Garfield) is on the east bank of the Musselshell River. It was named for William Henry Mosby, who settled here in 1891 after coming over the Rocky Mountains by team and wagon from Cottage Grove, Oregon. A post office was set up in the Mosby home in 1902 with Mary Mosby the postmaster. The community was formerly known as Baldwin, but the Mosby family — and the post office — moved on down the river with the post office set up in the Mosby home.In 1904 the name was changed to **Mosby**. Mail was brought once a week from Melstone and ranchers came from miles around to get their mail (Mrs. George Mosby in the Winnett Times).

"It is wild, rugged, spectacularly scenic, lonesome and harsh, but it's good country — very good country. Spring ice jams on the Musselshell turn loose raging floods that cover bottomlands, tear down fences and strew dead trees and other debris.' Byerly quotes residents as saying, "We're eighty miles from a doctor and the dirt trails can be knee-deep in mud or belly-deep in snow before the paved central Montana highway is reached that will whisk people to Lewistown, Winnett or Jordan." As in most central Montana towns, the homesteaders came, starry-eyed with their 160 acres of free land. But the pattern always repeated itself: either they sold out or they bought out others, and now the area is back to cattle ranges or, like the Cat Creek area, is dotted with oil wells.

Moschell (Sheridan) had a post office approved in 1918 with LaRuth Moschell as postmaster; it is possible the office was never in operation.

Mossmain (Yellowstone) had a post office 1916-35; Clora Fleming was the first postmaster. It was named for P. B. Moss of Billings.

Mouat (Stillwater) was called "Ghost Town, 1943" by Jim Annin: "The handsomest ghost town of World War II — **Mouat**, a $15 million investment in chrome — sat on a shelf of Montana's Beartooth Mountains . . . all but deserted" (They Gazed on the Beartooths). Before the government moved in, "**Mouat** was a wooded mountainside . . . its population consisted of jut-jawed old prospector Bill Mouat and his wife. Then the U.S., needing chrome sorely, found it at **Mouat**. The Japanese had choked off the chrome supply from the Phillipines; the Nazis blocked the Mediterranean route from Turkey. Nazi subs imperiled shipping from North Africa. The government moved in with old Prospector Bill. Production began June 1 . . . nine hundred construction workers and mill hands crowded into the five rows of new grey clapboard bungalows. Another thousand workers, wives and children moved into the upper town. . . . But Allied victories in North Africa and Sicily brought death to **Mouat**. Chrome could be shipped again more cheaply than **Mouat** could mill it. . . . The mill closed down. All that was left in **Mouat** three months after production began were guards, maintenance men . . . an occasional bear nosing through empty garbage cans . . . and old Bill Mouat and his wife."

Moulton (Fergus), near Grass Range, had a post office 1926-54 under Alta Gill. The dry years saw the exit of many dry land farmers and the acreage was combined into larger holdings by the few families that remained. A railroad siding and a grain elevator mark where **Moulton** used to be. Mail service is now out of Hilger. **Moulton** was named for Ben Moulton, a rancher and at one time county commissioner. During its best days, it was a siding on the Milwaukee; one man ran the store, post office and the grain elevators and his family lived in the only house in town. Twenty homestead families got their mail and groceries at **Moulton**, and a school operated here for about ten years. Now it is cattle and grain country (Byerly).

Mount Horeb (Silver Bow) had a post office 1882-83 with John Morrison as postmaster. The mail then went to Butte City. In the Bible Mount Horeb is "the mountain where God is said to have resided.... Mount Horeb and Mount Sinai seem (to be) the same" (*Columbia Encyclopedia*).

Mount Pleasant (Lewis and Clark) had a post office 1878-80 with Thomas Cotter as postmaster.

Muddy (Big Horn) is west of Lame Deer near where Muddy Creek runs into Rosebud Creek. The town was named for the former creek, which was named because of the character of the water. A post office was established in 1884 with Hiram Young as postmaster; it closed in 1901.

"Special U.S. Indian Agent R. L. Upshaw arrived at his dugout headquarters at the confluence of the Muddy and Rosebud creeks in January 1886 as the first resident Agent (of the Cheyenne). This was also the first agency headquarters" (Shane). Old correspondence indicates that the agency address on June 15, 1886, was listed as "Tongue River, **Muddy**, Montana."

Muir (Gallatin) This post office operated 1882-83 with Alvin McCray as postmaster; the office was also open 1923-27. It was named for John Muir, contractor on the Bozeman Tunnel.

Muir (Park) was a post office 1896-1906 that was formerly called Vaters, after postmaster Ernest Vater.

Mullan (Lewis and Clark) had a post office March 1882-April 1883; the mail was then sent to Helena. The town and the nearby tunnel were named for Lt. John Mullan, the first white man to explore the pass that came to be known as Mullan Pass. The first postmaster was James Morrison.

Muriel (Richland) was a post office 1917-27; Daisy Clark was first postmaster. **Muriel** was near Fairview.

Murn (Custer) was a Northern Pacific station established in 1906 near Miles City and named for Pat Murn, a roadmaster on the railroad.

Murray (Flathead) was briefly the name of a post office named for first postmaster Isaac Murray. It was open March-November 1900.

Muscleshell Road was a 180-mile-long military supply route sometimes called the Helena-Muscleshell Road. Later it was used as a mail route and goods were transported by ox team from the mouth of the Musselshell to Helena and Virginia City. This was especially true during low water, when river steamers were unable to reach Fort Benton. The route was eventually replaced by the Carroll Road, and in 1868 the Helena *Weekly Herald* reported that 300 Sioux, Blackfeet, and Bloods were "... just in back of Diamond Camp ... commanding the **Muscleshell Road**."

Muset was an 1897 post office later called Jocko. Mary Rowan was postmaster.

Musgrave (Carbon) was named for Richard Musgrave, the first postmaster (1916) and a homesteader. **Musgrave** is two miles west of a Burlington siding called Wade. The office was closed in 1921 and mail was sent to

Warren, but **Musgrave** still appeared on a Montana Railroad Commission map of 1945.

MUSSELSHELL (Musselshell) is east of Roundup on the river of the same name, which earned its title from Lewis and Clark on May 30, 1805. Lewis wrote in his diary: ". . . the stream which we suppose to be called by the Minetarus, the Musselshell River. . . ." Quantities of mussel shells (bivalves) were found along the river bed. An old stockman's landmark was the Musselshell Crossing, where herds of Texas longhorns, driven north in the 1880s, were bedded down for the last time before being fanned out in smaller herds to their ultimate Montana owners. The crossing was established in 1877 on the north bank of the Musselshell River opposite the present townsite. The trail between Fort Custer and Fort Maginnis passed through it. In 1880 a store which later housed the post office in 1883 was opened for business and settlement of the valley began. Lawrence Reed was the first postmaster.

Musselshell County was created in 1911 from parts of Fergus, Meagher, and Yellowstone counties. Another part of Fergus was annexed to **Musselshell** in 1911 and a part of **Musselshell** was taken to form part of Golden Valley in 1920. Roundup is the county seat. The Milwaukee Railroad, following the Musselshell River, traverses the entire county, and every town is located on this river-railroad path. The Bull Mountains in the southern part feed the streams that empty into the Musselshell. The county was named for the river and the river was named for the many mussel shells found along its banks.

"On April 10, 1866, the second or 'bogus' legislature, meeting in Virginia City, created a Muscle-Shell County and named Kercheval City as its county seat. The legislature and all its actions were later declared void by Congress and the one cabin in Kercheval City was washed down the Missouri by floodwaters. A permanent **Musselshell County** was finally created in 1911" (Winnett *Times*).

MYERS (Treasure), near Hysham, had a railroad station and was named after a civil engineer connected with the building of the Northern Pacific Railroad. The post office was established in 1911 with Clarence Beckstrom as postmaster.

Myersburg (see **Meyersburg**).

N

Nagos (Missoula) was a railroad siding. It was installed by a gang of Italian workers and first called Dagos, but the name was changed to avoid any unfavorable racial connotations.

Naismith (Toole) was a Great Northern station named for a superintendent of the old-time narrow-gauge Great Falls and Canada Railway. When this railroad was changed over to standard gauge, the station that had been located at Fort Conrad was named **Naismith**. It is located on the south bank of the Marias River (Jack Hayne).

Nantelle (Phillips) had a post office 1919-22 with Jessie Mitchell as postmaster. After that the mail was sent to Landusky.

NASHUA (Valley) is situated where Porcupine Creek runs into the Milk River. A few miles farther on, the waters of these two streams flow into the Missouri near Fort Peck Dam. **Nashua** is believed to be an Indian word meaning "Meeting of Two Streams." One of the first settlers here was Col. Charles Sargent, who had been at Fort Union in 1866 and returned twenty years later to take up a homestead near present-day **Nashua**, hoping that the land would be in demand as a division point on the Great Northern; the railroad chose Glasgow instead. By 1903 the town had a store, school, hotel and a saloon, but it boomed only when the dam was being built. The post office opened in 1888 with Charles Sargent as postmaster (Western Interpretive Services).

Natal (Fergus) was formerly called Pomo. The post office opened in 1905 with John Pratt as postmaster; it closed in 1929.

Navajo (Daniels) had a post office 1914-55; William Roufe was the first postmaster.

NEIHART (Cascade) was named for James L. Neihart, one of a group of prospectors who first discovered minerals in this part of the mountains. The discovery of silver-lead ore came in 1881 and proved to be one of the richest in the Little Belts. The igneous rock in which the ore is found is called pinto diorite because of its red-and-green spotted appearance. A town meeting was held in 1882 and the chairman, sitting on a rock, suggested the name of Farragut for the town. No one seconded the motion, but the next suggestion of **Neihart** was made and accepted. Main street was laid out to be eighty feet wide and all cross streets sixty feet.

Brother Van conducted the first church services in August 1882, ". . . free from tinsel, fuss and feather, or golden calf. Even St. Peter or St. Paul in working clothes would have felt comfortable" (Neihart *Herald*). One building still standing has a sign above the door reading
Wu Tang Laundry
Drugs
1882
For the first year there was no regular mail service; anyone coming over from White Sulphur Springs who wanted to bother with it would bring the mail sack. One sack took from November to June to make this forty-two mile trip. The post office was established in 1882 with Donald Mackintosh as postmaster. Sapphire mining proved profitable here, and it is estimated that more than $3 million worth sapphires ranging in color from pale to royal blue were taken from these mines.

Nelson (Blaine) had a post office 1891-96; Emma Schluter was the first postmaster. It was near Cleveland.

Nelson (Lewis and Clark) was named for Cy Nelson, one of the first settlers in the vicinity. The post office opened in 1904 with Robert Smith as postmaster; it closed in 1937.

Nelson Creek (Dawson) was near Watkins and had a post office 1914-15 with Louis Maves as postmaster.

Nevada City (Madison) was a mining ghost town until the recent restoration by Charles Bovey. It is now a tourist attraction with many original log buildings and an outstanding collection of old-time music boxes, player pianos and caliopes. A narrow gauge rail train connects **Nevada City** with Virginia City, which is about a mile to the north. The first Masonic Temple in Montana was at **Nevada City**. In 1865 the town held a

Fourth of July celebration and it was claimed that 5,000 people attended. At the time, **Nevada City** was the second-largest town in the area. George Ives was "hanged by the neck until dead" by the Vigilantes here. **Nevada City** was strung out all along the gulch — where prospectors carried on their search for gold — until it reached the western boundary of Virginia City. Adobetown and Junction City grew downstream, and near the head of the gulch were Highland, Pine Grove, and Summit. The post office operated 1865-1875 with Horace Harding as first postmaster. After the office closed the miners got their mail at Adobetown.

Newberg (Valley) was on the Milk River north of Malta and had a post office 1899-1902 with William Martin as postmaster.

New Caledonia was a settlement of clannish Scots miners and their families who worked the Anaconda Mine near Washoe. *Caledonia* is the old Roman name for Scotland. There was another settlement of Scottish immigrants at Bear Creek called Scotch Coulee.

New Chicago (Granite), south of Drummond, was named by William Dingwall, an old-timer who hoped the town would someday equal Chicago, Illinois. The area was formerly called Coberly. A post office was opened in 1872 with John Featherman as postmaster. Lucy Coberly came from Illinois and built a freighters' station on the Mullan Trail. Kate Dingwall, her granddaughter, recalled that when Lucy had to go for supplies, she would leave some food at the station and a small scales on the table so customers could themselves weigh the proper amount of gold dust to be left in payment (*Montana Standard*; July 5, 1976). **New Chicago** was once a bustling settlement and trade center. Featherman opened a mercantile business there on the old Mullan Trail. Nearby Henderson Gulch was named after a group of prospectors who arrived in 1865. The office closed in 1908.

New Deal (Valley) was settled during the time of President Franklin D. Roosevelt's New Deal program. The post office opened in 1935 with Abbie McClammy in charge; it closed in 1943.

New Dorsey (Meagher) was an old Montana Railroad station originally called just Dorsey, but when the station moved the name was adjusted.

Newhouser (Madison) was on postal records 1897-98 but never in operation, though Lawrence Harris had been appointed postmaster.

Newlon (Richland) was a station on the Northern Pacific near Sidney named for a pioneer, William W. Newlon, who was also the first postmaster when the office opened in 1881. It closed in 1901 but was active again 1902-13. The area around here was called Newlon Flats.

Newton (Yellowstone) was a station near Nibbe. Newton was the maiden name of the mother of H. N. Savage, who was the government's supervising engineer on the Huntley Reclamation Project.

Newton Grove (Yellowstone) had a post office 1914-27; Walter F. Newton was the first postmaster.

Newyear (Fergus), near Lewistown, had a post office 1899-1908 and 1911-12; the first postmaster was Nora Forest. **Newyear** was near Maiden. Gold was discovered here in 1880 but it was another twenty years before mining was commercially successful.

NIARADA (Sanders) is on Sullivan Creek some twenty miles west of the

Big Arm of Flathead Lake. The post office was opened in 1911 with Edmund Riley as postmaster.

Nibbe (Yellowstone), a station on the Northern Pacific, had a post office 1920-54 with Charles Treiber as postmaster.

Nichol (Phillips) was named for Martha Nichol, postmaster, and had an office 1906-07. **Nichol** was near Zortman.

Nicholia (Beaverhead) was a post office 1911-22; Lousette Dahlo was the first postmaster.

Nickwall (McCone) was on the Missouri River. The post office opened in 1909 with Tury Nelson as postmaster and closed in 1941.

Nielsen (Phillips) was a post office 1917-21 with Viggo J. Nielsen as postmaster. The postal name changed to Lowrane in 1921.

Nihill (Wheatland) was named for "Pat" Nihill, an early settler and landowner near this Great Northern station. The post office opened in 1910 with C. Justin Shanahan as postmaster; it closed in 1927.

Nile (Richland) was along the Missouri River. The post office was open 1911-12 with Inez Palmer as postmaster.

Niles (Judith Basin) was a settlement on Dry Wolf Creek above the old ranger station. The post office was established in 1904 and named for postmaster Solomon Niles; it closed in 1908. **Niles** was four or five miles up the creek past Geer. The mail was sent to Stanford after the **Niles** office closed.

Nimrod was a Great Northern station located on the Granite County-Missoula County dividing line. It had a post office 1903-10 and 1915-52; Amilia Moore was first postmaster. Nimrod was a Biblical character who was a mighty hunter; hence the term has come to mean an outdoorsman, particularly one interested in fishing. The Great Northern sought to give its stations tourist-attractive names. This station was formerly called Carlan.

Nimrod (Flathead) was formerly Java. It was also (see above) renamed by the railroad, hoping to promote the spot as a wonderland for fishermen.

Nina (McCone) had a post office 1914-23 with Alice Resech first postmaster. When the office closed, the mail was sent to Oswego, though it was across the Missouri River from **Nina**.

Nine Mile (Missoula) was named for George Brown's Nine-Mile House, which was just that distance from Frenchtown. The old Mullan Road crossed Nine Mile Creek at this spot. The post office opened in 1890 with George Brown as postmaster; it closed in 1930, but was open again 1934-35.

Nobleville (Madison) was a mining camp on the south fork of Wisconsin Creek where a mine was located in the 1870s. Dan Noble bought out the original prospectors and operated the mine until his death in 1899.

Nohly (Richland), a Great Northern station near the North Dakota border, was originally spelled Noble, but was named for A. F. Nohle, a landowner. The post office was established in 1916 with Merritt Johnson as postmaster; it closed in 1966. **Nohly** is just across the Missouri River from old Fort Union, which was erected at the junction of the Yellowstone and Missouri rivers. In 1805 Lewis and Clark, traveling in pirogues, passed by here. In 1828 the American Fur Company built Fort Floyd (later Fort Union) as a center for its trade with the Assiniboine and other Indians.

Nolton (Custer) had a post office 1880-81 with Call McLellan as postmaster.

Norbert (Chouteau) had a post office 1915-23. The name was then changed to Waltham. George Ellsworth was the postmaster in 1915.

Norheim (Blaine), near Chinook, had a post office 1914-35; the first postmaster was Halvor Groven.

NORRIS (Madison) was named for Alexander Norris, owner of the Norris Ranch. It is an old mining town situated where the railroad ends and a valley spreads out into the eastern part of the county. All the cattle from the rich pasturelands to the south had to be driven (now they are trucked) to **Norris** for shipment. It was about fifty miles from the summer pasture "up West Fork" to the station at **Norris**. The town is on Hot Spring Creek, and for years miners, cowhands, and travelers sought out a warm bath in the Norris Plunge behind the questionable privacy of its board fence. Recently the plunge has been taken over and improved by an individual owner. The **Norris** post office opened in 1891 with John Hoskins as postmaster. Shafts of old mines and coal outcroppings can still be seen around **Norris**.

Norrisvale (Flathead) was named for first postmaster Gustave Norris when the office opened in 1913; it closed in 1917. This town was near Polson.

North Great Falls (Cascade) had its own post office 1890-93 with Adelbert Kellison in charge.

Norwood (Silver Bow) had a post office 1882-93; John M. Parfet was postmaster.

Novary (Fergus) was established by Vincent Caroway midway between Cheadle and Grass Range. Caroway built his store and post office next to the railroad bed that was under construction by the Great Northern; the railroad project was abandoned late in World War I. The post office opened in 1917 but it and the town declined when Caroway went off to join the Navy. Caroway first named his town Wendt, after a nearby rancher, but the postal authorities, noting there was already a town by that name (postal records show it as Wint), would not accept it. Caroway then decided to name the town after a brand of groceries that he carried, called "Novary." Thus **Novary** was named "after a can of beans." The post office closed in 1934, the schoolhouse was moved, and now nothing remains to mark the site of **Novary** (Western Interpretive Services).

Novella (Dawson) was near the Missouri River. The post office opened in 1904 with Sallie Dawson in charge. When the office closed in 1907 the mail was ordered to Lismas, even though that office was several miles north across the Missouri River.

NOXON (Sanders) is on the Clark Fork River and the main highway to Spokane. It has had a post office since 1888 except for a few months in 1902-03; Thomas Smith was the first postmaster. **Noxon** is in a heavily forested area famous for trapping and the harvesting of huckleberries. It boomed during the construction of the railroad with railroading, mining and logging.

NYACK (Flathead) is nine miles south of the West Glacier entrance to

Glacier National Park. The station here is called Red Eagle. **Nyack** is on the Middle Fork River; for many years passengers have crossed in a basket hanging from a cable here. The post office was opened in 1912 under George Robertson; it closed in 1942.

Nye (Stillwater) is southwest of Columbus on the Stillwater River. The post office opened in 1887 and remained open most of time until 1965, when it became a rural independent station out of Absarokee. Thomas Ross was postmaster in 1887.

The town was first called Nye City, when it was a mining camp named for Jack Nye. "In the spring of 1883, Jack Nye and the Hedges brothers arrived from Big Timber . . . found an immense lead of copper-bearing ore 630 feet wide . . . traced it across two forks of the Stillwater for a distance of fifteen miles . . . this announcement started a 'run' to stake claims in the area. . . . The Stillwater Mining Company was incorporated . . . in 1884. . . . A smelter was built and the little town was called 'the new Butte. . . .' Later government surveyors found that Nye City . . . was actually on Indian lands . . . and by 1889 much mining activity had ceased" (Annin).

O

Oakno (Roosevelt) was the name given to a Sheridan County (originally) post office established in 1917 with John J. Lee in charge. It was in dry land homestead country and the office was open for less than a year. After it closed the settlers got their mail at Cuskerton.

O'Brien (Golden Valley) was near Barber. At a Knights of Columbus meeting in Sioux City, Iowa, a program was put on by a promoter who displayed huge vegetables raised in Montana. Father O'Brien, a priest with Cathedral Parish, and John Toole, a bookkeeper, were sufficiently impressed that they decided to go West to investigate free homestead land. They got off the train at Cushman, filed on land, and returned to encourage others to follow; thus began a Catholic settlement. The post office was active 1912-16 with Margaret Coleman as first postmaster. A church was built in 1917.

OILMONT (Toole) is in the lower end of the Sunburst Oil Field. The post office was established in 1925 with Prosper Gorham as postmaster. The name is a composite of that always exciting commodity, oil, and the name of the state.

Oka (Wheatland) Oka Bill Shiell was one of the Scotsmen who settled at East Buffalo Creek near Ubet. In 1879 a mail route was inaugurated between White Sulphur Springs and Martinsdale; later it was extended to Lewistown, passing through Judith Gap. Alf Stephens built a hotel and stables near the Musselshell Valley entrance to the Gap. The stage stop and post office (opened 1880) were named for Shiell. Business boomed and stage routes crossed and recrossed as the Yogo mines became active. **Oka** was the home station of the Billings and Benton stage line, and was also the stopping place for travel to and from the country to the north. Eliza Severance was the first postmaster. She had come from her home in Maine, traveling alone by train and riverboat. A. J. Severance met her in Fort Benton; they were married and started for his homestead at **Oka** in an open wagon. A spring blizzard hit and they were forced to camp for a week under the wagon with three other travelers (*In the Shadow of the Twin Sisters*). The better location of the Ubet station finally drew the traveling trade away from **Oka** and the office closed in 1895. It was open again 1896-1909 and 1913-23.

Olanda (Prairie) had a post office 1917-35. The first postmaster was John Braun. In 1934 Clell Bond and Paul McLarnon put on a rodeo at **Olanda**. They didn't charge an entry fee and only paid mount money: saddle broncs, $2.50; bareback, $1.50; and steers, $1.00 (*Wheels Across the Prairie*).

Old Agency (Teton) was the original name for Choteau. The post office was opened in 1875 with Alfred Hamilton as postmaster. The name was changed to Choteau in 1882.

Olden (Golden Valley) had a post office 1880-84 with T. B. Joliffo as first postmaster. When this office closed the mail was sent to Roundup.

Oldham (Hill) had a post office 1904-11. It was near Havre and named for Ina Oldham, the first postmaster. **Oldham** was the site of the famous Boundary Trading Post near the Wild Horse Trail.

OLIVE (Powder River) is ten miles north of Broadus on the Mizpah River. A post office opened there in 1909 with Arthur J. Smith in charge. "On March 17, 1919, the State Legislature created a new county and the first meeting of the County Commissioners was held at **Olive** 'a beautiful location on Mizpah Creek.' Later on in an election, **Olive**, with 198, lost out to Broadus, with 1624 votes, for county seat" (*Echoing Footsteps*).

Oliver (Beaverhead) had a post office 1872-74, with William Oliver as postmaster.

Oliver Gulch, (Sanders) near Camas, was a post office 1912-25 with Hugh Stephens the postmaster.

Ollie (Fallon) was a station on the Milwaukee named for the daughter of first postmaster Leander Greiner. The office opened in 1911 and closed in 1955. The **Ollie** school started in 1910 in a homesteader's shack. Later a 10-foot by 12-foot building was used with planks laid across nail kegs for seats. Everyone who had schoolbooks brought them. A railroad roundhouse, several stores, a bank, the United Brethren Church and two doctors were once a thriving part of **Ollie**. Now it's a ghost town.

OLNEY (Flathead) is between Whitefish and Eureka and was named for a local rancher. The post office was open 1907-08 with Elizabeth Dickerhoof as postmaster. It was open again 1914-17 and reopened in August 1918.

Olof (Wheatland) is in the northwest part of the county on Haymaker Creek. It was named for the first postmaster, Olof Olson; the office was open 1917-34.

Omholt (Toole) was named for first postmaster Ole Omholt. The office was open 1911-18; after that the mail was sent to Fowler.

O'Neill (Custer) was named for Frank O'Neill. The post office was opened in 1925 with Margaret O'Neill postmaster, and closed in 1944.

O'Neils (Beaverhead) was a stage stop for the Deer Lodge Stage on

Rattlesnake Creek.

Onge (Silver Bow) was named for the first postmaster, Frederic St. Onge. The office was open 1890-95.

Onondago was in Meagher County when the post office was open 1880-81 with Robert Finley as postmaster.

Ontario, in present-day Powell County, had a post office May-September 1896 with Lavinia Southmayd as postmaster. It was near Rimini.

OPHEIM, (Valley) ten miles from the Saskatchewan border, was named for Alfred S. Opheim, the second postmaster; John Opheim was the first. **Opheim** is a U.S. Port of Entry from Canada and is in the midst of a rich, wheat-growing region. The town had no railroad until 1926, when the Great Northern extended its Bainville-Scobey branch, one of the last examples of rail construction in Montana. During homesteading days **Opheim** was a beehive of industry: stores, banks, lumberyards, hotels, and bars did a profitable business. Wild grasses grew stirrup-high; sod-busters plowed it under and for a few years reaped huge profits from grain crops. They built large houses and barns and modern schoolhouses. But the drought years broke many of the farmers, and the land was left to lie fallow. Instead of the rich, native grasses returning to the range, thick, ugly mats of prolific Russian thistles grew; when mature, the plants break off and roll about the prairie like tumbleweeds, lodging in masses against fences and buildings. Old Opheim was a few miles from the present community. When the railroad came and built a station, the post office and the town moved to it. The office opened in 1910.

Ophir was the name of a mine, a creek, and finally, a post office in present-day Powell County. It was near Cemetery Ridge, a name that smacked of Gettysburg and the Civil War, and carried West by ex-soldiers turned prospectors. **Ophir** is a Biblical name for a land rich in gold. It was often used to name mines and that may be the source here. Blackfoot City, headquarters for the **Ophir** miners, was a rip-roaring town in 1876. When it was devastated by fire in 1896 the post office became known as **Ophir.** John Quigley was postmaster of an office that remained active until 1912.

Ophir. "In 1864 James Moore, captain of the stern-wheeler 'Cutter,' conceived the idea of founding a town to rival Fort Benton when trouble with his boat machinery tied him up for the winter thirty miles below Fort Benton. The town of **Ophir** was laid out. However, when Calf Shirt, a Blood chieftain, led 180 warriors to ambush a Negro and ten white men while they were cutting timber for the 'town,' the plan was abandoned" (Mockel).

Oraopolis. Granville Stuart wrote: "At the mouth of the Yellowstone, Judge W. B. Dance got off the steamer 'Welcome' to lay out a townsite which he caled **Oraopolis.** While thus engaged the boat pulled out and left him. After traveling for two days without food he managed to reach Fort Gilpin."

Orr (Cascade) was a post office 1896-1905. Bryon Porter was the first postmaster.

Orville (Sheridan) was almost at the end of the line when the Great Northern built its branch from Bainville to Scobey. The post office operated as **Orville** 1910-15 (Henry Lockrem, postmaster), when the name was changed to Madoc.

Osborn (Yellowstone) had a post office 1908-14. The first postmaster was Tora Robey.

Oscar (Hill) was named for the first postmaster, Oscar Eskew. The office was open 1912-26; the mail was then sent to Havre.

Ossette (Daniels) was a post office 1915-36. The first postmaster was Fay Miner.

Oswego (Valley) had a post office 1896-71. Warner J. Colwell was postmaster during the first year. **Oswego** was named by early-day settlers who had come from Oswego, New York. In the days of riverboats and before the town was begun, one of the boats, the Nellie Peck, was set adrift in a storm. Suddenly it struck a sandbar near present-day **Oswego** and almost immediately the boat was surrounded by "whooping savages" dressed in warpaint. The captain, realizing his crew wouldn't have a chance in a fight, made friendly gestures and all passengers were taken to the Indian camp. They were treated kindly, but after a few days dancing and ceremony began and the captives didn't know whether they were going to be adopted or massacred. A severe thunderstorm came up, frightened the Indians, and the crew and passengers escaped back to their boat. Years later a town grew up there serving the railroad and the cattle ranchers. The N-N Ranch was owned by the four Niedringhaus brothers: "Dutchmen from St. Louis, Missouri." In 1888 they began building a new headquarters ranch near **Oswego** for the herds they trailed in from Texas. Some years they shipped as many as 25,000 head to eastern markets. Supplies were hauled from Miles City, 150 miles away. A horse ranch was started near **Oswego** in 1928 and one time, eight hundred horses were shipped to Chappel Brothers Packing House in Illinois. There were as many as 12,000 horses in the area some years. In 1972 one of the worst prairie fires in northeastern Montana "swept **Oswego** off the map." Its seventy-five residents were forced to evacuate and only four homes survived the fire. Gradually some houses were moved in, two new ones were built, and the grain elevator still stands. About forty persons returned to live in **Oswego**.

Otis (Rosebud) was named after early settlers and had a post office 1900-03. Wallace Lyndes was the first postmaster.

Otter (Judith Basin) took its name from Otter Creek, named for the many otters found along its banks and in its waters. The post office was open 1882-83 and the mail was then ordered to Fort Benton. There weren't many post offices in those days, but Edgar Mann was in charge of the one at **Otter**.

OTTER (Powder River) is between Ashland and the Wyoming border. The post office opened in 1895 with Charles Bull as postmaster. Trappers and fur traders took thousands of otters from Montana's streams in the early days, and many creeks were named Otter. This office now serves the communities of Quietes and Sayle by rural mail routes. Before there was an **Otter** post office ranchers on Otter Creek took turns going to Birney for the mail. The first **Otter** office was located on the old Charles Bull ranch. It has since moved several times.

Outlook (Sheridan) opened a post office in 1910 with Bernard Dahlvang as postmaster. It is nine miles from Canada and about twenty-five from North Dakota. The story goes that in the early days a stranger rode into town, tied his horse to the hitching rack, and was just entering a saloon when someone yelled, "Lookout!" The stranger ducked a glass thrown at someone else, and they turned the words around to come up with **Outlook** to name the town.

OVANDO (Powell) is northeast of Missoula and was named for Ovando Hoyt, the first postmaster. The office opened in 1883. **Ovando** is a supply point for hay and sheep ranches and for small logging camps.

Overland (Fergus) had a post office 1881-85 with John Atchison as the first postmaster.

Oxford (Wheatland) had a post office 1909-16. When the office closed the mail was sent to Nihill. The first postmaster was Sherman Robinson.

P

PABLO (Lake) was named for Michel Pablo, a Flathead chief and a rancher and stockman who, by raising buffalo, is one of the individuals responsible for saving the bison from extinction. Walking Coyote, a Pend Oreille Indian hunting in the Milk River country, brought a few buffalo calves back to the Flathead Valley and sold them to Pablo and Charles Allard. They were the nucleus of the herd that now roams the Moiese Wildlife Preserve. **Pablo** is now a trading center for ranchers, and the Pablo Reservoir, made from Kerry Dam, is a bird refuge. The post office opened in 1917 with Bert Dimmick as postmaster.

Pacific City (Lewis and Clark) is a ghost town now, but there was placer mining there during the years 1864-75, when it was also known as McClellan Gulch.

Pacific Junction (Hill) takes its name from the fact that it was here that the Great Northern line to the Pacific coast was begun, branching out from what was then the main line from Havre to Butte. The discovery of Marias Pass made possible the westward extension of the railroad.

Pageville (Madison) was named for the first postmaster, Newton Page, and members of his family. The office opened in 1892 and closed in 1913. James Page was an early settler who was influential in getting a school started. He donated the land and the first classes were held in a log building on his ranch in 1883. **Pageville** was near Twin Bridges.

Painted Robe, (Golden Valley) a station on the Great Northern, was located on Painted Robe Creek, which got its name because the Indians, while hunting and trapping in that vicinity, often stopped by this creek to paint their robes with a certain clay found in the creek bed. The Montana Cattle Company, better known as the "79 Outfit," was also in the sheep business, and the country around **Painted Robe** was headquarters for wintering and lambing camps. One estimate places the number of ewes there one winter at 15-18,000.

Paola, (Flathead) near Essex, had a post office 1914-19 and 1920-28. The first postmaster was Marie Cameron.

Paradise was an office in Chouteau County 1901-02 with Joseph Birdwell as postmaster.

Paradise (Park) is also the name of a post office listed for this county April-November 1888 with Adelbert Whitney as postmaster.

PARADISE, (Sanders) was a division on the Northern Pacific and the spot where railway men, traveling westward, changed their watches from Mountain Standard to Pacific Standard Time before they streaked over the mountains forming Montana's western border. Not all historians — or even residents — agree, but the story is that the town's name is a modification of "Pair o' Dice," which was the name of a roadhouse on the trail through this area in the early days. The post office was established in 1907 with John Christenson as postmaster. A post office named **Paradise** is listed in postal records for a place in old Missoula County for the years 1890 to 1893. It is possible this is a forerunner of the existing town, since William Minor was postmaster of this office. Sanders County was created from a part of Missoula County in 1905.

Pardee (Mineral) is a mining settlement north of Superior. The name is a euphemism from the French *pardieu*, meaning "By God!"

Paris (McCone) is now just a deserted ranch surrounded by sunburnt range and red buttes and scarred with ravines. Some of the ranch buildings were made of stone, others are sod shanties. Drought years prompted most of the people of this settlement to move away. The post office was open 1914-37 with Lucy Ritchie, postmaster.

PARK CITY (Stillwater) was first known as Young's Point. In 1882 a colony from Ripon, Wisconsin, making the trip in prairie schooners, settled here. Young's Point was the landing place for boats on the Yellowstone River, but this was to be the settlers' future home, so they planted trees and a section of land was donated to them. They also planted elm and maple in a grove that is now a tourist park. After the settlers the railroad came and with the railroad came a station. The barren, sandstone bluffs north of town inspired railroad officials to christen the new station Rimrock, but the settlers, who had planted seedlings and started a city of trees, chose and clung to the name **Park City**. The general manager of the Northern Pacific resented this "stubbornness" on the part of the homesteaders and in retaliation he changed the location of the proposed railroad yards and shops from this townsite to Laurel (Annin). The post office was established in 1882 with Alonzo Young as postmaster.

Park County, which forms part of the southern border of the state, was named for its proximity to Yellowstone National Park. In 1882 the first business house was opened at Clark City (Livingston) and the Northern Pacific chose it for a division point. The growing city demanded a county seat closer than Bozeman. Gov. Preston H. Leslie approved a bill for formation of **Park County** and it was established in May 1887. A part of Gallatin was taken to form **Park**, and in 1895 parts of **Park** were taken to form parts of Carbon and Sweet Grass counties. Another part of **Park County** was annexed to Yellowstone Park in 1929.

Parker, (Broadwater) also known as Crow Creek City, was a small but bustling mining camp in 1896 near Crow (sometimes called Cow) Creek Crossing. The camp was named for John Parker, who had mines and a mill on Johnny Creek eight miles west of Radersburg (Western Interpretive Services).

204

Parker (Meagher) had a post office 1880-81 and was named for postmaster Amelia Parker. The name, according to postal records, was changed to Fort McGinnis in 1881.

Parkinson (Fergus) was a post office 1911-14 with Fred Martin as postmaster. The postal area had originally been called Weede, and after 1914 that name was used again.

Parnell (Jefferson) was a post office 1881-83 with Charles Howard as postmaster. After 1883 the postal name was Weber.

Parrot (Madison) had a post office in 1897 with Hardman Fleming as postmaster. It was located where the railroad originally crossed the Jefferson River. There was also a wagon bridge across the river there — the only one between Cardwell and Iron Rod. **Parrot** was named for R. P. Parrot, who built a mill here to process ore from the mines. In 1898 William S. Clark took over the Jefferson Valley Trading Company at **Parrot** and was postmaster until 1906, when the mill shutdown; when that happened stores as well as the post office moved to the railroad station at Renova.

Patcum (Sweet Grass) was a station named for Pat Cummings (Pat Cum), a former roadmaster of the Northern Pacific.

Patterson was a sidetrack in Gallatin County named for J. L. Patterson, who settled a homestead there in 1879.

Pattonhill, (McCone) named for the family of first postmaster Ruth Patton, had a post office 1915-25. It was in the northwestern section of the county about twenty-five miles from the Missouri River. The area was formerly served by a post office called Mathus.

Paxton (Dawson) is in the northwest corner of the county. Forest Hopkins was appointed postmaster when the office opened in 1909. It closed in 1938.

Pearl (Rosebud) was a settlement near the Wyoming border at Young's Creek named for Pearl Rogers. Pearl and her husband Tom used to drive a mule team hitched to a buckboard to Sheridan, Wyoming for the mail until they got a post office in 1904. Tom was the postmaster. The office closed in 1910 and thereafter they got their mail at the mining station of Dietz No. 5. Flat stones were used in the buildings at **Pearl** and remnants of the old dancehall remain. The land is now owned by Shell Oil (Elsa Spear Byron).

Pearmond, Piermond was an early post office and settlement on the south side of the Missouri River about thirty miles east of where the Milk River ran into the Missouri. The post office operated from 1891-98 and 1900-01. Jack Colwell was the first postmaster. The location would now be in McCone County. There was an N—N ferry here as early as 1896 (N—N was the brand of the Niedringhaus Brothers Cattle Company). The saloons in **Pearmond** were the Lone Star, the Bucket of Blood, and the Two Orphans.

Peasefort (Custer) had a post office 1879-80 with Fellow D. Pease as postmaster. Pease came to Montana in 1856 and found employment as an Indian scout for Gen. Sully and later as Chief of Scouts under Gen. Harney. His knowledge of the wilderness, the plains and the red man made him a valuable asset for the Army, and earned him approbation as "dean of the frontiersmen" and a life-long friend to the Indians. In 1859 Pease was married at Fort Union to Margaret Wallace, the daughter of a Crow woman and a French-Crow father. Pease was often called "Major" or "Colonel" by his friends because of his leadership qualities. With others he planned to form a colony known as Fort Pease on the Yellowstone River at the mouth of the Big Horn and establish it as a head of navigation; the idea was that the stable banks of the Yellowstone offered a better commercial route than that of the Missouri to Fort Benton. The Custer Massacre and constant Indian raids led to the abandonment of the project, but the settlement did manage to briefly acquire the status of a post office. After 1880 the postal name became Junction.

Pederson (Sheridan) is a community between Froid and Antelope. It was named for first postmaster Peder Pederson. The office operated 1908-10 and the name was then changed to Barford.

PEERLESS, (Daniels) west of Scobey, was originally named Tande, according to one historian, but due to the popularity of the Peerless Beer sold there people got into the habit of saying, "Let's go to **Peerless**," and this gave rise to the idea of changing the name. The Post Office Department in Washington, D.C. at first objected, but finally agreed (Perrin). **Peerless** was formerly called Battleson, and postal records show both names for a station on the Great Northern and Tande as a settlement about ten miles north. At any rate, it appears that Tande and Battleson combined forces and a post office under the name **Peerless** was established in 1926 with Paulina Brockway as postmaster.

PENDROY (Teton) was the terminal of a Great Northern branch line from Great Falls and a grain shipping point named for L. B. Pendroy, a personal friend of James J. Hill. The two met while Hill was scouting the country west of Devil's Lake, North Dakota in 1885 prior to the survey of the railroad. The post office opened in 1916 with Charles Sheble as postmaster.

Penfield (Silver Bow) was a station named for W. H. Penfield, maintenance engineer for the Milwaukee Railroad.

Peoples (Chouteau) was an early-day post office open 1890-93 with Julia Ereax in charge. It was on Peoples Creek and named for a family by the same name.

Peritsa (Big Horn) was a siding west of Hardin which took its name from an Indian word meaning crow or bird.

PERMA (Sanders) is on the Clark Fork River and the Flathead Indian Reservation. The Salish and Kootenai tribes came to **Perma** annually to dig the bulbs of the camas plant. A post office opened there in 1911 with James Carr as postmaster.

Perrysburgh (Chouteau) was an old post office in the days of the open cattle ranges. It was open 1884-88 and the first postmaster was William McElhinney. When that office closed the mail went to Fort Benton.

Pershing (Pondera) was a Great Northern siding built during World War I, when the railroads were operated by the U.S. Railroad Administration. It was named for Gen. John Pershing.

Peskan (Teton) was a post office 1906-09 (Abner Hall, postmaster), near Browning.

Peters (Chouteau) was named for Walter G. Peters, the first postmaster. The office was active 1902-04. It was near Big Sandy.

Petrie (Blaine) was named for postmaster Charles H. Petrie when this office was in operation, 1914-16.

Petroleum County is in the central part of eastern Montana, and was organized from a part of Fergus County in February 1925. Winnett is the county seat. The county got its name from the extensive petroleum production in the Cat Creek fields. The area of **Petroleum County** is 1,655 square miles; 1970 population was 711.

Petrolia (Petroleum) was a post office 1921-26. The first postmaster was Clara Svejkovsky. The name was coined for the rich oil deposits nearby.

Philbrook, (Judith Basin) one of the earliest post offices in the area, it was established December 1881 with Edward J. Morrison as postmaster.The office closed 1905-08 and then opened again until 1912, when it moved to the new, nearby town of Hobson. The railroad came through Hobson and the office took the station name. **Philbrook** was named by E. J. Morrison (Morison?) in honor of his grandfather, John Philbrook of Knox, Minnesota. It was an early stage station on the Great Falls-Lewistown route. In 1884 an elder of the Methodist Church here was in charge of the Helena District, which extended some five hundred miles from Helena east to Glendive and north to Sun River and Chouteau; Fort Benton, along the Missouri, **Philbrook** and Lewistown were also parts of his far-flung domain. The elder estimated the extent of his charge as 100,000 square miles (Adams). One of the main roundup camps of the Basin Cattle Pool was between **Philbrook** and Utica. Freight outfits traveling between Fort Benton and the Musselshell crossed the Judith River here. Between the two towns there were once two hotels, stores, saloons, a Community and a Presbyterian Church, where Brother Van Orsdel often preached. The stage stopped running in 1909 and as so often happened, the town moved to the railroad.

Philipsburg, (Granite) a county seat, was named for Philip Deidesheimer, the first superintendent of the St. Louis Montana Gold and Silver Mining Company, later known as the Philipsburg Mining Company. The settlement was first called Camp Creek, for the stream that meandered through town and furnished water for residents. **Philipsburg** was not incorporated until 1890, but in 1887 it had a population of 1,500 and was the trade center for 8,000 people. The oldest school building still in use in the state is the imposing brick edifice constructed in 1895 to serve grades one through twelve. The Peoples Hotel was built in 1890 but never used, even though upstairs rooms were furnished with fine furniture and Brussels carpets, and the downstairs saloon had huge mirrors and shining woodwork. Throughout the years it remained intact. The owners lived in a back room on $25 taken from their savings every month, but even during a World War I boom the hotel remained closed. In early days six-horse teams brought in wagonloads of ore for shipment on the Northern Pacific, which appeared in 1887. The post office, with Hugh Bell as postmaster, opened in 1868 (*Montana Standard;* July 6, 1976).

Phillips, (Phillips) near Malta, was named for B. D. Phillips, a big cattle owner whose ranch was near here. The post office was established in 1896 with Benjamin Phillips as postmaster. It was closed 1914-19 and then open until 1947.

Phillips County extends from the Canadian border to the Missouri River. It was organized from parts of Blaine and Valley counties in 1915 and named for Sen. Benjamin D. Phillips, who had used his influence to get Chinook named county seat of Blaine County, hoping that still another county would be created which would be named for him. Phillips was a principal owner of several mines in the Little Rockies and the Bear Paw Pool, and one of the largest sheep owners in the state; he had a vested interest in having a county tax assessor he could influence (A. J. Noyes, *The Story of Blaine County*). **Phillips** is one of Montana's largest counties, measuring 101 x 65 miles. The broad and fertile Milk River Valley cuts through the center and contains some of the finest range grass in the state. Homesteaders plowed up the prairie grass and settled on small tracts that proved inadequate to support them through the dry years. About fifty post offices were established in the little settlements during the homestead period and all but eight have been discontinued.

Phipps (Hill) was named for Emmet Phipps, postmaster when the office opened in 1914. It closed in 1926.

Phon (Garfield) had a post office 1915-36. Myron Wheeler was the first postmaster. "**Phon** on Woody Creek is near the area that is now being covered by Fort Peck Reservoir. **Phon** had a schoolhouse which doubled on Sunday as a church to serve the six families who then lived in that area" (Highland.

Piedmont (Jefferson) was so named because of its location at the foot (French: *pied*) of the twenty-mile grade up the east slope of the Rockies to Pipestone Pass Tunnel. The two percent grade was the maximum grade of the Milwaukee over the Continental Divide. The post office opened in 1910 with Mary Finn in charge; it closed in 1923.

Piegan (Glacier) was a post office 1877-1902 with John Billings as first postmaster. It is near Browning and the name comes from the Indian tribe.

Pike (Glacier) was a post office 1912-19. Frank A. Pike was the first postmaster.

Pikes Peak, in present-day Powell County, had an early post office in 1870 with John Meyer as postmaster; it closed in 1878.

Piltzville (Missoula) is a settlement a few miles east of Missoula named for William Piltz, a native of Maine who came to Bonner in 1896. It was first called Piltz Addition.

Pine Creek (Park) had a post office 1904-14. Alice Smith was the postmaster.

Pinegrove (Fergus) opened a post office in 1901. In 1910 a rural mail route was established with William Evans carrying the mail on the 110-mile round trip from **Pinegrove** to Lavina once a week — partly on horseback and partly in a three-seat spring wagon. Mrs. Shiftlet was postmaster at that time, but Annie McLean had been the first. The office closed in 1934.

Pineland (Missoula) was a post office 1882-83 with Edward Frank as postmaster. Much of far-flung, original Missoula County was indeed a land of pines.

Pineview (Yellowstone) was a post office 1909-42. The first postmaster was George Abel.

Piniele (Carter) was named for the twin buttes or pinnacles directly north of the townsite. When the name was submitted to Washington, it was spelled "Pinicle"and a government clerk further confused the issue by reading the "c" as an "e", so the new post office went on the official record as **Piniele**. The office was established in 1911 with Charles Einsel as postmaster. "In 1919 it was a fairly large town, with a flour mill, bank, doctor, post office, saloons, stores and a hotel. Between 75 and 100 people lived there. Tension ran high with competition to see if **Piniele** or Ekalaka would win the county seat for newly created Carter County. Ekalaka won and **Piniele** gradually faded away. About 1945 the store and post office were moved to Hammond, a location on the new highway, some eight miles away. All that is left at **Piniele** now is an old shed" (Pat Cunningham).

Pinto (Powder) was a post office 1914-22. It was near Broadus, and John BeDell was postmaster when it opened.

Pioneer (Powell) had a post office August-December 1870 with Nicholas Connolly as postmaster. The office was open again 1871-1907 and 1911-18, serving the area formerly getting mail at Gold Creek.

Piper (Fergus) is east of Lewistown and named for Harley Piper, owner of the townsite land and a farmer there since 1900. The post office opened in 1915 with James Lansley as postmaster. It closed in 1937. **Piper** was once a siding on the Milwaukee Railroad five miles from Heath. The depot has been gone since 1965. The train used to stop there to take on water from the creek. Once there was a stockyard and ranchers from Giltedge and Cheadle trailed their cattle here to load them up for faraway markets like Chicago, Sioux City, and St. Louis. The schoolhouse served as a church and a community hall. Thirty families once got their mail at **Piper**; in 1975 only five families were left (Byerly).

Pipestone (Jefferson) was named for nearby Pipestone Springs. The clay found along the creek bank was especially good for clay pipes, and the Indians came once a year to make them. Ollie Barnes was postmaster when the office opened in 1880. It closed but was reactivated in 1887 under the name **Pipe Stone Springs** with George Washington as postmaster. This office operated until 1928. There is also a Pipestone Pass and a Pipestone Tunnel at the Continental Divide near Butte.

Placer (Granite) was a post office 1896-98 with James Gillies as postmaster. Near Philipsburg, placer mining no doubt gave it its name, as well as to the town in Broadwater County (see below).

Placer, in Jefferson, now Broadwater, had a post office 1887-92 with John Kelly as first postmaster. Before that the mail was handled at the Beaver Creek office and after **Placer** closed, it was handled at Winston.

Plains, (Sanders) on the Clark Fork River, was called Horse Plains when it served as a wintering place for the Indians and their horses. Later, stockmen from as far away as Walla Walla, Washington drove their horses there for the winter, too. Wild horses congregated in great numbers to this protected, open pasture when snow covered many other ranges. The town was incorporated as Horse Plains, but the name was later shortened. The post office opened in 1883 with John McDiarnied as postmaster.

Plateau (Missoula) was named because of the several small tracts of tableland located west of this Northern Pacific station. **Plateau** is near the Mineral County boundary line.

Pleasant Valley (Flathead Valley) had a post office 1903-35 with Charles Lynch the first postmaster. The name is descriptive and could be just as easily applied to several valleys lying between the many streams and mountain ridges of Flathead County. Before this office opened the area was served by one called Meadow.

PLENTYWOOD, (Sheridan) a county seat, is the trading center for people living in the extreme northeastern corner of the state. The people around **Plentywood** have experienced prosperity, drought, and starvation — and prosperity and drought again. The economy has been boosted in recent years by oil exploration. The post office was established in 1901 on the ranch of William Stewart, who served as postmaster. By 1905 there seemed to be a need for a town and the post office was moved to Bolster House, a stopping place. George Bolster became postmaster and other businesses set up shop. The town was platted in 1909 and the railroad arrived. Charles Vindex (*Montana Magazine*, winter 1968) writes of the turbulent political history of this area: the citizens had become notably independent in politics, and in 1920 the town and surrounding country was widely known as the "only American community actually governed by practicing 'reds.'" The radicals proclaimed their ideology in the columns of a uniquely militant newspaper, the *Producer News*. But by 1932 the crest of power for the communistic group was over and by 1937 it had practically disappeared. This land, once prime hunting grounds for the Assiniboines, free pasture for the big cattle outfits, and after a fight, grazing land for sheep, succumbed in the early 1900s to the homesteader's plow. A few survived the bad years; most gave up and moved away.

Gary Sunsted of Antelope High School gives the following account of how **Plentywood** got its name: "In the early days, a cattle outfit driving across the treeless prairie met a couple of riders coming from the other direction. They asked if there was any place around where they could find water and firewood for a campsite. The cattlemen were told to keep going ahead for a mile or two and they would find "plentywood," as there was a growth of small timber along the bank of a creek at the point where the town now stands. The cattle outfit went on and made their camp where the town is now located.

PLEVNA (Fallon) was named after Plevna, Bulgaria, the scene of a great battle between Russians and Turks. There were a great many Bulgarians working on the Milwaukee Railroad, so officials approved the workers' choice for a name, although they had planned to call the station Edina. The post office opened in 1909 with Herbert Callin as postmaster. Many of the families who settled on small farms around **Plevna** retained their Old World customs. Russian feast days were kept and for a long time the women wore traditional black shawls on their heads. German immigrants settled here too, and in 1918 the Rev. J. E. Schatz wrote to Gov. Sam Stewart: "Sometime ago, the State Council of Defense made an order preventing the use of the German language in schools and churches . . . we have many . . . who are unable to understand the English language and it is hard for these people. . . . Every Sunday when I preach in English to these true citizens of our dear country my heart turns sad, for they are in tears and their hearts are heavy because they cannot understand what I say. Our church is a praying church. . . . Can we not hold our prayer meetings in German for these poor stricken emigrants?"

Plum Creek (Fergus) had a post office 1914-33 during the homestead era. The first postmaster was Ruth Luton. The Plum Creek that lent its name to the post office is a small creek, rising in the North Moccasins and emptying fifteen miles later into the Judith River. Its banks are lined with wild plum trees and the old Indians remember when they came there each year to pick plums. They chopped them up — one-third plum and two-thirds buffalo meat — and dried it to make pemmican, which was then stored in buffalo bladders to be eaten with relish during the winter months; nowadays the plums are used in jellies and jams. **Plum Creek** was once part of the huge Indian Reservation that stretched from the Yellowstone to the Missouri until 1875. Both cattlemen and homesteaders came, but horses were always the big thing on **Plum Creek** ranches. The area was also one of the early hideouts for horse thieves. They would steal horses and hide them out in the box canyons and breaks along the Judith River before trailing them up into Canada for sale. **Plum Creek** never had a store; early settlers went to Lewistown once a year and hauled home a wagonload of groceries and supplies. There was a log schoolhouse and later a frame one, which doubled as a community center for meetings and all night dances. The post office kept moving. The first one was at the present Lanzo Smart place; then Joe Benjamin moved it to where the old schoolhouse still stands; and finally it was moved to another place about a mile east. About forty families once got their mail at the **Plum Creek** office (Byerly & Byerly). "Horse thieves weren't all bad, though," recalled one old-timer, adding that a really poor family would often find a quarter of beef left hanging near their house, and besides, "They didn't steal much from **Plum Creek** settlers."

Plummerton (Teton) was named for the first postmaster, Guy B. Plummer. The office was open 1917-24; after that patrons got their mail at Cordova.

Point of Rocks "When the Montana gold rush started in 1862 and '63, **Point of Rocks** was the name of the promontory that puts a bend into the Beaverhead River about eleven miles southeast of the present town of Twin Bridges. **Point of Rocks** it was to old-timers. It was a long-time landmark. In recent years the name has been changed to Beaverhead Rock." Old-timers claim this is not the rock that Sacajawea pointed out to Lewis and Clark; that rock, they say, is seventeen miles south on the east bank of the Beaverhead River. "During the early gold rush days, slow-moving freight wagons hauling in supplies from Utah, and fast-going stages carrying passengers, mail and gold soon turned the old Indian trail that hugged close to the **Point of Rocks** into a well-traveled, deep-rutted road. The 'Point' provided an excellent place for robbers to hide while waiting for the stage. Early in the 1860s Mr. Gutchough built the **Point of Rocks** stage station. It consisted of a long, low building that housed the hotel, post office, and bar." The post office was officially on the records January-October 1873 and Sim Estes was postmaster. The "Point" was no doubt a mail drop for a much longer time. When this office closed, Blaine became the official postal station for the area (*Pioneer Trails and Trials*).

POLARIS (Beaverhead) is a mining ghost town near Grasshopper Creek. The Polaris Mine was an important silver property which was located January 31, 1885. It was worked steadily and the ore was shipped by team and wagon to Dillon. In 1892 it was sold to a New York syndicate. Later, the Silver Fissure Mining Company, organized with Harry Armstead in charge, bought the mine and planned extensive improvements. They built forty miles of road from the mine to Armstead, a station on the Oregon Short Line. The smelter was destroyed by fire in 1922 and by 1955 only a tavern called the Polar Bear, a two-story log house, and a shed were left (Wolle). **Polaris** was named by a mining engineers for the polar star (Rowe). The post office, with Mary Pierson in charge, opened in 1898 and has been maintained, even though the town's population has dwindled to only 5.

POLEBRIDGE (Flathead) is a summer post office at the northwestern edge of Glacier National Park. Benjamin Hansen was postmaster when the office opened in 1920. Today **Polebridge** consists of a scattering of houses, cabins, trailers and small ranches up and down the North Fork Road. At the heart of the community is the Polebridge Mercantile, a combination rural store, post office, gas station and a few rental cabins. The Northern Lights Saloon serves beer and meals beneath propane lights. The biggest question among citizens is how to improve the roads, and how to bring in electricity without also attracting a rush of housing developments. In 1914 a wagon road was built on the west side of the river, where the North Ford Road is now, and about a year later a bridge was built connecting both roads. The bridge was built of logs, and the little community that was growing up nearby adopted the name **Polebridge** (Peter Stark, the *Missoulian*; September 6, 1981).

Pollinger (Madison) was a few miles southeast of Twin Bridges and was named for Elijah M. Pollinger, a Kansan who arrived in Virginia City in 1863 with a stockload of merchandise in four wagons. Pollinger opened a store in Bannack and later purchased some ranch land east of Twin Bridges, where he managed a stage company as well as his own 2,000-acre cattle ranch. The **Pollinger** post office operated 1869-71 with Henry Morier and Owen Gaffney serving as postmasters. In 1871 the name was changed to Gaffney's Station.

POLSON (Lake), a county seat, was named in 1898 after David Polson, a stockman who lived south of town in the Mission Valley. **Polson** is located in a natural amphitheater at the foot of Flathead Lake. The post office was established in 1898 with Henry Therriault as postmaster. The town was the trading center for one of Montana's most fertile farming areas. The Cherry Regatta on Polson Bay has for many years celebrated the annual cherry harvest.

Polytechnic (Yellowstone) was opened in 1910 on the campus of the college by that name. Ernest F. Eaton, co-founder of the school, was appointed postmaster. The name of the school describes its original purpose; *i.e.*, to teach many techniques, or skills. Polytechnic merged with Intermountain Union College after a 1934 earthquake at Helena destroyed the latter's buildings; after the merger the schools became Rocky Mountain College. The **Polytechnic** post office was discontinued in 1955 and mail was handled thereafter from the main office in Billings.

Pomo (Fergus) was a post office established January 1905 with John Pratt as postmaster. In August of that year the name was changed to Natal.

POMPEY'S PILLAR (Yellowstone) is on the banks of the Yellowstone River. The town is named for the nearby rock which was sighted and named by Lewis and Clark on July 25, 1806. As the explorers were paddling down the Yellowstone, Clark noticed a huge, unusual rock several hundred paces from the river bank. He climbed to the top of the rock and viewed the distant mountains. He also saw ". . . emence herds of Buffalows, Elk and wolves," and pictographs carved in the rock's soft sandstone. He added his own name and the date to the markings and called the rock "Pompey's Tower," after Sacajawea's son, Baptiste, whom he affectionately called "Little Pomp" or "Little Chief."

Pondera (Liberty) is listed in postal records 1914-21; Andrew Pederson was the first postmaster.

Pondera (Pondera) was named for the Indian tribe. A post office was established there in 1892 with William Morison as postmaster. An old photograph reprinted in the Great Falls *Tribune* shows the Pondera Hotel with a train approaching on the narrow gauge track. The caption, dated 1903, says that **Pondera** is taking on a ghost-like appearance because businesses and residents are disappearing; and Frank Orr with his thirty-horse freighter team, the caption continues, is moving the Pondera Hotel to the new town of Conrad (Dean). Mail service was transferred to Conrad in 1903.

Pondera County is in the northwest section of the state just east of the Continental Divide. The name comes from the French *pend d'oreille*, meaning "hanging ear," and was first applied to an Idaho lake because in shape it resembled an earlobe. The name was later given to an Indian tribe that entered Montana. The county's name was changed to resemble the phonetic spelling of the French in order to avoid confusion with the Idaho town and lake of the same name. **Pondera County** was created in 1919 from parts of Chouteau and Teton counties.

Ponsonby (Beaverhead) was a post office 1893-95. It was near Dewey and Louis Fyhrie was postmaster.

PONY (Madison), near Harrison, was named for Tecumseh "Pony" Smith who arrived here in 1869. He acquired his nickname due to his small stature. **Pony** was once called by the *Madisonian* "the metropolis of the Madison Valley." In its heyday it boasted a population of well over a thousand. **Pony** is an old town; even before the Alder Gulch discoveries Smith had built a cabin on the stream that was to be called Pony Creek and was doing some placer mining. In the fall of 1875 quartz discoveries brought prospectors flocking, and by 1900 the town had many handsome brick buildings, including a $12,000 schoolhouse, a bank, newspaper, stores, hotels and saloons. It is now a cluster of summer homes with a few year-round inhabitants. The post office opened in 1877 with William Wart in charge.

Poplar (Roosevelt) is at the confluence of the Poplar and Missouri rivers, and was named because poplar trees grew abundantly along the banks. A toll ferry is maintained across the river. The town grew up around old Fort Peck, which was built to protect cattle ranchers from hostile Indians and was maintained until 1887. But before the bridge was built or the ferry established, the swains from town swam their horses through the spring ice floes on their way to go courting the girls living on the other side. The post office was established in 1892 with Howard Cozier as postmaster. The postal area was previously known as Poplar Creek Agency. **Poplar** is the agency headquarters for the Fort Peck Indian Reservation (1,525,537 acres), created in 1872. It was a fur trading post in the early days.

Poplar Creek Agency This forerunner of the town of Poplar had a post office under the agency name 1880-92; Charles D. Smith was the first postmaster.

Porcupine (Custer) was a post office 1878-80; the postmaster was George Murphy.

Porcupine (Park) was a post office 1908-17; Edward Ricketts was the first postmaster. Both this **Porcupine** and the one in Custer County (see above) were obviously named for the animal.

Portage (Cascade), near Flowerree, had a post office 1903-44; James Lennon was the first postmaster. It was a station on the Great Northern no doubt named because early explorers had to portage, i.e., carry their goods, around the falls and rough parts of the Missouri River.

Porter (Teton) was near Bynum in Teton County and had a post office 1910-15. The first postmaster was Mary Porter.

Post (Missoula) is an abandoned trading post near Missoula. It was named because it was close to Fort Missoula, a military post.

POTOMAC (Missoula) is at the confluence of Camas and Union creeks. It was named by R. S. Ashby, who came from a part of Virginia which borders the Potomac River. The post office was established in 1884 with Robert S. Ashby as postmaster. The town is now a crossroads store serving ranchers, lumberjacks, and miners who make weekly trips for supplies. The front porch of a ranch house served as the first post office.

Potosi is usually called Potosi Hot Springs and is now a campground and swimming pool. Large tungsten deposits are located a few miles away. Potosi Canyon is in the Tobacco Root Mountains, where Potosi Peak rises to a height of 10,096 feet.

Powder, Powder River, (Powder River) had a post office as **Powder** 1879-80 with Leopold Hohman as postmaster. A. L. Huffman, the famous pioneer photographer of eastern Montana, came to Montana Territory in 1878 to be post photographer at Fort Keogh. One of his pictures is entitled, "Interior of An Old-Time Ranch House, **Powder River**, Montana." An old cemetery here contains crumbling markers for the men who came "up the trail" from Texas.

Powder River County is almost in the southeast corner of Montana. The river from which it takes its name traverses the county from its Wyoming border to the northeast corner. For years historians have supposed the Powder River took its name from the dark, gunpowder-colored soil and sand along its banks; but Capt. William Drannan, an early scout, says in his book of reminiscences that a group of soldiers were four hundred miles from Bent's Fort when they were attacked by Indians; a Frenchman, Vierres Roubidoux, shouted "Cache la poudre!" or, "Hide the powder!" and since then the often dry river has been called the Powder (*Thirty-One Years on the Plains and in the Mountains*). The river has also been aptly described as "a mile wide and an inch deep." Lewis and Clark first called it the Red Stone because of the red rocks near it. Some historians believe that the Verendryes, a family of French explorers, reached this river in 1743 while seeking a route to the Pacific. In 1805 Francois Larocque journeyed almost the entire length of the stream, presumably from Broadus to Terry, where it runs into the Yellowstone River. Indians were the only people living along the river until cattlemen came with their herds in the 1880s. **Powder River County** was organized in 1919 from a part of Custer County. Broadus is the county seat.

Powderville (Powder River) is in the northeast corner of the county on the Powder River. It was once a stopping station for stagecoaches between Deadwood, South Dakota, and Miles City. There was a large stable, a dance hall, and a hotel; the town's largest building housed the bar downstairs and the hotel upstairs. Everything was torn down at the old townsite, and the post office was moved to its present location about a half mile from the original one. The town now consists of only one building which houses the post office, the postmaster, and his family, but the office serves a vast area in southeastern Montana (Pat Cunningham).

Powell County, in west central Montana, is a long, narrow county slanting along the west side of the Continental Divide. Deer Lodge is the county seat. **Powell County** was organized in 1901 from a part of Deer Lodge County. A part of **Powell County** was annexed to Missoula County in 1915.

Power (Lewis and Clark) was a post office 1881-82 with Henry McDonald as postmaster. It was near Centerville.

POWER (Teton) started as a wheat-shipping point on the Great Northern. "Its clustered grain elevators stand like lighthouses in a sea of wheat" (*Montana, A Guide Book*). The post office opened in 1910 with Frank Steers as postmaster.

Pownal (Fergus) was a station on the Milwaukee in the corner of the county that touches both Chouteau and Judith Basin counties.

Prague (Yellowstone) Postal records shows an office by this name in 1898 with John Staffek as postmaster.

Prairie City (Chouteau) had a post office 1913-17. Henry Messick was the first postmaster. The mail was sent to Burnham in present-day Hill County after the office closed.

Prairie County is in east central Montana. Terry is the county seat. The county was named after the topography of the region, and was organized from parts of Custer, Dawson, and Fallon counties in 1915.

Prairie Elk (McCone) had a post office 1914-33. Joseph Himrod was the first postmaster. The name derives from an area creek which, in turn, was named for the plentiful wild game of the early days. The Pioneer Cattle Company, owned largely by Conrad Kohrs, ranged its herds around here. Kohrs purchased the N—N outfit and in 1882 bought 12,000 head of cattle for $400,000 from Granville Stuart — said to be the largest cattle transaction that had occurred in Montana Territory up until that time.

PRAY (Park County) is a post office south of Livingston on the Yellowstone River. The office opened in 1909 with Valentine Eggers as postmaster.

Preston, (Fallon) near Baker, had a post office 1900-01 with Frank Preston as postmaster. It was open again 1903-14.

Prickly Pear (Jefferson) was a post office 1866-72, after that the area was served by the Clancy office. Abraham Ackerman was the first postmaster. The prickly pear is a common Montana plant: "The prickly pear is now in full blume," said Meriwether Lewis, "And forms one of the beauties as well as the greatest pests of the plains." Lewis and Clark found it particularly troublesome after their leather shoes wore out and they had to resort to moccasins. There are Prickly Pear Flats near Big Sandy.

Priest's Pass R. Alexander MacDonald and Valentine Thomas Priest pioneered paths across and over the Rocky Mountains. "Priest had come to the divide country with Jim Bridger in 1864 and after 15 years of prospecting and other work had determined to find a new way across the mountains." The Priest and McDonald Pass tollroads charged a dollar for a horse and wagon, $3 for a wagon train, 25c for a man on horseback, and 75c for a buggy. In 1883 the Northern Pacific laid its rails across the Divide at the summit of Mullan Pass and the whole freighting and travel picture changed (Willard).

Priest's Point is near the present railroad station in Zurich. Fr. Philip Popaglas, who had come to minister to the Cree half-breeds, became sick, died and was buried here in February 1877. A cross now marks the spot. In the Great Eastern Ecumenical Division of the West, the Fort Belknap area had been assigned to the Methodists — but no one ever came.

Primrose (Missoula) was a substation on the electrified Milwaukee a few miles from Frenchtown. "Probably named for primrose flowers growing profusely in this part of Grass Valley" (Omundson).

Primus (Gallatin) was a post office 1882-83 with Charles Reimig as postmaster. When the office closed the mail was ordered to Pony in Madison County.

Princeton (Deer Lodge) was a post office 1884-86 with John Taylor as postmaster. The office, which was open again 1892-1918 would now be in Granite County.

PROCTOR (Lake County) was established in 1910 and named for the first postmaster, Clarence Proctor.

Profile (Fergus) was a post office 1885-88. George Carrill was the first postmaster.

Progress (Sweet Grass) was a post office 1911-19. James Folson was the first postmaster. **Progress** was near Shawmut, and is a euphemistic name typical of those often chosen by eager settlers.

Project (Cascade) was a post office 1917-20 with Arthur Briggs as postmaster. The office was open again 1921-35. It was near Power.

Prospect (Liberty) was the optimistic name chosen for a homestead area post office. It opened in 1911 with John Valentine as postmaster and closed in 1938.

PRYOR, (Big Horn) south of Billings, takes its name from the creek and the mountains, which were named by Lewis and Clark for Sgt. Nathaniel Pryor, a member of the expedition. **Pryor** is on the Crow Indian Reservation and is the site of the Plenty Coups Memorial State Monument and Plenty Coups' two-story log house. Plenty Coups, who was the last of the great Crow war chiefs, died in 1933 at the age of 84; he represented the Indian nations at the dedication of the Tomb of the Unknown Soldier in Washington, D.C., and his short speech on war and peace is regarded as a masterpiece of oratory. The Will James ranch, a few miles from **Pryor**, was the working locale for the famous cowboy author-artist. The post office opened in 1892 with Emma Stoeckel as postmaster.

Pryor Gap, near the Montana-Wyoming border in the Pryor Mountains, was so important for the religious rituals of the Crows that the area was considered sacred. "The castle rocks, now penetrated by the railroad tunnel, were a favorite fasting place for the medicine men until the tunnel released the medicine" (Shane). Plenty Coups, chief of the Crows, once told his people, "Education is your most powerful weapon. With education you are the white man's equal. Without education you are his victim." When Plenty Coups died the Crows decided that no one could take his place, so they never again elected a chief.

Puett (Gallatin) had a post office 1881-82 with Mary C. Puett as postmaster.

Puller Springs (Madison) had a post office 1879-81 with James Puller as postmaster. The office was open again December 1881-1906. It was about three miles below the junction of the Sweetwater and Ruby rivers where several natural hot springs were found, and on the direct wagon train route of pioneers coming from the south toward Virginia City. Later, ranchers moved to the area. Jim Puller got some land from the government and developed the springs; he also built a hotel, a dancehall, a saloon, and applied for a post office. For many years people visited **Puller Springs** to enjoy the therapeutic benefits attributed to the hot water and mud baths. Now the springs are a part of the Maloney Brothers Ranch (*Pioneer Trails and Trials*).

Pure Water, (Garfield) near Watson Flats, had one store and the post office, which operated 1917-30. Hattie Kribs was the first postmaster.

Putnam (Rosebud) had a post office established in 1883. The name was changed to Hathaway in 1887. Henry T. Smith was the first postmaster.

Putman (Valley) had a post office established in 1883. The name was changed to Hathaway in 1887. Henry T. Smith was the first postmaster at **Putman**.

Pyrenees (Deer Lodge) was a post office 1887-91 with Hetman Davis as postmaster. It was near Cable in a mountainous area.

Pyrtees (Ravalli) was a post office 1890-1907. Frank Jamieson was the first postmaster. Originally named for the iron pyrite there, the community later became known as the Eight Mile area because of the creek by that name.

Q

Quam (McCone) was a short-lived post office named for the family of postmaster Cornell Quam. The office was open May 1918-August 1919, and was near Welton.

Quartz, Quartz Creek (Mineral) was a station near Rivulet which received its name from D. S. Dickson, a merchant, after the extensive quartz mining there. The post office was established as **Quartz Creek** in 1871, but the name was shortened to **Quartz** and the office was listed as such 1882-1916. The first postmaster was George Sandy.

Queen (Jefferson) was on postal records March-July 1888. Isaac Kipp was postmaster. **Queen** was no doubt the name of a mine.

Quietus, (Big Horn) in the southeast corner of the county, had its post office application approved in 1917 with Ada Rigby as postmaster. Frank Brittain had been the postmaster in a Wyoming community before he came here, so he filled out the forms and sent in a list of about fifteen suggested names for the new town — all were rejected by the officials in Washington, D.C. Brittain told his wife, "Well, they put a quietus on that." Almost in fun, the Brittains sent the word "quietus" to Washington; it was accepted and the office opened in 1917 (*Echoing Footsteps*). The post office was discontinued in 1960 and the mail ordered to Otter in Powder River County. **Quietus** is near Hanging Woman Creek.

Quigley (Granite) was named for Mr. Quigley from Chicago who promoted this mining camp. **Quigley** had a post office 1896-1900; Addison Sterling, postmaster.

Quinns (Sanders) was named for Dr. M. C. Quinns, according to J. . Rowe. A station named **Quinn** is shown on a contemporary map near the Silver Bow and Beaverhead county lines.

Quitmeyer (Sheridan) was named for postmaster William Quitmeyer while the office was open 1912-13. It was near Dagmar.

R

Race Track (Powell) was named for a racetrack that was built there. The post office opened in 1879 with Philetus Hoyt as postmaster; it closed in 1935. During the heyday of the Copper Kings, horse racing was popular in both Butte and Anaconda. The Montana Hotel in Anaconda had a mosaic of Marcus Daly's racehorse, Tammany, inlaid in the floor.

Radersburg(h) (Broadwater) is southwest of Townsend and named for Ruben Rader, a large landowner who donated the property for the townsite. **Radersburg** is an old mining town which sprang up in 1866 when John Keating opened his Keating Mine; the town boomed the following year when the East Pacific claim was discovered north of town. The post office was established in 1868 with Robert Mimms as postmaster; at the time it was in Jefferson County and for awhile the county seat, complete with courthouse and jail. The two-story Freemont Hotel, made of squared logs and square nails, was described as "a first-class hotel" in 1871. A now-decaying frame church was dedicated by Brother Van in 1917. **Radersburg** was the birthplace of movie star Myrna Loy, whose real name was Myrna Williams. The post office was changed to a rural independent station in 1966.

Radio (Lake) is on White Creek. There was a post office 1927-42 with Victor Nelson, postmaster. Before that the office was called Seines.

Ragus, (Powder River) near Ashland, was a post office 1917-18 and 1926-27. Abraham L. Young was the first postmaster.

Rainbow (Cascade), a small settlement of people who worked on the dam the Montana Power Company was building, according to writer, Dorothy M. Johnson, who was living there in 1913. **Rainbow** was seven miles from Great Falls and drinking water had to be hauled from there in barrels, but residents of **Rainbow** had electricity and it was free because the Company made it right there (*When You and I Were Young, Whitefish*).

Ralston (Silver Bow) was an office 1888-96, and was named for the family of first postmaster Alexander Ralston (see **Ralston** below).

Ralston Postal records also list an office for Deer Lodge County 1910-11 with William Ralston as postmaster. Quite possibly this was the same place as the above entry, because a part of Silver Bow County was annexed to Deer Lodge County in 1903 (see **Ralston** above).

Ramburg, Ramberg (Blaine) was named for a rancher, George Ramberg, who came with his family to take up land along Clear Creek, filing on acreage near the Bear Paw Mountains in 1893. The post office operated 1919-28 and Edward Welling was postmaster.

RAMSAY, (Silver Bow) west of Butte, originated as a Northern Pacific station. The post office opened in 1916 with John Frank in charge.

Ranch Creek, in the extreme southeast corner of Powder River County, was a post office 1918-55; May Dennis, postmaster.

Rancher, (Treasure) near Myers, had a post office 1888-1927. James Struthers was the first postmaster.

Randall Billy Cochran, Indian fighter and buildier of the first trading post in what is now Blaine County, tells of getting in a skiff and going to **Randall** from Fort Union. Cochran, who had hired out as a scout and courier for Capt. Otis, carried mail between the two posts ". . . 'til the spring of '72, when I bought two four-mule teams and began to freight between **Randall** and the Spotted Tail Agency — 300 miles to the head of White River."

No post office was ever recorded for **Randall** but presumably it was in the home of Billy Randall, an Iowa bachelor who drifted West in 1873. He was fifteen years old, and had a new suit of clothes, a carpet bag and $15. In 1881 he settled at a lovely spot at the mouth of Cow Creek on the north side of the Yellowstone River, ten miles east of Pompey's Pillar. Billy envisioned a big future for the cattle industry in Montana because of the seemingly unlimited open range; he took up a homestead in what is now Yellowstone County and by 1914 was running 1,000 head of cattle and controlling an empire of some 15,000 acres — though only 160 acres of it was actually his as deeded land. He set up a flood irrigation system that was often copied in the future; and he lived alone on his homestead for seventy years and watched the nester farmers move in, plow, plant, starve, and finally give up. Billy felt sorry for them and treated them kindly; he knew they were bleeding the land of its best resource, natural grass, and that no man could make a living on 160 acres.

Randolf, Randolph was a Dawson County post office 1914-1919; Daniel Patterson was postmaster. The office was at the Patterson homestead and named for their son, Randolph. The location now would be in Garfield County between Jordan and Baxby.

Ranous (Sheridan) was a post office 1914-15 with George Mills as postmaster. After that the postal area was called Daleview.

RAPELJE (Stillwater) was named for J. M. Rapelje, the general manager and vice-president of the Northern Pacific Railroad. The post office was established 1917 with Clara Norton as postmaster. The area was formerly called Lake Basin and had a post office by that name a few miles east. **Rapelje** fared better than most of the dry-land towns because it was at the end of the line for the Northern Pacific and drew trade from several outlying areas.

Rapids (Yellowstone) is near "a hard-running ripple in the Yellowstone River" which gave rise to the name. The post office was established in 1880 when it was still a part of Gallatin County. Isaac Hensley was postmaster. The office closed in 1886 but was active again 1892-97.

Rattlesnake (Blaine) was a post office 1917-32. Minnie Cureth was the first postmaster and the office, near Cleveland, was first called **Cureth**. It didn't amount to much, but the reptile for which it was named certainly did. Poisonous rattlesnakes plagued Lewis and Clark not only in this part of the state but also in Beaverhead County, where great dens of rattlers still exist. In the Big Dry country of old Dawson County, a cowboy was found dead in his bed with the snake still with him. According to Highland, "One of the biggest rattlesnake dens found . . . was near a schoolhouse on Little Breed Creek. In 1929-30 there were nine children attending this school. . . . The snakes were in a 'dog town' right at the schoolhouse, and the children hunted snakes from the first day of school . . . until cold weather drove the snakes down the prairie dog holes. No estimate is available of the number killed, but the record for one noon hour was 116 good rattles. Rules set up by the youthful snake hunters did not permit counting 'buttons' or broken rattles."

RAVALLI (Lake) is at the junction of roads coming from Polson, Thompson Falls, and Missoula. It is named for a Jesuit missionary to the Indians, Fr. Anthony Ravalli, who arrived in the Bitterroot Valley in 1845 and later went north to minister in the Flathead Valley. **Ravalli** had a post office open in 1887 with Charles Stillinger as postmaster.

Ravalli County is in the extreme western part of the state. The Bitterroot Mountain Range on the western edge of the county is the natural boundary between Montana and Idaho. Named for Fr. Anthony Ravalli, S.J., it was formed from a part of Missoula County in 1893. Hamilton is the county seat.

Raveena was an electrical booster station for the Milwaukee Railroad which was established when the line was electrified from Harlowton to Avery, Idaho.

Rayfield was a Fergus, later a Golden Valley County, post office 1920-37. The first postmaster was Newland Stubbs.

RAYMOND, (Sheridan) in the state's extreme northeast corner, is nine miles from Canada and the border port station, also called **Raymond**, at the International Boundary. The post office was established in 1914 with William Dodds as postmaster.

Raymond (Teton) was a post office 1891-1910 when the name was changed to Blackleaf. Daniel Hoy was the postmaster.

RAYNESFORD (Judith Basin) was the maiden name of a woman who boarded the Great Northern survey crew while the railroad was being built. The new station was between Stanford and Belt. Land for the townsite was obtained from Edmund Higgins, who homesteaded the land around here in 1891. In 1907, when the railroad was coming through, supplies for the workers came from Higgins and his wife, for whom the station was named. The post office was established in 1909 with Charles Hay as postmaster. Before that the mail was handled at Spion Kop.

Raynolds Pass (Madison) was named for Gen. William Franklyn Raynolds, who in 1859, under orders from the War Department, examined land in Yellowstone and Tongue River country. With great difficulty he took his long wagon train through the gullies and chasms adjacent to the two Powder rivers, over the heights at the head of Mizpah Creek, and across the Tongue to the Rosebud. The command reached Armells Creek, almost where Colstrip is now, traveled down the Armells Valley, and went up the Yellowstone to Fort Sarpy near the present town of Sanders.

Rea (Rosebud) was named for Samuel Rea, director of the Northern Pacific Railroad 1901-05.

Red Bluff (Madison) was named for the iron-stained bluffs behind the store and post office building in the former boom town. In the early days settlers in Madison County freighted supplies from **Red Bluff**, and from 1864 on it was a midway stop for stages traveling between Virginia City and the Bozeman area. The discovery of gold in the area made it boom overnight. A mine at the edge of town named Red Bluff had its own mill and boarding house. The post office, opened in 1874 (Sylvester Hurst, postmaster), was connected to a store; the other store was a hotel. The quality of life varied: some people had nice houses, others lived in dugouts. **Red Bluff** thrived until 1890; the post office survived until 1901. All that remains now of the original site is a large stone house and a few smaller buildings around it. The buildings and surrounding land are owned by Montana State University and are operated as an agricultural experiment station.

Red Deer (Toole) had a post office established in June 1926 with Cora Grass as postmaster. In 1926 the name was changed to Ferdig.

Red Eagle (Flathead) was a Great Northern station formerly called Nyack, which is an Indian word for the mountains in Glacier Park. **Red Eagle** was a prominent chief of the Blackfeet Indians.

RED LODGE, (Carbon) a county seat, is fifteen miles from Wyoming on the highway that leads to the Cooke City entrance to Yellowstone National Park. "The history of **Red Lodge** and its colorful name date far back to the time nomadic Crow Indians were first attracted to its fertile valley. The most romantic and generally accepted story is that the lodges of the Crows were colored by red clay found in the area. A legend, not so romantic, is that it was originally called Bad Lodge by the Crows because a supply of meat spoiled and ruined one of their festivities. John Webber, an early pioneer, always insisted that the name evolved because so many red man's lodges, not necessarily red in color, covered the area" (Leona Lampi). A gold prospector, James "Yankee Jim" George came to the Red Lodge country in 1866 looking for gold, but he found black gold instead; many European immigrants came to work the coal mines at **Red Lodge**, and it has been estimated that as many as 6,000 people lived there while the mines were in full operation. A Festival of Nations has been held here each year since 1951 with idea of nurturing the cultures and traditions of the community's varied heritages. The settlement was first known as Rocky Fork because of its location where two smaller creeks combine to form Rock Creek. The post office was established in 1884. At the time Ezra Benton was postmaster, surveyor, assayer, caretaker for the coal lands owned by Walter Cooper of Bozeman, and the lone resident of **Red Lodge** old town. Here is another idea concerning the origin of the name: "On the side of the mountain west of **Red Lodge** is a huge outcropping of mineral-bearing rock of a reddish hue and a big stream of water comes out of it. This red formation, viewed at a distance of 10 or 12 miles, presents a striking resemblance to a huge Indian Tepee or Lodge. From this the Indians called the stream 'Red Lodge Creek' " (Livingston *Enterprise*; May 12, 1888; reprinted *Red Lodge, Saga of a Western Area*).

Red Mountain (City) had a post office 1867-83. When the office closed mail was ordered to Butte City. It was named for nearby Red Mountain in the southeastern part of Silver Bow County.

Red Rock, (Beaverhead) between Dillon and Dell, was a stopping place for persons involved in the building of the Utah and Northern Railroad. The post office opened in 1879 with John Shineberger as postmaster; it closed in 1923 and mail was ordered to Armstead. The town, valley and river were named because of the predominately red rocks in the bluffs. Irrigated fields in the Red Rock Valley help raise fine crops, and Red Rock Creek supplies the reservoir, lake and swan refuge.

Red Root (Fallon) had a post office 1913-16. Charles Schneider was the first postmaster. **Red Root** was near Willard.

REDSTONE (Sheridan) is fifteen miles from Canada, and was started before the land was opened up to homesteading. The people that came later just stopped and sat down, knowing they had a right to stay and use the surrounding land so as they didn't trespass on another "squatter." Probably the first squatter in the **Redstone** area was Elmer "Hominy" Thompson, who was cowboy, rancher, and camp cook. "Dutch" Henry was another colorful character in the town's history; he was a rough, tough, bronc rider and the leader of a gang of unsavory characters. One of his camps was near Harry Gray's ranch, and Gray recalled that often his mother and the children would be alone when Dutch came by to ask for a bucket of milk; when the bucket was returned, there was always a dollar or a half-dollar in it — Dutch and his type may have been unsavory, but they respected a decent woman. Early settlers were homesteaders, farmers, stockmen, sheep shearers, and ranch hands. Judd Matkin belonged to one of the earliest school boards in the area and had to travel to Froid, fifty miles away, for the meetings. Supplies had to be freighted from Culbertson or Plentywood. In 1903 **Redstone** got its first store and in 1905 a post office with Elmer Bergh as postmaster. Bill Ator was a freighter and the first mail carrier. The name was suggested by the wife of Olaf Bergh, who noted the profusion of red shale in the area. Olaf built a stone structure to house a store and opened a mine to supply settlers with coal (Geraldine Bantz).

Redwater (McCone) is on the Northern Pacific spur on the way to Brockway, and was named for nearby Redwater Creek, which takes its name from the abundant red shale which lines the banks and often colors the water. The **Redwater** post office opened in 1911 with Frederick Lambie as postmaster. It closed in 1928.

Reed and Bowles Trading Post was one of the primary stopping points for travelers in the Judith Basin and for freight traffic on the Carroll Road, a gathering place for hunters, trappers, Indians and explorers. The post was sometimes described as a ranch, consisting of a square blockade with large entrance gates and four or five log cabins inside. One was the trading store, another was for Reed and for Bowles and his wife; the others were travelers' quarters or dining rooms. The whole place was "very untidy and dirty." Once, after a drinking bout, Bowles and Reed got into a knife and fist fight which ended the partnership and closed the post in 1880 (Western Interpretive Services).

REED POINT (Stillwater) was first listed on postal records as Reed, with a post office 1901-06. The first postmaster was John MacPherson. In 1906 the name was changed to **Reed Point** and William Young was appointed postmaster. "The Lewis Guthrie family had a store and post office in **Reed Point** about the turn of the century, but it was not until drylanders started to flock in that any thought of establishing a town came to mind. A townsite was platted in 1911," according to Annin, who also quotes from a report by Mrs. Guthrie concerning the town's history: "We had built a large store . . . with a full basement right in front of the old building about 1910. In this we had new shelves and counters, new post office fixtures for about 150 boxes — all these new and shining . . . with a cement approach to our store and big windows . . . and a sign, 'A. L. Guthrie, General Merchandise.' We had a steam heating system installed and also a fine big coal and wood stove, a must in case the steam heating would not be adequate for the very cold days, and of course, the chairs and spitoons were moved up so the fellows could continue sawing their wood or putting up their hay around that stove, much as they had around the old one. We were now working quite a crew, a man clerk on the grocery side, a woman clerk in dry goods and hats, and an assistant girl in the post office. . . . Mr. Guthrie was general manager and sold implements, J. I. Case, Moline plows, McCormick binders and Deering mowers. . . . We were carrying a full line of shoes, also overshoes . . . we were buying flour and salt by the carload . . . 1919 was the driest year ever known . . . there wasn't enough moisture to wet a light blanket, and in vain did we try to collect our accounts . . . soon we gave up. The people had nothing and in 1920, farmers and merchants alike folded up. The farms were worth nothing . . . families that had been prosperous and happy were in despair . . . and went out via the drought."

Reedsfort (Meagher), established as a post office in January 1881, was named for first postmaster Alonza Reed. When the office moved a couple of miles away the community that grew up around it became Lewistown, and the county became Fergus in 1885. The **Reedsfort** office was discontinued the same year.

Reese Creek, (Gallatin) a sidetrack, was named for John Reese, who settled here in 1864.

Reeta (Richland), near present-day Savage, operated 1901-05. J. E. Kiehl was the first postmaster. When the **Reeta** office closed mail was ordered to Tokna. Postal records also list the spelling as Retah.

REGINA (Phillips) is near Beaver Creek. The post office by this name was established in old Dawson County in April 1893 and discontinued the following year, when the mail was ordered to Balmont. A **Regina** office also opened in 1915 in Blaine (now Phillips) County with Joseph Gauthier as postmaster. This was during the era of the dry-land farmer — the 1893-84 office marked the era of the big cattle outfits, although by 1890 the best years of open range and free grass were over. By 1900 practically all of the big cattle pools and their cowboys were gone.

Reichle (Beaverhead) was named for the family of first postmaster Margareta Reichle. The office was open 1913-50, but in 1878 the settlement was called Willis Station, after Ozias Willis, an early settler who operated a stage station and post office here. That office was discontinued in 1879 but reopened the following year. William Reichle was appointed postmaster in 1882, and in 1913 the name was changed to **Reichle**. When the railroad came through, Glen — the station serving this community — became the post office.

Reina (Valley) had a post office 1893-94 with Lorana Marshall as postmaster. Mail was then sent to Arp.

Rema (Carter) was a post office 1915-20. Henry Schultz was the first postmaster.

Renova, approximately on the Madison-Jefferson county line, was formerly Parrot. The post office was active 1906-23, with William S. Clark as postmaster.

RESERVE (Sheridan) is near the North Dakota border and was named because the town was established on the Fort Peck Indian Reservation. It began as a siding on the Great Northern branch line when it was built in 1910. The post office opened in 1912 with Estelle Kallak as postmaster.

Retah is listed in postal records as a post office 1910-18. Lill Mae Ward was the first postmaster (see **Reeta**).

Revenue (Madison) had a post office January-December 1887 and May-December 1888 with James Johnson as the first postmaster. Prior to that, the post office for the area was Margana.

REXFORD (Lincoln) is near the Kootenai River seven miles from Canada. The post office was established in June 1903 with William Fewkes as postmaster. The giant Libby Dam built near here sounded the death knell for **Rexford**; residents were told they must move to a new townsite two miles away to avoid the water that would back up behind the dam and flood the area. **Rexford's** one business street had a tavern, two stores, and a church; these, along with the schoolhouse, city hall, and several houses were moved or replaced in 1969.

Reynold's City was a mining camp of the '60s in old Deer Lodge County (now Powell). It was named for Jack Reynolds, who discovered "pay dirt" there.

Rhodes (Custer) was named for Winifred Rhodes, who became postmaster when the office opened in January 1912. "Winnie was known as the best-looking gal in that wide open cattle country. She got up the petition for a post office, located it at her house, and got herself appointed postmaster. Winnie had an eye for business so she put up a sign out front: ALL ROADS LEAD TO RHODES . . . and soon they did! The only trouble was that when the postal authorities came to check things over, Winnie's books were quite out of balance. She was put in jail for mishandling government funds. Her daughter was born while Winnie was in jail. As soon as she got out, she took off for South Dakota. The little girl grew up to be as pretty as her mother" (from Dick Williams, Sturgis, South Dakota). The post office was discontinued in 1913 and the mail ordered to Alzada.

Riberdy (Missoula) was a post office 1901-03 with Edward Riberdy as postmaster. It was near St. Regis.

Riceville (Cascade) was named for the founder, Daniel Rice. A post office was established in 1890 with Mary Rice as postmaster. It was discontinued in 1928 and mail was sent to Campsite.

RICHEY (Dawson) is between Sidney and Circle and was named for the first postmaster, Clyde Richey. The station served as terminus for the Great Northern when it arrived in 1916. The post office opened in 1912. The Shell Oil Company discovered oil near here on July 13, 1951, in Williston Basin. By the end of that year, oil companies had leased more than 60,000,000 Montana acres.

Richland (Flathead) had a post office 1892-95 with William Orr first postmaster. Mail was then ordered to Kalispell.

Richland (Gallatin) was a post office 1881-82 with George Allen as postmaster. When it closed the mail was sent to Livingston.

RICHLAND (Valley) This town's post office opened in 1913 with Legrand Steele as postmaster. It closed in 1919 and reopened in 1926. **Richland** is on the west fork of the Poplar River, and was named by promoters hoping to attract settlers to the region.

Richland County borders North Dakota. Sidney is the county seat. The county, named to advertise this section of the state to prospective settlers, was organized in 1914 from a part of Dawson County, some of **Richland County** was taken in 1914 to form Wibaux County and some was taken in 1919 to form McCone County.

Ridge (Carter) was previously in Custer and Fallon counties. It is near Powder River country and the Wyoming border. The post office established in April 1898 with James Somers as postmaster; it was discontinued in March 1959 with orders to send the mail to Biddle.

Ridgelawn (Richland) had a post office 1883-93 and 1899-1914. Alex P. Ayott was the first postmaster.

Ridgway (Carter) had a post office 1911-54 and was named for the family of first postmaster Salome Ridgway. The mail was later sent to Hammond. **Ridgway** was on Box Elder Creek.

Riebeling, (Lewis and Clark) a station on the Great Northern, was named for Henry J. Riebeling, a rancher from whom the GN purchased land for the townsite. A post office operated there 1913-18 (James Gray, postmaster) and 1920-37.

Riedel (Blaine) was named for the family of first postmaster Ida Riedel and was open 1902-43; after that the mail was ordered to Leroy. The office was established to serve settlers on Sour Dough Flat and Gold Bench, as well as the other long benches that slope down from the Bear Paw Mountains to the Missouri River. **Riedel** had a country store, and all supplies were freighted in from Chinook or Big Sandy. Black Coulee School and later on, Cow Island Trail School, served the community and outlying farms.

Rimini (Lewis and Clark) is an old mining town said to be named by Lawrence Barret for the character in the tragedy *Francisca da Rimini*. The post office was established in 1884 with Brace Wilson as postmaster; it closed in 1936.

Rimroad (Dawson) was a post office 1928-34. Wallis Russell was the first postmaster. It was a station on the Northern Pacific named because of its location on the trail along the summit of the rim of Sheep Mountain.

Rimrock (Yellowstone) was the name the railroad chose for its station because of the Rimrock Bluffs. Residents objected and the name of the community remained Park City.

Rim Rocks (Rosebud) was the area post office after the Almberg office closed and the one in Davidell opened in 1928. Marie Nelson was postmaster.

RINGLING (Meagher) is between Livingston and White Sulphur Springs. It was named for John Ringling, of the Ringling Brothers of circus fame, as well as president and builder of the Yellowstone Park and White Sulphur Springs Railroad, which later became a branch of the Milwaukee. The station was first called Leader and was established in 1908. The post office opened in 1911 with Charles Allison as postmaster. The Ringlings owned ranch properties in this area amounting to more than 100,000 acres. The town became an important shipping point for Smith River Valley wheat and cattle. The Yellowstone Park and White Sulphur Springs line was a twenty-three-mile railroad, its own company, running one train a day and paying dividends to investors.

Ripley, (Lincoln) on the Great Northern, had a post office 1908-09 with Joseph Cechlovsky, Jr. as postmaster. It was near Libby.

Rising Wolf (Glacier) was a Great Northern station bordering Glacier National Park. The name honors Hugh Monroe, the first white man to explore the park; he spent so much time with the Indians that they came to call him Rising Wolf and named Rising Wolf Mountain in the park after him. The station was formerly called Lubec. The name change came in 1926.

River (Flathead) had a post office 1900-01 with Martin Coulin as postmaster. It was near Lasalle.

Riverside was the name of a Dawson-McCone County post office which closed in 1934.

Riverside (Gallatin) was an early post office between Chico and West Yellowstone that operated June 1882-December 1884 and again 1908-09 with Oliver Byam as postmaster; it would now be in Park County. The office was moved to Yellowstone and the name changed to West Yellowstone. Rivers have always been important to Montana, and this post office and settlement, like several others, were named for their location at the side of a river.

Riverside was an early post office in Missoula, now Ravalli County, which was open 1889-95. The first postmaster was John Hyle. Postal records also show an office for Flathead County 1896-97 with Arthur Lindsey as postmaster — it seems likely these two references are to the same place.

Riverview (Carbon) had a post office 1901-06 with Mary Hallas postmaster. After that the area was served by a new office at Belfry. **Riverview** took its name from its location along the Clark Fork River.

Riverview (Richland) had a post office 1909-13 with John Dean as first postmaster. This station on the Northern Pacific was sometimes called Riverview Spur because it was the end of the "spur" going north from Glendive. **Riverview** commands a view of the Yellowstone River.

Rivulet (Mineral) was named because of the many small streams in the vicinity. It had a post office 1903-54; Anna Schasser was the postmaster.

Roanwood (Valley) was a post office 1914-26 with Theodore Rosholt as first postmaster.

Robare (Pondera) was named for Henry Robert (Robarre), an employee of the American Fur Company who died on the Blackfeet Reservation. The town's name is a phonetic spelling of how the French trader pronounced his name. The post office was established in 1886 — Hiram Upham was postmaster — under the spelling, Robarre. The office closed in 1894 and was open again briefly in 1899. "The lawless frontier town of **Robare** on Birch Creek flourished during the years 1870 to 1900 partly on illicit whiskey trade. In 1885 a party of horse thieves was hanged from a cottonwood tree on Birch Creek" (Shane).

Robbers Roost (Madison) began as a stage station about 1864 and was first known as Pete Daly's Place. Mrs. Daly was a hospitable and charitable host who often accepted payment from her lodgers in the form of gold dust. Legend has it that Robbers Roost was the hangout for Sheriff Henry Plummer and his cutthroats, and that it was here they planned many of their holdups — hence the name. But old-timers say that even though the outlaws probably came here from time to time for drinks and recreation, there is no supportable evidence that it was their headquarters. Now the rambling, two-story log building, which still stands (as does the old log hitching rail where desperadoes and travelers tied their horses), is in a fenced grove next to a farmhouse. The ground-level porch, supported by logs, extends the length of the house and a similar veranda is accessible from the second story. In a large room on the first floor is the bar at which many a dusty traveler of the 1860s quenched his thirst. The **Robbers Roost** school operated 1892-44.

ROBERTS, (Carbon) on Rock Creek between Red Lodge and Laurel, is at the same location as a railroad station called Merritt. The post office was established in 1896 with John Summay as postmaster. Old-timers say that the town was named for one of the first baggage men on the train that came through there, who was said to be so obliging that he endeared himself to everyone along the route. Others say it was named for W. Milnor Roberts, chief engineer on the Northern Pacific 1870-73 (Maryott).

Robinson (Meagher) had a post office open in 1888, and Hiram Edwards for a postmaster. It closed in 1894.

Rochester (Lewis and Clark) was formerly called McClellan Gulch. The post office opened in 1890 with Alex Hamfield in charge. It closed in 1892.

Rochester, (Madison) near Virginia City, had post office opened in 1868 with William Wann as postmaster; the office closed in 1876 but was open again 1888-89. The Watseca vein in Rochester Gulch was often claimed to be the richest in the area, and the fortunes of this camp rose and fell with its operations. During 1891-92 the post office was listed as Watseca; then the name **Rochester** was restored with John Chapman as postmaster; it closed in 1918. The site for the camp, chosen in 1865, was three miles from Rabbit Springs. The Hardesty Hotel, a log schoolhouse, even an opera house, were built. Miners moved in, but left when water could not be stopped from flowing into the mine, even after the best engineers were called in. But for a decade, "**Rochester** was the liveliest, most prosperous town in Madison County and was reported to have a population of 5,000" (Grace Roffey

Pratt, *Trails and Trials*).

Dr. Paul Adams recalled his first Methodist pastorate when he was sent to Virginia City in 1902: "I got off the train at Alder and boarded a platform buggy or express wagon for Virginia City . . . also on the wagon was a girl that the sheriff had put on the train earlier and asked that I 'keep an eye on her.' The sheriff had picked her up at a mining camp called **Rochester** because she and another inhabitant of the camp brothel had gotten into a fight and this one had hit the other one over the head with a beer bottle. I sat in the front seat with the driver, and the girl and her escort sat in the back seat. She sang 'Only a bird in an iron bound cage. That's me,' and depicted her downfall from the dancehouse to the hockhouse and then to the jailhouse. These with profanities and obscenities filled the hour's journey to Virginia City which we reached about mid-night. . . . Her face was red and scarred with a long continued life spent in temper, drink and devil passions. . . . It was an experience which made a deep impession on this tenderfoot preacher."

Rochester became a ghost town in 1952 when Lucy Ziegler Miller and her sister Henrietta Ziegler Fisher, who for more than twenty years had been the only inhabitants, moved away. Their homes were about a quarter of a mile apart; "There wouldn't be enough work for two women in just one house," they explained. Lucy owned a car, but neither of them knew how to drive, so they seldom got to town, but they visited each other often (*Pioneer Trails and Trials*).

Rock Creek (Park County) was a post office 1902-37. The first postmaster was Martha J. Kelley. After 1937 the postal address was Criswell. Rocky creek banks and beds are an important part of Montana's geography and economy, and many names were derived from them.

Rocker (Silver Bow) is near Butte. It grew up because of the Bluebird Mine, faded when the mine shut down in 1893, and was revived when the Butte, Anaconda, and Pacific Railroad between Butte and the Anaconda smelter chose **Rocker** as its division point where all ore trains were made up. The postal record reflects this sporadic history: the post office opened in 1887 under Charles Carvey, closed in 1896, opened again 1901-09 and again 1917-19. The mining camp was named for a cradle-like machine called a rocker which was used by early-day miners to wash gold from gravel.

Rockford, (Fergus) near Moore, had a post office 1899-1906 with Albert Barney, postmaster. It was located at the crossing on Rock Creek.

ROCK SPRINGS (Rosebud) had a post office established in 1911 with Joseph Langdalen as postmaster. It is still run in conjunction with a general store and gas station. It takes its name from Rock Springs Creek, which is fed by a spring that comes out of the rocks.

Rockvale (Carbon) was near Silesia and had a post office 1894-14 with Orren Clawson, postmaster. **Rockvale** was settled in 1893 along the Northern Pacific tracks near the place where Rock Creek drains into the Clark Fork River, and its name comes from its location in Rock Creek Valley.

Rocky Boy (Hill) was named for the Rocky Boy Indians. The post office opened in 1919 with James Corcoran as postmaster. It was discontinued in 1943.

Rocky Fork (Carbon) was the original name of a settlement on the fork of

Rock Creek that later became known as Red Lodge.

Rocky Point, Montana was a wolfer's town ... "along with nearby Carroll, it had flourished briefly in the '70s while an effort was underway to make Carroll a rival of Fort Benton as head of navigation on the Missouri River. It was 70 miles east of Fort Benton and would have avoided navigation of a shallow and tricky channel. This would have lengthened the shipping season" (*Montana, High, Wide and Handsome*). It was also called Wilder's Landing for a time. "**Rocky Point** was built on the cliffs above the Missouri some distance upstream from Fort Musselshell," according to Highland who goes on to say that "it may never have had more than 75 inhabitants, but these folks, many of them, and others in the surrounding country, were engaged in profitable tri-territory and two-nation horsetrading of cayuses not their own. ... Horses were taken at night, moved to the badlands, brands were altered, herds were shuffled and reshuffled and then moved again between sundown and sunrise. Dakota horses often moved to Wyoming; Wyoming horses moved to Montana and Canada; Canadian horses moved southward. ... **Rocky Point** was a cluster of adobe-chinked huts along the Missouri. They were occupied by wolfers, trappers and whiskey traders." There was one hotel and several saloons. Never a "nice" place, the town got worse as river traffic dwindled and unsavory characters out of a job began hanging around. Cattle rustlers and thieves came. They were organized, tough, efficient, and courageous. To fight these organized thieves, Granville Stuart organized his Stuart Stranglers who took justice in their own hands and meted out swift punishment to offenders. In 1884 Bill McKenzie stole Spud Murphy's horse down on the Missouri River and headed for Fort McGinnis, 60 miles away. Lee Scott at **Rocky Point** started out to look for McKenzie and the missing blue mare. Lee and his cowboys caught McKenzie, shot him and hanged him on a big cottonwood tree about one and a half miles below the fort on Hancock Creek. For some years after that, the "strangling" of horse thieves and road agents was the way of "justice" throughout northern Montana and along the Missouri River.

For a time, regular freight lines were run betwen **Rocky Point** and Fort Belknap.

Rogers (Fergus) was named for the family of first postmaster Edith Rogers. The office opened in 1901 and closed in 1910. The mail was then ordered to Pinegrove.

Rohner (Lewis and Clark) was a post office 1890-1902 and took its name from first postmaster John Rohner.

Rolefield (Phillips) had a post office 1919-23; the mail was then sent to Lovejoy. Ole R. Field, the postmaster, created the town's name from his name and initial.

ROLLINS (Lake) is on the west shore of Flathead Lake. It was named for the postmaster, Rehenault Rollins, when the office opened in 1904.

Romola (Gallatin) was a post office 1901-1902 with Henry Vossers as postmaster.

RONAN (Lake) was named for Maj. Peter Roran, who wrote a history of the Flathead Indians. His wife was the first white woman to reach Alder Gulch. Ronan was the first Indian agent for the Flatheads. The area around **Ronan**, once part of the Flathead Reservation, was thrown open to white settlement in 1910 and thousands of people came into to establish small farms and ranches on the irrigated land. The post office opened in 1894 with Ludger Twott as postmaster.

Roosevelt (Chouteau) had a post office approved in 1900 but the order was rescinded in 1901. Theodore Roosevelt was vice-president then and a familiar figure in the West. The namesake "town" didn't materialize, but the county that was named for him did. Edward Chappell was to have been the postmaster.

Roosevelt County is in northeastern Montana, and much of the county is made up of the Fort Peck Indian Reservation. Wolf Point is the county seat. The county was named for Theodore Roosevelt, who had a ranch across the line in North Dakota and often came to this section of Montana. The county was organized in 1919 from part of Sheridan County.

ROSCOE (Carbon) was formerly called Morris, and under that name a post office had been established in 1901. The name was changed because of confusion in sorting mail for Morris and for Norris in Madison County. It had been named for the Morrises, early settlers in the region. Mrs. Morris was postmaster and was asked to select a new name for the town, so she chose **Roscoe**, which was the name of her favorite horse. That was in 1905.

Rosebranch, (Hill) near Marias, had a post office 1917-18 with Albert Panzram as postmaster.

ROSEBUD, a name inspired by the wild roses that grow profusely in Montana, is the name of a town, a county, and a river. The **Rosebud** post offices make for a confusing bit of history: the original **Rosebud** in old Custer County, present-day Rosebud County, is the place that became Albright in 1884; when the Northern Pacific came through, there was a station called **Rosebud**, but the post office was then called Beeman; in 1884 the Beeman office became the present-day **Rosebud** with James Hay the postmaster; meanwhile the old Custer County town of **Rosebud** opened a post office in 1880 with Malcolm Maples as postmaster and in 1884 that name was changed to Beeman.

Rosebud County is a long, narrow county extending from the center of the state (north-south) almost to the Wyoming border. Forsyth is the county seat. **Rosebud County** was organized in 1901 from a part of Custer County; a part of **Rosebud County** was taken to form a part of Big Horn County in 1913; and another part was taken for Treasure County in 1919. The county took its name from the creek along whose banks the wild roses grew profusely. Much of the Cheyenne Indian Reservation lies within the borders of this county.

Rosemont (Ravalli) had a post office 1898-1929 with Horace MacKnight postmaster. The mail was then sent to Stevensville. According to Vonnie Bugli of Stevensville High School, **Rosemont** began as a post office building put up by O.B. MacKnight. It was never much more than the post office and a few scattered homesteads. Mrs. Charles Derby was the mail carrier for **Rosemont** and Sunset Bench. She traveled three days a week to Stevensville for the mail and brought it to **Rosemont** to be postmarked and sent out on a rural route to the dry-land farmers. The school, built about 1908, was attended to by ten to fifteen pupils until 1928, when it consolidated with Burnt Fork. In 1919 the post office building burned and the daughter-in-law of O.B. MacKnight moved the office to her house where it remained until it was discontinued.

Rose Valley (McCone) had a post office 1916-20 with Otto Chapek as postmaster. It was near Redwater.

Ross (Garfield) is along the Musselshell River. The post office was established in 1906, and Mr. and Mrs. Thomas Gilfeather were the postmasters for many years. It was discontinued in 1935. Mail came in on Tuesdays and Thursdays. Patrons who traveled over many miles of gumbo roads and did not find the hoped-for package or letter in Tuesday's mail often just stayed over at the Gilfeather home until Thursday's mail came in. Mrs. Gilfeather also reported that she had probably fed more horse thieves than most people, becuse this isolated country in the breaks of the Missouri and Musselshell Rivers was a favorite place for rustlers to bring their stolen stock. A 1968 case involving some $300,000 worth of valuable racehorses centered around a modern-day operation of horse thieves hiding out in this same area.

Ross Fork (Fergus) is at the fork of the Judith River and Rock Creek. The place was named for a pioneer family named Ross and the location in the fork of the river. It was also a station on the Great Northern "spur" from Moccasin to Lewistown. The post office was established in 1913 with John Brady as postmaster. A covered wagon cook car was the first **Ross Fork** school. It was moved around for a couple of years to whatever spot was closest to the most children. The next schoolhouse was an abandoned lumberyard. The large front room was used for the school and the teacher lived in the back. The kids walked to a nearby spring to wash their hands at lunchtime. The abandoned Brown's Saloon was taken over next and finally an unused schoolhouse south of Moore was moved to **Ross Fork**. The Great Northern built into there in 1912 and caused a spurt of growth for the town. Not much is left now, not even the post office.

Ross Hole "Received its name from Alexander Ross, a Scotsman turned mountain man whose trapping party was caught in snow in the upper Bitterroot in 1823. . . . Later Ross camped at Hell Gate for several days where his men shot four wild horses, 27 elk and 32 deer for their party of over 100 people" (Western Interpretive Services). The March 12, 1824 entry in the diary of Alexander Ross, a clerk of Hudson's Bay Company, was, "We are at the end of the river, and impossible mountains surround us in every direction. This gloomy and discouraging spot we reached on the 12th of March, 1824, and named the place 'The Valley of Troubles, Ross Hole' " (*Not in Precious Metals Alone*).

Rothiemay (Golden Valley) was named by George Pirrie for a place near his old home in Scotland; Rothiemay is south of Greenrock, where the ships are built in Scotland and near Glasgow at the end of the channel going out into the bay. Pirrie was an early stockman in this part of Montana. The town had formerly been called Halbert, and a post office under that name was opened in 1885. George Pirrie founded the Rothiemay Ranch and after the Halbert office closed the post office was moved to the ranch and Annie Pirrie was postmaster of the newly named **Rothiemay** office. It was later moved from the Pirrie ranch to Rothiemay Flat and Rosa Lunceford became postmaster. Dan Gannon was appointed postmaster when it was moved to his general store . In 1917 Hubert Morsanny took over the store and became postmaster the next year after serving one year as an assistant postmaster. The **Rothiemay** post office was discontinued in September of 1952, the year that H. A. (Bert) Morsanny retired after serving thirty-four years as postmaster. The location of the old **Rothiemay** post office is twenty miles directly north of Ryegate. It has been in Fergus, Musselshell, and Golden Valley counties (Mary Morsanny). An authentic replica of **Rothiemay**'s post office is now housed in the Musselshell Valley Historical Museum at Roundup.

Round Butte (Garfield) had a post office January-November 1915. The name came from a nearby hill that had been named thus because of its shape. The post office was on the south bank of the Missouri and mail was carried from Jordan. One mail carrier was killed by an outlaw who had escaped from the Glasgow jail and was hiding out in the river breaks. In the heyday of the "160 acres of free land," "homesteaders' shacks popped up like mushrooms." Over thirty families came in; there were dances, picnics, and hunting trips — and hard work. By 1922 the drought and depression had forced most of them to sell out and leave.

Round Butte (Lake) was a post office 1920-54. Margaret McKittrick was the first postmaster. The community had formerly been known as Horte.

ROUNDUP (Musselshell) is a county seat forty-six miles north of Billings. The post office opened in 1883 with Alexander McMillin as postmaster. There was a small settlement and stock range trading center known as **Roundup** which was a short distance west of the present town. When the Milwaukee Railroad was located the town moved in to be near the station. The name comes from the fact that it was once the gathering point for great herds of cattle that had grazed up and down the valley. It remained a cowtown until 1903 when homesteaders arrived, fenced the ranges, and crowded the stockmen behind barbed wire. The railroad came in 1907 and later it became a coalminers' town as mines were opened up in the area.

Rouse's Point (Yellowstone) had a post office 1877-80 with D. E. Rouse as postmaster.

ROY (Fergus) was named by W. H. Peck, an early settler. The name was supposed to be Ray, for a member of his family, but through a mistake in the Post Ofice Department, the name **Roy** was assigned. The office opened in 1892 with Walter H. Peck as postmaster. The P—N Cattle Company ran its herd in this area. **Roy**'s peak population was about four hundred and that was in 1915 when there was a homesteader on every 160 acres. Saturday night dances were the big thing. People came by horseback or in a buggy. One man ran the general store for fifty years and never sent out a statement. "People paid when they could," he said, and always voluntarily. Some accounts ran for twenty years. Most homesteaders left when World War I broke out and only a few returned, so their 160-acre holdings were bought up and consolidated into big ranches, mostly cattle (Byerly & Byerly).

Royal (Granite) had a post office 1894-99 and again 1903-05. It was near Philipsburg. Henry Neal was appointed postmaster in 1894.

Royston, Montana was the heading on a letter written September 20, 1886 by Roy Cobban to the girl he had left behind in Wisconsin: "There is as yet only one lady in the place but we hope very soon to have several families, a store and a post office. . . . Occasionally we ride to Butte to church." Evidently Roy's town never developed as he had hoped. The community may have been named for Richard Royston, who came from Missouri to Butte. After a week working in the smelter and watching men dying from the gas and fumes from the furnace, he moved on to Virginia

City and Whitehall. One winter he worked a prospect hole; the ore looked pretty good, so in the spring he went to look for a team and wagon to haul the ore, but when he got back with them, someone had hauled the ore away (*Not in Precious Metals Alone*).

Ruby (Madison) was a thriving community in the early 1900s. It was headquarters for the Conrey Placer Mining Company and remained so until the end of the dredging days, about 1923. The largest dredge boat in the world at that time, Conrey's No. 4, worked the area 1911-22. **Ruby** was in the mouth of the canyon and the company dredged Alder Gulch as far as Adobetown, and it is said they took out twenty-two tons of gold. "I can remember in the early days when the sweeping of a saloon was offered for sale to the highest bidder. Once it was bid in for $12 and netted the bidder $64 (Daems)." The old mining camp grew from a cluster of cabins to a prosperous town when the dredges came in and declined just as fast when they went out. The post office opened in 1901 with Lawrence Booker as postmaster. It closed in 1924. The name comes from the Ruby Mountains, so called because the garnets found there were first thought to be rubies. The valley and river also took the name.

Ruby Gulch (Fergus) was a community at the foothills of the Judith Mountains. A company called the Ruby Gulch Sawmills supplied much of the lumber for buildings in Lewistown. At one time there were two schools in the Gulch to educate the homesteaders' children, but there was never a store or a post office at **Ruby Gulch**. People went over the muddy trails to Lewistown by wagon or buggy. Some worked in the New Year and Maiden gold mines.

RUDYARD (Hill) is on the High Line between Chester and Havre. It is said that it was named for Rudyard Kipling. The post office was established in 1910 with Rosell Miner as postmaster.

Ruger (Chouteau) post office from 1879-81 with Charles McNamara as postmaster.

Rumble Creek (Missoula) had a post office 1919-33. Mary Drury was the first postmaster.

Rumsey (Granite) was a post office 1888-97. William Buskett was the first postmaster.

Rumsey is near the present Rosebud-Treasure county line. It was named for Fay Rumsey, postmaster while the office was open 1910-12.

Russell (Chouteau) had a post office established 1914 with Sam Leach as postmaster. The office was closed in 1947.

Russell (Dawson) had a post office February-November 1887, with John Abrams as postmaster.

Ryan (Beaverhead) began as Ryan's Station, a tollgate for the "Great Beaverhead Wagon Road" which shortened by many miles the road between the Overland Trail and the mining camps at Helena and Butte. The place was also known as the Henneberry and Ryan Toll Gate and at one time was called Barret's Station (Western Interpretive Services). A **Ryan** post office was established in 1869 with James M. Ryan as postmaster. It closed in 1870 and postal records note that the area was formerly called Sturgis.

Ryegate (Golden Valley) is a county seat. A fine field of rye attracted the attention of one railroad official and suggested the name for the station.

Ryegate was built at the base of rimrocks which are three miles long and once a part of the shore of a large lake. Marine fossils are found in abundance there. Prehistoric inscriptions can still be seen on the exposed rocks. One crudely drawn picture, a mile west of town shows six men and three antelope. The **Ryegate** post office was established in 1908 with Erwin E. Kemp as postmaster. The first woman sheriff in Montana had her office in **Ryegate**. Ruth Lane Garfield was appointed to fill out her husband's term. She served two years and after that as undersheriff and probation officer. Her husband, who was shot by a demented farmer in 1920, had been appointed sheriff when Golden Valley became a county. The site of **Ryegate** was originally a part of the Sims-Garfield ranch; it was the rye field of Mr. Sims that inspired the name.

S

Sabra was in old Custer County when the post office opened in 1891 with William Goodwin as postmaster. The office closed in 1913.

SACO (Phillips), on the Great Northern in the center of the rich, irrigated Milk River Valley, owns its own natural gas system. The post office was established in 1892 with Helen Parker as postmaster. H. L. Willard says, "This picturesque town got its name either from Sack-ow, an Indian tribe in Maine, or from a contraction of the name Sacajawea." The Phillips County News of Malta says **Saco** is another railroad siding town named at the railroad's St. Paul office by a blindfolded employee, who spun a globe, and putting his finger down — according to the News — found it had landed on Saco, Me.

"South and east of **Saco** are the Larb Hills, a wild tangle of rough country where the cowpunchers used to rope grizzly bears for fun. . . . Saco Hot Springs' warm water flows from a pocket in the hills . . . the Sleeping Buffalo Rocks nearby resemble buffalo lying down if they are viewed from a distance . . . there are many legends about these big glacial boulders . . . the Gros Ventres and Assiniboine Indians knew of the rocks . . . once a hunting party advanced upon this herd of sleeping buffalo by the crossing, only to find the animals turned to stone. The largest rock was for years covered with picture writings . . . young Indians pinched pieces of flesh from their bodies and placed them on the stone to get Good Medicine for the hunt" (Willard).

Chet Huntley, the late television news commentator and developer of Big Sky, attended the **Saco** country school.

Sadie (Custer) had a post office established 1882 with Corrydon Wilson as postmaster. It was open off-and-on until a final closing in 1909; the mail was then sent to Calabar.

Sage (Hill) was named after the wild plant and Sage Creek. The post office opened in 1912 with Ole Selmyhr as postmaster, in his ranch home fourteen miles north and two east of Inverness. Early settlers mined their own coal and "made-do," hoping that the next year would bring a good dry land crop. Children walked five miles to the school at Minnetaka until one was built at Grassy Butte. After the bad year of 1917, most homesteaders left (*Tumbleweeds and Tarpaper Shacks*). The post office closed in 1918.

Sagebrush was to have been the name of a post office in Dawson County with Thomas Gilfeather the postmaster, in 1904, but the office was never activated.

Sagedale (Rosebud) was a post office 1916-18 with Carolyn Kaufman as postmaster. The office operated a year earlier under the name Sagdel — no doubt the result of an unfortunate mistake by postal authorities.

Sahara (Golden Valley) had a post office 1930-45. Ilah Dorrel was the first postmaster.

Sahara was in Meagher County when the post office was established in 1884 with Hugh Cameron as postmaster; it was in Fergus County when the office was discontinued in 1890.

St. Clair (Cascade) was the name of a mission near Cascade along the old Lewis and Clark Trail when the post office was operating 1889-93 with James Erskine in charge.

ST. IGNATIUS (Lake), in the center of the Flathead Reservation a few miles south of Ronan, is the home of a reservation sub-agency. It was named in honor of St. Ignatius of Loyola, the Spanish priest who founded the Society of Jesus. The Roman Catholic mission of the same name — now a National Historic Landmark — was founded there in 1854 by Frs. De-Smet, Hoecken, and Menestrey, all Jesuits. The **St. Ignatius** post office was opened in 1872 with Isidore Cohn as postmaster.

Saint Joe (McCone) was the name of a post office 1911-12 with Joseph Breitback as postmaster. After 1912 mail was received at Horse Creek.

St. Joseph (Hill) was a post office 1914-24. After that the mail was sent to Havre. Joseph Morris was the first postmaster.

St. Labre is an Indian school founded in 1884 after the Catholic Church had bought the land as a camping place for the homeless Cheyennes. The school managed to survive and was serving about a hundred Indian children in 1954. At that time a factory was built nearby and a concerted appeal — via ten million letters — was launched. Now an annual budget of over $2 million supports the school and other Catholic missions, and by 1976 **St. Labre** was educating 450 Cheyenne children in grades one through twelve and eighty children from the Crow tribe. **St. Labre** adjoins the town of Ashland. The new trend among Native Americans toward preserving and learning of their heritage and traditions recently was exemplified in an American Indian Day: legends were told, dances were taught, and old games were played. The title of one student's painting echoed the reviving Indian philosophy: "The Earth and Myself Are of One Mind" (Joel Pease, Billings *Gazette*).

St. Louis was in present-day Broadwater County. The post office opened in 1869 with David Linebearger as postmaster, and was open intermittently until 1895, when the name was changed to Hassel. Gold was discovered nearby at Indian and Crow Creeks in 1866; a town boomed into existence and was named **St. Louis** in honor of some prospective investors from St. Louis, Missouri. Placer mines were worked profitably around **St. Louis** for about twenty years. The name was changed to Hassel to prevent further confusion with the Missouri city, as mail often got mixed up, especially when the names of the states were abbreviated (Western Interpretive Services).

St. Mary (Glacier), near Glacier National Park, had an on again-off again post office beginning in 1898 with John J. Judd in charge, to its final closing in 1915. Lower St. Mary Lake is in Glacier County, Upper St. Mary Lake is in the park, and the town of **St. Mary** is between them.

St. Mary's Lake, near the St. Ignatius Mission, was called "The Waters of the Forgiven" by the Indians, who had a legend which told of beautiful spirits inhabiating deep waters and luring careless warriors to their destruction.

St. Mary's Mission (Ravalli), near Stevensville, played an important part in Montana history. Luther E. Stanley of Stevensville gives this account of the naming: "Fr. DeSmet was returning from St. Louis (Mo.) and bringing with him Frs. Mengarini and Point and three lay brothers because the Flatheads had asked for more 'Black Robes' to teach them. The party followed downriver to Missoula, then southward up the Bitterroot River about twenty-eight miles. At a spot between the present Stevensville and Fort Owens, they came to rest. The date was September 24,1841, the day the Church honors the Blessed Mother. . . . Fr. DeSmet was struck by the coincidence and named the clear river, the big mountain across from it, the mission and the valley, **St. Mary's**. They cut down two trees to construct a large cross, symbol of all their hopes.

Another version is in the form of an Indian legend remembered by Chief Big Face and retold here by Denise Rae Livergood of Stevensville High School: "Several years before the arrival of the Black Robes, a girl, about thirteen years of age, named Mary, became seriously ill. At her request she was baptized by one of the Iroquois Indian converts, who had inspired the Flatheads to seek the Black Robes. After being baptized she said, 'Listen to the Black Robes when they come. They will build a house of prayer where I am dying.' " This story has since been put to canvas by a missionary; the painting hangs in the old mission church.

Several other buildings were constructed around the church, including a pharmacy believed to be the first in Montana.

On the first Christmas Day that Fr. DeSmet spent in **St. Mary's Mission**, he held mass continually from 7 a.m. to 5 p.m., without rest; he baptized 115 Flatheads and thirty Nez Perces, as well as a Blackfeet chief and his entire family. The mission, sometimes called St. Mary's Village, was closed and restored in 1866 and closed and reestablished again after that, though now, instead of being an Indian mission, it is an attraction of historical interest.

St. Paul's Mission (Blaine), in the same mountain range as Landusky, was founded in 1886 by Fr. Frederick Hugo Eberschweiler, who also served as postmaster when the office opened in 1890. Eberschweiler was a Jesuit priest whose knowledge of the Gros Ventres language won the Indians' respect. His request for help in building his mission went unheeded by the men at Fort Benton, who were afraid to venture into the Little Rockies while the Gros Ventres and the Bloods of Canada were at war; so Eberschweiler turned to the prospectors swarming into the Landusky diggings and there mustered a volunteer crew. The stone buildings still stand, and the mission, which serves Gros Ventres and Assiniboines, is still administered by Jesuit priests. The post office was discontinued in 1944. Noyes adds that the walls and ceiling of the church are entirely covered with paintings designed to help the Indians learn Bible stories.

Besides the large church there were two four-story buildings, one for boys and one for girls, for the education of Indian children. There were also shops, stables, and farm equipment. The founding father, the Reverend Eberschweiler, had come a long way — all the way from Prussia — to find this beautiful spot, in rolling hills that formed a natural amphitheater. During his service there, Fr. Eberschweiler translated the Catholic liturgy into the Assiniboine language.

St. Peter's Mission (Cascade) had a post office 1885-1938. Thomas Moran was the first postmaster. This mission and the Ursuline Academy were established when nuns came from Miles City in 1884. Fr. L. Smith, chaplain at Fort Keogh, had sent to Ohio for the sisters to come and establish a mission; from there some went on to **St. Peter's** (Sr. Genevieve McBride, *Birdtail*), where they established a Mother House in log cabins, and an academy which was the first school in the area for the children of both Indians and settlers. The church still stands but other buildings were burned.

There was an "opera house" at the mission where entertainments were held, but there was never any opera. The Indians, some of whom had mandolins and guitars, formed an orchestra. **St. Peter's Mission** was also the site of the first definite effort to introduce breeding flocks of sheep into Montana; in 1867 the Jesuit fathers who had established the mission trailed three hundred head in from Oregon over the Mullan Road.

St. Phillip (Wibaux) had a post office 1913-34. Frank Lasinski was the first postmaster.

ST. REGIS (Mineral) is named for the St. Regis River, which flows in from the west to join the Clark Fork here; the St. Regis was named by Fr. DeSmet in 1842 in honor of St. Regis de Borgia, who belonged to the same Jesuit order as DeSmet. The post office was established in 1896 with John Dowling as postmaster. **St. Regis** is a shipping point for lumber industry products. The center of town is a bridge over the Clark Fork River.

ST. XAVIER (Big Horn) is on the Crow Indian Reservation along the Big Horn River. In 1887 Fr. Prando, a Jesuit missionary, and two companions founded a mission here and named it. The post office was established in 1891 with Joseph Bandini as postmaster. "In February 1877, Gen. Miles sent Sweet Woman, one of the four women who had been captured on January 7, 1877, in the battle at the mouth of Hanging Woman Creek, and an interpreter with tobacco and presents to the Cheyenne winter camp at the mouth of Rotten Grass Creek near **St. Xavier**. They were to ask the Indians to come into Fort Keogh and surrender. If they surrendered peacefully they were promised a choice of where they wanted to be located. This band of 350 decided to surrender. Little Chief was the orator and spokesman. He said the Indians were weak, the Army was strong, and they felt forced to place themselves at the mercy of the Army. They consented to remain at Fort Keogh with Gen. Miles and many joined up as Army scouts. This group became known as Two Moons' Band" (Ralph Shane).

Salem (Cascade) was a station named for Salem, Massachusetts. The post office, originally named Underdahl, was established in 1927 with Andrew Underdahl in charge; Underdahl was an employee of the Winston Brothers grading contractors, who built the railroad there.

Salesh (Flathead) was a small community that grew up east of Somers in 1880.

Salesville (Gallatin) was named for Zach Sales, who had a mill there in the 1860s, and for his brother Alan, a farmer and storekeeper. **Salesville** had a post office established in 1880 with Norman Webb as postmaster; it was closed 1888-90 then open again until 1927, when the name was changed to Gallatin Gateway.

Salisbury (Madison) was about two miles southeast of Twin Bridges. A post office under the name Pollinger had operated at this stage stop 1869-71; when Owen Gaffney moved his Planters Hotel (named after the famous hotel in St. Louis, Missouri) from Virginia City to Pollinger, the name was changed to Gaffney to honor this optimistic businessman. In 1875 it was changed to **Salisbury** — after one of the founders of the celebrated stage firm of Gilmer, Salisbury and Co. — with John Closton as postmaster. It was discontinued in 1883.

Saltbrook (Fergus) had a post office established 1884 with Henry Burke as postmaster. The fact that there was a Salt Creek in the area and that early homesteaders included the Brooks brothers (John and Anthony had come from Germany in 1870 and owned the Bar L Ranch), suggest the possible origin of the town's name. At the turn of the century one could ride from the Bar L to Lewistown or to the Missouri River without seeing a fence (Byerly & Byerly). In 1885 the name was changed to Christina to honor the wife of David Hilger, who had been appointed postmaster that year.

SALTESE (Mineral) is a mining town almost on the Idaho border and named in honor of Chief Saltese, a Nez Perce leader from the area. **Saltese**, whose main street and railroad tracks string out along a narrow canyon, is a supply point for the many small silver and gold mines in the nearby mountains. As a gesture of Western hospitality, **Saltese** keeps the doors of its small jail always open as a welcome to weary hoboes (*Montana, A Guide Book*). The town was first known as Silver City but renamed in 1891. Even before the silver boom, the site was known to packers, trappers, and prospectors, who called it Packer's Meadow. It was a good campground and stopping place on the difficult trail to the Mullan Road. The post office opened in 1892 with Presley T. Lomax as postmaster.

Sampson (Powder River) had a post office 1898-1902. William Moorehead was the first postmaster and the office was at this ranch. In 1901 the office was moved to James Slayton's ranch, near Otter.

Sandcliffs (Blaine) was established 1895 with A. S. Lohman as postmaster. When the office closed in 1918 mail was ordered to Cleveland. The name, no doubt, came from the topography of the region.

SANDCOULEE, SAND COULEE (Cascade) was established before Great Falls. Farmers from Iowa came by emigrant train to Corrine, Utah (the end of the railroad) in the early 1880s and hired freight wagons to take them and their household goods from there to **Sandcoulee**. The first settlement was called Giffin, after the Nat McGiffin family, who were area pioneers; when the McGiffins moved further up the coulee the name was changed to describe the terrain. The area boomed when coal was found in commercial quantities, attracting miners who supplied some of the railroads for several years. The post office was opened in July 1884 with Thomas Allen as the first postmaster.

Sand Creek (Madison) had a post office 1897-1902 with Charles Sherwood as postmaster. When the office closed the mail was ordered to

Ferguson, a stage stop and ranch near the present community of McAllister.

Sand Creek (McCone) had a post office 1913-43. Jane Olive Ward was the first postmaster. **Sand Creek** is between Vida and Weldon.

SANDERS (Treasure) is a community along the Yellowstone River. Rowe says it was named for pioneer and U.S. Senator W. F. Sanders. The post office opened in 1904 with Ollie Smith as postmaster. It was closed in 1905 but reopened the following year.

Sanders County is in the northwest part of the state, along the Idaho border. Thompson Falls is the county seat. It was organized in 1905 from a part of Missoula County and named for U.S. Senator W. F. Sanders, pioneer, vigilante, and statesman. Sanders was also a nephew of Sidney Edgerton, the first territorial governor.

SAND SPRINGS (Garfield) gets its name for the wide expanse of sandy soil and the life-giving springs in the area. "On the present site of **Sand Springs** was a little trader's cabin, where travelers and roundup riders stopped overnight back in the '80s. Sometime during the '90s a saloon was added. In 1910 Fred Allen established a residence in a little log cabin. The town began to grow. Two more log cabins were put up and joined to the first one by frame work halls. Then came the big event of a two-room frame house being built and joined to the original log cabin by another hall. A dance was given each time to celebrate the completion of a new building. After the establishment of the post office in 1911 (Fred Allen was postmaster) the town really began to grow. Cabins were put up, a store was built, and the log cabins were turned into rooms for rent. A large hall was built to house a restaurant, pool room and dancehall. Two newspapers were flourishing, the **Sand Springs** *Star* and the *Prairie Breeze*. A flour mill was started . . . it later burned down" (from a history of Garfield County written by high school students in 1947). **Sand Springs** was once part of the N—N range. Later, Fred Allen, the first settler, became U.S. Commissioner and eager homesteaders poured in. Allen had a store, a rooming house, and a dancehall. The homesteaders met with dry years and many left; Joe Dutton bought out Allen's store and the land around it. **Sand Springs** now consists of this general store and post office, a schoolhouse and a church to serve the farmers and ranchers who stuck it out.

Sandstone was in Custer County when the post office was opened in 1899 with William Haley as postmaster. The office was discontinued in 1907. The name comes from the type of rock found there.

Sanford (Garfield) was a post office in the house of Aldo Sanford, who served as postmaster when the office opened June 1899. Some of the acreage owned by Thomas Cruse's N—N outfit were in this area; Sanford's post office-home is mentioned in a deed that Cruse made. Postal records show the name was changed to Belfast.

SANTA RITA (Glacier) is on the road to the rich Cut Bank oil and natural gas fields. The post office was established in 1937 with Alta Anstey as postmaster.

Santee was listed as "county unknown' when an office was authorized for it in 1880 with Charles Aubrey the postmaster. It closed a year later.

Sapphire (Fergus) was named for local sapphire mines which produced gemstones ranging in color from a pale to a crisp, royal blue. The post office opened in 1902 with James Sites as postmaster. It was closed 1903-05 and then open again until 1907.

Sappington (Gallatin) was once a busy stock shipping point. The Northern Pacific sent a spur line from this point to Norris. There was a post office 1892-96 with Richard Wellever as the first postmaster; the office opened again in 1908 and remained so until 1957. The town was named for Henry Hiter Sappington, a pioneer from Sappington, Missouri. His farm was known as the Sappington Ranch, and when the railroad built a siding there, the name was adopted.

Sarpy (Big Horn) had a post office 1907-43. "Upper Sarpy's first settlers arrived in 1877 — two bachelor brothers, Al and Frank Clark. Later they were married, and two other families, the Cooleys and the Frazers, came. William Cooley served as the first postmaster; Frank Clark built a schoolhouse. Six children went to it for the four months term. The nearest white neighbors were at Lame Deer. Mail and supplies had to be hauled from Forsyth on a road that crossed the Sarpy Mountains. **Sarpy** was first in Custer County, then in Rosebud, and now in Big Horn" (*Crow Country*).

Satchwell (Rosebud) was a post office 1903-09 and was named for first postmaster Theodore Satchwell.

Saugus (Prairie) was at one time one of the biggest cattle and horse shipping points in eastern Montana. Jacob Shepherd was postmaster when the office opened in 1909; at the time it was in Custer County. Bill Woodcock, the first settler, lived in a large log house on the riverbank. The schoolhouse doubled as a dancehall and people came by wagon from Calypso for the Saturday night dances (*Wheels Across Montana's Prairies*). The post office was discontinued in 1925. Leafie Ulrich of Fallon writes that the Milwaukee Railroad changed the name of its station there after a terrible accident: in 1938 a cloudburst flooded Custer Creek and washed out the bridge, resulting in the wrecking of the crack Olympian passenger train — there was great loss of life and some bodies were never recovered. According to the daughter of Mrs. Haughian — a woman who owned considerable land around **Saugus** — the railroad wanted to change the name so people would not associate the place with the tragedy; so they changed it to Susan, which was Mrs. Haughian's first name.

Savage (Richland) is named for H. M. Savage, supervising engineer for the U.S. Reclamation Service, and is on the Yellowstone River near North Dakota. The post office opened in 1910 with Clark Brooks as postmaster. For many years it was a busy shipping point for grain farmers and river-bottom beet growers.

Savannah (Missoula) had a post office in operation 1886-87 with George Bussoa as postmaster.

Savoy (Blaine) is ten miles east of Harlem. The post office opened in 1909 with Chester Boardman as postmaster; it closed in 1958.

Sayle (Powder River) is in the southwest corner of the county between Otter and Moorhead. The post office opened in 1917 at the W. K. Smith ranch on Indian Creek. Janet Smith was postmaster. The name was chosen from a list of suggested names sent to the Post Office Department. The office later moved to Bliven ranch, then to Ed Clark's, the mail incoming from Clearmont, Wyoming. In 1938 the office moved again, this time to the Bert Phillips ranch. It was discontinued in 1955.

Schatz (Powell) was a post office established 1915 with Orlie Coats as postmaster. In 1950 it took the railroad station name Blossburg. It is in the southeastern part of the county along the Continental Divide and border of Lewis and Clark County.

Schley was a Fergus County post office 1898-1901 with William V. Lewis as postmaster. The area is now in Judith Basin County. When the **Schley** office was discontinued the mail was handled at Philbrook.

Schley (Missoula) was established as a Northern Pacific in 1899 and was named in honor of Rear-Admiral Schley, U.S. Navy, who had just become famous for his part in the war with Spain. The station was about ten miles northeast of Frenchtown.

Schott (Sheridan) had a post office March-September 1918. It was named for Mary Schott, the postmaster. After the office closed the area was served by Wolf Point.

SCOBEY (Daniels), a county seat, is in the northeast corner of the state, fourteen miles from Canada and the port of entry called Port of Scobey. The name was chosen by Mansfield A. Daniels — a pioneer rancher for whom the county was named — after Maj. C. R. A. Scobey, agent at the Fort Peck Indian Reservation, who was living in Poplar about 1900. A post office was established in 1901 with Joseph Bonnes as postmaster. The area was known as Old Scobey, and the settlement that grew up around the Great Northern station was called East Scobey. In 1915 the Old Scobey post office was closed and the name changed to Daniels; East Scobey became the present **Scobey**, and the office, still active, opened in 1917 with Mary Burke in charge. This is grain and cattle country.

Scott (Fergus) was named for an engineer of the GN Railroad. The name was later changed to McDonnell, for Edward McDonnell, a rancher.

Scribner (Carbon) had a post office July-August 1911. George Town was postmaster. The office was moved to Warren a station on the Burlington.

Scribner (Missoula) had a post office in February 1872 with Angus McLeod as postmaster. It was the first settlement north of Flathead Lake and named for Wiley S. Scribner, Secretary of Montana Territory, Missoula newspaper publisher, and later, a Chicago attorney. In November 1873 the name was changed to Flat Head Lake (*Somers, Mont., a Company Town*).

Sears (Richland), originally in Dawson County, had a post office 1909-10 with John Johnson in charge. After that mail was sent to Newton.

Sedan (Gallatin), was an early post office 1891-1915. James Woosley was the first postmaster and after the office closed patrons were served from Wilsall.

SEELEY LAKE (Missoula) This post office opened in 1918 with Ruth Rogers as postmaster. Both town and lake were named for J. B. Seeley, the first white man to live here. The area was formerly served by Corlett. **Seeley Lake** is a popular recreational area and the post office now serves those who dwell in cabins and summer homes around the lake as well as several dude ranches in the vicinity. The lake is a part of the chain of Clearwater Lakes.

Seines (Flathead) had a post office established in 1916 (John Lyons, postmaster); it closed in 1922 and reopened in 1923. After 1927 the area was known as Radio and served by an office with that name.

Seips (Roosevelt) was a settlement originally in Sheridan County whose post office was open 1915-29. Robert Maxten was the first postmaster.

Selish (Flathead) was in Missoula County when the post office opened in 1881 with John Dooley in charge; it closed in 1891. The name is from the Salish (Selish) Indians.

Selma (Liberty), originally in old Chouteau County, had a post office 1912-36 with John Miller postmaster.

Selway (Powder River) was named for the Selway brothers, who were early cattlemen. Robert Selway was first postmaster of the office, which opened in 1899. In 1902 the office was relocated to the south on George Mitchell's ranch on upper Pumpkin Creek. Mail came by carrier three times a week from Stacey. In 1910 the **Selway** office was moved to the William McBridge ranch on Fifteen Mile Creek, where the Sampson post office had been established in 1898. Claude Adams was one of the first carriers on this route; leaving Stacey as soon as the mail arrived from Beebe, he went by horseback to **Selway**, arriving sometime in the night. In 1932 the **Selway** office moved to Luella Block's home in the Custer National Forest and was finally discontinued in 1937. One of the first stores in this area was located at the Selway ranch; it stocked mens' work clothes and sheep camp supplies, all brought in by freight teams from Arvada, Wyoming; Belle Fourche, South Dakota; and Miles City.

Senate (Fergus) was a post office 1914-15; after that the area was served by the Kendall office.It was named for James P. Sennot, the first postmaster, but the postal authorities evidently "corrected" the spelling.

Senia, Camp Senia was one of the early dude camps, developed by Al Croonquest in 1917 and named for his wife. The camp was twelve miles above Red Lodge on the West Fork of Rock Creek in the Beartooth Mountains. The camp was discontinued and cabins were sold to private owners.

Setter (Cascade) originally in Judith Basin County, was open 1910-11, and named for John Setter, the postmaster. When it was discontinued mail was sent to Monarch.

Seventynine was in old Yellowstone — later Musselshell, still later Golden Valley — County, when the post office opened in 1909 with James Baillie as postmaster. It developed into a settlement composed largely of southern Russian immigrants from Odessa who spoke both Russian and English; for many years they continued to observe the customs of their homeland. They came along with some other farmers about 1912 when the "79" Ranch, one of the largest of the old-time spreads in Montana, was broken up. The ranch, and subsequently the post office, took the name from the brand of John T. Murphy, the president of the Montana Cattle Co., who started the ranch on Sweet Grass Creek in 1879. The post office was discontinued in 1916 and the mail was ordered to Ryegate.

Seville (Teton) was a short-lived post office 1911-12. Arthur Bloomer was postmaster.

Sexton (Gallatin) was a post office 1902-04 named for William Sexton, postmaster.

Shambo (Hill) was named for Louis Chambeau, a scout and packer with Gen. Phil Sheridan. Once Chambeau was assigned to carry the Fort Assiniboine payroll from Denver to the fort — he made the trip by horseback with a money belt worn next to his skin. Chambeau's own first paycheck was made out to "Louis Shambo," so he decided to leave it that way. Later he scouted for Gen. Nelson Miles and still later for General Pershing. He married a Gros Ventre Indian woman who gave him five children, then moved to Bull Hook Bottoms (Havre) and there became a good cowboy; later he raised horses and worked as a bartender. A Texan once offered Louis $1,500 for his life's story, but he was told to go away — he wasn't money-hungry, and besides, it might hurt some of his relatives. A school and community were named for him (*Grit, Guts, and Gusto*). The post office opened in 1922 with Glennie Malitor as postmaster and was closed in 1955.

Shambow (Madison) had a post office 1889-90 and was named for one of the postmasters, Levi Shambow. The name was changed to Magdalen.

Shannon (Meagher) was named for postmaster John Shannon. The post office was active 1897-1911; mail was then sent to Lewis.

SHAWMUT (Wheatland) was a part of old Meagher County when the post office opened in 1885 with Francis Shaw as postmaster. The town is named for a local rancher and was once a station on the Milwaukee. It is now a country store and post office between Harlowton and Ryegate along the Musselshell River.

Sheds (Gallatin) had a post office 1896-98. Mary Severns was postmaster.

Shed's Bridge (Custer) was later called Bonfield.

Sheep Dip (Stillwater) ". . . Was a lively burg . . . drinking, games of chance, gambling and a hurdy-gurdy joint, all open, ran 'til after the NP track passed below that town, and it ceased to exist a few years later" (Annin). "Sheep dip" was the term used to describe the booze that was sold there. Later the settlement moved to the railroad and became known as Columbus.

Sheffield (Custer), a station on the Milwaukee, was almost on the Rosebud County line. The area had been known as Calabar, but the name changed and a post office was established in 1929 as **Sheffield**. Cecilie Jensen was the first postmaster and the office remained active until 1949.

SHELBY (Toole) is a county seat named for Peter P. Shelby, general manager of the Montana-Central Railroad. **Shelby** came into existence in 1891 when the Great Northern was forging across the prairie towards Marias Pass; the builders threw off a boxcar at the crosstrails in the coulee and called it a station. Shelby, who at that time was working for the GN, is said to have remarked, "That mudhole, God-forsaken place . . . will never amount to a damn." But he was wrong, his namesake becoming a distribution center for a trade area extending for more than fifty miles in every direction. Chuck wagons drove in from the south from points up and down the Marias River, and from the Sweetgrass Hills to the north — then went home loaded with supplies. Cowboys and sheepherders, after months on the range, rode in for a fling at the honky-tonk night life offered there. In the late 1890s **Shelby** was a "cowboy town." Old-time stockmen of the area once boasted of being able to drive their cattle from **Shelby** to the North Dakota line without cutting a fence, but the homesteaders changed all that.

It was one of the last prairie and grassland areas to be settled in the U.S. "In **Shelby** in 1913 there were 5,000 homestead entries in one land office. The land was a magnet; photos of new land to be settled and advertising by the railroads made it seem attractive; the hardships were omitted in this advertising. The backgrounds of pioneers differed; the influx of settlers continued for several decades; ethnic groups were intermixed. . . . By 1921 the once-hopeful homesteaders were desperate. No federal or state aid was available to assist drought victims. Bankrupt and destitute homesteaders turned to the Salvation Army and Red Cross for help. Helpless to aid the thousands of homeless, officials of these agencies argued that drought sufferers were a state concern. **Shelby** attorney W. M. Black witnessed the disaster and wrote to Gov. Joseph M. Dixon about its proportions. Unable to hang on, many people left in despair, one with a poetic sign on his wagon:

> Twenty miles from water;
> forty miles from wood;
> We're leaving old Montana,
> and we're leaving her for good."
>
> (*Not in Precious Metals Alone*).

Then in 1921, in the midst of the homesteaders' exodus, Gordon Campbell, a geologist, discovered oil in Montana and successfully drilled the field that stretched from **Shelby** to the Canadian border. The town grew by leaps and bounds, even hosting the World Heavyweight Championship fight between Dempsey and Gibbons in 1923. The post office dates back to November 1892 with Charles Wittmeier as postmaster.

Sheldon (Missoula), then in Flathead County, had a post office 1887-1903. It was near Kalispell and named for Sarah Sheldon, the first postmaster.

Shepherd (Chouteau) was named for the first postmaster, Newton Shepherd. The post office was opened in 1887 and in 1892 the area name was changed to Yemen.

SHEPHERD (Yellowstone) is sixteen miles northeast of Billings. It was named for R. E. Shepherd, president of the Billings Land and Irrigation Co. and the Merchants National Bank. The post office opened in 1915 with Fern French as postmaster. The area was originally peopled with Dutch, German, and Scandinavian farmers who arrive in emigrant trains. The land, which had once been cattle country, became farmland after the Billings Bench Water Association canal, a sixty-five mile lifeline for crops, opened in 1905. Homesteaders came, dreamed and hoped, but as in much of eastern Montana, they finally succumbed to drought, grasshoppers and coyotes. In 1936 grasshoppers destroyed the sugar beet crop. By the mid '30s the plowed and deserted fields were overgrown with sunflowers and Russian thistles; fences were down and the entire area was one endless chain of prairie dog towns. By 1950 the land was back to cattle range, with crested wheat planted under the Montana Grass Conservation Act. Now another influx of population threatens to squeeze out cattlemen as **Shepherd** becomes suburbia for Billings.

Sherburne (Glacier) was in Teton County when the post office operated 1914-18. Preston Booker was postmaster. Later the area was served by the Babb post office.

Sheridan (Madison), in the fertile Ruby Valley, had a post office established May 1866, when mining activity was attracting many Civil War veterans to the gold fields. The town, as well as the eastern Montana county, was named for Gen. Phillip H. Sheridan, a noted Union cavalry leader; the name was chosen by Rozelle P. Bateman, who took up some land and built the first cabin there in the early 1860s. The first post office was in 1866 in the ranch house of Dennis Sullivan, some five miles northwest of town; Phillip Evans was official postmaster. In 1868 the cigar box which contained all the postal supplies was moved to Bateman's cabin, who took over the job.

Sheridan County is the most northeasterly county in the state, bordering Canada and North Dakota. It was named for Gen. Philip H. Sheridan, a Civil War cavalry leader and military commander during the Indian Wars. The county seat, Plentywood, saw a flurry of communistic political activity around 1932, but it eventually died down. More recent excitement has been caused by oil drilling in some parts of the county (Carl Friedrich, Antelope High School). **Sheridan County** was organized in 1913 from a part of Valley County; parts were taken to form Roosevelt County in 1919 and Daniels County in 1920.

Shields (Park) was originally called Shields River, and under that name a post office, then in Gallatin County, operated September 1877-May 1878 with David Carpenter as postmaster. The name was shortened to **Shields** and a post office operated intermittently 1882-1911; Isaac W. Butler was the first postmaster. Shields River and Shields Creek, both of which run by Wilsall, were named for a member of the Lewis and Clark expedition.

Shilling (Missoula), a siding on the Northern Pacific, was named for the president of the pulp mill there who used it to ship out his products. The place was previously called Gaspard and was also once known as Mellady.

Shiner (Dawson) was a post office 1898-99 with Rose Golden as postmaster. After that, mail was handled at Tokna.

(The) Shining Mountains On May 26, 1805, Capt. Meriwether Lewis climbed the hills on the shore of the Missouri some distance beyond where the Musselshell flows in. Looking westward, he saw the snowy crests of a huge mountain range shining in the sun, and thought what a terrific obstacle they were going to be to his expeditionary force on its way to the Pacific. Lewis called them the "**Shining Mountains**" in his journal. Officially speaking, of course, they became the Rocky Mountains; but romantically speaking, Montana has long been known as the Land of the Shining Mountains.

Shirley (Custer) was a station named after a U.S. Army officer who camped here during the Indian troubles of 1876, according to one writer. But a local historian says that the station, built in 1882, was first named Tillie, then Ainslie for a railroad division superintendent, and then in 1891 was named **Shirley** by Ainslie himself, after his daughter. The town had a post office 1905-45; the first postmaster was August Birkholz.

SHONKIN (Chouteau) was named for Shonkin Creek, which in turn was named for John Shonk, an early settler. This was cow country in the early days of white settlement in Montana. Supplies came upriver to Fort Benton and cowboys from the Judith Basin pool wintered here (Elizabeth Cheney). What was to develop into the Shonkin Ranch Company began as a single ranch around here. Nearby Shonkin Lake is fed by streams from the Highwood Mountains. The first post office was established in 1886 with Ernest Leaming in charge; it was closed and reopened a couple of times before 1908, when it was reestablished, and has been active ever since. Shonkin was once a station on the Milwaukee.

Shorey (Yellowstone), a station on the Northern Pacific, was named for a rancher who settled here.

Shriver (Carbon), named for Netti Shriver, first postmaster, had an office on Sage Creek 1915-38 for the convenience of homesteaders.

SIDNEY (Richland) is a county seat and the center of a wheat and sugar beet growing area — but cattlemen were trading cows there as early as 1888. In October of that year a post office was granted for the community. Maggie Crossen, wife of Charles Crossen — a soldier from Fort Buford — and daughter of the Reverend and Mrs. Moses Polley, was first postmaster; residents are still fond of referring to their community as "Maggie's Town." The settlement was originally called Eureka but there was already a post office by that name, so the neighbors decided to name the town for Sidney Walters, a young man whose parents were area pioneers. The boom years came 1904-09 after the completion of the big irrigation ditch. **Sidney**'s sugar beet industry — comprised of crops and the Holly Sugar refinery — has kept its economy at a high level when other parts of the state were experiencing lean times. Said a newspaper release, "**Sidney** sits on beds of coal, and in parts of Richland County, cattle graze over pools of oil."

Sieben (Lewis and Clark), once a Great Northern station, was an early stage station on the freight route between Fort Benton and Helena, and was called Mitchell. The name was changed to **Sieben**, after a family who owned a ranch near there, and under that name a post office was active 1925-28 with James Linderman appointed first postmaster. The Mitchell office was established in 1900.

Sifton (Fergus) was a post office June 1888-February 1890 with Annie Campbell as postmaster. When that office closed the mail was ordered to Stanford.

Sigmund (Powder River) When the settlements in newly-created Powder River County were voting to see where the county seat would be located, Broadus, with 1,624 votes, beat out Olive (198) and **Sigmund** (221). Just where **Sigmund** was has since been forgotten, but records indicate that a Max Sigmund inherited a homestead in Powder River County from his father.

Signal Butte is an historic point overlooking the old Fort Keogh Military Reservation and Miles City. In the early days the top of the butte was used to send heliograph signals and for fires, warning people for miles around about Indian trouble.

SILESIA (Carbon) is named for Silesia Springs, a mineral springs which got its name from Julius Lehrkind, who came from the eastern German province of Silesia. The Lehrkind family started a brewery in **Silesia**, but after a few years it burned down and some of the family moved to Red Lodge to start another one. **Silesia** is at the junction where the Northern Pacific Railroad branches off towards Red Lodge and Bridger. The post office was opened in 1900 with Charles Buzzetti as postmaster.

SILVERBOW (Silver Bow) is west of Butte. The post office was established in 1869 (R. C. Allen, postmaster) while the area was still Deer Lodge County, and the office was active on-and-off until 1907. On August 10 of that year Frank Lindborg was appointed postmaster — the office has been open ever since — but the spelling was changed to a single word.

Bannack and Virginia City were booming in the 1860s, but by '64 some prospectors with itchy feet were seeking new fields. One group included William Allison, Bud Parker, Frank Ruff, Joe and Jim Heiser, and Peter

Slater; according to one newspaper account they tramped cross-country in the spring of '64 and discovered gold on a straggling stream southwest of what is now Butte.

There are several stories about the discovery of **Silverbow** and its naming. "Seven-Up Pete tells it this way: 'Me and two others, a Scotsman and an Englishman, crossed the Min range with our pack critturs through Pipestone Pass. We were up on a prospectin' tower for placer diggins. . . . The crick was full of curves and bends and the sun a-glacin' along its waters made these curves, as we looked eastward, to look like so many silver bows' " (Mockel).

In 1891 Thomas Miles, a resident of **Silverbow**, addressed a letter to the Hon. J. K. Toole, requesting that something be done about the Indians who kept coming back and appropriating his pasture lands.

Silver Bow County is bordered on the west by the Continental Divide. It is Montana's smallest county in area, but was for many years the most populous. Butte, the county seat, is still known as "the richest hill on earth," and when the mines were in full operation, **Silver Bow County** was first in the state in wealth taken from the earth — automobile license plates here still bear the numeral "1". The county gets its name from Silver Bow creek, named by prospectors in 1864. It was organized in 1881 from a part of Deer Lodge County; a part of **Silver Bow County** was annexed to Deer Lodge County in 1903.

Silver Camp (Lewis and Clark) had a post office 1917-18 with Henry Johns as postmaster; after that the mail was directed to Flesher.

Silver City (Lewis and Clark), called Silver until 1888, was a station on the Great Northern. The post office was active most of the time 1867-1912. John Green, the first postmaster, was appointed when the area was still called Edgerton County. The name was chosen in 1869 because a man named Silver lost his wife while they were traveling by horseback through this country and he buried her along a stream later named Silver Creek — where gold was later discovered — to commemorate her interment (Perrin). When the GN built its line through here they called the station **Silver**, but confusion in reading the name on a train order caused a head-on collision at Sieben, and on August 25, 1925, the company changed the name to **Silver City**. It was not uncommon for the railroad and the postal department to be at odds over names assigned to an area.

SILVER GATE (Park) is almost on the Wyoming border. It is a summer town for tourists entering Yellowstone Park via Cooke City. The post office was established in 1937 with Sylvia Vincelette as postmaster. Early-day silver mining camps were located on nearby Silver Mountain, a part of the Beartooth Range; **Silver Gate** takes its name from the mountain and its location in the "gateway" between the mountains.

Silver Lake (Deer Lodge) was approved for a post office in 1895, but it was never in operation.

SILVER STAR (Madison) is between Whitehall and Twin Bridges on a branch line of the Northern Pacific serving the irrigated valley around it. **Silver Star** is one of the oldest towns in the state, and was named when it was a supply point for silver miners and the only town between Virginia City and Helena. Natives claim that Edward, Prince of Wales, the son of Queen Victoria, spent three days at the Silver Star Hotel in 1878. Green Campbell discovered gold in the hills near here in 1866 — his claim bears the number "1" in state patent records. **Silver Star** developed into a booming mining camp as other rich mines were established. George and Bill Boyer called their mine the "Silver Star." Prospectors, miners, and other residents gathered at the general merchandise store one Saturday night to name the two main camps; one they called **Silver Star**, and the other Rag Town, which later became Iron Rod. The **Silver Star** post office opened in June 1869 with John Couna as postmaster.

Simla (Toole), near Ethridge, had a post office 1915-25; Lydia Smith was the first postmaster.

SIMMS (Cascade) is on Little Muddy Creek. It was once a cattlemen's town, but now is dominated by farmers. **Simms** was named for an early settler who promoted the post office petition in 1909. William Curley was appointed postmaster.

Simpson (Hill) is near the Wild Horse port of entry on the Canadian side of the International Boundary; a gravel road connects the two. **Simpson**, with its post office, general store, and scattered farms, was almost cut off from the rest of the world during winter. Since 1972 even the post office has been gone, and now Russian thistles and wild mustard grow on fields that were originally tilled by hopeful wheat farmers. The post office (Edwin Fitch, postmaster) was opened in 1915, but now residents have to go thirty-eight miles to Havre for postal service. One of the first settlers in the area was Billy Sims; two other pioneers were the Simpson brothers, Barney and Ernie, who ran their sheep from the Canadian border to the Milk River — the community is named for them.

Sioux Pass (Richland) is a farming and ranching community halfway between Sidney and Culbertson. Because this was the home of the Sioux Indians in early days, the pass between the hills and the junction of the Yellowstone and Missouri rivers were named for them; when the community was established in the 1900s it was also called **Sioux Pass**. At one time the town, which was about three miles east of the pass, had a general store, dance hall, telephone switchboard, church, and a school. Some of the children rode six miles horseback to class. The Ellis family handled the mail; a son, Melvin, brought it once a week from a stage stop at Java. The post office became official in 1909 with Edgar Ellis the postmaster. When enough homesteaders had moved in, a three-times-a-week mail service was started; a man who broke mustangs took the route and used it as a training ground for his horses. Later the office moved about from one homestead cabin to another; at one time it was in a lean-to attached to the blacksmith shop. The town grew and a proper office was provided in a store; it remained there until it was discontinued in 1955 (*Courage Enough*).

Sipple (Judith Basin) is near the Fergus County border. John Sipple, who lived near Moore, put in an elevator stop beside the Milwaukee tracks when the line went through in 1909.

Sixteen (Meagher) was a station on the Milwaukee in the extreme southwest corner of Meagher County.

Skaar (Sheridan) was named for Ed Skaar, who came from Norway and was one of the first settlers in the area. Pierre Wibaux set up a bull camp three miles north of **Skaar** and had as many as four hundred bulls there at a time. The camp couldn't be seen from a distance, so cowboys used a nearby butte for a landmark which is still called Bull Butte. A history of Sheridan

County says that a post office was the result of the efforts of twelve-year-old Clarence Lund, who in 1912 took petitions around to be signed — but that the office didn't open until 1955, when Clarence was 43. At any rate, postal records show no office for **Skaar**.

Skalkaho (Missoula) This post office was established in March 1872; William Burnett was its first postmaster. The name was changed to Grantsdale in 1888.

Slayton (Golden Valley) was once a station on the Great Northern where there passed through every day as many as four passenger trains plus many freight trains as well; the area was also served by four Milwaukee trains daily. The settlement was named for D. W. Slayton, a prominent sheepman and state senator who established the Slayton Mercantile in Lavina. The **Slayton** post office operated 1915-31 and the mail was then sent to Cushman.

Sloan (Sanders) was named for Hattie Sloan, the first postmaster; he office was open 1910-37.

Smead (Sanders), near Noxon, had a post office 1891-95 and 1902-04; Winfield Hair was the first postmaster. **Smead** was once a station on the Northern Pacific.

Smelter (Cascade) had a post office 1888-1901; Val Laubenheimer was the first postmaster. It was the site of the smelter near Great Falls.

Smiley (Flathead) had a post office approved September 1897 with John Smiley to be in charge; however, the order was rescinded a year later and the office was never in operation.

Smith (Petroleum) had a post office 1911-20 and was named for postmaster Samuel Smith.

Smith Creek (Richland) was in Dawson County when the post office opened in 1913, and in Wibaux County when it closed in 1917; Samuel Gabel was the first postmaster.

Smithtown (Dawson) was named for Gov. Clay Smith. The idea had been to make it the county seat.

Smoke Creek (Sheridan) was approved for a post office in 1918 with Frank Neuman as postmaster, but it was never in operation.

Smoky Butte (Garfield), west of Jordan, is a well-known landmark that towers high above the surrounding hills and contains many rattlesnake dens. Much of the butte is made of basalt rock, some of which was used to riprap the Fort Peck Dam. The name comes from a kind of haze that seems to hang around the butte. C. J. Taylor, the first postmaster when the office opened in 1914, built a dance hall on his homestead which became a community center. The office was closed in 1920. **Smoky Butte** was once a contender to be the county seat, but now nothing by that name remains on the map but a creek.

Sneath (Chouteau) had a post office 1906-07 with John Sneath as postmaster; after that the mail was sent to Everson.

Snider (Sanders) had a post office opened in 1949 with Mrs. O'Tillie Evans in charge.

Snowbelt, Snow Belt (Garfield), south of Edwards, had a post office established 1913 with Henry Rup as postmaster; Frank Powell, keeper of the general store, was a later postmaster. The office closed in 1920. The name is descriptive of an area where the headwaters of several creeks are found.

Snowshoe (Lincoln) had a post office for several years. One record gives it as 1896-1912 with Patrick Pope in charge, but another states the office was only open 1904-13. The name is an obvious reflection of a popular means of transportation in the area.

Snyder (Flathead) had a post office established 1905 and named for postmaster George Snyder. The name was changed to Glacier in 1909.

Sober-Up (Pondera) was a line camp on the early cattle range. It was named for the many times when a cowboy, hoping to recover from a long drunken spree, went to the camp; it is still known by this name.

Soda Springs (Garfield) was named because their chemical content included some sort of soda or sodium. The N—N, or Niobrara Cattle Company, which was owned by Zeke and Henry Newman, managed to get control of the large range and water supply around the area for their stock, and in 1885 they built a cabin near the mouth of Sand Creek; this is thought to be the first dwelling in the Big Dry area (Highland).

Sollid (Chouteau) was named for Sam Sollid, a land locater during the coming of the homesteaders. Anton A. Dyrud, who arrived from Minnesota in the spring of 1909, started a store and a post office the next year. The office was closed in 1917 and mail was sent to Gates.

SOMERS (Flathead) is a sawmill town at the north end of Flathead Lake. It grew when the lumber industry boomed, hitting its peak in 1901. The lumber company there owned 122 houses. A Great Northern spur once ran to **Somers** from Kalispell. The post office opened in 1901 with John Sawyer in charge. The mail was dumped into a large basket and patrons sorted through it. By 1948 the sawmills were closed and boat traffic was gone.

Sonnette (Powder River), near Broadus, is an isolated community at the edge of the Custer National Forest. Citizens who applied for the post office chose the name when the office opened in 1926. Charles Smith was the first postmaster. The office was moved to Richardson's store in 1931 and to Pyrl Melville's ranch in 1962. A young man named Charles Oscar Mason — who had been a trapper and buffalo hunter — pioneered the first permanent settlement in this area about 1880. Before the establishment of the post office, **Sonnette** was known as Selway, and before that much of the area was called Camps Pass. The office closed in 1967 and the town became a rural independent station out of Broadus.

Soo (Daniels), in the northeastern corner of the county, was named for the Soo Line Railroad that entered Montana from North Dakota, paralleling the Canadian border across Sheridan County into Daniels County as far as Whitetail. There was a post office in **Soo** 1918-38; Stephen Kaniewski was the first postmaster.

South Butte (Silver Bow) had a post office 1885-95 with William Shirley as first postmaster.

Southern Cross (Deer Lodge), in the extreme northwest corner of the county, had a post office 1910-42 with James Hawks in charge.

Southvale (Lewis and Clark) had a post office February-July 1879 with Alvira Walrath as postmaster.

Spain was a siding on the Milwaukee branch line to Menard named for a prominent Bozeman family.

Spalding (Madison) was an early settlement. The post office, with Don Spalding in charge, operated 1883-86.

Spanish (Madison), near the Gallatin County line near Salesville, was named for Spanish Peaks and Spanish Creek. Joachim Kundert was postmaster when the office opened in 1901; it closed in 1911.

Spion Kop (Judith Basin), sixteen miles east of Belt on Williams Creek, was a Great Northern station named for a South African site where the British had won a famous and decisive victory in the Boer War. A rocky Montana ridge six miles long which served as a landmark for early travelers reminded some veterans of the militay engagement of a ridge at the South African battle site, and it was suggested that the new settlement be called **Spion Kop**. Cyril Colarchik says that in Afrikaans, the language of the Boers, spion means a view or lookout, while kop is a head or hill.

A relay station was established in **Spion Kop** for the tri-weekly stage and freight wagons. The Matthews family home soon became a hotel, charging 50c per night for lodging and the same for meals. The family opened a saloon; whiskey was a dime a glass, beer was a nickel.

Postal records are a bit confusing, but it seems that **Spion Kop** in its original location had an office 1906-09 or -08 when the post office boxes were moved to Raynesford. But in 1909, after the railroad was completed, a new **Spion Kop** sprang up along the track six miles east of Raynesford; a depot, section house, store, schoolhouse and stockyards were built. The new **Spion Kop** lasted about a decade (*Furrows and Trails in Judith Basin*), but postal records show a post office 1909-33.

Spokane (Jefferson) is listed in postal records as having an office June-December 1882 with Thomas B. Warren as postmaster. Also listed is Spokan, with an office 1867-68 with Stephen Reynolds as postmaster.

Spotted Horse (Fergus) was a post office 1890-92 with William Denner in charge. After 1892 the mail went to Maiden.

Spotted Robe (Glacier) was a station on the Great Northern. Formerly it was Kilroy; the name was changed in 1926 to honor a former chief of the Blackfeet. It was part of the railroad's policy to name or re-name stations with romantic-sounding names to attract tourists and settlers.

Spring (Valley) had a post office 1911-12 with Jonas Erickson as postmaster.

Spring Creek (Lewis and Clark) had a post office February-August 1878 with August Kruger in charge.

Springcreek (Stillwater) had a post office 1914-16 or -17; the mail was then sent to Absarokee. The postmaster was Homer R. Gray. Since most of Montana's rivers are fed by creeks, and many of them originate as mountain springs, the name **Spring Creek (Springcreek)** is common in the state.

Springdale (Park) was a railroad station and a stopping place for people on their way to Hunter's Hot Springs. It was named for the many springs which originate in the region. Near this place in 1806, Indians stole all of Capt. William Clark's horses, forcing him and his party to travel down the Yellowstone in bull boats. The **Springdale** post office was established in 1885 with Alexander Yule as postmaster.

Springhill (Gallatin) is a small farming community twelve miles north of Bozeman. It was settled in the 1860s and at the height of the development in the 1880s boasted a church, a school, two flour mills, a sawmill, a sash and door factory, a distillery, and a blacksmith's shop. The spring which flows from the Bridger Mountains down Mill Canyon supplied the community with water power for its mills and gave it its name (*Montana Historian*). Lewis Howell was postmaster when the office opened in 1876; it closed in 1894.

Spring Lake (Richland) had a post office 1911-18; Albert Retzlaff was the first postmaster. It was near Lambert.

Springtime (Stillwater) was platted in 1917 by the Miller brothers, who chose the name for this group of summer homes. The area was formerly known as Merrill. The **Springtime** post office opened in 1916 with Nelson Miller as postmaster and closed in 1932.

Springville (Jefferson) was one of the first-named towns in Montana Territory and was located at the source of a warm springs three miles northwest of what is now Townsend — or so it is depicted on an 1855 survey map made by Isaac Ingall Stevens as he pioneered a route for the railroad across Montana and the Northwest. Early trailblazers, hunters, trappers, and later, freighters and stage drivers, stopped at **Springville**. The first stage came in 1869. Tough and not easily discouraged, prospectors began drifting in, hoping to find another Eldorado or Montana Bar. They were so greedy in staking out claims for miles around that **Springville** soon became known as "Hog 'Em"; neighboring settlements and camps were known as "Beat 'Em" or "Cheat 'Em." Only a few crumbling foundations, some broken glass and rusty square nails now mark the spot where **Springville** once flourished. The post office was active 1869-79 (Wellington Stewart was first postmaster); thereafter Bedford became the postal station.

Sprole (Roosevelt) was a Great Northern station named for Major Sprole, an Indian agent who at one time was in charge of the Fort Peck Reservation.

Square Butte (Chouteau), in the southern tip of the county, is a landmark visible in central Montana and north to the Missouri River for a radius of seventy-five miles in many directions. It is also a town, located at the foot of a mountain where a big spring supplies everyone with water. The post office was moved here in 1913 when the railroad came through. Before that mail service had been at Lone Tree, five miles to the northwest, and before that at Hawarden. The town sprang up around the Milwaukee station and **Square Butte** reached its population peak (100) during World War I. There was a lumberyard, livery stable, department store, candy and ice cream shops, a drugstore and a bank. The blacksmith shifted to car repairs in 1918 and Trixie's Girlie House burned down in 1922, never to be replaced (Byerly). The post office opened in 1914 and later was replaced by a rural independent station at Fort Benton. The landmark **Square Butte** is unique in that there are some 650 acres on its flat top. Charles Russell frequently used this butte as a background in his pictures.

Staats (Carter) A post office was active here 1914-15 with William Staats as postmaster. It is near Ekalaka and used to be in Fallon County.

Stacey (Powder River) had a post office 1888-1959 except for one year, 1917-18. It is in the northwest corner of the county once a tributary of Pumpkin Creek. **Stacey** was named for L. W. Stacy (the "e" was added by the postal department), who lived at the Cross 5 Ranch. Charles Pring was the first postmaster and the office was originally near Big Pumpkin Bridge on Camp Creek Road. Mail contracts were let every four years and drivers carried the mail from **Stacey** to Selway and Beebe. It took two fresh teams each way. There were usually two or three passengers, 500-1,000 pounds of freight, plus a jug or so of whiskey. Passenger fare was $3, meals en route 50c; drivers' wages in 1915 were $40 a month (*Echoing Footsteps*).

Staff (Petroleum) had a post office established 1915 with Olaf Eike as postmaster. The office closed in 1933.

Stafford (Fergus) was named for a member of the Stafford family. Peter Stafford was postmaster when the office opened in 1911; it closed in 1914 and the mail was sent to Hilger.

Stahlville (Fergus) had a post office 1915-18. Joseph Stahl was the first postmaster; his name was combined with the French word for "town" to create the name.

STANFORD (Judith Basin) is a county seat. In 1880 Calvin and Edward Bower came here with a thousand head of sheep and acquired 100,000 acres. A post office was established in January 1882 (Robert Rabley, postmaster) at the site of what was later known as Old Stanford. The Bowers named the settlement for their old home, Stanfordville, in Duchess County, New York. **Stanford** was a station on the Fort Benton-Billings stage route and a meeting place for cowboys from the Judith Basin Pool and other cattle companies whose stock grazed the rich Judith Basin before homesteaders and sheepmen arrived. One time in Old Stanford a young cowboy named "Kid" Amby Cheney provided a Sunday afternoon's entertainment by riding a horse that the assembled cowhands insisted couldn't be ridden. But "Kid" Amby stuck with the cayuse, and after the ride, someone passed the hat and handed him a $65 collection.

For years stories of white wolves of prodigious strength and cunning grew and multiplied among folk living in the Judith. One particularly huge wolf known as Old Snowdrift became a legendary outlaw. A white wolf is mounted in the county courthouse in **Stanford**.

Another little community called Dubuque had grown up near Old Stanford and had a post office established in 1890. When the Great Northern brought its line through, they established a station at Dubuque, so it became a "town." The general merchandise store and other buildings were moved to Dubuque from Old Stanford and after 1892 this consolidated community was known as **Stanford**. Allen Stough was appointed postmaster.

Stark was in Missoula County when the post office opened in 1890 with Mary Menges in charge. The location is now on the border of Mineral County. The office closed in 1959.

Stearns (Lewis and Clark), near Wolf Creek, had a post office 1891-1921.

Steele (Chouteau) seems to be a forerunner of the Lonetree post office and stage stop. An office was established here in 1888 with John M. Steele as postmaster. In 1914 either the name was changed to Lonetree or the mail service was moved to the stage stop.

Stellar (Rosebud) was to have had a post office in 1931 with Joseph M. Huhl as postmaster, but records show that his appointment was rescinded in 1932.

Stemple (Lewis and Clark) was named for Stemple Pass over the Continental Divide and is between Canyon Creek and Lincoln. A post office opened in 1884 and was active on-and-off until 1923. Henry Jacob was first postmaster.

Sterling (Madison) was once a thriving mining town — more than five hundred people lived there in the 1860s. There were four quartz mills made of square stones cemented together with a mixture of lime and horsehair; the remains of one are still standing. The town was three miles west of Norris on Hot Spring Creek. The post office opened in 1867 with Andrew Hall as postmaster.

"The culmination of every miner's dream was to locate a mine comparable to the Monitor on Richmond Flats. Someone had grubstaked two miners to drive a tunnel and they had worked all winter unknowingly along the side of this rich vein. Then one day, while they were outside in the sunshine eating their lunch, a cave-in occurred, exposing this vein. . . . It was four feet in width with six inches of wire gold in the center. The ore assayed at $6,000 a ton after all specimens were picked out and at the old price of $19 an ounce. A sample of the ore sent to the World's Fair in San Francisco in 1895 received first prize. It took four years to mine this body of ore. My dad hauled seven tons of ore a trip to Norris and a ton-and-a-half of coal back to the mine. Old Rock and Him were the lead horses of his six-horse team. Many a cold and windy day, Dad would tie the reins to the dash board and get down out of the wind. The horses knew just where to go" (Cecil M. Reel, *Trails and Trials*). By 1872 most of the ore had been mined and people had left Sterling. W. R. Reel, a Montana miner, bought the land and claims including the townsite where he built his ranch home. The land is now in hay and pasture. The post office closed in 1883.

Sterrenberg (Pondera), named for postmaster John Sterrenberg, had a post office 1919-23. After that the area was called Ledger (see **Ledger**).

STEVENSVILLE (Ravalli) was in Missoula County when the post office was established in 1868. John Waislett was postmaster. **Stevensville** was named for Isaac Ingle Stevens. Luther E. Stanley says, "When Isaac Ingle Stevens was ordered to Fort Owen in 1853, he came to what he supposed would be a military fort but much to his surprise, it was a trading post. General Stevens, for the past year, had been in charge of military operations and Indian affairs in the Northwest Territory. . . he moved his government and military material to Fort Owen. This fort became the territorial capital in 1853 and served as that until 1858, when Stevens was called back to active duty with the Union Army. He was killed in action in 1862 at Chantilly. . . . Stevens laid out the new town near the ruins of St. Mary's Mission and Fort Owen. . . . It was named **Stevensville** in his honor and authorized by President Lincoln on May 12, 1864. Two weeks later, Lincoln signed the Act that made portions of Dakota, Idaho, and Wyoming into the new Territory of Montana. . . . In 1893 Ravalli County was established when the southern part of Missoula County was cut off and the new county was made. . . . **Stevensville** was the first county seat. After Marcus Daly had founded Hamilton in 1893, much of his time and money was spent in getting the county seat moved to his town. He succeeded in 1895.

Steve's Fork (Garfield) had a post office 1917-18 with Lula B. Sory as postmaster. A Baptist church was built there, and there was once a school, a blacksmith shop, and a couple of stores.

Stewart was a station on the Northern Pacific near Opportunity. Freight was unloaded here and hauled to the Anaconda smelter. Railroad company rules restricted building and forbade saloons. Some ten-acre farms were settled around here, but very few are left.

Stickley (Stillwater) was located on what later became the John Leuthold ranch. It was established as a post office in 1909 with Arthur Kraft as postmaster. Jeffe Keefer carried the mail without pay for a long time in order to get the office approved. In 1918 the office was moved to its present location and the name was changed to Molt.

Stickney (Cascade), originally in Meagher County, was named for first postmaster Benjamin F. Stickney. The office was established in May 1884; in 1888 it was moved across the river to Craig.

Stillwater (Stillwater) was in Gallatin County when the post office opened in 1877, but the area was later a part of Yellowstone and then Stillwater County. Horace Countryman, who operated a stage station and line, was the first postmaster. The name was changed in 1893 to Columbus because the railroad had another station in Minnesota named Stillwater and it caused some confusion. Later the name was used for another community in the same county.

Stillwater (Stillwater) operated a post office 1914-16 with Joseph Rainville as postmaster. It was near Stickley.

Stillwater County is an elbow-shaped county tucked in between Sweet Grass County to the west and Yellowstone and Carbon counties on the east. The county seat is Columbus. **Stillwater County** was organized in 1913 from parts of Carbon, Sweet Grass, and Yellowstone counties, and was named for the Stillwater River, which flows across its southern border from Wyoming headwaters to join the Yellowstone at Columbus.

Annin retells an Indian legend that explains why ". . . A stream that rushes along mile after mile . . . dashing over giant boulders, or whirling in arching riffles under some overhanging bushes, with never a cessation in its mad sprint for the Yellowstone . . . should have been christened, 'Stillwater.' " Many centuries ago, long before continental civilization, a tribe of Indians made their home in the beautiful Yellowstone Valley . . . theirs was a peaceful existence. Weeluna was an Indian maiden, so delicate of feature, so beautiful, that every Indian brave wanted her for his bride. Weeluna (Little Moon) had a heart full of love, friendliness, and happiness; her presence shed soft rays of contentment and peace whenever she entered a tepee. Young braves fought for her hand, dissensions arose. Finally she chose Nemidji. The others were jealous; more trouble arose. The tribe was desperate, no longer was there peace. Storms came, and food was short. Weeluna herself offered to lead a group of Indian girls in search of food, for the young men had all left the camp. She found elk and moose, but the exertion was too much for her, and she died. Her body, which had been placed high in a tree, was washed down by a violent storm and carried through the raging waters of the river. Nemidji jumped into the swirling waters to rescue the body of his betrothed and he, too, was swept away, with her body clasped in his arms. As the flood receded, there remained a bayou where the speed of the water was absorbed and distributed into riffles to flow through that portion of the stream. The tribe called it the "Hallowed Place" or, **Stillwater.**

Stipek (Dawson) was a station on the Northern Pacific along the Yellowstone River. Rose Stipek was named postmaster when the office opened in 1910; it closed in 1942.

Stockade (Stillwater) was in Sweet Grass County when the post office opened in 1916 (Fred Larimore, postmaster), but in Stillwater when it closed in 1923. Since it was near Absarokee, this very likely was a stockade built for protection from, or trade with, the Crows.

STOCKETT (Cascade), about fifteen miles south of Great Falls, had a post office in 1898 with Frank W. Bishop in charge. This coal mining town was named for Lewis Stockett, manager of the Cottonwood Coal Company. When the major mining operations were moved from Sand Coulee to Cottonwood Coulee, the name of the company was changed from the Sand Coulee Coal Company to the Cottonwood Coal Company. Mines later opened at Giffin and Lehigh. The company not only owned the mines, but also ran a company store and meat market where the miners were required to do most of their trading; they were issued coupons for the company store on pay day. There was also a miners' boarding house for bachelors. Elizabeth McGiffin Cheney, who was the first white girl born in this area, said that when she was a child there were only about a hundred English-speaking people out of more than a thousand miners, who were mostly of Italian, Polish, or other Slavic descent. The three Homan brothers and their large families made up much of the English-speaking population.

Stone Shack (Custer) was about twenty miles northwest of Miles City. A post office by this name opened in 1903 with Charles Snyder as postmaster. It closed in 1917, but opened again 1926-29; after that the mail was ordered to Meredith. Highland says that Mr. and Mrs. William McRae operated a roadhouse there; it was the first ranch on the road north of Miles City. A light rig could make it there in half a day, but it took a freight outfit all day. Mrs. McRae ran the post office 1904-07. The stone shack from which the place takes its name was built in the '70s or '80s by buffalo hunters; the McRaes used the old building for an ice house. An Englishman named "Old Man" Butcher also ran the Stone Shack Roadhouse, probably before the McRaes.

Stone's Precinct (Beaverhead) had a post office in 1868 with John Stone as postmaster. Voting precincts were set up at a centrally located ranch and the post office was often located there, too. The office closed in 1869.

Stone Station, Stone (Granite) had a post office under the name **Stone Station** in 1879 with Benjamin Horton in charge. The name was shortened to **Stone** in 1899, and the office was discontinued in 1906. A stage stop or station was built here in the 1860s. The railroad came through in 1887 and hay from this valley was shipped to distant points.

Stoneville (Custer) This post office opened in 1880 and was named for first postmaster Lewis Stone. The name was changed to Alzada in 1885 after Alzada Sheldon, wife of a pioneer rancher, because there was another town in Montana with a similar name which caused some confusion. Lou Stone owned the saloon here while General Miles was building telegraph lines from Fort Keogh to Fort Meade, South Dakota; the **Stoneville** telegraph station was a rock-covered dugout at the top of a hill.

Stony Butte (McCone), originally in Dawson County, had a post office 1904-08. Samuel McClatchie was the first postmaster. It was near Brockway.

Storrs (Gallatin) was near Chestnut and had a post office 1904-08. Will Evans was the first postmaster at this station on the Yellowstone Park Railroad.

Story (Gallatin), a siding between Bozeman and Belgrade on the Northern Pacific, was named for Nelson Story, who drove the first herd of Texas cattle into Montana in the spring of 1866. Story purchased six hundred head at Dallas and started north, bringing them into the Gallatin Valley and camping where Fort Ellis was later located. A new high school in Bozeman now stands where the Story Mansion used to be.

Stowman (Blaine) was near Chinook. It had a post office 1914-17. Ross Stowman was the first postmaster.

Strabane (Teton) had a post office 1909-19 except for the year between January 1917-18. James Peebles was the first postmaster. It is near Choteau.

Straders (Rosebud) was named for John Strader, postmaster when the office opened in 1881. The office was moved to Birney later that year.

Strater (Valley) was to have a post office in 1910 but it was never in operation because the appointed postmaster, Horace C. Cowan, declined the job.

Strauss (Pondera) had a post office June 1915-July 1916 when the mail was ordered to Brady. Walter H. Strauss was postmaster.

Straw (Fergus) is between Moore and Judith Gap almost on the Judith Basin County line. It was named for William O. Straw, who owned six thousand acres including the townsite. Straw, originally from Maine, came West with the railroad to make a preliminary survey — escorted and protected by the military — through the Judith Basin country. He liked the country so much he later returned and became a rancher and stockman. The post office opened in 1904 with Benjamin Gordon as postmaster; it was discontinued in 1954. A photograph taken about 1908 of the Gaugler store at **Straw** shows bedsteads, Monarch kitchen ranges, round heating stoves, boxes of fruit, and a wooden game table with net pockets in the corners. Customers' teams were tied to the hitching rack on the side (*In the Shadow of the Twin Sisters*).

Strawberry (Madison), near Pony, was the site of Montana's first quartz mill and by 1875 a camp of four hundred people, but it was short-lived.

Stringtown (Carbon) circa 1898 was a settlement of mines not far from Bearcreek. Before Bridger was located the settlement at that site was known as **Stringtown**, though some people claim the name was Georgetown, after George Town, who promoted the Bridger coal mines.

Stringtown (Madison) developed in the 1870s, when John Roberts built a flour mill about two miles east of Harrison. He also built — across South Willow Creek — a store and a two-story frame house and later, log barns for the horses used on the stage that stopped here en route to Virginia City. A one-room log schoolhouse and a few more houses were also constructed. Ranchers from Ennis, Cardwell, Pony and Willow Creek brought their wheat to this mill and went home with flour.

Stroud (Sheridan), near Middle Creek, had a post office from 1895 until about 1905 with J. E. Hanley, postmaster (*Courage Enough*). No record of this office is found in postal lists, so it may have been registered under a different name. The community was named for Robert and Joe Stroud, who came in 1888 with a herd of Texas cattle for the Reynolds Brothers Ranch; this ranch was the site of the first post office.

STRYKER (Lincoln) was named for a family: Frank Stryker was the first postmaster and Dave kept a stage station on the old Fort Steel Trail. **Stryker** is between Whitefish and Eureka; it was once a station on the Great Northern.

Stuart (Deer Lodge) had a post office intermittently (1882-1914) when mail was sent to Anaconda. Said "Brother Riggin," a Methodist preacher: "I would make my trips to Missoula and the Bitter Root on horseback, riding hundreds of miles, and organized the churches at **Stuart**, Anaconda, Philipsburg, New Chicago and Drummond in the Deer Lodge Valley" (Adams).

Sturgill (Chouteau) was granted a post office in April 1915 with Emma Larsen as postmaster. The name was changed to Discovery Butte the next month.

Sturgis (Beaverhead) was named for William Sturgis, the man appointed postmaster when the office opened in January 1868; in December James M. Ryan was appointed to the position and the name was changed to Ryan. William Sturgis arrived with the first Fisk Expedition, in 1862, and built Montana's first commercial sawmill, near Bannack. Later, James Ryan and he were granted a charter by the territorial legislature to build a tollroad through Beaverhead Canyon; the "Great Beaverhead Wagon Road" opened for business in 1866.

Suffolk (Fergus) was named for the owner of the Suffolk Ranch. Clara Nelson was postmaster when the office opened in 1914.

SULA (Ravalli) was named for Ursula "Sula" Thompson, the first white child born in this area. The post office opened in 1889 with William Whetstone postmaster. Despite the official name **Sula**, the area is often referred to as Ross Hole. The "hole," or basin, was named for Alexander Ross of the Hudson's Bay Company (see **Ross Hole**). The huge Charlie Russell painting which hangs behind the speaker's desk in the House of Representatives chamber in Helena depicts Lewis and Clark's meeting with the Flatheads at Ross Hole in September 1805. Near **Sula** is a sacred "medicine tree," with a ram's horn embedded in its side; explanations of how it got there are the source of many Indian legends.

Sullivan (Dawson) operated 1914-26, when the mail was sent to Richey. Dora Olson was the first postmaster.

Sumatra (Rosebud) was a station on the Milwaukee and the highest point between Miles City and Harlowton. When trains were still run by coal engines it was necessary to put on a "pusher engine" to make it up the hill to **Sumatra**. The station was first called Summit, and just how the name evolved into **Sumatra** is unclear. In the days before the railroad, **Sumatra** was on the the old trail that connected Fort Musselshell with Fort Custer in Big Horn County. The post office opened in 1910 with Jesse Haynes as the first postmaster. Some years ago a fire destroyed the schoolhouse and many residences. The town was never rebuilt, and now only a white church and a few tumbledown buildings along the tracks mark the place where this once-active community stood. Farmers were hard hit by the Depression. One in **Sumatra** wrote the governor in 1931: "Is there any place in the state where we could get work? . . . We have only one baking of flour left and one pound of coffee. We have no credit and no work. Our 400 acres of crop is utterly destroyed. We had no crop last year and only a very poor yield in 1929. In 1928 hail destroyed our crop and no insurance. . . . We have lived here for 20 years and paid $3500 in taxes. . . . What can you or anyone do about it?" (*Not From Precious Metals Alone*).

Summit (Chouteau) had a post office 1891-93 with Robert Turner as postmaster. Presumably this place and others with the name were so called because of their location.

Summit (Glacier) This post office was open 1903-05 with John McVay as postmaster.

Summit (Madison) was the last settlement up the Gulch. It's only a ghost town now, but between 1864-80, $500,000 worth of gold was taken from the mines of the Summit Mining District. The company was organized in 1863 and all provisions were packed in from Virginia City. By 1901 an estimated $1 million worth of gold had been shipped out. The Ora Cache Mine was the richest in the area. The 1901 boom reactivated the mines and the Kearsage properties were reworked. Buildings sprung up — and gradually fell down. By 1956, not one was left. The post office was established in 1867 with Nathaniel Sibley in charge. It was discontinued in 1881 (Wolle).

Summit (Meagher) was near Ringling and had a post office 1915-18. Nora Sill was postmaster.

Sunbeam (Missoula) had a post office 1887-88 with Ada Ferguson in charge.

SUNBURST (Toole) is twenty-seven miles north of Shelby near Canada. The name was suggested by William George Davis, who noted that the sun, as it rose, burst over the Sweet Grass Hills and shone down in the valley where the little town was begun. A post office was established at **Sunburst** in 1912 with John Mars as first postmaster. It became a boom town in 1922 when oil was discovered in the rich Kevin-Sunburst oilfields.

Sundance (Glacier) was a Great Northern station originally named Seville. The name was changed in 1926 to commemorate the Sun Dance ceremony of the Indians; the new name was obviously in line with the railroad's policy of assigning more romantic names to stations in order to attract settlers and tourists.

Sunnyside (Cascade) was named because it was beside the Sun River. A post office was established in 1893, and the name was changed to Vaughn in 1911.

Sunnyside (Park) had a post office established in 1885. The original name came from "Madame Bulldog," who put up a roadhouse — a sort of combination stage stop and travelers' resting place — on the present site of the O. L. Lee Ranch (Dorothy Pattyn). The name was changed to Clyde Park in 1887.

Sun Prairie (Phillips) had a post office 1913-36. Edward Cloe was the first postmaster.

SUN RIVER (Cascade) was in Lewis and Clark County, Montana Territory, when the post office was established in 1868 with John Sargent as postmaster. It is eighteen miles west of Great Falls and one of the oldest settlements still active in the state. The crossing here was used by travelers going from Fort Benton to the gold fields in western Montana. Before the railroads came this was a lively place where miners, trappers, and bull-whackers met. A great stampede for what proved to be false gold discoveries occurred in the winter of 1866; scores of prospectors were caught in a freezing blizzard which resulted in loss of fingers, limbs, ears and toes. It was this tragedy that led to the establishment of the first public hospital in Montana, because the dire need for one was realized when the men were brought to Helena for treatment. An improvised hospital which was set up in a cabin later became the county hospital. The post office at **Sun River** opened in 1868. An Indian name for the river, *Natae-oueti*, was translated by French trappers to mean "medicine" or "sun."

SUPERIOR (Mineral) is a county seat about ten miles from the Idaho border as the crow flies, and forty-eight miles by mountain road. Someone gave the name to a settlement at the mouth of Cedar Creek in 1869, after his hometown of Superior, Wisconsin; and when that little village disbanded, the post office, located a mile to the east, took the name. Frank Burke wrote from Crow's Nest, Montana, in 1881, "The country . . . is very thinly settled . . . the place that bears the pretentious name of Superior City, and which is the post office for the country within a radius of fifty miles, consists of a log house and a barn. You can never judge anything in these Western places by their names, for the people seem to have a peculiar habit of giving high-sounding names to the most insignificant places" (*Montana Magazine*; Winter, 1969). The **Superior** post office was established in January 1871 with Silas R. Smith as postmaster. The Northern Pacific station at this location was first called Iron Mountain, and a mill was built there to refine the ore taken from the nearby mountain by that name. The Clark Fork River bisects the town.

Susan (Prairie) was a Milwaukee station named for Mrs. Susan Haughian, who owned much of the land around here. According to Leafie Ulrich of Fallon, the name was changed from Saugus.

Sutherland (Prairie) is along the Powder River just below the mouth of Coal Creek. The post office opened in 1909 with Clara Sutherland in charge and was named for her family. It was discontinued in 1936.

Swan (Flathead) A post office opened here in 1904 with Bettie Waters as postmaster. Her successor was Emmett Swan, and the place seems to be named for him. Postal entries say the name was changed to Marion in 1906, but later on it was back to **Swan** again.

Swan Lake (Lake) had a post office 1915-60 (first postmaster was Albert Millett) when it became a rural station out of Big Fork. It may be named for the swans that often visit here, or for Emmett Swan, an early resident.

Sweeney (Rosebud) had a brief post office 1911-12 with Julia Barrett in charge. The office took its name from Sweeney Creek, which runs into the nearby Yellowstone River. Very often creeks took their names from an early settler along its banks — and in Montana, quite a few of them are Irish!

Sweetgrass (Park) had a post office 1878-92 with William Bramble postmaster for this entire period. Either the name was then changed to Howie, or the Howie office was moved here.

SWEETGRASS (Toole) is a port of entry very near the Canadian border. In 1890 a narrow-gauge railroad called the Turkey Track was built across the border between Great Falls and Lethbridge, and in 1900 **Sweetgrass** became a booming trade center as the dry land farmers arrived. The name comes from the abundance of "sweet" grass which grows around here. The town gave its name to the Sweetgrass Arch, a series of oil fields that extends south to Sunburst. The post office was established in 1902 with Samuel Griffith in charge.

Sweetgrass, Sweet Grass County is in south central Montana. Big Timber is the county seat. It was named at the suggestion of Mrs. Paul Van Cleve, Sr., for the abundant "sweet" grass seen on the vast prairies around Melville, where she lived. Sweet Grass Creek also runs through the northern part of the county. Organized in 1895, **Sweet Grass County** was formed from parts of Park, Meagher, and Yellowstone counties; a part of **Sweet Grass County** was taken in 1913 to form part of Stillwater County; a part was taken to form Wheatland in 1917; and in 1920 another part went to form Golden Valley County.

Sweetland (Deer Lodge) existed as a post office 1876-77 and was doubtlessly named for postmaster Nathan Sweetland.

Swiftcurrent (Glacier) operated a post office 1906-08 with Charles Matson as postmaster. It was near Electric.

Swingley (Park) had a post office 1921-37. Margaret Swingley was the first postmaster.

Sykes (Carter) had a post office 1909-23. The mail was then ordered to Belltower. Anna Pannill was the first postmaster.

Sylvanite (Lincoln) was an old mining town named for the gold-bearing mineral. As an ore, sylvanite appears silver-white with a metallic lustre. The town was once larger than Troy, which is twenty miles south. When ore was discovered about 1895 by two trappers, a stampede immediately followed. A mine opened on Fourth of July Creek and **Sylvanite** sprung up along the Yaak River. The town once boasted a hotel, a saloon, grocery store, and feed stable. During the first winter, all supplies were brought in by pack train; the going freight rate was 5¢ a pound. By 1897 the town had a newspaper. Travelers, woodsmen and miners could take a bath on Wednesday, Saturday, or Sunday night if they made arrangements ahead of time at the barber shop. In August 1910 a devastating forest fire swept through the town and burned **Sylvanite** off the map. The mining companies rebuilt some of the mills but the town never revived. A ranger station and a schoolhouse were later built on the old townsite. The **Sylvanite** post office operated 1896-1903 (Charles Bartlett, postmaster); it re-opened in 1910 and was active until 1913.

T

Tabiola (Deer Lodge) In 1896 the Post Office Department granted — but later rescinded — a petition to change the name of Blackfoot City to **Tabiola**. The new name that was eventually chosen was Ophir.

Tacy (Stillwater), near Rapleje, had a post office 1915-29; Dexter Harper was the first postmaster.

Taft (Mineral) was eighty miles west of Missoula and according to the Chicago *Tribune* (1909), ". . . the wickedest city in America . . . plague spot of vice." Before it became so wicked, it began as a "railroad construction camp on the Idaho-Montana border when the Chicago, Milwaukee and St. Paul was building its transcontinental line from Chicago to the Pacific Coast" (Virginial Weisel Johnson, *Montana, the Magazine of Western History*; Autumn, 1982). The little settlement served Chicago, Milwaukee and St. Paul Railroad workers as a headquarters, supply point, and operations center during construction of the 8,750-foot-long tunnel through rugged, mountainous country. The population of **Taft** swelled from 30 to possibly 2,000 with the arrival of construction workers. There were said to be from 200 to 500 prostitutes and only one "decent" woman in town. There were 27 saloons, one grocery and one drug store — a real rough-and-tough boom town. But workers began leaving in 1909, when the tunnel was completed, and by 1962, according to Johnson, "all that remained of **Taft** was the Taft Bar and Hotel with the original mahogany bar backed by mirrors, but now even that is gone as the highway buried Main Street and only a sign reading '**Taft** Area' marks the spot of one of Montana's last railroad construction boom towns."

Taft had a post office off-and-on 1907-1917; the mail was then ordered to Saltese. David Stewart was the first postmaster. The town was named after U.S. President William Howard Taft.

Tampico (Valley) is ten miles north of Glasgow on the Milk River. It began as a siding on the Great Northern and was granted a post office in 1908 with George Lohr in charge. The office was closed in 1973.

Tande (Daniels), near Scobey, had a post office 1915-22. It was named for Andrew Tande, the first postmaster.

Tango (Valley), near Opheim, had a post office 1914-18. Floyd Hevener was first postmaster.

Tarkio (Mineral), between Alberton and Superior, was a station on the Milwaukee. The post office operated 1913-59; Anderson Metz was the first postmaster.

Tattnal (Phillips) was a Great Northern station on Whitewater Creek.

Tawopa (Dawson), near Buford in Montana Territory, had a post office granted just before the territory became a state. The office was open October 1889-91 and Thomas Cushing was postmaster.

Taylor (Hill), originally in old Chouteau County, was named for first postmaster Mattie Taylor. The office was open 1904-07 and 1909-10; the mail was then sent to Alma.

Taylor (Lincoln), near Libby, was named for Mary Taylor, postmaster while the office was operating 1912-13.

Taylor Creek (Garfield) was east of Jordan. Cora Jacobson, postmaster, had the post office in her home for most of the years that it operated, 1922-34 (Highland).

Teedee (Carter), in the extreme northwest corner of the county, had a post office 1899-1942, when the mail was ordered to Ekalaka. Addiel Olsen was the original postmaster.

Teepee Rocks (Carbon) are also called Haystack Rocks and Hottentot Village. This group of rocks near Joliet has interesting and often fantastic sandstone formation due to erosion. The area, through which an old stage road used to run, is known as the Montana Monument Valley (Maryott).

TEIGEN (Petroleum) sprang into life when the Milwaukee Road put a station here in 1914. The town is named for Mons Teigen, a major landowner and sheep rancher. In 1883 Teigen and his partners, Knute and Ole Opheim, bought a band of 3,200 sheep in Gallatin County and wintered them near Anceney. The following spring they trailed them down the Musselshell Valley, looking for a place to locate, finally settling amid the broad valley and rolling hills near the present location of the **Teigen** post office and store. Each took a pre-emption claim on 160 acres and the sheep were turned loose to graze on the open ranges (Bard and Ann Teigen in the Winnett *Times*). Ole drowned in a creek seven years later and Teigen bought his and Knute's interest in the enterprise. Fort Maginnis was the trading post in those early days before the railroad. The post office, with Thomas Peterson in charge, was established in 1914. Now, almost a century after the first Mons Teigen settled in this valley, his grandson, also named Mons Teigen, is a rancher there.

Telegraph Creek (Phillips) This name indicates the importance of telegraph lines in early-day Montana Territory. Before railroads and telephones connected the territory with the states, and the territories to the west and south, telegraph lines crossed the area and linked the East and West coasts. The Army built the lines, and the Signal Corps sent men to operate the stations and maintain the lines. Charles T. Burke has letters written by his uncle, Frank Burke, whose job it was — not to hunt buffalo, build roads, mine gold or fight Indians — but to get messages through. From Crow's Nest, Montana Territory, Burke wrote in 1881: "I am stationed . . . Mullan Road . . . very near the boundary line between Montana and Idaho. . . . My duties are entirely connected with the military telegraph line which runs through (here), and as this part of the line is the chief connecting link between the eastern and western posts, it is a position of considerable importance" (*Montana Magazine*; Winter, 1969). And indeed it was; it took weeks for a letter to cross the continent, but communication by telegraph was almost instantaneous. And Burke was justifiably proud that he had a part in getting the news of the shooting of President Garfield across Montana Territory and into the papers of Portland and Walla Walla the same day it occurred.

By 1883 the railroads had pushed their tracks across the territory, and when the golden spike was driven on September 8, the East and West coasts were connected by rail. The same year, the telegraph offices at Billings, Bozeman, Deer Lodge, Ellis, Froze-to-Death, Keogh, Livingston, Missoula, New Chicago, Radersburg, and Superior City were officially closed.

Annie Barnard was the first postmaster at **Telegraph**.

Telstad (Toole) had a post office 1910-35. It was named for Ralph Telstad, the first postmaster.

Terminus (Beaverhead) was the original name of what is now Dillon. In 1880, the Utah and Northern Railroad had reached this point, but a farmer who owned the land needed for the right-of-way refused to sell, and for a time, construction of the line was terminated — railroad officials called the place **Terminus**. Many workers decided to settle here, so they applied for a post office, set up some stores, and began developing a town. The post office was established March 1880 and a year later the name was changed to Dillon.

Terminus (Custer) had a post office May-June 1882 with T. C. Kurtz the postmaster. The mail was then sent to Rosebud.

Terrace (McCone) had a post office 1914-19 with Paul Puffer as first postmaster. It was near Vida.

TERRY (Prairie), a county seat, is on the Yellowstone River half way between Miles City and Glendive. The post office was established in 1882; Benjamin Bowen was the postmaster. The town is named for Gen. Alfred H. Terry, who commanded an 1876 expedition in connection with Custer's campaign against the Indians. The sheep industry has flourished around **Terry**; in 1897 the Northern Pacific built its own wool house here. Before that the wool storage shed was also the schoolhouse and it was possible to hold class only when the place wasn't full of wool (Bob Murray).

In 1908 the **Terry** Chamber of Commerce extolled the virtues of the community in a brochure: "**Terry** is in the heart of the fertile Yellowstone Valley . . . hundreds of thousands of acres . . . open to homestead and desert land entry . . . on these lands immense crops of grain, hay and vegetables can be raised without irrigation. . . . It has a large wool house. In 1906-07, 1,000,000 pounds of wool were shipped for which nearly $275,000 were paid out. . . . It is one of the finest horse, cattle and sheep range sections of the West. . . . Within two miles of town it has a coal mine with one of the finest veins of lignite coal in the state. Coal runs from $3 to $4.50 a ton and the supply is inexhaustable" (*Wheels Across Montana Prairies*).

Terry's Landing was on the Yellowstone River. Granville Stuart, in his journal for May 9, 1880, writes, "Went about two miles up the Yellowstone River (from the fork of the Yellowstone and Big Horn rivers) to **Terry's Landing**. There is a telegraph and a post office here. Eelevation 2930 . . . got $250 from a gambler, B. F. Williams . . . with a check on the First National Bank in Helena . . . only man in town with any money. Buffalo by the thousands in every direction." The nearest telegraph station would have been Froze-to-Death, the nearest town possibly Big Horn or Junction City.

Teton (Chouteau) had a post office July 1884-October 1885 with J. D. Weatherwax in charge. The office was reestablished in 1896 with Arthur Engel as postmaster; it closed in 1917 and the mail went to Loma. The town took its name from the Teton River, on which it was located.

Teton Bench (Chouteau) was probably located on a bench above the Teton River near Carter. The post office operated only for 1911-12, and thereafter the mail was sent to Carter. Max Jahnke was postmaster.

Teton County lies just east of the Continental Divide and north of the state's center line. Choteau is the county seat. It was named for Teton River and Teton Peak. Popular opinion has it that the widespread use of the word "Teton" for place-names came originally from French trappers who gave the word to a mountain; in French *teton* means "breast." However, there was an Indian tribe belonging to the Sioux Nation called Tetons which lived along the Missouri River. A report by Maj. J. W. Powell to the Smithsonian Institute says that "Titon" or "Teton" is from the Indian word *titan*, "at or on land without trees," and came to refer to any of the Indians who lived on the prairie, rather than any specific tribe. This explanation for the origin of the name should at least be considered.

The county was organized in 1893 from a part of Chouteau County; in 1914 parts of **Teton County** were taken to form Toole County, and parts were taken to form Glacier and Pondera counties in 1919; a part of Chouteau County was annexed to **Teton County** in 1921.

Thale (Meagher) had a post office 1951-56, Eugene Parenteau was postmaster.

Thoeny (Valley) was named for first postmaster Jacob Thoeny. The office was in operation 1915-53.

Thomas (Missoula), near DeSmet, had a post office 1903-06 with Rufus Leahy as first postmaster. **Thomas** was in Meagher County while the post office was open June-December 1878 with Albert Brackett in charge.

Thomas (Prairie) had a post office 1909-11; the mail was then sent to Fallon. **Thomas** was named for postmaster Ernest Thomas.

THOMPSON FALLS (Sanders) is a county seat named for David Thompson, a Northwest Fur Company employee who traded in this area in 1809, and for the natural falls in the Clark Fork River here. The post office was first called Thompson, and continued under that name October 1882-May 1883. The mail was then ordered to Horse Plains. The Thompson office was reestablished in 1885, and in 1912 the name was changed to **Thompson Falls** to conform with the railway station. The Northern Pacific Railroad came through in 1883, and Thompson and Belknap were bitter rivals as train stops. At one time the NP refused to stop the train at Thompson, so the local citizens put huge logs on the tracks; while the crew was removing the obstructions, people from Thompson boarded the trains and tried to persuade immigrants to settle there instead of going on to Belknap. In 1883, 10,000 people on their way to the Idaho gold fields wintered at Thompson; twenty saloons opened to accommodate them, and all operated at a profit.

Thompson River, Thompson River Spur (Sanders) was a station on the Northern Pacific a few miles east of Thompson Falls. It was named for nearby Thompson River (Creek). **Thompson River** had a post office April 1870-July 1871 while it was still a part of Missoula County. Henry Hall was postmaster.

Three Buttes (Richland) had a post office 1904-32 with James MacKenzie as postmaster. The name, like many in Montana, describes the landscape.

THREE FORKS (Gallatin) is located near the forks formed by the Madison, Gallatin, and Jefferson rivers as they join to become the Missouri. Meriwether Lewis came upon this river junction on July 27, 1805. "This is a very handsome place, fine bottoms of timber etc.," wrote Whitehouse, a member of the Lewis and Clark party, in his journal; and Sacajawea recognized the place as the one at which four or five years earlier the Gros Ventres had attacked her people. As they looked at the three rivers flowing together, Lewis and Clark were unable to decide which of these "three noble streams" was the real Missouri. They named the first fork for Albert Gallatin, Secretary of the Treasury; the second for James Madison, Secretary of State; and the third for Thomas Jefferson, President of the United States (Salisbury). A few years after Lewis and Clark recorded their experiences here, Pierre Menard wrote his brother-in-law, Pierre Chouteau, Esq., that their trappers had been set upon by the Blackfeet — traps and horses were stolen and two men were killed: ". . . Unless we can have peace with these (Indians) or unless they can be destroyed, it is idle to think of maintaining an establishment at this point" (*Not in Precious Metals Alone*).

An "English Nobility Colony" was located near the present town of **Three Forks**. In 1884, a group of Englishmen, John A. Chater and Co., bought a large block of land and built several log cabins.

The post office at **Three Forks** was established in 1882 as the town developed. Asher Paul was the postmaster.

Three Mile (Ravalli) seems never to have had a post office, but it has survived for more than a century. It was begun in 1858 by Thomas Harris, who married an Indian woman and then "squatted" on the land. Harris built the first house in the area to be put together with nails instead of wooden pegs; he also dug a well, inducing the water into his house, by piping it into a big wooden tub and "Thus having the first house in the Pacific Northwest with running water." In 1859 he pioneered the raising of small, cultivated fruits; in 1871 the Three Mile School — one of the first in the territory — was begun after he built a schoolhouse in his backyard by the creek. Both community and creek got their name "because the creek entered the Bitterroot River three miles below the first St. Mary's Mission, located where Fort Owen Inn is now" (Bev Grier, Stevensville High School). Three Mile School was later known as Lone Rock School because of an unusually large glacial rock nearby. The community was developed by Eastern speculators who bought the land for $7 to $12 an acre, advertised it in the East, and sold it for "outrageous prices.",This same group of speculators formed the Bitterroot Valley Irrigation Company; apple orchards were planted and the area became known as the home of McIntosh Reds. In 1909 a large inn was built, but it burned down and a dancehall was put up in its place. Once there was a Lutheran church and a golf course (Mary Murray).

Thurlow (Rosebud) had a post office from 1915-1942; Walter Hawley was postmaster.

Thurza (Yellowstone) had a post office operating 1890-92 with John Coombs as postmaster.

Tiber (Liberty), near Chester, had a post office 1917-27. Hiram Caster was postmaster.

Tiger Butte (Cascade) had a post office 1908-12 with Fred Gustafson as first postmaster. The mail was thereafter sent to Great Falls. The office was named after a nearby mountain. There is also a Tiger Butte Mountain in Valley County, formerly called Panther Mountain.

Timberline (Gallatin) had a post office 1885-98. It was near Chesnut and the first postmaster was James Heron.

Timber Ridge (Blaine), near Hays, had a post office 1925-35. Joseph Watson was the first postmaster.

Tindall (Garfield), on the south fork of Lodge Pole Creek, was named for first postmaster Raymond Tindall. The office was established in 1914 in the Tindall home, where Olive Tindall served as postmaster for twenty-one years. She not only handled the mail, but also milked the cows, did church work, and conducted funeral services when no minister was available. At one time there were about a hundred families getting their mail at **Tindall**. Before the office opened some of the patrons had to go forty miles. The Reverend T. E. Mack, Baptist minister from Steve's Fork, held services in the schoolhouse at **Tindall**. The dry land farmers gave up and moved away and the post office closed in 1937 when the Tindalls left. Now only a few scattered farms are still occupied (Highland).

Tobacco (Lincoln) was opened in 1894 with John Leonard as postmaster; it closed in 1905 and the mail was sent to Eureka. It was a Great Northern Station named for its location on the Tobacco River.

Tobison (Valley) had a post office granted in 1916 with Edward Mahony as postmaster. The office closed in 1933.

Toddlake (Valley) had a post office 1919-20 with Henry Quiring in charge.

Tokna (Richland) had a post office 1884-92 with Jennie Dunlap as postmaster. The office was also open 1893-1909.

Toledo (Hill), "seven miles east of Bull Hook Bottoms where the railroad turned south to the Assiniboine Station, was an important center" (Allison). The railroad built a section house every six miles, not so much for the convenience of settlers as for the maintenance and construction crews. However, many of them grew into towns or centers where homesteaders gathered. The name here was changed to Pacific Junction, presumably when the railroad found it could push its line on to the West Coast by way of Marias Pass.

Toluca (Big Horn), once a station on the Burlington Railroad, had a post office established in May 1914. Legend has it that a train carrying a group of Swedes developed a hotbox and had to stop near here. The Swedes got out, and when they were asked why they did, answered, "Yust to looka." This story was frequently retold and the station named **Toluca** (Charles Cheney).

Tongue River, in old Big Horn County, was the name of a post office established December 1876 with Nelson A. Miles its first postmaster and William O'Toole its second. In January 1878, according to postal records, the name was changed to Fort Keogh. The river from which the name derives heads in Wyoming and flows through Big Horn and Rosebud counties to join the Yellowstone at Miles City. John Morgan, who lived near Miles City, developed his theory concerning the origin of the name by consulting old-timers and local historians: "The river, which is an exceptionally crooked one, was named thus by the Indians because it was like the white man's tongue — crooked — and could not be depended on." Granville Stuart wrote in his journal for April 1880: "We followed up Tongue River twenty-four miles and crossed the river twenty times, it being the crookedest stream in Montana, with long high spurs or points of mountains putting down into every bend." Pioneer Wyoming resident and historian Elsa Spear Byron says that the Indians told her father that they named the river for a peculiar tongue-shaped formation of trees and rocks that appears on the mountainside just above the headwaters of the Little Tongue and Tongue rivers. This "tongue" can be seen from the highway, and this seems to be the most generally accepted version concerning the origin of the name. But still another old-timer claims the Indians called it the "Talking River," which was loosely translated by the whites as Tongue River. In any case, the Indians seem to have named it.

Tongue River (Big Horn) was the name of a post office established 1937 with Leland Droese as postmaster. It closed in 1940. This one was near Decker.

Tonjun (Hill), near Havre, had a post office 1914-15 with Stella Johnson as postmaster.

Tony (Carbon) was a post office established near the Tony Early homestead on West Red Lodge Creek in March 1902. The mail came to **Tony** three times a week from Red Lodge, fifteen miles away. The name changed or the mail center changed to Fairbanks in 1906.

Toole (Mineral) was a little railroad station named for the manager of the Big Blackfoot Milling Company.

Toole County borders Canada. Shelby is the county seat. It was organized in 1914 from parts of Hill and Teton counties and named for J. K. Toole, Montana's first governor. **Toole County**'s once-dry prairies are now productive oil fields.

Top O' Deep (Granite), near Drummond, had a post office January 1893-August 1894 with Tillie Kreuzberger as postmaster.

Torbet (Gallatin) was a Milwaukee sidetrack named for a local rancher.

Tortona (Park) had a post office 1890-93 with Matilda Stocker in charge.

Tosland (Hill) was a post office 1914-17 with George Tosland as postmaster.

TOSTON (Broadwater), on the banks of the Missouri River, was named for Thomas Toston, an early homesteader and the first postmaster. The post office opened in 1882 and operated from his ranch. Toston built the Toston Ferry; an anchor post was still visible as late as 1946 but has since been washed away by the river. He bought his land from John Karns, a private who had served in the Virginia Militia in the War of 1812, receiving the land from the government for "meritorious service." Such grants were called "bounty land." The giant Toston Smelting Company, which operated 1883-99, brought a short-lived prosperity to **Toston**. Six-horse teams pulled loads of ore from Radersburg, and coal from the Big Springs area. Later, the Riverside Stock Farm, which featured pure-bred stock and racehorses, grew from three thousand to eleven thousand acres and included fancy buildings and a racetrack. Mining, smelting, trading, and land development marked **Toston** as a marketing center and helped it grow. But when the community found itself plagued by earthquakes, fires, and closing mines it nearly died (Eleanor Marks in *Broadwater Bygones*).

TOWNSEND (Broadwater) is a county seat advantageously "surrounded by the grandeur of the great Missouri River and its valley" and under the protection of the Big Belt Mountains. The first passenger train to travel from St. Paul to Portland (September 1883) stopped at **Townsend**. The town had been laid out and developed in anticipation of the coming of the railroad, and it was named by railroad officials, reportedly in honor of the wife of Charles B. Wright, president of the Northern Pacific 1874-79 — her maiden name was Townsend. The post office opened in May 1883 with William Woods, a watchmaker, the postmaster. A $10 thousand hotel, the Townsend House, was built. Town lots sold for $5 apiece and pioneer families built fine houses, giving the new town a dignity that it has maintained throughout the years. W. E. Tierney opened a merchandise center on the ground floor of a big building. The upstairs served as a hall for church, theater, school programs, dances and suppers. Agriculture gradually replaced the railroad as the dominant economic factor. The early post office moved back and forth across the street as postmasters changed and took the office to their places of business (Grace Holloway in *Broadwater Bygones*).

Tracy (Cascade) was near Sand Coulee. Abner and Nat McGiffin opened the first coal mine at Tracy in 1882. This led to the discovery of coal at Sand Coulee and to Jim Hill building the railroad to the mines in order to get coal to run the Great Northern engines. Nat McGiffin and his family moved to a new ranch "up the coulee" about 1885 or '86. The little town of Giffin developed as the coal mines were expanded and was named for this family. **Tracy** joins the long list of deserted mining camps in Montana (Elizabeth McGiffin Cheney).

Trailcreek (Flathead) is on the edge of Glacier National Park just a few miles from Canada. Both trails and creeks are important parts of the landscape around here, so the name is a logical descriptive one. A post office was granted in 1921 with Benjamin Price as postmaster. It closed in 1954.

Trapper City (Beaverhead) is a mining ghost town. There were probably never more than two hundred people living there, though the Beaverhead country attracted lots of trappers and miners in the early days. "City" used to be liberally used to describe pioneer settlements, but few would qualify for the term by today's standards.

Treasure County was named in order to attract settlers to the area. It was organized in 1919 from a part of Rosebud County. Hysham, the county seat, and all other towns in the county are located on the Yellowstone River, which cuts through its center. Fort Manuel Lisa, Montana's first trading fort, built in 1807, was in what is now **Treasure County**.

TREGO (Lincoln), south of Eureka, began as a Great Northern station and was named in honor of Mrs. A. H. Hogeland, wife of a former chief engineer of the railroad; her maiden name was Anna Trego. The post office opened in 1911 with Charles Miller as postmaster. It closed in 1919.

Trenton (Valley) had a post office 1903-05 with Charles Hill as postmaster. It was near Glasgow.

TRIDENT (Gallatin) is near the three forks of the Missouri River. The pattern of the rivers here resembles a trident, with the big Missouri the handle and the Madison, Jefferson and Gallatin rivers the tines. A cement company located here uses a red devil and his trident as commercial symbols. The post office opened in 1909 with Donald Morrison as postmaster.

Trine (Phillips) had a post office 1917-33. Ray Warren was postmaster.

Trommer (Liberty) had a post office 1910-16 with Vivian Irvine, postmaster. The mail was then sent to Lothair.

Trotter (Jefferson) was a brief (1880-81) post office with Rich Swarbrick as postmaster.

Trotters (Sheridan) developed after three men built a small stockade log building on a dry river bottom. The building also served as the first schoolhouse; with a table of planks and benches serving as desks. There was no designated playground, but a big hill served the purpose well. One day Arthur Elkis broke his leg jumping over a snowbank. His brothers took him home and his father set his leg. Ruth Smith was the first teacher.

Trouble was in present-day Garfield County. The name was something the homesteaders had plenty of, but evidently someone felt it was too pessimistic, because the post office that was granted in 1917 (Bert Duncan, postmaster) had its name changed to Hazny the following year.

Trout Creek (Fergus) had a post office 1867-76. P. T. Williams, and later Lewis Rativitt, served as postmasters the first year. The office reopened 1882-83. Montana is famous for its trout streams.

TROUT CREEK (Sanders) was a thriving town in the 1800s. "Old Trout Creek" was upstream across the creek where Larchwood is now. Logging, railroading, and mining were the principal activities. In 1910 Jim Hylent bought forty acres of timbered land and the town moved to its present location, where he built the Hylent Hotel; some say he had hoped the town would be named after him. In fact, postal records show that it was called Hylent after he became postmaster, but in 1910 the name was changed back to **Trout Creek**. There was a boom here during 1955-56 while the Noxon Rapids Dam was being built. The post office was first established in 1885 with W. J. Davis as postmaster.

TROY (Lincoln) is in a mountainous area in the northwest corner of the state, less than ten miles from Idaho and about fifty from the Canadian line. It is also just a few miles east of the line where Mountain Standard becomes Pacific Standard Time for westbound travelers. **Troy** was a freight division on the Great Northern and headquarters for silver mining outfits working in the Cabinet Mountains. Railroad construction crews and miners set up a camp at the mouth of Lake Creek east of the present town and called it Lake City. By 1891 the crews had moved on and remnants of the town moved over to the site chosen by the railroad for a freight division. The origin of the town's name is disputed; some say it was named for a civil engineer who worked for the GN when the railroad was locating track through this part of Montana. E. L. Preston, surveyor for the railroad, laid out the new townsite, including plans for the ten-stall roundhouse and freight yards. Wolle says that Preston named the town after Troy Morrow, the son of the family with whom he was boarding at the time; the late Troy Morrow, descended from the one above mentioned, became a pharmacist in and agrees with this claim. Another suggestion is that the town was named for the Troy weight system used for gold, silver, and other precious metals. The post office was established in 1893 with Henry Tatom as postmaster.

Truffley (Golden Valley) had a post office 1912-19. It was fifteen miles northwest of Ryegate and named for the family of Christopher Truffley, the first postmaster. The soil in the area was rich in potash and volcanic ash. Homesteaders settled on railroad land.

Truly (Cascade) had a post office July 1884-1905 (Belinda Hopkins, postmaster); thereafter the mail was ordered to Great Falls.

Tunis (Chouteau) was a Great Northern station west of Fort Benton. It had a post office 1910-18 (Othelia Johnson, postmaster) until the office was closed and mail was ordered to Carter.

Turah (Missoula), near Bonner, was a stage station on the Mullan Road, then an NP station. It was established in 1883 and named for Keturah, daughter of N. C. Thrall, an assistant vice-president of the Northern Pacific.

Turkey Track was the nickname given to a narrow-gauge railroad built in the 1890s which extended from Great Falls to Lethbridge, Alberta. Officially named the Great Falls and Canada, the **Turkey Track** took the place of the old bull teams on the Whoop-Up Trail, hauling coal from the Lethbridge mines to the smelters in Great Falls. In 1901 the Montana and Great Northern Railroad was formed; they purchased the **Turkey Track** and changed it from narrow gauge to standard. In 1907 the Great Northern took it over.

Turner (Blaine) is twelve miles south of the Trelon port of entry on the Canadian side, and was named in honor of Mr. and Mrs. H. C. Turner. Turner was a cattleman who, in 1912, built a store to serve settlers; in August of that year he became postmaster when a post office opened. Turner's store was an immediate success and other people came to also establish businesses. The Turners' son, Clyde, freighted supplies and mail once a week from Harlem (Trish Travis, Antelope High School). When the railroad came through in 1928, the town was moved two miles to its present location.

Tuscor (Sanders) was a station on the Northern Pacific down the valley and west of old Trout Creek (Larchwood Creek). In 1921 the entire town consisted of a combination store and post office which operated 1914-56. Margaret Kay was the postmaster.

Tusler (Custer), near Miles City, was a Northern Pacific station established in 1881 while track was being laid. It was first called Dixon, but the name was changed to honor an early settler and cattleman in the area. The post office operated 1898-1904; the postmaster was Meta Gorneman.

Twete (Blaine), near Hogeland, was named for Hans Twete and his wife, who served as postmasters for many years. The office opened in 1910. Mrs. Twete also managed the country store and was a practical nurse for the Big Flat country. Community spirit was high in **Twete** — neighbors helped each other, and for one day each year everyone gathered to pick rocks off the roads. In 1928 the railroad came through and **Twete** briefly boomed, declining just as fast with the exodus of disenchanted homesteaders. In 1929 the post office was moved to Hogeland (Highland).

TWIN BRIDGES (Madison) has had a post office since July 1869. The town was either named for the two bridges that spanned the Jefferson River nearby (*Montana, A Guide Book*), or for two bridges over the Beaverhead and Big Hole rivers built by the Lott brothers in 1865 (*Significance of County Names*). The town is near the confluence of the tributaries of the Jefferson River, which were named by Lewis and Clark in 1805. The explorers chose to commemorate the "three cardinal virtues" of President Thomas Jefferson with the names Philosophy, Wisdom and Philanthropy; these small rivers were later renamed respectively, the Beaverhead, the Big Hole, and the Ruby. The Lott brothers, who are credited with establishing Sheridan, built their bridges and charged their tolls. Then they set to work improving roads by closely following old Indian trails.

The settlement was first known as The Bridges. The Lotts donated land for public buildings and to individuals who promised to build homes on them. By 1884 **Twin Bridges** was being served by three daily stagecoaches from Virginia City, Dillon, and Whitehall.

"An imposing" brick building was built for the Twin Bridges Normal School in 1889, the only normal school in Montana at the time; but it finally lost out to politics and the legislature moved the normal college to Dillon. The **Twin Bridges** facility became the state orphanage and housed some five thousand children before its final closure in 1975.

Twin Buttes (Yellowstone) was near Newton Grove. Its post office was operating 1916-18; the postmaster was Thomas Smith.

Twin Creeks (Missoula), near Bonner, had a post office 1911-19; the first postmaster was J. William Davis.

Twist (Powder River) was the name of a post office 1931-34; Minnie Lawrence was the first postmaster.

Twitchell (Garfield), near Weldon, had a post office from 1919-21; Gladys Twitchell was postmaster. Bill Twitchell owned a horse ranch on the Big Dry in the early 1900s.

TWO DOT (Wheatland) was named for H. J. "Two Dot" Wilson, a cattleman who got his nickname because his brand was two dots, a large dot on the shoulder and another on the thigh, which made it very difficult for a thief to alter the brand. Two Dot was never one for dressing up, and one time in Chicago, having arrived with a load of cattle, he was arrested for vagrancy because he was so dirty and unkempt. He asked the policeman to accompany him to the bank, and when it was verified that Wilson had just deposited more than $10,000 he was set free. The incident had begun as a practical joke; a couple of cowhands who had accompanied Wilson to Chicago thought it would be fun to play a trick on the boss — they were the ones who pointed him out to police as a vagrant. But Two Dot found out about their conspiracy and went them one better — he took the next train home and left them in Chicago with neither money or a return ticket.

In 1900 a post office was opened with Edward Orr in charge and that same year the Montana Railroad reached **Two Dot**; it was later taken over by the Milwaukee. The weather-beaten station still sits along the track, and the post office remains in the front room of the postmaster's home.

Twoee (Dawson) had a post office 1910-12 with William Wood as postmaster.

Tyler (Deer Lodge) was a popular creek crossing and stage stop. There was also a toll bridge here during the era of the Mullan Road; travelers could either pay up or pull up Medicine Tree Hill and ford at Carlan (Murray).

Tyler (Fergus) had a post office 1909-40. Charlie Tyler, the postmaster, also ran the saloon — at least until Prohibition — and a few sheep. The saloon was in the middle of Tommy Cruse's N Bar Ranch. **Tyler** is still on the map, located where gravel roads from Forest Grove and Grass Range continue down the creek to hit Highway 87 about twenty-five miles north of Roundup. Charlie built a dancehall and a bunkhouse in Byrley before he got restless and left for Alaska (Byerly).

Tyndell (Carbon) was a stock loading yard and station on the Burlington Railroad near Bridger. It was built about 1912 when the track was owned by the old Big Horn Railroad.

Tyner had a post office January-August 1880. Cadmus Kendall is listed as postmaster, but no county is mentioned — the records just note that the office was on an Indian reservation.

U

Ubet (Fergus) was once the best-known stage station in Montana Territory. Skeletons of the old log buildings still remain, and were providing shelter for sheepherders as late as the 1920s.

The story of **Ubet** is told in a book (John R. Barrows, *Ubet*) by a man whose father, A. R. Barrows, established the settlement in 1880. There was a two-story log hotel (elaborate for the time), a post office, a blacksmith shop, an ice house, a saloon, and a stage barn with a stable. The name was a frontier improvisation inspired by the expression "You bet!" used by the elder Barrows when he was asked if he could think of a good name for the post office. Citizens pointed out that the name was short and unique, even if it wasn't very dignified. In the 1880s there were hardly half a dozen human habitations along the stage route between Billings and **Ubet**. The post office opened in 1881 and Augusta Barrows was appointed postmaster. Subsequent appointments show different members of the Barrows family managed the office during most of its existence. Mrs. Barrows' cooking and the comforts of the hotel made this a favorite stopping place for stage travelers and cowboys.

But even the Barrows couldn't cope with the rigors of a Montana winter. The icy winter wind howled through a gap allowing north and southbound traffic near the stage station. One time a salesman who was staying at Ubet found himself so cold that he got up at 3 a.m. to go down to the dining room and sit by the fireplace. An hour later the stage driver came in after fighting a blizzard most of the way; icicles hung from his beard and his hands looked like they were frozen stiff. The startled salesman, who had been dozing, looked up and saw the snow-encrusted man. "My God," he exclaimed. "Which room did you have?" (Stearns).

Ubet lasted as a stage station until the railroad was extended from Harlowtown to Lewistown and the "iron horses" replaced the stage teams. The post office was closed in 1904 and the mail handled at Garneill. **Ubet** was a one-man town; there were never any private residences, but the post office served an immense area that was later, in 1931, served by offices at Garneill, Judith Gap, Buffalo, Straw, Moore, and Beaver Creek.

Uebra (Garfield), on Indian Creek, got its unusual name through a misinterpretation of handwriting. Mrs. McGlumphey, who operated the post office in Dilo, circulated the petition and made out the application for an office. But she wrote very fast, abbreviated throughout, and made her "N's" like "U's", so that patrons, who had wanted to call their settlement Nebraska — in honor of their home state — found themselves with an office officially recorded as **Uebra**. Wilson Cory was the first mail carrier and used a horse and buggy. The post office was opened in 1919 with Clara Showyer as postmaster; it closed in 1936.

Ulidia (Cascade) had a post office in 1880, and for the next few years it was the mail center for a wide area, including Sand Coulee, which was a day's horseback ride away. It was named by Postmaster General Key's friends for his dusky, maiden sweetheart of that name (Rowe). The postal area was changed to Gorham in 1885.

ULM (Cascade), twelve miles southwest of Great Falls, was named for William Ulm, who had a ranch here, and whose land included the present townsite. The post office opened in 1883 with Ulm as postmaster, closed in 1901, and was restored in 1903. The Great Northern built its line through here in 1887, purchasing the right-of-way from Ulm. The town became a shipping center for wheat from the surrounding benchlands.

Underdahl (Cascade) was named for first postmaster Andrew Underdahl, an employee for Winston Brothers Grading Contractors, who were connected with the building of the railroad. The post office opened in 1921; a year later the name was changed to Salem.

Unger (Valley), near Glasgow, had a post office 1903-08. It was named for first postmaster Charles Unger.

Union (Dawson) had a post office 1909-44; the first postmaster was Albert Skillestad.

Unionville (Lewis and Clark) was granted a post office in 1869 with Philip Constans as postmaster. The office was closed 1887-92, then open again until 1894.

Unity (Meagher), near White Sulphur Springs, had a post office 1880-1912; Charles Cook was the first postmaster.

University Place (Lewis and Clark) had a post office 1891-95; first postmaster was James Johnson.

Uoll Heights (Garfield), located at the head of You All Creek, was a simplified spelling for the Southern expression. "Those responsible for naming the town were weighing several possibilities and finally decided on You All, but changing the spelling to Uoll. . . . My father, Thomas Karns, moved from Oregon to **Uoll Heights** in 1926 when I was nine years old" (Kermit Karns). **Uoll** was near Big Dry House and Little Dry House creeks, named because the Indians used to dry their buffalo meat there. Later it became sheep country. William Milroy told of losing 1,500 lambs in one spring blizzard as he was trailing his band to **Uoll** to be sheared. At one time, there was a little Catholic church in **Uoll**. The post office known as **Uoll Heights** was opened in 1916 with Benjamin Haas as postmaster. It was discontinued in 1935.

URAL, once a station on the Great Northern in Lincoln County, is along the Kootenai River. The post office was established in 1905 with Oscar Gibbler as postmaster. In December 1908 Clarence Lawrence was appointed postmaster. The office was discontinued in 1959.

Utica (Judith Basin), on the Judith River, was a hangout for cowboys and headquarters for the Judith Basin Cattle Pool in the early 1880s. There was a storehouse for saddles, bridles, and other gear for roundups from one season to the next. "Biggest problem," said old-time cowboy "Kid" Amby Cheney, "was how to winter a slicker and summer a girl." When the riders came to town, **Utica** was the liveliest town around.

Jake Hoover discovered a sapphire mine in Yogo Gulch above **Utica**; that's the same Hoover who gave Charlie Russell a home and some grub while the artist was fiddling around with painting. Four New York prospectors heard about Yogo Gulch and came rushing out. But there wasn't enough money in the mining game for all four, so some settled on the land. Their names were J. D. Waite, Frank Wright, John Murphy, and Joseph Cutting, and all came from Utica, New York. The story is, that during a blizzard they all decided that must have been crazy to have come here and should name the place in fond memory of their hometown because that was the location of the New York insane asylum.

The story of the **Utica** post office is typical of many early Montana towns. In 1879, James Cutting started the first store in a little log building which also housed the post office, which opened in 1881; Cutting was the first postmaster, running the office in connection with his store. Later, Dr. Gaylord McCoy built an office building on Main Street and used half of it for his medical practice, while his sister ran the post office in the other half. Then, for a while, the office was run in connection with the hotel; and still later, a man named Jacobsen tended the store in one part of a building while his wife served as postmaster in the other part. Sometimes the post office had a building of its own, but in later years it was usually kept in the homes of the postmasters, most of whom were women.

An incident in 1881 created a lot of excitement in **Utica.** Before the town had an official postmaster, John Murphy's cabin served as post office for the convenience of settlers. It was winter time and the roads were often blocked with deep snow. The mail carrier's buckboard broke down and when he left on horseback, he took only the letters and left a heavier sack for the next trip, which would be in a couple of months or so. The sack got kicked under Murphy's bunk on the dirt floor of the cabin and the dog slept on it for several months. The sack became covered with dust and was forgotten. When the snow was gone, along about the middle of May, a detachment of soldiers from Fort McGinnis rode into **Utica** from the North. They were trailing a sack of money lost several months previously and asked if any had been found. It was the $40,000 payroll for the soldiers at Ft. McGinnis which had disappeared. Murphy said sure, go ahead and search the cabin and then he remembered the sack the dog had been sleeping on all winter. "That's it," gasped the soldier as Murphy pulled it out from under his bed. "That's the $40,000 we've been moving heaven and earth to find."

Utica is Charlie Russell country and much of the artist's work bears memories of this area and its people. Here are some lines from the *Charles Russell Suite* composed and produced during Montana's Diamond Jubilee in 1964:

> We never leave the dance
> With money in our pants
> While the fun holds out,
> We'll hoot and shout
> In **Utica** Saturday night.

After spending a winter with Jake Hoover, Russell decided to establish a little place of his own, so he picked out a homestead in Pagel Gulch above **Utica.** Timber was handy so he could cut logs for his cabin and snake them in with the aid of his saddle pony, Monte. The project was begun with enthusiasm and optimistic plans to get it done before winter set it. But it soon became plain to his Judith neighbors that the young cowboy was considerably more adept at drawing pictures than he was at building a home, and his cabin became almost as laughable as the yarns he told. When the misfitted and rather crooked side walls were hardly half as high as they should have been, Charlie decided to put the roof on. Inside, a circle of stone in a corner served for heating the cabin and for cooking; the cracks in the roof let the smoke escape. A heap of boughs supplied a place to spread blankets. This cabin was not only Charlie Russell's first home in the West, it was also his first studio (Mildred Tourman, *Utica, Montana*).

Blackfeet and Crow Indians often camped near **Utica** as they traveled cross-country between the Hardin and Browning areas. Sometimes they pitched camp in the Belden's hay field or near the school. Often they had a string of ponies with them. The route the Indians followed through central Montana was generally the same one used by stage and freight drivers.

P. W. Korell, an early settler, established a store which was still being run by his son in 1971. **Utica** was cattle country back in the early days, and is getting back to it now. The town had a renewal of activity when the sapphire mines re-opened, attracting tourists as well as summer homeowners. Today **Utica** stands as a relic to the past, a place where, more than any other in Montana, the romantic vision of the Old West still survives in cowboy sagas and tales.

Utopia (Liberty) was near Chester. Certainly the name indicates the hopes of homesteaders, but its one-year existence (1911-12; Carrie Heaton, postmaster) also points out the rapid disillusionment of settlers.

V

Valentine (Fergus) is near the Petroleum County line thirty miles east of Roy and thirty north of Winnett. There are two legends concerning the origin of the name. One is that it was named for a Valentine family who settled in the hills northeast of the community. They had a good spring of water on their land which was called Valentine Springs, so when the post office began in 1903 (Maud Lorimer was the postmaster), it was also called **Valentine**. The other theory, maintained by Mary Bean, agrees that the town took its name from the springs, but suggests that they were named because they were discovered on Valentine's Day (Marguerite Cook).

Ben and Mary Bean started their sheep ranch on Blood Creek in the early 1900s. "Mrs. Bean worked hard to establish the **Valentine** post office, carrying the mail herself on horseback from the Leslie Sheep Ranch, where the closest post office was located." In 1906 she was successful in getting the route through from Grass Range to **Valentine**. William Lane was the first mail carrier. The Beans built a hotel which consisted of six or seven log rooms joined end-to-end and for years they accommodated the weary traveler and eager homesteader pressing eastward through Fergus County. The post office was in one corner of the hotel and much of the time Mary Bean was postmaster. The **Valentine** *News* was edited by George Budwieser during the homestead boom. In the 1930s the Valentine Dam was built, but before it filled and was ready to supply irrigation waters to dry lands, most of the farmers had given up and moved away. **Valentine** dwindled to two buildings and a ranch (Mrs. Sam Conolly in the Winnett *Times*).

Valentine, in its heyday, had a hotel, general store, livery stable, community hall, school and several houses. Dovetail people went there to trade. Now nothing is left but the deserted school building and a few scattered shanties. The post office closed in 1943, so the Paul Pitmans, who are area ranchers, take turns carrying the mail three times a week from Roy. The homesteaders gave up, most of the sheepmen moved out, and the country is back to cattle. This is the typical story of so many central Montana settlements and areas. "It was survival of the fittest; many left; those who stayed bought up the land, built fences, improved the range, developed reservoirs to make the area one of the best ranching ones anywhere" (Byerly).

VALIER (Pondera) was named for Peter Valier of LaCombre, Wisconsin, who supervised the building of the Montana Western Railroad (Dorothy Floerchinger). **Valier** is northwest of Conrad on the shores of Lake Francis, a reservoir now used for irrigation. The Montana Western, with a total length of 22.2 miles, connected **Valier** with the main line of the Great Northern. It was built in 1909. The post office was established in that year, too, with John Pettyrove in charge. The **Valier** area was settled mainly by a group of Belgian immigrants; a trainload of them arrived in 1913.

Valleux (Chouteau) This post office opened in 1884 with Nelson Valleux as postmaster. It closed in 1885 and mail was sent to Fort Benton.

Valley (Deer Lodge) had a post office 1880-1883 with Allen Pierse as postmaster. This part of southwestern Montana is made up of mountains and valleys, so the name is most likely descriptive. **Valley** was near Silver Bow.

Valley County, one of the largest counties in the state, is bordered on the north by Canada and on the south by the Fork Peck Reservoir. Glasgow is the county seat. **Valley County** was named for the area's topography and was created in 1893 from a part of Dawson County. Parts of **Valley County** were taken in 1913 to form Sheridan County, in 1915 to form Phillips County, and in 1920 to form a part of Daniels County. Joe Culbertson came to this part of the Missouri River country in 1830, when what is now **Valley County** was buffalo range and favorite hunting country of the Gros Ventre, Blackfeet, Piegan, and Blood Indians.

Valleytown (Phillips) had a post office established 1908 with Sarah Whitbread as postmaster. The office was closed in 1942.

Valleyview (Sanders) was near Lonepine and had a post office 1912-13 with Norman Rockhill as postmaster.

Van (Toole) was named for first postmaster Mary Van Buskirk. The office opened in 1912 and closed in 1935.

Vananda (Rosebud) was once a station on the Milwaukee, with a post office 1912-1959. Vena (Vevia?) Smith was the first postmaster.

VANDALIA (Valley) is on the Milk River between Glasgow and Saco near the site of an old trading post called Campbell's Houses or Hammett's Houses. The post office opened in 1904 with Henry H. Nelson as postmaster, who had already established his ranch in the area; the house was built of huge cottonwood logs and patterned after manor houses in Nelson's native Denmark. It took from 1898 to 1902 to complete the structure, because each log had to be peeled and seasoned. St. Mary's Lodge, at the eastern entrance to Glacier National Park, is said to be patterned after Nelson's house. Two years after his death, Nelson's widow married the foreman, John David, who ramrodded the ranch into an empire of nine thousand acres and two thousand head of cattle. Many buildings in Glasgow were built of brick from the brick plant at **Vandalia** (Murray).

Vanderpool (Glacier) is a community near Babb.

Van Norman (Garfield) is on Dry Creek. The post office was active 1914-63; Helmer Hoverson was first postmaster. **Van Norman** was named for Elija William Van Norman, who came here from Canada before any other settlers to herd sheep. His nickname was "Pack Rat" Van Norman, because he seemed to always be packing something home. Two mail routes later serviced the area, one from Jordan and one from Rock Springs; the post office moved betweeen various ranches as different settlers took their turn as postmaster. In 1958 the post office burned with the Haight house, but Mrs. Haight was able to save the mail and most of the supplies and she moved herself and the office into a sheep wagon until a new house could be built.

Van Orsdel (Fergus), the famous and beloved circuit-riding minister of frontier days, was almost immortalized by having a post office named for him; one was authorized in April 1924, but the order was rescinded. William Wesley Van Orsdel arrived in the West as a Methodist missionary and an inspired young man of twenty-two, and came to be one of the most respected and influential men in Montana Territory, devoting his life to his far-flung mission field. The following story typifies his beginning ministry: "The blase proprietor of the Four Deuces Saloon in Fort Benton looked up one day and was surprised to see a stocky young man wearing a white vest, a long, black frock coat, and a black Stetson hat. The young man marched up to the bar and demanded to know where he could hold a preaching service. Without a moment's hesitation, the bartender banged on the bar and announced, "This bar and the games will be closed for an hour. Go ahead, preacher." Van Orsdel gulped — this wasn't what he had in mind as a place to hold a service. He looked over the "congregation" of bearded miners, cowhands, and dancehall girls, then he mounted a chair and began to sing in his mellow, baritone voice. After several songs, he was encored again and again. By then the listeners were interested enough to ask him his name. When he told them, the gamblers all greed that it was too complicated and decided to call him "Brother Van."

Vanstel (Rosebud) had a post office 1916-34. Simon Bibitzke was the first postmaster.

Varney (Madison), south of Ennis on the Madison River, was named for O. B. Varney, who settled on Trail Creek and ran a large herd of horses. Varney kept his corrals at Eight Mile House, which were named because it was eight miles from Virginia City. Varney ran cattle, too, and his brand was a "V" on the left shoulder. Later he and a man named Farrell bought a huge tract of land and ran up to two thousand horses on it, selling the stock to both the American and Italian governments for use as cavalry mounts. Farrell was also county sheriff and operated a freight line between Virginia City and Corinne, Utah.

Harry Daems, from whose "memoirs" the above information was taken, was an early settler and postmaster at **Varney** for many years. He was the son of Doctor L. Daems, Virginia City medical man, druggist, and apothecary, carrying a full assortment of pure drugs, medicine, assay supplies, chemicals, oils, paints, perfumes, fancy articles, flavoring, and extracts. Daems brought his "store" by bull team from Denver and set up the City

Drug Store. The **Varney** post office opened in 1914 with William Wilcox, the sawmill operator, as postmaster. The office closed in 1944.

Vaters (Park County) had a post office 1889-96. It was named for Ernest E. Vater, first postmaster. Postal records say the name was changed to Muir in 1896, but it is quite possible the postal area shifted to the Muir office for a few years, because the **Vaters** office was reopened in 1916 and remained active for twenty-two years.

VAUGHN (Cascade) is twelve miles west of Great Falls and named for Robert Vaughn, the author of *Forty Years On the Frontier*. Vaughn came to Montana in 1860. A post office here was established as Sunnyside in 1893; in 1911 it was changed to **Vaughn** and James C. Morgan was appointed postmaster.

Vaughn (Lewis and Clark) was the name of a post office 1887-89.

Vebar (Golden Valley) was a Great Northern station named for the V-Bar brand used by a nearby cattle ranch.

Velma (Valley) was to have been the name of a post office in 1903 with David Folson as postmaster, but the order was rescinded a year later.

Vermilion (Sanders), near Trout Creek, had a post office 1889-1905 with the exception of 1894-95. Alfred Brile was postmaster.

Verneil (Musselshell) had a post office 1915-17 with Lorena Kock as postmaster.

Verona (Chouteau) had a post office 1914-35 with Frank Worstell the first postmaster. **Verona** is near Big Sandy and began as a station on the Great Northern on the run between Fort Benton and Havre.

Vestal (Deer Lodge) was a post office 1878-81 with James Root as postmaster.

Viall (Garfield) had a post office April 1905-1908. It was named for first postmaster John Viall, who also owned a small cattle outfit.

VICTOR (Ravalli), near Stevensville, was named for a great Flathead Indian chief. The post office opened in 1881 with John L. Sloane as postmaster, closed briefly that same year, then reopened.

Vida (McCone) is an isolated prairie town between Circle and Wolf Point. The post office opened in 1911 with August Nefzger as first postmaster, whose pay was about $150 quarterly, based on cancellations and money orders at the **Vida** office. In 1939 Ed and Helen Schillinger opened a store and took over the postal duties.

Vincent (Dawson) had a post office June 1898-October 1899, with Walter Looke in charge. The mail was ordered to Sanford when the office closed.

Vincent (Gallatin) was a sidetrack named for Webb Vincent.

Violet (Fallon) was near Webster. The post office was established in 1908 with Elijah Mulkey as postmaster; it was closed in 1915.

Vipond (Beaverhead) was a mining settlement near Deweys named for John Vipond, who discoverd a lode there in April 1868. At first Vipond hauled the ore by mule team to the railroad in Corinne, Utah; later he built a well-equipped mill on his own land, but a decrease in the price of silver forced it to shut down in 1895. A post office was established in 1878 with William Spurr in charge; the office closed in 1888.

Virgelle (Chouteau) had a post office with Edward Stehley as postmaster which operated from 1902 until 1961. The town's name was coined from the first names of Virgil and Ella Blackenbaker. Mr. Blackenbaker was a prominent sheep rancher and at one time was elected state senator. For many years a free ferry operated across the Missouri at **Virgelle** from March to October.

VIRGINIA CITY (Madison), a county seat, was the first town incorporated in Montana (1864). This famous Montana town was first named Varina, in honor of the wife of Jefferson Davis, President of the Confederacy. But a local judge, G. G. Bissell, refused to write the name on a legal document, declaring he would "be damned first," a sentiment which would likely have been echoed by many Civil War veterans in the area, for whom the memory of the conflict was still a fresh and emotional memory. Bissell wrote "Virginia" at the top of the legal document, and so the name was established — later it became known as **Virginia City**.

In May 1863 six prospectors led by young Bill Fairweather arrived in the hills along the Madison River. Henry Edgar, a member of the party, wrote in his journal, "We crossed the Madison and came up . . . Wigwam Gulch . . . camped beside Bald Mountain . . . killed an elk . . . remained during the afternoon and overnight to dry and smoke the meat. On May 26, 1863 about 4 o'clock in the afternoon. . . . Fairweather and I were to make camp and stand guard. . . . About sundown, Bill went across the creek to picket the horses . . . saying 'There's a bit of bedrock projecting . . . we'd better go over and see if we can get enough money to buy a little tobacco.' So Bill took the pick and shovel, and I took a pan, and we crossed the creek . . . while I was washing down the dirt, he scratched around in the bedrock with his butcher knife. . . . 'I've found a scad!' I called back, 'If you have one, I have a thousand' and so I had. We spent the next morning measuring the ground and staking it off. 'What shall we call the gulch?' I asked. 'You name it,' Barney Hughes said. So I called it Alder Gulch on account of the heavy clump of alders along the . . . creek." This strike caused a gold rush to the gulch and **Virginia City** sprung up and boomed. The town was laid out in June 1863, and within eight months there were five hundred dwellings, including stores and saloons. By the fall of 1864 the population was about 18,000. The post office was established in May 1864 with George Parker in charge. At this time **Virginia City** was still in Idaho Territory.

The first Episcopal Church in Montana was begun here in 1868 by Bishop Tuttle, whose assigned territory included Utah, Dakota, Montana Territory, and this bit of Idaho. Montana's oldest newspaper, the *Madisonian* was started by Thomas Deyarmon and has been published since November 13, 1873 and continues to operate weekly. It's masthead stated: "The *Madisonian* is devoted to the advocacy of the principles of the Democratic Party and to local news."

Vista (Flathead) was a station on the Great Northern named because of the beautiful view of Whitefish Lake and the mountains.

Volberg (Custer) is a country store and post office on Pumpkin Creek, a large stream which attracted many stockmen to its banks, where they noted the vast, unfenced and unclaimed ranges on both sides and often decided to settle. But the ranches were miles apart and it was a lonely life, particularly for women. Theodore Roosevelt, who came by occasionally from his northern ranch, once remarked, "The frontier is hard on women and horses." Occasionally families and cowboys got together for a dance; the men outnumbered women ten to one and the children slept on quilts in the corner. Music often lured cowboys to travel many miles. "The Hotch-kiss family on Pumpkin Creek had a piano. . . . The first year the assessor came into their house he said he just wouldn't list the piano, it was the 'only one he had found in the country outside of Miles City.' Custer County then occupied half the state north and south and more than one-fourth of it east and west" (Brown and Felton). The post office was opened in 1915 with Charles Allen as postmaster.

Volcour (Lincoln) was a Great Northern station.

Volt (Roosevelt) had a post office established 1917 with Jacob Schultes as postmaster. It was discontinued in 1941.

W

Waco (Yellowstone) was a station on the Northern Pacific Railroad. The post office was in operation 1907-18 (Gena Bergum, postmaster). It was near Custer.

Wade (Carbon) was a projected townsite on the Burlington Route be-tween East Bridger and Warren. There was a store for surrounding ranch-ers, but the country was dry, ranchers did not prosper and neither did the store.

WAGNER (Phillips) is on the Milk River. At nearby Exeter Creek on July 3, 1901, the Kid Curry gang held up the Great Northern train; they grabbed a case which they thought contained $40,000, but as they found out later, they had only stolen a stack of papers. The **Wagner** post office opened in 1901 with John Ebaugh as postmaster. Except for one year, it has been in operation ever since.

Waldheim (Musselshell) was the name of a settlement with a post office in 1909 under Hugh McCoy. It may have been called Waltham for awhile. Around 1919, after the end of the First World War, many citizens sug-gested changing the name, which sounded a bit too German for their tastes. So Wahoma was suggested and sent to the national postal department. The change was approved in April 1919, but rescinded a couple of months later, when the town became Bundy. William Davis was postmaster.

Waleston (Phillips) is some twelve miles north of Wagner. It had a post office 1919-34 with Joseph Snider in charge.

Walkerville (Silver Bow), a suburb of Butte, had a post office estab-lished in 1878 while it was still a part of old Deer Lodge County. The postmaster was Francis P. Carey. The town was named for the Walker Brothers of Salt Lake City, Utah, who owned and operated the Alice Mine at **Walkerville**. The town was settled mostly by miners from Cornwall, England. Now tumbledown houses sprawl around ore dumps and mine tipples. The post office was closed in 1959. In a little country cemetery in Pensilva, Cornwall, there is a stone that says:

In Memory of _____
Gone to Butte, U.S.A.

Wallace (Meagher) had a post office for four months 1895-96 with Elizabeth Cooper in charge.

Wallace (Missoula) was granted a post office in 1892 with Elias Bryan as postmaster. Postal records say the name was changed to Clinton in 1892 but actually, the postal business for this area was merely transferred to Clinton, which is nearby.

Wallis (Wheatland) was near Two Dot. The post office opened in 1912 with Wallis Huidekoper, a pioneer stockman, as postmaster. It closed in 1923.

Wallum (Golden Valley) was the name of a post office and rural settlement 1917-33. Wilbur Warn was the first postmaster.

Walsh (Phillips) was near Valleytown. The post office operated 1913-18. Garrett Ahern was the first postmaster.

Waltham (Chouteau) had a post office beginning in 1923. It was originally called Norbert, but they were actually two different places. **Waltham** began as a Milwaukee station. The post office was discontinued in 1962.

Waltham (Musselshell) was the name used for a short time by a community originally named Waldheim (see **Waldheim**). **Waltham** was never retained as a name because there was all ready another town by that name in Montana.

Walton (Flathead) was named for Izaak Walton, author of *The Compleat Angler and Outdoor Man*. The name is a result of the railroad's efforts to attract visitors and settlers with appealing names. Later the station adopted the post office name, Essex.

Wanetta (Yellowstone) had a post office 1915-34 with George Cook as postmaster. Edith Reid took over in 1926.

Wanso (Sheridan) had a post office 1922-34. Sigurd Swanson was the first postmaster, and the name may have been created by deleting the first and last letters of his name.

Wapka Chug'n is an old buffalo jump, or *pishkun*, near Havre, and now a National Historic Site. Native Americans used the site to process buffalo, the staple commodity of their culture. Plants used in making pemmican still grow here. "Chug" is the sound sometimes used to describe the sound a buffalo makes, and a town in Wyoming is named Chugwater, because it is where buffalo used to come to drink.

Warland (Lincoln) had a post office 1907-57. The first postmaster was Dean Good.

WARMSPRINGS, Warm Springs (Deer Lodge) was named for the nearby hot water springs. The post office opened in 1871 with Luther Barnard as postmaster. Prior to 1873 the name was spelled as two words. In 1895 the State Hospital for the Insane was established here.

Ward (Ravalli), near Hamilton, had a post office 1910-12 with Andrew Cavanaugh as postmaster.

Ware (Fergus) began as a station on the Milwaukee. Abe Hogeland came to this area in 1881 as a surveyor for the Great Northern; he left when his job was done, but returned in 1893 with a wife and son and settled at what is now **Ware**. His daughter was the first white child born in the vicinity. At the time, Fort Crow, on the Judith River near **Ware**'s railroad station, was a trading post popular with the Indians. The railroad brought more settlers, especially after the passage of the Homestead Act. The community needed a name; some suggested Acuashnut but others, not fond of this Indian name, held out for Barre. In 1915 a post office was applied for, and the government chose the former name, spelling it Acushmet. John Woolhiver was first postmaster. The railroad, however, disapproved of the name Acushmet and renamed the station **Ware**, a name not accepted by the community until 1950, when Ulysses Stevens was appointed postmaster. At one time, **Ware** had two grain elevators, a service station, a post office, a school, two saloons, and a population of about 350. By 1952 all but two or three families had moved away, and the post office was closed in 1954 (Gene Comes, as told by Marguerite Cook).

War House Lake This appears to be a lake in the Judith Mountains which is possibly misnamed on contemporary maps. According to Ruth Hoffman, who lives in Pyramid Gulch, what is shown as War Horse Lake is actually **War House Lake**, named because there was an Indian war house on the butte above it in the 1800s. These war houses were stone walls behind which the Indians hid to watch their enemies. Ms. Hoffman says that the remains of an old war house here could be seen as late as forty or fifty years ago, and that there were still traces of signal fires on a butte near Teigen.

Warren (Carbon) was a Burlington station from which the Big Horn Calcium Company shipped limestone from the Pryor Mountains to various sugar factories. **Warren** is on the main highway between Bridger, Montana, and Lovell, Wyoming. When the post office here was closed in 1953, the mail was ordered to Frannie, Wyoming. The office was originally established in 1911 with George Town as postmaster.

Warrick (Chouteau) had a post office 1890-57. "At the NL Horse Ranch on Birch Creek on the south side of the Bear Paws, the Texan manager, Dan Arnold, got tired of sending a cowboy to Big Sandy for the mail. Arnold wrote to Washington, D.C. requesting a new post office to be named **Warrick**. That was his wife's maiden name" (Allison). The new office opened in April 1890 with Mowny Arnold as postmaster.

Warsaw (Liberty), near Chester, had a post office 1912-57. The area was largely settled by Polish and Russian immigrants and presumably was named for the Polish capital. Antoni Koloski was first appointed postmaster but was not commissioned, so Lucas Bauer got the job.

Warwick seems to be the name of a Fergus County post office, but no date is listed. A notation says that the name was changed to Danvers in 1914.

Washington Bar (Madison) had a post office July 1884-1896. George Cope was the original postmaster; later, Esther Pinckney also served. Washington Bar was a mining camp of the gold rush days.

Washington Gulch (Powell) had a post office established in 1869 when prospectors rushed from the diggings around Virginia City to Gold Creek. The first postmaster was Patrick White. The office closed in 1907.

Washoe (Carbon) is near Red Lodge. The post office opened in December 1907 with Earl Lombard as postmaster. The Anaconda Copper Mining Company and its subsidiary, the Washoe Coal Company, developed a company town at the headwaters of Bear Creek in 1907. Two years later the Montana, Wyoming and Southern Railroad came through, and shipments of twelve hundred tons a day went to Anaconda smelters. However, with the formation of the Montana Power Company in 1912, it wasn't long until electric power helped slow the demand for coal, and the Washoe Mine closed. The name was chosen by the Anaconda Company, which had a Nevada mine by that name and also a smelter with the same name at Anaconda (Maryott). Washoe is also the name of a county and a valley in Nevada; it comes from an Indian tribe native to that state.

Waska (Roosevelt) had a post office 1917-35 (Arnold Lund, postmaster). Its life, like many Montana towns, spanned the eager, then finally disappointing, homesteading years in the eastern part of the state.

Wason Flats (Garfield) was first called Wason. The post office was established in 1913 in the home of Sam Wason. Effie Wason was postmaster. It was discontinued in 1939.

WATERLOO (Madison) is on the Jefferson River. The post office opened in 1900 with James H. Gordon as postmaster. Settlers came to Waterloo beginning in 1864. There were farmers, doctors, miners, surveyors, and some people who started a woolen mill which failed; a pottery mill, however, was successful. Mrs. Foster sold "soft soap" which she made from beaver fat. Stock raising became the top industry in the area and a boxcar served as the first depot. A dancehall and a combination store-post office were built. "It is said that the town got its name due to a lot of friction over the location of the post office. It was almost like a battle, so the early settlers decided upon **Waterloo** as a suitable name" (*Trails and Trials*).

Watkins (McCone) is south of Circle near the headwaters of the Redwater River. It was named for Mary Watkins, who was appointed postmaster in 1912. The office opened in 1910 with Ellen Spires in charge and closed in 1959.

Watseka was the original name of this Madison County settlement. In 1891 the post office opened with John Chapman as postmaster. The following year the name was changed to Rochester.

WATSON (Beaverhead) was an early day settlement. A post office opened in 1870 at the Simon Estes stage station. Estes operated a wayside station where horses could be changed, dinner had for passengers, and a bed for the night if needed. It was on a branch line of the "Great Beaverhead Wagon Road." (Murray) The first postmaster was Philip Lovell. The office closed in 1881.

Watson (Meagher) had a post office established in 1900 and named for first postmaster Alexander Watson. The office was discontinued in 1948.

Waive (Cascade) was a station on the Great Northern between Belt and Great Falls.

Wayne (Cascade) was a station on the Great Northern between Belt and Great Falls. The post office operated 1913-16 with Joseph Gailbraith as postmaster.

Wayne (Rosebud) was named for postmaster Wayne Newell. The office was open 1900-01; after that the mail was ordered to Lee.

Weber (Jefferson) had a post office established July 1883 with Mathias

Weber in charge. The name was formerly Parnell.

Webster (Fallon) was named for postmaster Alfred Webster. The office was opened in 1910 and remained active until 1965.

Weede (Petroleum) This post office was established in 1901 and named for the Weede family. Sarge Weede and Mrs. W. Boyle were early postmasters. The office was inactive 1911-14 and then opened until its final discontinuance in 1926. For a time the community was known as Parkinson. "Before 1910, Ed Weede from Yellow Water and Button Butte located on a piece of land south of Flatwillow Creek near the mouth of Box Elder on the Circle Bar Ranch and established a post office there. He carried the mail from Melstone by pack horses once every week . . . called it the **Weede** post office. Ed Weede was an old-timer who lived with the Indians and learned to make clothing out of buckskin . . . trimmed with beads and fringes . . . and then he sold them" (Edward Degner in the Winnett *Times*).

Welch (Jefferson) was named for James Welch, the first postmaster. The office was open 1902-11. When it closed, the mail went to Homestake.

Weldon (McCone) had a post office 1915-53. Frank McGurren was the first postmaster.

Welliver (Sheridan) was named for the first postmaster, Margaret Welliver. The office was open 1911-18. The mail was then sent to Plentywood.

Welter (Petroleum), northwest of Winnett, was named for Nicholas Welter, the first postmaster and an early homesteader. The post office was in operation 1915-26. The mail was sent to Staff when this office closed.

Wendell (Valley) had a post office established in 1914 with Tilly Holmes in charge. The office was discontinued in 1933.

Westbutte was in Chouteau County when the post office opened in 1901. It was in Toole County when the name was changed to McDermott in 1925, soon after Peter McDermott became postmaster. "Our family started homesteading on the South Slope of West Butte in 1898. My grandmother, Mary Knoble, was the first postmistress of **Westbutte** when the office opened in 1901" (Mary Knoble Young, *Montana Magazine*; Winter, 1973). Postal records incorrectly show the name spelled "Knobel." The name of the town is one of many in Montana derived from its geographic location and description.

WESTBY (Sheridan) is Montana's most northeasterly town located on the North Dakota border some ten miles from the Canadian line. It got its name when it was actually in North Dakota. The incorporated town moved across the border into Montana when the railroad came through. The town was originally settled by Danish people "By (pronounced bee) in their language means "town," and since this was the most westerly town in North Dakota, the citizens named it **Westby**. The post office opened in 1910 (in North Dakota) with James Hanson as postmaster.

West Fork (Daniels) had a post office established in 1914 with Hagen Hayenga in charge. It was discontinued in 1934. West Fork Creek cuts across the southwest dorner of Daniels County and flows into Cottonwood creen and then to the Poplar River.

WEST GLACIER (Flathead) is the western entrance to Glacier National Park, so the name describes its location at the southern tip of Lake

McDonald. In 1949 a **West Glacier** post office was established with Helen Gibb as postmaster. Before that the postal area was called Belton.

Westmore (Fallon) had a post office 1910-42. Clara Lowry was the first postmaster.

WEST YELLOWSTONE (Gallatin) serves as the western entrance to the famous national park. A post office was recorded in 1920 with Samuel Eagle as postmaster. During 1909-20 it was called Yellowstone, and before that there was a Riverside office (Oliver Byam, postmaster) 1882-84 and 1908-09. The original Yellowstone office was located a few miles away from the present townsite, but moved to contemporary location in 1883. **West Yellowstone**'s first school began in 1914, and the pupils came to school on skis. Though comparatively quiet during winter, **West Yellowstone** booms in the spring, when summer residents return and tourists come to visit Yellowstone National Park.

Wetzel (Glacier) was named for first postmaster Maggie Wetzel. The office opened in 1900 and closed in 1904; thereafter the mail was ordered to Browning.

Wheat Basin (Stillwater) had a post office 1918-36. Frances Rionel was the first postmaster. The town was platted by John Stolte in 1919.

Wheatbelt (Hill), near the Canadian border, had a post office 1924-29 — good years for wheat farmers. The mail was then sent to Simpson. Maud S. George was the first postmaster. The name was descriptive of the area.

Wheatland (Valley) was the name of a short lived post office 1913-14 with Harry R. Stockton in charge.

Wheatland County is a small county slightly south and west of the geographical center of the state. Harlowton is the county seat. The county was organized in 1917 from parts of Meagher and Sweet Grass counties and was named for the rich wheat lands it encompassed.

Wheaton (Musselshell) is a settlement near Roundup. It had a post office 1911-28. Tillie Smith was the postmaster.

Wheeler (Valley) is on the western edge of the Fort Peck Indian Reservation. The town lived and died with the influx of workers who built the dam, which forms the huge Fort Peck Reservoir on the nearby Missouri River. **Wheeler** is now the Buckhorn Club and a scattering of houses and mobile homes beside the highway just above Fort Peck Dam. It once had a population of 850. Now the Buckhorn cashes in on memories of better days by lining the walls with reproductions from the first issue of *Life* magazine, which featured construction of, and life around **Wheeler** and the Fort Peck Dam. The town was named for Burton K. Wheeler, a U.S. Senator from Montana who was instrumental in getting the dam approved and built. The post office opened in 1935 with Albert Hole as postmaster and closed in 1953.

Whelan (Golden Valley) was an early-day community near Irene. Daniel Whelan was appointed postmaster when the office opened in 1903 and his name was adopted for the official record. The office closed in 1906.

Whitcomb (Phillips), near Zortman, had a post office 1906-13 with Arthur Darland as postmaster. It was open again 1915-16.

White (McCone) in the southern part of the county, had a post office

1914-17 with Anton Liver as postmaster. When this office closed the mail was sent to Watkins.

WHITEFISH (Flathead) was named for its location near Whitefish Lake, and the lake got its name because of the great catches of whitefish taken from its waters at certain times of the year. The post office was established in 1903 with John Skyles in charge. **Whitefish** was chosen as a division point on the Great Northern Railroad after Jim Hill could not come to terms with Columbia Falls landowners on the price for rights-of-way. The area is now famous for skiing, but just a century ago it was entirely uninhabited, except for bands of Indians roving through the Flathead Valley. Settlement began about 1890 and by 1905 there were 950 residents. The early community was nicknamed Stump Town because it was built on harvested forest land and wagons going down the street had to go around the stumps on Central Avenue.

Whitehall (Jefferson) takes its name from a large white ranch home, originally owned by E. G. Brooke, which was used a stopping place for stages running from Helena to Virginia City. Brooke named his station Old Whitehall, after a similar structure in Whitehall, Illinois (E. Carroll Speck). The original station and post office were about four miles from where **Whitehall** is now. The modern community developed after the railroad came through in 1889 with a branch line between Garrison and Logan. Postal records show the name was first spelled as two words; e.g., White Hall. The post office opened in 1869 with Edward Brooke as postmaster. Before that the area was served by the Milk Ranch office. "In January 1926, Dad bid in the second trick at **Whitehall**, located forty miles east of Butte," wrote Chet Huntley in *The Generous Years*. "Consequently, my secondary education . . . was derived in **Whitehall** High School. . . . **Whitehall** was a Butte satellite . . . during the summers, **Whitehall** youngsters frequently worked in the copper mines . . . but I always found employment on a ranch."

White Pine (Sanders) is on the highway north of Thompson Falls. It was named for the trees surrounding it and for White Pine Creek. The nearby station on the Northern Pacific is called "Childs" and serves as a shipping point for the Jack Waite Mine. **White Pine** had a post office from 1903-1965; Paul McCarthy was the first postmaster.

Whites, White City (Broadwater) was an old mining town in Broadwater County during the frantic gold rush days of the 1870s. A post office operated at **White City** 1875-1909; after that the mail was routed to Canyon Ferry. All that remains is a little marker with the inscription:

This is the site of **White's City**,
population in 1875, 15,000 souls.

WHITE SULPHUR SPRINGS (Meagher) is the county seat and was one of the original counties in Montana. **White Sulphur Springs** was the headquarters for a county that included most of central Montana. The town was named because of the white deposits around the hot sulphur springs that were found there. The Indians used to come great distances to use the medicinal waters from these springs. Many white people have followed their example. The place was first called **Brewer Springs** because it was James Brewer who started a resort there and claimed that the water had the same chemical content as Baden Baden Spa in Germany. This Smith River Valley with **White Sulphur Springs** as its trading center was once the home of buffalo, later of prospectors working the Castle Mountain lead and silver mines, and since the days of Fort Logan has been famous for its fine cattle. Henry Brainerd was appointed postmaster when the office opened in 1876.

Whitetail (Daniels) is seven miles from the Big Beaver port of entry into Canada. The post office was established in 1911 with Wade Dunn as postmaster. Presumably it was named for the native whitetail deer.

WHITE WATER (Phillips) is named for Whitewater Creek, which runs through town. The creek gets its name from the milky look of its water. A few miles to the south it runs into the Milk River, where the whitish coloring is even more pronounced. **White Water** is in the northern part of the county, sixteen miles from the Morgan port of entry into Canada. The post office opened in 1912 with Severt Simonson as postmaster.

WHITLASH (Liberty) is a port of entry at the Canadian border. The post office was established in 1892 with George Bourne as postmaster.

Whitney (Prairie) was named for its location on Whitney Creek. The post office opened in 1899 with Charles Boulter as postmaster, and was active most of the time from then until 1921, when the postal service for this area was transferred to Mildred. An active community club had as its motto, "Whitney Creek, the Garden Spot of Montana, where crops do grow." The first club meetings were held in the schoolhouse. Then Mr. Faus suggested they build a hall and each man contributed fifty dollars in cash or labor. The first picnic was held there June 16, 1915. They set up lemonade and hot dog stands, sold candy, had a baseball game, and a dance that night. The club cleared $1200, which not only paid the lumber bill, but also bought a piano and opera chairs (*Wheels Across Montana Prairies*).

Whoop-Up Trail In 1870 the U.S. Government outlawed selling whiskey to the Indians. The marshals and their deputies set out to see that the law was respected. Fur traders regarded whiskey as the first requisite of their business. Where whiskey was, there the trade was, so they built posts in less restricted territory across the Canadian border.

One of the first of these trading posts was built by Captain John Healy and A.B. Hamilton at the confluence of the St. Mary and Belly Rivers eight miles from where Lethbridge now stands. It was named **Fort Hamilton** but flourishing business soon led to its rechristening as **Fort Whoop-up**. So the north country came to be known as Whoop-up country and the 230 mile trail that led from there to Fort Benton was called the **Whoop-up Trail**. Freight trains pulled by oxen or mules with crews of bull whackers and mule skinners took the furs and whiskey to the trading posts in Canada.

The trade continued to "whoop it up" until 1874. Then Fort MacLeod was built by the Royal Mounted Police on Oldman's River 28 miles from **Fort Whoop-up**. The Mounties put an end to the traffic. Today, only those who know where to look can trace its route in faint, broken scars on stretches of virgin prairie between Fort Benton and MacLeod, Alberta. (Harry Stanford, *Great Falls Tribune*, May 1, 1932). For a few years after the whiskey traffic was stopped, the trail continued to be used as a supply route between Fort Benton and Canada.

Whoop-up Country, a book written by Paul F. Sharp, was first published in 1955 and has gone into two more editions. "The trail provides Sharp the vehicle by which he explores and explains the varied economic, cultural and political manifestations of this buffalo region. Fur men, whiskey traders, bullwackers, buffalo robe and wolf hunters, cattlemen, cavalrymen and red-coated Canadian Mounties people the saga, as do the Blackfeet, Assiniboine and Gros Ventre." (Review by I.D. Hampton) Locale for *Danger Trail*, a recent book of fiction by Robert McCaig, is the **Whoop-Up Trail** of 100 years ago as the Circle C wagons got their freight through despite a desperate battle with hired guns. History and fiction keep alive the story of the **Whoop-up Trail.**

WIBAUX (Wibaux) (pronounced WEE-boh) is a county seat named for Pierre Wibaux, a Huguenot who came to eastern Montana, liked it, and stayed. Wibaux became one of the largest cattlemen in the state, making a fortune during the hard winter of 1890 by buying cattle at bargain prices at a time when many stockmen were forced to sell. His own herd had been wiped out during the blizzards of 1886-87, but he got more financial backing from French investors and eventually built his herd up to 75,000 head. His humor and sagacity are remembered in many legends. The **Wibaux** post office was established in January 1895 with Luther Allen as postmaster. The place had first been callled Keith and later Mingusville; the present name was chosen in 1895.

Wibaux County (pronounced WEE-boh) is a small county along the North Dakota line. Contemporary maps show only two towns in the county besides the county seat, Wibaux. The Northern Pacific Railroad crosses the narrowest part of the county, and Beaver Creek runs its entire length. The county was named for Pierre Wibaux (see **Wibaux**) and was organized in 1914 from parts of Dawson, Fallon, and Richland counties; a part of **Wibaux County** was annexed to Fallon in 1919, and a part of Fallon was annexed to **Wibaux County** the same year.

Wickes (Jefferson) was a station on the railroad and named for W. W. Wickes, engineer and promoter of the Alta Mining Company. The post office opened in 1878 with Ezekial Dean as postmaster. It was discontinued in 1964.

Wilborn (Lewis and Clark) was named for William Wilborn. Postal records indicate a post office opened in 1908 with Ruth Bradley as postmaster, and the very next entry shows Ruth Wilborn as postmaster. Maybe she married William.

Wilder (Fergus) had a post office 1886-1939. Robert Richie was the first postmaster. This town was named for Amhert H. Wilder, a St. Paul, Minnesota businessman who was a partner in many of the Montana enterprises of C. A. Broadwater. **Wilder** was on the Missouri River about fifteen miles above and on the south side of the Musselshell (Montana Historical Society Library). There was also a station on the Great Northern railway between Butte and Helena in Jefferson County named **Wilder**, named after one of Broadwater's daughters who, in turn, had been named after Wilder.

Wilder's Landing was the name sometimes given to Rocky Point, a Missouri River settlement. Fred Whiteside's journal records an election held there in November 1878. A gunnysack was nailed to a log in a log building to serve as the ballot box. One candidate's sign on the whiskey keg read:

> Have a drink with Tom Irvine, Democrat for Sheriff,
> and vote as you damn please.

Whiteside and 120 others cast their votes and were surprised to read in the election returns that **Wilder's Landing** had cast four hundred votes for Tom Irvine (Montana Post).

WILLARD (Fallon) is south of Baker. The present townsite was once the home range of the 101 Ranch, established by the Standard Cattle Company of Texas in 1888. Longhorns were brought in from Texas in herds of three to four thousand head, summered and fattened at **Willard**, then driven fifty miles to Wibaux for shipment to Chicago markets. In an autograph letter dated July 24, 1944, Fred W. Anderson of Kirkhoven, Minnesota, relates the town's name history: "I was one of fifteen who came from the same community in Seif County, Minnesota, and homesteaded in the **Willard** community. My homestead happened to be located on the road to Ekalaka. As soon as we landed with our first carload of goods, the businessmen of Baker were after me to take the post office on my claim and told me to name it. I took my middle name, Willard, and so it was named and opened in 1910. I had the post office for fourteen years before I sold out to C. J. Anderson. I also had a store in connection with it."

Williams (Park) was in old Gallatin County when a post office operated briefly from January-April 1887; Henry Williams was the postmaster.

Williams (Pondera) is a ghost town on the Lake Frances Reservoir Project. It was named for William Cargill who purchased the Conrad Investment Company from W. G. Conrad (Floersinger). **Williams** had a post office from 1910-1958; Cloie Evans was the first postmaster. In the very early days this was a stopping place on the Fort MacLeod trail.

Willis (Beaverhead) was originally called **Willis Station**. A post office under that name operated there from October 1878-Januay 1879. The **Willis** name was used from 1880 on. Ozias Willis was the postmaster and ran the stage station. The name of the town was eventually changed to Reichle in 1913. Later still the postal service for this area was centered at Glen where the railroad station was built.

Willow Creek (Gallatin) was named for the creek on which it is located, and the creek was named for the many willows along its banks. The first pioneers arrived in the area in 1864, among them the Green, Tinsley, Williams, Smart, and Hale families. The Reverend Lerner Statler, a Methodist minister, and his wife arrived the same year. Each of them had driven a covered wagon and the Statlers joined up with a Jim Bridger caravan for protection against the Indians. A small frame church was built in **Willow Creek** and Mr. Statler served the area from there to Virginia City, averaging 200 miles a week for the 30 the thirty years he was there. When he was off preaching, Mrs. Statler milked six cows and made butter to sell.

School was first held in the log cabin home of the Greens, who had seven children of their own and hired the teacher. In 1867 a school district was organized and a schoolhouse was built.

The post office opened in 1867 with Richard Reeves as postmaster. Later the office was moved to Ben Wells' store and he became postmaster in 1873. The mail came through by stagecoach between Helena and Bozeman and on to Virginia City and Bannack.

When the Northern Pacific Railroad came through the valley about 1882, the community was moved to its present location. The Jack Cooper ranch is now on the original townsite.

Willowglen (Deer Lodge) had a post office 1882-85 with John Eardley as postmaster. After that the mail was dispensed at Anaconda.

Willow Rounds (Pondera), the oldest white settlement in the county, was named by Indians for the willow-circled parks near the Marias River. For centuries this was a winter campsite for the Piegans, so it was selected as the site for the first fur trading post above the mouth of the river in 1848; Augustin Armell built the post. Later it was a stopping place on the Healy Trail between Fort Shaw and Canada's Fort MacLeod.

Willow Springs (Meagher) had a post office April-August 1892 with Herbert James as postmaster.

Will's Creek (Fallon) had a post office established in 1910 with Reuben Yates as postmaster. The office was discontinued in 1917.

Wilma (Granite) had a post office opened in 1903 with Thomas Parks in charge. The office was closed in 1905 and the mail was sent to Philipsburg.

WILSALL (Park) began as the terminus of a Northern Pacific spur line. The community, which is on Shields Creek, was laid out by Walter B. Jordan, who combined the names of his son Will, and his daughter-in-law Sally, to coin the town's name. The post office opened in 1910 with Albert Culbertson as postmaster.

Wilson (Cascade) had a post office 1910-14. John Johnson was the first postmaster.

Windham (Judith Basin) was named for the Vermont home (Windham County) of Leslie Hamilton, who owned the Sage Creek Ranch near **Windham**. The first choice for a name was Hamilton, after L. H. Hamilton, who came to the Sage Creek Valley in 1880 and began a large sheep and farming operation. But there was all ready a town by that name. The post office was established in 1907 with Leona Miner in charge. In 1910 William Peters was appointed postmaster. The office was made a rural station out of Stanford in 1966. When the railroad came through in 1907, Hamilton and others laid out the town. "Duncan Gillespie and his drug store spanned the periods of growth and decline in **Windham**. The homesteaders, the rail-roaders, and coal miners from nearby Lehigh boomed the town for awhile. Mike and Fred Reed promoted rodeos. Now the town is about gone, but productive grain and cattle ranches surround it" (Byerly).

Windville (Gallatin) had a post office very briefly, August-December 1881 with George Hutchinson as postmaster. The name seems to indicate it was located in a very windy area around Livingston.

WINIFRED (Fergus) is a small town along Dog Creek north of Lewiston. It began as a railway station. Some say it was named for Winifred Sewall, the daughter of E. D. Sewall, but most authorities insist it was named for Winifred Rockefeller, the daughter of Percy Rockefeller. The post office opened in 1913 with Laurence Porter as postmaster. An old map shows the area around **Winifred** platted into seventeen townships of 712 square miles, bordered on the north by the Missouri River. Homesteads of 160 acres were laid out and about a thousand families proved up on them, struggled for a few years, then gave up. The northern half of this area now contains about twenty-five productive ranches, and natural gas seems to be a promise for the future. **Winifred** continues to be an active town, with churches, schools, community clubs, and beautiful scenery (Byerly).

Winnecook (Wheatland) had a post office 1885-1897 and 1901-33. The first postmaster was Ralph Berry.

WINNETT (Petroleum), a county seat, was named for Walter John Winnett, who was born in the Crystal Palace — now Queen's Hotel — in Toronto. Winnett ran away from home as a boy, seeking adventure in "Indian country." His excellent marksmanship abilities helped him get jobs with outfits who were always looking for someone who could keep them in fresh meat. When he was captured by the Sioux Indians and later adopted into the tribe, he was given the name Eagle Eyes because of his remarkable shooting skills. Winnett established a ranch in Montana Territory in 1879 near an active trading post and the Hangman's Tree used by vigilantes in the area. The massive ranch house, which he built in 1900, housed his own family and served as a gathering place for the community. Dances, weddings, funerals, church services, and school were all held here. Billings was the closest town, so Winnett built up a freight line business to haul supplies. Each of his outfits consisted of ten to twenty horses and huge wagons. In 1910 he built a store and petitioned for a post office — and with that, **Winnett** became an official town. John Hughes was the first postmaster. By 1913 the railroad had reached Grass Range and supplies were subsequently hauled from there. Ed Fleury, Winnett's best driver, was a half-breed Indian who could handle thirty-two horses with a jerkline. Winnett also built the Log Cabin Saloon, because his many ranch hands and freight wagon drivers kept stealing horses out of his barn to ride over to Grass Range to get a drink — he figured it would be a lot easier on his horses to have a saloon close at hand. When the the land was opened for homesteading in 1914, dry land farmers poured in. The few that stuck it out through the dust storms, drought, and grasshoppers of 1917-20 saw the parched land yield black gold and the town boom when the Cat Creek oil wells gushed following the 1919 drillings (Mirth Winnet Kiehl, *Winnett Times*). Rudy Glatz, the venerable editor of the *Winnett Times*, has continued to keep the town and the county informed and entertained.

Winston (Broadwater) is between Townsend and Helena. Among the early settlers there was the Beatty family, ancestors of Norma Beatty Ashby, who currently hosts "Today in Montana," a statewide television program. **Winston** began with Fred Goudy's Saloon, which was followed by the Duncan Hotel, a combined restaurant and rooming house. The Duncans worked to promote the town after it was platted by the Northern Pacific Railroad, and farmers and ranchers settled the area. The Dodge brothers operated a rooming house in a rock building that still stands, though deserted and crumbling. Mines in the area were active 1908-18 and 1926-28, producing gold, silver, copper and lead. The biggest mine was the East Pacific, which was almost a town in itself, with shops, offices, two saloons, and a three-story bunkhouse for 150 workers. This place was sometimes referred to as Eagle City (Barbara Baum in *Broadwater Bygones*).

The post office was established in 1892 with Warren Dodge as postmaster, but another record shows George Lamb in the position — annual compensation, $304.21. **Winston** was named during the railroad-building days for P. B. Winston, a contractor for the NP. Previously the area was known as Placer; the depot known by that name was loaded on a flatcar and moved to **Winston**. There was also a railroad siding and community near here called Beaver Creek and later, Placer.

One of the very first settlers around **Winston** was George Beatty. He was a young New York man who was "doomed to die" — presumably from tuberculosis — who set out for Montana in the 1860s, hoping the mountain air would add a year or two to his life. He even brought his tombstone with him, and carved on it:

> My mother's prayers kept me out of Hell.
> Thank God for a blessed hope beyond the grave.

Beatty stored the tombstone in a back shed and when he died — at age ninety-two — they put it on his grave in Helena, where it can still be seen.

Wint (Fergus) was a post office 1915-17 with Mae Meadors as postmaster. After that the postal area was known as Novary.

Wiota (Valley) was originally named Milk River. The name was changed in 1910 when a post office was granted — it is an Indian word meaning "many snows." The office was discontinued in 1912 and the mail was sent to Nashua. William Ivey was the first postmaster.

WISDOM (Beaverhead) was named for the Wisdom (now the Big Hole) River that flows through the town. In 1805 Lewis and Clark, at the confluence of the tributaries of the Jefferson River near the present site of Twin Bridges, decided to name the three streams for the three "cardinal virtues" of their President and benefactor, Thomas Jefferson. But Philosophy, Philanthropy and Wisdom proved to be too much for later settlers, who changed the names to the Big Hole, Beaverhead, and Ruby. But the town kept the name **Wisdom** and later, a nearby waterway was named the Wise River. The other two virutes seem to have been lost entirely in the renaming process. The **Wisdom** post office was established in 1884 at the William Geery ranch four miles from the present townsite. James Gerry was postmaster. The office was moved to the Noyes ranch when Mrs. Noyes was appointed postmaster; then Minnie Ballard took the job and moved the office to her ranch; and later it was located at the ranch of George Stewart — all before it finally settled in its present location. The name of Noyes was considered for the town, but it had too much of a resemblance to the name Norris. The settlement was originally called Crossings.

Wise River (Beaverhead), in the extreme northern part of the county, is located where the Wise River flows into the Big Hole. Since the Big Hole was originally named the Wisdom River, it is possible the tributary's name was derived from it. The post office opened in 1913 with Ellen Pyle as postmaster.

Withee was a siding on the Great Northern south of Conrad and was named for Ted Withee, an associate of the Cargills in the Valier Land and Water Company (Floerchinger).

Wold (Dawson) was named for first postmaster Richard Wold. The office was open 1909-12 and the mail was later sent to Bloomfield.

Wolf Butte (Judith Basin) is a mountain near Stanford which was an important landmark on the overland trail from Billings to Great Falls. And even before that, it was well known as the site of Indian signal fires. A. V. and Melvin Cheney bought ranches and settled at the foot of **Wolf Butte** in 1902. Many stone tepee rings were uncovered when the fields were plowed. The Cheneys also found arrowheads, pemmican hammers, and hieroglyphs on canyon walls.

WOLF CREEK (Lewis and Clark) is north of Helena and an important recreation center which includes a general store, service stations and tourist courts. It was named for the large creek that flows by it, and is derived from the Indian phrase, "Creek - Where - the - Wolf - Jumped - Too" (Rowe). However, *Montana, A Guide Book* spells the last word "to," which gives an entirely different picture of the incident which apparently prompted the

Indians to choose such a name. Files of the Great Northern Railroad give the name origin as "Creek - That - The - Wolf - Jumped - In." Regardless of what the wolf did, he left his stamp on a rushing mountain stream and a town. A post office under the name **Wolf Creek** was opened in 1888 with George Houghton as postmaster. The settlement was first called Carterville.

Wolfdene (Meagher) had a post office January-May 1881 with John Woodhurst as postmaster. Perhaps the name was meant to be Wolf Den.

WOLF POINT (Roosevelt) is a county seat in the northeastern part of the state where Wolf Creek flows in the Missouri River. An old trading post was established here in fur trading days which later developed into a cow town as the herds were trailed in. The most generally accepted version concerning the naming of the town is the one related by old trappers: One winter a party of wolfers — who made up the lowest rung of the social ladder in frontier life — captured several hundred grey wolves in very cold weather. They hauled the carcasses into camp and stacked the frozen wolves in huge piles, facing the river where the steamboats came in — the grisly mound of wolves gave the town its name (Willard). Bill Bent, whose father established Bents Fort on the Arkansas, says, "The point received its name from a large number of wolves piled up by Charlie Conklin and two other fellows, but the Indians came, and they never got to skin them" (A. J. Noyes, *The Story of Blaine County*). A post office was established in Wolf Point in 1882 with Charles Aubrey as postmaster.

Wolfspring (Yellowstone) had a post office 1904-06 with Irvin Wood as postmaster.

Wolsey (Meagher), near White Sulphur Springs, had a post office established 1891 with William Woolsey as postmaster. Postal officials must have dropped an "o" from the name when they recorded the office. It closed in 1915.

Wood Coulee (Blaine) had a post office 1914-21 except for February 1917-March 1918. The first postmaster was Olaf Isfeld, and when the office closed in 1921 the mail was sent to Zurich.

Woodman (Missoula), near Lolo, had a post office established in 1898 with Frank Bradley as postmaster. Except for 1907-08 the office was active until 1918, when it was discontinued.

Woodrow (Dawson), near Lindsay, had a post office in 1913 with Amy Nye as first postmaster. Like so many other eastern Montana offices, this one spanned the homestead years. It closed in 1930.

Woods Bay (Lake) was approved for a post office in 1950. Juanita Micken was to have been postmaster, but the order was rescinded the following year.

Woodside (Ravalli) had a post office 1890-1938. Lambert Wood was the first postmaster.

Woodville (Jefferson) had a post office open in 1882 with Thomas Wright as postmaster. The mail was sent to Meaderville when the office closed in 1912.

Woodworth (Missoula) was in old Deer Lodge County when the post office was approved in 1889. It was named for Chauncey Woodworth, the first postmaster, and was active until 1945.

Woody (Dawson) was to have been the name of a post office approved in 1901 with Mack Hunter to be in charge. But the order was rescinded the following year.

Wooldridge (Valley) was probably named for the Wooldridge family that lived in the area. The post office opened in July 1910. The postal area was changed to Bowdoin and the **Wooldridge** office closed in 1917.

WORDEN (Yellowstone) was named for Sen. Joseph Dixon's wife, whose maiden name was Worden, and possibly for her father as well, who was a prominent Montanan. The post office was established in 1910 with William Dodds in charge. The land surrounding **Worden** has been richly productive ever since the Huntley Irrigation Project brought water to it.

Wordensville (Missoula) was the name sometimes applied to Hell Gate. Worden and Higgins had a general merchandise business there in one of the state's first commercial buildings (see **Missoula**).

Works (Blaine), near Cleveland, had a post office 1915-17 with Henry Jess, Jr. as postmaster.

Wormser (Sweet Grass) was named for a wealthy man named Wormser who came to the area to establish a settlement for Dutch immigrants. Though he built a large house on Big Timber Creek he mismanaged things so badly that he went broke. The **Wormser** post office opened in 1896 with Arnold Onwersloot as postmaster. It was discontinued in 1903.

WYOLA (Big Horn), ten miles from Wyoming on the Little Big Horn River and the Crow Indian Reservation, is a shipping point for cattle from valley ranches. The post office was established in 1911 with Robert Colvard as first postmaster.

X

Xenia (Hill) was a station on the Great Northern between Kremlin and Gildford. Residents of **Xenia** got their mail at Fort Assiniboine.

Y

Yaak (Lincoln), the most northwestly town in Montana, was named for the nearby Yaak River. *Yaak* is an Indian word meaning "arrow," and this river cuts like an arrow across the bow of the Kootenai River in northwest Montana and Canada. The post office was established in 1914 with Charles B. Weber as postmaster; the office closed in 1917 and was open again 1920-53.

Yakt (Flathead), a Great Northern station, is almost on the Idaho border. The post office opened in 1920 with Phoebe Lang as postmaster and closed in 1949.

Yale (Wheatland) was a railroad station first called Hedges, but the post office which opened at the Hedges ranch (Ida Hedges, postmaster) was named **Yale**. In 1910 both the office — which by then had moved to town — and the station were officially named Hedgesville.

Yankee Jim Canyon (Park) "For over a quarter century, Yankee Jim made his living from the toll road that still bears his name and from the roadhouse hotel that was the only stopping place for travelers into the mining area and through the upper Yellowstone Valley. He carved out a crude, makeshift wagon road along the rocky cliff ledge which was the only available pass. His road opened the upper Yellowstone Valley to wagon travel, where prospectors with pack animals had located gold quartz and veins of coal. . . . Yankee Jim enjoyed the complete domination of the area and this entrance to Yellowstone Park until the Northern Pacific Railroad started building their branch line up the valley from Livingston in 1883. When they came to his tollroad, Yankee Jim was there to meet them with his old .50-caliber buffalo gun. After much dickering and many bitter words, a right-of-way was agreed upon for a specified sum. The railroad tracks utilized most of Yankee Jim's toll road through the canyon.

"But Yankee Jim never forgave this intrusion of his private domain. Even twenty years later, every day when the train went by, he could be seen, his white beard and hair flying in the wind, shaking his fist and uttering choice cuss words at the engineer" (*Footprints Along the Yellowstone*).

Yantic (Blaine) was a station on the Great Northern where the railroad crosses Clear Creek. A post office operated 1889-97 with Robert Main as first postmaster; after that the mail was handled in Chinook.

Yarnell (Lincoln) was a Great Northern station on the Kootenai River.

Yates (Wibaux) began as a Northern Pacific station. A post office was open 1908-20; William Oleson was the first postmaster.

Yegen (Fergus) began as a railroad station and was named for the Yegen brothers, who were Swiss immigrants. They began life in Montana as sheepherders, later operated a store in **Yegen**, and finally became prominent sheepmen and bankers in central Montana.

Yellowstone (Yellowstone) had a post office 1886-87 with William Bracken as postmaster.

Yellowstone City (Park) was a short-lived mining town near Emigrant Gulch. A strike was made here in 1864. Supplies had to be brought in from Virginia City. There were about 300 people, fifteen of them women who stuck out the winter and watched their property to keep it safe from claim jumpers. The mines were worked the following summer, but they proved to be of minor importance; people started leaving in the fall and by 1866 it was deserted (Wolle). The camp was named for its location on the Yellowstone River.

Yellowstone County is in the south central part of the state and is one of Montana's most populous counties. Billings is the county seat. The name was first given to the river, which French trappers called *Roche Jaune*, or "yellow rock." **Yellowstone County** was organized in 1883 from a part of Custer County; parts of it were taken to help form Carbon and Sweet Grass counties in 1885, Musselshell in 1911, and Big Horn and

Stillwater in 1913; in 1919 and 1925 **Yellowstone** and Carbon counties annexed parts of each other.

Yellowstone Crossing (Gallatin) A post office with this name was established in 1874 with Hugh Hoppy the postmaster; it was closed the following year. In 1883 the nearby Riverside office was moved to Yellowstone and in 1920 the name was changed to West Yellowstone. These several variations on the same name and the slightly different locations all served a singular purpose — to furnish some kind of postal service to the area just west of Yellowstone National Park.

Yemen (Chouteau) had a post office 1892-93 with Charles Lacy in charge. It was near Fort Benton and was formerly called Shepherd.

Ynot (Phillips) had a post office 1917-31 with Mary McMullen as postmaster. It was near White Water.

Yogo (Judith Basin) began as a prosperous gold mining camp located on the eastern slope of the Little Belt Mountains. When the gold played out, minerals of lesser value were mined and taken by horse freight team to Armington, where they were shipped to the Great Falls smelter. The old freight rail ran along Upper Wolf Creek and Surprise Creek, then along Lone Tree Creek towards Geyser. **Yogo** was the home of "Black Millie," who came to Montana as a nurse for the family of an Army officer. For some reason she wandered over to the diggings at **Yogo** and settled, where she became famous for her excellent cooking and the table she set for boarders, always spread with a white linen cloth. When the mines were closed and the miners had moved on to richer fields, Millie found herself alone with her empty table. The Great Falls sheriff (at that time **Yogo** was in Cascade County) came and took her to a poor farm, but she was unhappy there, and eventually she wandered back to **Yogo** and her little cabin in the hills. There — so the legend goes — she spread her table each day with a spotless, white linen cloth and waited for the miners who never returned (Elizabeth Cheney).

However, in later years, there was a rebirth of activity in the **Yogo** mines. The first post office was in a little log cabin of postmaster Emmett Carroll. The office operated 1890-92 and 1894-95, and the mines were reopened around 1930. But in 1933 Charles T. Gadsden, the resident manager for the New Mine Sapphire Syndicate, wrote from "Yogo Mines, Montana: . . . I know of only one man who would be in a position to buy the Mine. . . . I explained to him that any reasonable offer would be submitted to the shareholders and I would like to see the property all kept in one block so that it would be possible for it to be worked again someday for the good of the surrounding country. . . . I was unable to pay this last installment of the 1932 taxes."

Yogo sapphires are world-famous for their superior cornflower-blue color and high brilliance; gemologists consider them to be the standard by which sapphires the world over are judged. However, they are ordinarily mined in such small sizes that they are used industrially more often than for jewelry.

The name Yogo was also given to a mountain, Yogo Baldy, and is still used frequently throughout Montana, but the origin of the name is unknown.

York (Lewis and Clark) was a mining camp a few miles north of Canyon Ferry. The post office opened in 1887 with Henry Kincaid as postmaster; it was discontinued in 1917 and the mail was then handled at Nelson. **York** was named for New York City; a nearby camp was called Brooklyn.

Younger (Rosebud) had a post office opened in 1886 with Charles Younger as postmaster. In December 1888 the postal area name was changed to Basinski.

Young's Point (Stillwater) was a landing point for boats that came up the Yellowstone River. Alonzo Young, who ran a boat landing here, was appointed postmaster when the office opened in 1878. In 1882 the office moved to Park City, on the railroad.

Yreka (Powell), near Beartown, had a post office 1871-82; William Ferguson was the first postmaster.

Z

Zenon (Phillips) had a post office established in 1916 with Alphonse Durocher as postmaster; it was discontinued in 1919 and mail was served out of Phillips.

Zero (Prairie), south of Terry, had a post office under this name in 1915; Gotlieb Kalfell was appointed postmaster. **Zero** was built around the facilities of the Northern Pacific depot, consisting of a depot, water tank, and coal dock. Passenger cars and converted box cars were used for living quarters. There was also a pumping plant and pumper's house by the river. Coal and ice were free, but water had to be brought in by train. The station was later called Benz (*Wheels Across Montana's Prairies*). This community was originally called Blatchford; a post office by that name opened in 1885. When the name changed, Kalfell just moved his office to his ranch, where it stayed until 1918. That same year James Collins, the NP pumper, became postmaster and moved the office to the pumphouse, where it remained, even after Collins was killed in an accident in 1920. The new pumper distributed the mail until 1926, when Fannie Galbraith took over the job and moved the office to her store. In 1932 the office was moved to the Erny home, where it occupied a corner of the living room and later a corner of the closed-in front porch. Discarded boxes from the Terry office served patrons at **Zero**. When the office finally closed in 1957, it had served the area for seventy years. This story of a much-moved post office is typical of many 19th Century Montana farm communities. The reason for the 1915 name change to **Zero** is not known.

Zortman (Phillips) is in a little patch of forest in the Little Rocky Mountains. It was named for Pete Zortman, who ran a mine in Alder Gulch. After Fort Browning was completed, the construction workers found themselves out of a job, so many went prospecting in the nearby hills. Area mines flourished in the early 1900s and there was profitable gold production from this town until 1903, when the Zortman Cyanide Mill was completed and the mining activity changed. In the same year a post office was established with Susan Brown as postmaster. The second largest cyanide mill in the world was once in the gulch above **Zortman**. After gold was discovered in 1864 this area, which also included Landusky and

Beaver Creek mines, produced some $25 million in gold. Most of the mines closed during World War II and the last one shut down in 1949. Though the town started to fade after that, it has since gained a new lease on life as a tourist attraction. Its historic past, superb scenery, and modern accommodations — plus the promise of renewed mining activity — are once again attracting people to **Zortman** (Byerly).

Zosel (Deer Lodge) had a brief postal career with an office 1892-93; the postmaster was Wiley Mountjoy.

Zuley (Fergus) was named for Adam Zuley, the first postmaster. The office was open 1915-18 and the mail was then handled at Roy.

ZURICH (Blaine), on the High Line between Harlem and Chinook, was named for the famous Swiss mountain city (Willard). It was here, along the Milk River, that westbound travelers got their first look at the Bear Paw Mountains to the southwest. The post office opened in 1907 with John Archer as postmaster.

Mountains

Montana was named for her mountains. They have been a major influence in her history and her economy. The Continental Divide was the greatest challenge to explorers who sought a passage to the Pacific; prospectors and miners rushed into take the rich minerals from the hills; and the snow-capped peaks have fed the life-giving streams for agriculture.

The main range of the Rocky Mountains was first called "Shining Mountains" by Lewis and Clark. The sobriquet of "Land of the Shining Mountains" was for a long time applied to the state. Later Montana was called the "Treasure State" because of the mineral deposits in her mountains. **Rocky Mountains** is an appropriate name for rocky they certainly are.

Lesser ranges bear a variety of names, some in honor of men, but many more describe a natural feature. The **Mineral Range** in the western county by the same name; the **Sapphire Mountains** between Missoula and Deer Lodge; the **Ruby Range** in Madison County (though the stones were really garnets); the **Granite Mountains** near Philipsburg; and the **Cinnabar Mountains** north of Yellowstone Park were named for the ore they contained.

Beartooth Range in Stillwater County has tall white limestone cliffs that reminded the early day explorers and settlers of the teeth of one of their animal adversaries. The **Wolf Mountains** in southern Montana, the **Big Horns** that cross the state line into Wyoming, and the **Whitefish Range** are other animal origin names. A scrubby, stocky pine tree grew on the slopes of the mountains in Musselshell County and was called "Bull Pine." From that the name of **Bull Mountains** evolved.

Tobacco Root Mountains in Madison County were named for a plant that grew there. The **Rosebuds** honor one of Montana's most abundant native flowers.

The Mission Range, rising like a vast blue wall in the Flathead Lake region and ending north of Missoula, takes its name from St. Mary's Mission. One ridge behind **Troy** is called **Preacher Mountain** because a Methodist minister from England borrowed a gun to go hunting there in 1895. The gun was found the next day leaning on a tree, but nothing was ever found of the preacher. In the Bob Marshall Wilderness area is a fifteen mile long escarpment that rises 1000 feet in sheer cliffs and is called the **Chinese Wall.** Glacier Park, containing mountains of ice, is aptly named for them. The **Castle Mountains** are made up of unusual rock formations that viewed from some angles look like castles on the mountain top.

The story behind the name for the **Crazy Mountains** in Park, Meagher, and Sweet Grass Counties is told in the Montana Guidebook: "The sharp, rugged **Crazy Mountains** glittering in the clear air are an isolated and geologically young range; they form an almost incredibly jagged upthrust of rock more than 11,000 feet high. Before white men ever saw them, Indians knew them as the **Mad Mountains,** feared and avoided them. Their terrifying steepness, their awe-inspiring structure and the demoniac winds that blow continually out of their strange canyons impressed white men as much as it had their coppery brethren, though with less superstitious awe. The epither 'Mad' became the more familiar 'Crazy.' The weird range is rarely visited."

The **Judith Mountains**, like the river and the county, owes its name to Meriwether Lewis' girl friend, and the **Pryor Mountains**, to a member of the

Lewis and Clark expedition. **Gallatin** and **Bridger Ranges**, like the county and town, were named indirectly for men. The first postmaster, Emmett Swan, helped secure a post office for the little community near a beautiful lake. Later the lake and a mountain range were also given his name.

Lesser mountains and individual peaks have interesting and descriptive names, but they are as numerous as the towns and can only be sampled here. **Mount Jumbo**, behind the University of Montana campus, viewed from certain angles looks like a huge elephant. During the later 1870s Barnum had a circus elephant named "Jumbo" who was billed as the largest one in captivity. The Indian name for this mountain was **Si nim koo** meaning in Salish "big bump or something in the way." Next to it is **Mount Sentinel** which also had an Indian name, **Eshmock**, indicating a high point or look out. The **Flathead Range** takes its name from the tribe of Indians native to the area.

The **Belt Mountains** and the **Little Belts** owe their name origin to an unusual rock formation that seems to encircle one part of the mountain as it is seen from the town of **Belt**.

The **Cabinet Mountains** are in northwestern Montana. The Oregon Steam Navigation Company began operations in 1862 as the **Mary Moody** came up the Clark's Fork River to Cabinet Landing just inside the Montana border. This was the first steamboat that navigated waters of western Montana. The next boat, **The Cabinet**, came up the Clark's Fork and ran from the upper end of Cabinet Falls to the Rapids at Rock Island. The river boats did a profitable business for two or three years.

As Stephen Douglas concluded, after much debate about a name for the territory, the Spanish word "montana" meaning a mountainous country did "suit" that land up north.

301

Rivers

Rivers were the first highways and the first freightways of Montana, great landmarks appearing on the earliest maps that guided explorers and trappers through the wilderness. The first names given to the rivers came from the Indians as they described their hunting grounds, so most had a name before there was a town or even a fort.

The giant of them all is the **Missouri**. Explorers entered Montana riding its waters, and from its tributaries discovered the rest of the state. Although the **Missouri River** did not take Lewis and Clark to West Coast as they had hoped, its headwaters nevertheless led them over the Continental Divide and into a land where the waters merged with the Columbia, and thence to the Pacific. The **Missouri** was used by Indians long before the white man came, and each tribe had its own name for the big river. The Gros Ventres called it *Amahte Arzzha*, or "The River That Scolds All Others" according to *Montana, A State Guide Book*. Other historians claim that phrase was used to describe the Marias River. White men had trouble pronouncing Indian words and simplifed the name to **Missouri**. J. P. Rowe says the name came from an Indian word meaning "muddy waters," and Senator Engalls' famous comment that "Its waters are a little too thick for a beverage and a little too thin to farm," would bear out this description. It has also been claimed that the **Missouri** was named for a Sioux tribe living near the river called by Illinois Indians *Emessourite*, meaning "dwellers on the Big Muddy." On early French maps, the name is given severally as *Emossouritsu*, *Oumossourits*, and *Le Missouri de R. de Pekatenoui*.

From the **Missouri River** explorers and fur traders branched off to follow the **Yellowstone** through the southern part of Montana. The name is a translation from the French *Roche Jaune*, meaning "yellow rock." Annin says that local Indians called it the Elk River. Many early trading posts were established along the **Yellowstone River** and its tributaries. A steamboat from St. Louis named the Yellowstone arrived at the junction of the **Missouri** and **Yellowstone** rivers on June 17, 1832, the first boat to come that far up the **Missouri**. Supplies were brought in and furs were taken back to the states on these riverboats.

The three major tributaries of the **Yellowstone**, the **Big Horn**, the **Tongue**, and the **Powder River**, drain the southeast corner of Montana. The **Big Horn** was named by Lewis and Clark in honor of the remarkable mountain animal they had discovered. The **Tongue River** was named by Indians because of the peculiar, but very definite, tongue-like formation on the mountain in Wyoming whose springs form the headwaters of the river. For years people have said that the **Powder River** took its name from the dark gunpowder-colored soil and sand along its banks. Capt. William Drannan, in *Thirty-One Years on the Plains and in the Mountains*, writes that once in 1841, when the Army and its scouts were some four hundred miles from Bent's Fort, they came under a sudden Indian attack. A Frenchman named Vierre Roubidoux yelled, "Cache la Poudre!" or, "Hide the powder!" — thus giving the river its name. The **Powder River** has often been described as being "a mile wide and an inch deep." Lewis and Clark called it Red Stone after the red rocks nearby.

The **Musselshell River** is a natural boundary between Garfield and Petroleum counties which flows into the Missouri. It was named by Lewis and Clark in 1805 for the quantities of mussel shells found along its banks, but in his Journal, Lewis gives the Indians credit: "The stream which we suppose to be called by the Menetarus, the Musselshell River."

Lewis and Clark followed the Missouri northward to the mouth of the **Milk River**, which is fed by Whitewater and Frenchman creeks, both of which arise in Canada. They gave it its name after noting the whiteness of the water. At a large fork further up, Lewis, uncertain which was the main branch, explored the northern fork, which he found went too far north to be the route to the Pacific that they were seeking. He named it Maria's River, after Maria Wood, a cousin with whom he thought he might be in love, although its muddy waters "but illy comport with the pure celestial virtues and amiable qualifications of that lovely fair one." Later the apostrophe was dropped and the name became the **Marias River**.

Meriwether Lewis's romantic inclination named another river, too — the **Judith**, for another cousin, Judith Hancock. The explorers camped near the mouth of this river on May 29, 1805, and ever since this spot has been important in Montana history. In 1833 Maximillian of Wied visited this place and visited with a party of Indian chiefs. And on the opposite side of the Missouri River from the mouth of the **Judith** there was erected in 1843 Fort Chardon, a post of the American Fur Trading Company, which was open for one year. In 1855 Gen. I. E. Stevens held a famous parley with several northern Indian tribes opposite the mouth of the **Judith**; the site was chosen largely because of the bountiful game in the Judith Basin. Camp Cooke just above the mouth was the first U.S. Army fort in Montana; it was established in 1866 and garrisoned for three years. Later, cattlemen often crossed the river here when they were moving their great herds from the Judith Basin to the Milk River country.

The **Smith River** heads in the mountains near White Sulphur Springs and joins the Missouri near Ulm. It was named by Lewis and Clark in 1805 in honor of Secretary of the Navy Robert Smith.

The explorers, still hoping to find a river that would lead them to the Pacific, came to a big division of the Missouri near a place now called Three Forks. They explored each branch, only to find that each river came from headwater streams in the mountains on the east slope of the Rockies, and that not one went on to the Pacific. They named the rivers for the three men in the U.S. Government who were instrumental in promoting the expedition: the **Jefferson**, for the famous President; the **Madison** for Secretary of State James Madison; and **Gallatin** for the Secretary of the Treasury.

Continuing up the **Jefferson River**, Lewis and Clark came to another fork, this one near the present town of Twin Bridges. They decided to name these tributaries after what they considered the "three cardinal virtues" of Pres. Thomas Jefferson: **Wisdom, Philosophy**, and **Philanthropy**; nice names, perhaps, but too much for the prospectors who arrived later and renamed them, respectively, the **Big Hole**, the **Beaverhead**, and the **Ruby River**. Still, the name Wisdom has survived as a town, and may have given its name to the **Wise River** in Beaverhead County. The **Ruby** took its name from nearby mountains with mines that produced garnets which were at first mistaken for rubies.

The **Sun River** comes from Teton Peak on the Continental Divide, running through Lewis and Clark and Cascade counties before it joins the Missouri near Great Falls. The Indians called this river *Natae-osueti*, which French trappers took to mean "Medicine" or "Sun River." When Lewis and Clark came upon it on July 18, 1805, they called it the **Dearborn**, after Henry Dearborn, Secretary of War, but this name was later used instead for a smaller river to the south.

Even though these explorers were responsible more than any other group for naming and mapping the rivers of Montana, only two rivers bear a name to commemorate them. The **Clark Fork (Missoula River)** in Western Montana was named for Wiliam Clark as was the Clark's Fork of the Yellowstone.

The **Flathead River** and the crystal clear **Blackfoot River** were named after Indian tribes. Before the white man came, there was a trail along the **Blackfoot** where the road now runs which was used for the annual buffalo hunt; it was called *Coakahlerisk kit*, or "River of the Road to the Buffalo." Nez Perces, Shoshones, and Flatheads headed east on it each year, hoping to avoid their Blackfeet enemies. White men recorded the river as the Big Blackfoot Fork on an 1865 map.

The **Jocko River**, which flows through Lake County, was named for Jacque ("Jocko") Raphael Finley, a trader and trapper for the Northwest and Hudson's Bay fur companies. Jocko was an associate of the famous explorer David Thompson, and a half-breed who once used his influence and diplomacy to prevent a bloody conflict between Indian factions camped on the bank of the river; to commemorate his role as mediator, the river was given his name. It was first called Jacque's River, but later it was changed (Omundson).

The **Kootenai River** was also named after an Indian tribe. They saw it as a bow, because it makes an arc in the northeast corner of Montana as it meanders into Canada. The **Yaak River** appears to cut across the **Kootenai** like an arrow, and so was given the Indian word for arrow.

The **Bitterroot River** was named for the abundant and useful plant that later became the official state flower.

There are several smaller rivers in Montana, but this is a book of towns, and this brief review of rivers is included only to show their influence on the naming of communities and counties. Most of the rivers were given names before there were any settlements, and even during those very early days, about half were named for topographical features and the other half for people. Naturally the influence of Indian words is stronger in the naming of rivers than of towns.

The great river which was the ultimate goal of the Lewis and Clark expedition, was named in 1792 by Capt. Robert Grey, a Bostonian who had sailed around Cape Horn to the Pacific coast and anchored in a harbor of the Oregon-Washington rivers; he called it the Columbia, because that was the name of his ship that had brought him there.

Creeks

Man marks down his story in many ways — by journals kept, by pictures drawn, and by place names he leaves upon the land and the streams. The scattered bits of regional history gleaned from creek names can yield a fascinating and fairly accurate account of the land and its inhabitants.

This is a summary of the tabulation of 475 creek names in Montana which now appear on most state maps.

Montana was a wilderness, unmapped and unnamed when Lewis and Clark entered it in 1805. President Thomas Jefferson had charged the Corps of Discovery to explore the land, map it, study the flora and the fauna, and give names to the creeks, rivers, and mountains. So the first wave of "naming" and recording came with these early explorers. Lewis honored Sacajawea by naming a creek for her when she saved their supplies from a sinking boat. He named another creek for his Sergeant Pryor who explored it, but for the most part, Lewis and Clark gave descriptive names to the physical features of the land as they mapped it. They were impressed by the Big Horn sheep, a species of animal entirely new to them. Creeks, mountains, and rivers bear this name, as well as that of other animals the explorers found.

Some creeks were named for dates or events like "Fourth of July Creek," where they camped on that holiday in 1805, or "Bull Creek" because a big buffalo bull charged into their camp and left chaos in his wake, or "Blowing Fly Creek" in Eastern Montana where the flies were so annoying that the men couldn't rest. They had to spend the whole evening "blowing flies off."

The Indians had given names to many creeks and some of them like "Rotten Grass Creek" and "Lodgepole Creek" were preserved and recorded on the white man's maps.

After Lewis and Clark came the fur traders; many of them were Frenchmen. The influence of this group remains in such names as "Chouteau Coulee Creek," "Dupuyer," "LaValle," "LaMarsh," "Beauchamp," and "Beauvais" creeks. Following the trappers and traders, the prospectors poured into Montana as each new gold field was discovered and mined — the Gold Creek development, then Alder Gulch in 1863 and others in quick succession. Some creeks were named for the minerals found there, but more often they were named for the men who discovered the precious metal. "Callahan Creek" in Lincoln County was named for an old silver miner who struck it rich there.

The Civil War influence was felt in many Montana names during the Gold Rush Era. Adventurous young men released from the army sought excitement or escape in the rush to Montana. They left such names as "Confederate Creek" and "Union Creek" to commemorate their loyalties, and these names were often used for the post office when it was established.

Sometimes colorful individuals lent their names to creeks, such as "Bloody Dick Creek" in Beaverhead County, which was named for an Englishman living there in the 1860's and who was known only by that nickname, or "Crandall Creek" in Carbon County in memory of a man killed there by the Indians in 1876.

Then came the settlers: first the pioneers and cattlemen, then the dryland farmers. Often a creek was named for the first man who settled near it. We find a generous sprinkling of Scandanavians as indicated by four "Thompson" creeks, and Irishmen with "O'Brien" and "O'Fallon"; the Scotsmen left such names as "McDonald," McGinnis," "McGuire," and "McHessor" on the maps of the state. There were Englishmen and Cousin Jacks who came to work in the copper mines of Butte and named the creeks "Chapman," "Carter," "George," and "Morgan."

Indian influences are seen again as white men named creeks for them as a group or for individuals: there are "Squaw" creeks in Gallatin and Madison Counties; there are "Indian" creeks in many areas. "Big Knife Creek" in Missoula County was named for an Indian chief.

Descriptive names tell us that the water in Montana's streams was "Bitter" in Yellowstone and Valley Counties, "Clear" in many areas, "Hell Roaring" in Park County, "White" in Phillips County and "Stinking" in one part of Beaverhead County. "Mud" creeks in Phillips and Wheatland, and "Muddy" in Big Horn and Sheridan Counties indicate the erosion of soil and spring run-offs. Pipestone Springs and creek were named by the Indians because the white clay there was excellent for making pipes.

"Mill Creek," "Corral," "Cabin," "Ranch," and "Home Creek" take their names from something man has built along the creek. "Mill" could indicate a saw mill for processing logs, a flour mill for grinding grain, or as in the case of "Mill Creek" in Madison County, the mill was one which processed hides. A tanning mill was located about twenty-five miles from Virginia City and the creek took its name from that. Bark was ground by water power and used to tan as many as 2,000 cow hides per summer. The mill was in succcessful operation for about five years and turned out an excellent quality of leather.

"Sleeping Child," "Tincup," "Tomato Can," "Cache," "Razor," "Arrow," and "Black Cannon" are hints of history that has passed this way as the creek took its name from an object found there.

What kind of animals were in Montana when the white men came? There are nine of these 475 creeks named "Bear," eight named "Beaver," ten "Deer," and six "Elk." Only three were named "Buffalo," perhaps because his kind had almost disappeared before the great influx of place-naming-settlers came. Fish of some kind account for fifteen of the creek names. The wolf which was plentiful in Montana as long as there were buffalo and deer for him to feed on became a problem for the cattlemen when the wolf's natural prey was gone and he turned to killing cattle. He has left his imprint on at least eight creeks. Other animals recorded in this name history are antelope, badger, otter, cows, horses, dogs, sheep, fox coyote, grasshoppers, rattlesnakes, and a variety of birds.

Cottonwood and willow trees led all others as native to the state. Ten "Cottonwood" creeks are in six counties and the evergreens include "Cedar" creeks and several kinds of pine trees. "Ash," "Camas," "Poplar," "Sage," and "Rosebud" enlarge the picture of the native flora.

Of the 475 creeks categorized in this survey, 142 were named for people; 105 were named for animals; sixty-one were named for nearby plants; fifty were given environmental or descriptive names; and at least eighteen carried an Indian influence. Five creeks were named because of their shape — "Moon," "Elbow," "Crooked," and "Dovetail." Sources such as "Lake," "Warm Springs," and "Geyser" appear in eight names. Nine creek names describe the appearance of the water — "Clear," "Milk," "Yellow Water," and "White Water Creek." The rest of the names fall into a group that has been called "Miscellaneous" — "Careless," "Chippy," "Froze-to-Death," "Hell," "Sawtooth," "Smoke," Whiskey," and many more.

The categories used in this summary are purely arbitrary ones. The survey was made to get an over-all picture of the trend of naming creeks in relation to the trend in naming towns. A thorough study on the origin of creek names would require another year of research and another book. They are listed here because so many of them developed into town names, and because even a superficial survey records some history of the state.

Roughly forty-two percent of the towns were named for people, and about thirty percent of the creeks were. On the other hand, about thirty-four percent of the creeks were named for plants and animals and only five percent of the towns were. Physical features accounted for about eighteen percent of the names in both groups. The other categories were not easily compared.

Name origins are valuable only to the extent that they record regional history. Since creeks were often the first things named in a new area, their naming history is seldom recorded as in the case of towns when settlers have come together into some kind of organization. But a broad look at the names of the creeks in a state can reveal many things about the original conditions and about the people who passed by or settled there. These creek names exerted an influence on the town names that came later.

The story of Montana is related to such words as "Sacajawea" and "Pryor;" "wolf" and "beaver;" "cottonwood" and "willow;" "gold" and "coal;" "Custer" and "Commanche;" "Chouteau," "Thompson," and "O'Brien." In these name-words we can glimpse a century and a half of history in the Territory and the State — what was here, who came, and why they came. The explorers, the trappers, gold miners, pioneers, cattlemen, Indians, and the dry-land farmers recorded history as they named the life-giving streams of water.

Maps

The following maps reveal, as words never could, the rapid changes in the counties of the state. From an original nine counties in 1864 to the present 56, Montana presents an almost bewildering pattern of shifting county boundaries. Needless to add, these changes have made the job of locating towns an extremely difficult one. Don McKay, Montana's leading "county buster," could never have known the problems he would cause the chronicler of Montana towns. Some towns have been in as many as three different counties! I hope — I trust — they have all been accurately placed.

R. C. C.

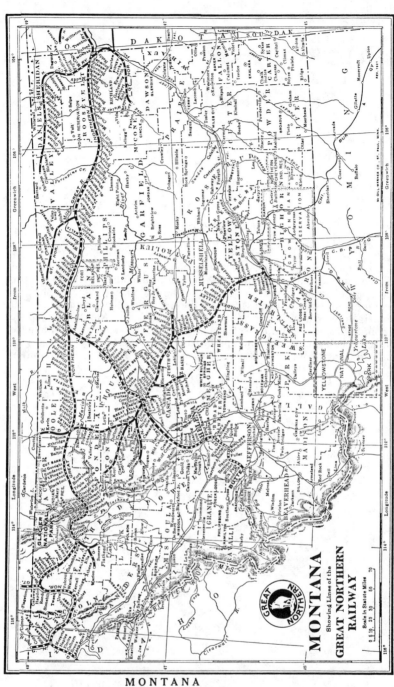

MONTANA

Great Northern Railway Lines in Montana

A glance at this Great Northern railway map published in 1921 shows that many Montana towns were the direct result of the coming of the railroads — many were little more than stations or sidings which sprang up along the tracks. Settlements that had previously centered in an area a short distance for the main line sometimes moved the country post office and maybe a store to the nearest station and retained their original name; but because so many of the towns were established first as stations or sidings, they were often named by railroaders — thus the railroads had a great influence on the choice of names that came to dot Montana's maps. Railroad officials, members of the families, even construction workers, were often honored by having a station named for them. (Map courtesy Chuck Nelson; Walla Walla, Washington).

Before there were counties, Montana was divided thus:

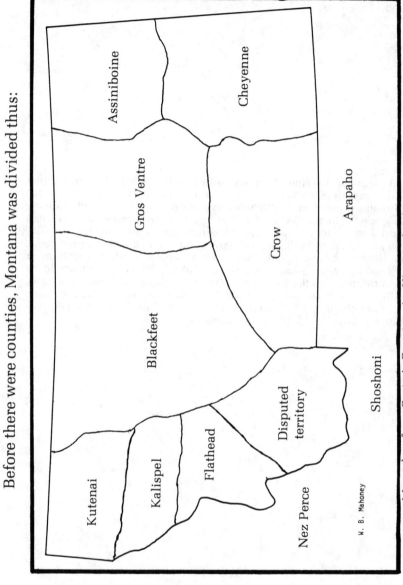

Map taken from *Custer's Country, An Historical Atlas*, by George Kurkowski.
A Bicentennial Publication. Star Printing Co., Miles City 1976

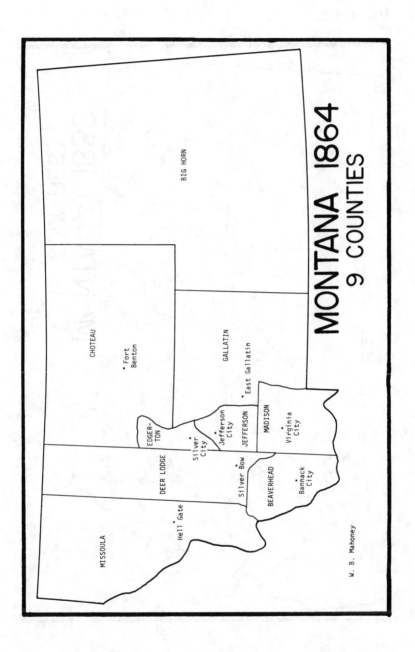

MONTANA 1864
9 COUNTIES

BIG HORN

CHOTEAU

• Fort
Benton

GALLATIN

• East Gallatin

EDGER-
TON

Jefferson
City

JEFFERSON

MADISON

• Virginia
City

• Silver
City

Silver Bow

BEAVERHEAD

• Bannack
City

DEER LODGE

MISSOULA

• Hell Gate

W. B. Mahoney

313

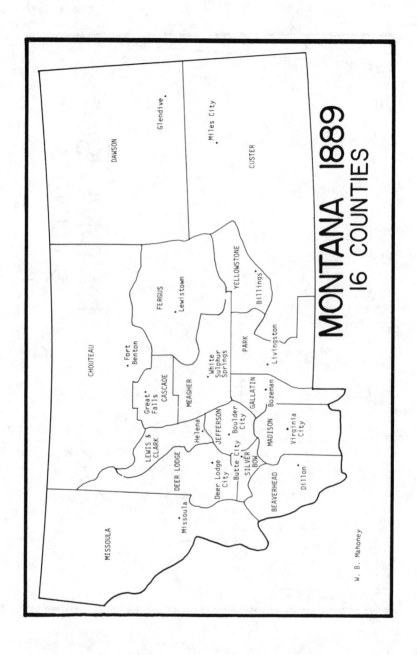

MONTANA 1889
16 COUNTIES

W. B. Mahoney

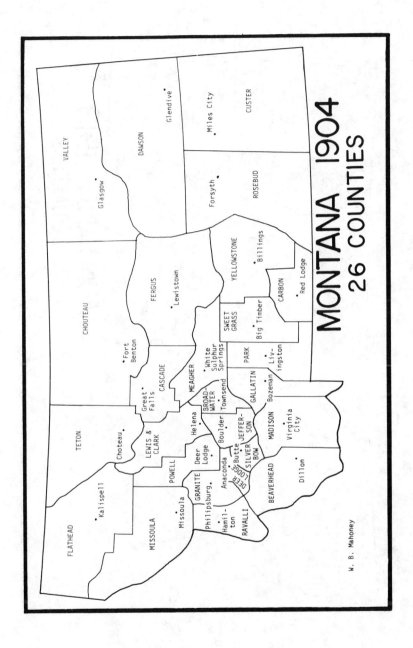

MONTANA 1904
26 COUNTIES

W. B. Mahoney

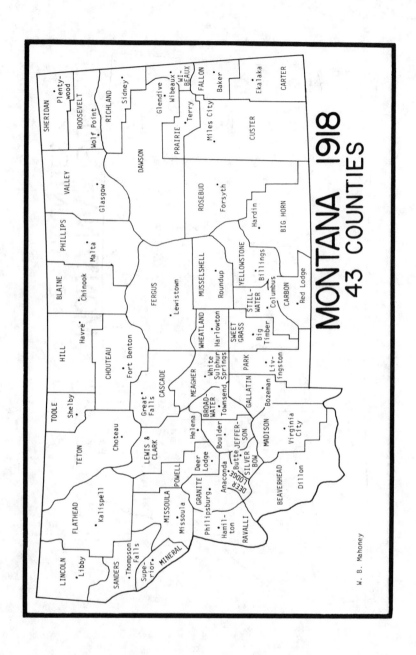

MONTANA 1918
43 COUNTIES

W. B. Mahoney

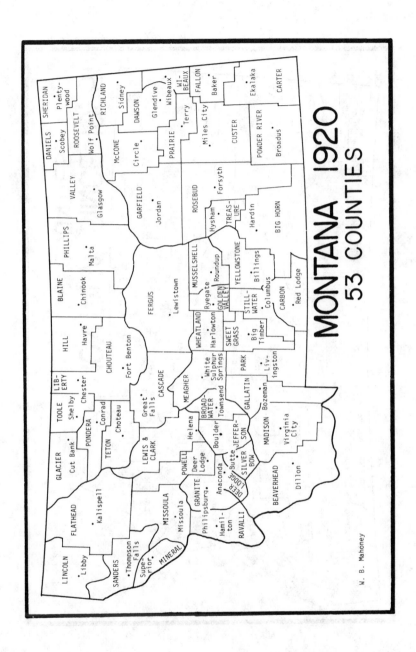

MONTANA 1920
53 COUNTIES

W. B. Mahoney

317

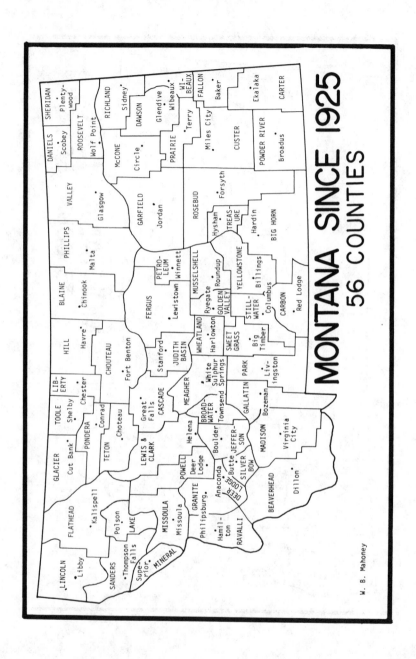

MONTANA SINCE 1925
56 COUNTIES

W. B. Mahoney

Bibliography
BOOKS

Aasheim, Magnus. *Sheridan's day break; a story of Sheridan County and its Pioneers.* Compiled and collated by Magnus Aasheim. Sheridan County Historical Association, 1970.

Abbott, Newton Carl. *Montana in the Making.* 6th ed. Billings, Montana: Gazette Printing Co., 1938.

Adams, Paul M. *When Wagon Trails were Dim.* Montana Conference Board of Education of the Methodist Church, 957.

Allison, Janet S. *Trial and Triumph: 101 Years in North Central Montana.* Chinook, Montana, 1968.

Annin, James. *They Gazed on the Beartooths.* 3 vols. Billings, Montana: Reporter Printing and Supply, 1964.

Barrows, John R. *Ubet.* Caldwell, Idaho: Caxton Printers, 1934.

Barsness, Larry. *Gold camp; Alder Gulch and Virginia City, Montana.* New York: Hastings House, 1962.

Berry, Gerald L. *The Whoop-up trail; Alberta-Montana relationships.* Edmonton, Alberta, Canada: Applied Arts Products, 1953.

Berthold, Mary Paddock. *Turn Here for the Big Hole.* Detroit: Harlo Press, (c 1970).

Bicentennial Committee, Bonner School. *A grassroots tribute: the story of Bonner, Montana.* Missoula, Montana: Gateway Printing, (c 1976).

Broadwater County Historical Society. *Broadwater Bygones: A history of Broadwater County, Montana since 1897.* Bozeman, Montana: Color World, 1977.

Brown, Mary and W. R. Felton. *Before Barbed Wire.* New York: Holt, 1956.

Burlingame, Merrill G. *Gallatin Century of Progress.* Bozeman, Montana: Artcraft Printers, 1964.

Burlingame, Merrill G. and K. Ross Toole. *A History of Montana. Vol. II.* New York: Lewis Historical Publishing Company, 1957.

Byerly, Ken. *Central Montana's communities . . . yesterday, today, and tomorrow.* Lewistown, Montana: Central Montana Publishing Company, n.d.

Charlton, Wavie. *Cry of the homestead.* n.p., 1976.

Culbertson diamond jubilee, 1887-1962: seventy-five years of progress. Culbertson, Montana, n.p., 1962.

Davis, Jean. *Shallow Diggin's.* Caldwell, Idaho: Caxton Printers, 1962.

Dearborn Homemaker's Club. *Dearborn country, a history of the Dearborn, Wolf Creek and Craig areas.* Fairfield, Montana: Fairfield Times, 1976.

Dimsdale, Thomas J. *The Vigilantes of Montana.* Norman: University of Oklahoma Press, 1966.

Dufresne, Lorraine. *A Heritage Remembered: early and later days in the history of western Sanders County, Thompson Falls, Montana.* Sanders County Ledger, 1976.

Eckelberry, Henry. *Yesterday was Demersville.* Kalispell, Montana: Thomas Printing, 1974.

Egly Country Club, Egly, Montana. *Trails, Trials and Tributes.* n.p., 1958.

Elwood, Henry. *Somers, Montana – The Company Town.* Kalispell: Thomas Printing, 1976.

Extension Homemakers Council, Powder River County. *Echoing Footsteps.* Butte, Montana: Ashton Printing and Engraving Company, 1967.

Fanning the Embers. Billings, Montana: Gazette Printing Company, 1971.

Fitzpatrick, Lilian L., *Nebraska Place Names.* Lincoln: University of Nebraska Press, 1967.

Florence community. *Some Bitterroot Memories, 1860-1930.* Missoula, Montana: Gateway Printing, 1976.

Florin, Lambert. *Montana-Idaho-Wyoming Ghost Towns.* Seattle: Superior Publishing Company, 1971.

Frazer, Robert W. *Forts of the West.* Norman: University of Oklahoma Press, 1965.

Frenchtown Historical Society. *Frenchtown Valley Footprints.* Missoula, Montana: Mountain Press, 1976.

Fulmer, Genie P. *Cabins and Campfires in Southeastern Montana.* Forsyth, Montana, 1973.

Furrows and Trails in Judith Basin County. Judith Basin Press.

Garfield County, Montana High School. *Garfield County 1919-1969.* Jordan, Montana, 1969.

Geraldine Bicentennial Committee. *Spokes, Spurs and Cockleburs.* Fort Benton, Montana: River Press Publishing Company, 1976.

Gordon, Albie, Margaret Lehfeldt and Mary Morsanny. *Dawn in Golden Valley, a county in Montana.* n.p., 1971.

Harlowton Woman's Club. *Yesteryears and Pioneers.* Harlowton, Montana, 1972.

Henry, Ralph C. *Our Land Montana.* Helena, Montana: State Publishing Company, 1962.

Highland, Geneva. *Big Dry County.* Billings, Montana: Billings Printing Company, 1960.

Hill County Bicentellial Commission. *Grit, Guts and Gusto: a history of Hill County.* Havre, 1976.

Huntley, Chet. *The Generous Years.* New York: Random House, 1968.

Iverson, Ronald J. *The Princess of the Prairie: History of Belgrade.* Montana State University: McGill Museum Publications, 1965.

James, Don. *Butte's Memory Book.* Pictures by C. Owen Smithers. Caldwell, Idaho: Caxton Printers, 1975.

Johnson, Dorothy M. *When You and I Were Young, Whitefish.* Missoula, Montana: Mountain Press, 1982.

Johnston, Lloyd and Mabel Johnston. *We Called Them Back; Montana homesteaders and pioneers of the old Wilson Post Office country.* Fairfield, Montana: Fairfield Times, 1974.

Lambert, Eloise and Mario Pei. *Our Names: Where They Come From and What They Mean.* New York: Lathrop Lee and Shepherd Company, 1961.

Leakey, John, as told to Nellie Snyder Yost. *The West that Was: from Texas to Montana.* Lincoln: University of Nebraska Press, 1958.

Lehigh, Rufus Wood. *Five Hundred Utah Place Names.* Salt Lake City: Deseret News Press, n.d.

Lolo History Committee. *Lolo Creek Reflections.* Missoula, Montana: Economy Publishers, 1976.

Madison County History Association. *Pioneer Trails and Trials: Madison County, 1863-1920.* Blue Print and Letter Company, 1976.

McCracken, Harold. *The Charles M. Russell Book.* New York: Doubleday and Company, Incorporated, 1957.

Miller, Joaquin. *History of Montana.* Chicago: Lewis Publishing Company, 1894.

Minnesota Friendly Club, Minneota, Montana. *Tumbleweeds and Tar-paper Shacks.* Iowa Falls, Iowa: General Publishing and Binding, 1971.

Missoula, Montana. *Church of the Holy Spirit.* Centennial celebration, September 18-20, 1970. Missoula, Montana: Gateway Printing, 1970.

Mockel, Myrtle. *Montana, an Illustrated History.* Chicago: Swallow Press, 1969.

Mockel, Myrtle. *Montana's Song, and Poems of the West.* Philadelphia: Dorrance, 1964.

Historical and Arts Society. *Courage Enough: Mon-Dak family histories, Richland County, Mt.,* Bismarck, N.D., 1975.

Montana Almanac. ed. 1958, 1959-60. Missoula, Montana: University of Montana Press.

Mountains and Meadows, a Pioneer history of Cascade, Chestnut Valley, Hardy, St. Peters Mission, and Castner Falls, 1805-1925. Compiled by Mrs. Clarence Rowe. Great Falls, Montana: Blue Print and Letter Company, 1970.

Murphy, James E. *Half Interest in a Silver Dollar*. Missoula, Montana: Mountain Press, 1983.

Murray, Henry Thomas. *Judith Basin Pioneers; a story of early days in central Montana together with the genealogy of the Murray family*. n.p., 1965?

Murray, Robert A. *Military Forts in the Powder River Country of Wyoming*. Lincoln: University of Nebraska Press, 1968.

Musselshell Valley Pioneer Club, History Committee. *Horizons O'er the Musselshell*. n.p., 1974.

Noyes, Alva Josiah. *In the Land of Chinook; or, the story of Blaine County*. Helena, Montana: State Publishing Company, 1917.

O'Fallon Historical Society, Baker, Montana. *O'Fallon Flashbacks*. Western Printing and Lithography, 1975.

Olson, Lenore. *Since Homesteading Days: histories of the Larslan, Avondale and Sunnyside communities*. 1976.

Pace, Dick. *Golden Gulch: the story of Montana's fabulous Alder Gulch, being a true, quite partial and somewhat humorous history*. Virginia City, Montana, n.p., 1962.

Paladin, Vivian A. *From Buffalo Bones to Sonic Boom*. Glasgow, Montana, 1962.

Pearce, Thomas Matthew, ed. assisted by Cassidy Pearce. *New Mexico Place Names: A Geographical Dictionary*. Albuquerque: University of New Mexico Press, 1965.

Penake, Judy, ed. *In the Shadow of the Twin Sisters: Ubet, Garneill, Straw Buffalo, Montana*. Lewistown, Montana: Montana Business Services, 1973.

Phillips, Paul C. ed. *Forty Years on the Frontier: as seen in the Journals and Reminiscences of Granville Stuart*. Glendale, California: The Arthur H. Clark Company, 1957.

Plentywood: Golden Years, 1912-1962. Plentywood, Montana: n.p., 1962.

Price, Adelia M. and Horace M. Lane. *Montana Driftwood*. Mesa, Arizona: Richard Glen Lane Publishing Company.

Randall, Leslie Watson. *Footprints Along the Yellowstone*. San Antonio: Naylor Company, 1961.

Russell, Charles M. *Trails Plowed Under*. New York: Doubleday and Company, 1927.

Salisbury, Albert and Jane. *Two Captains West*. Seattle: Superior Publishing Company, 1950.

Schafer, Betty and Mable Engelter. *Stump Town to Ski Town*. Whitefish Library Association, 1973.

Shepherd Historical Book Committee. *"Lest We Forget . . ."* Shepherd, Montana: Frontier Press, 1976.

Sealock, Richard A. and Pauline E. Sealock. *Bibliography of Place Name Literature*. Chicago: American Library Association, 1948 and 1967.

Smith, Albert. *The Place Names of Westmoreland*. London: Cambridge University Press, 1967.

Stahlberg, John, ed. *Montana: the American Guide Series*. Federal Writers' Project. New York: Viking Press, 1939. Hastings House, 1955.

Stearns, Harold Joseph. *A History of the Upper Musselshell Valley of Montana*. Harlowton, Montana: Times Clarion, 1966.

Stevensville. *Montana Genesis: a history of the Stevensville area of the Bitterroot Valley*. Missoula, Montana: Mountain Press, 1971.

Stewart, George R. *Names on the Land*. New York: Random House, 1954.

Toole, K. Ross. *Montana, An Uncommon Land*. Norman: University of Oklahoma Press, 1959.

Toole, K. Ross. *The Rape of the Great Plains: northwest America, cattle and coal*. Boston: Little, Brown Company, 1976.

Tuttle, Daniel Sylvester. *Reminiscences of a Missionary Bishop*. New York: Thomas Whittaker, 1906.

Urbanek, Mae. *Wyoming Place Names*. Boulder, Colorado: Johnson Publishing Company, 1967.

Utica Historical Society. Utica, Montana: n.p., 1968.

Waldron, Ellis. *An Atlas of Montana Politics Since 1864*. Missoula: University of Montana Press, 1958.

Whithorn, Bill and Doris Whithorn. *Photo History of Aldridge.* Minneapolis: Acme Printing and Stationery, 1965.
Willard, John. *Adventure Trails in Montana.* Sponsored by Montana Historical Society, 1971.
Wolle, Muriel Sibell. *Montana Pay Dirt.* Denver: Sage Books, 1963.
Woodson, Warren. *Pioneering Tales of Montana.* New York: Exposition Press, 1965.
Writers' Program, Montana. *Copper Camp.* New York: Hastings House, 1945.

BOOKLETS

Johnson, Coburn, John Mason, Minnie Paugh and Katherine Schaefer. *Bibliography of Montana Local Histories.* Published by Montana Library Association and University of Montana, 1977.
Cockhill, Brian and Dale L. Johnson. *Bibliography. A Listing of Masters Theses and Doctoral Dissertations of an Historical Nature, University of Montana. Montana segments.* University of Montana Library, 1977.
Bell, William S. *Old Fort Benton, what it was and how it came to be.* Helena, Montana: n.p., 1909.
Bicentennial, Golden Valley County, *Heritage '76.* Roundup Record, 1976.
Centennial Committee of Deer Lodge. *Historical sketch of Deer Lodge City, Montana.* n.p., 1964.
Home Demonstration Club of Big Horn County. (Montana) *Crow Country.* Billings: Western Litho Print, 1955.
Carver, Frank. *Significance of County Names.* Dillon, Montana: Reprinted from Butte Post, February 5, 1916.
Glasgow Jubilee Committee, Vivian Paladin, ed. *Glasgow.* McKee Print, 1962.
Houston, E. L. *Early History of Gallatin County.* Bozeman, Montana: Bozeman Daily Chronicle, 1933.
Kerin, Tom. *Dutton Golden Jubilee.* Great Falls, Montana: Great Falls Leader, 1959.
Fletcher, Bob and Irvin Shope. *Montana Historical Markers.* Montana State Highway Commission. Helena, Montana: n.d.
Kuhlman, Fay. *Bearcreek, Montana.* Bearcreek Banner.
deSmet, Pierre-Jean. *Origin, Progress, and Prospects of the Catholic Mission to the Rocky Mountains.* Philadelphia: Fithian, 1843. Reprint: Fairfield, Washington: Ye Galleon Press, 1967.
Railroads to Rockets 1887 to 1962. Diamond Jubilee, Phillips County (Montana). Malta, Montana, 1962.
Golden Jubilee History Committee. *Wolf Point.* Wolf Point, Montana: Herald News, 1965.

PUBLIC DOCUMENTS

"Origin of Geographic Names in Montana National Forests of Gallatin County." National Forest Service. Missoula, Montana, n.d. (typed).
"Origin of Geographical Names in Montana National Forests of Absaroka and Flathead." Missoula, Montana, n.d. (typed).
From Journals housed in the National Archives Building, Washington, D.C. Record of Appointments of Postmasters:
   Volume 1855 to 1867
   Volume 1864 to 1878
   Volume 1877 to 1884
   Volume 1885 to 1900
   Volume 1900 to 1930

From Post Office Department Building:
    Volume 1930 to present.
Microfilm copies of above records at State Historical Library, Helena.
Montana Geographic Names Branch of Geographic Names, U. S. Geological Survey,
    National Mapping Division, Reston, Virginia. Two volumes, total 569 pages.
    March 23, 1982.

INTERVIEWS AND LETTERS
See Acknowledgments.

ARTICLES AND PERIODICALS

Ashley, James M. "The Naming of Montana," *Montana* July 1952.
"American Names." *Life* January 31, 1944.
Billings Gazette. Information from feature stories in many issues.
Chamberlain, Alexander F. "Geographical Terms of Kootenay Origin." *American Anthropologist*. April-June 1902.
Croy, H. "Let's Name the Town for Me." *Saturday Evening Post* June 8, 1964.
Childears, Lucille. "Montana Place Name Records," *Western Folklore*. January 1954.
Garver, Frank H. "Montana as a Field for Historical Research," *Mississippi Valley Historical Association Records Vol. VII* pp. 99-112. 1913.
Great Falls Tribune. Information from feature stories in many issues.
Heaney, Kevin. "Montana's Fabulous Ghost Towns" *Montana Outdoors*. July-August 1980.
Hogen, M. "Turn Left at Spring Creek," (Wyoming) *American Forester*. September 1964.
Karsch, Carl C. "Montana Land of Ranchers and Vacationers," *Presbyterian Life*. May 1968.
Missoulian. Information from articles, news notes and feature stories.
Montana Standard (Butte). Information from news and feature stories.
Madisonian (Virginia City, Montana). Special editions and historical features.
Marmont. "Old Fort Whoop-up Trail" as described by Harry Stanford *Great Falls Tribune*. May 1932.
Montana, the Magazine of Westen History. All back issues were scanned and information used from many of them.
Montana Postal Cache. Information about Montana post offices, lists and dates and maps of eastern Montana counties.
Park County News (Livingston). Information from several issues.
Postal History Quarterly, "Montana" by Robert Dalton Harris.
Posthorn, Montana Branch of National League of Postmasters. May 19, 1982. "Montana's postmasters and towns."
Stewart, G. R. "How Cities Get Those Funny Names," *Science Digest*, May 1946.
Winnett Times. Anniversary Edition. July 16, 1964.

MAPS

Custer's Country, historical Atlas by George Kurkowski. Miles City; Star Printing, 1976.
Garfield County map drawn by Gardner Hays and included in Big Dry Country by Geneva Highland.
Montana. Great Northern Railway Co. St. Paul: McGill Graphic Arts, 1967.
Montana Gold Strikes, Ghost Towns, Frontier Military Outposts. Altadena, California: Cooper Enterprises, n.d.
Montana, the Big Sky Country. Montana Highway Commission. Helena: 1968.
Montana. Northern Pacific Railway. St. Paul: Mc Gill Graphic Arts, 1966.

Montana Postal Cache. County maps by Dennis Lutz showing early day post offices. Published in Montana Postal Cache 1976.

    Map 1 Dawson County 1869-1893
    Map 2 Valley County 1893-1913
           Dawson County 1893-1914
    Map 3 Valley and Sheridan counties 1913-1919/1920
    Map 4 Valley, Sheridan, Daniels and Roosevelt counties. 1920 to date.
    Map 5 Dawson, Richland and Wibaux counties. 1914-1919.
    Map 6 Dawson, Richland, Wibaux, McCone and Garfield counties 1919 to date
    Map 7 Custer County 1877 to 1883
    Map 8 Custer County 1883-1901
    Map 9 Custer and Rosebud counties 1901-1913
    Map 10 Big Horn, Custer, Fallon, Prairie and Rosebud counties 1913-1917
    Map 11 Big Horn, Carter, Custer, Fallon, Powder River, Prairie, Rosebud and Treasure counties 1917 to date.

Rocky Mountain Division. Chicago, Milwaukee, St. Paul and Pacific Railroad Co. Deer Lodge, Montana, n.d.

Shane, Ralph M.
    Early History of the Northern Cheyennes, an illustrated historical map of Montana, 1966.
    Early History of Blackfeet Indian Reservation, 1966.
    Historical Map of the Crow Indian Reservation.

Waldron, Ellis, County maps in An Atlas of Montana Politics since 1864.

UNPUBLISHED MATERIAL

Bue, Olaf J. "A Guide to Pronunciation of Place Names in Montana."

Charlo Community School Project. (Duplicated, stapled).

Daems, Harry Beauregard. "Early Days on the Madison." (typed).

Historical Library Clipping File:
    Garver, Frank.
        "Early Emigrant Roads and Trails into Montana."
        "Marking Historical Sites in Montana."
        "Montana Counties in 1865."
        "Place Names in Jefferson County."
        "Significance of County Names in Montana."
    O'Donnell, D. (of Billings) "Names of Rivers and Creeks in Montana."
    Wheeler, W. F. "Montana Names."
    Willard, John. "Westward from North Dakota Line on Highway 2."

History of Garfield County by students of Garfield County High School. Jordan, Montana. 1947-48 (typed).

Hysham and Treasure County by students of Hysham High School. 1963 (duplicated, stapled).

Noyes, A. J. "How the Big Hole Basin got its Remarkable Name."

Omundson, Don. "A Study of Place Names in Missoula County, Montana." Missoula: University of Montana, 1961. M.A. Thesis.

Perrin, F. F. "Statement of Origin of Station Names, Montana." Great Northern Railway Co. 1952 (duplicated).

Rowe, J. P. "The Origin of Some Montana Place Names." Missoula: University of Montana, 1933 (mimeographed).

Spray, Jimmie. "Early Days in the Madison Valley" (typed).

Student papers from high schools in Antelope, Willow Creek, Grass Range, Dutton, Redstone and Stevensville.